Major
Libraries
of the World
A SELECTIVE GUIDE

Major Libraries of the World

A SELECTIVE GUIDE

Colin Steele

BOWKER
LONDON & NEW YORK

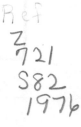

Contents

Preface

This book is essentially a practical guide to 300 'Major Libraries of the World'. The final responsibility for the selection of the libraries lies firmly with the author, who realises any such selection is invariably subjective. A small number of libraries were excluded because they did not reply either to the questionnaire on which the *Guide* is based or to subsequent letters. Some libraries did not wish to be included, e.g. the Matenadaran in Yerevan (USSR) considered itself a 'research institute with scientific staff' rather than a library, while the International Labour Office Library in Geneva was in the process of moving between buildings during the writing of the book. Certain libraries have been included as being representative of 'special' libraries, e.g. the International Jugendbibliothek at Munich, the Lyndon Baines Johnson Library at Austin, and the Library of the Institute for Sex Research, Bloomington. A certain number of libraries have been included almost by reason of their geographical location. A general library of 400,000 volumes may not rank very highly in the United States or Europe but in Africa or Asia the impact of such a collection can be completely different.

In terms of the published literature on the subject it could be said that this book occupies a sort of halfway house between publications such as the *Internationales Bibliotheks-Handbuch* (Munich, 1974), which provides a comprehensive but very brief listing of libraries and Anthony Hobson's *Great Libraries* (London, 1970), which by format, although not by content, falls under the heading of a 'coffee-table' book. The present work is probably nearest in style and layout to *World Libraries and Librarians* (London, 1939), which was issued in looseleaf format apparently for updating, but which does not seem to have survived World War II.

My work has also been made easier by the existence of Arundell Esdaile's *National Libraries of the World,* 2nd edition revised by F.J. Hill (London, 1957) and Esdaile's earlier work with M. Burton, *Famous Libraries of the World.* The idiosyncratic, but informative, pamphlets by the late Melba Berry Bennett, *Historical Libraries* (Palm Springs 1958-69) have also proved useful. Space precludes documenting the numerous national, regional and individual library guides consulted, but my debt to the authors of these works is just as real as it is to the individuals who follow in the 'Acknowledgements'.

Acknowledgements

First thanks must go to all the librarians throughout the world who answered the original questionnaire. In an era when questionnaires must almost seem to cascade onto the desks of chief librarians, it is reassuring that so many took the time and trouble to reply. I must next thank Mrs. Janet Page, who provided research assistance with calm efficiency and enthusiasm. My wife, Anna, was, as usual, a major support, not only in tolerating my many lapses from parental duties but also in reading, checking and criticising entries. Ian Laurie of Bowker provided the original idea for the book and I am grateful to him for his continued help and for ensuring that I completed the manuscript more or less on time. Mrs. Jackie Hennesy produced an admirable typescript from an, at times, extremely illegible manuscript. My warmest thanks to her and to the following who, of course, bear no responsibility for the faults that remain. Within the Bodleian Library, Oxford, I should like to thank Mr. G.P.M. Walker for advice on Eastern Europe and translations from the Russian; Mr. J. Brister for translations from the Italian; Mr. W.G. Hodges for translations from the Greek; Mr. D. Barrett for translations from the Turkish; Mr. A.D.S. Roberts for information on Japanese libraries; and Mr R. May, Mr. H.W. Alderman, Mr. C. Braybrooke and Mr R. J. Roberts. Others in Oxford to whom I am indebted include Mr R. Waterfield, Mr M. D. Deas, Dr. D. Hopwood, Dr. and Mrs R. Evans, Mr J. S. G. Simmons and Mr. D. J. Gilson (whose review of A. Hobson's *Great Libraries in Library History,* vol. 2, no. 3, Spring 1971, was, perhaps, the best to appear).

Outside Oxford I must thank Señor Luis Villalba, former Minister for Cultural Affairs, Spanish Embassy, London; Dr. Mario Montuori, Director of the Italian Institute, London; Senhor José Ferreira Lopes, Head of the Cultural and Information Office, Brazilian Embassy, London; Dr. L. Hallewell of the University of Essex Library; Dr. D. Rhodes of the British Library; Mrs. L.M. Newman of Lancaster University Library, whose *Libraries in Paris* (Scorton, 1971) is a model of its type; A.E. Jeffreys of the University of Newcastle-upon-Tyne Library; the staffs of the British Library (Library Association Library) and College of Librarianship, Aberystwyth, Wales, particularly Messrs. A. Thompson, D. Ball and J.S. Parker; Mr. Roger Howard for advice on China; Mr. F. Walton, Librarian of the Gennadius Library, Athens; Dr. P. Xuereb, Librarian of the Royal University of Malta; Professor J. Freudenthal of Simmons College, Massachusetts; Mr. J.M. Wells of the Newberry Library, Chicago, and Dr. Pedro Grases of Caracas.

Oxford 1975   Colin Steele

Photographic Credits

The publishers wish to thank the many librarians who provided illustrations for this book, and in particular, the following. Page numbers appear in parentheses after each name.

Richard and Sally Greenhill (I,58); Österreichische Lichtbildstelle, Vienna (13); Bilderdienst der Stadt Wein (19); Verlag Richard Pietsch, Vienna (14); Loiseau S.A. Brussels (22); Bibliothèque Royale, Brussels (22,23); Dave H. Ottignies (26); Musée de Mariemont (29,30); Juan R. Freudenthal, Simmons College, Boston, USA (49,50); Sanchez (59); Filip Lašut (63); Jan Tachezy (64,65); Stanislav Nemec (67,68); Morten Bo, Copenhagen (70); W.B. Paton (77); Piccardy, Grenoble (83); P. Jahan (86); André Leconte (89); Chevojon (92); Salaun (96);Marc Lavrillier, Paris (100); Photothèque Musée de L'Homme (100); Landesbildstelle Berlin (118); Archiv Verkehrsamt der Stadt Köln (119); Jupp Falke (124); Hans Wilder, Göttingen (128); Beuroner Kunstverlag, Beuron (139); Graphokopie H· Sanders (105); St Jacob (107); Herbert Strobel (111); Kwasi Andoh (143); Dean and Chapter, Durham Cathedral (154); The British Library Reference Division (167, 168); LSE Information Office (171); Photo Reportage Ltd., London (172); B.J. Harris (183); Country Life, London (186); Bakonyi Béla (200); Tulok Ferenc (202); Hordur Vilhjalmsson, Reykjavik (203,204); UNESCO (210); The Green Studio, Dublin (218); M. Rix (228); F. Barsotti, Florence (229, 231); Publifoto, Naples (239); Marcel Schroeder, Luxembourg (262); Ammex Asociados, Mexico (267); Leiden Universiteitsbibliotheek (278); Jan E. Sajdera, Cracow (300,301); Jorge Alves (311); Antonio Passaporte: LOTY, Lisbon (313): Microfilm Unit, Library, University of Singapore (326); Editorial Patrimonio Nacional (337); Ed. Pergamino, Barcelona (339); L. Roos (346); J. Arlaud, Geneva (354); Hildegard Grubenmann-Morscher, Muttenz (356); F. Diethelm Mosen, Galgenen-Siebnen, Switzerland (357); Photoglob-Wehrli AG, Zürich (359); D. Smirnov (369,372); M. Sakalausko (392); Daniel Bartush, Troy, Michigan (394); Charles R. Collum (396); Linda Wolfe (398); University of California, Berkely (402); National Library of Medicine, Bethesda, Maryland (406); Johnson Litho Colour, Glenview, Illinois (414); Bob Wyer, Delhi, NY (416); Allen Stross (422); The Friends of The Dartmouth Library (425); Sol Goldberg (426); Geo. E. Watson (430); Bob Serating Photo, New York (442); Ezra Stoller©ESTO (444); Association of Fellows, The Pierpont Morgan Library, New York (444-446); United Nations (446); Henry E. Huntington Library and Art Gallery (454,455); Keller Color Inc., Clifton NJ (462); Alterocca (468).

Background to the entries

Arrangement of the Entries. The entries, which are arranged in alphabetical order of (a) country and (b) town, are based on a questionnaire circulated to libraries in the course of 1974. Completed entries were submitted to the libraries for their final approval during the summer of 1975.

Photograph. Wherever possible a photograph of each library has been provided. This is usually of the outside of the library but occasionally of the inside. In a few instances it has not proved possible to obtain a photograph.

Preliminary Information. Each entry begins with basic information about the library concerned, i.e. full address and telephone number.

Historical Description. The short historical passage which follows the preliminary information attempts to survey, in very general terms, the development of the library concerned. Figures of holdings are quoted wherever possible but these can sometimes only be regarded as approximations, and it must be added that it is often the largest libraries that find it most difficult to make an exact numerical assessment of their holdings. Also it must be remembered that the figures quoted relate mainly to the time of compilation, late 1974 to mid-1975, and not to the date of publication of this book.

Special Collections and Treasures. This section is intended to provide an impression of the riches of a particular library. It is not intended to be exhaustive, and for the collections and treasures of the larger libraries, such as Harvard or the Bibliothèque nationale, Paris, it cannot be other than extremely selective. To make a wine comparison, the effect might, perhaps, be compared to sampling the 'bouquet' of a fine claret, i.e. gaining the impression of depth and quality but without becoming drunk with detail.

Exhibition Areas. This brief section describes the major exhibition areas of the library, and should be of particular value to the tourist-type visitor to libraries.

Hours. Hours of opening and closing are indicated wherever possible.

Transport. Information is provided on how to reach the library by public transport and by car (when public transport is not readily available). It is assumed that in practically every case taxis are available from hotels, transport centres, etc.

Parking. Parking facilities are indicated wherever possible for those who visit the library by car.

Admission. This section briefly outlines the procedure laid down by each library for (a) the submission of a request to use its collections and (b) the rules regarding visitors, who just wish to look around the buildings and exhibition areas.

Information. Details of where general and specific information on the library concerned can be obtained.

Sales. Information is provided on where publications, postcards, reproductions, etc. can be obtained. If no sales desk exists this fact is indicated.

Guidebooks. Guides to the library are indicated in this section, with cost if applicable.

Restaurant/Snack Facilities. Details of where these can be found in, or near, the library.

Services. This section states very briefly the existence and location, where possible, of such facilities as cloakrooms, lavatories, pay telephones, etc.

Catalogues. A brief listing is provided of the major catalogues of the library.

Classification. Details of the library's classification scheme or schemes.

Copying/Photography. This section mentions the facilities available for the copying of material. Readers ought to be prepared to encounter restrictions on the copying of fragile materials, to be required to pay in advance for the provision of photocopies, and in some cases to have to sign an undertaking to respect copyright provisions. Details are provided, when supplied, of the rules governing private photography (e.g. by flash camera) within the library.

Friends of the Library. Details are provided of the organisations of 'friends' which support the work of a library. If none exists, or the information has not been provided, this section is left blank.

The above headings have been applied as far as possible to each library throughout the book for the sake of uniformity but there are a small number of instances where they are necessarily invalidated (e.g. in the USSR and China, where the use of a car is prohibited for foreign visitors).

Albania

TIRANA
Biblioteka Kombëtare (National Library) Tirana
Tel. 58-87

History. The origins of the Library date back to 16 April 1917, when it was opened in the town of Shkodra. On 10 July 1920 the Library was transferred to Tirana, with the stock growing mainly through donations. On 10 December 1922, when it was officially designated the National Library, it contained 6,000 volumes. By 1938, the total had risen to only 12,000 volumes and the collections had been housed in several locations in Tirana. After the liberation of Albania, the development of the Library was encouraged by legal deposit laws of 31 May 1948 and 2 April 1951. In 1966 the Library occupied part of the new Pallatit të Kulturës (Palace of Culture), retaining its original building for technical processes and pre-1960 foreign books. Current holdings total 697,511 items, comprising 623,117 books, 68,059 periodicals, 2,713 maps and 3,622 microfilms.

Special Collections and Treasures. The main collection is the archive on Albania, containing 42,800 items. It includes writers published outside Albania such as De Rada, Naim and Sami Frashëri, Vaso Pasha, etc., as well as native productions. The Rare Books and Manuscripts Section contains a comprehensive collection of the works of Albanian humanists, such as Marin Marleti, Beçikemi, Lek Matranga, Kostandin Kristoforidhi, etc. A particular collection is devoted to the national hero, Georges Kastrioti-Scanderbeg.

Exhibition Areas. In the Palace of Culture.

Hours. Daily 0800-2000 (summer to 2100). Closed national hols.

Transport. Buses to the Palace of Culture.

Parking. Palace of Culture car park.

Admission. *Readers* and *Visitors:* free of charge.

Information. In the Reading Room.

Sales. At the Library entrance.

Guidebooks. *Biblioteka Kombëtare* (guide in French and Albanian).

Restaurant/Snack Facilities. None.

Services. Cloakrooms, lavatories.

National Library, Palace of Culture, Tirana, Albania

Catalogues. Alphabetical and subject card catalogues. Various special catalogues.

Classification. Universal Decimal Classification.

Copying/Photography. Dry-copying and microfilming facilities available through Library staff.

Algeria

ALGIERS
Bibliothèque nationale d'Algérie
1 avenue du Dr Frantz Fanon, Alger
Tel. 63-06-32/63-10-49

History. The Bibliothèque nationale d'Algérie was founded in October 1835, the first librarian being Louis-Adrien Berbrugger (1801-69). The Library's stock grew slowly in its first years. By 1853 it had 2,100 titles and several hundred manuscripts, which were housed in several unsatisfactory locations. In 1862 the Library moved to the architecturally impressive palace of Dey Mustapha Pacha, which provided Berbrugger with 32,000 square feet of floor space. By the middle of the 20th century, however, space was at a premium. Therefore on 12 May 1958 the Library moved into its present modern building, near the top of the Tagarins Hills, southwest of the older part of the city. Holdings currently total 750,000 books, 3,000 MSS, 1,038 current periodicals, and 1,775 reels of microfilm.

Special Collections and Treasures. Collections include the Algerian Collection (the Library now possesses legal deposit privileges); the music library of the former Société des Beaux-Arts d'Alger; the Africana Collection, dealing with the history and culture of North Africa, which contains rare items of the 17th and 18th centuries; the Brazza and Gsell Collections.

Exhibition Areas. The Library possesses an exhibition hall, while the entrance hall can also be used when required.

Hours. Mon.-Sat. 0830-2030. Closed Sun. and hols.

Transport. Buses pass in front of the Library.

Parking. Available nearby.

Admission. **Readers:** To obtain a permanent reader's ticket one must produce two photographs and proof of residence (e.g. rent receipt). Tickets are renewable each January.
Visitors: Must produce proof of identity, and are granted

Bibliothèque nationale
d'Algérie

use of the Library for two weeks. Visitors are given access to the reading rooms and all Library materials, but may not borrow books.

Information. At issue and reference desks.

Sales. None.

Guidebooks. Brochure: *Bibliothèque nationale d'Algérie.*

Restaurant/Snack Facilities. Refreshment room open 0830-1230 and 1430-1800.

Services. Lavatories, smoking-room, telephones.

Catalogues. Alphabetical author and subject catalogues.

Classification. Own.

Copying/Photography. The Library has a copying service, providing photocopies and microfilms, but machines are not available for individual use. Private photography inside the Library is allowed, but those wishing to use cameras must hold a 'provisional authorisation' (which is granted to temporary readers and visitors to the Library).

Argentina

BUENOS AIRES
Biblioteca Nacional
Calle Mexico 564, Buenos Aires
Tel. 34.7370

History. In 1796 Manuel Azamor y Ramírez, Bishop of Buenos Aires, left his collection of books for the establishment of a public library in Buenos Aires. The provisions of the will were not carried out until 1810, when the *Junta Revolucionaría* authorised its establishment. Other libraries were added to it and on 16 March 1812 it was formally opened as the Biblioteca Pública de Buenos Aires. Progress was slow until the latter half of the 19th century. On 9 September 1884 the Library was renamed the Biblioteca Nacional and, under the administration of Paul Groussac, developed its bookstock from 32,000 volumes in 1885 to nearly 230,000 in 1930. Holdings in 1974 totalled 1.6 million volumes. The present National Library building was dedicated on 27 December 1901, but by the middle of the century had become overcrowded. Construction of a new building began in 1970. The new Library will be situated on the Avenida del Libertador General San Martín and completion is expected in 1977.

Biblioteca Nacional, Buenos Aires

Special Collections and Treasures. Collections include the Pedro Denegri Collection, strong in French authors; the library of Dr. Ezequiel Leguina, which includes a second edition of *Don Quixote;* and the Lynch-Gorostiaga MS Collection of 6,800 pieces. Individual treasures include Jose de Hernández, *El gaucho Martín Fierro* (1872), the first edition; A. Ortelius, *Theatrum orbis terrarum* (1570); a fourteenth century MS of Jean Buridan; and the first edition of Sarmiento's *Civilización i barbarie* (Santiago, 1845), a high point of the Library's extremely strong Río de la Plata Collection.

Exhibition Areas. Display cases in the main corridor leading to the reading rooms.

Hours. Mon.-Fri. 0700-2200. Closed Sat., Sun. and public hols.

Transport. The Library is located in the centre of the city, and hence accessible by all forms of transport.

Admission. Readers: Proof of identity is required. *Visitors:* No restrictions.

Information. Information desk in main hall.

Sales. None.

Guidebooks. None.

Restaurant/Snack Facilities. None in Library, but several cafés and restaurants in nearby streets.

Services. Cloakroom in the main hall. Washrooms next to the reading rooms. Lifts. Telephone on the ground floor.

Catalogues. Alphabetical and classified catalogues.

Classification. Brunet.

Copying/Photography. Dry-copying machines located to the left of the central corridor. Photo-duplication department on the 3rd floor. Permission must be obtained for private photography.

Friends of the Library. Association of Friends of the National Library. Small annual subscription.

LA PLATA

Biblioteca Pública de la Universidad Nacional de la Plata
Plaza Rocha No. 137, La Plata, Provincia de Buenos Aires
Tel. Secretariat 2-4109

History. The Library was founded on 19 September 1884, as the new Biblioteca Pública de Buenos Aires (the old one having been renamed the Biblioteca Nacional).

Its original stock owed much to the first Director of the Library, Dr. Francisco P. Moreno, who donated his own 2,000 volume collection on natural science, prehistory and American history. The Library grew with other donations, such as those of Ortiz de Rozas, Mayer y Curutchet, and more importantly with the purchases of the libraries of Antonió Zinny (3,700 volumes) and Nicolas Avellaneda (5,600 volumes). With the foundation of the Universidad Nacional in 1905, the Library's 36,575 volumes were transferred to the control of the University. By 1909 holdings had risen to 51,579 volumes, thanks to the donation of material from the President and Vice-President of the University. In 1938 the Biblioteca Pública moved into a new building; its stock at the end of 1973 totalled 434,495 volumes.

Special Collections and Treasures. The Library has one of the best collections of newspapers and periodicals relating to independence movements in Latin America, particularly in the Río de la Plata area, as well as the printings of the famous *Imprenta de niños expósitos de Buenos Aires.* Special collections include those mentioned above, plus those of J.V. González; Alejandro Korn (history and philosophy of Argentina); J.A. Farini (history, geography and travel); Arturo Costa Alvarez (philology and linguistics); the collection of translations of Cervantes, and the collection of 17,000 volumes on the early exploration and history of South America.

Exhibition Areas. Temporary exhibitions are housed in display cases in the entrance hall.

Hours. Mon.-Fri. 0700-2200. Sat. 0800-1300. Closed Sun. and public hols.

Transport. Easy access by public transport.

Parking. Available in neighbouring streets.

Admission. Readers: Free admission for city residents and members of the University. All users of the Library must provide evidence of identity plus photo.
Visitors: Must apply in advance to the Librarian.

Information. Information service provided by the Documentation Centre of the Library.

Sales. None.

Guidebooks. None.

Restaurant/Snack Facilities. None.

Services. Public telephone in entrance hall. Lavatories.

Catalogues. Up to 1968 author and thematic catalogues. Since 1968 author, title, and subject catalogues.

Classification. Dewey (except for medicine).

Biblioteca Pública de la Universidad Nacional de la Plata

Copying/Photography. Photocopying service provided next to Documentation Centre. Apply to the Director for private photography.

Australia

CANBERRA
National Library of Australia
Parkes Place, Canberra, ACT 2600
Tel. 62 1111

History. The Library has its origin in the Parliamentary Library and Joint Library Committee established in 1901. While primarily serving the needs of the Australian Parliament, then located in Melbourne, the Committee conceived the idea of nationwide library services once the Parliament was established in the national capital. In the period 1901-27 it laid the foundations of the present collections, adopting in 1923 the name 'Commonwealth National Library'. The Library in its present form has its genesis in the National Library Inquiry Committee established in May 1956. The Library was subsequently established under the National Library Act 1960, which came into operation on 23 March 1961. It occupies a building which was begun in May 1964 and opened in August 1968 and stands on the southern shore of Lake Burley Griffin. Current holdings total 1,439,976 volumes, 72,662 current serial titles, 5.3 million metres of moving picture films, 283,172 maps, 829,561 microforms and 3.1 million data records.

Special Collections and Treasures. Many special collections are devoted to Australasia and the Pacific area, such as the E.A. Petherick Collection comprising 10,000 volumes and 6,500 pamphlets, maps, MSS, etc., and the Sir John Ferguson and Rex de C. Nan Kivell Collections. The books collected by Gregory Matthews comprise the finest collection ever assembled on Australian ornithology. Other special collections include those of J.H.L. Cumpston on public health in Australia; E.A. Crome and Norman Ellison on the history of aviation; F.J. Riley on trade unionism; K.J. Kenafick on left-wing and anti-conscription movements; M.H. Ellis on political movements; Ian MacLaren on local history; and the Phil Whelan Collection of autographed, or annotated, copies of books by Australian authors. The Library holds a number of items relating to James Cook, the most precious being the journal, in his own hand, of the voyage of the *Endeavour,* 1768-71, during which he charted the eastern coast of Australia. The collection of Leon Kashnor has 4,775 books, 5,995 pamphlets and nearly 2,000 MSS on the political economy of Great Britain; the collection of David Nichol Smith is strong in first and early editions of writers of the Restoration

National Library of Australia, Canberra

and the 18th century; the collection of Dr. C.T. Onions comprises 4,000 works on English philology, and the library of the Clifford family of Ugbrooke Park, England, is a notable collection of a more general scope with some 10,000 books and 1,500 pamphlets.

Exhibition Areas. Major exhibitions are mounted in the mezzanine area on the first floor, and the Nan Kivell Room on the lower ground floor 1. Smaller exhibitions are mounted in the main entrance foyer, the theatre foyer on the lower ground floor 1, and the entrance foyer to the Rare Book and Manuscript Reading Room on the second floor. Exhibition areas are open Mon.-Fri. 0900-2200; Sat. Sun. and public hols., 0900-1645.

Hours. Main Reading Room Mon.-Fri. 0930-2200. Sat. and public hols. 0930-1645. Sun. 1330-1645. Books cannot be obtained from the stack on Sun. Map, Oriental Studies, Pictorial and Rare Book and Manuscript Reading Rooms Mon.-Fri. 0930-1645. Closed 25 Dec., and reading rooms are closed Good Fri. and Anzac Day (25 April).

Transport. Bus to the Library.

Parking. Available near the Library.

Admission. Readers: Free to all reading rooms. A reader's ticket is required for the Petherick Special Studies Room and the Rare Book and Manuscript Reading Room.
Visitors: Admitted free.

Information. In the main foyer and the Catalogue Bibliography Room on the ground floor.

Sales. The Print Shop in the main foyer. Greetings cards, prints, colour transparencies and the Library's publications are for sale.

Guidebooks. A brochure in English on the Library is available free.

Restaurant/Snack Facilities. A Readers' Lounge providing light refreshments is located on the fourth floor. Open Mon.-Fri. 1130-1530.

Services. Typing rooms adjacent to the Main Reading Room (ground floor) and the Petherick Special Studies Room (first floor). Cloakrooms on ground floor and lower ground floor 1. Toilets on all floors. Ramp entrance and toilet for handicapped persons. Public telephones on ground floor and fourth floor. Smoking is permitted in the Readers' Lounge.

Catalogues. Dictionary card catalogues for accessions up to 1967. Author/title and subject card catalogues for accessions from 1967 onwards.

Classification. Dewey.

Copying/Photography. No machines are available for

Captain James Cook's journal of the voyage of the Endeavour, page for 19 April 1770, in the National Library of Australia

individual use, though the Library provides a copying service through its Photographic and Reproduction Units. Readers may use their own cameras in public areas.

CANBERRA
The Library, Australian National University
PO Box 4, Canberra, ACT 2600
Tel. (062) 49.5111

History. The Library collections date back to the formation of the Canberra University College in 1929, and the foundation of the Australian National University, with its four original Research Schools, in 1946. When, in 1960, the Canberra University College became associated with the Australian National University as the University's School of General Studies, its collections, along with those of the Australian National University, formed the nucleus of the existing Library collections, which have continued to grow in a co-ordinated plan of development under a single Librarian. Holdings in July 1975 totalled 780,000 volumes, housed in two general libraries: the Advanced Studies Library in the R.G. Menzies Building, and the General Studies Library in the J.B. Chifley Building. There are also ten other libraries serving specialised subject areas. The General Studies Library is the undergraduate library for the University, though it also holds research material, mainly in language and literature.

Special Collections and Treasures. The most significant special collection is the Asian Studies Collection comprising some 120,000 volumes in Chinese and Japanese. It comprises the largest Oriental collection in an Australian university.

Exhibition Areas. The Exhibition Room is located on the ground floor of the Menzies Building. Books are displayed on a rotational basis.

Hours. Menzies Building: Term, Mon.-Fri. 0900-2200. Sat. 1000-1700. Chifley Building: Term, Mon.-Fri. 0830-2300. Sat. 1000-1800. Sun. 1000-2200. Out of term usually Mon.-Fri. 0900-1700. All libraries closed normal public hols and 25 Dec.-1 Jan. inclusive.

Transport. Bus from the Civic Centre, Canberra. On foot, a ten minute walk.

Parking. Parking is available on campus.

Admission. *Readers:* Members of the University. Non-members of the University are admitted at the discretion of the Librarian. Written application in advance is preferred.
Visitors: Must apply to the Librarian.

Information. Adjacent to the entrances of the main buildings.

Sales. None.

Guidebooks. Guidebooks in English are available free.

Restaurant/Snack Facilities. None.

Services. Lifts, lavatories, smoking areas, typing rooms. Carrels with lockable cupboards. Public telephones are installed in the cloakroom of the Chifley Building, and telephones for calls within the University are provided on the stair landings on the first and second floors.

Catalogues. Divided author-title and subject catalogues.

Classification. Library of Congress.

Copying/Photography. Copying machines are strategically placed throughout the Library buildings. In the Chifley Building coin-operated machines are on the first floor. There are no restrictions on private photography of open areas.

SYDNEY

State Library of New South Wales
Macquarie Street, Sydney, New South Wales 2000
Tel. 221-1388

History. The State Library of New South Wales is the 'national' library of the state. It was founded in 1826 as the Australian Subscription Library and is the oldest library in Australia. It was acquired by the state in 1869 as the Free Public Library, Sydney, a name changed to the Public Library of New South Wales in 1895, when the Trustees were constituted as a body corporate. They became the Council of the Library of New South Wales, when the Library's name was changed again in 1969. The building now housing the Library was built in four stages: the Mitchell wing was occupied in 1910, the Dixson wing in 1929, the main building in 1942, and the south-east wing in 1964. The Library is a research and reference library covering the whole field of human knowledge. Its holdings now total 1,294,776 items.

Special Collections and Treasures. The special collections of the General Reference Library contain the N.M. and H.M. Richardson Collection of Bibles and the Donald MacPherson Collection of Art and Literature. The Shakespeare Tercentenary Memorial Library is the most comprehensive collection of Shakespeareana in Australia with a total of well over 3,000 volumes. The Mitchell Library of over 260,000 volumes is named after David Scott Mitchell, who bequeathed his collection in 1907. The geographical scope of the Library, housed in the Mitchell wing, covers the Australian and Pacific region. The Dixson Library, named after Sir William Dixson, is similar in scope to the Mitchell Library but smaller in

The State Library of New South Wales, Sydney

size, with just over 20,000 volumes.

Exhibition Areas. The Dixson Galleries on the first floor. Hours Mon.-Sat. 1000-1700. Sun. 1400-1800.

Hours. General Reference Library: Mon.-Sat. 1000-2200. Sun. 1400-1800. Mitchell Library: Mon.-Fri. 1000-2200. Sat. 1000-1700. Dixson Library: Mon.-Fri. 1000-1700. Closed 25 Dec., Good Friday, and until 1300 on Anzac Day (25 April).

Transport. All means of public transport provide services that pass close by the Library. (The Library stands on the corner of Macquarie Street and Shakespeare Place, adjoining Parliament House and facing the Royal Botanic Gardens.)

Parking. No special parking facilities are available.

Admission. Readers: Admission to the Library is free, but readers' tickets are required for certain departments, notably the Mitchell and Dixson Libraries, and Special Collections of the General Reference Library. The Library is strictly a reference library.
Visitors: The casual visitor is allowed to see the Reading Room of the General Reference Library, the vestibule and the galleries.

Information. Reference desk in the General Reference Library.

Sales. In the Vestibule, at the entrance to the Mitchell wing.

Guidebooks. The Library of New South Wales. Information for Readers. Free.

Restaurant/Snack Facilities. The cafeteria on the roof is open to the public. This may be reached by using the lift, accessible from the eastern corridor.

Services. Lifts, lavatories.

Catalogues. Dictionary catalogue housed in the Main Reading Room. Separate catalogues detail the Mitchell and Dixson collections which are housed in the respective libraries.

Classification. Dewey.

Copying/Photography. The Library provides its own photographic service. Dry-copying orders will be completed within 24 hours. Other orders, e.g. microfilm, within the week. There is a minimum charge of 20 cents, and payment is in advance, except in the case of a written order on letterhead from a department, firm or institution with a regular account.

SYDNEY

University of Sydney Library
Sydney, New South Wales 2006
Tel. 660 8996

History. The University of Sydney was established in 1850, the first University in Australia. The first books were acquired in 1851, and in 1885 substantial growth in the collections was made following a £30,000 gift by Thomas Fisher to the University for library purposes. In a matching gift the State Government erected the University's first separate library building, which was opened in 1909 and which was named the Fisher Library. In 1963, the library moved to a new building, and the name Fisher Library was transferred along with the collections. The University of Sydney Library now comprises the central (Fisher) library and fourteen branch libraries serving various faculties and departments. Total holdings, which are all under central bibliographical control, amounted to 1,923,433 items at 31 December 1974. The Library is the largest academic library in Australia.

Special Collections and Treasures. The Rare Book and Special Collections Library is situated on Floor 2 of the central block of Fisher Library, immediately below the main entrance hall. The Library is particularly strong in seventeenth and eighteenth century English literature and history, much of which is contained in the Macdonald Collection. The library's holdings include 36 incunabula; 37 medieval MSS; the Dalley-Scarlett and Richardson music collections, which include a number of first editions of Handel; and the W.H. and Elizabeth M. Deane Collection. Outstanding individual items are a 15th century French manuscript *Book of Hours;* a Hebrew Torah scroll of the early 13th century; and the first edition of Isaac Newton's *Principia Mathematica,* 1687, with annotations by Roger Cotes, and possibly by Newton himself.

Exhibition Areas. The Rare Book and Special Collections Library is situated on floor 2 of the central block of Fisher Library, immediately below the main entrance hall.

Hours. Lent Term: Mon.-Fri. 0800-2200, Sat. 0900-1700, Sun. 1400-1800. Trinity and Michaelmas Terms: Mon.-Fri. 0800-2300, Sat. 0900-1700, Sun. 1400-1800. May and August Vacations: Mon.-Thurs. 0900-2200, Fri. and Sat. 0900-1700, closed Sun. Long Vacation: Dec. Mon.-Fri. 0900-1700; Jan/Feb. Mon. Tues. Thurs. Sat. 0900-1700, Wed. 0900-2200. Closed: Good Friday, afternoon of 24 Dec., 25-26 Dec., afternoon of 31 Dec., and 1 Jan.

Transport. The University is approximately 2 miles south-west of the centre of Sydney. Numerous buses along George Street in the city pass the campus.

Fisher Library, University of Sydney

Parking. Private cars are generally restricted.

Admission. *Readers:* The Library is open without restriction for reference purposes. Only members of the University and certain others may borrow.
Visitors: No restrictions.

Information. In the Reference-Catalogue area on the entrance level (floor 3).

Sales. None.

Guidebooks. *Guide to the Library,* issued annually, in English. Free of charge.

Restaurant/Snack Facilities. Vending machine room, just outside the Library, open during the same hours as the Library. There are University catering facilities in nearby buildings (generally closed at weekends).

Services. Typing rooms, but no typewriters provided. Lifts. Lavatories on all floors, off the central corridor, including facilities for people in wheelchairs. Smoking permitted on open-air roof area and in small areas in the Research Library. Public telephones on Floor 3, in corridor. Lounge area equipped for listening to music through headphones.

Catalogues. Card catalogue in three parts: author, serial, and subject. The subject catalogue is supplemented by a computer-printed book-form catalogue. There is also a computer-produced catalogue for the Undergraduate Library.

Classification. Dewey.

Copying/Photography. Fisher Library 3rd floor copying area has several coin-operated machines. Each branch library has at least one coin-operated machine. Private photography only possible with the permission of the Librarian.

Friends of the Library. Friends founded in 1962, give voluntary donations of money, donate books to the Library, are invited to exhibitions and lectures, etc.

Austria

ADMONT
Stiftsbibliothek
A-8911 Admont
Tel. 03613/2312 Nebstelle 24 (extension 24)

History. The Library's history is linked to the founding

of the Monastery at Admont, which was consecrated by Archbishop Gebhard von Salzburg in 1074. Gebhard brought with him various ecclesiastical and liturgical MSS which provided the basis of the Library, although unfortunately this collection was to be ravaged, as was the Abbey, in the War of Investitures just over a decade later. The reorganisation of the Library owed much to Abbot Gottfried, who assumed office in 1137. A catalogue of the Library's holdings, drawn up in 1370, contains 320 volumes, while a second catalogue begun in 1380, but recording accessions into the 15th century, records 640 volumes. With the spread of printing in the 15th century the collections gradually increased, being housed over the Lady Chapel. Under Abbot Urban Weber (1628-59) the books were moved to a hall 111 ft. long, and then in the mid-18th century, the present rococo hall was designed by J.G. Hayberger. Declining revenues forced the Library to sell some of its major treasures in the mid-1930s, and then under the German Reich, its contents were dispersed. After World War II the Benedictines returned, and today most of the books and MSS have been recovered. Current holdings total 150,000 printed works, 1,500 MSS and 900 incunabula.

Special Collections and Treasures. Treasures include an 11th-century Italian Bible given by Archbishop Gebhard; a 13th century copy of Gratian's *Decretum,* the standard compilation on canon law; an illuminated *Evangeliarum* (Codex 511); a huge 2-volume Bible, lavishly illustrated, probably the chief example of book illustration from Salzburg in the 12th century; Abbot Irimbert's commentary on the *Book of Joshua* (Codex 17); *Liber matutinalis* (Hs. 18), which was begun by Prior Johannes and completed by the monk Udalrich; and an illuminated *Missale* by the monk Magnus.

Exhibition Areas. The Exhibition Room is on the first floor of the Monastery in the south wing.

Hours. Open daily from Easter to All Saints' Day 0800-1200, 1400-1700.

Transport. The Library is accessible by train, car and bus.

Parking. Parking is permitted at the Monastery.

Admission. Readers: Apply to the Librarian. *Visitors:* Tours are provided at a small cost.

Information. At the Library desks.

Sales. None.

Guidebooks. Die Stiftsbibliothek Admont by P.A. Krause, 7th edition, in German.

Restaurant/Snack Facilities. None.

Stiftsbibliothek, Admont

Services.   Lavatories.

Catalogues.   MS   catalogues   of   manuscripts   and incunabula. Author and subject catalogues for printed books.

Classification.   Own.

Copying/Photography.   Dry-copying machine. Apply to Library staff for private photography.

MELK
Bibliothek des Benediktinerklosters (Stiftsbibliothek)
A-3390 Melk
Tel. A 027252/2312/21

History. The Benedictine monastery and its Library were founded in 1089 by Leopold II and then in 1111 Leopold III gave the castle at Melk and extensive land holdings to the Order. In 1297 the Castle was destroyed by fire and was slowly reconstructed between 1303 and 1429 as a fortified monastery. In the 15th century the monastery gained importance through the 'Melk Reform', especially under Abbot Nikolaus von Matzen (1418-26) and Prior Petrus von Rosenheim. The influence of Melk spread over the whole of Southern Germany and lasted almost a century. The holdings of the Library increased proportionately. The monastery was again damaged by fire in 1683. The work of reconstruction pressed forward under Abbot Berthold Dietmayr (1700-39). He had the damaged buildings pulled down and in 1702 the foundation stone was laid for the present baroque building above the Danube. The Library is situated in the north wing of the building and currently contains 80,000 volumes, 2,000 MSS and 1,105 microforms.

Special Collections and Treasures. The Library contains 868 incunabula. The oldest MS dates from 840 AD, and from Melk's own scriptorium are several rarities including the *Annales Mellicenses,* c. 1123, and Boethius's *De consolatione philosophiae,* 1033.

Exhibition Areas. Treasures are displayed in cases in the main baroque hall.

Hours. Mon.-Thurs. 0700-1200, 1300-1700, Fri. 0700-1200. Closed Sat. and Sun. Prior application to the Librarian is advisable.

Transport. Westbahnstation, Melk. Taxis available from the station.

Parking. Car park in front of the entrance.

Admission.   Readers: Free of charge.
Visitors: General admission charge — Sch. 15.

The Benedictine Abbey, Melk

Information. From the Librarian.

Sales. At the entrance.

Guidebooks. General guide — Sch. 15

Restaurant/Snack Facilities. Cellar room by the entrance.

Services. Washroom, lavatories, telephone in the Reading Room.

Catalogues. Author catalogue, special catalogues for manuscripts and incunabula.

Classification. Own.

Copying/Photography. Dry-copying machine in the Monastery School. Special permission is required for private photography.

VIENNA
Österreichische Nationalbibliothek
Josefsplatz 1, A-1014 Wien
Tel. 0222/52-16-84, 52-69-41, 52-52-55

History. The origins of the Austrian National Library date back to the 14th century. Known as the Imperial Court Library until 1920, it owed much to the support of the Habsburg Emperors Frederick III (1449-93), Maximilian I (1493-1519), and Ferdinand I (1531-64). Prior to 1623 the Library was housed in the Minorite Monastery, which was totally unsuitable for housing the 10,000 books and 1,600 MSS. In 1626 it moved to the Imperial Palace and then in 1726 to the present building, with its famous baroque hall. The collections benefited in the 18th century from the acquisition of books from the Old University Library, founded in 1365, and material from monasteries dissolved in 1783. During the Revolutionary Wars Vienna was constantly under threat of capture by the French, but when in 1809 Vienna was occupied, the major treasures had already been evacuated from the Library. By the end of the 19th century the growth of the collection had slowed down, but was revived by the vigorous policy of Directors such as von Hartel and von Zeissberg. After the break-up of the Austro-Hungarian Empire in 1918 the Library became the property of the Republic of Austria, and since 1945 has been called the 'Österreichische Nationalbibliothek'. Space problems loomed large after World War II and the main possibility for extension presented itself in the form of the so-called Neue Hofburg, an immensely long, broad wing, added shortly before the turn of the century to the old Imperial Palace and built at right angles to the Ringstrasse. A large part of this wing was assigned to the National Library in 1956. Work began in 1962 and the wing housing parts of the Dept. of Printed Books was

Österreichische National-
bibliothek, main building
(1723-6)

officially opened to the public on 28 September 1966. In 1949 the Library had 3.3 million items, including 1.4 million printed books. Today holdings total nearly 5.4 million items, including 2,188,000 printed books and 301,000 MSS and autographs.

Special Collections and Treasures. Collections include those of the humanist scholar Wolfgang Lazius, acquired in 1565; the 15,000 volume Fugger Library (1655); the Library of Prince Eugene of Savoy (1738); the Oriental Collection of Joseph von Hammer Purgstall; the Fidei-commiss Library of the Austrian Imperial family (1921); part of the Library of Emperor Maximilian of Mexico (1924); and the Chinese collection of Rosthorn (1949). The Music Department is rich in autographs and finest prints of Haydn, Mozart, Beethoven, Bruckner and Strauss, while individual treasures in the Manuscript Department include the *Vienna Genesis,* an early 6th century fragment which is one of the most famous of early Christian manuscripts; the *Dagulph* or *Golden Psalter,* c.783-95, presented by Charlemagne to Pope Hadrian; the German Bible of King Wenceslaus, Prague (1401-2); *Hortulus Animae,* c.1510, by Simon Benning in the Flemish school of illumination; the Prayer Book of William IV of Bavaria, 1535, by Albert Glockendon of Nürnberg; Boccaccio's *Theseide,* c.1470, illustrated by the Maître de roi-René. The Map Collection is the most important in Central Europe. The Globe Museum is one of the largest in the world.

Exhibition Areas. Special exhibitions are held in the Prunksaal (Hall of State), Josefsplatz entrance, and there are permanent exhibitions of special collections.

Hours. Main reading room: Mon.-Fri. 0900-1945, Sat. 0900-1245 (shorter opening hours during summer). Closed: Sun, public hols. and from 1-21 Sept.

Transport. Trams: Line 52 (to Westbahnhof), Line D (to Südbahnhof), all circular routes (Lines A, AK, B, BK, D, J,T). Bus Route 2.

Parking. Short-term parking near Josefsplatz entrance. A large car park in Heldenplatz, but this is usually full.

Admission. Readers: No-one under 16 years of age may use the Library. Applicants must prove their identity (with photograph, etc.); they receive a Reader's Ticket and must observe the Library rules.
Visitors: Entry charge to permanent exhibitions, ÖS.2; to large special exhibitions in Hall of State during summer seasons, ÖS.10.

Information. At the Heldenplatz entrance.

Bible of King Wenceslaus of Bohemia (1401-2), in the Österreichische National-bibliothek

Sales. At the Josefsplatz entrance. Guides, photo-graphs, slides etc., available.

Guidebooks. Die   Österreichische   Nationalbibliothek

— *History, Resources and Functions* (in German, with short summaries in English, French and Italian, cost ÖS 25.00). *Anleitung für Benützer* (guide for users) — free of charge.

Restaurant/Snack Facilities. Next to the Main Reading Room (Heldenplatz). Open Mon.-Fri. 0900-1900.

Services. Typing rooms, cloakrooms, smoking room, telephones, all near the Main Reading Room.

Catalogues. Author and subject card catalogues. Special catalogues for individual collections.

Classification. Own.

Copying/Photography. Photographic and microfilming service. Copying machines for readers' use, in the Main Reading Room. Readers may use their cameras in the reading rooms only with special permission. A charge of ÖS 10.00 is made to those wishing to take photographs in the exhibition rooms.

VIENNA
Universitätsbibliothek Wien
Dr Karl Lueger-Ring 1, A-1010 Wien
Tel. 0043 222 42 76 11

History. The Library can trace its origins back to the foundation of the University in the 1365. It developed steadily until the 16th century, when it entered a period of decline that lasted for several centuries. By 1756 wars and neglect had reduced the Library to almost complete disarray, and such volumes as had not been destroyed or dispersed were presented to the Vienna Hofbibliothek. The new University Library was founded in 1775 and opened in 1777. The collections of the suppressed Jesuit Order, and personal gifts of the Empress Maria Theresa, made up its first stock. Until 1815 the Library received a flood of accessions from the sequestrated monasteries, the more important of which went to the Royal Library (see above, Austrian National Library). The collections moved into the present building, designed by von Ferstel, in 1884 and by 1923 they totalled over one million volumes. The Library suffered damages during both world wars. Restoration was not completed after World War II until 1951. 1964 saw further extensions and alterations to accommodate the increasing size of the collection, now totalling 1,786,317 volumes and 1,226 MSS.

Special Collections and Treasures. The Library has built up special collections relating to Austrian studies. Its 652 incunabula include Johannes Balbus, *Catholicon* (Strassburg, Rusch, 1470); Johannes Nider, *Praeceptorium divinae legis* (Cologne, Zell, 1472); Diomedes, *Ars grammatica* (Venice, Jenson, 1475); Antoninus, *Summa*

University of Vienna

theologica 1-4 (Nürnberg, Koberger, 1477-9); Petrarch, *Opera Latina* (Basle, Amerbach, 1496); Johannes Widmann, *Rechnung auf alle Kaufmannschaft* (Leipzig, Kachelofen, 1498).

Exhibition Areas. Showcases in the lobbies exhibit recent accessions and special displays.

Hours. Reading Room and Catalogue Hall: Mon.-Fri. 0900-2000, Sat. 0900-1300. Closed Sun., 2 Nov., 24-31 Dec., the week before Easter to Easter Tues., Whit. Sat. to the following Mon. week, and the whole of the month of Aug.

Transport. Trams: nos. 38, 41-44, A, B, Ak, Bk, D, T, 25. Bus Line 1.

Parking. No parking areas at the Library.

Admission. Readers: On production of suitable identification and payment of a deposit.
Visitors: No special regulations.

Information. In the Catalogue Room.

Sales. None.

Guidebooks. Die Universitätsbibliothek Wien, ed. H. Alker is available in German.

Restaurant/Snack Facilities. None in the Library, but available in the University main building.

Services. Cloakroom, tape recorder, microfilm and microcard reading machines.

Catalogues. Author catalogue in book form for works up to 1931; on cards for works from 1932 onwards. Subject card catalogue in 3 parts: (a) works published up to 1931 (b) works published 1932-1971 (c) works published since 1972.

Classification. Classed catalogue (own system).

Copying/Photography. There are 4 dry-copying machines in the main office to the right of the cloakroom. Apply to the Library staff for private photography.

VIENNA
Wiener Stadtbibliothek
Rathaus, A-1082 Wien
Tel. 0222/42800/809

History. A municipal library existed in Vienna in the 15th century, but in 1780 it was sold to the Court Library. On 29 April 1856 the Vienna Stadtbibliothek was re-founded by a decree of the Municipal Council. Its field of collecting covered Viennensia, Austriaca, and works on constitution and administration. The Library began to purchase valuable private collections and to benefit from various legacies. With the acquisition of the MS score to Beethoven's overture *Die Weihe des Hauses* came the real birth of the music collection, which now contains large numbers of autographs by the composers Franz Schubert, Johann Strauss (father and son), Hugo Wolf, Josef Lanner, and numerous Viennese composers. Today the Library with its three spheres of collections — printed matter, manuscripts, and music — ranks among the most important Austrian libraries. Current holdings total about 300,000 printed volumes, 200,000 MSS, 15,000 music MSS, and 60,000 items of printed music.

Special Collections and Treasures. Collections include printed matter relating to the Turkish sieges of Vienna (1529 and 1683); posters, periodicals and pamphlets from the year 1848; Vienna playbills and theatre literature, especially of the 19th century. The MSS collections include copious autographs in the fields of Austrian (and in particular Viennese) literary, musical, cultural and political history, particularly from the 19th century. Apart from the music holdings mentioned above (the most important Schubert and Johann Strauss collections in the world) there is hardly an Austrian composer who is not represented in the collection with an original MS.

Exhibition Areas. Eight display cases in the corridor opposite the Library entrance.

Hours. Mon.-Thur. 0900-1830, Fri. 0900-1630. Music and Manuscript collections 0900-1500. Closed Sat., Sun., and public hols. The Library also closes from 1-15 Aug; from then until 31 Aug., all collections are only accessible from 0900-1500.

Transport. Tram routes to the Rathaus: A, B, D, E$_2$, G$_2$, H$_2$, J, T, 38, 39, 41, 42, 43, 44.

Parking. In front of the Rathaus, on the Ringstrasse side, is an underground car-park.

Admission. Readers: Free admission. An identity card with photograph must be shown in order to receive a Reader's Ticket. Proof of academic work must be given to consult the Manuscript and Music collections. *Visitors:* Free admission.

Information. In the Catalogue Room (Rathaus, staircase 4, 1st floor, door 333).

Sales. None.

Guidebooks. Forthcoming.

Restaurant/Snack Facilities. None.

Reading Room of the Wiener Stadtbibliothek

Services. Lift next to staircase 4. Cloakroom in the reading room. Smoking permitted in the hall in front of the Library entrance.

Catalogues. Author, keyword and systematic catalogues.

Classification. Own, based on the Prussian classification rules.

Copying/Photography. A dry-copying and microfilming service is available. Permission must be obtained and a fee paid for private camera photography.

Belgium

ANTWERP

Museum Plantin-Moretus
Vrijdagmarkt 22, B-2000 Antwerpen
Tel. 33.06.88

History. The origin of the Museum dates back to the Plantin printing office, which was founded in 1555 and continued by the Moretus family until 20 April 1876, when it was sold to the city of Antwerp for 1.2 million francs by Edward Moretus-Plantin. It was opened to the public on 19 August 1877. The refurbished house, where Christopher Plantin conducted his trade as printer and publisher, contains thirty-three rooms. Although other museums and historical buildings have similar period rooms, this is not the case with those rooms in the Museum which are a reminder of its real purpose — the original workshop character of the old Plantin house: the printer's, the foundry, the correctors' room and the bookshop are unique. These collections and displays have been particularly emphasised in the twentieth century by Dr. Leon Voet, Director of the Museum since 1950. During World War II the artistic treasures were evacuated to the castle of Lavaux-Sainte Anne near Namur. On 2 January 1945 a flying bomb exploded near the Museum, which was not officially re-opened until 28 July 1951. The Museum is supported by the City of Antwerp and local benefactors and continues to add to its collections. The Library currently contains 30,000 volumes (20,000 printed before 1800) and 500 MSS.

Special Collections and Treasures. The archives of the Museum contain the ledgers, letters and other documents of Plantin and the Moretus family. They constitute a rich source for the history of the Plantin printing shop, and of printing in general. The Library contains most of the editions produced by Plantin and the Moretus family, a magnificent collection of Antwerp prints, a comprehensive collection of Antwerp publications, a selection of

Museum Plantin-Moretus

works by foreign typographers, and about 150 incunabula, the most precious being the only 36-line Gutenberg Bible in Belgium. The Museum also contains about 15,000 carved wooden blocks and about 3,000 copper engravings which have illustrated the works of Plantin and the Moretus family. Among the many instruments for type-casting are about 15,000 matrixes and about 5,000 punches. A major 20th-century bequest has been received from Max Horn (1882-1953), whose collection focused on finely bound French literature of the 16th-18th centuries.

Exhibition Areas. The Museum itself is, in effect, one large exhibition area.

Hours. Daily 1000-1700. Reading Room open Mon.-Fri. 1000-1600. Closed 1-2 Jan., 1 May, Ascension Day, 1-2 Nov., 25 and 26 Dec.

Transport. Trams and buses.

Parking. Blue zone disc parking available.

Admission. *Readers* and *Visitors:* Free of charge.

Information. At the Porter's Desk.

Sales. At the Porter's Desk. Various guidebooks and postcards available.

Guidebooks. Guide by L. Voet available in English, French, Dutch and Flemish — Belg. F. 10. Other books on the history and holdings of the Museum available. Visitors can hire portable tape-recorders for Belg. F. 50 each.

Restaurant/Snack Facilities. None.

Services. Lavatories.

Catalogues. Card catalogue of Old Library and reference books. Manuscripts, archives and drawings in book catalogue.

Classification. Own.

Copying/Photography. No machines in the Museum, but facilities available in the City Library and the Town Hall. Private photography only with the permission of the Curator.

Friends of the Library. (*Vereeniging der Antwerpsche Bibliophielen*). Membership Belg. F. 300 yearly. The Society was founded in 1877 by Max Rooses, the first director of the Museum, and Pieter Génard, archivist of the City of Antwerp. The Society aims at promoting the knowledge of old books, especially from and in the Low Countries. It publishes the periodical *De Gulden Passer* and membership of the Society includes a subscription to this review.

BRUSSELS
Bibliothèque royale Albert Ier/Koninklijke Bibliotheek Albert I
boulevard de l'Empereur 4, B-1000 Bruxelles/
Keizerslaan 4, B-1000 Brussel
Tel. (02) 5136180

Bibliothèque royale Albert Ier, Brussels

History. The Bibliothèque royale Albert Ier (Koninklijke Bibliotheek Albert I) is the national library of Belgium. Its origins date back to the 15th century and the Library of the Dukes of Burgundy, notably Philip the Good (1419-67). In 1559 the 'Burgundian Library' was converted into a Royal Library by Philip II, who ordered all the collections to be transferred to the Coudenberg Palace in Brussels. This Royal Library had a turbulent history until the 19th century. In 1830 Belgium became independent and, on 19 June 1837, a royal decree was issued establishing, under the name of the Bibliothèque royale (Koninklijke Bibliotheek), a national library for Belgium. This was based on the Burgundian Library, the Charles van Hulthem collection of 64,000 books and MSS, and the Public Library of the City of Brussels, comprising 100,000 volumes and 3,192 MSS. Since 1837 the Library has grown steadily, until today it has over 3 million volumes and 33,000 MSS, housed in new buildings which were formally opened in 1969 and dedicated to the memory of King Albert I.

Special Collections and Treasures. Treasures include the 'Burgundian Library', with the famous *Chroniques du Hainaut* comprising 40 miniatures in the purest style of the great Flemish school; the Breviary of Philip the Good; the *Conquests of Charlemagne* by Aubert, whose grisaille miniatures constitute one of the principal characteristics of Flemish books; and the *Belles Heures* of the Duc de Berry. Collections include the van Hulthem Collection, which is particularly rich in early editions and in works dealing with the history of Belgium, the sciences, the origin of printing and philology; the F.J. Fétis Collection of musical texts, some of them unique copies; the Count de Launoit Collection of material on Voltaire; Madame Louis Solvay's Collection of more than 1,400 rare books and MSS; and the Max Elskamp Collection.

Jacques de Guise, Annales hannoniae, translated into French by Jean Wauquelin, vol. 1 (Mons, 1448), in Bibliothèque royale Albert Ier, Brussels (MS 9242). Detail of illumination from folio 1: presentation of the manuscript to Philip the Good, Duke of Burgundy

Exhibition Areas. A permanent exhibition of MSS and printed books is maintained in the Musée de Livre (Museum van het Boek) (Book Museum). Various temporary exhibition rooms within the Library.

Hours. Reading Room: Mon.-Fri. 0900-2100, Sat. and the day before a holiday 0900-1900. Different departments in the Library open for shorter hours and some close on Sat. The Library closes on Sun., the last week in August, 1 Jan., 1 May, Ascension Day, Whit Mon., 21

July, 15 August, 1-2, 11 and 15 Nov., 25-26 Dec.

Transport. Trains to the Central Station. Numerous buses and trams.

Parking. No facilities available.

Admission. Readers: Readers must obtain a reader's card. The Library is open to every Belgian and to all foreigners resident in Belgium. Readers must be at least 21 and must prove their identity and pay an annual fee of F. 20. Provisional membership is free. The conditions of age do not apply to students but they must prove their identity. Readers' tickets are renewed every year. It is possible to obtain a permit to read, valid for one day only, at a cost of F. 5. Foreign visitors may obtain a temporary reader's card on presentation of identifying material. The admissions office is located in the Catalogue Hall and is open from 0900 to 1600 hours. *Visitors:* Free admission to the exhibitions and the Book Museum.

Information. At the main entrance (Mont des Arts-Kunstberg).

Sales. At the entrance to the Chapelle de Nassau/Nassaukapel (selling Library publications, catalogues and reproductions of documents).

Guidebooks. Readers' guide, in French and Dutch, free of charge.

Restaurant/Snack Facilities. Self-service restaurant on the upper level of the central aisle of the Library, open 1000-1645.

Services. Guided tours, audio-visual displays, lavatories, lifts, telephone, cloakroom.

Catalogues. Alphabetical catalogue of authors and titles of anonymous works. Alphabetical subject catalogue (subject headings adapted from the Library of Congress).

Classification. Own.

Copying/Photography. Automatic copier for use by readers in the General Reading Room. The Library has its own photographic service. Apply through Library staff. Readers and visitors are forbidden to take photographs inside the Library.

Friends of the Library. Les Amis de la Bibliothèque Royale Albert Iᵉʳ (Vrienden van de Koninklijke Bibliotheek Albert I). Annual subscription F. 500.

Ovid, Metamorphoses, translated by Colard Mansion (Bruges, 1484), in the Bibliothèque royale Albert Iᵉʳ, Brussels. Illumination from folio 348, verso: Glaucus greeting the sorceress, Circe

GHENT

Bibliotheek van de Rijksuniversiteit te Gent
Rozier 9, B-9000 Gent
Tel. (091) 233821/257571/257611

History. In 1817, when Ghent State University was founded by King William I of the Netherlands, the town of Ghent handed over the municipal library to the University. This foundation collection included material from various abbeys such as Saint-Bavo, Saint-Peter, and Baudeloo, and lay institutions such as the Oudburg of Ghent and the Council and States of Flanders. Pierre Lammens, Librarian from 1818 to 1836, sold his own large collection to the University in 1818, while another later Librarian, Baron F. Vander Haeghen, gave his collection of 10,000 books in 1872/3. The Library remained in the old building of Baudeloo Abbey until 1938, when it gradually transferred the collections to its present tower block, designed by Henry van de Velde, currently housing over 2 million items.

Special Collections and Treasures. Collections include the Vander Haeghen Collection (see above) of books and MSS relating to Ghent, or printed there; the Tiele-Meuleman Collection of 19,000 pamphlets relating to the history of the Low Countries 1490-1800; and the literary collections of Snellaert (acquired in 1872), of Heremans (acquired in 1884), and of de Bast-Armelini (acquired in 1908). The Library's holdings of Dutch literary works of the 16th-18th centuries are particularly strong. Treasures include the 26 MSS of the abbey of Saint Maximin at Trier and many of the MSS of the abbey of Saint-Bavo, written and decorated for Abbot Raphael de Marcatellis, natural son of Philip the Good.

Exhibition Areas. 20 exhibition show cases are located at the entrance to the Library.

Hours. 1 Oct.-15 May: Mon.-Fri. 0900-2100. 15 May-14 July and 16 Sept.-1 Oct.: Mon.-Fri. 0900-1900. 15 July-15 Sept.: Mon.-Fri. 0830-1330. Closed Sat., Sun., 1 Jan., East. Mon., 1 May, Ascension Day, Whit Mon., 21 July, 15 Aug., 1-2, 11, 15, Nov., 25-26 Dec.

Transport. Tramway 4, or buses 9 and 5 from the railway station.

Parking. Parking in St. Pietersplein.

Admission. Readers and *Visitors:* Anyone over 18 may use the Library free of charge but enrollment is necessary to borrow books.

Information. At the Lending Desk.

Sales. Postcards and catalogues of bookbindings, Erasmiana and treasures of the Library are sold at the Entrance Desk.

Library of Ghent State University

Guidebooks. A free guidebook in Dutch is available.

Restaurant/Snack Facilities. None.

Services. Cloakroom and lavatories at the entrance.

Catalogues. An alphabetical catalogue of authors and anonymous books; a systematic UDC catalogue; published catalogues of periodicals, journals, geographic maps and manuscripts.

Classification. Own.

Copying/Photography. Copying machines are at the Library entrance. Microfilms, microfiches, photographs and photostats are provided upon written demand. Permission must be obtain in advance for private photography.

LIÈGE
Bibliothèque générale de l'Université de Liège
place Cockerill 1, B-400 Liège
Tel. (04) 420080, extension 206

History. The University of Liège was founded in 1817. The University Library's collections were based on the library of the city of Liège, totalling 7,000 volumes, and several local religious libraries. A gift from William I of books, MSS, etc., plus a special acquisition grant of 18,000 guilders, enabled the Library to enrich its basic stock. In 1818 the Library moved into a wing of the former Jesuit college, where University teaching had just begun. By 1840 the collections totalled 62,000 volumes and 400 MSS. Rapidly growing stock, and inadequate accommodation in the General Library, partly accounts for the development in the early 20th century of separate Law and Arts Libraries. The General Library vacated its old Jesuit college quarters in 1932, eventually to return to them, suitably modernised, in 1949. Current holdings of the General Library include 1.5 million volumes, 4,000 MSS and 560 incunabula. A rationalisation of the total University book stock is taking place to coincide with the continuing move of the University to Sart Tilman, an area close to the city, and to this end a University Library annex was officially opened at Sart Tilman on 14 October 1965.

Special Collections and Treasures. The main special collection is on material relating to the history of Liège (*Leodensia*). Another important separate collection is the Léon Graulich Library, founded in 1921 by a group of lawyers. Treasures include the following MSS: the 12th-century *Evangéliaire d'Averbode;* a 15th-century Book of Hours; and the 15th-century *Tacuinum Sanitatis.*

Exhibition Areas. None cited.

Bibliothèque générale de l'Université de Liège, Loan Department

Hours. Reading Rooms: Mon.-Fri. 0900-2200, Sat. 0900-1700. Closed Sun. and public hols.

Transport. Bus Routes 1 and 4: From Gare des Guillemins to Pont d'Avroy, plus 5 minutes' walk. Bus Route 20: From Gare des Guillemins to place Cathédrale, plus 4 minutes' walk.

Parking. Route: Guillemins — rue des Guillemins — parc d'Avroy — place Cathédrale — rue Charles Magnette. Parking in place du 20-Août, place Cockerill, or quai sur Meuse.

Admission. Readers: Apply to the Secretary of the Library between 0900-1200, with a passport-type photograph. Anyone may borrow books, but a refundable deposit of F. 200 is required.
Visitors: May not borrow books. Free access to the reading rooms.

Information. In the lending department and in the Secretary's office.

Sales. None.

Guidebooks. Readers' guides, in French, are available free from the Secretary's office.

Restaurant/Snack Facilities. A cafeteria on the first floor open 1030-1730 during term, 1000-1400 during holidays.

Services. Cloakroom on the ground floor of the Philosophy and Letters building, next to the Library. Toilets and smoking room at the cafeteria.

Catalogues. Alphabetical catalogue on slips up to 1969, computer produced lists since that date. Various other catalogues, e.g. MSS, theses, periodicals.

Classification. Own.

Copying/Photography. One photocopier for individual use on the landing of the first reading room. Three self-service photocopiers in the lending department. Two more photocopiers are available in the Secretary's office.

LOUVAIN
Bibliothèque centrale de l'Université catholique de Louvain Mgr Ladeuzeplein 21 (Postal address: Blijde Inkomststraat 1), B-3000 Louvain Tel. (016) 222311/231235

History. The University of Louvain was founded in 1425 by Pope Martin V at the request of John IV, Duke of Brabant. For more than two centuries the University was without a general library. The University Library owes its

Université catholique de Louvain, Bibliothèque des Sciences exactes, Louvain-la-Neuve

origin to a former Louvain student, Laurent Beyerlinck, canon of the Cathedral of Antwerp. In 1627 he bequeathed to the University his library of 852 volumes, rich in history and theology. In 1635 it was followed by a legacy of 906 volumes from the Professor of Medicine, Jacques Romanus. The University Library publicly opened on 22 August 1636, with Professor Valerius Andreas, an historian, as first Librarian. The initial stock totalled 1,700 volumes installed in the Old Clothmakers' Hall in the Faculty of Medicine. The death of Andreas in 1655 ushered in a period of decline which lasted until the 18th century. The subsequent steady growth of the Library has been punctuated by several severe setbacks. In 1795 and 1797, under the French régime, 5,718 volumes were removed. The Library was destroyed by fire in August 1914. It was restocked and rebuilt only to be destroyed again in May 1940 during World War II. By 1970 the stock had been rebuilt to 1.5 million volumes, when the University split into Dutch- and French-speaking parts (see next entry). It is intended that the 'French' Central Library will move to Louvain-la-Neuve in the middle 1970s to join the Bibliothèque des Sciences Exactes, which is already there. Holdings currently include 1.5 million books, 220 MSS, and 156,000 microforms.

Special Collections and Treasures. The Library has 98 incunabula, several printed in Louvain, and the oldest printed in Venice, 1472. MSS include a 15th-century *Hore beate Virginis Marie.* Collections include microfilms of MSS of Mount Sinai and Mount Athos, and the *Filmothèque Paternostre de la Mairieu.*

Exhibition Areas. The exhibition of incunabula, MSS and rare items can be visited (Local 00.28) on request.

Hours. Mon.-Fri. 0830-2130, Sat. 0830-1730. Closed Sun., 1 Jan., 2 Feb., the afternoons of the last three days of Holy Week, Easter Mon., 1 May, Ascension Day, Whit Monday, 21 July, 15 Aug., Mon.-Wed. following 1st Sun. in Sept., 1 and 11 Nov., 25 and 26 Dec.

Transport. All forms of public transport serve the Library.

Parking. There are adequate parking facilities.

Admission. Readers: Access to the Library is reserved for members of the University. However, visiting researchers can obtain a Reader's card for a limited period without charge.
Visitors: Apply to the Librarian in advance.

Information. At Library staff desk.

Sales. None.

Guidebooks. Pour le Lecteur, a guide to the Library in French.

Hore beate Virginis Marie, attributed to Thomas Louth (15th century) in the Bibliothèque centrale de l'Université catholique de Louvain

Restaurant/Snack Facilities.   None.

Services.   Cloakroom and lavatories.

Catalogues.   Author, title and classified card catalogues. Separate catalogues for periodicals and theses (cards and listings).

Classification.   Own, particularly running number.

Copying/Photography.   Copying machines are available in the Reading Room, the Periodical Room, and the Bibliography Room. Readers may use their own cameras only with prior permission.

LOUVAIN
*Katholieke Universiteit te Leuven, Bibliotheekcentrale
Mgr Ladeuzeplein 21, B-3000 Leuven
Tel. (016) 238678*

History.   See above entry for Bibliothèque centrale de l'Université catholique de Louvain. Holdings of this Library serving the Dutch-speaking University currently total 800,000 volumes in the Central Library. (The University Library is formed out of a central library and departmental libraries scattered over three campuses. Total of all these libraries is 1 million volumes).

Special Collections and Treasures.   Many of the treasures were lost in the fires of 1914 and 1940. Those that remain are not yet available for detailed listing, because of the problems caused by the division of the University Library.

Exhibition Areas.   The Museum of Flemish Students Folklore (3rd floor).

Hours.   Main Reading Room: Mon.-Fri. 0830-2130, Sat. 0830-1730. Closed Sun., 2, 11 Nov., 25 - 26 Dec., 2 Feb., the afternoons of the last three days of Holy Week, Easter Mon., 1 May, Whit Mon., 21 July, and Mon., Tues. and Wed. following the first Sun. in Sept.

Transport.   The Library is in the centre of Louvain, and is accessible by bus or on foot from the railway station.

Parking.   In the neighbouring streets.

Admission.   Readers: Registration in Library. Free.
Visitors: Must obtain the Chief Librarian's permission (through the Sub-Librarian).

Information.   Inquiries should be made to members of staff.

Sales.   None.

Katholieke Universiteit te Leuven

Guidebooks. Guidebooks in Dutch and in English (forthcoming). Free of charge.

Restaurant/Snack Facilities. None.

Services. Cloakroom, lavatories, microform reading room, lifts.

Catalogues. Author, alphabetical subject, and foreign dissertation catalogues. File of corporate bodies and serial titles. Catalogue Hall is located on the first floor.

Classification. Own.

Copying/Photography. Coin-operated copying machines for individual use are in the main reading room and the periodicals room. Those wishing to use private cameras should apply to the Chief Librarian (via the Sub-Librarian).

MORLANWELZ-MARIEMONT
Bibliothèque du Musée royal de Mariemont
chaussée de Mariemont, 100
B-6510, Morlanwelz-Mariemont
Tel. (064) 221243; (064) 226563

History. The Mariemont Museum and Library were left in 1917 to the Belgian nation by Raoul Warocqué, a great patron of the Hainaut province. Warocqué (1870-1917) began collecting, at 16, rare editions of Greek and Latin texts. The subsequent development of his Library owed much to the advice of his friends Franz Cumont and George van der Meylen, particularly the latter, who imposed on Warocqué's collection its character of *haute bibliophilie.* Between 1895 and 1914 Warocqué purchased a superb collection of rare books and precious bindings, dating from the end of the 15th to the beginning of the 20th century. In 1910 he commissioned a new wing to the chateau of Mariemont to house his collection. This was completed in 1913. After Warocqué's death in 1917 the collections were completed by the Curators of the Royal Museum of Mariemont. The chateau was destroyed by fire on 25 December 1960 but a new museum — comprising the library — was built in 1968. Nevertheless the Library did not occupy its present new buildings until February 1972. Collections now total 70,000 volumes, 400 periodicals and 5,000 autographs.

Special Collections and Treasures. The *Fonds précieux* totals 15,000 volumes and includes Justinian, *Instutiones* (Mainz, Schoeffer, 1468); F. Villon, *Les oeuvres de maistre Francoys Villon* (Paris, 1532); *Missale romanum ex decreto sacrosancti Concilii Tridentini restitutum* (Antwerp, Christopher Plantin, 1571), one of the 10 copies printed on vellum; Victor Hugo, *L'Art d'être grand-père* (Paris, 1877), one of the 20 copies printed on 'papier de Chine'; various superb bindings on such works

Musée royal de Mariemont

as Procopius, *De bello persico* (Rome, 1509) and Justus Lipsius, *Opera omnia* (Antwerp, 1637). Collections have been developed on works of Victor Hugo, Anatole France, Beethoven, Bach, Schumann, Saint-Beuve, Baudelaire and bindings signed by J. Weckesser and Ch. de Samblanx, apart from collections developed in the Library's main areas, i.e. history, history of art, archaeology, history of the book, classical philology and the history of Hainaut.

Exhibition Areas. The 'Réserve précieuse' and the galleries surrounding it.

Hours. Mon.-Sat. 1000-1230, 1330-1800. Closed Sun. and holidays.

Transport. Rail: From Brussels lines 108 and 122 (direct, or changing at Haine-Saint-Pierre). From Charleroi line 112. From Mons line 118 to La Louvière, then line 112 or tram (nos. 30, 31, 80, 82 — stop at La Hestre-Écoles).

Parking. Parking spaces opposite the main entrance to the park.

Admission. Readers: Must obtain an admission card. This is available free to any Belgian, or to any foreign reader, who has proof of identity.
Visitors: Free of charge.

Information. The Museum's information service also covers the Library.

Sales. The Museum has a sales department. Catalogues and postcards are available.

Guidebooks. A reader's guide in French, free of charge.

Restaurant/Snack Facilities. Readers may use the Museum's cafeteria, open 1000-1230, 1330-1800.

Services. Cloakrooms, lavatories, lifts, smoking lounges, telephones.

Catalogues. Alphabetical author catalogue. Subject catalogue since 1971. Catalogues are located at the entrance to the Reading Room.

Classification. In the Reading Room, books are shelved according to subject. Reserve books according to accession number and size.

Binding from the workshop of Claude de Picques executed by Thomas Mahieu (c. 1545) on Procopius, De bello persico (Rome, 1509), in the Bibliothèque du Musée royal de Mariemont

Copying/Photography. Library staff fulfil readers' copying orders. Readers may not use cameras inside the Library.

Friends of the Library. Amis de Mariemont: an association common to the Museum and the Library. Minimum annual subscription Belg.F. 200.

Brazil

RIO DE JANEIRO
Biblioteca Nacional
Av. Rio Branco, 219-31-ZC-21, Rio de Janeiro GB
Tel. 222-6199 or 232-0520

History. The National Library of Brazil has its origin in the volumes which the Portuguese Prince Regent, later João VI, brought to Rio de Janeiro after fleeing from Lisbon in 1807. The 60,000 volumes were installed initially in the Hospital da Ordem Terceira do Carmo which was opened in 1810 to scholars, and then in 1814 to all students. When, in 1821, João returned to Portugal, the Royal Library remained in Rio, only the *Manuscritos da Coroa,* which had never been part of the Royal Library, or accessible to the public, being removed. In 1847 legal deposit privileges were obtained. From 1853 to 1870, the Library was housed in the Casa do Largo de Lala, where for the first time reading room space was provided. In 1910 the Library moved into its present building, which, though re-equipped and refurnished from 1948-50, is now badly overcrowded. By 1895 the collections totalled 231,132 volumes, by 1930 500,000 volumes, by 1956 1.5 million volumes, and current holdings include 1.8 million volumes, 600,000 MSS and 20,000 periodicals.

Special Collections and Treasures. Collections include the library of José Bonifácio de Andrada e Silva, given in 1838 by his heirs and rich in scientific material; that of the noted Argentinian bibliophile Don Pedro de Angelis with 2,700 volumes and 1,300 MSS, principally related to the history of the Rio de la Plata; those of the bibliophiles Manuel Ferreira Lagos and João Antonio Marques; and 48,236 volumes from the private library of the ex-Emperor Pedro II (1891) forming the so-called *Coleção D. Thereza Christina Maria.* In 1911 Dr. Júlio Benedito Otoni bought the private library of José Carlos Rodrigues and donated it to the National Library. In the MSS section the Alexandre Rodrigues Ferreira and Freire Alemão Collections relate to botany, while other collections include the Archives of the Casa dos Contos, material related to history of Minas Gerais; the Rio Branco Collection; and the Arquivo de Mateus Collection relating to São Paulo. Treasures include letters of notable Jesuits of the colonial period such as Anchieta and Manuel da Nobrega; the 1462 Latin Bible of Fust and Schoeffer; Xisto Figueira, *Arte d'rezar as horas canonicas* (Salamanca, 1521); João de Barros, *Grammatica da lingua portuguesa* (Lisbon, 1539), a unique copy; Luis de Camões, *Os lusiades* (Lisbon, 1572), first edition; Pedro Magalhaes de Gândavo, *Historia da provincia sacta Cruz* (Lisbon, 1576), the first Brazilian chronicler; and José da Silva, *Guerras do Alecrim e*

Biblioteca Nacional, Rio de Janeiro

Mangerona (Lisbon, 1737), believed to be the only example known.

Exhibition Areas. Main Hall: selected exhibitions. Display cases in the various sections, such as Manuscripts and Music Departments.

Hours. General Reading Room: Tues.-Fri. 1000-2100, Sat. 1200-1800. Closed Sun. and Mon. and public hols.

Transport. By bus or taxi. The Library is located on one of the main thoroughfares of Rio de Janeiro.

Parking. No parking facilities at the Library but available is nearby streets.

Admission. Readers: Readers need not register but must produce some form of identification.
Visitors: Should make application to the administration in advance. Tours for groups can be arranged.

Information. In the General Reading Room and special sections.

Sales. In the publications sales room, where editions of the *Instituto Nacional do Livro* and of the *Biblioteca Nacional* can be purchased.

Guidebooks. Information brochure, in Portuguese, available free.

Restaurant/Snack Facilities. None.

Services. Cloakrooms, lavatories and lifts.

Catalogues. Dictionary catalogues in both the General Reading Room and the special sections.

Classification. Dewey (for the main holdings of the General Reading Room).

Copying/Photography. Microfilm and copying facilities are provided by the Library but there are no machines for individual use. Permission must be obtained for private photography.

SÃO PAULO
Biblioteca Municipal Mário de Andrade
Rua da Consolação, No. 94 (Caixa Postal No. 8170),
São Paulo
Tel. PBX 36.7126-9 (Director: 34.7880)

History. The Library has its origins in the Biblioteca da Secretaría da Camara, founded on 17 October 1907. In 1925 the then Prefeito (Mayor), Firminiano Pinto, authorised the opening of the Library to the public. Its initial stock of 15,000 volumes was significantly increased in 1937 by the addition of the State Library's collection of 40,000 volumes. The Library moved to its present tower building in the centre of the city on 25 January 1942. Its collections then totalled 120,000 volumes, with the stack tower housing the bulk of the volumes. After financial cutbacks in the 1950s and the early 1960s, the Library's collection has again expanded to the present total of 911,260 volumes in the Central Library and 192,520 in the twelve branch libraries.

Special Collections and Treasures. Special collections include the Carvalho Franco Collection; the Felix Pacheco Collection of Brasiliana; the Pereira Mattos Collection; and those devoted to ONU and UNESCO publications. MSS include those of Pedro I, Feijoo, Machado de Assis and Conçalves Crespo. Books include Claude d'Abbeville, *Histoire de la mission des pères capucins en l'isle de Maragnan* (Paris, 1614); Richard Hakluyt, *The Principal Navigations* (London, 1598-1600); Damião de Gois, *Chronica de felicissimo rei Dom Emanuel* (Lisbon, 1566-67); Abraham Ortelius, *Épitomé du théatre du monde* (Antwerp, 1588); Marc Lescarbot, *Histoire de la Nouvelle France* (Paris, 1609); Sebastião da Rocha Pita, *Historia da America Portugueza* (Lisbon, 1730); and Charles Brockwell, *The Natural and Political History of Portugal* (London, 1726).

Exhibition Areas. Located in the entrance hall of the Library.

Hours. Mon.-Fri. 0800-2400, Sat. and Sun. 0900-1800. Closed public hols.

Transport. By bus.

Parking. No parking facilities at the Library itself, but they are available nearby.

Admission. Readers and Visitors: The Library is open, free of charge, to all.

Information. On the first floor.

Sales. None.

Guidebooks. None.

Restaurant/Snack Facilities. None on the premises, but restaurants, cafeterias nearby.

Services. Lavatories and telephones on first floor, lifts.

Catalogues. Author and subject catalogues.

Classification. Dewey.

Copying/Photography. Photocopies, microfilm and mimeograph facilities available. Prior permission must be sought for private photography.

Biblioteca Municipal Mário de Andrade, São Paulo

Bulgaria

SOFIA

Cyril and Methodius National Library
Blvd Tolbuhin II, Sofia
Tel. 88-28-11

History. The Bulgarian National Library was founded on 10 December 1878 immediately after the liberation of the country from the Turks. The initial stock came, for the most part, in the form of gifts from Bulgarian patriots and from Russian friends of Bulgaria. This initial enthusiasm soon waned, however, and it was only through a copyright law of 1897 that the collections continued to grow in the early 20th century. During World War II the Library building was entirely destroyed, with only 200,000 books surviving. A new building was opened on 16 December 1953 and today it houses 2,833,179 units (of which just over 1 million are books and periodicals). At present the National Library is the largest scientific public library in Bulgaria, a national repository and the archive of Bulgarian literature. At the same time it is the national centre for bibliography and methodical guidance of the country's libraries. Since 1953 it has also been functioning as a research institute in the fields of library science, bibliography, bibliology, archival science and paleography, and it publishes a considerable number of materials in these fields.

Special Collections and Treasures. The more important special collections of the Library were started at its very foundation and have since been extended. They include Old Slavonic and Old Bulgarian MSS and books; archival documents connected with the Bulgarian Renaissance; Ottoman and Turkish documents; Persian and Arabic MSS; maps; portraits; photographs; prints and music.

Exhibition Areas. There are no special exhibition rooms due to an overall shortage of space in the Library.

Hours. Mon.-Fri. 0800-2100, Sat. 0800-1900, Sun. 0800-1300. Closed: 1 Jan., 1-2 May, 9-10 Sept., 7 Nov.

Transport. Trams: nos. 4 and 10. Trolley-buses: nos. 1 and 4.

Parking. Limited facilities.

Admission. *Readers:* Readers must be at least 18 years old and engaged in serious research. A reader's card may be obtained for a small charge, and this entitles the holder to use the Library. Registration takes place on the ground floor at the Library entrance.
Visitors: The Library is open to any visitors, individually or in groups, and there is no charge.

Cyril and Methodius National Library, Sofia

Information. At the general information desk in the Catalogue Hall. There are also information desks in the specialised reading rooms.

Sales. The Library's publications are available from the Publishing Department on the ground floor.

Guidebooks. A guidebook in English is available.

Restaurant/Snack Facilities. There is a snack-bar in the basement of the Library.

Services. Lavatories on each floor, cloakroom on the ground floor, typing in carrells on the first floor, smoking areas on each floor, and several lifts. There is a telephone booth at the Library entrance.

Catalogues. Alphabetical, systematic, subject, and union catalogues.

Classification. The Library uses a classification which is based on the scheme used in the Lenin Library in Moscow.

Copying/Photography. There is a copying service which can supply xerographic copies, photostats and micro-films. Apply to Library staff for private photography.

Friends of the Library. The Society of the Friends of the Cyril and Methodius National Library. Members are, for example, scientists, research workers, writers, fellows of the Bulgarian Academy of Sciences. No subscriptions are paid.

SOFIA

Central Library, Bulgarian Academy of Sciences
1,7 Noemvri, Sofia
Tel. 87-77-31

History. The Library was founded in 1869 in the town of Brăila, as the library of the Bulgarian Literary Society. It moved to Sofia in 1879, and in 1911 was renamed the Library of the Bulgarian Academy of Sciences. From September 1944 onwards the Academy of Sciences was entrusted with an overall scientific research function, and the Library was remodelled on the Library of the Academy of Sciences of the USSR. Substantial acquisitions were made under the 1946 legal deposit law, while at the same time special funds were allocated to the Central Library for the purchase of basic foreign literature, particularly in the sciences and social sciences. The Library now has holdings of 738,637 books and 295,314 periodicals.

Special Collections and Treasures. The archives of the Bulgarian Academy of Sciences are stored in the Central Library and contain highly important documents on the

Central Library, Bulgarian Academy of Sciences, Sofia

history of Bulgarian civilisation, such as a 10th century parchment, the 13th century *Triodion* from Bitola (Monastir), and the *Song-book of Ivan Alexander,* dating from 1337.

Exhibition Areas. A permanent exhibition room displays new acquisitions of the Library.

Hours. Mon.-Fri. 0800-2000. Closed Sat., Sun., and public hols.

Transport. Trams: 4 and 10. Trolley buses: 1, 2 and 4. Buses: 4, 80, 209, 106, 84, 9, 242, 75, 94, 200.

Parking. In front of the Library.

Admission. *Readers:* Academy, University and Research Institute staff, and University students working on theses are admitted to use the Library.
Visitors: No admission without permission from the Director.

Information. In the entrance hall.

Sales. None.

Guidebooks. None.

Restaurant/Snack Facilities. Snacks available 0830-1600.

Services. Cloakroom, lavatory and smoking room (adjacent to the Reading Room).

Catalogues. Alphabetical and classified catalogues of books. Catalogue of periodicals.

Classification. Own.

Copying/Photography. There is a copying service using Rank-Xerox 720 and 1360 machines. Microfilms can be provided. The Director's permission must be obtained for private photography.

Canada

HAMILTON
McMaster University Library
McMaster University, Hamilton, Ontario L8S 4L6
Tel. 416-525-9140, extension 4781

History. McMaster University and its Library were established in 1887. The University was named after Senator William McMaster, who had come to Canada in 1833 from Northern Ireland at the age of 21. A devout

McMaster University Library, Mills Memorial Building

Baptist, he was keenly interested in the development of education under religious auspices. He founded Toronto Baptist College and left his fortune to Woodstock College, institutions which united in 1887, the year of his death, to form McMaster University. In 1926 Woodstock College was discontinued for economic reasons and in 1930 the University moved from Toronto to Hamilton. The Library was located in the new University Hall, using two floors, one a reading-room and the other a stack area. In 1951 the Library occupied its own building, Mills Memorial Library, and since that time extensions have more than tripled the available space. In addition to this General Arts Library, the Science and Engineering Library is situated in the Physical Sciences Building, and the Health Sciences Library serves the large Health Sciences and Medical Centre complex. Current holdings total 3,028,000 units, including 750,000 books, 891,000 microforms and 1,260,000 archival items.

Special Collections and Treasures. The most important single collection is the Bertrand Russell Archive. Among the Library's rare books and incunabula there are fine copies of the 1493 Koberger *Nuremberg Chronicle* and the 1496 Basle *Opera Latina* of Petrarch, edited by Sebastian Brandt. Manuscripts include an 11th-century Boethius *De consolatione philosophiae,* an 1150 Psalter and a 1557 Book of Hours from Tours. The Barry Brown Collection is the most valuable part of a collection of 18th-century literature which contains over 20,000 items. The Library has the papers of a number of modern authors such as Vera Brittain, Sir George Catlin, Pierre Berton, Margaret Laurence and Farley Mowat, and a number of collections of first editions of such well-known authors as Samuel Beckett, Charles Dickens and D.H. Lawrence. There is also a large collection of original and ephemeral materials from Canadian radical and underground groups active in the 1960s. The Map Collection of 80,000 items includes 400 rare 18th-century Canadian maps. The Canadian Baptist Archives form one of the most important collections of church history in Canada.

Exhibition Areas. In the Russell Archive, and in Special Collections, both located on the third floor.

Hours. 0800-2400 daily. Closed 25 Dec., 1 Jan., Victoria Day, Dominion Day, Labour Day.

Transport. The city bus stops at the Library.

Parking. Available for a nominal charge.

Admission. Readers and *Visitors:* The Library is open, free of charge, to all responsible adults.

Information. Desk in Reference Reading Room, to the right of the main entrance. General information available from the attendant at the front door.

Bertrand Russell, MS of radio broadcast, 'What I believe' (1947), in McMaster University Library

Sales. Books and other materials published by the Library Press available through the University Book Store, or the office of the University Librarian.

Guidebooks. Guides in English are available free in the Library.

Restaurant/Snack Facilities. Coffee and cold drink machines in the student lounge in the sub-basement.

Services. Coin-op. typewriters, lavatories, lifts, smoking lounge in sub-basement, pay telephones in basement and sub-basement, wheel-chair entry for the handicapped, music room with sound recordings and players.

Catalogues. Divided card catalogue (author/title and subject). Computer circulation list.

Classification. Library of Congress.

Copying/Photography. Coin-op. machines: 4 in Mills Memorial, 1 in Science and Engineering, 1 in Health Sciences. Permission must be sought for private photography.

MONTREAL
Bibliothèque nationale du Québec
1700 rue Saint-Denis, Montréal, Québec H2X 3K6
Tel. 873-4553

History. The Library's origins date back to the middle of the 19th century when l'Oeuvre des Bons Livres was founded in 1844 by the Sulpicians. In 1860 it was suceeded by the parish library of Notre-Dame, which in turn, in 1884, was absorbed by the Cercle Ville-Marie. With the collections requiring more and more space the Bibliothèque Saint-Sulpice was built in 1912 at 340 (later 1700) rue Saint-Denis. In 1961 the Government of Québec created a Ministry of Cultural Affairs, to which the Library was attached, and then re-named in 1967 as the Bibliothèque nationale du Québec. Holdings currently total 260,000 volumes of books and manuscripts, 9,000 microfilms and 6,000 periodicals.

Special Collections and Treasures. Apart from the collections on the Québec area, the most significant collection is perhaps the Cinematographic Documentary Collection, which includes some 10,000 volumes and 110,000 cards.

Exhibition Areas. Exhibitions of books and manuscripts are held in the Main Reading Room.

Hours. Usual timetable: Tues.-Fri. 0900-2100, Sat. 0900-1700. Closed Sun. and Mon. Summer timetable: Mon.-Fri. 0900-1700. Closed Sat. and Sun.

Bibliothèque nationale du Québec

Transport. The Library is close to a métro junction. Buses are available.

Parking. In neighbouring streets.

Admission. *Readers:* Must be at least 16 years old. Free admission. A reader's ticket issued at the entrance.
Visitors: Visitors may be shown round by a member of the Library. Group visits can be arranged on request.

Information. From the superintendent's office at the entrance. A reader's information service in the work room.

Sales. The Library's publications are either sold or provided free of charge.

Guidebooks. A reader's guide is available free on request.

Restaurant/Snack Facilities. No restaurant or snack-bar on the premises, but several in the vicinity of the Library.

Services. Cloakroom, lavatories, smoking lounge, telephone, on the level of the main reading room and on the ground floor.

Catalogues. Author and subject catalogues.

Classification. Dewey and Library of Congress.

Copying/Photography. Photocopying and microfilming machines. Requests to be made via the reading room staff. Cameras may be used inside the Library, but readers must not be disturbed.

MONTREAL
McGill University Libraries
c/o The Director of Libraries, 3459 McTavish Street,
Montreal, Quebec H3A 1Y1
Tel. (514) 392-4953

History. McGill College was founded under Royal Charter in 1821. In 1823 the first library developed as the Medical Library, organised by the Montreal Medical Institution, which later became part of the College. In 1855 a book budget was created to purchase a number of items on science and literature. By 1893 the collection had grown to 37,000 volumes and occupied its first permanent building, the Redpath Library, donated to the University by Peter Redpath. The continuing expansion of the library stock, however, necessitated extensions to the stack area, both in 1900 and again in 1922. By 1953 major construction was required and a large wing was added south of the central library complex. Continued growth led to the planning of the McLennan Library in 1962. It was formally opened on 21 January 1969, being

McLennan Library, McGill University

named after a generous benefactor to the University, Miss Isabella C. McLennan. The *raison d'être* of the McLennan was that it should serve the research needs of the humanities and social sciences, while the modernised Redpath building would meet the needs of the undergraduates. In 1973, the University's 22 libraries were organised by subject into five broad areas (Humanities-Social Sciences, Law, Life Sciences, Physical Sciences-Engineering and Undergraduate) in order to facilitate and coordinate future development. Current holdings total some 3,075,000 items.

Special Collections and Treasures. Collections include the William Osler Library and manuscripts on the history of medicine; the Dr. Casey Wood Collection of ophthalmology; the Lyman Collection of entomological publications; the Wainwright Collection of French legal history; the John Humphrey Human Rights Collection; the Air and Space Law Collection; the Ivanow Collection of Persian MSS; the Lande Collection of Canadiana; the Gurney Collection on crustacea; 5,000 letters from naturalists of the late 19th and early 20th centuries; and over 5,000 original drawings, mostly of birds. In addition the Rare Book Dept. in McLennan has a number of distinguished special collections of books, prints, maps and MSS.

Exhibition Areas. No specifically designated exhibition areas.

Hours. Main Library: Service — Mon.-Fri. 0900-2145, Sat. 0900-1645; Study — Mon.-Sat. 0830-2300, Sun. 1000-2300. Summer hours (June-August) curtailed: closed on statutory holidays.

Transport. The campus is in the centre of the city and can be easily reached by bus, metro or taxi.

Parking. Campus parking is available for a fee.

Admission. Readers: Readers may register at any library. A scale of fees applies to various categories of readers who need to use the libraries for an extended period.
Visitors: No special provision is made for visitors.

Information. Information desks are centrally located in all libraries.

Sales. None.

Guidebooks. A directory to the McGill University Libraries is available without charge to visiting scholars.

Isaac Newton, Opticks (London 1704). Newton's own copy with his bookplate and marginal annotations, in the Rare Book Department of McGill University Libraries

Restaurant/Snack Facilities. Vending machines are available in, or near, the premises of most of the libraries.

Services. Cloakrooms, lavatories, lifts, smoking lounges, public telephones and typing rooms are available in, or near, the premises of most of the University libraries.

Catalogues. The main entry Union Catalogue is in McLennan Library. Each individual library maintains author/title/subject catalogues.

Classification. Library of Congress, Cutter, Dewey, National Library of Medicine.

Copying/Photography. All libraries have self-service photocopiers. Readers should ask permission before using their own cameras.

Friends of the Library. The Libraries have a number of memberships with varying fees.

OTTAWA

National Library of Canada/Bibliothèque nationale du Canada
395 Wellington Street, Ottawa, Ontario K1A 0N4
Tel. (613) 996-4852

History. The National Library of Canada was established on 1 January 1953, as a result of the 1952 Canadian National Library Act. Initially, space was provided for the Library in the Public Archives Building and Records Centre, but, on 20 June 1967, the present National Library building was officially opened. The building currently houses both the National Library and the Public Archives, and a number of services are shared by both institutions. The National Library is a depository library for books, phonorecords, government documents and periodicals published in Canada. In addition it buys, on an extensive scale, material published outside Canada in the fields of the humanities and social sciences (scientific material is collected by the National Science Library, now Canada Institute for Scientific and Technical Information, see next entry). Current holdings include 39,062 linear feet of monographs, 29,820 linear feet of serials, 26,537 linear feet of government documents, and 31,463 reels of microfilm.

Special Collections and Treasures. Major special collections include the music libraries and collections of Percy Scholes, Healey Willan, Alexis Contant, Hector Gratton, and Claude Champagne; the Judaica library presented by the Canadian Jewish Congress; the Georges Alphonse Daviault collection of Canadiana; the Canadian textbook collection; the philately collection from the Royal Philatelic Society; the Vanier Institute collection on marriage and the family; and the C.J. Gougeon collection of 8,000 popular songs.

Exhibition Areas. The major Exhibition Room is on the first floor of the Library. The sunken foyer in the entrance hall and the auditorium foyer can be used as supplementary space when necessary.

National Library of Canada

Hours. Mon.-Fri. 0830-2100, Sat. 0900-1700. Reading rooms open 24 hours, 7 days a week; after regular working hours their use is restricted to holders of passes. (Apply to Circulation Desk.)

Transport. Various city buses pass reasonably near the Library.

Parking. There is little space and the use of public transport is recommended.

Admission. Readers: Casual users may use library materials in the Reading Room on the 2nd Floor. Graduate students and researchers must register at the Circulation Desk on the 2nd Floor and may be assigned a locker if one is available.
Visitors: May be admitted to the ground floor and exhibition rooms only. Those wishing for a tour of the Library must give advance notice to the Public Relations Office, and must come during working hours.

Information. General information and directions: Commissionaires' Desk on main floor and first basement level. Library information and assistance: French and English reference desks in the Reference Room, 2nd Floor.

Sales. There is no sales desk but sales of publications are handled by the Information Canada Bookstore (171 Slater Street). Free publications are distributed by the Public Relations Office of the Library.

Guidebooks. Basic guidebook, in French and English, free to users.

Restaurant/Snack Facilities. Cafeteria on the 5th Floor (open c.0730-1530). In the first basement there is a small canteen with vending machines.

Services. Main cloakroom and lavatory on the ground floor; central lifts serve the 1st-5th floors, which contain the public areas; pay phones on the 1st and 2nd floors; typewriters and dictating machines may be used in the Newspaper Room and in the individually-assigned study rooms.

Catalogues. The card catalogues in the Reference Room are: the main author-title catalogue, the in-process catalogue, and a subject (classified) catalogue which was closed in 1975, to be replaced by a catalogue using Library of Congress subject headings. There are English and French indexes to the classified catalogue, and the new subject catalogue will also have headings in both languages. The National Library maintains a union catalogue of the holdings of over 300 major Canadian libraries. Application to use this service must be made at the Information Desk.

Classification. Library of Congress for shelving monographs; Dewey in the classified catalogue.

Copying/Photography. Xerographic, photostat and microfilm copying is controlled by staff. Apply to the Circulation Desk. Private camera photography by permission.

OTTAWA

Canada Institute of Scientific and Technical Information (formerly National Science Library), National Research Council of Canada, Ottawa, Canada K1A 0S2
Tel. 993-1600

History.   Development of a central scientific library for Canada began in 1924 with the formation of a library at the National Research Council of Canada. When the Canadian National Library Act became effective on 1 January 1953, the National Library formally recognized the National Research Council Library's role as a national science library. These responsibilities were confirmed by Act of Parliament in 1966. In October 1974 the National Research Council of Canada created the Canada Institute for Scientific and Technical Information (CISTI), combining its two major information services, the former National Science Library and its Technical Information Service. CISTI is the focal point of the Canadian national scientific and technological information system. Its activities are designed to provide resources and services not available locally and to initiate services of value to Canadian scientific research and development, such as its computerized current awareness service. CISTI is housed in a new building on the Montreal Road campus of the National Research Council in Ottawa. CISTI has nearly 1 million volumes, housed in the main and nine branch libraries, apart from many non-print forms (e.g. microfiche (700,000), microfilm, punched card and magnetic tape). Depository collections include technical and research reports issued by a number of national and international information agencies.

Special Collections and Treasures.   A major archive of historical importance is the Collection of Faraday letters.

Exhibition Areas.   An exhibition of early scientific works is maintained on the main floor, Room 175.

Hours.   Mon.-Fri. 0800-2100. Closed Sat., Sun. and public hols.

Transport.   By bus: no. 2 from downtown Ottawa. By car: east on Queensway to Blair Road and north on Blair to National Research Council, or east on Montreal Road to NRC.

Parking.   Parking lots at the Library.

Admission. Readers and *Visitors:* Free of charge.

Model of the Canada Institute for Scientific and Technical Information

Information. Desk near the entrance on the main floor.

Sales. Information Desk.

Guidebooks. A free English/French information brochure is available at the Information Desk.

Restaurant/Snack Facilities. Cafeteria on the second floor, quadrant A, is open Mon.-Fri. 0830-1530.

Services. Telephones and washrooms on the main floor — other washrooms on the stack floors. Study carrels, lounge area on the stack floors.

Catalogues. Dictionary card catalogue.

Classification. Library of Congress.

Copying/Photography. Copying facilities are provided. Enquiries should be made at the Information Desk. No restrictions on private (camera) photography.

QUEBEC

Bibliothèque de l'Université Laval
Cité Universitaire, Ste-Foy - Québec G1K 7P4
Tel. (418) 656-3126

History. The Library was founded in 1852 with a stock of 15,000 volumes, taken from the old Jesuit College (founded in 1635) and the Québec Seminary Library. By 1863 it had 35,000 volumes, by 1888 100,000, 1921 145,000, and 1946 260,000 volumes. In this latter year the first serious attempts at modernisation were made and reforms included the introduction of the Library of Congress classification. In 1962 the Williams-Filion Enquiry was the starting point for an even more fundamental reorganisation, which resulted in the movement of the Library to a new building, 'Le Pavillon de la Bibliothèque', on the Sainte-Foy campus in 1968. Holdings currently total 1,712,842 items in the Main Library and the Scientific Library housed in the 'Pavillon Vachon'.

Special Collections and Treasures. Special collections focus on French folklore, and the history of Québec art. The map collection is particularly strong on the cartography of Québec and Canada in the 17th, 18th and 19th centuries.

Exhibition Areas. Occasional exhibitions are held on the 1st floor of the Main Library, with a permanent exhibition in the Rare Books Section on the 5th Floor.

Hours. Mon.-Fri. 0830-2300, Sat. 0830-1700, Sun. 1400-1700. Closed public hols.

Bibliothèque de l'Université Laval

Transport. Public transport available to the Library. (The campus is located at Ste-Foy, a suburban area west of Québec.)

Parking.   6,000 parking spaces.

Admission.   *Readers:* Open to members of the University and researchers with suitable identification.
Visitors: No charge.

Information.   Information Office at the main entrance to the General Library.

Sales.   None.

Guidebooks.   A guidebook in French is available free of charge.

Restaurant/Snack Facilities.   Snack-bar in the basement of the General Library.

Services.   Typing rooms on the 2nd, 3rd, 4th and 5th floors. Cloakroom in the basement, lavatories on all floors, six lifts. Smoking rooms on the 2nd, 3rd, 4th and 5th floors.

Catalogues.   Author-title and subject card catalogues. Computerised catalogue for periodicals.

Classification.   Mainly Library of Congress.

Copying/Photography.   Machines on the 1st, 3rd, and 5th floors and in the basement. Xerographic, photostat, microfiche, microfilm copying available.

TORONTO
University of Toronto Library, Toronto, Ontario M5S 1A1 Tel. (416) 928-2294 (general enquiries)

History.   The University of Toronto was founded in 1827 as King's College, the name being changed to the University of Toronto in 1849 when much of the original book collection went to Trinity College, founded at that time. The rest was reorganised and finally housed in the East Hall of University College. In February 1890, however, a fire destroyed much of the building and almost totally destroyed the collection of 30,000 volumes. A library restoration committee was formed and within sixteen months had collected no less than 31,000 volumes and 5,000 pamphlets, housed in the new University Library, which was officially opened in 1892. With the growth in collections, additions were made to the building in 1910 and 1954. In December 1972 the Thomas Fisher Rare Book Library (120 St. George Street) opened, and in August 1973 the John P. Robarts Research Library for the Humanities and Social Sciences (130 St. George St.) followed suit. These developments allowed the older section to be renovated and it was subsequently renamed the Sigmund Samuel Library

John P. Robarts Research Library, University of Toronto

(9 King's College Circle), housing the duplicate-copy collection. The Science and Medicine Library is located at 7 King's College Circle. Total holdings of the more than fifty campus libraries include 4,057,000 volumes, 1,015,000 microforms and 8,085 MSS.

Special Collections and Treasures. The Thomas Fisher Rare Book Library houses the Dept. of Rare Books and Special Collections and the University of Toronto Archives. On the occasion of the dedication of this Library in April 1973 it received the magnificent collections of Shakespeare, Hollar, Kipling, Dunsany and Norman Douglas, formed by Sidney and Charles Fisher of Montreal, which were placed on long-term loan in the Library by the Ontario Heritage Foundation. Other special collections include the Library of the non-conformist minister James Forbes (1629-1712); the Charles Darwin Collection, the major part of it being assembled by Richard B. Freeman; the James L. Baillie Collections on the birds of North America; the Albert Einstein Collection; the Jason A. Hannah Collection of works of medical and related sciences; the Hobbes, Locke and Rousseau Collections; the A.T. De Lury Collection of Anglo-Irish literature; the Juvenile Drama Collection collected by D. Seaton Reid; and, while not forming a separate collection, the Library's holdings of Canadian material are extensive.

Exhibition Areas. Second floor of the Robarts Library and foyer of the Fisher Rare Book Library.

Hours. Robarts, Sigmund Samuel, Science and Medicine Libraries: Winter Session (Oct.-May); Mon.-Fri. 0830-2400, Sat. 0900-1700, Sun. 1300-2200. Summer Session (May-Sept.); Mon.-Thurs. 0830-2100, Fri. 0830-1800, Sat. 0900-1700, closed Sun. Thomas Fisher Rare Book Library: Oct.-May, Mon.-Sat. 0900-1700; May-Sept., Mon.-Fri. 0900-1700. Closed on Thanksgiving, 25 Dec., 1 Jan., Good Fri., Victoria Day, Dominion Day, Civic Holiday and Labour Day.

Transport. By subway: get off at St. George Street stop and walk one block south on St. George Street. By bus: Spadina Bus, get off at Harbord, walk two blocks east. Wellesley bus, get off at corner of St. George and Hoskin.

Parking. Parking is available off Sussex and St. George Streets, north of the Library.

Admission. Readers and *Visitors:* Visitors may use the reference collections at any time without registering. On showing identification at the loan desk they may ask to see material from the stacks. If they wish to borrow they should register at the Readers' Service Office on the third floor of the Robarts Library. Registration fee as an Extra-mural Reader costs $15 p.a.., plus a returnable deposit of $10. Visiting faculty members, upon showing university identification, may apply for a Visitor's card (up to one month) or Extra-mural or Research Reader's card (over one month) which all provide stack access and borrowing privileges. A Research Reader pays a refundable deposit of $25 plus a fee of $20 for four months or $50 a year (for a University of Toronto graduate, a fee of $15 for four months or $40 a year).

Information. At entrance level and on the second floor of the John P. Robarts Library and at the entrance of the Sigmund Samuel Library.

Sales. None.

Guidebooks. Available in English at most service desks.

Restaurant/Snack Facilities. 2nd floor and 14th floor cafeteria in the Robarts Library.

Services. (Robarts Library) Washrooms on 1st, 3rd, 5th and stack floors. Coatcheck on the 2nd floor. Telephones on 2nd and 3rd floors. Photocopy and microtext readers on the 3rd floor. Typing rooms on 4th and 5th floors. Also escalators, lifts, and smoking areas.

Catalogues. Main (union) catalogue is divided author-title and subject. Old catalogue, of pre-1959 acquisitions which have not yet been reclassified, is also divided. The Science and Medicine Library has a computer-produced book list of its monographic and periodical holdings.

Classification. Central Library and the majority of other libraries use Library of Congress.

Copying/Photography. Xerographic and microfilm copying facilities are available. Apply to the staff. Readers may use their own cameras in the Library, provided they do not disturb other readers.

VANCOUVER
University of British Columbia Library
2075 Westbrook Place, Vancouver, BC V6T 1W5
Tel. 228-3871

History. The University of British Columbia was founded in 1908 and is now the second largest university in Canada. Early buying for the Library was undertaken in Europe by the University of Minnesota Librarian James T. Gerould. A major influence on the subsequent growth of the collections was the Chief Librarian, John Ridington, who fought effectively against inadequate funding in the early years. In 1925 the Library moved to its present site and has now grown to a bookstock of just over 1.7 million volumes and 2 million non-book items (records, maps, microforms, etc.), housed in the Main Library, 12 branch libraries and about 50 departmental reading rooms. The Library is the largest

Main Library, University of British Columbia

university library in Western Canada.

Special Collections and Treasures. Collections include the F.W. Howay and Robie L. Reid libraries of Canadiana; the A.J.T. Taylor Collection on the Arctic; the P'u-Pan Collection of Orientalia; the A.M. Donaldson Collection of Burnsiana; the 40,000 volume N. Colbeck Collection of English literature; and the P.A. Woodward and H. Sinclair Collections on the history of medicine and science. Manuscript collections include the Tolmie Collection, the Alan B. Plaunt Collection, and the Malcolm Lowry papers.

Exhibition Areas. Main Library. Display cases are also available for exhibits.

Hours. Winter Session (10 Sept.-30 April): Mon.-Fri. 0800-2300, Sat. 0900-1700, Sun. 1000-1800. Summer Session (3 July-17 Aug): Mon.-Fri. 0800-2100, Sat. 0900-1700, Sun. closed. Between the Winter and Summer sessions times of opening can vary.

Transport. Bus No. 10 (to the University of British Columbia, via Chancellor Boulevard, or via University Boulevard). Bus No. 49 (to 41st Avenue, along SW and NW Marine Drive). (The University is located in a suburb of Vancouver, six miles from the centre of the city.)

Parking. There are two visitors' car-parks off East Mall, opposite the main Library building.

Admission. Readers: There is no charge for the use of Library materials by registered readers. Apply to the Circulation Office (Main Library entrance hall) for Readers' Cards.
Visitors: There is no charge for the use of the Library.

Information. Desk in Main Library Concourse.

Sales. None.

Guidebooks. Library handbook and various brochures, in English. Apply to the Information Desk.

Restaurant/Snack Facilities. Vending machines in the basement down the stairs inside the main entrance. There are several cafeterias on the University campus, which are open from morning to early evening on weekdays. There are two which also open at weekends.

Services. Cloakrooms, lavatories, lifts, smoking lounges, telephones (just inside the north entrance to the Main Library). Typewriters are available free in the Curriculum Lab. (3rd. floor, Education Building) and in Sedgewick Library. The Main and Woodward Libraries each have one coin-operated electric typewriter: see the Information Desk in either Library.

Catalogues. The card catalogue in the Main Library Concourse lists materials in all libraries on the University campus. Branch libraries have card catalogues of their own holdings.

Classification. Library of Congress.

Copying/Photography. There are several coin-operated self-service photocopying machines throughout the Library system. Change for photocopiers is available from the Xerox Room at the rear of the Main Library entrance hall (Mon.-Sat. 0900-1700). Staff operated service also available in Woodward Biomedical Branch Library. No restrictions on private photography.

Friends of the Library. Friends of the University of British Columbia Library. Anyone who donates money to the Library automatically becomes a member.

Chile

SANTIAGO
Biblioteca Nacional
Avenida Bernardo O'Higgins 651, Santiago
Tel. 381151

History. The National Library of Chile was founded by the Junta Revolucionaria on 19 August 1813. It closed in October 1814, following the Spanish reoccupation, with the stock consisting of only a few hundred volumes. It was re-established by a decree of 5 August 1818, Manuel de Salas y Corbalán (1754-1841) being the first librarian. The Library remained in the old building of the University of San Felipe (today the Teatro Municipal), its holdings totalling 8,000 volumes, derived mainly from the University of San Felipe and the Jesuit Library in the Convictorio de San Carlos. Copyright deposit laws of 1825, 1834, 1844 and 1846, albeit inadequately enforced, stimulated the growth of the Library, which also received several large donations. Housed in several locations during the 19th century, the Library moved in 1925 to its present location, occupying the city block formed by Bernardo O'Higgins, Moneda, MacIver, and Miraflores Streets. Current holdings total 1.5 million items, including 5,000 manuscripts.

Special Collections and Treasures. Collections include the 10,000 volume library of the Chilean statesman Mariano Egaña (1793-1846); the libraries of José Miguel de la Barra, Benjamín Vicuña Mackenna, Don Ignacio Victor Eyzaguirre and José Toribio Medina (1852-1930), the eminent bibliographer and historian, which comprises nearly 22,000 volumes and hundreds of copied and original MSS (now housed in the José Toribio Medina

Biblioteca Nacional, Santiago

Room); the Archivo del Escritor, which attempts to collect any material by or about Chile's most outstanding literary figures; the Archivo del Compisitor Chileno, which performs the same function in the musical sphere; and the Fondo Bibliográfico Raúl Silva Castro, devoted to one of Chile's most outstanding literary critics and bibliographers. The National Archive, housed in one wing of the Library, partly grew out of the Library's manuscript section and contains many important collections.

Exhibition Areas. The Exhibition Room is located in the centre of the building, main aisle.

Hours. Not cited (at least 0900-1700 daily).

Transport. Any bus marked Alameda (Bernardo O'Higgins).

Parking. Adjacent streets, or in parking lots not far from the Library.

Admission. Readers: Open to all. Foreign scholars should contact the Director or his Assistant in order to ensure faster service, etc.
Visitors: The Library is open to the public without cost.

Information. An information officer is generally available at the two main entrances in B. 0'Higgins and Moneda Streets.

Sales. Immediately to the right of the Moneda Street entrance. Pamphlets, monographs and reprints, published or sponsored by the Library, are on sale.

Guidebooks. None.

Restaurant/Snack Facilities. None on the premises but available nearby.

Services. Lavatories, lifts and telephones. Typing rooms are available with special permission.

Catalogues. Author, title, and subject card catalogues located at the entrance to the Main Reading Room.

Classification. Bibliothèque nationale (Paris).

Copying/Photography. Facilities available through Library staff. Private photography requires the special permission of the Director's Assistant.

The first Chilean printed book, Modo de Ganar el jubileo santo (Santiago, 1776)

China

NANKING
Nan-ching t'u shu kuan (Nanking Library)
Nan-ching, Kiangsu
Tel. (not available)

History. The Library was founded in 1933 as the National Central Library, with its initial stock comprising 40,000 volumes from the Documents Department of the Ministry of Education. The reading rooms were opened to the public on 1 September 1936. The Sino-Japanese War broke out in July 1937, forcing the evacuation of the Library in February 1938 to Chungking, the war-time capital. The Chungking premises of the Library were completed in January 1941 and the reading rooms opened a month later. After the Japanese surrender in August 1945, the Library closed its branches and various departments scattered in the villages near Chungking and in May 1946 returned to its original seat at Ch'eng Hsien Chieh, Nanking. 1949 saw the Communists gain control of the Chinese mainland and the removal of the rarest items of the Library to Taipei, Taiwan (see entry for National Central Library, Taipei). The bulk of the collections, however, totalling about 1 million volumes, remained in Nanking. Today holdings are estimated to total nearly 3 million volumes, with emphasis being placed, in recent years, on collecting in the natural sciences. Since the Library is no longer a national library it is today run by the Municipal Revolutionary Committee.

Special Collections and Treasures. The Library has a rich collection of material on the province of Kiangsu and strong collections of material in the humanities, natural sciences, engineering, medicine and agriculture.

Exhibition Areas. No details available.

Hours. No details available.

Transport. Nanking is accessible by direct train from Peking. Public transport is available within Nanking. (The Library is situated near the centre of Nanking, to the north-east of the central square (Hsin Jie Kou Square) and beneath the Ming dynasty city walls.)

No further details are available on this Library.

PEKING

Pei-ching t'u shu kuan (National Library of Peking)
Peking 7
Tel. (not available)

History. The Library was founded in 1909, with its stock formed from books formerly preserved at the Hall of Classics and at the Library of the Grand Secretariat, with over 8,500 Buddhist manuscripts of the T'ang dynasty. On the establishment of the Republic in 1912, the Ministry of Education assumed responsibility for the Library, which reopened in August 1912. The Library now received numerous collections and, in addition, by order of the Ministry, the Government printing offices in the various provinces had to send in their publications. In June 1929 the Library merged with the Metropolitan Library, which had been established in 1926 by the China Foundation. The new institution, named the National Library of Peking, occupied in Spring 1931 a new building of traditional Chinese design, erected on a 6½ acre site in the western part of Peihai Park. The Library was formally opened on 25 June 1931, the building consisting of several connected units. Legal deposit privileges helped swell the collections from 400,000 volumes in 1931 to 1.2 million volumes in 1949, to 6 million volumes in 1961 and to the present total of over 9 million volumes. The Library was closed during the 'Cultural Revolution' (c. 1966-8) but today, as the largest library in China, occupies a key place in the national library structure. Plans are in hand to build a Library annex to relieve the present serious overcrowding, which has led to much of the pre-1949 holdings, being scattered around Peking.

Special Collections and Treasures. Collections include 8,500 MSS from Tun Huang, consisting mainly of Buddhist sutras written during the T'ang Dynasty, though some were written as early as the 4th century AD. These manuscripts were discovered in Tun Huang and transferred to the Library by the Government in 1909. The collection of over 3,000 provincial and district gazeteers is believed to be the largest in China, with many unique copies, particularly of those printed in the Ming Dynasty. Other collections include the Map Collection; the Tangut Sutra Collection; the Manchu, Mongolian and Tibetan Collection; the Liang Ch'i Ch'ao Depository Library of over 41,000 volumes; the Mollendorf Collection of 3,300 foreign works on general linguistics; the Cheng Chen-to Library of nearly 100,000 volumes; and a set of the Jehol Palace copy of the *Ssu k'u ch'üan shu*, the Imperial Library of Emperor Ch'ien Lung, in 36,300 manuscript volumes bound in silk. Treasures include 215 volumes of the Ming manuscript encyclopaedia *Yung-lo ta tien;* 4,500 rolls of the Buddhist *Tripitaka*, printed in Chao-ch'eng, Shansi, between 1118 and 1173; a 5th-century MS from Tun Huang; and several rare editions of Marxist-Leninist works.

National Library of Peking

Exhibition Areas. Available but no details provided as to location.

Hours. Sept. to May: Daily 0900-2200. June to Aug.: Daily 0800-2100.

Transport. The Library is in Wen Jin Jie Street, west of the Peihai, just beyond the bridge. Bus 14 northwards from the Liupukou stop on West Changan Avenue to Wen Jin Jie Street. Bus 5 from west side of Tien An Men Square, northwards to Peihai Park, then short walk. Trolleybuses 1 and 9 from China Art Gallery or the Palace Museum westwards. Trolleybus 3 from Wangfuching Street northwards. Taxis from all hotels. The chief taxi rank is at 54 Dong an men nan jie (tel. 55 76 71).

Parking. In forecourt.

Admission. Readers: The Library is open to researchers with letters of recommendation from their organisations. Foreigners have access (but not necessarily physical access) at all times (see also general regulations in entry for Peking University Library).
Visitors: Free of charge.

Information. At entrance and all staff desks.

Sales. None.

Guidebooks. No details available.

Restaurant/Snack Facilities. None.

Services. No details available.

Catalogues. Dictionary card catalogue.

Classification. Chinese material is classified by several schemes, notably that designed by Liu Kuo-Chün, the *Ta hsing t'u shu kuan fen lei fa* (The Classification Scheme for Large-Scale Libraries) and the *Chung-kuo jen min ta hsüeh t'u shu kuan fen lei fa* (The Classification Scheme of *the Chinese People's University Library*).

Copying/Photography. No details available.

PEKING
Pei-ching ta hsueh t'u shu kuan (Peking University Library), Peking
Tel. (not available)

History. The Library was founded in 1902 and was originally located near the city centre. Mao Tse-tung worked in the Library in 1918 as an assistant, coming under the influence of the Chief Librarian, Li Ta-chao, one of China's first Marxists. After the 4 May Movement of 1919, which began at Peking University, the Library was used by students to help distribute revolutionary material. In 1925 holdings totalled 80,000 volumes, by 1936, 238,370 volumes and in 1949, 724,894 volumes. In 1953, four years after the Communist takeover in China, Peking University moved to its present suburban site and the Library went with it. In moving, it incorporated a number of other libraries, notably the library of Yenching University, which had a stock of 403,221 volumes. Rumours of mass destruction of books during the 'Cultural Revolution' were apparently unfounded. Some of the departmental libraries and possibly the main University Library were raided but most of the books have been recovered and holdings now include 2.8 million volumes. The Library currently occupies a traditional stone style building with overhanging eaves but construction of the New University Library, located in the centre of the campus, began in 1973 and was scheduled for completion by early 1976. The new building will house all the collections, which are at present scattered around the campus in 17 departmental libraries, as well as in the present main Library building.

Special Collections and Treasures. The Rare Books Section totals 120,000 volumes. The Library has a collection of ancient MSS, scrolls and early printed works, including a collection of illustrated books and scroll paintings. The paintings include local scenes and landscapes (one of these features the old formal gardens on which the University was built). The Library specialises in acquiring the publications of the 'capitalist world' in the humanities and natural sciences.

Exhibition Areas. Exhibition area on the ground floor, where exhibits in glass cases show Mao's works and Lu Hsun's works, including early and rare editions of both; books and pamphlets, mainly new, in support of current political and production movements; special selections of works related to students' current reading programmes, chosen by their teachers and Library staff; and new acquisitions, mainly foreign books. Students are permitted here. On the first floor is an Exhibition Room, open only to invited guests including foreign visitors, where a changing exhibition, in glass cases, consists of samples of the Library's special collections, usually old MSS, paintings, examples of calligraphy, historical records, etc. A guide may be asked to introduce these to the visitor. The new Library building will have vastly greater exhibition areas.

Hours. Mon.-Sat. 0800-1700 but can close unexpectedly, e.g. for meetings.

Transport. The University campus is in the northwestern suburbs of Peking in Haitien District, lying on the main road to the Summer Palace. Bus 32 northwards from the Capital Gymnasium at Paishihchiao (White Stone Bridge) stops at Chungkuantsun, near the new main South Gate of the University. It also stops outside

Peking University Library, Old Building

the old traditional-style West Gate. Taxis from all hotels.

Parking. Available but at present limited. Facilities, however, will be improved outside the new Library building.

Admission.   Readers: Foreign students studying at the University may join the Library as ordinary readers by obtaining library tickets. Three books may be borrowed at a time. Proscribed catalogues are not open to such students; neither are the special collections (though they may be taken on a visit to the latter). Foreign teachers working at the University are entitled to up to ten books at a time (as are Chinese teachers at the University), and they are permitted to use the proscribed catalogues if they request to do so and they have good reason, but not the special collections. Foreign teachers (but not foreign or Chinese students) may use the Teachers' Reading Room containing newspapers, magazines and journals from abroad. This Reading Room is attached to the languages departments. Other reading rooms in other departments are open to students under the supervision of teachers. Foreign readers and researchers would have the same reading rights as foreign teachers working at the University. They could also obtain access to that part of the special collections relevant to their subject but only if that were part of the agreement which permitted them access to China to read or research in the first place. This stipulation is true for all the major libraries in China.
Visitors: Visitors may be permitted to see the Library as part of a larger visit to the University as a whole (i.e. no visitor sees only the Library, as it would be considered a discourtesy to the rest of the University). Such visits are arranged with the University's Revolutionary Committee (the administrative body) and, in the case of foreigners, are fixed by the Chinese organisation that has sponsored or invited the foreigner to visit China, at the request of the visitor. For scholars this would be a specialist organisation. For other visitors it would be the Chinese People's Association for Friendship for Foreign Countries (for friendship delegations), the China Travel Service (for tourists), or another government department.

Information. Library assistants at the Borrowers' Counter. In general, apply to the Revolutionary Committee, Peking University.

Sales. None.

Guidebooks. None.

Restaurant/Snack Facilities. None.

Services. No details available.

Catalogues. Author and subject card catalogues.

Classification. The Chinese National Classification

System. At present foreign language books are classified by Dewey but they will be classified by the CNS in the new Library.

Copying/Photography. The Library cannot at present offer any photocopying or microfilm facilities. This may be remedied in the near future with the development of China's own photocopier.

PEKING
Chung-kuo k'o hsueh yuan t'u shu kuan (Central Library of the China Academy of Sciences)
3 Wen-chin-chieh, Peking
Tel. (not available)

History. The Academia Sinica (China Academy of Sciences) was founded in October 1949 from the merger of the Academia Sinica of Nanking (founded in 1928) and the National Academy of Peiping (founded in 1929). The Central Library was founded in 1951, with 330,000 volumes from the Institute of History and Philology of the Academia Sinica. Various branch libraries were soon established, e.g. in Shanghai (1953) and Lan-Chou (1955). By the end of 1958 there were 113 branches and reading rooms in the various research institutes of the Academy. The Library specialises in acquiring material in the natural sciences and technology, which includes national responsibility for acquiring the publications of the 'capitalist world' in mathematics, physics, chemistry, biology, the basic theory of technology and 'new sciences', such as automation, jet technology and atomic energy. The Central Library, which has legal deposit privileges, currently has holdings which include 2.5 million volumes.

Special Collections and Treasures. The Library has strong collections in its designated areas of acquisition and is particularly noted for its holdings of foreign material, e.g. reports of the US Atomic Energy Commission and proceedings of international conferences.

Exhibition Areas. No details available.

Hours. No details available.

Transport. By bus or trolleybus to the Library, which is located in the north-west suburbs of Peking, close to Peking University.

Parking. No details available.

Admission. Readers and *Visitors:* See information in entry for Peking University Library.

Information. No details available.

Sales. No details available.

Guidebooks. No details available.

Restaurant/Snack Facilities. No details available.

Services. No details available.

Catalogues. Author and subject card catalogues. Union list of periodicals in Western languages.

Classification. Own.

Copying/Photography. No details available.

PEKING
Ch'ing-hua ta hsueh t'u shu kuan (Tsinghua University Library), Peking
Tel. (not available)

History. The Library was founded in 1912, following the establishment of Tsinghua College in 1911. The first Librarian was Tai Chih-ch'ien, who had received his professional library education in the United States. By 1925 holdings totalled 87,000 volumes and by 1936, 251,478 volumes. The Library suffered during World War II, when a significant proportion of the stock disappeared. Today holdings include 1.3 million volumes, housed in the now rather out-dated purpose-built building, erected in the early part of the 20th century. Tsinghua is ranked amongst the most prestigious universities of China.

Special Collections and Treasures. The Library's collections are particularly strong in science and technology, especially civil engineering. It buys foreign publications extensively on these subjects.

Exhibition Areas. No details available.

Hours. No details available.

Transport. The University is situated in the north-west suburbs of Peking and can be reached from the city centre by bus no. 31 from Pinganli (near Peihai Park). The University campus is a little to the east of that of Peking University. Taxis are available from all hotels.

Parking. Adequate parking facilities outside the Library.

Admission. Readers: See the regulations under entry for Peking University Library.
Visitors: Visits can only be arranged through one's sponsoring organisation and Tsinghua's Revolutionary Committee.

Information. Tsinghua Revolutionary Committee.

Tsinghua University

Item from Tsinghua University Library

Sales.   None.

Guidebooks.   None.

Restaurant/Snack Facilities.   None.

Services.   No details available.

Catalogues.   Author and subject catalogues.

Classification.   For Chinese material: own. For Western material: Dewey.

Copying/Photography.   No details available.

SHANGHAI

Shang-hai t'u shu kuan (Shanghai Library), Shang-hai Tel. (not available)

History.   The Library's origins date back to the founding of the Shanghai Library in 1849, but in its present form it dates from 1952, when it was formed from an amalgamation of the old Shanghai Library, the People's Library of Shanghai, the Sciences and Technology Library of Shanghai, the Historical Literature Library and the Newspaper and Periodical Library. The Library organised a network of community or street libraries in the 1950s which by 1958 totalled some 3,400 units. The Library has also been responsible for the production of numerous useful bibliographical tools. Current holdings include 6 million volumes, housed in the combined building of the Shanghai Library and Museum.

Special Collections and Treasures.   The Library has an outstanding collection on China, both nationally and regionally, while important collections have been developed in engineering, medicine and agriculture.

Exhibition Areas.   No details available.

Hours.   No details available.

Transport.   The Library, located south of Nanking Road, the busiest thoroughfare of Shanghai, is accessible by taxi or public transport. Shanghai is on a direct train route from Peking.

Parking.   No details available.

Admission. Readers and *Visitors:* See details in entry for Peking University Library.

Information.   From the Revolutionary Committee.

Shanghai Library and Museum

No further details are available on this Library.

Colombia

BOGOTÁ

Biblioteca Nacional de Colombia
Calle 24 No. 5-60 (Apartado Aéreo No. 27600), Bogotá
Tel. 41 40 29

History. The National Library has its origins in the Royal Library of Santa Fé de Bogotá, founded on 9 January 1777. This resulted from the initiative of Francisco Moreno y Escandón, who saw a use for the libraries left by the Jesuits after their expulsion from Spanish territories in 1767. The Royal Library occupied the building which is today used by the Presidents of Colombia, i.e. the Palacio de San Carlos. It remained there until 1822 when it was relocated in the Colegio de San Bartolomé. It was closed during the Independence movement until 25 December 1823, when it reopened as the National Library, with a stock of 10,000 volumes. In 1938 a five-storey Library building was opened, which was renovated in the early 1970s. The Library has legal deposit privileges, although many books published outside Bogotá seem to escape the net. Holdings currently total some 360,340 items, including 300 MSS and 40 incunabula.

Special Collections and Treasures. The Library is particularly strong on books and items relating to Colombia and surrounding countries. Rare book holdings amount to some 25,000 volumes. The Fondo Anselmo Pineda and the Fondo José María Quijano Otero contain much valuable material, particularly in pamphlet form, on 19th century Colombian history. The Library also houses the national newspaper collection (with a printed catalogue available up to 1936). Individual treasures include notable works on the history and discovery of South America in general and New Granada in particular, such as J. de Laet, *Novus orbis* (Antwerp, 1633); Juan Flórez de Ocáriz, *Genealogias del nuevo reino de Granada* (Madrid, 1674); Pedro Simón, *Primera parte de las noticias historiales de las conquistas de tierra firme en las Indias occidentales* (Cuenca, 1627); Lucas Fernández de Piedrahita, *Historia general de las conquistas del nuevo reino de Granada* (Antwerp, 1688); and Antonio Rodriguez de Leon Pinelo, *Epítome de la biblioteca oriental i occidental* (Madrid, 1629), one of the first bibliographies to relate to the New World.

Exhibition Areas. The Exhibition Room is situated on the first floor.

Hours. Mon.-Sat. 0900-1900. Closed Sun. and normal public hols.

Transport. Buses pass close to the Library, which is

Biblioteca Nacional de Colombia, Bogotá

✤
HISTORIA
DE CHRISTO PACIENTE

traducida del Latin al Castellano:

Por el Doctor Don Josef Luis de
Asula, y Lozano.

Tomo segundo.

Con las licencias necesarias:

En Santa Fè de Bogotá
En la Imprenta Real de Don
Antonio Espinosa de los Monteros.

Año de 1787.

The first book printed in Colombia, Historia de Christo Paciente (Bogotá, 1787), in the Biblioteca Nacional de Colombia

Biblioteca Luis-Angel Arango, Bogotá

located in the centre of downtown Bogotá.

Parking.   There are *parqueaderos* in front of the Library.

Admission. Readers: Must show some form of identification, e.g. passport, student card, letters etc. *Visitors:* No restrictions.

Information.   First floor at the Reception Desk, or in the Reference Reading Room (Room 106).

Sales.   None.

Guidebooks.   None.

Restaurant/Snack Facilities.   None within the Library but various restaurants are located in the neighbourhood.

Services.   Typewriters can be used in Room 210. Cloakrooms at entrance to Library. Telephone in the Porter's Lodge. Washroom on the first floor.

Catalogues.   Author card catalogue.

Classification.   Dewey.

Copying/Photography.   Copying facilities available in Room 210 (Sala de Investigadores).

Friends of the Library.   It is the Library's intention to form such a group.

BOGOTÁ
*Biblioteca Luis-Angel Arango,
Calle 11 4-14, Bogotá
Tel. 439100*

History.   The Library, which is operated and supported by the Banco de la República, is primarily a reference rather than a loan collection. It has been called 'the library showplace of Colombia', with facilities for many cultural activities. The Library began to be formed in 1932 as a specialised library for the bank. In 1933 it had 4,000 volumes, largely of an economic nature. Gradually the scope of the collections widened until today it has 130,000 volumes, 15,000 microforms, 1,000 MSS and 8,000 periodicals covering most disciplines. The Library moved into its present building in the old 'La Candelaria' quarter in February 1958, when it took the name of Dr. Luis-Angel Arango, a former President of the Bank, and was opened to the public in general.

Special Collections and Treasures.   The Sala Colombia serves the extensive Colombian collection whose riches include the Laureano García Ortíz Collection of 25,000 volumes and the Carlos Lozano y Lozano Collection. The Library also has an important collection of 18th-century printing of Santa Fé de Bogotá, a collection of 373 works of art and a collection of maps relating to Colombia in particular and the world in general.

Exhibition Areas. Exhibition Rooms on the 1st and 3rd floors.

Hours. Mon.-Fri. 0800-2100, Sat.-Sun. 0800-1800.

Transport. The Library can be reached by bus or taxi.

Parking. There are several *parqueaderos* within easy walking distance of the Library.

Admission. Readers and *Visitors:* Free. An identity card, or for foreigners a passport, must be produced.

Information. In the entrance hall.

Sales. None.

Guidebooks. None at present.

Restaurant/Snack Facilities. None on the premises for readers, but available nearby.

Services. Cloakrooms, lavatories, music room in which weekly concerts are held.

Catalogues. Author and subject catalogues. Printed catalogue also available.

Classification. Dewey.

Copying/Photography. Xerographic and microfilm copying available through photocopying section at the back of the Reading Room.

Cuba

HAVANA
Biblioteca Nacional José Martí
Plaza de la Revolución, La Habana
Tel. 7-3613

Biblioteca Nacional José Martí, Havana

History. Under the pressure of important Cuban personalities of that time, the Library was established on 18 October 1901 by the U S Military Governor, Leonard Wood. Its first quarters were the inadequate La Fuerza Fortress and its first Director was Domingo Figarola Caneda who gave to the Library his private book collection. He served in this capacity until 1918 although he ceased officially in 1920. Later it was moved to the second floor of the Maestranza building which was also inadequate. There it remained until 1938. In this year the Library returned to La Fuerza. On 21 February 1958 the Library moved into its present building, costing 2.8 million dollars, with space for a million volumes. The overthrow of President Batista on 1 January 1959 by Fidel Castro led to a total revision of the role of the National Library, e.g. the collections were improved and made more accessible to the general public. New departments were created, and for the first time the Library assumed the publication of the National Cuban Bibliography. The reorganization was put under the care of Maria Teresa Freyre de Andrade. The years since 1959 have seen great progress in the exploitation of the collections. The National Library is also the head of the Cuban network of public libraries. Current holdings total over 500,000 volumes, not including maps, engravings, etc. The present Director is the Cuban poet Luis Suardíaz.

Special Collections and Treasures. The Cuban Collection, directed by the Cuban Bibliography Department, has collections of printed books and MSS by and on famous Cubans, collections of old Cuban engravings and photographs, and cuttings from periodicals. Other collections include the Antonio Bachiller y Morales Collection; the Antonio Sánchez de Bustamante y Sirvén Collection of international law; and the Fernando Ortiz Collection of 30,000 volumes rich in Cuban history, literature, anthropology and ethnology. Treasures include a Lord Albemarle MS of 14 July 1762, written just prior to the taking of Havana by the English; Terence, *Comedies,* 1497 and other incunabula; P. Heyn, *Beschreibung von eroberung der Spanischen silber flota,* 1629, MSS of J.M. Heredia; the *Papel periodico de la Habana* (1790-1804); and the first series of *Revista bimestre cubana,* 1831-4 (the Library also has the second series, 1910 onwards).

Exhibition Areas. Various exhibition areas, e.g. the Martí Room commemorating the Cuban writer and national hero, José Martí; the Music Dept.; the Map Room, etc.

Hours. Reading Rooms: Mon.-Fri. 0805-2300. Sat. 0805-1900. Sun 0805-1300.

Transport. Bus to the Library, which occupies a central site in the Plaza de la Revolución.

Parking. At the back of the Library.

Admission. *Readers* and *Visitors:* Free of charge.

Information. At Loan Desks and specialised reading room desks.

Sales. None.

Guidebooks. Brochure in Spanish, available free of charge.

Restaurant/Snack Facilities. In the Basement.

Services. Lavatories, cloakrooms, film shows, concerts and readings are held in the Library on a regular basis.

Catalogues. Author and subject card catalogue.

Classification. Own and Dewey.

Copying/Photography. Copying available through Library staff. Apply to the Director for private photography.

Czechoslovakia

MARTIN
Matica Slovenská, Mudroňova 13, 03601 Martin
Tel. Martin 2346 (4 lines)

History. The Matica Slovenská was founded in 1863 as a cultural institution, library and museum. From 1875-1919 the institution was closed, but re-opened in the latter year, and from then until 1954 continued to fulfil the same functions. In 1954 legislation passed by the Slovak National Council raised the status of the Matica Slovenská to that of a National Library and centre of bibliographical research for Slovakia. Its holdings of books, periodicals and special prints total 2,136,000 items. A new Library building, with 7,000 square metres of stack space, is currently nearing completion.

Special Collections and Treasures. No details available.

Exhibition Areas. No details available.

Hours. 0900-1800 daily.

Transport. The Library is served by the city bus service.

Parking. There is parking space for cars.

Admission. *Readers* and *Visitors:* Free of charge.

Information. Library staff desks.

Sales. None.

Guidebooks. None.

Restaurant/Snack Facilities. There are restaurants near the old Library. A snack bar is planned for the new Library building.

Services. Cloakrooms, lavatories and smoking lounges

Matica Slovenská, Martin. New building under construction

are located near the Reading Room and Lending Office.

Catalogues.   Author, subject and classified catalogues.

Classification.   Dewey

Copying/Photography.   Copying machines available in central locations. Private photography requires the Director's permission.

PRAGUE
Státní knikhovna České socialistické republiky (State Library of the Czech Socialist Republic)
Klementinum 190, 110 01 Praha 1
Tel. Main switchboard: 26 65 41, or 26 72 41;
Director: 22 51 92

History.   The State Library is an organisation which encompasses the following institutions: the National Library, the University Library, the Slavonic Library, the French Library, the Central Economic Library and the Central Scientific-Methodic Cabinet for Librarianship. Most of these institutions are located in the Clementinum (a complex of buildings built by the Jesuits and dating 1578-1727). The history of the oldest unit — the University Library — can be traced to the foundation of Charles University in 1348. The first record of the Library occurs in 1366, when the Emperor Charles IV, the University's founder, bestowed on it 48 volumes. Its first catalogue appeared in 1370 and listed 204 volumes. In 1777 it was combined with the libraries of the Law and Medical Faculties and opened to the public. Since 1782 all Bohemian books and periodicals have been deposited with the Library, and the 1935 Copyright Act ensured legal deposit of all publications published throughout Czechoslovakia. The second most important unit of the Czech State Library is the National Library which was originally a department of the University Library. In 1949 it became an independent institution and in 1959, with the establishment of the Czechoslovak State Library (confirmed by a new statute of 29 December 1973), it became one of its main units. Current holdings total 4.5 million volumes, a figure which includes 62,000 volumes of MSS and early and rare printed books.

Special Collections and Treasures.   Probably the most precious book in the Library is the *Vyšehrad Codex,* the coronation gospel book dating from the first royal coronation c.1085. Other treasures include the *Passional,* c.1314, of Abbess Kunhuta, illuminated by Canon Benes of St. Georges Convent; the *Velislav Bible,* c.1340; the *Břevnov Breviary,* 1195, which is the earliest example of Czech neumatic notation; the *Gradual of Malá Strana,* 1572, a beautifully illuminated Catholic book of great size; and the commemorative volume by the humanist Nagonius written at the end of the 15th century to the glory of King Vladislav Jagellonský. Various illuminated

University Library, Prague

Bibles have survived from the Husite period, the most outstanding of which is the Old Testament in Czech. Collections include the J.A. Comenius Collection, the collection of the writings of John Wycliffe, largely brought to Prague by Czech students on their return from Oxford; the Lobkowicz Library of near 53,000 volumes; a large collection of material on John Hus; and the libraries of Theresa Koseová-Dubrouská, Vlastimil Tusar, F.X. Šalda and Viktor Dyk. The Music department holds an outstanding Mozart collection; the MSS of the old Czech composers Rejcha, Voříšek, Miča; and some examples from the works of the classic composers Smetana, Dvořák, Novák, Suk and Martinu.

Exhibition Areas. The Baroque Hall, completed in 1727, which still houses the original Jesuit Library; the Mathematics Hall, used for occasional small exhibitions; the Hall of Mirrors, used for large exhibitions and concerts.

Hours. General Reading Room: Mon.-Sat. 0700-2200. Other reading rooms: Mon.-Fri. 0700-1900. Closed Sun. and public hols.

Transport. Trams no. 2, 20, 17, 30. Buses no. 155, 134, 197. Stops on the Náměstí Krasnoarmějců. (The Clementinum occupies about 5 acres in the centre of Prague and is opposite the Town Hall.)

Parking. Access to the Library by car is from Náměstí prim. Vacka, Praha I, Staré Město. Parking on Kaprova ul., Praha 1.

Admission. Readers and *Visitors:* The Reader's Certificate is valid for the whole of the Library and is issued by the Service Department in the main hall, or by the Slavonic Library on the 3rd floor of the Clementinum, or by the Central Economics Library. Readers require an identity card, or, if foreign, a valid passport. Non-resident visitors and foreigners are supplied with a short term permit to enter the reading rooms.

Information. The Porter's Lodge of the Library. Bibliographical information in the main hall.

Sales. Publications issued by the State Library of the ČSR are sold in the Distribution Office of the State Library in Liliova ul. 5, Praha 1 (ground floor); open daily, except for Sat. and Sun., 0715-1600.

Guidebooks. None.

Restaurant/ Snack Facilities. The buffet on the ground floor of the Library is open Mon.-Thurs. 0830-1600, Fri. 0830-1230. Closed Sat.

Services. Cloakroom to the right of the entrance hall. Telephone booth in the entrance hall. Lavatories on the ground floor, left of the Porter's Lodge. Lift.

The Vyšehrad Codex (1085), in the Czech State Library. The codex was written in a Prague scriptorium and used by the kings of Bohemia when they took their coronation oath in St. Vitus's Cathedral

Catalogues. Author catalogue, systematic catalogue (public and official) and subject catalogue. Various special catalogues. Cumulative catalogue of foreign literature acquired by libraries and institutions in and outside the ČSR.

Classification. Universal Decimal Classification.

Copying/Photography. Copying facilities are provided by the Technical Department on the first floor. Open: Mon., Wed. and Fri. 0800-1200, 1300-1400; Tues. and Thurs. 0800-1200, 1300-1800. Closed Sat. and Sun. Readers may not use their own cameras inside the buildings without the permission of the Director.

PRAGUE
Knihovna národního muzea (Czech National Museum Library), Václavské nám.68, 115 79 Praha 1
Tel. 26 94 51-9

History. The National Museum was founded on 15 April 1818, a symptom of the revival of interest in Czech culture. The Library's purpose was to collect Bohemian and Czech literature, prints, maps and the exact sciences. The first acquisition of importance was the Kašpar Šternberk Collection of Bohemica, which was soon followed by many other donations and bequests. By 1840 the Library possessed about 12,939 books, predominantly in literature and the natural sciences. In 1846 the Library moved from the confined premises of the Šternberk palace to new premises in Na příkopě. The growth of the collection necessitated a further move in 1892 to Wenceslas Square, where it still remains, although the demands on available space have necessitated some outhousing for example, the collection of; periodicals dealing with Bohemica has been moved to the former Governor's castle in Královska and the literary archives to the Strahov (see following entry). One of the most important tasks the Library has been entrusted with in recent years is the administration of castle libraries, which the National Museum took over in 1954. Current holdings total 1.5 million books, 9,000 MSS and a rich collection of old prints.

Special Collections and Treasures. One of the most treasured of the MSS is the 13th century *Mater verborum,* which contains the earliest examples of written Czech. Others include the prayer book, *Liber viaticus,* written for the Bishop of Litomyšl, Jan Stréda, c.1364, a fine example of the Bohemian school of illumination; MSS of John Huss; the *Life of Aesop the Wise* (Olomouc, 1557); Comenius's *Didaktika,* 1630, with his own MS supplements and corrections; the MSS of all the poems in the first edition of the *Songs of Silesia* by Bezruč; the MS of A.S. Puškin's poem, *O, Delija dragaja,* 1811-17, the only Puškin MS in Czechoslovakia; and the *Jistebnice Hymnal,* with the

Czech National Museum Library, Reference Room

Hussite song, 'Ktož sú boží bojovníci' (Ye who are God's warriors).

Exhibition Areas. In 1957 the Library opened the Muzeum knihy (Book Museum) at Žďár nad Sázavou devoted to the history of the book. Hours, 1 April-30 Oct. daily 0800-1700 except Mon. In winter by previous appointment to the Castle's administrative office.

Hours. 0800-1900. Closed Sat., Sun. and public hols.

Transport. By tram and by underground railway. (The National Museum is located at the top end of Wenceslas Square.)

Parking. Available nearby.

Admission. *Readers* and *Visitors:* No charge.

Information. At the Library staff desks.

Sales. Common with the National Museum sales desk.

Guidebooks. Knihovna národního muzea, with summaries in German, Russian, French and English, published 1959.

Restaurant/Snack Facilities. Snack-bar in the building of the National Museum.

Services. Cloakrooms, lavatories.

Catalogues. Author catalogue.

Classification. Own.

Copying/Photography. Microfilm copying facilities available.

PRAGUE
Památník národního písemnictví, Strahovská knihovna
(*Museum of National Literature, Strahov Library*)
Strahovské nádv 132, 118 38 Praha 1
Tel. 53 14 51

History. The Strahov Monastery and its Library were founded by Prince Vladislav II in 1140 for the reformed Order of Premonstratensian monks. In 1258, however, the precious collection of MSS was destroyed by fire; the second collection was almost totally destroyed during the Hussite Wars of 1420 and then the third was removed by the Swedish general, Königsmark, during the Thirty Years' War. The foundations of the present collection were laid by Abbot Frank, who purchased the Freisleben library of Jihlava in 1665. In 1671 the baroque Theological Hall was built and the Philosophical Hall was added in 1783-93. By 1756 the catalogue had recorded

Museum of National Literature, Theological Hall of Strahov Library

12,000 volumes. The collections benefited from the librarianship of Jan Dlabač at the end of the 18th century. The collections grew only slowly, however, during most of the 19th and early 20th centuries. By 1950 the holdings totalled 130,000 volumes. After considerable alterations to the building, the Library was opened to the public in 1951. On 8 May 1953 the Literary Archives of the National Museum Library (see preceding entry) were transferred to the Strahov monastery, which was designated the Museum of National Literature. Current holdings total 800,000 volumes and 5,000 MSS.

Special Collections and Treasures. Treasures include the *Strahov Evangeliary,* 9-10th century MS, from St. Martins Monastery at Trier — it contains the gospel teachings of Christmas, Easter and Whitsun, written in Latin with gold on purple parchment; the *Jarloch Chronicle,* 1220, written at Milevsko, Bohemia, in Latin on parchment, by the Abbot; the *Bible of Doksany,* 13th century, in which the entire Bible has been transcribed in the most minute handwriting in Latin on parchment; the *Schellenberg Bible* 1440; and the *Missale of Louka,* MS, 1483, written at Brno and encased in a Renaissance binding. Of the 1,200 incunabula the oldest book is the 1456 *Nürnberg Fust,* while the *Chronicle of Troy* was the first book printed at Pilsen in 1468. The Library has 16 of the 32 Czech incunabula, 7 of them unique copies. The Library also has a set of the four volume *Le Musée français* (Paris, 1803-9) which came from Napoleon's own library and P.J. Redouté's *Les Liliacées* (6 volumes, Paris, 1802-12) presented by the Empress Marie Louise, wife of Napoleon, in 1812. The Literary Archive of the Museum of Czech Literature has within it many important collections relating to Czech cultural and literary life.

A 16th-century Book of Hours of the Virgin Mary and the Holy Cross, in Strahov Library

Exhibition Areas. Cabinet of Book Culture. Theological and Philosophical Halls and adjoining corridors and rooms.

Hours. Study Room: Mon.-Fri. 0800-1800, Sat. 0800-1200. Closed Sun. and public hols. Historical rooms: Every day 0900-1700.

Transport. Tram no. 22 (terminal station 'Památník písemnictví). (The Strahov is situated on the summit of the hill of Petřín above the Vltava River.)

Parking. Strahov courtyard.

Admission. Readers: Free of charge. Registration in the Study Room. *Visitors:* Entrance fee Kčs 2 per person.

Information. In the entrance hall or in the Study Room.

Sales. At the gate or in the entrance hall.

Guidebooks. Available in Czech, Russian, Polish, German, English, French, Italian, Swedish and Spanish.

Restaurant/Snack Facilities. None, but several nearby.

Services. Lavatory, smoking lounge, telephone.

Catalogues. General author catalogue. Special catalogues of MSS, early prints etc.

Classification. Own.

Copying/Photography. Xerographic and microfilm copying facilities available through staff. Photography in the Library halls is only permitted if no camera stands are used.

Denmark

ÅRHUS
Statsbiblioteket (State and University Library)
Universitetsparken, DK-8000 Århus C
Tel. (06) 122022

History. The history of the State and University Library of Århus may be said to have begun with the fire which destroyed Christiansborg Castle in 1884. During this fire the Danish Royal Library, in the immediate neighbourhood of the Castle, was in great danger. Since the Royal Library had been receiving both legal deposit copies of Danish publications, it was decided to build a major library outside Copenhagen. Thus, on 17 June 1902, the Statsbiblioteket at Århus was opened. The Library received books from several sources, the nucleus being formed from 19th century duplicates of the Royal Library, the Regenburg Collection on Schleswig-Holstein, and part of the Wegener historical library. Legal deposit privileges began in 1902, and by the end of 1973 the Library had approximately 1,254,000 volumes, housed in a new building opened on 17 December 1962. It serves as the library for the University of Århus and as a central lending library to all Danish public libraries.

Special Collections and Treasures. Apart from the special collections mentioned above, the library possesses a collection of records and documents concerning the history of feminism, as well as a collection of books and articles by and on the 19th century Jutland author S.S. Blicher. Since December 1971, the State Library has undertaken national responsibility for the collection of literature on the mass media. The official name of the newspaper collection is The State Newspaper Collection and it is the main Danish collection of newspapers. About 1,200 titles are represented with 100 still current.

Exhibition Areas. Exhibition Room.

Statsbiblioteket, Århus

Woodcut (trial scene) from
the first printing of the Jutland
Law in the Danish language
(Ribe, 1504), in the Statsbiblioteket, Århus

Hours. Reading Room and Catalogue Hall: Mon.-Fri.
0900-1900, Sat. 0900-1400. Closed Sun. and public hols.

Transport. Buses from Tirstrup Airport to the air
terminal in Århus will stop at the Library (Lange-
landsgade) on request. The main entrance to the Library
is from the University Park, facing south.

Parking. In the University Park and opposite the Library
(Gustav Wiedsvej).

Admission. *Readers:* Free of charge.
Visitors: Guided tours can be arranged.

Information. In the Catalogue Hall, on the first floor.

Sales. In the cloakroom in the vestibule. Postcards and
library publications available.

Guidebooks. A reader's guide, free of charge, in
Danish only.

Restaurant/Snack Facilities. The canteen is open for
staff and readers Mon.-Fri. 1130-1330. Closed Sat.

Services. Microfilm reading room, typing room,
listening room (for records and tape-recordings), research
rooms, cloakrooms, telephone booths.

Catalogues. Card catalogues for books, periodicals and
various special collections.

Classification. Local system primarily based on the
Library of Congress.

Copying/Photography. Various kinds of copying
machines available. There is a coin-operated photocopying machine in the Reading Room. Private
photography unrestricted in public parts of the Library.

COPENHAGEN
Det Kongelige Bibliotek (The Royal Library)
Christians Brygge 8, DK-1219 Copenhagen
Tel. (01) 15 01 11

History. As early as the 16th century Danish kings had
a fairly comprehensive library housed in the Copenhagen
Castle but in 1605, during the reign of King Christian IV,
the whole collection was handed over to Copenhagen
University. This old Royal Library was subsequently
destroyed in a fire in 1728. King Frederik III (1648-70)
founded a new Royal Library in about 1665 and by the
time of his death it had 20,000 volumes. The collections
were housed in a building, erected 1667-73, near the
Royal Castle (the building now houses the National
Archives). Legal deposit privileges began in 1697. In 1793
the Library was opened to the public and in 1849 it

The Royal Library,
Copenhagen

became state property. By 1906 the Library had grown to 800,000 volumes and moved into its present building, which is currently being remodelled and extended. In accordance with the general library reforms in the early 20th century the Royal Library became the country's main library for humanities and social sciences and the library for Copenhagen University in the same fields. At the same time the University Library of Copenhagen took over the responsibility for medicine and science (see next entry). In 1943 the Royal Library and the two sections of Copenhagen University Library were organised as one administrative unit under the management of the National Librarian. Current holdings of the Royal Library total 1.8 million volumes and more than 2 million items of music, maps and prints.

Special Collections and Treasures. The Danish Department of 700,000 volumes is the most complete collection of Danish literature in existence. The Library's Judaica Collection has its core in the David Simonsen and Lazarus Goldschmit Libraries. Other collections include the Count Otto Thott Library, rich in medieval and other MSS, and early printed books; the Henrik Hielmstierne Collection of Danish literature of the 16th and 17th centuries; the papers of Hans Christian Andersen and Søren Kierkegaard; and Svend Grundtvig's Collection of Danish ballads and folklore. Individual treasures include the *Dalbybogen* (c. 1050-1100), possibly the oldest book written in Scandinavia; *The Angers fragment,* an original part of the *Gesta Danorum* by Saxo Grammaticus; F.G. Poma de Ayala, *Nueva corónica y buen gobierno* (c. 1600), a MS survey of the Incas prior to Spanish conquest; *The Kristina Psalter* MS (c. 1230); the world-famous *Flatøbogen,* written 1387-94 by two Icelandic priests, containing the sagas of the Norwegian kings and according to a special law from 1965 transferred to Iceland; Aeldre Edda, *Codex Regius* (c. 1270), the only complete copy in existence of the old Norse religious and heroic poems; *Ta-pen-nich-p'an ching,* a Chinese MS written before 1028 containing a translation from Sanskrit to Chinese of the Mahaparinirvana-Sutra; and renowned collections of Tibetan and Mongolian MSS, Avesta MSS, etc.

Exhibition Areas. At the moment the Library is undergoing modernisation and rebuilding which has limited exhibition space. Nevertheless exhibitions are held on a regular basis.

Hours. Mon.-Sat. 0900-1900. Closed Sun. and public hols.

Transport. The Library is situated near the centre of Copenhagen, opposite Christiansborg Castle and within reach of many bus routes from the Town Hall square.

Parking. Streets adjoining the Library.

Admission. Readers: No special regulations, except for

loans.

Visitors: Visitors are welcome to the Library. There is a public relations department which deals with group visits.

Information.   At the Library staff desks.

Sales.   Library publications, postcards etc. are sold in the cloakroom.

Guidebooks.   An information booklet, in English, is available free of charge.

Restaurant/Snack Facilities.   Canteen which provides coffee, tea, snacks etc.

Services.   All usual facilities available.

Catalogues.   Various author and subject catalogues.

Classification.   Own. Modern Danish books are classified by Dewey.

Copying/Photography.   Copying service provides dry copies and microfilms, etc. Copying machines are also available for individual use. Permission must be obtained before readers can use their own cameras.

COPENHAGEN

University Library, 2nd Dept., Scientific and Medical Library
49 Nörre allé, DK-2200 Copenhagen, N
Tel. 01 39 65 23

University Library, 2nd Department, Copenhagen

History.   The University of Copenhagen was founded in 1479 and its library in 1482. For many years the collections were housed in the loft of *Trinitatis Kirke* (Holy Trinity Church), until the collections were destroyed by fire in 1728. The most important factor in the subsequent development of the Library was the Ministry of Education Report of 1926, which recommended that the Royal Library (see preceding entry) should concentrate on the literature of the humanities, while the University of Copenhagen Library was to specialise in medicine and the sciences. The University Library 2nd Dept. (to differentiate it from the 1st Dept., the old University Library in Frue Plads) was therefore built during 1935-37 on the corner of Tagensvej and Nörre allé in the centre of the scientific/medical research area. Under copyright laws the Library may claim any Danish work it requires. Current holdings total 522,000 books and 448,000 foreign dissertations.

Special Collections and Treasures.   Special collections include the J.F. Classen Collection and a comprehensive pictorial book collection of birds and their eggs.

Exhibition Areas. Exhibits are located in several glass show-cases in the entrance hall.

Hours. Sept.-May: Mon.-Fri. 0900-2000, Sat. 0900-1600. June-Aug.: Mon.-Fri. 0900-1800, Sat. 0900-1600. Closed: Sun. official hols, 24 Dec., 31 Dec., Sat. before Easter Sun., Sat. before Whit Sun., Queen's birthday (16 April), Constitution Day (5 June).

Transport. Bus nos. 10, 84, 24, 43.

Parking. In the Library grounds.

Admission. *Readers* and *Visitors:* Free.

Information. In the cloakroom or secretariat (ground floor).

Sales. In the cloakroom — postcards available.

Guidebooks. Guide for borrowers, in Danish, no charge.

Restaurant/Snack Facilities. Hot drinks are available from a vending machine in the smoking lounge.

Services. Six studies — on the 1st and 2nd floors. Lavatories, cloakrooms, smoking lounge, telephone next to the hall staircase on the first floor.

Catalogues. Alphabetical author and title catalogues. Systematic catalogue with subject index.

Classification. Own.

Copying/Photography. There is a copying service but machines are not available for individual use.

Ecuador

QUITO

Biblioteca Ecuatoriana 'Aurelio Espinosa Pólit'
Apartado 160, Quito
Tel. 530-420

History. The Library was founded by the famous Ecuadorean humanist, Father Aurelio Espinosa Pólit, in 1928 and has been called 'the finest library of Ecuadorean imprints presently in existence'. Pólit, the first director of the Library, was also the first Rector of the Catholic Pontifical University of Ecuador. It is located in the northern suburb of Cotocollao and, although it is a private institution run by the Jesuits, its collections are open to all serious researchers. Originally housed in an old Jesuit building, the Library has been located in a new

Biblioteca Ecuatoriana 'Aurelio Espinosa Pólit', Quito

colonial style building since 1972. Holdings currently total 60,000 volumes, 100,000 pamphlets and 18,000 MSS.

Special Collections and Treasures. The Library has special collections of the colonial chroniclers and Ecuadorean authors. The Library possesses 1,400 periodicals and 1,800 newspapers, many of them little known. The map collection is one of the best in Ecuador.

Exhibition Areas. A special Exhibition Room displays historical objects and documents, such as the MS of the *Historia del reino de Quito* by Father Juan de Velasco.

Hours. Library Archive: Wed.-Fri. 0900-1200, 1500-1800. Closed Sat.-Tues. Museum: Wed.-Fri. 1000-1200, 1500-1800. Sat.-Sun. 1500-1800. Closed Mon.-Tues. and public hols.

Transport. By bus: Cotocollao no. 7, or Turismo: Mitad del mundo.

Parking. Available.

Admission. *Readers:* Admitted on production of suitable identification to the Director. It is preferred if new readers ring up in advance (530-420). A blue library ticket is issued, which details identity card or passport number. Payment of S/.5,00.
Visitors: On payment of S/.10,00. Special concessions for educational institutions.

Information. At the Information Office.

Sales. In the Bookshop next to the Information Office.

Guidebooks. None.

Restaurant/Snack Facilities. None.

Services. Cloakrooms, lavatories, telephones.

Catalogues. Alphabetical author and subject catalogues.

Classification. Modified Dewey.

Copying/Photography. Apply to the Director. Flash photography prohibited.

Egypt

CAIRO

The Egyptian National Library, General Egyptian Book Organisation, Nile Corniche, Boulac, Cairo
Tel. 900232

History. The National Library (Dar-ul-Kutub) was founded in 1870 by Ali Mubārak, Minister of Education, as part of the general modernisation movement in Egypt, in the second half of the 19th century. A basement of the Darb al-Jamāmīz Palace was provided for the collection, then named the 'Khedival Library'. The collection was formed from books and MSS obtained from various government offices, mosques and waqf properties, and then in 1873 a valuable collection of European books was presented to the Library by the earliest 'Egyptological Association', which had been founded in Cairo in 1836. In 1889 the Library transferred from the basement to the first floor of the Palace and in 1904, because of increasing growth of the collections, to a building at Midan Ahmed Maher. Legal deposit privileges were received in 1954 (amended in 1962) and these have helped swell holdings to the current figure of 1.5 million volumes. In 1970 the Library occupied its new building on the east bank of the Nile, with storage space for 5 million volumes. It is currently part of the Ministry of Culture of the Arab Republic of Egypt. The old building in Midan Ahmed Maher continues to be used as a general public library; the new building functions as a research library.

Special Collections and Treasures. Collections include the 3,458 vol. library of Mustaphan Fadil Pacha, brother of Khédive Ismaïl, one of the prime movers in the foundation of the National Library; the libraries of the former royal family; and the collections of Ahmad Taymour Pacha (18,147 vols.), Ahmad Zaki Pacha (18,625 vols.), Ahmad Talaat (30,000 vols.) and Ali Jalal Husseini (8,638 vols.). The Library has been endowed, since 1920, with a printing section which has contributed much to the revival of fine printing in Egypt. The Library also contains one of the finest collections of Arabic MSS in the world.

Exhibition Areas. No details provided of location of Exhibition Room, but exhibits include a collection of Arabic papyri and MSS illustrating the evolution of Arabic writing through the first four centuries of the Hijra, and a precious collection of handwritten copies of the *Qur'an*.

Hours. Daily 0900-2000. Closed public hols.

Transport. Public transport is often crowded. Taxis are

relatively cheap. Old Building: about 1½ miles east of the Nile Hilton, towards the old part of Cairo. New Library: located on Nile Corniche (east bank of the Nile) about one mile north of Nile Hilton.

Parking.   No details available.

Admission.   Readers and *Visitors:* Open, free of charge, to all. The Library at Midan Ahmed Maher functions as the main public library for Cairo.

Information.   At Library staff desks.

Sales.   No details available.

Guidebooks.   In Arabic and English.

Restaurant/Snack Facilities.   Available in the New Library.

Services.   Lavatories, cloakrooms, facilities for the blind and visually handicapped.

Catalogues.   The Library maintains two groups of card catalogues: one for Arabic and one for foreign collections. Each group is divided into three separate catalogues: author, title and classified. Various printed catalogues.

Classification.   Modified Dewey (16th edn), with extensions for Islamic religion and Arabic and Egyptian language, literature and history.

Copying/Photography.   Microfilming and dry-copying through Library staff. Private photography forbidden.

GIZA

Cairo University Library, Orman Gardens, Giza
Tel. 848426 and 845747

History.   Cairo University Library was established with the University in 1907. In 1928 it became the State University and moved into its present building in 1930. While the number of students that it serves has risen enormously in recent years (currently 75,000 students and 14,000 teaching staff), the funds available to the University Library have not risen proportionately, so that current holdings only total 215,000 volumes, 4,000 MSS and 200 fragments of papyri.

Special Collections and Treasures.   Collections include the Ibrahim Helmi Collection of 18,000 volumes, the Kamal ed Din Hussein Collection of 4,000 volumes, and the Sybold Collection of 3,000 volumes.

Exhibition Areas.   Occasional exhibitions are held, but there is no permanent exhibition area.

Cairo University Library, Giza

Hours.   Oct.-May: 0900-1900.   June-Sept.: 0900-1400. Closed during national and Moslim hols.

Transport.   Buses pass close to the Library.

Parking.   Available on campus.

Admission.   *Readers* and *Visitors:* Free admission. A deposit of L.EG.5 must be made by any non-registered student or non-teaching staff member wishing to borrow books.

Information.   Near the main entrance.

Sales.   On the second floor. University publications for sale.

Guidebooks.   A guide in Arabic, published in 1965, free of charge. A new guide, also free of charge, is in preparation.

Restaurant/Snack Facilities.   Not in the Library itself but in the vicinity and on the University campus.

Services.   Cloakroom, lavatories.

Catalogues.   Author and subject.   Bound   catalogue (1907-1972). Card catalogue (1973-).

Classification.   Dewey (1907-1972). Library of Congress (1973-).

Copying/Photography.   Facilities on the ground floor. Prior   permission   must   be   obtained   for   private photography.

Ethiopia

ADDIS ABABA
Haile Selassie I University Libraries
PO Box 1176, Addis Ababa
Tel. 115673 or 110844

History.   The Haile Selassie I University Library is the largest library in Ethiopia. It was created in December 1961 out of a number of previously autonomous institutions of higher learning, each with its own book collection. However, a degree of centralisation was gradually introduced, so that a more homogenous library system began to take shape. The largest and oldest library in the system was that of the University College of Addis Ababa, founded in 1950. In August 1969 the Central University Library moved into a new building given by the United States Agency for International

The John F. Kennedy Library, Haile Selassie I University, Addis Ababa

Development. It was dedicated to the late John F. Kennedy on 23 July 1970, by the then Emperor Haile Selassie and Mrs. Rose Kennedy. Today the two-storey Library contains 326,509 volumes, 1,269 manuscripts and 45,819 microforms.

Special Collections and Treasures. The major special collection, housed in the Institute of Ethiopian Studies, with a stock of over 12,000 volumes and 500 manuscripts, covers all aspects of Ethiopian history and culture. The Law Library possesses a fine collection of African legal materials, completed where necessary on microfiche.

Exhibition Areas. The John F. Kennedy Memorial Library has an exhibition area on the first floor.

Hours. Term: Mon.-Fri. 0800-2250, Sat. 0830-2130, Sun. 1500-2130. Vacation: Mon.-Sat. 0830-1830. Closed Sun. July-Aug: Mon.-Sat. 0830-2130, Sun. 1500-2130.

Transport. Buses 11, 13, 17, 23, 31 to Siddist Kilo. Any 'Seicento' taxi for 25 cents.

Parking. Ample parking facilities available.

Admission. Readers: Students, faculty and staff, and the general public may use the Library but outside readers must deposit Eth.$ 10 per book for borrowing. *Visitors:* Free of charge.

Information. Reference Dept. and Ethiopian Collection — ground floor. Periodicals and Documents — first floor.

Sales. None.

Guidebooks. Library guides in Amharic and English available, free of charge.

Restaurant/Snack Facilities. None.

Services. Telephone on ground loor. Lavatories on ground and first floors. Smoking lounge first floor. Typing facilities by arrangement.

Catalogues. Author, title and subject card catalogues.

Classification. Library of Congress for general collections. Dewey 16 for Ethiopian collections.

Copying/Photography. Copying and microfilming facilities available.

Finland

HELSINKI

Helsingin yliopiston kirjasto (Helsinki University Library)
PO Box 312, 00171 Helsinki 17
Tel. 191 2742

History. The Library of the University of Helsinki acts as the general research library of the University and as Finland's national library. Historically its origins may be traced back to 1640, when the University of Turku was founded. Growth of the Library was steady, but in 1827 a fire destroyed the Turku University building and the 40,000 volumes in the Library. The Library, re-founded in Helsinki, occupied in 1844 its present building, designed by Carl Ludwig Engel in the neoclassical style. The growth of collections was then rapid. The Library had enjoyed copyright deposit privileges for Finnish books since 1707 and from 1820-1917 it was a copyright library for Russian books. In 1857 the collections totalled 100,000 volumes and by the 1910s some 400,000 volumes. Increased book accommodation was provided by structural alterations in 1893, in 1906, when a tower was added, and again during 1954-8. In 1974 the Library was united with the Undergraduate Library, the former Student Union Library. Current holdings total 1.6 million volumes, 1,200 shelf metres of MSS and 22,000 rolls of microfilms.

Special Collections and Treasures. The Finnish national collection comprises the archives of Finnish literature. Other collections include the America, Estonica, Georgica, Hebraica, Lettonica, Lithuanica and Turcica Collections consisting of Russian literature in the language of the minorities, received from Russia as deposit copies during 1820-1917; the Monrepos Collection of about 9,000 finely bound volumes, mostly from the Age of Enlightenment; the collection of 19th century Russian literature, the best outside the USSR; the Enckell Collection of 547 maps printed before 1800; the Adolf Erik Nordenskiöld Collection of 4,000 volumes on geography, cartography, geology and science, particularly relating to the arctic regions, including over fifty different editions of Ptolemy's *Cosmography.* The MSS Collection contains various documents and manuscripts estates of persons belonging to Finnish cultural history; a collection of 10,000 vellum fragments; the collection of Slavonic MSS; and musical composition MSS, notably those of Jean Sibelius.

Exhibition Areas. Exhibition Room, to the right of the entrance hall.

Hours. Reading rooms: Mon.-Sat. 0900-2100, Sun. 1200-1800. 1 June 31 —31 Aug: Mon.-Sat. 0900-1800,

Helsinki University Library

Title page decoration of the first Finnish translation (by Mikael Agricola) of the New Testament (1548), in Helsinki University Library

Sun. 1400-2000.

Transport. The Library is ten minutes' walk from both the bus and the railway stations.

Parking. Parking facilities are provided between 0800 and 1700. A small charge is made.

Admission. Readers: Admission is free to every person of 18 years of age, or younger persons studying at the University. For home loans, foreign students must produce a guarantee (the guarantor's signature and two witnesses), but foreign teachers at the University are not required to produce such a guarantee.
Visitors: Free of charge. The Library is shown to groups of visitors on request. Arrangements for a tour may be made with the Head of the Service Division (tel. 191 2745).

Information. In the Catalogue Hall. Hours: Mon.-Fri. 1000-1600 (tel. 191 2742).

Sales. The attendant in the entrance hall has guide-books, postcards and slides for sale. The printed publications of the Library can be bought at the Government Printing Centre, Annakatu 44.

Guidebooks. Helsinki University Library. A short survey (in English), 2 Fmk. *Helsinki University Library Guide* (in English), free.

Restaurant/Snack Facilities. The café in the basement is open weekdays 0900-1700 (in summer 0900-1530).

Services. Two machines in the typing room for readers. Cloakroom in the entrance hall, telephone and lavatories in the basement. Smoking is only allowed in the café and the stairway leading there.

Catalogues. Alphabetical and systematic catalogues.

Classification. Universal Decimal Classification.

Copying/Photography. The Library supplies photo-copies, microfilms, enlargements and xerographic copies. There are two photocopying machines in the Lending Office for the use of readers. The assistants in the Lending Office and the attendant in the entrance hall will change money.

France

AVIGNON

Muséum Calvet, Bibliothèque
65 rue Joseph-Vernet, F-84000Avignon
Tel. (90) 810860

History. The Library was founded in 1810 by Dr. Esprit Calvet (1728-1810), a former Professor of Medicine at Avignon University, who not only bequeathed his collections, but also his fortune for the establishment of an independent museum administered by a Board of Trustees. Calvet's collections, initially housed in the convent of St. Martial, included 1,382 volumes, rich in material on history, archaeology and classical history. In 1826 the stock of the Library was amalgamated with that of the town library, which in 1833 moved into the Hôtel de Villeneuve-Martignan, constructed between 1741 and 1754. The official opening took place on 3 April 1835. The 20th century has seen the development of a lending library in 1937, a children's library in 1948, and, since 1970, branches in the suburbs. Current holdings total 270,000 volumes, including 700 incunabula, 6,600 MSS, 40,000 prints, 12,000 pieces of music, and 30,000 coins.

Special Collections and Treasures. Treasures include manuscripts from the 10th-12th centuries (relating to St. Isidore, St. Ambroise and St. Thomas Aquinas); the *Book of Hours* of the Blessed Cardinal Pierre de Luxembourg; the *Psalter* of Maréchal Boncicault; 17th-18th century sacred and secular music from the city's former Académie de Musique; and eighty operas of late 17th-early 19th centuries from the library of Castil-Blaze. Among the incunabula are *Juvenalis et Persii Satyrae* (Paris, 1472), a very rare work); *Breviarum Romanum* (Venice, 1478); St. Augustine, *De civitate Dei* (Toulouse, 1488); St. Augustine, *Meditationes* (Paris, c.1500), a work of which only two copies are known; *La vérité des miracles ... de M. de Paris* (1737), a copy which belonged to Schopenhauer, with his MS notes. Collections include the original Calvet Library; the Requiem Collection on local and natural history; the Marieton Collection of 19th century French literature; and the Raynolt Collection.

Exhibition Areas. No permanent exhibition rooms.

Hours. Mon.-Sat. 0830-1200, 1400-1830. Closed Sun. and public hols.

Transport. No public transport available.

Parking. In nearby streets.

Admission. *Readers* and *Visitors:* Admission free of

Muséum Calvet, Avignon

Decorated initial from Missal of Pope Clement VII (1478-1534), in the Muséum Calvet, Avignon (MS 136). Showing portrait of Pope Urban V

charge.

Information. At muséum entrance.

Sales. None.

Guidebooks. None.

Restaurant/Snack Facilities. None, but available in the neighbourhood.

Services. Lavatories.

Catalogues. Author, subject and systematic catalogues of printed books. Printed catalogue of MSS (7 vols.).

Classification. Own.

Copying/Photography. Xerographic microfilm copying through Library staff. Private photography only with official authorisation.

BESANÇON

Bibliothèque municipale
1 rue de la Bibliothèque, F-25000 Besançon
Tel. (81) 81 20 29

History. The Library was founded in 1694 by the Abbé Jean-Baptiste Boisot, who left his collections to the abbey of Saint-Vincent of Besançon on the condition that they were made available to the public two days a week. This initial stock, comprising in large part the library of Cardinal Granvelle, was seized during the French Revolution and subsequently enriched with other sequestrated material. It became town property in 1803 and in 1817 occupied its present quarters. Current holdings include 280,000 volumes, 1,215 periodicals 3000 manuscripts, and 1,011 incunabula.

Special Collections and Treasures. Collections include the *Fonds Granville* (illuminated manuscripts, State Papers of Cardinal Granville, incunabula, fine bindings, etc); the Local History Collection, including the town archives from 1290 onwards; and the manuscript collections of Baverel, Castan, Chifflet, Dunand, Duvernoy (notably on the Franche-Comté); P.A. Paris (drawings of the 18th Century) and Weiss.
Treasures include the *Bonmont Psalter* (13th century); the *Froissart Chronicles* (early 15th century); the *Prayer Book* of Maximilian I (1514); while among the printed book treasures are the *Bréviaire* (Salins, 1484), the first typographic work executed in Franche-Comté; the *Regimen sanitatis Salernitanum* and the *Speculum* of Rodrigue de Zamora, printed in Besançon in 1487 and 1488 respectively.

Bibliothèque municipale, Besançon

Exhibition Areas.   Exhibition room

Hours.   Mon.-Sat.   0900-1200,   1330-1800   (July-Sept. 1400-1800). Closed Sun. and public hols., 1-8 July.

Transport.   The Library is located in the centre of Besançon, at the joining of la Grande-Rue and rue de la Bibliothèque, and is easily accessible on foot.

Parking.   In neighbouring streets.

Admission. Readers: Free admission to the Reading Room and for the use of modern printed material. Proof of identity and permission from a member of staff are necessary for whose wishing to consult manuscripts and rare items.
Visitors: Free of charge.

Information.   Apply to Library staff desks.

Sales.   None.

Guidebooks.   None.

Restaurant/Snack Facilities.   None.

Services.   Cloakrooms, lavatories.

Catalogues.   Card catalogues: alphabetical author, alphabetical subject (since 1900). Printed catalogues: printed books (4 vols., 1842-5), manuscripts incunabula, etc.

Classification.   Details not provided.

Copying/Photography.   Copying facilities available through Library staff. Permission must be obtained for private photography.

GRENOBLE

Bibliothèque municipale
boulevard maréchal Lyautey, F-38000 Grenoble
Tel. 440156, 444250, 444276

History.   The Library has its origins in the 34,000 volume collection of Mgr Jean de Caulet, Bishop of Grenoble (1726-1771), which was not dispersed at his death, thanks to the initiative of the printer André Faure. Faure launched a subscription appeal on 15 January 1772 to preserve Caulet's library, which was opened to the public in 1773 on the 2nd and 3rd floors of the Lycée Stendhal. The 6,000 volume collection of the 'Bibliothèque de l'Ordre des avocats de Grenoble' was soon added and then in 1803 the Library received 3,543 volumes from the Grand Chartreuse monastery. In 1872 the Library occupied a building, constructed 1865-72, to the east of the place de Verdun. Collections totalled 160,000

Bibliothèque municipale, Grenoble

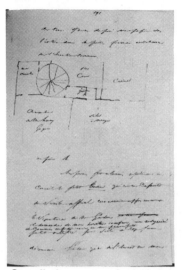

Stendhal, manuscript of La
Vie d'Henri Brulard (1835-6),
in the Bibliothèque municipale,
Grenoble (MS R299, vol. 1).
Folio 191

volumes in 1872, 213,000 in 1920, 237,000 in 1938, and currently include 573,226 books, 20,068 MSS and 2,560 maps and plans, housed in the new library building opened in 1970.

Special Collections and Treasures. Special collections include that of Caulet, mentioned above, which is strong in first editions of French authors such as Ronsard, du Bellay, Montaigne, Descartes, Molière, Corneille, etc; the Crozet Collection on Stendhal; the Rey Collection on Socialism; the de Beylié Collection on Indo-China; the Blanchet Collection on paper-making; the de Manteyer Collection on Provence, les Hautes-Alpes and Italy (10,000 volumes); the Pelloux-Prayer collection of first editions and 'editions de luxe'; and the Guitton Collection on contemporary French and Italian literature. Treasures include the first books printed at Lyon (1473), at Abbeville (1486), and at Grenoble (1490); *Le Champion des Dames,* MS of Martin Lefranc, 15th century; the *Poésies* of Charles d'Orléans (c. 1461) transcribed by his secretary, Antoine Astesan; François Villon, *Oeuvres* (Paris, 1533) first edition; Blaise Pascal, *Pensées* (Paris, 1670); and Jean Racine, *Esther* (Paris, 1689).

Exhibition Areas. Exhibition Room has several exhibitions per year.

Hours. Tues.-Sat. 1000-1200, 1400-1900. Closed Sun., Mon., during spring holiday (Easter) and the whole of Aug.

Transport. Public transport passes close to the Library.

Parking. In front of the Library.

Admission. *Readers* and *Visitors:* Free of charge.

Information. At Library staff desks.

Sales. None.

Guidebooks. Guide de la Bibliothèque, currently being reprinted, will be available free of charge.

Restaurant/Snack Facilities. Vending machines.

Services. Lavatories, lifts.

Catalogues. Author and subject card catalogues. Various special catalogues.

Classification. Dewey (reference works).

Copying/Photography. Facilities available. Private photography only permitted with authorisation.

LYON

Bibliothèque municipale de la Ville de Lyon
30 boulevard Vivier Merle, F-69431 Lyon Cedex 3
Tel. (78) 628520

History. The Library has a continuous history from about 1530, when it formed part of the College of the Trinity. In 1565 the College was given to the Jesuits and the development of the Library really dates from this time. The Library had two main sources of growth: support from the Council (Consulat) of the town, and gifts and bequests, notably the 1693 bequest of the famous library of Camille de Neufville-Villeroy, Archbishop of Lyon for 40 years. The Library suffered losses following the suppression of the Jesuits in 1762, and then during the French Revolution when it was damaged by shells and by pillaging. The Library did receive, however, various collections of dissolved religious houses, totalling 30,000 volumes in all. The Library had occupied the same building since 1530, but in 1912 it was installed in the ancient palace of the Archbishops, built in the 15th century and renovated in the 18th century. The Bibliothèque du Palais des Beaux Arts, founded in 1831, was added at the same time. In 1973 the entire collections, including 500,000 books, 11,200 MSS and 1,000 incunabula, were transferred to a new building in the 'Part-Dieu' section of the city.

Special Collections and Treasures. The Library has the richest collection of manuscripts of any provincial library in France. There are, for example, 13 MSS of the 5th-8th centuries and 40 MSS of the 9th century, including texts from St. Augustine, St. Jerome and Bede, and autographed MSS of the Deacon Florus. Collections include the Coste Collection, covering the history of Lyon; the Charavay Collection, particularly rich in autographs of the Reformation period; the Marat Collection of first editions and journals; the Becker Musical Collection of 1,500 volumes; the J.B. Vuillermoz Collection on Freemasonry; the Arthaud Collection on numismatics; the Thiollière Collection on paleontology; and the Bricaud Collection on the occult in the 19th and 20th centuries.

Exhibition Areas. Three rooms on the ground and first floors, totalling 600 sq. yards.

Hours. Tues.-Sat. 1000-1800. Closed Sun., Mon. and public hols.

Transport. By bus: nos. 26, 36, 37, 40B, 41, 46, 58B. (After 1978 by subway 'Part Dieu'.)

Parking. 'Parc des Cuirassiers' (1500 cars).

Admission. Readers: The Library is open to all, but readers wishing to consult ancient books (before 1800), manuscripts and engravings must make a special

Bibliothèque municipale, Lyon

Barthélemy de Chasseneux, Catalogus gloriae mundi (Lyon, 1529), in the Bibliothèque municipale, Lyon

application to the Chief Curator.
Visitors: By appointment.

Information. At the Desk in the hall of the Library.

Sales. At the Information Desk: posters, catalogues of exhibits, postcards and various publications are sold.

Guidebooks. A French folding guidebook is available free of charge.

Restaurant/Snack Facilities. Numerous cafeterias and restaurants nearby in the commercial centre.

Services. Telephones, lavatories, cloakrooms in the basement; smoking lounges and escalator on ground floor; lavatories on all 5 floors.

Catalogues. Author and subject catalogues. Special catalogues for the 'ancient reserve'

Classification. Dewey for reading room material, otherwise classified by entry.

Copying/Photography. Xerographic and microfilm copying can be obtained through the staff. Special permission is needed for private photography.

Friends of the Library. The *Societé des Amis de la Bibliothèque du Lyon* is open to all. Benefactor 100F; Honorary member 50F; Friend 10F.

PARIS

Bibliothèque nationale
58 rue Richelieu, F-75084 Paris Cedex 02
Tel. 266-62-62

History. The Bibliothèque nationale, which until the French Revolution constituted the Royal Library, has no precise date of origin. It can however be stated that it is the oldest of the European national libraries and that its continuous history dates from the reign of Louis XI (1461-80), who brought together some MSS and printed books by confiscation. His successors. Charles VIII and Louis XII, were both bibliophiles and radically improved the collection. Francis I (1515-1547) brought additional prestige to the Royal Library and his reign also witnessed the *Ordonnance de Montpellier* of 28 December 1537, which provided legal deposit privileges, the first such privileges granted in Europe (although they were not strictly enforced till the 19th century). In 1666 Colbert, an enthusiastic supporter of the Library, had it moved to La place rue Vivienne just opposite its present site. The Library was opened to the public in 1692, a concession which soon lapsed, only to be restored in 1736. In 1789 the Royal Library was effectively nationalised and became state property. During the revolutionary period

Bibliothèque nationale, Paris

the Library acquired some of its rarest items, in addition to some 300,000 volumes from the *dépôts littéraires*. By 1818 holdings totalled 800,000 books. The Reading Room, designed by Labrouste, in the style of his previous work at the Bibliothèque Sainte-Geneviève, was opened in 1868. Further extensions were made to the Library, in the 1930s, 1950s and 1960s, although the early part of the twentieth century, especially during World War I, witnessed a decline in the Library's fortunes. Current holdings total over 20 million items, including 8 million books and pamphlets, 800,000 maps and 180,000 MSS. The *Réunion des Bibliothèques nationales de Paris* (National Libraries Group), formed in 1926, now includes the Bibliothèque nationale, the Bibliothèque de l'Arsenal (see next entry), the Bibliothèque du Conservatoire and the Bibliothèque de l'Opéra.

Special Collections and Treasures. Collections in the Department of Printed Books include those of Renan covering the Bible and philology; Le Senne on the history of Paris; Payen on Montaigne; Bengesco and Beuchot on Voltaire; Seymour de Ricci on books of *haute bibliophilie;* Henri de Rothschild on first editions and precious bindings; and Châtre de Cangé on the military administration of the Ancien Regime. The Manuscripts Department has the collections of Baluze on the 16th and 17th centuries; Clairambault, Gaignières, Dupuy Fontanieu, Moreau, and Joly de Fleury on the history of France; and the Rothschild Collection of valuable MSS. The Oriental Section has the Pelliot Collection on China and Central Asia; the Mondon-Vidailhet Collection on Ethiopia; and the Griaule Collection on the Mission Dakar-Dijbouti. The Music Section has the Fonds Jean-Baptiste Weckerlin and Patrice Coirault on the French song; the *Fonds ancien* of the Conservatoire national de musique; the 18th century Philidor Collection; the Blancheton Collection on instrumental music of the 17th-18th centuries; and the Schoelcher Collection on Handel.

Exhibition Areas. The Mansart and Mazarine Galleries. Smaller exhibitions are held in the Dept. of Prints and the Dept. of Music.

Hours. Mon.-Sat. 0900-1800. Some of the special departments open later or close earlier. Closed Sun. Annual closure for a fortnight starting the second Mon. after Easter. In addition the Library is closed on legal holidays: 1 and 2 Jan., Easter Sat.-Mon., 1 May, Ascension Day, Whit Mon. and Tues. in Whitsun week, 14 July, 15 Aug., 1-2 Nov., 11 Nov., and 25 Dec.

Transport. Metro: Bourses, Halles, Opéra, Palais-Royal, Quatre-Septembre, Richelieu-Drouot. Bus: nos. 39, 48, 67, 74 and 85.

Parking. In the neighbouring streets. The Library is near to the Bourse and Pyramides parking on the right bank

Detail from Portuguese atlas attributed to Lopo Homem (1519), in the Bibliothèque nationale, Paris.

of the Seine.

Admission.   Readers: To obtain a reader's card apply at the Service d'accueil. A *'carte régulière',* valid for one year, or a *'carte de 24 entrées,* or a *'carte dispensée de frais'* (8 days maximum) may be issued to those over 18, with a degree and engaged in work requiring the use of the library. A foreigner will need his passport together with a letter of introduction from the cultural services of his embassy or a French university professor. For the first two payment of a small fee and two passport photographs are also required. A two-day ticket may be supplied to those who do not fulfil the required qualifications, and whose research is limited, on production of a passport. A reader's card for the BN is also valid for the other libraries of the *Réunion.*
Visitors: Guided tours are arranged by the *Service des Monuments historiques,* 62 rue St. Antoine, 75004 Paris.

Information.   At the Reception Desk (Service d'accueil) in the main entrance of the Library.

Sales. There is a sales service for the Library's publications: Catalogues, catalogues and posters of exhibitions, postcards etc. Open Mon.-Fri. 0930-1230 and 1400-1600. (Price list on request.)

Guidebooks. La Bibliothèque nationale 62pp.   3F. Various free departmental guides in French.

Restaurant/Snack Facilities.   None in the Library, but there are numerous restaurants, with and without self service, in the immediate vicinity of the Library.

Services. Lavatories, telephones, lifts to Depts. of Prints and Music, microfilm readers in Depts. of Printed Books, MSS, Music and Periodicals. Studios for listening to gramophone records and for sightreading of music.

Catalogues. Each Department has its own catalogues. For example, in Printed Books the published author catalogue is *Catalogue général des livres imprimés* which began appearing in 1897. This must be supplemented by various card and sheaf indexes, plus the *Catalogue des livres imprimés...* 1960-69 (Paris, 1972-5), 20 vols. already published. Various printed subject catalogues are available, as well as a card index of keyword entries e.g. 1925-35, 1936-59, 1960-70, 1970-. See particularly *Les Catalogues du Department des Imprimés,* 1970, 55p. and plans and *Les catalogues du département des Manuscrits: 1 Occidentaux,* 1974, viii-103p'.

Classification. Own.

Copying/Photography. There   are   photocopying machines in most departments. Photocopies, photographs, microfilms and slides can be supplied against payment in advance. Professional photographers may be allowed, on payment of a fee, to photograph certain items, providing no copyright regulations are infringed. The Service photographique is located on the north side of the Cour d'Honneur. This service, of which the photocopying sections in the Departments are largely independent, can reproduce documents from any of the libraries in the *Réunion.*

Friends of the Library. Société des Amis de la Bibliothèque nationale, founded in 1913, with a categories of membership.

PARIS

Bibliothèque de l'Arsenal
1 rue de Sully, F-75004 Paris
Tel. 277-44-21, 272-19-09, 272-33-14

History. The Library was founded in 1757 when Antoine-René de Voyer d'Argenson, marquis de Paulmy (1722-1787), Minister of War, was given a lodging in the erstwhile residence of the chief of the royal artillery. A fervent bibliophile, he brought his library there. Enriched by many acquisitions, especially by part of the well known collections of the duc de la Vallière, it was sold to the comte d'Artois, the King's brother, on 20 June 1785, the marquis reserving for himself the full use of the library till his death. During the French Revolution, the library of the comte d'Artois was one of the first to be seized and its 190,000 volumes constituted the 8th *dépôt national littéraire de Paris.* Accordingly, it received manuscripts and books from other Parisian *dépôts litteraires.* In April 1797, a decree proclaimed the Arsenal a 'bibliothèque nationale et publique', and on 25 April 1816 the Arsenal was formally returned to the comte d'Artois, although it was managed, in fact, by the Home Office. In 1824, Charles Nodier was appointed Librarian to the comte d'Artois (who became King of France shortly afterwards). Nodier filled this office until his death in 1844. During the 19th century, the Library received many large gifts, notably the Saint-Simonian collection of manuscripts and printed books from Prosper Enfantin. By 1877 the stock totalled 350,000 volumes and rose to 610,000 volumes in 1908, partly aided by legal deposit privileges in the field of literary texts. It became part of the Réunion des Bibliothèques nationales in 1926 and a Department of the Bibliothèque nationale in 1936 see preceeding entry. Recent growth has concentrated on material in the performing arts. Current holdings include 1,530,000 printed books, 15,000 manuscripts, 150,000 prints.

Special Collections and Treasures. The Manuscripts Collection includes 200 illuminated manuscripts; original documents relating to the marquis de Paulmy's duties; part of the archives of the Bastille; the records of the *dépôts littéraires;* papers relating to the Arnauld family and the history of Saint-Simonism; and the Lambert Collection on Huysmans. The Library possesses one of

Bibliothèque de l'Arsenal, Paris

the largest collections of Romance literature in existence, particularly rich in mystery plays and early French poetry. The Theatre Collection has the extensive private libraries of Georges Douay (50,000 volumes) and Auguste Rondel (300,000 volumes), supplemented by the archives on Antoine, Baty, Copeau, Jouvet, Pitoëff and E.G. Craig. Individual treasures include the *Tropary* from Autun, a 10th century manuscript with a 3rd century ivory panel in the binding; the *Terence des ducs* (1405-10), a manuscript which belonged to the duc de Berry; the *Bible of Charles V* (early 14th century), a fine example of the Paris school; the *Charlemagne* and *Celestin Gospels* (both 9th century); and the *Psalter of Blanche de Castille et de Saint-Louis* (c. 1200-1223); perhaps one of the most beautiful manuscripts of the 13th century.

Exhibition Areas. There is no permanent exhibition room, although there are areas, such as the *Cabinet la Meilleraye,* a fine example of a decorated 17th century suite of rooms, the 18th century *Salon de Musique,* the apartments of Charles Nodier, and the office of José-Maria de Heredia, within the Library, which can be visited.

Hours. Mon.-Sat. 1000-1700. Closed on public hols. and the first fortnight in Sept.

Transport. Nearest Métro station: Sully-Morland. By bus: no. 86 or 87.

Parking. In adjoining streets.

Admission. Readers: Serious research students only are admitted. A reader's card for the Bibliothèque Nationale is valid. For a reader's ticket for the Bibliothèque de l'Arsenal alone, prior application in writing to the Conservateur-en-Chef is required. A temporary pass is available for brief visits.
Visitors: Wednesday 1400-1600. Visits by parties can be arranged.

Information. At the Bureau de renseignement on the 1st floor.

Sales. Postcards on sale at the Bureau de renseignement.

Guidebooks. None.

Restaurant/Snack Facilities. None in the Library.

Services. Lavatories.

Catalogues. Various printed catalogues, with card supplements, to the MSS, prints and music. Several sequences, in guard-book, sheaf and card index form for the books and major collections.

Classification. Own.

Copying/Photography. Dry-copying through staff for readers only. For microfilming, or more specialised works, the services of the Bibliothèque nationale or a private photographer may be used.

PARIS
Bibliothèque de la Sorbonne
47 rue des Écoles, F-75230 Paris Cedex 05
Tel. 325-24-13

History. In 1253, Robert de Sorbon, Chaplain to Louis IX, founded a college for students of theology, which, under the name 'La Sorbonne', later extended to the whole University. The MSS and books built up by the original foundation were dispersed in 1794, teaching in the college having been suspended in 1791. The basis of the present Library was a bequest of 8,000 volumes in 1762 by a former university rector, J.G. Petit de Montempuis. It was supplemented by a stock of books, acquired in 1765 from the Collège Louis-le-Grand, on the expulsion of the Jesuits from Paris. The collections managed to survive the French Revolution and in 1812 they were designated the 'Bibliothèque de l'Université, a title retained until 1968 (when it was renamed under the University of Paris reorganisation to differentiate it from the other faculty libraries). During the intervening period the original collections were systematically enlarged until today they total 2 million volumes.

Special Collections and Treasures. Collections include the Fonds Beljame (Shakespeare in France); the Fonds Eugène Manuel (19th century French poetry); the archives of the University of Paris from the 14th-18th centuries; 400,000 theses from French universities; and a collection on the history of French universities.

Exhibition Areas. Exhibition cases in the Salle de Documentation.

Hours. Academic year: Mon.-Sat. 0900-2200. Summer: Mon.-Sat. 1000-1145, 1400-1745. Closed Sun. and public hols.

Transport. Métro: nearest stations Odéon, St. Michel, Luxembourg, Bus routes: 21, 27, 38, 63, 81, 85, 86, 96. (The Library extends along the east side of the Cour d'Honneur.)

Parking. 'Panthéon' (entrance from the rue Soufflot), 'Saint-Sulpice' (entrance from place Saint-Sulpice).

Admission. Readers: Must hold a reader's ticket. Foreign readers can obtain these on presentation of their passports and proof of membership of a university. If foreign readers wish to borrow books, they must produce a letter of recommendation from their embassy. *Visitors:* Temporary authorisation to use the Library can

Church of the Sorbonne (1629)

be granted, for a limited period, on production of identity papers and letters of recommendation from a professor or embassy.

Information. At the enquiry desk in the Reading Room.

Sales. None.

Guidebooks. The guide to the Library is no longer available but a new, enlarged and revised edition is planned.

Restaurant/Snack Facilities. Automatic sandwich and drinks machines are in the Library building and there are several cafés and restaurants nearby.

Services. Lavatories. Telephone kiosks in the University grounds.

Catalogues. Author, subject and periodical card catalogues. Printed catalogues for MSS, incunabula and 16th century books.

Classification. Own.

Copying/Photography. 'Monnayeur' (self-service) photo-copying machines in the Reading Room. Microfilm copying through Library staff. Written applications must be made to the Chief Librarian at least a week in advance for private photography.

PARIS
Bibliothèque historique de la Ville de Paris
24 rue Pavée, Paris 4
Tel. 272-10-18 or 508-89-99

History. The first collection of material on the history of Paris was bequeathed to the city by Antoine Moriau in 1759 and housed in the Hôtel de Lamoighon, where he had been living. In 1795 the collection of 20-30,000 volumes was transferred to the Institut de France. Another library was built but its 120,000 volumes were destroyed by fire in 1871. The present collection was founded in 1872, its rapid growth owing much to the able librarianship of Jules Cousin. By 1893 the stock was 100,000 volumes and, as a result of this growth, the books had to be moved from the Hôtel Carnavalet to the nearby Hôtel le Pelitier Saint-Fargeau. Continued expansion in the 20th century led to the Library's return in 1968 to its original quarters at the Hôtel de Lamoignon, suitably renovated and extended. The Library was formally reopened on 30 January 1969. Current holdings total over 500,000 books, 6,000 MSS volumes, 12,000 maps and 50,000 photographs.

Special Collections and Treasures. Collections are devoted to the French Revolution, *La Ligue, La Fronde,*

Bibliothèque historique de la Ville de Paris

Dreyfus, feminism and the theatre. The collection of engraved plans of the city and individual houses, dating from the 17th century, is apparently unique. MSS include the papers of notable Paris historians, such as Théodore Vacquer, Marcel Poëte and Lucien Lambeau. Other collections include the Fonds Michelet, Sand and Flaubert. The collection of posters on Paris is particularly valuable for the 19th century. The Library administers *La Maison de Balzac* at 47 rue Raynouard, Paris 16e and *La Maison de Victor Hugo* in the former Hôtel Rohan-Guéménée.

Exhibition Areas. Rare material is displayed in display cases, e.g. on the main staircase.

Hours. Mon.-Sat. 0930-1800. Closed Sun., public hols. and 1-15 Aug.

Transport. Métro: nearest stations Saint Paul, Chemin Vert. By bus: nos. 29, 67, 69, 76, 96.

Parking. In nearby streets.

Admission. Readers: Passport or identity card must be shown in order to gain a reader's ticket.
Visitors: Apply to Librarian.

Information. There is an information service for readers engaged in research. Also an indexing service.

Sales. None.

Guidebooks. La bibliothèque historique de la ville de Paris. In French only.

Restaurant/Snack Facilities. None on premises.

Services. Lavatories.

Catalogues. Alphabetical and subject card catalogue. Separate card catalogues for official publications, maps, microfilms etc., periodicals, manuscripts, special collections.

Classification. Own.

Copying/Photography. Apply to Library staff.

PARIS

Bibliothèque de l'Institut de France
23 quai de Conti, F-75270 Paris Cedex 06
Tel. 326-85-40

(For photograph see next entry)

History. The Institut de France was formed from various academies by a decree of 25 October 1795.

It was given part of the buildings of the Collège Mazarin in 1805 for its meetings and also to house the Library, which was based on the collection bequeathed to the 'Ville de Paris' by a Parisian magistrate and bibliophile, Antoine Moriau (1699-1760). Besides the Moriau collection the Library received material from the *dépôts littéraires,* built up as a result of French revolutionary confiscations. The collections totalled 70,000 volumes in 1825, 600,000 in 1926 and currently 1.5 million books with 22,000 periodicals and 60,000 microforms.

Special Collections and Treasures. Collections include the Godefroy Collection of historical MSS, formed in the second and third quarters of the 17th century by Théodore and Denis Godefroy, historiographers of France; the papers and correspondence of such 'académiciens' as Condorcet, Cuvier, Maxime du Camp, Hennin, Maspero and Henri de Régnier; the Barth Collection on Alsace; the Delessert Collection on botany; the Duplessis Collection on the history of art; the Huzard Collection on the history of the *Institute;* the Rodocanachi Collection on the Renaissance in Italy; the Schlumberger Collection on Byzantium; and the La Pinte de Livry Collection of precious books.

Exhibition Areas.   No details available.

Hours.   Mon.-Fri. 1200-1800. Closed Sat., Sun. and from 15-31 Aug.

Transport.   Métro: nearest stations Odéon, Mabillon, Pont Neuf, Louvre. Bus routes: 24, 27, 58, 70, 95.

Parking.   Near the Library.

Admission. Readers: The Library is reserved for members of the Institute but people with two academic sponsors may read there, as well as foreigners with a reference from their embassy.
Visitors: Visitors are not permitted in the Library.

Information.   At Library staff desks.

Sales.   None.

Guidebooks.   None.

Restaurant/Snack Facilities.   None, but available nearby.

Services.   Cloakrooms, lavatories.

Catalogues.   Dictionary catalogue.

Classification.   Own.

Copying/Photography.   Orders for copies of manuscripts should be addressed to the Chief Librarian. Microfilms and photocopies are carried out by the Centre national de la Recherche scientifique (CNRS).

PARIS
Bibliothèque Mazarine .
23 quai de Conti, F-75006 Paris
Tel. 033 8948

History. The Library was founded in 1643 by Cardinal Mazarin, with Gabriel Naudé as Librarian. It is the oldest public library in Paris. With Mazarin's fall from power the Library was sold in 1652, Naudé himself purchasing the medical items. When Naudé died on 29 July 1653, he left his medical collection to Mazarin, who, pardoned in 1653, also purchased the remainder of Naudé's extensive collection. Queen Christina of Sweden, who had purchased numerous MSS at the forced sale of Mazarin's library, now returned them, as did many other purchasers. By 1660 Mazarin had amassed 45,000 volumes, which he bequeathed to the Collège des Quatre Nations. During the reign of Louis XIV many of the MSS were taken by Jean Baptiste Colbert for Louis XIV's Royal Library. In 1926 the Mazarine was incorporated into the *Réunion des Bibliothèques nationales de Paris,* but in 1945 was attached to the Institut de France (see preceding entry), which had occupied the buildings of the college since the 19th century. The Reading Room, which dates from the 17th century, has been recently restored. Current holdings total 500,000 volumes, 4,500 MSS and 1,800 incunabula.

Special Collections and Treasures. Collections include those of Prosper Faugère on Pascal and Jansenism; the Pièrre Lebrun Collection of MSS and 19th century French literature; the Faralicq Collection on books and book collecting; the most important collection of MSS and printed works relating to Jansenism and the Port Royal 'Movement' of the 17th century; a large collection of Spanish and Italian works of the 16th and 17th centuries and one of the best collection of *Mazarinades* in the world. Other collections cover old medical books and French provincial history.

Exhibition Areas. None.

Hours. Mon.-Fri. 1000-1800. Closed Sat., Sun. and on national hols.

Transport. Métro: nearest stations Odéon, Mabillon, Pont Neuf, Louvre. Buses: 24, 27, 58, 70, 95. (The Mazarine Library is in the first court of the Palais de l'Institut.)

Parking. Near the Library.

Admission. *Readers:* Must present their national identity cards, or passports.
Visitors: No special regulations.

Information. At staff desks.

Bibliothèque Mazarine, Paris

Sales. None.

Guidebooks. None.

Restaurant/Snack Facilities. None in the Library, but several nearby.

Services. Cloakrooms, lavatories.

Catalogues. Author card catalogue. Printed catalogues for manuscripts, incunabula and Mazarin material.

Classification. Own, begun in 17th century.

Copying/Photography. Copying service available through the staff. Photography permitted within the Library.

PARIS
Bibliothèque de l'Institut national des Langues et Civilisations orientales
2 rue de Lille, F-75007 Paris
Tel. 260-34-58

History. The École des Langues orientales vivantes was founded on 30 March 1795, a small general library being established at the same time. Its stock, housed in the Bibliothèque nationale, was woefully small, totalling only 300 volumes in 1867. The development of the collection really occurred only after the move to the present premises in 1873, when a succession of able Librarians, such as Auguste Carrière and E. Lamprecht, were in charge. The Slavonic Collection was developed by Professor Paul Boyer between 1908 and 1935, when the Library was itself modernized. Current holdings total over 500,000 books and 1,200 MSS.

Bibliothèque de l'Institut national des Langues et Civilisations orientales, Paris

Special Collections and Treasures. The Russian Collection of 68,000 volumes includes many reviews of the 19th century, e.g. *Sovremennik, Otecestvennye zapiski, Vestnik Evropy* and *Russkaja Starina;* newspapers of the Russian Revolution; the complete works of Tolstoy, Gogol, Doestoevsky and Gorky; and many works in the regional languages of the USSR. Other collections include the Derembourg Collection and important Arabic and Korean Collections.

Exhibition Areas. None.

Hours. Mon.-Sat. 0900-1900 (15 July-30 Sept. 1400-1900). Closed Sun. and public hols. Also closed from 25 Dec.-1 Jan. and 2 weeks during the university Easter hols.

Transport. The Library is in the centre of Paris and well served by public transport.

Parking. In neighbouring streets.

Admission. Readers and *Visitors:* Free access on presentation of suitable identification.

Information. At staff desks.

Sales. None.

Guidebooks. A guide to the Slavonic Section was published in 1975.

Restaurant/Snack Facilities. None in the Library.

Services. Cloakrooms, lavatories.

Catalogues. Catalogues of the Arabic, Chinese, Japanese and Korean Collections. Catalogue on cards (bound) for books received pre-1966. Systematic card catalogue for books received post-1966.

Classification. The older collections are classified in order of accession. Since 1935 collections have been divided according to languages.

Copying/Photography. Through the Library staff.

PARIS
Bibliothèque Sainte-Geneviève
10 place du Panthéon, F-75005 Paris
Tel. 633.05.15-17

History. The bookstock of the Library dates from the 17th century, although the Abbaye Sainte-Geneviève can trace its history back to the 6th century. Its original collections were dispersed and François, Cardinal de la Rochefoucauld, undertaking a reorganisation of the Abbey in 1619, donated several hundred volumes and encouraged a vigorous acquisition policy. In 1710 the size of the Library was doubled with the bequest of 16,000 volumes by Charles Maurice Tellier, Archbishop of Rheims, making it the largest in Paris next to the Royal Library. In 1790 the Library became state property and was named the Bibliothèque du Panthéon, which title it retained until 1815, when its old name was restored. Its collections grew during this period with material received from the *dépôts littéraires.* Legal deposit privileges were gained in 1828, although these were not totally effective until 1926. The present building, designed by Henri Labrouste, was completed in 1850 and gained attention through its innovatory use of iron and stone. Alterations and extensions were carried out in 1933, 1954 and 1961. In 1930 the Library was attached to the University of Paris system, without losing its character as a public library. Current holdings include 1.5 million books, and 4,052 MSS.

Bibliothèque Sainte-Geneviève, Paris

Special Collections and Treasures. The major collection is the Bibliothèque nordique, reached through the entrance at 6 rue Valette. Based on an 1868 gift of 1,500 volumes from the consul Alexandre Dezos de la Roquette, it now comprises one of the richest collections outside Scandinavia on that area. Current holdings total 140,000 books, 1,210 current periodicals and 9,300 theses. The *Fonds Rómain Rolland* is another separate collection, comprising the books and personal papers of Rolland. Other collections include those of Cossman (geology); Guénin (shorthand); Mareuse (history of Paris); Denis (South America); and Delaunay (editions and translations of *De Imitatione Christi*).

Exhibition Areas. None.

Hours. Public Room: Mon.-Sat. 1000-2200 (1 July-30 Sept. 1400-2200). Réserve: 1000-1200, 1400-1800. (The Réserve to the right on entering the main building from the place du Panthéon, contains most of the pre-1800 books as well as MSS, fine bindings etc.) Closed: public hols., 2 Jan., from the Thurs. before until the Wed. after Easter, 1-15 Aug., 24-26 and 31 Dec.

Transport. Métro: nearest stations Maubert, Mutualité, Luxembourg, Saint-Michel. Bus routes: 21, 27, 38, 81-2, 84-5, 89.

Parking. Underground car park in rue Soufflot (there is a charge).

Admission. *Readers:* Main Room: minimum age 16. To gain Reader's ticket, two photographs, proof of identity, proof of domicile, passport or visa, must all be presented. Réserve: the same conditions of access and authorisation justifying the reader's work.
Visitors: Visits are not permitted, except in groups with permission of the Chief Librarian.

Information. From the assistant in the Reading Room.

Sales. None.

Guidebooks. Reader's guide, in French, free of charge.

Restaurant/Snack Facilities. None.

Services. Lavatories.

Catalogues. Alphabetical author catalogue. Systematic subject catalogues with alphabetical index. Special catalogues for periodicals, collections, congresses.

Classification. Own.

Copying/Photography. Xerographic and microfilm copying available but controlled by the Library staff, particularly the assistant in the Salle de Lecture. Private photography not allowed.

PARIS
Bibliothèque littéraire Jacques Doucet
10 place du Panthéon, F-75005 Paris
Tel. 6.330515 [poste 22]

History. The Library has its origins in the personal collection of the famous couturier, Jacques Doucet, who, with the advice of André Suarès and later André Breton, built up a collection of manuscripts and first and rare editions of contemporary works, many enriched by marginal notes and dedications. On Doucet's death in 1929 the Library was bequeathed to the University of Paris, which housed it in part of the wing designed for the Réserve of the Bibliothèque Sainte-Geneviève (see preceding entry), where it still remains. The original legacy encouraged many gifts to the Library in the spheres of modern literature, art and the avant-garde. The number of volumes and MSS in the Library doubled in the period 1958-68 and currently totals over 25,000 volumes and 50,000 MSS and autograph letters.

Special Collections and Treasures. Collections include those of Henri Bergson; Henri Mondor, Mallarmé; André Gide (MSS and about 15,000 letters received by him); Marcel Jouhandeau (300 MSS, 5,000 letters); François Mauriac (c. 1,200 MSS); Paul Valéry (more than 12,000 items covering his printed works, material about him, etc.); Robert Desnos; Pierre Reverdy; Tzara; the Archives Jean Schlumberger; the Archives Natalie Barney (on Americans in Paris). The Library has a comprehensive series of Surrealist and Dadaist publications, modern book bindings (e.g. by Pierre Legrain, Rose Adler and Germaine Schroeder), MSS of Apollinaire and Max Jacob, while Matisse deposited a copy of each of the books he illustrated, sometimes with the original design and preliminary sketches.

Exhibition Areas. Exhibition rooms with cases devoted to Bergson, Valéry, Mondor, Mallarmé, and Barney.

Hours. Mon., Tue., Thurs., Fri. 1400-1800. (It is possible, however, to apply to the Director for admittance outside these times.) Closed in Aug. and Sept., the week before and the week after Easter and from 24 Dec. to 2 Jan. inclusive.

Transport. Metro: nearest stations Maubert, Odéon, Luxembourg, Saint-Michel. Bus routes: 21, 38, 81-2, 84-5, 87, 89.

Parking. Underground car park in the rue Soufflot.

Admission. *Readers:* The Library is intended for serious research in modern French literature. Students must produce a letter of recommendation from their tutor, listing qualifications, subject to be studied etc. Access to the letters and manuscripts is subject to the written agreement of their authors, or to that of their owners.

Bibliothèque littéraire Jacques Doucet, Paris

Binding by Pierre Legrain of the manuscript of Le Poète assassiné by Guillaume Apollinaire, in the Bibliothèque littéraire Jacques Doucet, Paris

Visitors: Casual visitors are not encouraged.

Information. At staff desks.

Sales. Free distribution of exhibition catalogues of the Library.

Guidebooks. None.

Restaurant/Snack Facilities. None.

Services. Lavatories.

Catalogues. Alphabetical, subject, title and periodical card catalogues. Various special catalogues. Published catalogues by G.K. Hall & Co.

Classification. Own.

Copying/Photography. Photocopying is possible (providing the necessary consent has been obtained) but often may be suspended due to staff shortages. Periodicals may be microfilmed through the ACRPP.

PARIS
Bibliothèque du Musée de l'Homme
Palais de Chaillot, place du Trocadéro, F-75116 Paris
Tel. 704: 53-94

History. The Musée d'Ethnographie du Trocadéro was founded on 23 January 1878, with its particular subject fields being physical anthropology, human palaeontology, prehistory and ethnography. The Library collections grew slowly at first but developed more rapidly in the 20th century. On 1 January 1929 the Museum was totally reorganised, and took its present name in 1937, when it occupied the building overlooking the Champ de Mars and the Eiffel Tower. Current holdings total 260,000 books, 3,500 periodicals, 7,500 maps and 48 MSS.

Bibliothèque du Musée de l'Homme, Paris

Special Collections and Treasures. Collections include those of Marcel Mauss, Lévy-Bruhl, Paul Rivet, Alfred Métraux, Stresser-Réan, Louis Marin, Jeanne Cuisinier, Henri Breuil, Harper Kelley, and those of the Société des Américanistes, Société des Océanistes, Société pre-historique française, Institut d'Ethnologie, and Société d'Ethnographie de Paris.

Exhibition Areas. No details available.

Hours. Mon., Wed.-Sat. 1200-1800. Closed Sun., Tues, public hols.

Transport. Metro: Trocadéro. Bus routes: 29, 30, 32, 63, 82.

Parking. Available near the Library.

Admission. Readers: About 15,000 volumes, not including periodicals, are in the reading room on open access to readers, who are admitted without formalities. Access to the rest of the holdings depends on proof of identity at the lending desk.
Visitors: Apply to the Librarian.

Information. Readers may consult reference librarians.

Sales. None in the Library but sales desk in the entrance hall to the Museum itself.

Guidebooks. Reader's guide, in French. Free of charge.

Restaurant/Snack Facilities. A bar ('Le Totem'), open all the time.

Services. 5 carrels, 2 lavatories and 2 lifts.

Catalogues. Author, subject and periodical catalogues.

Classification. Library of Congress (adapted).

Copying/Photography. Dry-copying through the staff.

PARIS
Bibliothèque centrale du Muséum national d'Histoire naturelle
38 rue Geoffrey Saint-Hilaire, F-75005 Paris
Tel. 331-71.24, 331-95.60, 336-00.70

History. The Library was founded by the decree of 10 June 1793 which reconstituted the 'Jardin national des plantes et le Cabinet d'histoire naturelle de Paris' under the name of 'Muséum d'histoire naturelle'. Provision was made for a library in a series of articles regulating the selection of books, the building etc. The decree ordered that the collection of paintings on vellum (after plants cultivated in the *Jardin,* or animals belonging to the *Ménagerie* at Trianon), which was deposited at the Bibliothèque nationale, should be taken back to the Museum and become part of the newly created library, which was moreover able to receive a large number of items from the *dépôts littéraires.* It was opened to the public on 7 September 1794, and by 1825 it had 10,000 volumes. The Library was initially housed in the old buildings of the 'Jardin du roi', then from 1822 to 1840 it took over the first floor of the Maison Buffon, before moving in 1840 into the building it occupied until 1963. By 1963 the collection had grown too large for the old building and it moved to its present location on the rue Geoffroy Saint-Hilaire. Today holdings total 610,000 volumes, 8,000 periodicals, 2,667 MSS and 5,480 maps and plans.

Bibliothèque centrale du Muséum national d'Histoire naturelle, Paris

Special Collections and Treasures. Treasures include paintings on vellum, dating from 1640, of rare plants in the garden of the Duke of Orléans, at Blois. The collection was continued by various artists until the end of the 19th century. Collections include the Charles Lucien Bonaparte Collection, rich in ornithology; the Michel Chevreul Collection, rich in works of chemistry and alchemy; the Mandl Collection of works of chemistry and physiology; the Lacroix Collection on meteorites and mineralogy; the MS collections of explores and naturalists such as Commerson, Bonpland, Buffon, etc.

Exhibition Areas.   None.

Hours.   Mon.-Sat. 0930-1730. Closed Sun., the week before and the week after Easter, from 15 July to 15 Sept. (opening to the public on Tuesday and Friday afternoons).

Transport.   Metro: Jussieu, Censier-Daubenton, Austerlitz. Bus routes: 67, 89, 47.

Parking.   No facilities at the Museum but available in nearby streets.

Admission.   *Readers:* The Library is open to researchers in the Museum laboratories, at the university, at the Centre national de Recherche scientifique, to students studying for degrees, and to members of the public doing temporary research.
Visitors: In groups and by previous appointment only.

Information.   In the General Reading Room.

Sales.   None.

Guidebooks.   Out of print but a new edition is to be published soon.

Restaurant/Snack Facilities.   None.

Services.   Cloakrooms, lavatories, lifts.

Catalogues.   Author card catalogue and subject catalogue for works published after 1888.

Classification.   Own.

Copying/Photography.   Available through Library staff. Private photography forbidden.

STRASBOURG

*Bibliothèque nationale et universitaire de Strasbourg
Direction de l'Établissement et Service de Droit, Section
des Alsatiques, and Section centrale (Sciences humaines
et sociales, 6 place de la République (B.P. 1029), F-67070
Strasbourg Cedex
Tel. (88) 360068
Section Médecine: 6 rue Kirschleger, F-67085 Strasbourg
Cedex
Tel. (88) 362323
Section Sciences: 34 boulevard de la Victoire (B.P.
1037), F-67070 Strasbourg Cedex
Tel. (88) 613323
Cedex
Tel. (88) 613323*

History. On 24 August 1870 the town libraries of
Strasbourg were destroyed by bombardment during the
Franco-Prussian War. The new library that resulted was
called the 'Kaiserlische Universitäts und Landesbibliothek'.
It was initially located in the Château des Rohan and
then in 1895 it transferred to the building it still occupies.
A decree of 29 July 1926 conferred on the library the
unique title of the 'Bibliothèque nationale et universitare'.
On 25 September 1944, during the Second World War, a
bomb hit the Library causing great damage to the
reading rooms and book stacks. Reconstruction of the
damaged areas took place between 1950 and 1960. In
1964 the medical library was established in the Medical
Faculty Building and in 1968 the science library on the
University campus 'de l'Esplanade'. In 1975 the 'Fonds
regional' et 'Fonds de Droit' were decentralized in
buildings close to the 'Section centrale'. Holdings today
total over 3 million volumes, 30,000 maps, 1,984
incunabula and 5,832 MSS, most of these located in the
Main Library.

Special Collections and Treasures. Special collections
include the Drioton Egyptology Collection of some
10,000 items; the Gobineau Collection comprising
manuscripts, printed books and memorabilia relating to
Comte A. de Gobineau (1816-1882); a substantial
collection on the Alsace region, comprising 3,000 maps
and plans and over 100,000 volumes; the Goethe
Collection; a selection of the books which belonged to
the German lyric poet Uhland; the Goldstücker Collection
of over 2,000 items on Sanskrit philology and Indian
archaeology; and the Law Collection of M.A. von
Bethmann Hollweg. Treasures include St. Augustine,
Cité de Dieu, a 16th century MS in the translation of
Raoul de Presles written on vellum; and 36 Latin and
Low-German MSS from the convent of Frenswegen.

Exhibition Areas. The Exhibition Hall is in the Main
Library, next to the entrance hall. Several exhibitions are
held each year.

Hours. Affaires générales et Service de Droit: Daily

*Bibliothèque nationale et
universitaire de Strasbourg*

0900-1200, 1400-1800 (except Sat. from July-Sept.). Section des Alsatiques: 0900-1200, 1400-1800 (except Sat. from July-Sept.). Section centrale: Mon.-Fri. 0900-2200, Sat. 0900-1200, 1400-1800. Closed Sat. from July to Sept. Section Médecine: 1000-2200 (except Sat. and Christmas and Easter hols.). Section Sciences: 0945-2100 (except Sat. and Christmas hols.). The Library is closed public hols. and a few days between Christmas and 1 Jan. During University vacations the Library stays open only to 1800.

Transport. All the sections of the Library are in Strasbourg itself and are served by the public bus system.

Parking. No reserved parking for readers but it is possible to park near the Library.

Admission. Readers: Access to reading rooms on presentation of either a student's card of Strasbourg University or suitable Library authorization. An annual payment of 15F is made for loans to non-student *Visitors:* A provisional pass to the reading rooms is given to occasional readers or visitors.

Information. In the Public Information Office in the Catalogue Room.

Sales. Various publications available, e.g. *Bibliographie alsacienne.*

Guidebooks. A short guide is available free of charge.

Restaurant/Snack Facilities. None.

Services. Cloakroom and lavatories in all sections of the Library.

Catalogues. Alphabetical author and subject catalogues.

Classification. Section centrale: own. Science Section: CDU. Medical Section: Cando.

Copying/Photography. Xerographic and microfilm copying service (within the limits of French copyright laws). Private photography only with official authorization.

German Democratic Republic

BERLIN

Deutsche Staatsbibliothek
DDR-108 Berlin, Unter den Linden 8, Postfach 1312
Tel. 20 78 0

History. The Library is the central academic library of the German Democratic Republic, and its activities, under its successive titles of Churfürstliche Bibliothek, Königliche Bibliothek and Preussische Staatsbibliothek, date from 1661. (For its history from 1661-1939 see Staatsbibliothek Preussischer Kulturbesitz, p. 116). World War II proved to be a traumatic period: the building was severely damaged in 1943-44 and the partition of Germany meant the division of the Library's collection. The Soviet authorities encouraged the restoration of the Library, which reopened, with legal deposit privileges, on 1 October 1946 under the designation of Öffentliche Wissenschaftliche Bibliothek, only to be renamed the Deutsche Staatsbibliothek in November 1954. Growth has accelerated since then and current holdings in East Germany total 3,437,679 items. (Total overall holdings, including material 'illegally' held in West Germany, are given as 5,237,679.) The Library acts as a central clearing house for loans in the DDR and is responsible for the union catalogues of incunabula and MSS.

Special Collections and Treasures. Notable collections include the Asia-Africa Collection and the Map Collection, while the Deutsche Fotothek, Dresden, Zentrales Bildarchiv für Wissenschaft, Forschung and Lehre (Central Picture Archive for Science, Research and Education), as well as the Theodor-Fontane-Archiv, Potsdam, are all connected to the Deutsche Staatsbibliothek. The Library has 990 incunabula in East Germany including H. Schedel, *Weltchronik* (Nürnberg, 1493); Franciscus Columna, *Hypnerotomachia Poliphili* (Venice, 1499); and Nikolaus van Wyle, *Translationen* (Esslingen, 1478, one of the earliest German language incunabula. Manuscripts include the musical MSS of Bach, Beethoven, Handel, Haydn, Mendelssohn, Mozart, Schubert, Schumann and Weber; the *Itala Fragmente,* 5th century, the oldest MS in the Library's possession; the *Salaberga-Psalter* 8th century; the *Codex Wittekindeus,* 10th century; the *Hippiatricorum Collectio,* a Byzantine MS of the 10th century; the MS of G.E. Lessing's *Minna von Barnhelm;* and 125 letters of I.S. Turgenev to the Berlin art critic Ludwig Pietsch. Other treasures include the *Deutsch-Französische Jahrbücher* (Paris, 1884), in which Karl Marx wrote and of which only one issue appeared; issues 1-52 of Lenin's *Iskra;* the 1650 map of Berlin and its environs by Johan Gregor

Deutsche Staatsbibliothek, Berlin

Memhard; and the first edition of F. Engels' *Der Ursprung der Familie des Privateigenthums* (1884).

Exhibition Areas. In the vestibule, the rest room and in all special departments.

Hours. Mon.-Fri. 0900-2100, Sat. 0900-1700. Closed Sun. and public hols.

Transport. Railway station: Friedrichstrasse. Underground stations: Stadtmitte or Hausvogteiplatz. Trams: routes 22, 46, 70, 71. Bus routes: A18, A57, A9, A32, A59.

Parking. At Unter den Linden, Friedrichstrasse station, Charlottenstrasse.

Admission. *Readers:* Minimum age 16, annual charge M.1. Apply to Admissions Department.
Visitors: Organized tours on the first Sunday of each month, 1030. Other tours can be arranged. No charge.

Information. At the entrance, in all catalogue and reading rooms and in the Institute for Loans.

Sales. Library publications and postcards are sold in the Admissions Department.

Guidebooks. Readers' guide, in German, M.1. Directions to readers, in German, M.0.50. Information leaflet, in German, English, Russian, French, Spanish, free of charge.

Restaurant/Snack Facilities. On the ground floor, open 0900-1600.

Services. Microfilm and microfiche readers in the reading rooms. Cloakroom, telephones on the ground floor. Rest-room, typing rooms on the second floor. Lift, lavatories, washrooms, first aid facilities.

Catalogues. Systematic, alphabetical and key-word catalogues, as well as special catalogues for the separate collections, (e.g. music, children's books, manuscripts, incunabula, maps, orientalia). Various union catalogues, e.g. for periodicals and foreign monographs.

Classification. Universal Decimal Classification for technical sciences, mathematics, geography and forestry. Own classification for other subjects.

Copying/Photography. There is a copying service. Apply to Library staff. Permission must be obtained for private photography.

BERLIN

Humboldt Universität zu Berlin
Universitätsbibliothek DDR 108 Berlin, Clara-Zetkin-
Strasse 27
Tel. 2078 240

History. The University of Berlin opened in 1810 but the University Library was not established until 1831 (opening in 1833). In the intervening years the former Royal Library (the Deutsche Staatsbibliothek) performed the necessary library service to the University. Library holdings increased rapidly: in 1839 there were about 15,000 volumes, in 1890 137,000 and by 1913 there were about 263,000 volumes and about 300,000 dissertations. The Library moved into its present building in 1922, having previously been housed in the Royal Library and in rented premises. Losses during World War II were relatively small. After 1945 the contents of the Library were further increased when other libraries were incorporated into the Humboldt University under one management. At present the University has one Central Library and 24 departmental libraries, with holdings of 3.6 million volumes.

Special Collections and Treasures. Collections include the Portrait Collection (portraits of the professors and lecturers at the Berlin University, later the Humboldt University, since 1810); the Fontane Collection and Archive of the 'Tunnel over the Spree'; 1 million dissertations and school prospectuses; and various collections devoted to Celtic philology and Caucasian languages.

Exhibition Areas. None.

Hours. Mon.-Fri. 0800-2000, Sat. 0800-1200. Closed Sun. and public hols.

Transport. Trams: Nos. 46, 70, 71, 22 (nearest stop: Friedrichstrasse). Buses: No. A57.

Parking. At the Friedrichstrasse stop and on the corner of Clara-Zetkin-Strasse and Universitätsstrasse.

Admission. Readers: Anyone over 16 may use the Library. A registration fee of M.1 is payable.
Visitors: Free of charge.

Information. In the Central Information Department, on the ground floor of the Central Library.

Sales. None.

Guidebooks. Humboldt-Universität zu Berlin — Wegweiser (1973). Other guides (in German) are available.

Restaurant/Snack Facilities. None.

Humboldt Universität zu
Berlin, Universitätsbibliothek

Services. One public telephone, one washroom and toilets, on the ground floor.

Catalogues. A central catalogue of the holdings of the departmental libraries. Alphabetical (book form) catalogue of literature published before 1963. Alphabetical card catalogue (1909-). Systematic card catalogue. Alphabetical card catalogue of dissertations. Key-word catalogue of dissertations (1960-).

Classification. BBK (Bibliothekarisch-bibliographische Klassifikation).

Copying/Photography. Photocopying Department on the ground floor of the Central Library. The use of cameras within the Library is governed by Library regulations.

DRESDEN
Sächsische Landesbibliothek
DDR-806 Dresden, Marienallee 12
Tel. 52677 and 57097

History. The Library dates from 1556 when the Elector August of Saxony began to build up a collection in Dresden Castle. By 1580 the collection comprised 2,354 volumes. In 1590 the 3,000 volume library of Dietrich von Wertherns was acquired, a collection which included 500 incunabula. During the Thirty Years' War the Library came under ecclesiastical control and library development slowed. During the second half of the 18th century the Library grew rapidly with the purchase of several extensive private libraries, notably of von Bünau (42,000 volumes in 1764) and Brühl (62,000 volumes in 1768). Johann Michael Francke, who had been in von Bünau's service, now joined the Court Library and reclassified the entire holdings, which, in 1786, received a new home in the Japanese Palace. Francke's work was continued with vigour by Adelung and then Ebert. By the mid-19th century, however, an inadequate budget had slowed down growth once more. Between 1927 and 1933 the Japanese Palace was modernised, but on 13/14 February and 2 March 1945 it was burnt out during the severe bombing of Dresden. About 450,000 volumes, 45 per cent of the holdings, were destroyed. In 1947 the Library moved into former barracks, which were subsequently converted for library purposes. Holdings currently include 1,055,000 volumes.

Special Collections and Treasures. 783 incunabula, 2,000 rare books, 900 precious bookbindings, 21,300 MSS, about 100,000 autographs, 60,000 maps and city views, the Stenographische Bibliothek (former' Bibliothek des Stenographischen Landesamts', since 1966 a department of the Sächsische Landesbibliothek) with 40,000 views and 1,000 MSS, in shorthand, and the Music department with 48,000 scores 11,000 MSS,

Sächsische Landesbibliothek, Dresden

22,000 textbooks and theoretical literature, 26,000 records and tapes. Treasures include the *Codex Dresdensis,* the most important Maya manuscript; Albrecht Dürer's Sketchbook; the block-book *Ars memorandi,* c. 1465; the first edition of Sebastian Brandt, *Narrenschiff* (Basle, 1494); dookbindings of the famous Dresden bookbinder Jakob Krause; a set of original parts of the B Minor Mass by Johann Sebastian Bach; and the most important collection of manuscripts of the Italian composer Antonio Vivaldi outside Italy.

Exhibition Areas. The 'Buchmuseum' has 38 display cases in three rooms, displaying some of the many treasures of the Library. 13 exhibition cases in the Library.

Hours. Mon.-Sat. 1000-1900. Closed Sun. and public hols.

Transport. Trams: lines 7 and 8 to Dr.-Kurt-Fischer-Platz; line 11 to Forststrasse or Waldschlösschen. Buses: lines 71 and 91 to Dr.-Kurt-Fischer-Platz. The Library is no more than 15 minutes' walk from any of these stops. Motorists should approach the Library from Dr.-Kurt-Fischer-Allee or from Forststrasse.

Parking. Outside the Library.

Admission. Readers: All citizens of the DDR over 16 years of age are eligible to use the Library. Foreigners with visas for visiting the DDR can use the Library and permission may also be granted to foreigners without residence permits. Registration takes place in the Lending Department on the first floor. After filling in an application form and proving identity, the reader receives a user's ticket. The charge is M.1 per annum.
Visitors: Apply to Library staff.

Information. In the General Information Department, on the first floor opposite the stairs.

Sales. The Library's own publications are on sale in the Lending Department.

Guidebooks. Einführung in die Benutzung (introduction for use of the Library), in German. *Das Buchmuseum der Sächsische Landesbibliothek,* in German.

Restaurant/Snack Facilities. Coffee bar and buffet (in the dining room, Mon.-Fri.), ground floor, on the left. Open 1000-1500. Smoking is only permitted in the ante-room of the dining room. A small coffee room, first floor, open Sat. 1000-1500.

Services. Cloakroom with self service lockers in the lobby on the first floor. Lavatories, ground floor and first and second floors, on the left hand side. Restrooms in the left hand corridor of the first floor and in the small coffee bar on the first floor on the right of the landing. Telephone in the small coffee bar on the first floor.

Catalogues. Author and subject card catalogues. Various special catalogues.

Classification. Own.

Copying/Photography. Quick copying service available through Library staff, as are other reproduction facilities. Prior permission must be sought for private photography.

HALLE
Universitäts- und Landesbibliothek Sachsen-Anhalt
DDR-401 Halle/Saale, August-Bebel-Strasse 13 und 50
Tel. 88147

History. The University of Halle was founded in 1694, with the University Library being formed from the acquisition of two important learned libraries in 1696. Growth of the collections improved dramatically at the beginning of the 19th century, first with material from the secularised monasteries and then from the library of Wittenberg University, which merged with that of Halle in 1817. Otto Hartwig became director of the Library in 1876. Under his management a new alphabetical and systematic catalogue was begun and a new library building erected. The Library's collections continued to grow in the 20th century and survived World War II intact. The purpose of the Library was extended in 1948, when it was allotted the additional function of a regional library for Sachsen-Anhalt (now for the districts of Halle and Magdeburg). Since 1969 the Library system has been centralised with that of Martin-Luther University. Current holdings total 3,340,000 volumes, of which 315,500 are MSS and autograph letters.

Special Collections and Treasures. Collections include the Ponickau Collection on the history and geography of Saxony and Thüringia; the Hungarian Library comprising the collection of the Hungarian Exulant Cassai; and the branch library of the German Oriental Society. Treasures include a pre-825 *Codex* from Tours; a fragment from Priscian's *Institutiones grammaticae;* the Frehersche *Codex der Petersberg-Chronik;* the *Hallische Schöffenbücher;* 100 letters of Leibniz; and letters of Martin Luther, Philipp Jacob Spener, Christian Wolff and Lavater.

Exhibition Areas. Exhibitions held in various parts of the Library.

Hours. Catalogue Room and Information: Mon.-Fri. 1000-1900. Main Reading Room: Mon.-Fri. 0800-2200, Sat. 0800-1700. Closed Sun. and public hols.

Transport. No details available.

Parking. In nearby streets.

Universitäts- und Landes-
bibliothek Sachsen-Anhalt

Admission. Readers: Minimum age of 16. Readers between 16 and 18 must produce written authorisation from their place of education. Members and students of the University of Halle and residents in the area are eligible to borrow from the Library. Others may work in the reading rooms.
Visitors: A public tour takes place on the first Saturday in each month at 1100. Other tours can be arranged.

Information. In the Information Department on the first floor of August-Bebel Str. 13.

Sales. None.

Guidebooks. A guide, published 1967, in German. A new guide is in preparation.

Restaurant/Snack Facilities. None.

Services. Cloakrooms, lavatories, microfilm readers.

Catalogues. Alphabetical, systematic and key-word catalogues. Alphabetical central catalogue covering the holdings of the libraries in the Halle and Magdeburg area (Zentralkatalog Sachsen-Anhalt).

Classification. Own.

Copying/Photography. There is a photographic and copying service (third floor of August-Bebel Str. 13, room 90, open Mon.-Fri. 1000-1500, closed Wed.). Machines are not available for individual use.

LEIPZIG
Deutsche Bücherei
DDR-701 Leipzig, Deutscher Platz
Tel. 8470

History. The Deutsche Bücherei (DB) was founded at Leipzig on 3 October 1912 on the initiative of the Börsenverein der deutschen Büchhändler (German Booksellers Association) and began its activity on 1 January 1913. It received, by voluntary agreement, a copy of every work published in Germany or German-speaking countries. By 1941 it had widened its scope to include items of German relevance published anywhere in the world, although during the years of Nazi rule (1933-45) its collecting functions became somewhat distorted. Its intake enabled it to publish the *Deutsche Nationalbibliographie* and various German bibliographies of special materials. During World War II the DB's stock suffered only minor damage, although various rooms within the building were damaged. On 24 November 1945, the DB reopened and on 17 August 1946 began republishing the *Deutsche Nationalbibliographie.* Since 1949 the DB has widened its scope considerably and is now under the direct supervision of the Ministry

Deutsche Bücherei, Leipzig

for Universities and Technical Colleges of the DDR. On 1 August 1960 a new legal deposit law ensured the receipt of two copies of all works published in the German Democratic Republic. Books published abroad are sent, as before, as complimentary copies. The main building, erected from 1914-16, received an additional annex in 1934-36 and then a second annex was completed in 1965. Current holdings total 6,077,831 items.

Special Collections and Treasures. The *Deutsche Buch- und Schriftmuseum* became a special division of the DB in 1950. The scope of its collection comprises documents concerning the history of the book, writing and paper of all times and nations. The Museum is unique within the German Democratic Republic. Collections include the *Klemm-Sammlung,* the collection of the bibliophile H. Klemm on the German and foreign art of the book; the Collection of Fine Prints; and the German Paper Museum, with its large collection of watermarks, consisting of 213,532 original papers. The Museum also has charge of the remains of the *Ehemalige Bibliothek des Börsenvereins der Deutschen Büchhändler zu Leipzig,* which had been damaged during World War II. This includes 19,200 volumes of special literature, 17,200 plates, some 65,000 circulars, about 20,000 second-hand bookshop and publishers' catalogues and nearly 60,000 records concerning the history of the booktrade.

Exhibition Areas. Exhibition rooms of the German Book and Writing Museum and the vestibule of the DB.

Hours. Mon.-Fri. 0800-2200, Sat. 0900-1800. Closed Sun. and public hols.

Transport. The Library is easily accessible by public transport (trams).

Parking. The DB has its own parking area for staff and readers.

Admission. Readers: Readers' tickets can be obtained on presentation of an identity card at the counter in the Lending Department. Anyone who is 'over high school age' may use the Library for research.
Visitors: (By appointment if possible) are admitted Mon.-Fri. 0800-1500. An appointment is obligatory for those wishing to see the special collections. General tours around the Library cost M.0.50 for a single person and groups may tour the Library at a cost of M.0.10 per person. There are also free tours.

Information. Can be obtained in all rooms where readers have access (catalogues, Information Department, reading rooms etc.). Readers with special problems may also apply in person or in writing to every Library department.

Sales. Counters of the Lending Department.

Guidebooks. Various guides in German at small cost.

Restaurant/Snack Facilities. Basement snack bar, where light meals are available to staff and readers. Open Mon.-Fri. 0830-1100, 1200-1600.

Services. Free lavatories with washing facilities; smoking is permitted in the vestibule; public telephone.

Catalogues. Author, subject (alphabetical), and publishers' and institutions' catalogues. Alphabetical catalogue 1913-1973; 1974-. Subject catalogue of monographs 1913-1945; 1945-1973; 1974-. Separate subject catalogues for periodicals, for the same periods as above.

Classification. Own.

Copying/Photography. Copying facilities are available. Cameras may be used only with the permission of the General Director.

LEIPZIG
Karl-Marx-Universität, Universitätsbibliothek
DDR-701 Leipzig, Beethovenstr. 6
Tel. 34 391

History. Leipzig University was founded in 1409 but the University Library was not established until 1543, when Caspar Börner assembled 4,000 volumes and 1,500 MSS following the dissolution of the monastic foundations in Saxony. Börner, who also bequeathed his own private library, rich in early printed Greek books, was succeeded in 1547 by Joachim Camerarius (1500-74), an eminent humanist who encouraged the Library's growth. The Thirty Years' War, 1618-48, marked a period of decline, but matters improved under Joachim Feller, Librarian from 1676-91, who produced a printed catalogue of the Library's MSS in 1686. During the 18th century, Leipzig occupied an important place in European culture but the Library did not develop significantly. The 19th century, however, marked a period of great expansion with the number of volumes rising from 120,000 in 1850 to 500,000 by 1900. This growth necessitated a move in 1891 from the old Paulinerkloster building (Bibliotheca Paulina) to the present building, the Bibliotheca Albertina. The Library suffered severe bombing in 1945, but by 1950 the damaged buildings had been rebuilt and the services returned to normal. Current holdings total 3,050,000 books, 8,700 MSS, 169,000 autographs and 2,713 incunabula.

Karl-Marx-Universität, Leipzig, Universitätsbibliothek

Special Collections and Treasures. Collections include the 360 Aldines from the Library of Petrus Mosellanus, acquired by Caspar Börner; the Camerarius and Sleidanus Collections; the Hirzel Goethe Library; the Richard

Wülker Goethe-Frankfurt Collection; the Faust and Schiller Libraries of Bode and Dürr; the Chinese Collection of Wilhelm Grübe; the Library of the former Veterinary Surgeons' College in Dresden; the correspondence of Johann Christian Gottsched; the MSS collections of Professor J.H. Bobbart and Constantin Tischendorf, the latter covering the Middle East; and the George Kestner Collection of letters and autographs. The most valuable item in the MS collection is the *Codex Friderico-Augustanus,* part of *Codex Sinaiticus* (now in the British Library).

Exhibition Areas.   Exhibits in show cases in the lobby.

Hours.   Reading Room: Mon.-Fri. 0900-2100, Sat. 0900-1800. Closed Sun. and public hols.

Transport.   Several tram lines run close to the Library.

Parking.   Parking lots are available.

Admission.   *Readers:* Students and university personnel admitted free, other readers pay an annual registration of M.1.
Visitors: Apply to the Librarian.

Information.   In the Catalogue Department.

Sales.   None.

Guidebooks.   *Benutzungsführer* (1971) in German, available free.

Restaurant/Snack Facilities.   None.

Services.   Typing room next to Reading Room, microfilm and microfiche reading devices in the Reading Room. Cloakrooms, lavatories.

Catalogues.   Alphabetical, subject, systematic, biographical and dissertation catalogues.

Classification.   Own.

Copying/Photography.   Copying facilities through Library staff. Permission must be obtained for private photography.

Germany, Federal Republic of

BAMBERG

Staatsbibliothek Bamberg
D-86 Bamberg, Neue Residenz, Domplatz 8
Tel. 0951 23752

History. The Staatsbibliothek Bamberg was founded in 1803, its initial stock deriving from the libraries of local monasteries and religious foundations dissolved during secularization. Some of this material dates back to the 11th century library assembled by the Emperor Henry II in Bamberg Cathedral. The first Librarian, Heinrich Joachim Jaeck, quickly amalgamated the various collections, which were housed in the Jesuit college, whose origins dated back to 1648. A fairly stagnant period in the Library's history followed but in the 20th century fairly extensive growth was experienced after World War II. Since 1965 the Library has occupied parts of the renovated baroque Neue Residenz in the Cathedral Square. Holdings currently total 300,000 books, 4,500 manuscripts and 3,400 incunabula.

Special Collections and Treasures. Notable collections include the Zweibrücken Collection of 11,400 volumes, covering English and French literature of the 18th century; the library of Dr. Johann Theophil Hoeffel; the Josef Heller Collection of 70,000 drawings and 10,000 books, which form the basis of the art collection (this includes original drawings by Holbein and woodcuts and copper engravings from the time of Dürer); and the Marschalk of Ostheim Collection of regional, historical and genealogical writings and minor publications on the revolution of 1848. The most famous manuscript in the Library is the Bamberg *Apokalypse,* which originated from the collegiate foundation of St. Stephen.

Exhibition Areas. Exhibition rooms are located in the main entrance hall and the Scagliola Room. Permanent exhibitions of important manuscripts. Changing book and graphic art exhibitions.

Hours. Reading Room: Mon.-Thur 0900-1730, Fri. 0900-1800, Sat. 0900-1200. Closed Sun. and public hols. and each afternoon in Aug.

Transport. Bus, stopping at Domplatz.

Parking. Parking spaces in front of the Library.

Admission. Readers: For borrowing and for the use of manuscripts an identity card is required.
Visitors: Should apply to the Librarian.

Staatsbibliothek, Bamberg

ut manducent carnes regum · a carnes tribu
norum · a carnes fortium · a carnes equo&
& sedentium in ipsis · a carnes omnium li
berorum · a servorum · pusillorum & mag
norum ·

The Bamberg Apocalypse (c.
1000), in the Staatsbibliothek,
Bamberg

Information.   In the Reading Room.

Sales.   In the Exhibition Room.

Guidebooks.   None.

Restaurant/Snack Facilities.   None.

Services.   Typewriter and telephone in the Lending
Department. Cloakroom and lavatories at the main
entrance.

Catalogues.   Up to 1925 systematic book catalogue; after
1925 users' alphabetical and keyword card catalogues;
staff card catalogue of entire holdings; separate MS
catalogues (printed 1895-1966).

Classification.   Prior to 1925 own; after 1925 books have
been classified by running number.

Copying/Photography.   Photographic copies can be
obtained from the Library's Photographic Department.
Automatic dry-copying machine available (not for
individual use).

BERLIN
Staatsbibliothek Preussischer Kulturbesitz
*D-1 Berlin 30 (Tiergarten), Potsdamer Strasse 33, Postfach
1407*
Tel. (030) 2661

New building for the Staatsbibliothek, Berlin. Under construction. Photograph taken
in January 1974

History.   For the history of the Library from 1661 to
1939, see Deutsche Staatsbibliothek, p.105. The
Staatsbibliothek Preussische Kulturbesitz has its origins
in the former Preussische Staatsbibliothek founded in
1661 by the Great Elector Frederick William under the
name of Churfürstliche Bibliothek. Re-named the
Königliche Bibliothek in 1701, the Library was then
systematically and liberally enlarged under Frederick the
Great so that the collection amounted to approximately
150,000 volumes in 1786. In 1780 for the first time the
Library obtained a building of its own (known as the
'Kommode'). It was not until 1914 that the Library
moved into a larger building (Unter den Linden). In 1919
the Library was re-named the Preussische Staatsbibliothek. In 1939 the Preussische Staatsbibliothek was
the third largest library in Europe, with a collection of
approximately 3 million volumes and well over 70,000
MSS. During World War II the collections were
evacuated to less threatened areas of Germany, the
larger part, comprising some 1.7 million volumes, being
transferred to regions of the country that now belong to
the Federal Republic of Germany. After the war the
books and MSS in the western zones were stored in
Marburg and Tübingen. The Marburg collections were
maintained, at first, as the Hessische Bibliothek and then
from 1949 onwards as the West-Deutsche Bibliothek. In

1962 the Library became part of the Stiftung Preussischer Kulturbesitz and in 1964 the collections began returning to Berlin (West) (e.g. the MSS and incunabula stored at Tübingen were returned in 1967-8). The late Hans Scharoun designed a new Library building, currently scheduled for completion in 1977, which will be one of Europe's largest library buildings. Present holdings include 2.56 million volumes (of which more than half are in Berlin) and 83,000 MSS. The Staatsbibliothek Preussischer Kulturbesitz, together with the Deutsche Bibliothek, Frankfurt and the Bayerische Staatsbibliothek, Munich (see relevant entries), fulfil the function of a national library of the Federal Republic of Germany.

Special Collections and Treasures. The Manuscript Department contains over 9,000 Western MSS, 3,000 incunabula (e.g. the *Gutenberg Bible*) and 300,000 autographs (notably in the history of the natural sciences and technology: Kepler, Galilei, Einstein, etc.). Bequests have come from such figures as Herder, Fichte, Hegel, the brothers Grimm, Schopenhauer and Hauptmann. The Music Department has about 18,000 music MSS (including numerous original MSS by Bach, Haydn, Mozart, Beethoven, etc.). Of particular note is the Mendelssohn Archiv, a special collection of the Mendelssohn family. The Department of Maps, with 350,000 maps and 30,000 volumes of atlases and special literature, is by the scope and importance of its holdings the greatest Federal German collection. The Eastern European Department contains about 275,000 volumes and, next to the collection in the Bayerische Staatsbibliothek, is perhaps the most important Federal German collection. The Oriental Department, with 56,000 individual MSS and 27,500 microfilms of original MSS in Nepal, India and Ethiopia, has been termed the greatest Oriental manuscript collection of the Western world. The East Asian Department contains about 110,000 volumes and can be regarded as the greatest Federal German collection.

Exhibition Areas. Entrance Hall (on the completion of the new building).

Hours. Mon.-Fri. 0900-1900, Sat. 0900-1300. Closed Sun. and public hols.

Transport. Bus: nos. 24, 29, 48, 75, 83. Underground (U-Bahn) to Kurfürstenstrasse, and then by 48, 75 or 83 bus.

Parking. Parking facilities are available in the parking place of the Philharmonie, opposite the new Library building.

Admission. Readers and *Visitors:* In general, free of charge.

Information. In the Lending Department, the Reading Room and the Catalogue Room.

Sales. Sales desks will be available on the completion

of the new building.

Guidebooks. Information sheets, in German and in English, as well as a printed leaflet are available free of charge. A guidebook is in preparation.

Restaurant/Snack Facilities. There is a canteen in the completed section of the new building. Open Mon.-Fri. 0900-1600.

Services. Cloakrooms, lavatories, lifts, telephones, in the completed portion of the new building.

Catalogues. Alphabetical catalogues of monographs and periodicals. Subject catalogues: the old 'Realkatalog' (for literature acquired before 1945), the new subject catalogue (for literature acquired after 1945).

Classification. Old 'Realkatalog': the system used by the former Prussian State Library. New subject catalogue: the Eppelsheimer method, in modified form.

Copying/Photography. Copying machine in the Lending Department. Apply to Library staff for microfilming and photographing facilities.

BERLIN
Ibero-Amerikanisches Institut
Preussischer Kulturbesitz, Berlin 45, Gärtnerstrasse 25-32
Tel. (030) 7717017

History. The Institute, with its Library, opened on 12 October 1930 as a cultural institute of the Prussian state. Three important collections formed the nucleus of the Library: the 80,000 volume library of the eminent Argentine scholar Dr. Ernesto Quesada (donated to the Prussian state in 1927); a large collection of Mexican books donated by the Mexican government; and the Library of the Ibero-Amerikanisches Forschungsinstitut of the University of Bonn, this Institute having been dissolved in 1930. The Library contained 120,000 volumes at its inception. Some 40,000 volumes were lost during World War II. After the war the Library continued its work under the new name 'Latein-Amerikanische Bibliothek' and then from 1954-61 as the 'Ibero-Amerikanische Bibliothek'. In 1962 it readopted its original name when it became part of the Preussischer Kulturbesitz. After the completion of the new State Library building (see preceding entry) the Institute will move from its present premises to adjoining quarters. Current holdings include 460,000 volumes, 30,000 maps, 200,000 newspaper clippings, and 7,000 photograph records.

Ibero-Amerikanisches Institut, Berlin

Special Collections and Treasures. The Library is the German central library for literature in all fields of knowledge from the countries of the Iberian world, namely Spain and Portugal with their overseas territories, South and Central America, and the West Indies, including British, French and Dutch territories. Collections, other than those mentioned above, include the Walter-Lehmann Collection of books, MSS, photographs and drawings; the Folklore Collection with exhibits from Brazil; and the bequests of E. Seler, P. Ehrenreich, M. Uhle and R. Lehmann-Nitsche.

Exhibition Areas.   No exhibition room. Small exhibitions are held in the corridor outside the Reading Room.

Hours.   Mon., Wed., and Thurs. 0900-1700, Tues. and Fri. 0900-1900, Sat. 0900-1300. Closed Sun. and public hols.

Transport.   Bus: nos. 17 and 86.

Parking.   Adequate parking facilities available.

Admission.   *Readers* and *Visitors:* The Library is open to all free of charge.

Information.   At the desk in the Reading Room.

Sales.   Various publications available on application to Library, but no sales desk.

Guidebooks.   Pamphlet in English.

Restaurant/Snack Facilities.   None.

Services.   Lavatories on the ground floor. Occasional concerts and lectures.

Catalogues.   Author, title and subject catalogues.

Classification.   Own.

Copying/Photography.   Dry-copying is available through the Library staff. One dry-copier is available for the use of readers outside the Reading Room.

A page from a parchment manuscript in the Ibero-Amerikanisches Institut, Berlin. The manuscript was written, in black and red letters, in the mid 16th century and contains parts of the New Testament which were translated for missionary work into Cakchiquel, a Mayan language

COLOGNE
Universitäts- und Stadtbibliothek
D-5000 Köln-Lindenthal, Universitätsstrasse 33
Tel. (0221) 470-2260, 470-2214

History.   The University of Cologne dates back to a Bull of Pope Urban VI of 21 May 1388, which provided its foundation charter. The University was closed in 1798 and not re-opened until 29 May 1919. The Library, which serves the citizens of Cologne as well as the University, was established in the following year through the amalgamation of three existing libraries: the City Library, the Library of the Commercial Academy and the Library

Universitäts- und Stadtbibliothek, Cologne

of the Academy of Practical Medicine. The present main library has developed from the first two, while from the last has grown the medical library (now the Central Medical Library for the whole Federal Republic). The library building suffered some damage during World War II but no appreciable losses to its holdings. The growth of holdings after 1945 made even more urgent the need for new buildings. The main library was housed in the main university building between 1934 and 1966; in 1966 it moved into its present modern quarters. At the end of 1974 it contained 1,448,548 items, not including the holdings of the Central Medical Library. The medical library occupied its new building in 1973, and is now a separately administered library.

Special Collections and Treasures. Collections include the Wallraf Collection of over 14,000 printed works, including many incunabula and early printed works; the Gustav von Mevissen Collection of 25,000 volumes; the Johannes Fastenrath Collection of 10,000 volumes; and the church music collection of Wilhelm Bäumker of 3,000 volumes. Other collections focus on the history and culture of the Rhineland, Icelandic literature and Thomas à Kempis. Treasures include a Shakespeare First Folio (1623), two block books and 2,345 incunabula.

Exhibition Areas. Book and art exhibitions in the entrance hall.

Hours. Lending Department: Mon.-Fri. 1030-1300, 1430-1630, Thurs. 1430-1800. Reading Room: Mon.-Fri. 0900-2100, Sat. 0900-1200. Closed Sun. and public hols.

Transport. Any form of public transport to the University.

Parking. Library parking lot.

Admission. Readers and *Visitors:* Free of charge. Loans dependent on University and city status. (The University also has a number of departmental or Institute libraries, some of which are accessible only to members of that particular Institute.)

Information. At the Information Centre.

Sales. None.

Guidebooks. None.

Restaurant/Snack Facilities. Automatic drink dispensers in the entrance hall.

Services. Typing-rooms. Cloakroom and lavatories in the entrance hall. Lifts in the administrative area. Public telephone in Post Office opposite the Library.

Catalogues. Alphabetical catalogue and systematic catalogue with keyword index. Union catalogue of the Academic Libraries of North Rhine-Westphalia in the same building.

Classification. Own.

Copying/Photography. Copying machines located in the Reading Room. Permission to take photographs in the Library should be obtained in advance.

DARMSTADT
Hessische Landes- und Hochschulbibliothek Darmstadt
D-61 Darmstadt, Schloss
Tel. 06151-124424

History. The Library was founded in 1567 with the book collection of the first Landgraf of Hessen-Darmstadt, George I. During the 17th century the Library increased significantly, partly as a result of the legacies of the libraries of Count Philipp von Butzbach (1581-1643) and Johann Michael Moscherosch (1601-1669). By 1789 the Library contained 16,000 volumes. In 1790 the Landgraf Ludwig X increased the Library's annual budget. Ludwig also had his own library (Kabinettsbibliothek) and this grew steadily, while the Court Library benefited from the secularisation of the monasteries in the early 19th century. Grossherzog Ludwig I amalgamated the two libraries in the Darmstadt Schloss (Castle), with Andreas Schleiermacher undertaking the organisation and cataloguing. In 1817 the Library was opened to the public. Its holdings grew rapidly: by 1865 holdings totalled 376,000 volumes, by 1914, 575,000 and by 1932, 717,000. During World War II, on the night of 11/12 September 1944, the Schloss was burnt to the ground, with 400,000 volumes lost. The Library of the Technical College in Darmstadt also lost most of its holdings in the war, and so in 1948 it was decided that the two libraries should amalgamate. The restored rooms of the old castle were occupied in 1958. Current holdings include 917,500 volumes, more than 4,000 MSS, 2,050 incunabula and 2 million patent letters.

Special Collections and Treasures. Collections include the 'Günderrode' Library, an 18th century collection of 16,000 volumes on law, history and theology, which was endowed to the Library; the Baron Hüpsch Collection of printing and rare MSS; and the 19th century collection of medicine and natural sciences of Professor Baldinger of Marburg. Treasures include a fragment of the *Weingarten* prophet-MS of the 5th century; the 9th century *Seligenstädter Evangeliar* and the *Liuthard Evangeliar* from the palace school of Charles the Bald; the *Gero-Kodex,* c.960; the *Hitda-Kodex,* first quarter of 11th century; and the *Darmstadt Pessach Haggadah,* originating from the Hüpsch Collection, a richly illustrated early 15th century Hebrew MS. The Music Dept. has a collection of music autographs from the archives of the publishing firm Breitkopf and Härtel.

Hessische Landes- und Hochschulbibliothek, Darmstadt

Exhibition Areas. The 'Great Exhibition Room' contains 22 glass show-cases.

Hours. Reading Rooms: Mon.-Fri. 0900-1900, Sat. 0900-1230. MS and Music Rooms: Mon.-Fri. 0900-1230, 1330-1630, closed Sat. Closed Sun. and public hols.

Transport. Tram route 3, buses H and F.

Parking. In the 'Schlossgarage' beside the Library.

Admission. Readers: No charge. Borrowers must register in the Lending Department.
Visitors: Free admission, including use of the Reading Room.

Information. In the Catalogue Room, on the main floor.

Sales. None.

Guidebooks. A guide for readers is available in German. Free of charge.

Restaurant/Snack Facilities. None.

Services. Cloakrooms, lavatories.

Catalogues. Author and systematic catalogues. Separate catalogues for manuscripts, incunabula and music. Central catalogue of the libraries of Institutes in the Technical University.

Classification. The Eppelsheimer system.

Copying/Photography. Dry-copying service beside the Lending Department. Two copying machines for individual use (one in the cloakroom and one at the entrance to the Patent Records Room). Microfilming and photocopying service also available through Library staff. Apply to the Director for private photography.

ERLANGEN
Universitätsbibliothek Erlangen-Nürnberg
D-8520 Erlangen, Universitätsstrasse 4/Schuhstrasse 1a
Tel. 09131/852151

History. The University of Erlangen was founded on 4 November 1743 by Friedrich, Margrave of Bayreuth, and his consort, Friederike Sophie Wilhelmine, the sister of Frederick the Great. The Library's initial stock was formed from the inherited private library of the Margrave Friedrich (till then in the Christian-Ernestinum School in Bayreuth) and the book collection of the first chancellor of the University, the physician Daniel de Superville. In 1759, after the death of Wilhelmine, the donation of her private library containing a wealth of contemporary French literature was made. In 1748-1770 the valuable

Universitätsbibliothek
Erlangen-Nürnberg, Erlangen

library of the Cistercian monastery at Heilsbronn was obtained. In 1805-6 the major part of the library of the Margraves of Ansbach was handed over to Erlangen by the then sovereign of Ansbach-Bayreuth, King Friedrich Wilhelm III of Prussia. Storage space had now become a problem, especially after the collections of the University of Altdorf were united with those of Erlangen in 1818 (the University of Altdorf being suspended in 1809). The Library thus moved with other sections of the University from the 'Ritterakademie' to the larger (former) Margrave's Castle in 1825, where it remained until shortly before World War I, when it moved into a new library building. A period of recession occurred during and shortly after both world wars. Recent growth, however, has necessitated the building of a large extension to the University Library. Current holdings include 850,000 volumes, 610,000 dissertations and 4,150 periodicals. Special departments of the Library exist in Erlangen for the technical sciences (since 1966: Egerlandstr. 3) and in Nürnberg for the social sciences and economics (since 1961: Egidienplatz 23) and for humanities, especially pedagogics (since 1972: Regensburger Str. 160).

Special Collections and Treasures. Collections include the library (27,000 volumes) of the Nürnberg doctor and naturalist Christoph Jacob Trew (1695-1769), with 15,000 letters from the 16th-18th centuries; the libraries of different professors of the University, e.g. the Elias von Steinmeyer Germanic collection of 11,000 volumes; the graphic collection of the Margraves of Ansbach (1,666 pieces), 14th-17th centuries; and the Luthardt Collection (10,000 pieces), particularly of 19th century graphic art. There is also a collection of coins and medals. Treasures include a self-portrait of Albrecht Dürer (c. 1490), and, among the incunabula and MSS, the *Riesenbibel* and the *Fuldaer Evangeliar* from the Gumbertus Monastery at Ansbach.

Exhibition Areas. Combined exhibition room and lecture.

Hours. Reading Room: Mon.-Fri. 0830-2000, Sat. 0830-1230. Vacations: Mon.-Fri. 0830-1800. Closed Sun. and public hols.

Transport. The Library is in the centre of the town and is accessible by public transport.

Parking. Restricted.

Admission. Readers and *Visitors:* Free admission.

Information. At the information centre in the Lending Department in the new building.

Sales. None.

Guidebooks. Instruction for Service (1975).

Restaurant/Snack Facilities: On the upper floor of the new building.

The Fuldaer Evangeliar (c. 860), in the Universitäts-bibliothek, Erlangen-Nürnberg

Services. Typing rooms, studies, lift, public telephone and lavatories.

Catalogues. Different catalogues for all parts of the Library for internal use. For readers public alphabetical author and subject catalogues for books published after 1900.

Classification. Arrangement in the magazines following the main disciplines without subdivisions. A part of the holdings before 1924 was entered in a class catalogue (own classification).

Copying. Copying machines are available near the Lending Department. Dry-copying and microfilm facilities available through Library staff. Private photography allowed only with Director's permission.

FRANKFURT
Deutsche Bibliothek, Bundesunmittelbare Anstalt des Öffentlichen Rechts
D-6000 Frankfurt am Main 1, Zeppelinallee 4-8
Tel. (0611) 75661

History. The Library was founded in 1946, on the iniative of Professor H.W. Eppelsheimer, with the co-operation of the City of Frankfurt, the German Booktrade Association, and the British and American military authorities. Its function. was to provide a provisional bibliographical Archive and Centre for West Germany. The West German publishers agreed to deposit copies of all their publications. In 1952 the status of the Library changed, when, under the auspices of the West German Republic, the Hesse Provincial Government, the German Booktrade Association and the City of Frankfurt, the Library became a public foundation. In 1969 the Government of the West German Republic assumed full control of the Library. The obligation to deposit copyright copies of all books was confirmed by law, and from these books the *Deutsche Bibliographie* is compiled. Current holdings total approximately 2 million volumes, maps, sheet music, discs and microfilms.

Special Collections and Treasures. The Library contains the most comprehensive collection of German books published since 1945 in East and West Germany and abroad, German emigré works published abroad between 1933 and 1945, translations of German works into foreign languages, and foreign language works about Germany published abroad.

Exhibition Areas. The Exhibition and Lecture Room seating up to 200. Various other display areas.

Hours. Reading Room and book issue: Mon.-Fri. 0900-2000, Sat. 0900-1700. Closed Sun. and public hols.

Deutsche Bibliothek, Frankfurt

Transport. The Library is located near the city centre and can be reached by bus or tram.

Parking. None at Library, but available nearby.

Admission. Readers: Use of the Library is free to all over 18 years of age on presentation of identity cards. *Visitors:* Should make prior application.

Information. In the Reading Room and in the Catalogue Room.

Sales. None.

Guidebooks. A users' guide in German, French and English is available, free of charge.

Restaurant/Snack Facilities. Mornings: Mon.-Fri. 1000-1130. Afternoons: Mon.-Thurs. 1430-1600, Fri. 1430-1530.

Services. Cloakroom on the ground floor. Coin operated telephone in the basement. Smoking is only permitted in the restaurant and lobby in front of the Reading Room. Lavatories and washrooms on the ground floor.

Catalogues. Alphabetical author catalogue. Subjects may be traced in the *Deutsche Bibliographie: Schlagwort- und Stichwortverzeichnis.*

Classification. Own.

Copying/Photography. Copying facilities are available to the right of the entrance to the Reading Room.

FRANKFURT
Stadt- und Universitätsbibliothek
D-6 Frankfurt/M. 1, Bockenheimer Landstrasse 134-138
Tel. (0611) 79071

History. The City Library (Stadtbibliothek) was established in 1668 by a merger of two libraries, the Ratsbibliothek and the Bibliothek des Barfüszerklosters, the latter having been in receipt of legal deposit for Frankfurt publications since 1603. In 1728 the Library issued its first printed catalogue, which listed 13,000 titles. In 1825 the Library moved into its own building and then in 1914 it put its resources at the disposal of the newly founded University. During World War II 600,000 volumes were destroyed by bombing, as well as the entire Library building. In 1946 the Library was merged with the Rothschild-Bibliothek, the Bibliothek für Kunst und Technik, the Manskopfsches Museum für Musik- und Theatergeschichte and instituted as the Stadt- und Universitätsbibliothek. In 1964 the Library moved into a new building opposite the Frankfurt University campus. Present stocks total 1,737,000 items,

Stadt- und Universitäts-bibliothek, Frankfurt

including 9,800 MSS, 5,000 musical MSS and 2,500 incunabula.

Special Collections and Treasures. Major treasures include the 42-line Latin *Bible* printed by Johannes Gutenberg (Mainz, 1455); the 48-line *Bible* printed by Fust and Schöffer (Mainz, 1462); the 15th-century *Frankfurt Book of Armaments;* the original MS of Heinrich Hoffman's *Struwwelpeter;* and a *Lectionary,* bound in a late 10th century ivory front cover from the Reichenau monastery and an early 14th century back cover with an engraved and gilded copper sheet.

Exhibition Areas. None indicated.

Hours. Information services: Mon.-Fri. 0830-1900, Sat. 0900-1300. Reading rooms: Mon.-Fri. 0830-2000, Sat. 0900-1300 (or 1800). Closed Sun. and public hols.

Transport. Trams: Nos. 6, 8, 19, 23, 24. Buses: Nos. 32, 33.

Parking. Limited number of spaces off Zeppelinallee.

Admission. *Readers* and *Visitors:* Free of charge.

Information. At the desk in the entrance hall, on the left hand side.

Sales. None.

Guidebooks. Library guide in German, free of charge.

Restaurant/Snack Facilities. Common room in the basement (near the cloakroom), with vending machines for drinks.

Services. Study carrels, cloakrooms, lavatories, lifts, smoking lounges.

Catalogues. Alphabetical monograph, subject and periodical catalogues.

Classification. Eppelsheimer.

Copying/Photography. Seven machines are available for individual use (2 in the entrance hall, 3 in Reading Room I, and 2 in Reading Room II). Prior permission must be sought for private photography.

FREIBURG
Universitätsbibliothek
D-78 Freiburg, Rempartstrasse 15, Postfach 1629
Tel. 203-4503 (management); 203-4520 (enquiries); 203-4524 (Main Reading Room)

History. The Library's holdings stem from the book

collections of the individual faculties, which were responsible for the acquisition of books after the University was founded in 1457. Prominent among these was the Faculty of Arts, whose rooms probably housed all the other facultìes' books and became generally regarded as the University Library. The individual faculties kept records of their own books until 1756. The reorganisation of the University under Maria Theresa resulted in renewed activity for the Library. The first great increase in stock came in 1775 resulting from the taking over of the valuable and abundant holdings of various colleges, especially the Collegium Pacis and the Collegium Sapientae. The dissolution of the monasteries in 1773, 1782 and 1803 brought further increases. In 1783 the old rooms, which were in the college buildings of the Faculty of Arts, were abandoned and the Library was transferred to the former Jesuit college. In 1902 it moved to its present building which was partially destroyed in 1944 but rebuilt after World War II. It is, however, not large enough to meet present demands and as it is not possible to enlarge it, a new building was begun in 1973, which should be completed by the beginning of 1978. Current holdings total 1,154,700 printed items, 1,250 manuscripts and 558,025 dissertations.

Special Collections and Treasures. Various bequests of university professors, among them Perger (1792), de Benedictis (1800), Klüpfel (1811), Perlet and Hug (1845), Pfost (1846), and the Dr. Adolf Schaeffer bequest of old Spanish printing. The MS holdings include two codices focussing on ecclesiastical law : a *Dionysio-Hadriana* (9th century) and a *Decretum Burchardi* (*11th century*); a sacramentary of the abbey of St. Vitus, Mönchengladbach (c. 1070-80); a Cistercian psalter (13th century); a Franciscan bible (late 13th century), and a picture bible (late 15th century).

Exhibition Areas. These will only be available after the completion of the new building in 1978.

Hours. Catalogues, Reading Rooms, Information Department, bibliographic service: Mon.-Fri. 0830-2130, Sat. 0900-1900. (Opening times may be shortened during vacations.) Closed Sun. and public hols.

Transport. The Library is in the city centre and easily reached by public transport.

Parking. A very limited number of parking spaces is available.

Admission. *Readers:* Anyone may use the Library, free of charge.
Visitors: Guided tours can be arranged on application to the Secretary's office.

Information. In the Bibliography Department on the ground floor, on the right. Open Mon.-Fri. 1000-1630.

Universitätsbibliothek, Freiburg

Sales. None.

Guidebooks. Readers' guide, in German, free of charge.

Restaurant/Snack Facilities. None in the Library itself, but there is a cafeteria in the University building, and one opposite the Library.

Services. Individual study carrels and typing booths in the reading room. Cloakroom, lockers and lift in the hall. Smoking permitted in the entrance hall. Telephone in the college building I, opposite the Library.

Catalogues. Card catalogues: alphabetical catalogue, catalogue of dissertations, new systematic catalogue, Freiburg catalogue of periodicals. In book form: old systematic catalogue, Freiburg periodical index.

Classification. The new systematic catalogue is classified according to the Eppelsheimer method.

Copying/Photography. There is a copying service. Coin-operated machines are also available in the entrance hall. Private photography is permitted, provided other readers are not disturbed. Photography of MSS, incunabula, etc. requires special permission.

GÖTTINGEN
Niedersächsische Staats- und Universitätsbibliothek
D-34 Göttingen, Prinzenstrasse 1, Postfach 318
Tel. 0551-395212 (Secretariat)

History. The University of Göttingen was founded in 1734 by George II, King of England and Elector of Hanover. Its initial stock was based on the 8,912 volume library of Joachim Heinrich von Bülow, 2,200 volumes from the Hanoverian Royal Library and 800 volumes from the Göttingen Gymnasial Bibliothek. The Library grew rapidly with many gifts coming from England. Under the librarianship of Christian Gottlob Heyne (1763-1812) the collections grew from 60,000 to 200,000 volumes. Its acquisition policy and its catalogues and the facility with which a user had access to the books made Göttingen the first modern library in the 18th century and thus it set an example for the development of other libraries. It made its holdings accessible in a most liberal manner to the members of the University and to the scholarly world of all Europe. By 1875 the collection had reached over 400,000 volumes. The Library buildings were badly damaged on 24 November 1944 but book losses were relatively small. Within the limits of the current rebuilding of the University on the north-east edge of town the Library will also occupy new buildings. Two sections have already been begun, in medicine and mathematics/natural sciences, and the main Library will be located in the immediate vicinity of the arts faculties. While the Library is the central library of Göttingen

Niedersächsische Staats- und Universitätsbibliothek, Göttingen

University, at the same time it fulfils the library functions of the Lower Saxony State Library, whose name it has carried since 1949. Holdings currently total 2.3 million volumes and 12,000 MSS.

Special Collections and Treasures. Special collections fostered by the Deutsche Forschungsgemeinschaft (German Research Council) are: Mathematics, Theoretical Physics, Geophysics, Astronomy, Theoretical Chemistry, Geography, Geology, Mineralogy, Petrography, Forestry, Great Britain, United States, Canada, South Africa, Australia, Finland, Hungary, Korea, Ural-altaic Languages, General Knowledge, Library Science. Besides the above, the Library also owns collections of books, 15th to 19th centuries, covering all areas of knowledge, among them the renowned libraries of von Bülow, Z.G. von Uffenbach and Baron von Asch (presented between 1772 and 1806 and consisting mainly of Oriental MSS and Russian books). Treasures include about 5,000 incunabula, 1,500 16th century printed books, pamphlets written by Luther, and works from scholars active at one time at the University, notably G.C. Lichtenberg, K.F. Gaus, Bernard Rieman and David Hilbert.

Exhibition Areas. Temporary exhibitions are mounted in the foyer and in a series of display cases on the stairway to the first floor.

Hours. Reading Room: Mon.-Fri. 0900-1900, Sat. 0930-1700. Closed Sun. and public hols. (Times vary for other sections of the Library.)

Transport. The Library is very near to the railway station and the town centre. All buses go near the University.

Parking. There is ample parking space near the University. Parking in the special library parking lot available only after consultation with Library authorities.

Admission. Readers: Members of the University may use the Library free of charge. A small charge is made to non-University members for the use of lending facilities and the Reading Room.
Visitors: Free of charge.

Information. In the Catalogue Room, Reading Room, etc.

Sales. Postcards (e.g. coloured postcard reproductions of Göttingen MSS) can be purchased in the Reading Room.

Guidebooks. None.

Restaurant/Snack Facilities. Automatic vending machines for drinks in the entrance hall on the ground floor.

The Fuldaer Sakramentar (975), in the Niedersächsische Staats- und Universitätsbibliothek (MS theol. 231). Folio 4, verso

Services. Lavatories on ground floor, cloakrooms and typing room near the Reading Room. Lockers in the lower foyer near the Library entrance. Rest-room for readers in the upper and lower foyers (smoking permitted). Telephone kiosks outside the Library entrance and in the entrance hall.

Catalogues. Author catalogue in volumes up to 1929, on cards from 1930. Subject catalogue in volumes up to 1944, on cards from 1945. Keyword catalogue from 1920. Catalogues of incunabula, manuscripts, newspapers, etc.

Classification. Own.

Copying/Photography. Dry-copying machines are to be found in the foyer on the ground floor, in the Journal store and in the photographic studio. Permission is required for private photography.

HAMBURG
Staats- und Universitätsbibliothek
D-2000 Hamburg 13, Moorweidenstrasse 40
Tel. (040) 41 23 2213

History. The Library was founded in 1479, when Bürgermeister Hinrich Murmester enlarged, with his own books, a secular book collection from the town council of the 14th and 15th centuries. The holdings were increased through benefactions from Hamburg councillors, scholars and citizens, such as Joachim Jungius, Hermann Samuel Reimarus, Tassius, Lindenbrog, Holstenius, Langenbeck and Placcius. During the Reformation the Library acquired books from dissolved monasteries. In 1696 a law was passed under which all resident printers and publishers had to deposit in the Library a copy of each work they produced. A valuable acquisition in the 18th century was the bequest of the brothers Johann Christian and Johann Christoph Wolf, of which the most valuable examples of old manuscripts and printing have been preserved to the present day. After the University was founded in 1919 the Library took on the duties of a university library and its name was changed. In 1943/44, during World War II, the Library building was destroyed and 620,000 out of a total of 740,000 volumes were lost. By 1974 holdings had risen to 1,500,000 items, housed in a former grammar school taken over in 1945 and enlarged by a book tower and administrative block.

Staats- und Universitäts-bibliothek, Hamburg

Special Collections and Treasures. Collections are devoted to Hamburgensia and Holsatica (i.e. from Holstein, N. Germany); African literature; the language and culture of Spain, the Basques, Portugal and Latin America; politics; maritime law; sailing vessels; inland, coastal and deep-sea fishing. In the sphere of music the Library is strong in Händel MSS, and possesses the library of the Händel scholar Chrysander; and Brahms archive, and 450 libretti from the Hamburg Opera (17th and 18th centuries). 3,000 prompt books from the Hamburg City Theatre (18th century), and numerous bequests from most of Hamburg's authors, such as Jungius, Klopstock, Hagedorn, Claudius, Liliencron, Dehmel, Jahnn, Borchert and Heym, contribute to the significant number of local interest collections. Treasures include 7,150 old MSS, 1,000 papyri, 50,000 letters by scholars of the 16th-18th centuries (Supellex epistolica), and 14,500 autographs of the 18th-20th centuries (Campe Collection and Literary Archive).

Exhibition Areas. A permanent Exhibition Room houses various displays of the Library's stock.

Hours. Reading Room: Mon.-Wed. 1000-1800, Thurs. 1000-1900, Fri. 1000-1600, Sat. 1000-1300. Closed Sun. and public hols.

Transport. The Library is located near the Dammtor railway station, which can be reached by city railway, underground or tram.

Parking. Parking space in the Library grounds and nearby.

Admission. *Readers:* Tickets can be obtained free on application.
Visitors: Use of books in the Reading Room is free and no prior permission is needed.

Information. At the information centre in Room 11.

Sales. None.

Guidebooks. A small brochure in German, free of charge.

Restaurant/Snack Facilities. None at present but scheduled for the projected new Library building.

Services. Cloakrooms, telephones, lavatories and lifts are available. A typing room and smoking room are planned for the new building.

Catalogues. Alphabetical, subject and classified catalogues. North German union catalogue.

Classification. Own.

Copying/Photography. The Library has a laboratory for black and white and colour photography and dry-copying. There are also 2 automatic dry-copying machines. Permission must be sought for private photography.

11th/12th-century cover (with a 5th-century ivory relief) for an 11th-century parchment manuscript of the four Gospels, in the Staats- und Universitätsbibliothek, Hamburg.

HEIDELBERG
Universitätsbibliothek Heidelberg
D-6900 Heidelberg 1, Plöck 107-109, Postfach 1749,
Tel. [06221] 54 380

History. The Library of Heidelberg University dates
from 1386, the year of the University's foundation (the
oldest University on West German soil). It soon gained
the support of the Electors of the Palatinate, such as
Philip, Ludwig III and V, Friedrich II, and Ottheinrich, the
first Protestant Elector of the Palatinate, who resided in
Heidelberg from 1556-59. The 'Bibliotheca Palatina' was
further enriched in 1584 with the books and manuscripts
of Ulrich Fugger, one of the famous family of Augsburg
bankers. The Library suffered during the 17th century. In
1622 Heidelberg was captured by the forces of the
Catholic League and in 1623 3,542 MSS and 5,000
printed volumes were transferred to the Bibliotheca
Apostolica Vaticana. In 1693 a fire not only destroyed
the remaining library collection but also the town. The
Library was gradually rebuilt and, in 1816, 852 MSS were
returned to Heidelberg by the Vatican. The remaining
MSS were microfilmed by the Library after World War II,
a war which left the Library's holdings relatively
unscathed. The present library buildings date from
1901-05 and currently house 1,300,000 volumes, 6,000
MSS and over 700,000 doctoral dissertations, pamphlets
etc.

Special Collections and Treasures. The Library's
treasures include the largest collection of MS sources of
Middle High German literature but for those of Vienna
and Munich, among them the famous *Manesse Codex,*
the largest collection of German minnesongs, and the
illustrated MS of the *Sachsenspiegel* (1st half of 14th
century). Special collections include the library of Salem
Monastery; early Heidelberg prints and bindings; the
history of medieval and modern European art;
Egyptology; and modern German book design from 1900
onwards.

Exhibition Areas. Exhibition Room, opposite the General
Reading Room.

Hours. Catalogue and Information Desk: Mon.-Fri.
0900-1600, Sat. 1200-1300. Closed Sun. Reading Room:
Mon.-Fri. 0900-2145, Sat. 0900-1900. Closed Sun. and
reduced opening during Aug.

Transport. Trams: routes 1 and 2 (stopping at Universi-
tätsplatz).

Parking. Very little parking space in the vicinity of the
Library (during term).

Admission. Readers: No charge. Readers who are not
members of Heidelberg University or other institutions,
or not residents in Heidelberg, are free to use the

Universitätsbibliothek,
Heidelberg

Reading Room but may not borrow from the Library (except in exceptional cases). Special regulations govern the use of the Manuscript Department and previous application is necessary.

Visitors: No charge. The Reading Room, Catalogue Room and Exhibition Room are open to the public during opening hours. Visitors may see the Manuscript Department upon request.

Information. In the Catalogue Room.

Sales. In front of the General Reading Room. Colour slides of Library holdings, postcards and books are on sale.

Guidebooks. A guidebook, in German, is available at the Information Desk for a small charge.

Restaurant / Snack Facilities. None.

Services. Cloakrooms, lavatories. Smoking is permitted in the public hallway (seats available).

Catalogues. Alphabetical and subject catalogues.

Classification. Own.

Copying / Photography. There is a copying service: readers should apply at the Information Desk or in the Reading Room. Machines are also available for individual use in the hallway and in the Reading Room. No limitations on private photography in the rooms open to the public, except in the Exhibition Room, where visitors must ask a guide or a guard for special permission. To take photographs in the Manuscript Department visitors should apply at the desk. There is no charge.

The Codex Manesse (Zürich, c. 1310-40), in the Universitätsbibliothek Heidelberg. The most comprehensive collection of Middle High German lyrics with almost 6,000 verses and 138 full-page illuminated pictures of the minnesingers

KIEL

Bibliothek des Instituts für Weltwirtschaft an der Universität Kiel (Zentralbibliothek der Wirtschaftswissenschaften)
D-23 Kiel 1, Düsternbrooker Weg 120-122, Postfach 4309
Tel. (0431) 8841

History. The Institute was founded on 18 February 1914 by Bernard Harms, who wished to build up a collection of publications and primary sources to serve as a basis for research on problems of theoretical and applied economics. He thus intended to create a research institution in the field of economics and the social sciences to form a counterpart to those existing in the field of natural science. The Library's initial growth owed much to the activities of the late Dr. Wilhelm Gülich, who was Director of the Library from 1924-60. During World War II the Institute lost a great many of its research staff and all its technical equipment, but the Library's stock was saved thanks to its evacuation to

Bibliothek des Instituts für Weltwirtschaft an der Universität Kiel

Ratzeburg in 1942-3. The Institute resumed its activity in 1948 and in the following year the Library returned to Kiel. In 1966 the Library became, with the support of the Deutsche Forschungsgemeinschaft, the Zentralbibliothek der Wirtschaftswissenschaften of the German Federal Republic, i.e. the Central West German Library for Economics. Current holdings total 1,219,784 volumes and 20,566 periodicals.

Special Collections and Treasures. The Library is in itself a special collection, for in order to illustrate economic life in its many ramifications, it has become an all-encompassing research centre for the social sciences. History, politics, geography, anthropology — all the related fields are represented. The standard reference works for biology, psychology, science and philosophy are included, while material such as fiction, memoirs, or popular magazines shows the impact of economic factors upon daily life. Long runs of statistical, legal and governmental publications reach back to the beginning of industrialisation. In 1972 the Library acquired the 7,000 volume collection of a former Director, Erich Schneider.

Exhibition Areas.   None.

Hours.   Mon.-Fri. 0800-1630. Closed Sat., Sun. and public hols.

Transport.   Bus: no. 6 to the Institute. Buses run every 20 minutes.

Parking.   Car park opposite the Library.

Admission.   Readers: No charge.
Visitors: The Library is open to the general public, free of charge.

Information.   In the Catalogue Room.

Sales.   None.

Guidebooks.   Das Institut für Weltwirtschaft an der Universität Kiel (illustrated). A pamphlet in English also available.

Restaurant/Snack Facilities.   Canteen opens 0900-0930, 1145-1300. Restaurant (bookable in advance).

Services.   Typing room, cloakroom, lavatories and wash-rooms, one lift, one reading room for smokers, smoking areas in the hall, public telephone. The International House 'Welt-Club' serves as a dormitory and home to students and research workers.

Catalogues.   There is no 'main catalogue' for the Library. All catalogues, except the *Standortskartei* (shelflist), are alphabetically arranged and carry complete bibliographical information; only the headings change.

Catalogues include those of 'Person', Corporations, Administrative Authorities, Regional, Subject and Title. There are currently 5,421,155 cards analysing the collection.

Classification. Own.

Copying/Photography. Photographic Department catering for most needs. For individual use there are two photocopying machines. Private photography inside the Library is only permitted in exceptional circumstances.

Friends of the Library. The Society of the Friends of the Institut für Weltwirtschaft. Membership open to any person or corporation.

MUNICH
Bayerische Staatsbibliothek
D-8000 München 34, Ludwigstrasse 16
Tel. 089-21981

History. The Bavarian State Library was founded in 1558 by Albert V of Bavaria (1550-79), although much of the credit for its establishment must go to Johann Jakob Fugger (1516-1575). A number of great foundation collections placed it immediately in the front rank of contemporary libraries. These included the Widmanstetter Collection, rich in Orientalia, bought in 1558, and the 10,000 volume library of Fugger himself. After the death of Albert V the Library continued to receive the patronage of the rulers of Bavaria. For example, Maximilian I, when Tübingen fell in 1634, had the contents of the City Library sent to Munich, thus raising the stock to 17,046 printed volumes and 723 Latin and Greek MSS. From the end of the Thirty Years' War in 1648 to the middle of the 18th century the Library made little progress but revived under the directorship of A.F. Oefele, the historian, from 1746-80. With the sequestrations of the beginning of the 19th century the Library had to incorporate no less than 150 collections, among them those of the Bishop of Passau and the Augustinian Canons at Polling. The Library's present building was erected between 1832 and 1843, although it was badly damaged during World War II and 500,000 volumes were lost. Rebuilding began in 1946 and continued through to 1970. The Library, which has legal deposit privileges for Bavaria, currently contains 3.7 million volumes, 40,000 MSS and 16,300 incunabula.

Special Collections and Treasures. The manuscript collection is outstanding and includes such treasures as the *Breviarium Alarici,* an abstract from the laws of the Emperor Theoderic (AD 506); the poems of the nun Hrotsvith of Gandersheim, the first German poetess (died soon after 1001); the *Heliand,* the oldest complete MS of the Old Saxon Harmony of the Gospels (9th century); *Codex Aureus,* the four Gospels written in gold letters

Bayerische Staatsbibliothek, Munich

on purple parchment, conceivably the most magnificent Bible in the world, written at the command of the Emperor Charles the Bald; *Carmina Burana,* a collection of medieval poems; the *Muspilli,* a single MS poem of the end of the world and the Last Judgement, written by a Bavarian between 830 and 840. The Oriental Collection includes the Widmanstetter Hebrew, Arabic and Persian MSS; the K.F. Neumann and Onorati Martucci bequests of Chinese literature; the library of the Paris orientalist Étienne Quatremère, containing 12,000 MSS, 50,000 printed books and 2,000 volumes of Chinese, Manchurian and Mongolian literature; and Professor Haug's collection of 400 Iranian and Indian MSS. The Music Collection is founded on the Hörwart and Werdenstein Collections, rich in MSS and Renaissance vocal music, and on the musical contents of the Fugger Library, containing the famous Munich song book.

Exhibition Areas. The vestibule of the Reading Room, the Fürstensaal, and the 'Treasure Room'.

Hours. Main Reading Room: Mon.-Fri. 0900-2000, Sat. 0900-1700 (Aug.-Sept.: Mon.-Fri. 0900-1700). Closed Sun., public hols., and during Passion Week. Special hours of opening apply to Christmas until 6 Jan.

Transport. Underground: routes U3 and U6 (stop — Universität). Bus routes: 53 and 55 (stops — Ludwigstrasse, von-der-Tann-strasse, Schellingstrasse).

Parking. Public parking areas in the streets.

Admission. Readers: Admission is restricted to readers over 18 and those engaged in research. Foreigners must pay a returnable deposit of DM 60 (DM 30 for foreign students). Proof of identity is sufficient for occasional use of the Main Reading Room.
Visitors: Unrestricted access to the rooms open to the public; guided tours can be arranged on prior application.

Information. General information and information on catalogues is available, and there is also a postal information service. Separate information desks for the special collections (Manuscripts, Music, Eastern Europe, Oriental, Maps).

Sales. There are no sales desks. Guides and rules of admission are for sale at the pay-desk in the Loans Department. Exhibition catalogues are available from the exhibition supervisor. Library publications, especially of the Manuscript Department, are available through the book trade, and at the moment also from the Management Office.

Guidebooks. Irmgard Bezzel's guide to the Library (published 1967), in German, DM 15. Fritz Junginger's readers' guide (1972), in German, DM 0.80. Rules of use of the Library (1970), in German.

Restaurant/Snack Facilities. Cafeteria in the basement, in front of the Periodicals Reading Room. Open 0900-1700.

Services. 18 readers' carrels in the General Reading Room (2 with typewriters). Cloakrooms: on the ground floor between the entrance and the Lending Department, in the basement in front of the cafeteria and on the first floor in front of the Manuscript Department. Lavatories: on the ground floor, in the Reading Room, near the Manuscript Department and the Special Collections. Lift at the entrance and in the east wing in the Lending Department. Smoking is permitted in the hall of the main staircase and in the cafeteria. Telephone at the entrance.

Catalogues. Numerous author, title and subject catalogues.

Classification. Own.

Copying/Photography. Six dry-copying machines in the Reading Room. There is also a photographic service (for microfilms, photocopies etc.). Permission from the Director is necessary for taking photographs in the Library. Readers may photograph books for private purposes, as long as no damage is done to the books and other readers are not disturbed. MSS may not be photographed.

MUNICH
Internationale Jugendbibliothek
D-8 München 22, Kaulbachstrasse 11a
Tel. 28 52 61

History. The International Youth Library was founded in 1948 by Jella Lepman. In 1953 it became an associated project of UNESCO. During its first years special stress was laid upon activities with children, and later it became a research library, comprising not only systematically collected holdings of children's books, but also manuscript collections and a large section of professional literature and bibliographies. In 1969 UNESCO donated 28,000 volumes from the Bureau International d'Education in Geneva, so that the Library has now achieved a sound historical base. The Library's holdings now total 240,000 volumes in 65 languages.

Special Collections and Treasures. The Library claims to be unique in that it is the only special library in the world devoted to children's and youth literature. It has 15,000 children's books, dating from the 19th century and earlier, in addition to MSS, photographs, tape-recordings, etc. of leading authors and illustrators of children's books.

Exhibition Areas. Eight exhibitions are held each year in the Exhibition Hall, Youth Library.

Internationale Jugendbibliothek, Munich

Hours. Central Reference: Mon.-Fri. 1400-1800. (Circulation Dept.: Tues.-Fri. 1400-1800, closed 1 Aug.-16 Sept.) Closed Sat., Sun. and public hols.

Transport. Subway station: Universität.

Parking. Available in front of the Library.

Admission. Readers and *Visitors:* Open to all free of charge.

Information. At the Library staff desks.

Sales. None.

Guidebooks. Brochure, in German and English, free of charge.

Restaurant/Snack Facilities. None.

Services. Cloakrooms, lavatories and telephones. Analyses and reports of books on pre-payment of a fee.

Catalogues. Author, illustrator, title, classified and country catalogues. The catalogue is also available in 18 bound volumes (G.K. Hall).

Classification. Modified Dewey.

Copying/Photography. Xerographic copies can be made on cost-of-materials basis.

Friends of the Library. Private membership DM 30 annually.

STUTTGART
Württembergische Landesbibliothek mit Bibliothek für Zeitgeschichte
D-7000 Stuttgart 1, Konrad-Adenauer-Strasse 8, Postfach 769
Tel. 202-2724 (Director)

History. Duke Carl Eugen von Württemberg founded the Herzogliche Öffentliche Bibliothek (the basis of the present library) on 11 February 1765. Its stock consisted of older official libraries, private libraries (e.g. Uriot, Fromann, Nicolai), supplemented by extensive purchasing by the Duke and his envoys. The Library's collections grew rapidly during the 'Säkularisation' of 1803-6, which brought together in Stuttgart the manuscript and book collections of various monasteries and religious foundations. After 1806 the Library became a public responsibility and the collections developed under a succession of able librarians such as Christoph Friedrich Staelin and Wilhelm Heyd. In 1883 the Library moved into a new building, which was destroyed by fire in 1944 along with 580,000 volumes. It was only in 1970 that a

Württembergische Landesbibliothek, Stuttgart. Main Reading Room

new Library building was completed. It now houses 1.3 million volumes, 11,448 manuscripts, 6,536 incunabula and 19,000 newspapers.

Special Collections and Treasures.   The Library contains about 2,500 medieval and 8,500 modern manuscripts. Treasures include the *Itala-Fragmente* (5th century), which represents one of the oldest Latin translations of the Bible; the *Stuttgart Psalter* (820-830) a Carolingian manuscript with many illustrations; the *Evangeliar* of St.Gereon (Cologne c.1050); the greatest work of the Cologne school; the *Hirsauer Passionale* (1120-1140); *Landgrafenpsalter* (1213-1215), written for Count Hermann von Thüringen, the earliest and most important work of the Thüringen/Saxon school; and the *Weingartner* (song), manuscript, the most famous collection, after the Heidelberg *Manesse Codex* of German Minnesongs (courtly love songs). The most precious of the incunabula are the Ulmer incunabula. About 300 incunabula came from the Frommannische Bibliothek in 1785, and a collection from the Abbé de Rulle in Nancy was added in 1786. 315 items came from Tübingen in 1935. Incunabula from Ernst Kyriss were added in 1962, from Major J.R. Abbey in 1963, and the Savonarola collection was acquired in 1966. The collection of printing from 1501 to 1750 consists of about 10,000 volumes: about 6,500 from the 16th century, 4,500 from the 17th century and 2,000 from the first half of the eighteenth. Other collections include the collection of Württemberg authors of the 18th and early 19th centuries (about 550 volumes); the collection from the old Ellswanger Library (acquired in 1939) containing 17th century printing; and a very rich collection of Bibles totalling 8,500 items.

Exhibition Areas.   A book museum (some 280 metres from the Library) displays a permanent exhibition on the history of books and manuscripts.

Hours.   Main Reading Room: Mon.-Fri. 0900-2000, Sat. 0900-1300. Manuscripts, newspapers, maps and art collections, Hölderlin Archive: Mon.-Fri. 1000-1300, 1400-1700. Library of Contemporary History: Mon.-Fri. 0800-1700, Sat. 0800-1200. Closed Sunday and public hols.

Transport.   Trams: nearest stop is 'Charlottenplatz'.

Parking.   An underground car-park is planned.

Admission.   Readers: May use the catalogues, bibliographical material and the reading rooms without formal registration. Readers must obtain a borrower's card in order to take books out of the Library. There is no charge for this.
Visitors: Must pay a fee. Use of the catalogues, bibliographical material and the reading rooms without formality. Visitors are admitted to the other parts of the Library only when accompanied by a guide, and after prior arrangement.

St. Matthew's Gospel (Weingarten, 13th century), in the Württembergische Landesbibliothek. The beginning, showing the Christmas scene

Information. At the desk on the main floor, above the staircase from the cloakroom.

Sales. Postcards and Library publications are sold in the cloakroom.

Guidebooks. Reader's Guide, in German, DM 3.

Restaurant/Snack Facilities. Cafeteria in the lower hall, open 0900-1830.

Services. Lifts, two public telephones in the cloakroom. Smoking is permitted only in the Cafeteria.

Catalogues. Alphabetical catalogue. Subject catalogue with keyword index. Union catalogue for Baden-Württemberg.

Classification. Own.

Copying/Photography. Three copying machines for individual use in the large Reading Room. Copying and photographic requests can be fulfilled throughout the Library. Private photography only with special permission.

Friends of the Library. Württembergische Bibliotheksgesellschaft (for friends and benefactors) — annual subscription DM 20.

TÜBINGEN
Universitätsbibliothek der Eberhard-Karls-Universität
D-74 Tübingen 1, Wilhelmstrasse 32, Postfach 2620
Tel. (07071) 29 2577

History. The Library was founded soon after the founding of the University of Tübingen in 1477 and was first referred to as 'publica bibliotheca' in 1499. The Library was, at first, housed in a side room in the University building. In 1819 it moved to the Rittersaal (Knights' Hall) of the castle of Hohentübingen, where it remained until it moved into its first proper library building, designed by Stuttgart architect Paul Bonatz and built in 1912. The Bonatz building was adapted to the Library's need for more space by an extension built in 1963, which kept to the style of the original building. The Library's holdings were substantially increased during the course of time by a succession of valuable scholarly libraries and bequests. Valuable items from the secularized monasteries also came into the Library's possession. Holdings currently include 1.6 million volumes, about 5,360 MSS and 30,930 maps.

Special Collections and Treasures. Treasures include 1,654 incunabula. Special collections have been built up in theology and Oriental studies. Valuable older holdings also include material in legal (public law) literature, 17th century pamphlets and old German dissertations.

Universitätsbibliothek,
Tübingen

Exhibition Areas. Changing exhibits are displayed in glass cases in the passageway linking the old and new buildings.

Hours. Term: Mon.-Fri. 0800-2100, Sat. 0800-1600. Vacation: Mon.-Fri. 0900-1900, Sat. 0800-1215. Closed Sun. and public hols.

Transport. By bus from the Hauptbahnhof (main railway station) stopping at the Library. There is a taxi rank 200 metres from the Library.

Parking. Facilities in front of the Library.

Admission. *Readers:* Reader's card to be obtained on first use of the Library.
Visitors: No restrictions are placed on visitors.

Information. At the desk located on the first floor by the catalogue in the new University Library building.

Sales. None.

Guidebooks. Available at the Information Desk.

Restaurant/Snack Facilities. Restaurant opposite the Library.

Services. Cloakroom, lavatories, smoking area and newspaper corner in the foyer of the new building. Typewriting and microfilm reading rooms are approached through the Main Reading Room.

Catalogues. Alphabetical and subject card catalogues. Alphabetical catalogue of dissertations (on microfiches, with supplement on cards).

Classification. Own.

Copying/Photography. Seven copying machines for individual use are available in the entrance hall of the new building, in the passageway between the old and the new buildings, in front of the Textbook Collection in the old building and in the Main Reading Room. Reproduction of MSS and rare and valuable works is carried out in the Library's own photographic department. Permission must be obtained from the Librarian for private photography.

WOLFENBÜTTEL
Herzog August Bibliothek
D-3340 Wolfenbüttel, Lessingplatz 1, Postfach 227
Tel. 05331/22561 and 26652

History. The Library was founded by Julius, third son of Henry, Duke of Brunswick and Lüneburg, who on his succession in 1568, moved his own private library to

Herzog August Bibliothek, Wolfenbüttel

Wolfenbüttel. His son, Heinrich Julius (1564-1613), continued to expand the Library but in 1618, some years after his death, his successor presented the books and manuscripts to the University of Helmstedt. This University eventually closed in 1810 and most of the books were brought to Wolfenbüttel. The Library at Wolfenbüttel was refounded in 1644 by Duke August (1579-1666), who housed his personal library in the old armoury over the stables. He acted as his own Librarian and his purchasing developed the collection into what has been termed the richest in 17th-century Europe. At his death the Library numbered just over 28,000 volumes and 2,000 manuscripts. From 1690 until 1716 Gottfried Wilhelm Leibniz was Librarian. He divided his time between Wolfenbüttel and Hanover. The Library moved into a new building in 1723, and then into its present building in 1887. After World War II the Library came under the control of the provincial government of Lower Saxony and the buildings were enlarged and improved. The collections currently total over 500,000 items.

Special Collections and Treasures. Collections include the Helmstedt MSS, from the old Julian library returned to Wolfenbüttel in 1815; the Augustan MSS (collected by Duke August and numbering about 2,500); the Weissenburg MSS (acquired in 1689); the Gudiani codices (468 volumes including 114 Greek, collected by Marquard Gude, and bought in 1710); and the Blankenburg MSS, collected from the libraries of various members of the Ducal House, including that of Duke Ludwig Rudolf. Treasures include the *Codex Arcerianus* (5th or 6th century), dealing with the measuring and boundaries of lands under the agrarian system of Rome; the very fine illustrated *Bavarian Choirbook* of polyphonic masses, executed in 1519-20; *Annales Guelferbytani,* written 813-16; a lexicon of Tyronian Notes dating from the 9th century; Alexander Cortesius, *Laudes Bellicae,* a humanist Latin poem, with calligraphy by Bartolomeo Sanvito of Padua, c.1480-90; and the unique copy of Ulrich Boner's *Der Edelstein* (Bamberg, 1461), the first illustrated and the first dated book in German language printed with movable type.

Exhibition Areas. Four exhibition rooms in the centre of the building and in the north wing. In 1968 the library acquired the house where the poet and librarian G.E. Lessing lived at the end of his life and this is now a museum.

Hours. Reading Room: Mon.-Fri. 0800-1800, Sat. 0800-1200. Closed Sun. and public hols.

Transport. Many road and rail services to Wolfenbüttel. Taxis are available at the railway station.

Parking. There is a parking place at the Library.

Admission. *Readers:* Use of Reading Room and lending facilities of the Library free of charge.

Visitors: For visits or tours the charge for adults is DM 1, schoolchildren and students DM 0.50. Members of the Friends of the Library free.

Information. The Information Department is reached via a glass door on the right of the entrance hall, and then through the next glass door on the left hand side.

Sales. In the entrance hall: Library publications, guidebooks, exhibition catalogues, postcards, etc.

Guidebooks. A guidebook to the Library is available in German.

Restaurant/Snack Facilities. None.

Services. Typing room, cloakrooms, lavatories, smoking room.

Catalogues. Old and new alphabetical catalogues, in bound volumes and on cards. Subject card catalogue for new books. Printed catalogues for MSS, music, libretti and various special catalogues.

Classification. Own.

Copying/Photography. Copying machines are available to readers near the Lending Department. Microfilms, slides and xerographic copies can be made by the staff on request. Private photography is not permitted in the Library.

Friends of the Library. Gesellschaft der Freunde der Herzog August Bibliothek Wolfenbüttel e.v., founded in 1971. Subscription DM 50.

Ghana

ACCRA
Balme Library, University of Ghana
PO Box 24, Legon, Accra
Tel. 75381 ext. 410

History. The University College of the Gold Coast was founded in 1948. The Library, which opened in October 1948, was later named after the first Principal of the College, David Balme. The initial collection totalled 6,500 books, of which over half were borrowed from Achimota College. Gradually these were replaced, the borrowed books being returned, and by January 1950 the book stock totalled 17,600 volumes. Planning for a permanent building at Legon began in the 1950s and the present building was completed and occupied in 1959, by which time the collections had grown to 119,000 volumes.

Balme Library, University of Ghana

In 1961 the University College was upgraded to full university status, as a result of the Kojo Botsio Commission. The Library, like the University, responded to the new situation and an Africana Library was established to support the work of the new Institute of African Studies. In 1967 the Library appointed its first Ghanaian Librarian, the late E.Y. Amedekey. Current holdings total 275,000 volumes and 5,000 periodicals making it the largest research library in Ghana.

Special Collections and Treasures. Collections in the Africana Library include the Gold Coast Secretariat Library of 600 volumes, received in 1951, from the libraries of F.S. Newlands and F.W. Abbott, both former civil servants; and the library of J.T. Furley, received in 1953, comprising 200 items (including maps and MSS) relating to the history of Ghana. By September 1973 the Africana book collection included 11,976 volumes, 2,482 pamphlets and 1,356 periodicals. It contains over 900 rare items of Africana dating from 1556-1900. Other Balme Library collections include the Arabic Library; a Volta Basin Research Project Library; an Atoms for Peace Library; and a United Nations Documents Library.

Exhibition Areas. The Main Hall of the first floor constitutes the exhibition area, but some exhibitions are also mounted in the Catalogue Hall.

Hours. Term and all vacations except summer: Mon.-Fri. 0800-2200, Sat. 0800-1600. Summer Vacation: Mon.-Fri. 0800-1630, Sat. 0800-1200. Closed Sun. and public hols.

Transport. Bus 21 from Accra to Legon. The University lies 8 miles to the north-east of Accra. From the University main gate, University Avenue extends to Legon Hill; midway an open space is overlooked by the Balme Library.

Parking. Ample parking facilities available.

Admission. Readers: Those other than University members may be admitted at the discretion of the Library Board, or of the Librarian acting on their behalf. *Visitors:* Apply to Librarian.

Information. Information Desks are located in the Catalogue Hall, the Africana Library, and the Students' Reference Library.

Sales. None.

Guidebooks. A limited number of guidebooks are available free from the Librarian's Office.

Restaurant/Snack Facilities. None on the Library premises.

Services. Cloakroom, lavatories and telephone are

located by the main entrance.

Catalogues. Author and subject card catalogues.

Classification. Library of Congress.

Copying/Photography. Orders for copying may be placed with the Reader Services Librarian. Prior permission for photography must be obtained from the Librarian.

Friends of the Library. A 'Friends of the Balme Library' is in the process of formation and details may be obtained from the Librarian.

Great Britain

ABERYSTWYTH
National Library of Wales/Llyfrgell Genedlaethol Cymru
Aberystwyth SY23 3BU, Wales
Tel. Aberystwyth (0970) 3816/9

History. In the middle of the 18th century a group of Welshmen founded the Society of Cymmrodorion, whose constitution provided for a library at the Welsh School in Clerkenwell Green. The Librarian was to procure a copy of every book printed, or to be printed, in Welsh, and as many manuscripts as possible, but by the end of the century the Society had been dissolved. It was not until 1872, when the first University College of Wales was established, that the formation of a National Library became a real possibility. A Royal Charter was granted on 19 March 1907 and in January 1909 the Library was opened in the Old Assembly Rooms, Aberystwyth. Copyright privileges were received in 1911 and subsequently modified in 1956. The Library now contains over 2 million books, pamphlets, newspapers and journals, 30,000 manuscripts and 3.5 million deeds, which are housed in the Library building designed by Sidney Kyffin Greenslade and built in stages from 1911 onwards.

Special Collections and Treasures. The Library has a unique collection of Welsh books dating from 1546 to the present. The collection of Sir John Williams includes 19 of the 22 Welsh books printed pre-1600, notably the first book printed in Welsh, *Yn y Lhyvyr Hwnn ....* Other collections include the Bourdillon library of medieval French romance; the Hartland Collection of ethnology and folklore; the Witton-Davies library of Hebrew and Oriental literature; the Jones Collection on philosophy; the Jaffrennau Collection on Brittany, and the Owen Collection on America. The Library also possesses a

National Library of Wales, Aberystwyth

complete set, in fine bindings, of the Gregynog Press, presented by its founders the Misses Gwendoline and Margaret Davies. Manuscripts include the Hengwrt-Peniarth Collection, over 500 volumes, notably the *Black Book of Carmarthen* and the *Black Book of Chirk,* both early 13th century. Other outstanding treasures include the *Book of Llandaff;* the *Bangor Missal;* a fine 12th century copy of Geoffrey of Monmouth's *Historia regum Britanniae;* the *Sherbrooke Missal;* the *de Grey Book of Hours;* and a unique text of the Cornish play *Bevans Meriasek.*

Exhibition Areas.   Exhibition areas are located on the first and upper floors of the Central Hall, the Gregynog Exhibition Gallery on the upper floor within the South wing, and the Central Hall upper floor annexes.

Hours.   Mon.-Fri. 0930-1800, Sat. 0930-1700. Closed Sun. and Christmas, New Year and Easter public hols.

Transport.   Buses stop at the entrance to the Main Library drive. (The Library is approximately one mile from the centre of Aberystwyth.)

Parking.   Car park to accommodate 110 cars.

Admission.   Readers: By Reader's Ticket only (applications should be made in advance to the Librarian). There is an official application form which must be certified by a person of recognised standing. Applicants should normally be at least 18 years of age.
Visitors: Free admission. Parties of visitors should make prior arrangement. Admission to Gregynog Gallery Mon.-Sat. 1000-1700 (Spring Bank Holiday to end of Oct. only).

Information.   In the Main Central Hall and General Enquiries counter.

Sales.   Main Central Hall Desk and Gregynog Exhibition Gallery Sales Desk.

Guidebooks.   Guide to the Library (in Welsh/English). Price 10p.

Restaurant/Snack Facilities.   Ground floor (central) of the Main Central Hall — main administrative building.

Services.   Cloakrooms, lavatories, one public telephone in the Central Hall area. Smoking permitted in the restaurant only.

Catalogues.   Author, printed books catalogue. Handlist of manuscripts has appeared annually since 1941.

Classification.   Library of Congress adapted to local requirements.

Copying/Photography.   There is a copying service but

machines are not available for individual use. The Library can supply dry copy, microfilm, print-out, negative and positive photostats, photographs or transparencies. Private photography prohibited.

Friends of the Library. Friends of the National Library of Wales, minimum annual subscription 50p.

BIRMINGHAM
Birmingham Public Libraries, Central Libraries
Paradise, Birmingham B3 3HQ
Tel. 021-235 4511

History. The Free Libraries Act was adopted by Birmingham Town Council in 1860 and the first Central Library was opened on 6 September 1865. On 11 January 1879 this was destroyed by fire and replaced in 1882 by a second building, which contained the Reference and Central Lending Libraries. At the time the rebuilt Central Library was opened it contained 50,000 volumes, which had increased to 150,000 by 1900. By 1960 the stock of the Reference Library had increased to over 700,000 and demands on space necessitated the construction of the present Central Libraries building. Construction began in 1969 and was completed in 1973, the official opening ceremony taking place in January 1974. Possibly the largest non-national public library in Europe, it has a total floor area of 215,000 square feet and seating for more than 1,200 readers on eight floors. Holdings currently total in the Reference Library 963,000 volumes, 3,100 current periodicals, 170,000 MSS, 18,500 maps, 55,000 microcards, 33,000 microfiches and 6,500 microfilms, while the Lending Departments have 115,000 volumes, 375,000 illustrations, 10,000 35mm slides and 15,000 gramophone records.

Special Collections and Treasures. Collections include the Shakespeare Library with over 40,000 volumes in 86 languages; the Parker Collection of Children's Books; the Kings Norton and Sheldon Parochial Libraries; the J.B. Stone Collection of Photographs; the Diocesan Record Office for Birmingham; and collections on Milton, Johnson, Cervantes, Baskerville, Boulton and Watt and Priestley.

Exhibition Areas. Monthly exhibitions are located in the entrance hall and the Central Lending Library Readers Lounge, while on floor 6 there is a permanent exhibition of early printed books, fine bindings and private press books. Exhibitions are also arranged in other departments throughout the building.

Hours. Reference Library: Mon.-Fri. 0900-2030, Sat. 0900-1700. Lending Library and Music Library: Mon.-Fri. 0900-2000, Sat. 0900-1700. Children's Library and Visual Aids Dept.: Mon.-Fri. 0900-1900, Sat. 0900-1700. Closed Sun. and normal public hols.

Birmingham Public Library, Central Library Building

Transport.　Most bus routes terminate in or near the city centre, where the Library is situated. The main railway station (New Street) is five minutes away.

Parking.　No parking at the Library. Municipal car parks nearby at Cambridge St., Paradise Circus and Summer Row.

Admission. Readers: The Reference Department is open to everyone, free of charge. Admission tickets issued at the control counter on floor 2. Readers requiring books from the stack may need to provide proof of identity. Anyone living, working or being educated in Birmingham is eligible to borrow. Registration for borrowing is in the Lending Library on floor 1; proof of identity is necessary. There is no charge and other library authorities' tickets are accepted. Sound recordings may be borrowed from the Music Library on floor 3 on payment of annual subscription; no residential or other qualification required except proof of identity for registration.
Visitors: Organised parties may visit the Library on prior application to the City Librarian.

Information.　At the Reception Desk on the ground floor. Also in the Lending Library (Readers' Adviser counter) and in the Reference Library. There are enquiry counters in each subject department.

Sales.　Library publications (reprints, bibliographies etc.) available from appropriate departments.

Guidebooks.　Various guides to individual departments available, free, throughout the Library.

Restaurant/Snack Facilities.　A snack bar is being built on the Library concourse; it will be accessible from, though not part of, the Library building.

Services.　Waiting rooms for visitors on the ground floor (adjacent to the reception desk). Escalators: ground floor to floor 6. Readers' Lounge (Central Lending Library, floor 1) with general periodicals. Coats and bags counter (floor 1). Toilets (including facilities for disabled) on floor 2. Lifts (one for public use) ground to floor 6. Study carrels on floors 3 to 6. Pushchairs for young children in the Lending Library. Separate lift and entrance facilities for the disabled. No smoking in the Library.

Catalogues.　Reference Library: Author and classified catalogues in each department (except Quick Reference and Commercial Information), on cards up to 1973 and on microfilm from 1974. Complete catalogue of Reference Library on floor 3. Lending Library, Music Library and Children's Library: Author and classified catalogues, on cards, up to 1971. Author only (at present) computer print-out in book form from 1972.

Classification.　Dewey.

Copying/Photography.   Copying and photographic facilities are provided. Prior permission must be obtained for private photography.

BOSTON SPA
The British Library Lending Division
Boston Spa, Wetherby, West Yorkshire LS23 7BQ
Tel. Boston Spa (0937) 843434

History. The British Library Lending Division (BLLD) was formed on 1 July 1973 by the merger of the National Central Library (formed in 1916) and the National Lending Library for Science and Technology (established 1961). The stock and services of both former libraries are now maintained by the Lending Division of the British Library (for the British Library see also entries for British Library, Reference Division, and Science Reference Library). The total site is 60 acres but only a small proportion of it is occupied by buildings, which provide 72 miles of shelving. The Library provides a loan or photocopying service for organisations in the UK and abroad, enlisting the assistance of other libraries when it cannot satisfy requests from its own holdings. The development of the Library owed much to its first Director-General and former head of the NLLST, Dr. D.J. Urquhart. Holdings currently total 2.25 million volumes and over 1 million documents in microform.

Special Collections and Treasures. The Library has one of the world's most comprehensive loan stocks of recent scientific and medical literature.

Exhibition Areas. Front entrance hall.

Hours. Mon.-Fri. 0900-1700. Closed Sat., Sun. and public hols.

Transport. By bus: From Harrogate, bus 78 (Tadcaster). From Leeds, bus no. 41 or 42 (Wetherby/Tadcaster). From York, bus no. 43 — 46 (Tadcaster/Leeds). Change at Tadcaster for bus no. 78 (Harrogate). In all cases the stop for the Library is Walton Corner. By car: The Library is signposted from the A1 (Wetherby by-pass), which is reached from Leeds by the A58 and from Harrogate by the A661. From York the A64 runs to Tadcaster — follow signs to Wighill and then Thorp Arch. The Library is signposted on the left at the Trading Estate entrance. By train: York is the most convenient station from which to travel to the Library.

Parking. Large parking areas on site.

Admission. Readers: May consult any item free of charge.
Visitors: By prior arrangement.
(Any organisation may use the services of the BLLD in the UK. To do so registration and acceptance of

The British Library Lending Division, Boston Spa

conditions is necessary. No membership fee is charged. Any organisation or individual abroad can use the international photocopy service of the BLLD)

Information.   In Reading Room.

Sales.   Various publications available. List available on demand.

Guidebooks.   Brief Guide to Services, in English only. Free of charge.

Restaurant/Snack Facilities.   BLLD staff canteen available 0900-1700.

Services.   Cloakroom, lavatories, telephones, all situated near the entrance hall. Calculating machines available on loan to readers.

Catalogues.   Union card catalogue of books. Government publications, music and Slavonic union catalogues of books. Conference, translations and reports Indexes.

Classification.   A small part of the monograph collection is classified by Dewey; the rest is unclassified being principally arranged alphabetically.

Copying/Photography.   Xerographic   and   microfilm copying available through staff.

CAMBRIDGE
Cambridge University Library
West Road, Cambridge CB3 9DR
Tel. Cambridge (0223) 61441

History.   The University Library has had a continuous existence since early in the 15th century. It has seen its collections grow from a total of 76 volumes in 1424, in a single room in the Old Schools, to the extensive contents of its present building, completed in 1934 with a substantial enlargement added in 1972. Before the Reformation the custody of the Library was committed to the University Chaplain but after the office was abolished in 1570, the creation of a University Librarian followed in 1577. The Library almost totally depended for its early growth on donations and bequests, indeed the earliest recorded purchase of a book is in 1617. Copyright deposit, albeit of a somewhat erratic nature, began in 1662 and was confirmed by the Copyright Act of 1709. In 1715 the Library received by gift from George I the magnificent library of 30,000 volumes, collected by John Moore, Bishop of Ely. The 18th century and most of the 19th marked the gradual acceptance by the Library of its role as a repository of national literature. In 1934 the Library moved from its Old Schools site and today its holdings total 2.9 million volumes, 700,000

Cambridge University Library

maps, 67,000 microforms, 300,000 items of printed music and 16,000 volumes of manuscripts.

Special Collections and Treasures. Collections in Printed Books include: The Acton Library (historical, 60,000 volumes); Royal (Bishop Moore's) Library (30,000 volumes); Bradshaw (Irish books); Wade and Aston (Chinese and Japanese books); Madden Collection (ballads); the Harold Williams Collection of Swift; Darwin Library (books from the library of Charles Darwin containing his notes and annotations); and the Peterborough Cathedral Library (7,000 items, on deposit). *Manuscripts:* Baldwin Papers; Crewe Papers; Darwin Papers; Hardinge Papers; Jardine Matheson archives; Taylor-Schechter Genizah Collection; Templewood Papers; Cholmondeley (Houghton) MSS (on deposit); Ely Records (on deposit); MSS deposited by Cambridge colleges (Pembroke, Peterhouse and Sidney Sussex). The Library also houses the University Archives. Treasures include the *Codex Bezae,* a 5th century MS of the Gospels and Acts; the *Nash Papyrus,* a Hebrew papyrus of the Ten Commandments, dating from the 1st century; Bede's *Historia ecclesiastica gentis Anglorum* (the earliest known MS dating from c.AD 737); *Life of Edward the Confessor,* MS (c. 1245); the *Breviarium Secundum Usum Sarum,* written in France in the 15th century on vellum; the *Gutenberg Bible* (Mainz), printed before 15 August 1456; the first dated book printed in England, the *Dictes or Sayengis of the Philosophhres* by William Caxton, 18 November 1477; and some unique Caxton quartos.

Exhibition Areas. Exhibitions are held periodically in a special exhibitions area.

Hours. Full term and Vacation Mon.-Fri. 0900-1900 Sat. 0900-1300. Closed 24-29 Dec., New Year's Day, Good Fri.-Easter Mon., the weekday after 31 March, 30 June and 31 Dec. (although if one of those days is a Fri. the Library remains closed on the next two weekdays), 16-23 Sept.

Transport. The Library is situated on the west side of Cambridge, about 10 minutes' walk from the city centre. Buses no. 180 and 181 run from the railway station to the city centre. A plan of Cambridge showing principal routes to the Library is available on request.

Parking. The Library has its own car park (entrance to the Library grounds is from West Road, a turning off Queen's Road).

Admission. Readers: Members of the Senate are admitted whenever the Library is open. Other members of the University are admitted on presenting a valid admission ticket.

Visitors: Anyone wishing to use the Library should apply in writing to the Librarian.

Information. The Chief Information Desk is in the Main

The Codex Bezae (5th century), in the Cambridge University Library. The Codex Bezae is a manuscript of the Gospels and the Acts of the Apostles

Reading Room, in the centre of the Library. Information about specific Library material may be obtained in the Reading Room concerned.

Sales. Library publications are obtainable from the General Office on the 4th floor. A complete catalogue of publications is available.

Guidebooks. Information for new readers and *Readers' handbook,* free on request.

Restaurant/Snack Facilities. On the ground floor, opening onto South Court. Open: Mon.-Fri. 0930-1830, Sat. 0930-1155. Catering hours: 1030-1345, 1530-1655.

Services. Cloakroom with lockers; 7 passenger lifts; microfilm readers; smoking permitted only in a section of the Tea Room; public telephones; typing room; posting box (collections 1400 and 1800, Sat. 1215).

Catalogues. Main and supplementary author catalogues. Official publications catalogue is a subject catalogue.

Classification. Own, based largely on an early edition of Dewey.

Copying/Photography. Photocopiers stand in the North Front Ground Gallery (access from North Front, floor 1), but are not available for individual use. The Photography Department supplies bromide and photostat prints, microfilms, colour slides, etc. They must be ordered on the appropriate form. Readers and visitors are not permitted to use cameras within the Library.

CAMBRIDGE
Trinity College Library
Cambridge CB2 1TQ
Tel. Cambridge (0223) 58201

History. Trinity College was founded in December 1546 by King Henry VIII, who amalgamated two Colleges already existing on the site — the King's Hall and Michaelhouse. Both had libraries but most of the books had disappeared by the end of the 16th century. A new Library building was projected as early as 1556 but nothing was done for some forty years, during which time the old King's Hall Library continued to serve the new foundation. In 1598 a single room was fitted out as the new Library, in part of what is now the Great Court. The collections only totalled 500-600 volumes but they grew rapidly in the 17th century, reaching 2,705 volumes by 1667. This growth necessitated a new building, the Wren Library, designed by Sir Christopher Wren, which was built and furnished between 1676 and 1695. The grandeur of its interior is enhanced by carved woodwork by Grinling Gibbons and sculpture by Roubiliac, and

Trinity College Library, Cambridge

others. The flow of books into the Library, both by gift and purchase, led to a catalogue of duplicates for sale being compiled in 1784. By the late 1880's the Library contained 90,000 volumes. An extension was built in 1892-4, running at right angles to the Main Library along the ground floor of the North side of Nevile's Court. Twentieth century extensions include a new Undergraduate Reading Room, constructed in 1958 on the first floor of the same building. Current holdings total around 150,000 printed books, 1,500 MSS volumes (to the 17th century) and 125,000 MSS items since that date.

Special Collections and Treasures. Treasures include many illuminated books, notably the 10th century *Gospels,* the 12th century *Canterbury Psalter* and the 13th century *Apocalypse.* Post mediaeval MSS include Milton's shorter poems, numerous MSS of Isaac Newton and Richard Bentley, a large group of Tennyson's poetical drafts, Thackeray's *Henry Esmond,* extensive collections of letters of Edward Fitzgerald and Macaulay, and A.E. Housman's *Shropshire Lad.* The Library is rich in early printed books, e.g. 750 incunabula. Collections include the 'Gale Collection' of MSS; including a substantial number of Greek MSS; the Houghton Papers, totalling 30,000 items; the Milner-Gibson-Cullum Collection of autograph letters, and a large collection of *Adversaria,* printed books bearing MS marginalia. Substantial collections of printed books were given by James Duport (d.1679), Sir Henry Puckering, John Laughton (d.1712), Matthew Raine (bequest of 1831) and William Grylls (in 1863). Other collections include the Wyse Collection of classical pamphlets; the Capell Shakespeare Collection; a large Dante Collection; the Pascal Collection bequeathed by H.F. Stewart; the Arthur Cayley library of 19th century mathematical books; 800 volumes from the library of Sir Isaac Newton, the gift of the Pilgrim Trust in 1944; and Lord Rothschild's collection of 18th century English printed books and MSS, of which the Swift section is of major importance.

Exhibition Areas. The Wren Library: permanent exhibition of MSS and printed books in six showcases. (The Wren Library contains the MSS and the printed books up to 1820.)

Hours. Wren Library. Readers: Mon.-Fri. 0900-1700. Sat. 0900-1300 in full term only. Visitors: Mon.-Fri. 1415-1645 (in summer), 1415-1545 (in winter). Sat. in full term only 1045-1245. Longer hours for Reading Room and Lower Library, which are private. Closed Sun., 24 Dec. and following four days, 1 Jan., Good Fri. and the three following days, and Aug. Bank Holiday.

Transport. By bus or taxi from Cambridge railway station. (Trinity College is located in the centre of Cambridge and the Library can be reached through the College from Trinity Street or the Backs. The entrance to the Library is the north-west corner of Nevile's Court.)

The Canterbury Psalter (c. 1147), in Trinity College Library, Cambridge (MS R.17. 1). Illustration from folio 283, verso: the scribe, Eadwine, who wrote the manuscript at Christ Church, Canterbury

Parking.   There are no parking facilities at the College but there are meters and car parks in Cambridge itself.

Admission.   Readers: Readers should make a written application in advance.
Visitors: Free of charge. (No large groups.) Afternoons only. See hours above.

Information.   At the main entrance.

Sales.   Postcards etc. are sold at the main entrance.

Guidebooks.   The Library of Trinity College Cambridge, a short history, by P. Gaskell and R. Robson (Trinity College Cambridge, 1971) in English, £1.50 plus postage and packing.

Restaurant/Snack Facilities.   None in the Library but restaurants etc. in the town.

Services.   None.

Catalogues.   Card catalogue (author) of printed books and additional MSS; published catalogues of early MSS.

Classification.   Own.

Copying/Photography.   Photocopying   facilities   are available. Private cameras may not be used in the Library.

DURHAM
Dean and Chapter Library
The College, Durham DH1 3EH
Tel. Durham 62489

The Dean and Chapter Library, Durham

History.   The earliest monastic house at Durham was a continuation of the more ancient foundation at Lindisfarne where a scriptorium had been in existence. When the community left Lindisfarne in 875 they took with them some of the books, such as the *Lindisfarne Gospels* (now in the British Library). They eventually settled at Durham to build the first church on the site of the present Cathedral in about 995. The Library grew steadily after the Norman Conquest. An inventory taken in the middle of the 12th century records 436 volumes, while the catalogues of 1391 and 1395 reveal a collection of about 900 volumes. In the time of Prior Wessington (1416-1446) the Library was largely assembled in a room over the Parlour or Slype, between the south transept and the Chapter House. The Library remained undisturbed here until after the dissolution of the monasteries, but in the second half of the 16th century more than half the contents were lost in one way or another. In the 17th century Dean John Sudbury (1662-84) rebuilt and furnished as a library for the Dean and Chapter the building which was formerly the Refectory. This now houses books printed before 1800 together with antiquarian manuscripts and music books.

The 14th century Dormitory was restored between 1849 and 1854 to make a new library for modern books and a museum. Holdings currently total 40,000 volumes and 2,000 MSS volumes.

Special Collections and Treasures. Collections include those of Philip Falle, Canon of Durham (1699-1742), consisting of a valuable collection of Dutch scores of chamber music and books relating to musical subjects; Dr. Christopher Hunter's collection of about 150 MSS purchased in 1757, including the 12th century medical MS of Master Herbert (Hunter MS. 100), formerly part of Durham's mediaeval Library; the MSS of George Allan, obtained in 1832; the antiquarian and topographical papers of Longstaffe, Raine, Randall, Sharp and Surtees; the diaries of Bishop H.H. Henson; the letters and theological writing of Bishop J.B. Lightfoot; the notable collection of early music now known as the Bamburgh music, deposited in 1958. Treasures include the *Durham Gospels* (MS. A.II.17), its ornamentation closely related to the *Lindisfarne Gospels;* the *Commentary* of Cassiodorus on the psalms (MS. B.II.30), with two full-page miniatures of King David; St. Augustine's *Commentary* on the psalms (MS. B.II.13/14), pre 1088, four volumes of the handsomely illuminated *Bible* of Hugh du Puiset, Bishop of Durham 1153-95; and Gregory IX's *Decretals* (MS. C.I.9), late 13th century.

Exhibition Areas. The Dormitory museum, in the west cloister, contains displays and exhibitions of books and antiquities. It is planned to move the museum to a treasury at the southern end of the Dormitory undercroft, adjacent to the shop and restaurant.

Hours. Tues.-Fri. 0930-1300, 1415-1700. Closed Sat., Sun. and Mon. and Aug.

Transport. Buses: to the Market Place, two minutes' walk from Palace Green (and the Library). The Library is entered by the door in the south cloister of Durham Cathedral.

Parking. Multi-storey car park next to the Market Place. No parking in Cathedral precincts or on Palace Green.

Admission. Readers: Registration takes place in the Library Office (the Loft) and readers may work there, in the Dormitory, or in the search room of the University Department of Palaeography and Diplomatic. An intending reader should normally write to the Chapter Librarian.
Visitors: Visitors should give prior notice of their arrival.

Information. Staff on duty in the Loft will answer queries.

Sales. In the Loft, or in the Cathedral shop (south-west undercroft). Photographs, transparencies, books, postcards, etc. are available.

Illumination from Laurence of Durham, poems in Latin (c. 1140), in the Dean and Chapter Library, Durham (Cosin MS V.III.1). The manuscript was written in Durham Cathedral Priory during Laurence's lifetime

Guidebooks. Cyclostyled account of the library (6 pages) available free from the Loft.

Restaurant/Snack Facilities. The Cathedral restaurant is situated next to the shop in the southern part of the undercroft of the Dormitory.

Services. No lavatories in the Library; there are some through the west undercroft of the cathedral. Microfilm readers are available (through the University).

Catalogues. Typed catalogues of all printed book collections. Published catalogue of the printed music books.

Classification. Printed material post-1850 generally according to Dewey. Otherwise material is arranged by press-mark.

Copying/Photography. Photographic orders should be given to Library staff. Prior permission must be sought for private photography.

DURHAM
Durham University Library
Palace Green, Durham DH1 3RN
Tel. Durham 61262/3

History. The Library was established in January 1833, with an initial donation of 160 volumes by William van Mildert, last Prince Bishop of Durham and founder of the University. The bookstock was originally housed in a gallery, erected by van Mildert for the purpose, within Bishop Cosin's Library (1669) on Palace Green, between the Castle and the Cathedral. Cosin's Library itself was used by members of the University from an early date but the collection was not formally placed in the University's charge until 1937. The donation of collections, formed by Dr. Routh (1854), Bishop Maltby (1856) and Dr. Winterbottom (1859), resulted in the expansion of the University Library into the former Bishoprick Law Courts, dating from 1450. In more recent years an adjoining 19th century lecture block has been converted for library use and in 1967 a large reading room and stack extension was completed. In 1950 a separate Oriental Section was established and since 1955 this has been housed at Elvet Hill. The first stage of a new building to provide additional space for the Oriental Section, and to house the Middle East Documentation Centre, was completed in 1972. A new building for the Science Section was opened in South Road in 1965. Current holdings of the Library total 450,000 books and 100,000 microforms.

Durham University Library, Exchequer (c. 1450) and Cosin's Library (1669) with main entrance (1928)

Special Collections and Treasures. The Special Collections in the Palace Green and Science Sections contain some 55,000 items, including over 200 incunabula, some 2,000 STC books, about 10,000 Wing items and 4,000 MSS. The collections are particularly strong in contemporary printed material relating to English history and religion of the later Stuart period. Specific collections include Bishop Cosin's Library of 5,000 titles, rich in liturgy, theology and early French printing; the Library of M.J. Routh (1755-1854) of 16,000 titles, reflecting interests in patristics, classics and 17th century British history; the Bamburgh Library of 8,400 titles which was formed by John Sharp (1644-1714), Archbishop of York, and his descendants and is strong in early natural science; the Collingwood Collection, which focuses on 17th-19th century mathematics; the Observatory Collection on astronomy and physics; the Library of the Sunderland Meeting of Friends on Quakerism, 17th to mid-19th century; the Local Collection on the North East of England; and the Plomer Collection, consisting of books from the library of William Plomer (1903-73), poet, novelist and librettist, together with his literary MSS and correspondence. The Oriental Section administers the archive of MSS relating to the Sudan, 1881 onwards.

Exhibition Areas. No permanent exhibition. Special exhibitions are arranged from time to time at Palace Green, in the entrance hall, Bishop Cosin's Library, Bamburgh Library and at the Science Section.

Hours. Mon.-Fri. 0900-1700, Sat. 0900-1230. During term Palace Green and Science Section open to 2200. Closed 24 Dec.-1 Jan., Good Fri.-Easter Mon., Miners' Gala Sat., and the late Summer Bank holiday.

Transport. The Library is within easy walking distance of both Durham railway and bus station.

Parking. Multi-storey car park next to the Market Place.

Admission. Readers: Non-members of the University who wish to use the Library should write in advance to the Librarian for permission.
Visitors: Should apply at the Control desk inside the main entrance.

Information. At the Library staff desks.

Sales. Library publications and a small selection of postcards may be purchased on application to the Reference Librarian at Palace Green.

Guidebooks. Notes on the research use of the Library (1971) and *Special Collections in Durham University Library* (1974), available free from the Reference Librarian.

Restaurant/Snack Facilities. None.

Services. Typing room, lavatories, lift.

Catalogues. Name catalogues in sheaf form; classified catalogues on cards.

Classification. Dewey for modern collections at Palace Green; Library of Congress for Oriental Section; Universal Decimal Classification for Science Section.

Copying/Photography. Copying facilities are available through Library staff. Readers may use their own cameras but must ask the permission of the Librarian or a senior member of staff.

EDINBURGH
National Library of Scotland
George IV Bridge, Edinburgh EH1 1EW, Scotland
Tel. 031-226 4531
Map Room, NLS Annexe, 137 Causewayside,
Edinburgh EH9 1PH
Tel. 031-667 7848

History. The Library was founded in 1682, largely at the instigation of Sir George Mackenzie of Rosehaugh, the King's Advocate, as the library of the Faculty of Advocates. It was intended to be principally a legal library, but by the time the first catalogue was printed in 1692, it was clearly more than the working library of practising lawyers. Copyright privileges were received in 1710 and have been retained ever since. As a result the Library soon became the largest and most important in Scotland. Maintaining such a library, however, became an impossible strain on the Faculty's private resources and, eventually, under the terms of the National Library of Scotland Act 1925, it was transferred to the state, the Faculty retaining the legal collection and the right to future copyright legal material. Work began on a new building on a site adjacent to the old Library in 1938, and, after a wartime standstill, it was completed in 1955 and formally opened by Her Majesty the Queen in 1956. A Map Room was completed and opened in 1958 and in 1973 the Reading Rooms were enlarged and extended. Inter-library lending facilities in Scotland were administratively centred in the Library with the takeover of the Scottish Central Library in April 1974. In the same year the Map Room moved to the Library Annexe, about a mile away from the main building. Today the National Library of Scotland is one of the four largest libraries in Great Britain. Current holdings total about 3 million books and pamphlets and the equivalent of 30,000 volumes of manuscripts.

National Library of Scotland, Edinburgh. Crown copyright: reproduced by permission of the Department of the Environment

Special Collections and Treasures. Printed Books: a collection of over 400 widely representative incunabula including a *Gutenberg Bible;* many examples of early Scottish printing; a fine collection of private press printing, including a *Kelmscott Chaucer* and an *Ashendene Bible;* a collection of Scottish bindings, mainly of the 18th century; and a complete set of Gould's *Birds*. Among the special collections: Wordie (polar exploration), Rosebery (early and rare Scottish books and pamphlets), Hugh Sharp (English and American first editions in mint condition), Warden (shorthand), Lloyd and Graham Brown (Alpine and mountaineering literature), Lauriston Castle (chapbooks), Bute (17th and 18th century English plays), Dieterichs (German Reformation and academic theses), Mason (children's books), Newman (roadbooks), Glen and Inglis (Scottish music), Balfour (Handel) and Hopkinson (Berlioz and Verdi). Manuscripts: the last letter of Mary Queen of Scots; the Asloan, Auchinleck and Bannatyne MSS of early Scottish literature; the MSS of *Waverley, Heart of Midlothian,* and *Redgauntlet;* MSS of Barbour's *The Bruce* and Henry the Minstrel's *Sir William Wallace;* historical and family papers such as the Balcarres, Denmilne and Minto; and literary collections such as the Abbotsford, Blackwood and Carlyle.

Exhibition Areas. Exhibition rooms on ground floor. Main room — general exhibition of mediaeval MSS, early European printing and MSS illustrating the political, religious, social and literary life of Scotland. Annexe — touring and commemorative exhibitions. Small exhibitions are held in the show cases of the corridor leading to the main staircase. Large, multi-media exhibitions are occasionally held in the Laigh Parliament Hall.

Hours. Reading rooms: Mon.-Fri. 0930-2030, Sat. 0930-1300. Map Room: Mon.-Fri. 0930-1700, Sat. 0930-1000. Exhibition: Mon.-Fri. 0930-1700, Sat. 0930-1300, Sun. 1400-1700. (During the Edinburgh International Festival: Mon.-Sat. 0930-2000, Sun. 1400-1700.) The Library closes on Good Fri., 25 Dec. and 1 and 2 Jan.

Transport. Buses: nos. 23, 27, 41, 42, 45 to George IV Bridge; nos. 1, 34, 35, 43 to the Lawnmarket; no.ʳ 42 to Causewayside.

Parking. No parking at George IV Bridge. The Library is in a metered zone. Nearest car parks: Bristo Street and Johnstone Terrace.

Admission. Readers: 3-day or 6-monthly tickets are issued to readers wishing to use the Library for research and reference not easily carried on elsewhere. There are special conditions for the admission of undergraduates. *Visitors:* The Library is open to the public. No admission charge.

Information. In the Catalogue Hall, first floor.

Sales. In the Front Hall. Postcards, slides, Library publications and facsimiles are available.

Guidebooks. There is a free bookmark, in English, which lists the main details of the Library.

Restaurant / Snack Facilities. None.

Services. Cloakroom in the Front Hall; lavatories on the ground and first floors; passenger lift from ground floor to Reading Room; public telephone on the ground floor, outside the Map Room. Smoking is forbidden in the Library.

Catalogues. Printed books (card catalogues): main name catalogue of printed books pre-1968 imprints (British Museum cataloguing rules); main name catalogue of printed books post-1967 imprints (Anglo-American cataloguing rules 1967); title catalogue post-1967 imprints. Catalogues of maps and music. Subject index (sheaf catalogue) to foreign books.

Classification. Fixed location.

Copying / Photography. Copying service available through Library staff. The use of cameras is not allowed unless written permission is obtained from the Department of the Environment, Argyle House, 3 Lady Lawson Street, Edinburgh 3.

Friends of the Library. Friends of the National Libraries (see entry for British Library).

EDINBURGH
Edinburgh University Library
George Square, Edinburgh EH8 9LJ, Scotland
Tel. 031-667 1011

History. The origins of Edinburgh University Library date back to 1580, when Clement Little, an advocate, bequeathed 300 books for a 'public library' in Edinburgh. The Library was intended to serve the college, which was established in 1583 in Edinburgh. Most of the Little Collection remains in the University Library to this day. The Library depended greatly on donations for its early growth, such as the 500 volume collection of William Drummond of Hawthornden received in 1626. Purchasing grants were virtually non-existent in the 16th and 17th centuries, but from 1709 the Library received copyright deposit privileges (only to lose them again in 1837). By 1883 the Library possessed some 140,000 volumes and today contains 1.1 million printed volumes, 170,000 pamphlets, 18,000 volumes of manuscripts and 35,000 MS letters. About half of these items are housed in the Main Library building, opened in 1967, the rest in the sectional and departmental libraries.

Special Collections and Treasures. Special collections, other than those of Little and Drummond mentioned above, include the James Nairne collection bequeathed in 1678; the David Laing collection of MSS bequeathed in 1879; a large number of books from Adam Smith's Library; the Halliwell-Phillipps collections of Shakes-

Edinburgh University Library

peariana and dramatic literature; and MSS of contemporary Scottish writers, such as Hugh McDiarmid, Edwin Muir, Sydney Goodsir Smith, George Mackay Brown, Norman MacCaig, Thomas Carlyle etc. Medical history is illustrated in large collections of John Goodsir, T.C. Hope, Andrew Duncan (father and son), Lord Lister and many others. Scottish life and history is variously shown in documents of Alexander Carlyle, Jane Welsh Carlyle, William Carstares, Thomas Chalmers, Adam Fergusson, Francis Jeffrey, the folk-song collector Marjorie Kennedy-Fraser and many others.

Exhibition Areas.   Main Library Exhibition Room.

Hours.   Term: Mon.-Thurs. 0900-2200, Fri. 0900-1900 Closed Sat., Sun. Vacation: Mon.-Fri. 0900-1700. Closed Good Fri., Edinburgh, Spring and Autumn Holidays, 25 Dec. to the 3rd weekday in Jan.

Transport.   Edinburgh Corporation bus service to within 200 yards of Library.

Parking.   Parking meters in George Square.

Admission.   *Readers:* Must complete a registration form at the Main Library Service Desk. Applicants who are not members of the University should enquire by letter to the Librarian. Members of the General Council of a Scottish University may borrow books on payment of a subscription.
Visitors: Not encouraged (except to Exhibition Room). Otherwise apply in writing to the Librarian.

Information.   In the Main Library and in the other libraries in the system.

Sales.   Christmas cards are on sale during December, in the Main Library.

Guidebooks.   *Guide to the Library,* free on request. Also guides to sectional libraries.

Restaurant/Snack Facilities.   Coffee room in Main Library, open most library opening hours.

Services.   Main Library: typing carrels for certain registered users on application, lavatories, lifts, public telephones. Special access and cloakrooms for wheelchair readers. Cubicles for blind or partially sighted readers.

Catalogues.   Name catalogue, partial classified catalogue. Various other specific catalogues, e.g. manuscripts, Chinese books, Edinburgh University theses.

Classification.   Main Library is Dewey. Sectional libraries various.

Copying/Photography.   Photocopying service. Slides, microfilms, photostats, bromide prints, colour transparencies also available. Enquiries to Service Desk. Cameras may be used to photograph the interior of the building on application.

Friends of the Library.   Friends of Edinburgh University Library, modest subscription charge.

GLASGOW
The Mitchell Library (Glasgow District Libraries)
North Street, Glasgow G3 7DN, Scotland
Tel. 041-248 7121 (12 lines)

History.   The Mitchell Library was founded in 1874, following a bequest of £66,998 10s 6d from Stephen Mitchell (1789-1874), a tobacco manufacturer. The Library was opened on 1 November 1877, with a bookstock of 14,432, the nucleus coming from the libraries of Cosmo Innes, William Euing, Robert Napier, Dr. William Stevenson and Lord Neaves. By 1891 the Library's stock had risen to 89,000 volumes which were re-housed in Miller Street. This improved accommodation, however, resulted in increased use of the Library and by 1894 the accommodation was proving inadequate to meet the demands made upon it by an average daily attendance exceeding 2,000 persons. Therefore in 1904 a site was purchased with frontage facing North Street. Building operations began on 7 January 1907 and the Library was re-opened on 16 November 1911. Expansion has been steady throughout the 20th century. The Library's holdings currently total 950,000 items including MSS and microfilms.

Special Collections and Treasures.   Collections include the Glasgow Collection of more than 20,000 volumes; the Scottish Poetry Collection of approximately 10,000 volumes including 3,500 on Robert Burns; the Kidson Collection of 18th century English popular music in over 5,000 volumes; the Moody Manners Collection of 2,900 volumes including full scores, instrumental parts and vocal scores of about 100 operas; the Slains Castle Collection comprising the collections of James Drummond, Bishop of Brechin (d.1695), and the Earls of Erroll; a Private Press Collection of 1,350 volumes and the North British Locomotive Company Collection containing about 9,000 glass plate negatives of photographs of locomotives built by the company and its constituent companies together with a similar number of photographic prints.

Exhibition Areas.   The Jeffrey Library on the first floor is used for exhibitions and lectures.

Hours.   Mon.-Fri. 0930-2100, Sat. 0930-1700, Sun. 1400-2000 (Oct.-May). Closed on Scottish and local public hols.

The Mitchell Library, Glasgow

Transport. Electric train from Queen Street Station to Charing Cross Station. Bus from Queen Street Station to Charing Cross (Nos. 10, 10a, 56). Bus from Central Station to Charing Cross (Nos. 43, 44, 57, 59).

Parking. Streets to the North, South and the West of the Library are outside the parking meter zone.

Admission. Readers and *Visitors:* No admission restrictions.

Information. In the Main Reading Hall.

Sales. In the Main Reading Hall. Library publications on sale, e.g. *Glasgow Public Libraries 1874-1966.*

Guidebooks. None.

Restaurant/Snack Facilities. None.

Services. Carrells, lavatories, public telephone in main entrance hall.

Catalogues. Dictionary catalogue 1877-1915 (guard book). Classified catalogue 1915-1949 (printed). Dictionary catalogue 1950-1969 (card). Classified catalogue 1970-(card).

Classification. Dewey.

Copying/Photography. There is a copying service and a copying machine is available for individual use. Private photography only with the permission of the Librarian.

LEEDS
The University Library
University of Leeds, Leeds LS2 9JT
Tel. Leeds 31751

History. The University of Leeds achieved independent university status in 1904, but the origins of the Medical Faculty go back to the Leeds Medical School, founded in 1831, and of the other faculties to the Yorkshire College of Science (later Yorkshire College) founded in 1874. In 1885 the Library stock totalled 4,000 items and this rose to 85,000 items in 1919. Expanding from a single room under the Great Hall in 1894 into numerous separate adjacent rooms, the Library had outgrown its accommodation by the 1920s and had become difficult to supervise. A new central library, the Brotherton Library, circular in plan and built through the generosity of Lord Brotherton who had given £100,000 for the project in 1927, was opened in 1936. A mezzanine floor was inserted in the 1950s, but this accommodation was practically exhausted by the late 1960s. The opening in 1975 of the new South Library, costing nearly £1 million, has brought much needed extra space to house the main

University Library, Leeds. Main room of the Brotherton Collection

science and technological research collection of the University, together with a new collection of 50,000 undergraduate textbooks and 1,200 reading places. Holdings at mid-1973 totalled 1,116,022 volumes and pamphlets, 107,955 units of microforms and 340 metres of MSS material.

Special Collections and Treasures. The Brotherton Collection, located within the Brotherton Library building, is the principal rare book collection and its nucleus is the private library of Lord Brotherton which was presented to the University, in accordance with his wishes, by his residuary legatees. It contains some 48,000 printed books pamphlets, over 2,300 MSS, 4,000 deeds and 37,000 letters. Among the printed books are 252 incunabula, including the unique copy of the *Epitome Margaritae Eloquentiae* by Lorenzo Guglielmo Traversagni, printed by Caxton c. 1480. Other early printed books include Pynson's edition of Chaucer (1526); all four Folios of Shakespeare (1623-1685); and numerous 17th century pamphlets and Civil War tracts. First and other important editions of English literary authors are well represented. Special collections include the Icelandic Collection of over 12,000 volumes and pamphlets, formed by Mr. Bogi Melsted (d.1930) and since augmented; the Anglo-French Collection comprising 4,000 volumes of French translations of English books and French books on England, published before 1805; the All Souls Collection of early science and theology; the Blanche Leigh and J.F. Preston Collections of books on cookery and household management, containing some 2,000 items, many of them early printed books; the Harold Whitaker Collection of county atlases and printed maps of the British Isles; the Roth Collection of printed books and MSS on post-Biblical Judaica, formed by Dr. Cecil Roth (1899-1970); an Anglo-German Collection containing some rare German translations mainly of 18th century English literature. The Medical Library contains a valuable and extensive collection of old medical classics, mostly inherited from its constituent predecessors.

Exhibition Areas. Changing exhibitions of a bibliographical nature are held in both the Brotherton Collection Room and the entrance vestibule of the main Brotherton Library.

Hours. Term: Mon.-Fri. 0900-2200, Sat. 0900-1300, Sun. 1400-1900. Vacation: Mon.-Fri. 0900-2100 (Summer Vac. closed at 1700), Sat. 0900-1300 (Summer Vac. closed at 1230). Closed on Sun. during Vac. and for about a week at Easter and at Christmas.

Transport. Leeds Corporation Transport, services 1 and 4 from City Square. (For City Station — British Rail). Other services from Central Bus Station, Eastgate.

Parking. Limited parking for visitors is available on the campus. A parking fee is payable.

A.C. Swinburne, manuscript of Tristram of Lyonesse, in the University Library, Leeds

Admission. Readers: Registered members of the University and certain categories by special arrangement are eligible as readers. Others should apply in writing to the Librarian, stating their subject of study and producing a satisfactory recommendation.
Visitors: Organised groups of visitors are permitted but should apply in writing to the Librarian and should restrict their visit to the vacation, where possible.

Information. Enquiries desk in the Brotherton Library (in the Main Reading Room), Mon.-Fri. 0900-1700.

Sales. No sales desk as such but various guides for sale (also available by post).

Guidebooks. Notes for readers is available free of charge (a new edition is normally published annually). Also available: *The Brotherton Collection — a brief description* (1953).

Restaurant/Snack Facilities. None in the Library but catering facilities available on the campus.

Services. Within the Brotherton Library: study rooms suitable for typing, microfilm readers, microfiche and microprint videotape player, lavatories, lift. Immediately outside the Brotherton Library: self-service lockers, smoking area, public telephone.

Catalogues. Brotherton Library: Union name catalogue on slips for the whole of the Library system. Classified subject catalogue on cards for the holdings of the Brotherton Library.

Classification. Own.

Copying/Photography. There is a Photocopying Department which takes orders for microfilming and other forms of copying. Self-service, coin-operated, xerographic copying machine is available in the entrance vestibule of the Brotherton Library during opening hours. Self-service (but supervised) machines are in the Photocopying Department and are available Monday-Friday 0900-1700 and on Saturday mornings. Private photography occasionally permitted after written application to the Librarian.

LIVERPOOL

Liverpool City Libraries
William Brown Street, Liverpool L3 8EW
Tel. 051-207 2147

History. The first public library in Liverpool was opened in 1852 in Duke Street. On 15 April 1857 Sir William Brown, an American merchant in Liverpool, laid the foundation stone of the Brown Library to mark Liverpool's 650th anniversary as a borough. The circular Picton

Early 19th-century children's books, in the Hornby Library, Liverpool

Library, adjacent to the Brown Library, opened in 1879 and is named after Sir James A. Picton, who became the first local authority President of the Library Association in 1883. The Hornby Library was presented to the city by Hugh Frederick Hornby and opened in 1906. In 1941 the Brown Library was severely damaged by bombing, over 200,000 volumes being destroyed. Rebuilding began in June 1957 and restoration was completed in 1961. Together the Brown, Picton and Hornby Libraries form the nucleus of one of the largest public library systems outside London, with total holdings currently comprising 2,715,440 volumes.

Special Collections and Treasures. The Hornby Library is a special collection in itself with some 8,000 rare books, 8,000 prints and over 4,000 autographs. Treasures include Audubon's *Birds of America* (1827-38); original MSS of Robert Burns; *Le terze rime de Dante* (Venice, 1502), the first work from the Aldine Press to bear its mark; Fenelon's *Les avéntures de Télémaque* (Paris, 1730), being Louis XV's own copy; *Swift's Travels ... by Lemuel Gulliver* (1726), first edition; and a self portrait of Mark Twain etched in copper and inscribed.

Exhibition Areas. Exhibitions are held in the Picton and Hornby Libraries, as well as in the International, Art, Technical, Music, Record Office, Commercial and Commonwealth Libraries.

Hours. Central Departments: Mon.-Fri. 0900-2100, Sat. 0900-1700. Closed Sun. and public hols.

Transport. All city bus services pass close by. The Central Libraries are located in the centre of Liverpool near Lime Street Station.

Parking. There are a number of municipal car parks within walking distance.

Admission. Readers: All persons over 15 years of age can use the reference library. Lending facilities are free to those living, working or studying in Liverpool, or with tickets from other library authorities.
Visitors: Groups should make prior arrangements.

Information. Service points in all departments.

Sales. Books, postcards and prints relating to Liverpool are for sale.

Guidebooks. Guide to the Central Libraries — free on application to the City Librarian.

Restaurant/Snack Facilities. Coffee bar, open Mon.-Fri. 1030-1130, 1630-1730.

Services. Lavatories. Lift for the disabled.

Catalogues. Dictionary catalogue (authors, title, subject).

Classification.   Dewey.

Copying/Photography.   Electrostatic copying, photostat and microfilming service. Written permission for private photography should be obtained in advance from the City Librarian.

Friends of the Library.   The Friends of the Brown, Picton and Hornby Libraries (by election only). Also Associate Membership of the Friends.

LONDON
The British Library Reference Division (British Museum Library)
Great Russell Street, London WC1B 3DG
Tel. 01-636 1544

History.   The British Museum was founded by Act of Parliament in 1753 to bring together the collections of Sir Robert Cotton, already national property, and those formed by the two Harleys, first and second earls of Oxford, and by Sir Hans Sloane, both collections being on offer to the nation on favourable terms. Under the terms of the Act, which closely followed lines laid down in Sloane's will, a government lottery was held to provide funds both to pay for and to house these collections. The Royal Library was presented to the nation by George II in 1757, and added to the above collections in Montague House, a 17th-century building, which opened as the British Museum in 1759. With the Royal Library came copyright deposit privileges, which, with many donations, ensured a rapid growth in the collections. The Library of George III was presented to the nation by his son in 1823 and housed in the present King's Library finished in 1826, as the first part of a new building on the site. The new south wing, with the entrance portico in its present form, was completed in 1847, and the domed Reading Room in 1857. The Library benefited greatly at this time from the vigorous leadership of Antonio (afterward Sir Anthony) Panizzi (1797-1879), who became Keeper of Printed Books in 1837 and Principal Librarian in 1856. In the 20th century the continued growth of the collections has posed overwhelming space and organisation problems, despite the loss of 200,000 volumes during World War II. In 1973 the Library departments were detached from the Museum and joined with other libraries to form the British Library (see also entries for British Library, Lending Division and Science Reference Library). The holdings of the British Library Reference Division currently total nearly 8 million volumes, 75,000 Western MSS, 30,000 Oriental MSS and 100,000 charters and rolls.

Special Collections and Treasures.   Collections include the Thomason Civil War Collection; the Garrick Collection of plays; the Cracherode Library of fine printed books;

British Museum, south front (1852)

the Bagford Collection of fragments of early printing; the Burney Collection of early newspapers, classical manuscripts and printed books; the Sir Joseph Banks library of botanical, zoological and Icelandic books; the Egerton MSS; the Arundel Collection of English historical and literary MSS; the fine printed book library of Thomas Grenville, strong in English literature and early printing; the Rich Collection on the Near and Middle East; the Henry Davis Collection of bindings; the Ashley Library of English Literature; the Paul Hirsch Music Library of 15,000 volumes; the Stein Collection of Chinese material including the *Diamond Sutra* (AD 868), the oldest dated printed document in the world. Treasures include the *Codex Alexandrinus* (5th century); the *Codex Sinaiticus* (4th century); the *Lindisfarne Gospels* (c.698); the *Egerton Papyrus* (2nd century); the *Westminster Psalter* (12th century); the unique copy of *Beowulf* (c.1000); two of the four extant copies of *Magna Carta;* Azzogendi's first edition of Ovid (Bologna, 1471), a unique complete copy; the *Gutenberg Bible;* the First Folio of Shakespeare's plays (1623); and the only known autograph MS of Coleridge's *Kubla Khan.*

Exhibition Areas.   The four exhibition galleries are the Kings Library, the Grenville Library, the Manuscript Saloon and the Bible Room. All four galleries may have part of their permanent displays temporarily moved to house one of the special exhibitions mounted regularly in rotation, for example, to mark a centenary.

Hours.   Reading Room: Mon., Fri., Sat. 0900-1700, Tues., Wed., Thurs. 0900-2100. Closed Sun., Good Friday, 24-26 Dec. and the week beginning with the first Mon. in May.

Transport.   By underground: to Tottenham Court Road or Holborn tube station. Bus routes: Tottenham Court Road northward bound and Gower Street southward bound: 1, 14, 24, 29, 73, 176. Southampton Row: 68, 77, 77A-C, 170, 188, 239. New Oxford Street: 7, 8, 19, 22, 25, 38.

Parking.   Parking meters in the area.

Admission.   Readers and *Visitors:* By ticket only, obtainable from the Reading Room Admissions Office. Applicants must shown that they are engaged in serious research for which the materials are not easily available elsewhere, and must produce satisfactory evidence of identity. Tickets will only be issued to applicants in person, but advance application may be made in writing, in which case evidence of identity should be in the form of a letter of recommendation from an identifiable person of standing.

Information.·   In the main entrance hall of the Museum (general) and in the various reading rooms.

Sales:·   British Museum bookstall.

Cicero, De oratore, manuscript by Lupus of Ferrières, written either at Ferrières or Fulda (c. 836), in British Library Reference Division (Harley MS 2736). Folio 40, detail

Guidebooks. There are free leaflets in English, about the British Library, the Reading Room, Map Library, Music Library and Official Publications Library.

Restaurant/Snack Facilities. Available.

Services. Cloakrooms, lavatories and telephones at the entrance to the Reading Room. Typing room between the Reading Room and the North Library. Lost Property Office in the main entrance to the Museum.

Catalogues. Author and subject catalogues, mainly book form, but some card.

Classification. Own.

Copying/Photography. Photocopies, microfilm and photostat copying. Apply through reading room staff.

Friends of the Library. The Friends of the National Libraries. Minimum subscription £1.50. Life subscription £30. Apply to the Secretary, 21 Regnum Court, North Walls, Chichester, Sussex.

LONDON
*British Library Reference
Division, Science Reference Library
25 Southampton Buildings, Chancery Lane, London
WC2A 1AW
Tel. 01-405 8721*

History. The Science Reference Library is the largest public scientific and technological reference library in the United Kingdom. It provides literature resources in depth as a service to support current research and development in science and technology. It is also the national library for patents, trade marks and designs. The Library was known as the National Reference Library of Science and Invention until 1973, when the British Library came into being. It was formed in 1960 by the British Museum, which in 1968 added the Patent Office Library (founded in 1855), now the Holborn branch and headquarters of the SRL. The Holborn branch broadly contains the literature on the inventive sciences, engineering and industrial technologies, while the Bayswater branch (10 Porchester Gardens, Queensway, London W2 4DE) has all the rest of the scientific literature and is particularly strong in the life sciences and technologies, earth sciences etc., and also in material on any science in Slavonic and Oriental languages. Holborn has 15 million patents, 600,000 volumes, 18,000 periodicals, trade literature from 2,500 companies and major series of reports. Bayswater, founded 1966, has 210,000 volumes and 16,000 periodicals.

The British Library, Science Reference Library, Holborn branch

Special Collections and Treasures.   The Library in itself constitutes a special collection.

Exhibition Areas.   None.

Hours.   Holborn: Mon.-Fri. 0930-2100, Sat. 1000-1300. Closed Sun. and public hols. Bayswater: Mon.-Fri. 0930-1730. Closed Sat., Sun. and public hols.

Transport.   Holborn: by underground to Chancery Lane station, or bus or High Holborn. Bayswater: by underground to Bayswater or Queensway station, or bus to Porchester Gardens and Queensway.

Parking.   Meters in the area.

Admission.   Readers and *Visitors:* The collections are freely available to all for reference purposes. No reader's ticket required.

Information.   Staff are available at enquiry desks to answer a wide range of general queries. For specialised enquiries staff are prepared to provide assistance.

Sales.   None.

Guidebooks.   Guide to the Science Reference Library and various notes and aids to readers, in English. Free of charge.

Restaurant/Snack Facilities.   None, but available nearby.

Services.   Cloakrooms, lavatories, telephones, lifts. The SRL will compile, by arrangement, select bibliographies on specialised scientific and technological topics. Requests giving precise details of what is wanted should be addressed to the Deputy Director (Services) at the Holborn branch. Linguists available to help with foreign languages material.

Catalogues.   Author and subject. Indexes of bibliographies, dictionaries and periodicals.

Classification.   Own.

Copying/Photography.   Microfilm and photocopies available. Permission for private photography must be sought from the respective libraries.

Friends of the Library.   See preceding entry.

LONDON

British Library of Political and Economic Science
Houghton Street, London WC2A 2AE
Tel. 01-405-7686

History.   The British Library of Political and Economic Science was founded by public subscription in November 1896, following the establishment of the London School of Economics in October 1895. The initiative in establishing the School and the Library came from a group associated with Sidney and Beatrice Webb, the Library being envisaged as a 'new laboratory of sociological research'. It was first housed, with the School, in the lower floor of 10 Adelphi Terrace but in May 1902 the Library was rehoused in a new building in Clare Market. Here the Library, already containing 10,000 volumes, was provided with its first proper accommodation. The Library assumed substantially its present shape in 1931-3, when the present main buildings of the School flanking Houghton Street and Clare Market were erected. A new building is projected to relieve the current serious overcrowding. The British Library of Political and Economic Science is now probably the largest in the world devoted exclusively to the social sciences, with some 670,000 volumes, comprising over 2.5 million items.

Special Collections and Treasures.   Special collections include the Fry Library of International Law; the Schuster Library of Comparative Legislation; the Beveridge Collection; the Passfield papers; the Malinowski papers; the Mill-Taylor Collection, being the letters of John Stuart Mill, the Victorian economist and philosopher, to Mrs. Taylor who became his wife and to his step-daughter Helen; the Power Library on publishing and bookselling; and various papers and diaries of George Bernard Shaw.

Exhibition Areas.   Exhibition cases in the Library Hall.

Hours.   Mon.-Fri. 1000-2120 (1700 in Aug.), Sat. 1000-1700 (closed in July and Aug.). Closed for six days at Christmas, six days at Easter, 1 Jan., the Spring and Late Summer Bank Hols.

Transport.   Bus to Aldwych. Underground to Holborn, Strand or Temple. Entry to the Library is via the main entrance of the London School of Economics.

Parking.   Meters in Lincoln's Inn Fields.

Admission.   *Readers:* The Library is open to members of the London School of Economics, persons to whom permits have been issued and day visitors admitted at the direction of the Librarian. Permits are issued on completion of an application form, provision of references and payment of a fee, which, however, is normally remitted in the case of those engaged in advanced research.

Strand House, Portugal Street, London, in which the British Library of Political and Economic Science is to be rehoused (photograph taken in October 1972)

Visitors: Those not wishing to use the Library must visit at a time designated by the Librarian.

Information. At the Enquiry Desk within the Library.

Sales. None.

Guidebooks. A Self-Guided Tour of the Library and *Notes for Readers* are available, free, at the Enquiry Desk.

Restaurant/Snack Facilities. On the third floor of the main London School of Economics building.

Services. Typing room, with controlled access. Cloakrooms at entrance to London School of Economics. Lavatories at end of Room U. Telephones outside entrance to Library.

Catalogues. Author catalogue on cards. Subject catalogue (published as *A London Bibliography of the Social Sciences,* 35 volumes so far) with card supplement of recent accessions.

Classification. Open-shelf collections: Library of Congress. Closed access stack: monographs by size and running number, official publications by special schemes.

Copying/Photography. Main copying services on first floor of Library. Self-service machines in Main Hall of Library. Private photography by permission of the Sub-Librarian (Readers' Services).

LONDON
Guildhall Library
Aldermanbury, London EC2P 2EJ
Tel. 01-606 3030

Guildhall Library, London

History. The origins of the Guildhall Library cannot be referred to in the singular, since it has had two. In 1423 the merchant Richard Whittington died and the executors of his will, with those of one William Bury, set up the first Guildhall Library. The Library survived until 1549, when the whole collection was 'borrowed' by the Duke of Somerset. No attempt was made to re-establish the Library until 1824 when the Corporation of London established a reference library of material on the history and development of London. In the course of time collections were added in related subject fields, although it was not until 1873 that its holdings were opened to the general public. This move coincided with the Library's occupation of a neo-gothic building erected 1868-72. This building suffered war damage on the night of 29-30 December 1940, when many thousands of volumes were damaged or lost. The steady growth of the collections, which now total over 200,000 books, pamphlets, etc., MSS. in 68,924 archival units, and 60,000 prints, cuttings, etc., necessitated the move in late 1974 to new and larger premises.

Special Collections and Treasures.   The Guildhall Library is a general reference library housing the pre-eminent collection on London. It is particularly strong in the ephemeral political and social pamphlets of the 17th-early 19th centuries. The Department of Manuscripts is the official repository for deposited records relating to the City of London. Maps date from the 16th century and include the Agas plan of London (c.1570), of which only two other copies are known. The following libraries and collections have been either presented or deposited: libraries of the Worshipful Companies of Gardeners, Fletchers (toxophily), Glaziers and Clockmakers and of the Antiquarian Horological Society and Institute of Masters of Wine; Cock Collection (on Sir Thomas More); Gresham College Library; London Municipal Society Collection of Election literature and tracts; Tyssen Collection of 18th century sermons and theological works; and Hamilton and Chapman bequests of 19th century plays. Treasures include one of the only six known signatures of Shakespeare; the *Great Chronicle of London;* the 14th century *Missal* of St. Botolph, Aldersgate; the *Chronicles of France*, a 14th century illustrated MS; and a first edition of Sir Thomas More's *Utopia* (London, 1516).

Exhibition Areas.   The Whittington Room to the right and the Exhibition Room to the left of the main entrance.

Hours.   Mon.-Sat. 0930-1700. Closed Sun., 24 Dec. and bank hols.

Transport.   Nearest underground stations are Moorgate (Northern, Circle and Metropolitan lines) and Bank (Northern, Circle, District, Central and Waterloo and City lines). Buses from most parts of central London.

Parking.   There are no separate car-parking facilities.

Admission.   Readers: Readers of MSS, prints, maps and drawings must sign the readers' register and may need to provide some identification, as may readers of rare printed material.
Visitors: Casual visitors are discouraged from entering the main reading rooms.

Information.   Information desks in each of the three reading rooms.

Sales.   In the General Office on first floor, up the stairs on the left of the main entrance hall. Publications include catalogues of manuscript, printed books and print collections; portfolios of prints; and twice yearly magazine, *Guildhall Studies in London History.*

Guidebooks.   Free   guide   in   English   only,   copies displayed at entrance to Printed Books Reading Room.

Restaurant/Snack Facilities.   None.

Services.   Study carrels adjoining periodicals room on lower ground floor, lavatories on lower ground floor. Arrangements can be made to enable disabled readers to gain access to all the library's facilities.

Catalogues.   Name and classified card catalogues for printed books; classified and name card catalogue for MSS; topographical and subject catalogues for prints with article and engraver index; portrait index; chronological indexes of satirical prints and London maps.

Classification.   Special London classification used in all departments; in addition Dewey used for printed books.

Copying/Photography.   Copying facilities are available but not for individual use. Private photography by permission of the Library staff only. Flash permitted only when required to photograph books and documents for bona fide research purposes.

LONDON
India Office Library and Records
Foreign and Commonwealth Office, 197 Blackfriars Road, London SE1 8NG
Tel. 01-928 9531

History.   The India Office Library was founded in 1801 as the East India Company's repository for the printed books and manuscripts which had been presented to it. The Library's Indological resources greatly expanded after 1867 when it became a copyright deposit library for Indian publications. This privilege lasted until Indian and Pakistan Independence in 1947. The emphasis for collecting then shifted temporarily to western language materials and to the preservation of the private papers of former Secretaries of State, Viceroys, Governors, etc. The holdings of the Library currently total just over 300,000 volumes, 42,000 MSS, 3,700 periodicals and 50,000 prints, drawings and photographs. The India Office Records comprise the archives of the East India Company (1600-1858), the Board of Control (1784-1858), the India Office (1858-1947) and the Burma Office (1937-1948). These materials comprise some 200,000 volumes and files of original material, 20,000 maps and 100,000 official publications. The history of the Record Office goes back at least to 1771 when the East India Company appointed a 'Register and Keeper' to take charge of the Proceedings and other records received from India. Both the Company and Board of Control archives passed under the control of the India Office in 1858 and remained so until Indian and Pakistan Independence. The Library and Records, whilst to some extent necessarily retaining their separate identities, are

India Office Library and Records building, London

now administered as a department of the Foreign and Commonwealth Office. Both collections were moved from the former India Office building in Whitehall to new premises in Blackfriars Road in January 1968.

Special Collections and Treasures.   The first manuscript collection received in the Library was that of Robert Orme, historiographer to the East India Company 1769-1801. Other MS collections include those of Henry Thomas Colebrooke, who presented 2,749 MSS in 1819; Colin Mackenzie (1753?-1821), Indian antiquary and topographer; the Buchanan-Hamilton MSS (presented c.1820); the Sir Walter Elliott MSS (presented 1871); the Fowke MSS (presented in 1947); the Sir Thomas Stamford Raffles Collection; the Wellesley Correspondence (purchased 1936); the Clive Collection, with more than 11,000 folios, relating to the Indian career and administration of Robert, first Lord Clive, and of his son Edward; the Delhi Collection of 3,600 MSS, particularly strong in Indian Muslim mystical and religious works; the Irvine Collection which consists almost entirely of Indian histories; the Stein Collections, comprising the MSS brought back by Sir Aurel Stein (1862-1943) from three archaeological expeditions to Central Asia 1900-1, 1906-8 and 1913-16; and the Hoernle Collection consisting of the MS portion of the collection of antiquities from eastern Turkistan. The Library's Tibetan MSS, documents and xylographs derive from six principal sources: the Hodgson donation, the St. Petersburg Academy donation, the Lha-sa Collection, the Waddell donation, the Denison Ross purchase, and the Stein Collections.

Exhibition Areas.   Exhibitions are held in the Conference Room and remain on show for about a year.

Hours.   Library and Records: Mon.-Fri. 0930-1800, Sat. 0930-1300. Newspaper Reading Room (Bush House): Tues. and Thurs. 1000-1700. Closed Sun., normal public hols. Reading rooms closed annually for a fortnight beginning on the Mon. falling between 4 and 10 October.

Transport.   Underground: To Waterloo on the Northern and Bakerloo lines. Buses: 1, 1A, 4A, 68, 70, 76, 176, 188 and 196 and Red Arrow buses 501, 502, 503, 504, 505 and 507 stop or terminate at Waterloo. From Waterloo walk by the National Theatre and along the Cut. Buses 17, 45, 63, 109, 141, 155, 177 and 184 pass the building.

Parking.   None.

Admission.   Readers: Applications for Readers' Tickets should be made in writing, on a form to be obtained from the Director.
Visitors: Should fill in a pass form at the main entrance.

Information.   In the Catalogue Hall on the 4th floor.

Sales.   In Catalogue Hall on 4th floor. Colour postcards, prints and catalogues on sale.

Guidebooks.   S.C. Sutton, *A Guide to the India Office Library,* 2nd edition (HMSO 1971), £1.50.

Restaurant/Snack Facilities.   None.

Services.   Coats and cases must be left with the Attendant in the Catalogue Hall (4th floor). Readers who are doing long-term research in the building can apply at the Staff counter (4th floor) for a locker. Public lavatories on the 4th floor. Readers' typing room and public telephone on the 5th floor. Readers' common room on the 11th floor.

Catalogues.   Library: by language; published catalogues continued by author and subject card catalogues.

Classification.   Library: No classified arrangement (closed access). Record Office: By administration and series with mixed notation.

Copying/Photography.   Photocopying and microfilm facilities are available, as are Rank Xerox copyflo and prints from microfilm. Private photography not allowed.

LONDON
University of London Library
Senate House, Malet Street, London WC1E 7HU
Tel. 01-636 4514

University of London Library

History.   The University of London Library is a general library covering nearly all subjects studied in the University. The coverage in the humanities is wider and in greater depth than in law, science and technology. It was founded in 1838 when a gift of books was accepted by the University (founded in 1836). Growth was not rapid, however, until the late 19th century when some large donations were received, notably the Grote Collection of classical literature (7,000 volumes) and the De Morgan Collection of early mathematical books (4,000 volumes). When the University moved to South Kensington in 1900 the Library had grown to some 30,000 books. In 1903 it received from the Goldsmiths' Company the great 30,000 volume collection of early works on economics formed by Professor A.H. Foxwell, thus doubling the size of the Library. In 1938 the Library moved to its present location in Senate House in Bloomsbury. The Library then contained 300,000 volumes. Current holdings now total about 1 million items, filling to capacity the Library's tower stack.

Special Collections and Treasures.   Collections include the Goldsmiths' Library of source material for economic and social history mainly up to 1850 (see above); the Sterling Library of early and rare editions of English literature; the Durning-Lawrence Library of 16th and 17th century English literature, particularly Shakespeare and Bacon; the Quick Memorial Library of early education; the Harry Price Library of the occult; the Malcolm Morley Collection on British and American theatrical history; and the Belgian Library.

Exhibition Areas.   Display cases in the Library entrance hall.

Hours.   University Session: Mon.-Fri. 0930-2100, Sat. 0930-1730. Summer Vacation: Mon.-Sat. 0930-1730. Closed Sun., bank hols. and one or more days after the Christmas, Easter and late Summer bank hols. (Note: the General Open Access Library and the subject libraries are closed 15 minutes earlier than the Library closing times given above.)

Transport.   Underground: Northern Line to Tottenham Court Rd. or Goodge Street, Piccadilly Line to Russell Square. Various buses to neighbouring main thoroughfares. The Library is situated in Senate House, access by lift to the 4th floor.

Parking.   No private parking facilities for visitors. There are parking meters in Malet Street and Russell Square.

Admission.   *Readers:* Tickets for one year are issued to members of the University only. Non-members may be allowed tickets for certain periods if they apply in writing. Day tickets may be issued on personal application. There is no charge.
Visitors: Normally by prior arrangement only.

Information.   In the Catalogue Hall.

Sales.   In the entrance hall. Library publications and postcards are available.

Guidebooks.   *Introductory guide* and *Notes for new readers,* both free of charge.

Restaurant/Snack Facilities.   On the third floor of Senate House. Open to Library readers 1030-1130, 1300-1400, 1530-1700.

Services.   Lifts from ground floor, lavatories, telephones.

Catalogues.   Alphabetical author catalogue of books (on cards). Classified subject catalogue of books received since 1958 (on cards). Various special catalogues: e.g. periodical titles, manuscripts, music, maps.

Classification.   Bliss. (Some sections use Dewey or their own classification.)

Copying/Photography.   Self-service coin-operated photocopying machines. The Attendant at the entrance to the Library will give change for the machines. There are further facilities in the Photographic Section in the basement of Senate House. (Mon.-Fri. 1000-1645). Before taking any book or journal for photocopying, permission must be obtained from a member of the staff. For other photographic work (microfilming, enlargements, slides) enquiry should be made in the Photographic Section Office, in the basement (Mon.-Fri. 0930-1730). On Sat. enquiries may be made at the Enquiries Desk in the Library. Private photography requires the permission of a senior member of the Library staff.

LONDON
The Library, School of Oriental and African Studies
Malet Street, London WC1E 7HP
Tel. 01-637 2388

History. The Library of the School of Oriental and African Studies was founded in 1917, with its nucleus being formed by the collection of Oriental books owned by the London Institution. The University Library and the libraries of University and King's Colleges transferred their Oriental books (other than Hebrew and Syriac), in exchange for the Western books from the London Institution Library. Foremost among these collections were the printed books and MSS presented to King's College in 1835 by the Orientalist and numismatist William Marsden. Large donations subsequently came from the India Office, the British Museum and private persons. In 1961 the Hayter Report recommended that the Library should be regarded as a 'national lending library' for Oriental and African studies, with the result that growth has been particularly rapid in the last decade. In 1973 the Library moved into new accommodation with space for 1 million volumes. Current holdings include over 400,000 volumes, 2,000 MSS and MS collections, 10,000 sheets of printed maps and 20,000 photographs.

Special Collections and Treasures. The Library houses on deposit the archives of the Council for World Mission (formerly the London Missionary Society) and various papers relating to the Chinese Maritime Customs (1860-1943). Special collections absorbed in the main stack include those of Sir Reginald Johnston (rich in modern Buddhism); Henry McAleavy (China and Japan); B. Ponsonby-Fane and Sir Henry Partlett (Japan); William Marsden, Sir Thomas Arnold, R.C. Reed and C.J. Edmonds (Orientalia); and J.F. Fleet, Ernst Haas and Sir Dinshaw Petit (South Asian material). The Library also possesses the papers of Sir Frederick Maze, the letters of Sir Robert Hart, and other papers relating to Edward and Cecil Bowra, which together form a valuable source for the study of the history of China.

Exhibition Areas. None.

The Library, School of Oriental and African Studies

Hours. Term and Easter Vacation: Mon.-Fri. 0900-2030, Sat. 0930-1230. Christmas and Summer Vacations:

Mon.-Fri. 0900-1700, Sat. 0930-1230. Closed 24-26 Dec. and the working day immediately following; at 1300 on Maundy Thurs. until 1400 on the following Tues.; on the Spring Bank Hol. and the preceding Sat., on the Sept. Bank Hol. and the preceding Sat.

Transport. Underground: nearest stations Russell Square, Goodge Street, Warren Street, Euston Square. Bus: any service to Russell Square or Gower Street.

Parking. No facilities. Parking meters in neighbouring streets.

Admission. Readers: Registration is carried out at the Issue Desk. Ordinary members (i.e. students and teaching staff of the School and others at the discretion of the Librarian) will be required to pay a deposit of £5 if they wish to borrow books.
Visitors: Apply to the Librarian.

Information. At the Issue Desk at the main entrance, and in the Catalogue Hall, 1st floor.

Sales. No sales desk, but publications distributed through Publications Officer in the School.

Guidebooks. Library Guide, 2nd ed., 1973, in English, price £1.

Restaurant/Snack Facilities. Not in the Library but facilities in the School, open 1000-1730.

Services. Typing rooms, 1st and 2nd floors. Cloakroom, ground floor. Lavatories, lower ground, ground, 1st and 2nd floors. Lifts. Telephones, lower ground and 2nd floors. Smoking is not permitted within the Library.

Catalogues. Author, title and subject catalogues in Catalogue Hall on 1st floor. Published catalogues by G.K. Hall & Co., *Union Catalogue of Asian Publications* (Mansell).

Classification. Own.

Copying/Photography. Self-service coin-operated copying machines on two floors, while the School Photographer can advise readers on other services which are available. Private photography only with the permission of the Librarian or Deputy Librarian.

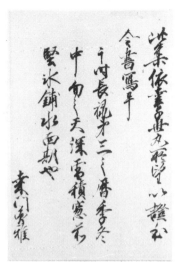

The Kokinwaka-shū, manuscript prepared by the priest, Enga (1459), in the Library of the School of Oriental and African Studies. Final page. The Kokinwaka-shū is an anthology of ancient and modern verse compiled by Ki no Tsurayuki and other notable poets in 905

LONDON
Wellcome Institute for the History of Medicine (Library)
183 Euston Road, London, NW1 2BP
Tel. 01-387 4477

History. The Library was established in about 1890 by the American born Sir Henry Wellcome (1853-1936) as a private undertaking within the international pharmaceutical company now known as the Wellcome Foundation Ltd. In 1936 when Wellcome died the collection totalled over 300,000 volumes, housed in a large warehouse in the London suburbs. Following the systematic weeding of the collection, it was formally opened to the public in December 1949 in the Wellcome Building erected in 1931. The Library is now the property of the Wellcome Trust set up under the terms of Sir Henry's will. It is one of the world's largest libraries dealing with its special range of knowledge, i.e. the history of medicine and the contributory sciences. The Library's holdings now total 350,000 books, 10,000 manuscripts, 100,000 autograph letters, 100,000 engravings and 38,000 photographs.

Special Collections and Treasures. The Library's holdings are particularly strong in Orientalia (containing MS and printed material) in the Sanskrit, Arabic, Persian, Hebrew, Syriac, Ethiopian, Chinese, Japanese, Tibetan and Batak languages, and Americana (including the León and Guerra Collections of Mexicana and Americana). The Library also possesses a significant collection of medical and scientific incunabula (632 items), based on acquisitions from three private libraries: William Morris (1898), Dr. J.F. Payne (1911) and Kurt Wolff (1926). Treasures include the *Nuremberg Chronicle* (1493), a magnificent copy which once belonged to William Morris, and letters by Pasteur, Florence Nightingale and Lord Lister.

Exhibition Areas. No permanent exhibition room. Occasional exhibitions in the Library.

Hours. Mon.-Fri. 0945-1715. Closed Sat., Sun. and public hols.

Transport. Underground to Euston Square, Euston and Warren Street stations. Also numerous London Transport buses to neighbouring main thoroughfares.

Parking. None. Meter parking in the neighbourhood.

Admission. Readers: Admission free to approved readers on written application.
Visitors: Not encouraged.

Information. In the Catalogue Room.

Sales. Books and pamphlets, exhibition catalogues, printed catalogues of the Library, published by the Institute, available from the Publications Department.

Guidebooks. A *Guide to the Reference and Periodical Collections in the Reading Room* is available free to readers.

Restaurant/Snack Facilities.. None.

Library of the Wellcome Institute for the History of Medicine

Services.   Cloakrooms, lifts and lavatories are available at the entrance to the Library. Telephones available in the building.

Catalogues.   Author card catalogues of printed monographs 1467 to present. Chronological catalogue 1467-1850. Subject, name and topographical catalogues covering monograph and journal entries from the Institute's bibliographical quarterly, *Current Work in the History of Medicine,* since its inception in 1954; these catalogues also cover the reference and secondary historical material on open access in the Reading Room. Also various printed catalogues.

Classification.   Wellcome Institute system, adapted, with additions, from the Barnard classification.

Copying/Photography.   Copying facilities are provided. Apply to Library staff. Private photography not permitted.

MANCHESTER
John Rylands University Library of Manchester
Oxford Road, Manchester M13 9PP
Tel. Main Library Building: 061-273 3333; Deansgate Building: 061-834 5343

History.   The present Library resulted from the merger in 1972 of the Library of the University of Manchester, founded in 1851 as Owens College, and the John Rylands Library, founded in 1900 as a memorial to the businessman John Rylands (1801-1881) by his third wife, Mrs. Enriqueta Rylands. The combination of one of the largest University libraries in the country and a famous rare books library created one of the most important research libraries in Great Britain. The day to day teaching and research material of the University in the humanities is concentrated in the main administrative building, opened in 1936, on the University campus. Extensive collections of scientific and medical literature are located in the Christie Science Library and the Medical Library respectively. The University's internationally famous collections of early printed and rare books and MSS are housed for all subjects in the Deansgate building, home of the original Rylands Library. The Library acts very much as the research library of the region and a considerable number of local libraries have been incorporated into its stock. It has a registered readership of over 30,000 users. Its holdings currently total well over 2½ million books, over 16,000 MSS in over fifty languages, some 500,000 deeds, charters and family muniments and over 400,000 titles in microform.

Special Collections and Treasures.   The policy of the University is eventually to focus all the MSS and rare books and special collections in the Deansgate building of the John Rylands University Library whilst

John Rylands University Library, Manchester

administering it as part of the whole from the main building on the campus. Collections include the 40,000 volume Althorp Library of the 2nd Earl Spencer, purchased in 1892, containing possibly the most complete collection ever formed of Aldine Press printings at Venice, and outstanding collections of Dante literature, French Revolution material and pamphlets dealing with the Civil War, Popish Plot, Revolution of 1688 etc. The Crawford Collection of Oriental and Western MSS is equally noteworthy. Extending from the third millennium B.C. to the present day it includes over fifty different languages and cultures on virtually all the materials ever used by man for his records. Many of the leading schools of Western and Eastern illumination are there represented. The Christie Library is extremely strong in French Renaissance literature and the Bullock Collection is composed almost entirely of Italian 16th century books. Literary MSS holdings range across authors such as Johnson, Dickens, Ruskin, Lander, Gaskell, Hugo and Monkhouse and extend to papers of Second World War leaders such as Field Marshall Sir Claude Auchinleck, General Dorman Smith and others. The J.R. Partington History of Chemistry collection, the extensive Manchester Museum Library, the old established former library of the Manchester Medical Society, and others, create a richness in Science and Medicine almost comparable with that in the Humanities.

Exhibition Areas. Exhibitions are held regularly in both the Main and Deansgate buildings. The latter is open ·to the public; the former can be seen by the public on application.

Hours. Main Library Building: Mon.-Fri. 0900-2130, Sat. 0900-1300 (during term, Christmas Vacation from 2 Jan. and Easter Vacation excepting Holy Week). Open without library services (i.e. for reading and study purposes only), Michaelmas and Lent terms: Sat. and Sun. 1300-1800. Summer term (until end of examinations): Sat. 1300-2130, Sun. 1200-2130. Spring Bank Holiday Mon. 0900-2130. Christmas Vacation up to 23 Dec., Holy Week and Summer Vacation the Library is open Mon-Fri. 0930-1730, Sat. 0930-1300. Otherwise closed on Sun., University hols. and public hols. Deansgate building: Mon.-Fri. 0930-1730, Sat. 0930-1300, except on the days when the Library as a whole is closed.

Transport. Frequent bus services. The Main Library (the University) is in Oxford Road about one mile south of the city centre. The Deansgate building (Special Collections Division) is in the centre of the city.

Parking. Main Library: university car parks available. Deansgate building: public car parks in the vicinity.

Admission. Readers: All members of the University are entitled to register as readers. Others wishing to use the Library must apply to the Librarian, normally two days before they require admission, and must not be less than 18 years of age.

Visitors: The Deansgate building is open in part to visitors. Visiting parties to Deansgate and all visitors to buildings on the campus must give prior notice.

Information. Enquiry desks near the entrances of all buildings.

Sales. Postcards, *Bulletin* of the Library, catalogues.

Guidebooks. The Pocket Guide to Facilities and Resources. Detailed guide to special collections in preparation. History of the Library in preparation.

Restaurant/Snack Facilities. The Main Library building has vending machines for drinks. Readers may use the University Refectory. No facilities in the Deansgate building. There are extensive public facilities in the area.

Services. Cloakrooms and lavatories in all buildings, public lifts in main building and in Christie Library.

Catalogues. Author card catalogue in each building. Partial union catalogue of all holdings and classified subject catalogue, with subject index, in main building. Various supplementary catalogues in published and card form.

Classification. Dewey for open access collections.

Copying/Photography. There is a copying service but machines are not available for individual use. Extensive photography services for all sorts of reprography available. Special rates for readers are offered. Private photography of any kind is forbidden.

OXFORD
Bodleian Library
Oxford OX1 3BG
Tel. Oxford 44675

History. The Bodleian Library is the main library of Oxford University, and in England is second in size only to the British Library (see entries for the British Library Lending and Reference Divisions and for the Science Reference Library). It has a continuous history from 1602. The first library was founded in the 14th century and housed in a room built for it, adjoining St. Mary's Church, Humphrey, Duke of Gloucester, younger brother of King Henry V, added a great collection of MSS between 1435 and his death in 1447 and this was housed in a library room specially built over the Divinity School and still known as Duke Humphrey's Library. By the middle of the 16th century the contents of this

Bodleian Library, Oxford. The New Library

Library had been dispersed and the Library owed its refounding to Sir Thomas Bodley, an Elizabethan diplomat and scholar. The restored University Library was formally reopened on 8 November 1602 with a stock of about 2,000 volumes. Deposit privileges were received from the Stationers' Company in 1610. Such privileges caused space problems. In 1612 Arts End was built onto Duke Humfrey's Library, and when the adjacent Schools Quadrangle was built 1613-1619, the top floor was from the first reserved for book storage. From 1789 the first two storeys around the Quadrangle were taken over, as in 1860 was the Radcliffe Camera, built by James Gibbs, 1737-1749. In the 1920s the Bodleian absorbed other special libraries: the Radcliffe Science Library (South Parks Road), Indian Institute Library and Rhodes House Library (South Parks Road). In 1939 the New Bodleian Library across Broad Street was completed as the main book-stack and processing section, thanks to a grant from the Rockefeller Foundation. Since World War II a separate Law Library has been built and the Indian Institute rehoused on the top of the New Bodleian. The Bodleian has recently occupied the Clarendon Building, situated between the Old and New Libraries. Current holdings total nearly 3.4 million volumes, 4,168 metres of manuscripts and 18,500 charters and deeds.

Special Collections and Treasures. Collections include the Barocci Collection of Greek MSS; the Laudian MSS numbering over 1,300 in 20 different languages; the libraries of Robert Burton, rich in ephemera, and John Selden, containing over 8,000 items; the Oriental MSS of Edward Pococke and Dr. Robert Huntingdon; the bequests of Thomas Tanner in 1736, Thomas Carte in 1753, and Richard Rawlinson in 1755, with the state papers of Edward Hyde, first Earl of Clarendon, received in 1759, enriching the already strong collections on English history; the bequest of Nathaniel Crynes in 1745, increasing the holdings of early printed books; the Gough Collection rich in topographical and liturgical works; the Malone Collection of Elizabethan and Jacobean plays and literature; the Douce Collection of 17,000 volumes of illuminated MSS, incunabula and other early printing; the Oppenheimer Hebrew Collection; the Sanskrit Collections of Professor Wilson and the Maharajah Sir Chandra Shum Shere; the Backhouse Chinese Collection; the Mortara Italian Library; the Shelley Collection; the Bywater Aristotelean Collection; the Henry Ward Poole Mexican Independence Pamphlet Collection; the John Johnson Collection of Ephemeral Printing; the Albert Ehrman Broxbourne Library (on deposit); the John Locke papers; the T.W. Bourne Handel Collection; and the Walter Harding Collection of libretti, plays, ballad operas, jest books and sheets music. Treasures include King Alfred's translation of Gregory's *Cura pastoralis* (late 9th century); *Chanson de Roland* (c.1130-40), the oldest known *chanson de geste*; *St. Margaret's Gospels* (c.1025); the *Kennicott Bible* (1476), one of the finest Hebrew illuminated manuscripts

P.B. Shelley, manuscript of original draft of Ode to the West Wind, in the Bodleian Library, Oxford (MS. Shelley add. e. 12, folio 63)

in existence; the *Codex Mendoza* (c.1541), perhaps the world's most famous Mexican pictographic MS; Shakespeare's *Venus and Adonis* (1593), the only known copy; *Bay Psalm Book* (1640), the only copy outside the USA; Tycho Brahe's *Astronomiae instauratae mechanica* (1598), a presentation copy to the Doge of Venice with additional MS table by Brahe; Kenneth Grahame's MS of *Wind in the Willows* (1908); and T.E. Lawrence's MS of *The Seven Pillars of Wisdom* (1920-1922).

Exhibition Areas. A selection of the Library's treasures can be seen in the permanent exhibition housed in the Divinity School (access via the Schools Quadrangle). Temporary exhibitions are housed in the Special Exhibition Room in the Old Bodleian.

Hours. Term: Mon.-Fri. 0900-2200, Sat. 0900-1300 (-1900 New Bodleian and Radcliffe Camera). Vacation: Mon.-Fri. 0900-1900 (sometimes 1700), Sat. 0900-1300. Closed Sun., Good Fri., Easter Mon., first Wed. after end of Trinity (summer) term, week including late Summer Bank Holiday, 24 Dec.-1 Jan.

Transport. Oxford City buses to Cornmarket or the High St. Access to the Bodleian is via Broad Street, Catte Street or Radcliffe Square.

Parking. Disc parking in Broad Street and St. Giles. Car parks in St. Aldates and Westgate Shopping Centre.

Admission. Readers: The Library is open to all members of the University upon registration in Arts End (Old Library) from 0930-1300 and 1400-1630. Gowns must be worn. Non-members of the University must produce a letter of recommendation.
Visitors: Currently restricted to the Old Library Proscholium and Divinity School. Mon.-Fri. 0900-1700, Sat. 0900-1230.

Information. Porters' desks for general information. Otherwise any staff desk.

Sales. Proscholium (Old Library). Library publications, postcards, slides, Christmas cards etc.

Guidebooks. Visitors' Guide. Various leaflets on particular parts of the Library, available free of charge.

Restaurant/Snack Facilities. Catering facilities are planned for the Clarendon Building located between the New and the Old Bodleian.

Services. Lavatories, telephones, in all sections of the Bodleian. Typing and Blind Readers' Reading Room in New Bodleian.

Kenneth Grahame, holograph first version (in one of a series of letters) of The Wind in the Willows (dated 12 August 1907), in Bodleian Library, Oxford (MS. Eng. misc. d. 281, folio 19)

Catalogues.   Author book form catalogues, divided at 1920. Separate card catalogue of foreign dissertations. Catalogues housed in Lower Reading Room, Old Bodleian.

Classification.   Own.

Copying/Photography.   Photocopying and other photographic services available through reading room staff. Private photography is not permitted.

Friends of the Library.   Friends of the Bodleian, £1 p.a. upwards. Bodley's American Friends, $5 p.a. upwards.

OXFORD

Taylor Institution Library
University of Oxford, St. Giles, Oxford OX1 3NA
Tel. Oxford 57917

History.   The Taylor Institution was established in 1845 following the bequest of Sir Robert Taylor (1714-1788), the sculptor and architect, who left the residue of his estate for establishing a foundation for the teaching of modern European languages (except English) in Oxford. The Institution and its Library occupy the east wing of the building erected between 1841 and 1844 by the University to house the Institution and the Randolph Galleries (now the Ashmolean Museum). The original neo-classical building designed by Charles R. Cockerell was extended along St. Giles and completed in 1938. The Taylorian Library now contains over 250,000 volumes, comprising the chief literary and philological works in the principal European languages, a large number of periodicals, together with a substantial supporting collection of foreign, historical, philosophical and topographical works and linguistic atlases. It has claims to be the largest separate collection of its kind in Great Britain.

Special Collections and Treasures.   Collections include the Finch Collection of 3,500 literary and linguistic works; the Fiedler Collection of 2,500 German literary, philological and historical works; the Dante Collection of 800 volumes; the Martin Collection of 1,000 Spanish and Portuguese books, which include early editions of Cervantes, Calderon and Lope de Vega; the Nevill Forbes and Morfill Collections of Slavonic books totalling nearly 6,000 volumes; the W.P. Ker Collection of Icelandic and Scandinavian books totalling 500 volumes; the Dawkins Collection of Byzantine and modern Greek books, totalling 2,000 books, several MSS and a large number of pamphlets. Dr. Theodore Besterman, the founder and sometime Director of the Institut Voltaire, signified in 1974 that he would bequeath the publications of his Voltaire Foundation to the Taylor Institution, which would also become his residuary legatee. This should

Taylor Institution, Oxford.
(*Photograph copyright*
Country Life)

firmly establish the Taylorian as a world centre for the study of the Enlightenment.

Exhibition Areas. None.

Hours. 1 Oct.-30 June: Mon.-Fri. 0900-1900, Sat. 0900-1300. 1 July-30 Sept.: Mon.-Fri. 1000-1300, 1400-1700, Sat. 0900-1300. Closed: Sun., Good Fri.-Easter Mon. inclusive, the week beginning with the Late Summer Bank Holiday, the first Mon. and Tues. after the first Sun. after 1 Sept., and one week at Christmas.

Transport. Oxford city bus services to St. Giles.

Parking. Disc parking in St. Giles.

Admission. Readers: Graduate members of Oxford University and graduates of other universities working for higher degrees at Oxford require no application form. Readers must sign the Admissions Register in the Main Reading Room. Regulations for admission and borrowing contained in the Library guide.
Visitors: Must apply to the Librarian in advance

Information. Desk in Main Reading Room.

Sales. None.

Guidebooks. Available to readers on registration (and others on request), in English. No charge.

Restaurant/Snack Facilities. None.

Services. Men's and ladies' lavatories. There are no public telephones in the building but some are to be found at the south end of St. Giles behind the Martyrs' Memorial. A portable microfilm reader is available for loan to graduate students upwards.

Catalogues. General catalogue in book form arranged alphabetically. Supplementary card indexes of recent accessions, offprints, etc.

Classification. Own.

Copying/Photography. Quick copy service. Enquiries to Main Reading Room staff. Photographing and micro-filming service also available. Apply to Librarian for private photography.

Greece

ATHENS
National Library of Greece
Panepistemiou Street, Athens
Tel. 614-413, 606-495, 608-597

History.   The foundation of the Library dates from 1828, the year when John Capodistrias, the first Prime Minister, established the Library on the island of Aegina. Its initial stock totalled 1,844 volumes, largely donated by those who had taken part in the struggle for Greek Independence. The Library was transferred to Athens, the new capital, in September 1834, when it contained 8,000 volumes. Legal deposit privileges were received in the same year and numerous gifts were received in succeeding years. Holdings were initially stored in the old Byzantine Church of Saint Eleutheriou but when in 1842 the University Library (founded in 1838) and the National Library were placed under the same administration, the collections were transferred to the upper floor of the newly erected University building. In 1866 a royal decree combined the two libraries into one, with the title 'National Library of Greece'. The growth of the collections necessitated the construction of the present building, begun in 1888 and finally occupied in 1903. Legal deposit privileges were confirmed in 1943, with two copies being deposited at the National Library, one for its own collection and the other for the University of Athens, which is housed in the same building. Current holdings total about 2.5 million items.

Special Collections and Treasures.   Collections include those of Demetrios Postolakas, 1,995 volumes of rare works, MSS, etc. of Greek authors; the Constantine Sakellarios Collection of 5,400 volumes, acquired in 1833; the Constantine Bellios Collection of 1,886 volumes, acquired in 1837; the Constantine Sathas Collection; the private library of King George I of Greece; the Mavrocordatos-Baltatzis Library, acquired in 1930; and the archives of the London Philhellenic Committee, donated in 1931. Individual treasures include the *Grammar* of Lascaris (Milan, 1476), the first book to be printed in Greek type; Sibthorp's *Flora Graeca* in 10 volumes; and an 8th century BC papyrus, *The Book of the Dead.*

Exhibition Areas. Small exhibition room in the Department of MSS.

Hours.   Mon.-Fri. 0900-1300, 1700-2000, Sat. 0900-1300. Closed Sun., whole of Aug. and 13 hols during the year.

Transport.   The Library can be reached by bus or trolleybus.

Parking.   No parking facilities at the Library itself.

National Library of Greece

Admission.   Readers: No charge but readers must leave their bags at the entrance to the Library and present an identity card to the clerk in the Reading Room when requesting books.
Visitors: Should ask permission to enter the Library.

Information.   At the various service desks.

Sales.   None.

Guidebooks.   None.

Restaurant/Snack Facilities.   None on premises but available nearby.

Services.   Lavatories at the right of the entrance. Telephones.

Catalogues.   Alphabetical author, classified subject and alphabetical subject catalogues.

Classification.   Own.

Copying/Photography.   Copying facilities are available through Library staff.

ATHENS
Parliament Library,
Palaia Anactora, Athens
Tel. 3235030

History. The Library was established in 1846 but suffered fire damage in 1854. During the period of rebuilding, 1862-75, the surviving stock of books was transferred to the house of the historian Polyzoïdes. From 1875 to 1934 it occupied the Old Parliament Building, now the Ethnological Museum of Greece. In that latter year it moved to its present site in the Parliament Building, where it functions as a reference and lending library. It was set up by resolution of the Chamber of Deputies but is now a library open to the general public. In fact its collections are perhaps more readily accessible to the public than those of the National Library (see preceding entry). The Library, which has legal deposit privileges, consists of two sections, the Central Library and the Benake Library. Current holdings total over 1 million volumes, with 450 MSS.

Special Collections and Treasures. The Library has the most complete collection in Greece of Greek newspapers and periodicals. It has a valuable collection of incunabula, codices, 11th-15th century MSS and archives relating to Greek history. It is especially rich in documents relating to the Greek Revolution of 1821. The Renan-Psichari library holds the 35,000 volume collection of the well known Greek linguist and language reformer, Jean Psichari (1854-1929). Other collections include the

Parliament Library, Athens

libraries of political figures such as General Metaxas (1871-1941), George Kaphandaris (1873-1946) and George Sideris (1886-1940). Treasures include *Sermones Peregrini de tempore et de sanctis per anni circulum* (Strassburg, 1495); a fine illustrated edition of *La vita de philosophi* (Florence, 1505); J.M. Tricaelius, *Dictionum Graecarum et Latinarum thesaurus* (Ferrara, 1510); a Plato in Greek printed at Louvain in 1531; an edition of Euclid in Italian published at Urbino in 1575; Léon Trippault, *Dictionaire françois-grec* (Orléans, 1577); Pappus of Alexandria, *Mathematicae collectiones* (Pesaro, 1588), and Andreas Demetrius, *Der Griecken Opganek ende Onderganck* (Dordrecht, 1599).

Exhibition Areas.   No details available.

Hours.   Mon.-Sat. 0730-1330. Closed Sun. and public hols.

Transport.   Bus. (The Parliament House is situated on rising ground east of Sindagma Square.)

Parking.   No details available.

Admission.   Readers: Free of charge.
Visitors: Apply to the Librarian.

Information.   At Library staff desks.

Sales.   None.

Guidebooks.   History of the Library (1846-1970) available in Greek.

Restaurant/Snack Facilities.   None.

Services.   Lavatories and lifts.

Catalogues.   Dictionary card catalogue.

Classification.   Munich system.

Copying/Photography.   Copying facilities are available.

Gennadius Library, Athens

ATHENS
Gennadius Library, American School of Classical Studies
61 Souidias Street, Athens 140
Tel. 710-536 (Director's residence 710-190)

History.   The Library (known also as the Gennadeion) was formerly the private collection of Dr. Joannes Gennadius (1844-1932), a distinguished scholar and erstwhile Greek Minister to Great Britain. Gennadius assembled some 27,000 volumes devoted to Greece and Hellenic culture from ancient times to the present day. Wishing to establish the Library as a permanent memorial to his father, George Gennadius, who played a notable part in the national renaissance, and also to make it more readily available to scholars, he gave it in 1922 in trust to the American School of Classical Studies in Athens. The Carnegie Corporation donated funds to house the collection and the Greek Government provided the site adjacent to the American School. The marble building, designed by W. Stuart Thompson, was dedicated on 23 April 1926. Two wings were added to the original structure in 1972. Holdings of the Gennadeion, which is maintained and supported by the American School, currently total 58,000 volumes but many more titles, 500 MSS and various archives. The Gennadeion is primarily a research library but its founder's passion for fine bindings, rare editions and association copies have made it also a bibliophile's delight.

Special Collections and Treasures. The focus of the collection is Greece but it is not simply a classical or Byzantine library. Greece is here conceived as a unity, from antiquity to the present, and perhaps nowhere else can the history and culture of Greece in its entirety be so readily studied. Gennadius realised that Greece (however defined geographically at any given period) could not be properly studied without reference to its neighbours. Hence his collection expanded to include the Balkans, Anatolia, Egypt and the Near East in general: early printed materials on the Ottoman Empire are a good example. He also recognised the cumulative importance of ephemeral materials, e.g. his collection of pamphlets on the early kingdom of Greece (1832-1864) which provides superb documentation on the reign of King Otto. Areas of particular strength: early editions of the classical, patristic and Byzantine authors, including most of the *editiones principes;* the Greek Bible, beginning with the *Psalterion* (Milan 1481) and the *editiones principes* of the New Testament (Basel, 1526); liturgical books; grammars beginning with the first dated Greek book, the *Epitomē tōn oktō tou logou merōn* of Constantine Lascaris (Milan, 1476) and ten others of the 15th century; early travellers to Greece and the Near East; the Korais collection; the Byron collection, including personal 'relics' as well as books by and about him. The Library has 68 incunabula, of which 40 are Greek. Pictorial materials include 200 sketches of Greece by Edward Lear. Among the many individual treasures are: illuminated copies of Homer (Florence, 1488) and the *Anthologia Graeca* (Florence, 1496); one of the two copies of the works of Lucian (Florence, 1496) printed on vellum; George Canning's copy of the Stephanus edition of Plato (Geneva, 1578); Louis XV's set of Sir William Hamilton's *Collection of Etruscan, Greek and Roman Antiquities* (Naples, 1766-67); Sibthorp's *Flora Graeca*, 10 vols. (London, 1806-1840); and Ath. Christopoulos, *Ta Lurika kai Bakhika* (Athens, 1825), the only known copy of the first book printed in Athens. Archives of major importance include: Ali Pasha, Ion Dragoumis, Dimitri Mitropoulos (autograph musical scores), Konst. Mousouros (Musurus Pasha), Heinrich Schliemann, George Seferis,

ΤΑ ΛΥΡΙΚΑ ΚΑΙ ΒΑΚΧΙΚΑ

ΤΟΥ

ΑΘΑΝΑΣΙΟΥ ΧΡΙΣΤΟΠΟΥ-
ΛΟΥ.

"Ἂν δὲν ἐλευθερωθῇ τὸ Ἔθνος μας ἀπὸ ταῖς μωρολογίαις τῆς σοφολογιω-τάτικης γλώσσας, εἶναι τῶν ἀδυνάτων νὰ προκόψῃ." ΣΠ. ΤΡΙΚ:

Ἐκ τῆς Τυπογραφίας τῶν Ἀθηνῶν

ΕΝ ΕΤΕΙ ΑΩΚΕ.

1825

The first book printed in Athens, Ta Lurika kai Bakhika (1825), in the Gennadius Library, Athens. This is believed to be the only surviving copy of the book

and Emm. Tsouderos.

Exhibition Areas. Ten display cases in the Reading Room and the West Wing hold a selection of rare books, MSS, fine bindings and Byronia. The West Wing serves also as a picture gallery and houses the Macedonian Room donated by Mme. Hélène Stathatos.

Hours. Mon.-Fri. 0900-1330, 1700-2000, Sat. 0900-1315. Closed Sun., official hols and month of Aug.

Transport. By bus: no. 50. By car: from Constitution Square take Queen Sophia Boulevard, turn left on Plutarch Street, then right on Alopekis Street, two blocks to dead-end and turn left on Gennadius Street, which ends at Souidias Street and the entrance to the Library.

Parking. Parking facilities very limited.

Admission. Readers: The Library is open to the public. *Visitors:* Visitors are welcome but should identify themselves to the Director or the staff. Groups can be accommodated only during hours when the Library is closed, by prior arrangement with the Director.

Information. At Library entrance desk.

Sales. A few items only on sale, notably copies of Edward Lear's sketches.

Guidebooks. None.

Restaurant/Snack Facilities. None.

Services. Cloakrooms, lavatories.

Catalogues. Author and subject card catalogues, plus title cards for anonymous works. Greek cards are interfiled with others in a single alphabetical arrangement (Roman). *Catalogue of the Gennadius Library,* 7 vols (G.K. Hall, Boston, 1968), *First Supplement* (1973). A two-volume catalogue of the travel collection, *Voyages and Travels,* edited by S.H. Weber, appeared in 1952-3.

Classification. Gennadius's own, partly adapted to Library of Congress system.

Copying/Photography. Copying facilities are available. Apply to Library staff. Private photography by special permission only.

Friends of the Library. Friends of the Gennadius Library: regular members $10-$25 annually (£2.10-£10.50); contributing members $100 or more annually (£31.50); life members $500 (£157. 50); patrons $1,000 or more (£315). Subscriptions from donors within the sterling area may be sent to the Society for the Promotion of Hellenic Studies, 31-34 Gordon Square, London WC1.

Hungary

BUDAPEST

Országos Széchényi Könyvtár (National Széchényi Library)
H-1827 Budapest, Muzeum krt. 14-16
Tel. 134-400. Information Department 341-684

History. The National Library of Hungary, founded in 1802, owes its establishment to the activity of Count Ferenc Széchényi (1754-1820). Széchényi's own library of 15,000 books and manuscripts was the cornerstone of the Library, which publicly opened its doors on 20 August 1803. Legal deposit privileges began in 1804. In 1808 the National Museum of Hungary was founded and the Széchényi Library was incorporated in it. By 1848 the Library's holdings totalled over 100,000 volumes, housed in the present building, designed by Mihály Pollack and completed in 1846. By 1902 the Library's bookstock had risen to 350,000 volumes but lack of finance prevented more rapid growth after World War I. In 1949 the Library was legally separated from the Hungarian National Museum and officially declared the National Library. At present holdings include 2,045,891 books, 219,682 periodicals and 482,286 manuscripts. A new Library building is under reconstruction in the former King's Palace.

Special Collections and Treasures. Collections include the libraries of Miklós Jankovich, Sándor Kisfaludy, Lajos Kossuth, Imre Madách, Sándor Apponyi and the old Hungarian book collection of Gyula Todoreszku and his wife Aranka Horváth. The Széchényi Library houses the best collection of the various editions of the works of the great personalities of Hungarian literature and science. The Library possesses the richest collection of incunabula in Hungary. Treasures include the *Chronica Hungarorum,* the first book printed in Hungary (Buda, 1473); Sebald Heyden, *Puerilium colloquiorum formulae* (Cracow, 1531), the earliest book containing texts printed in Hungarian; the *New Testament,* translated by János Sylvester (the Sárvár-Ujsziget Press, 1541), the first book in the Hungarian language printed in Hungary. Among other special collections, in the Newspapers Collection, some 70 per cent of the Hungarian holdings are unique copies. In the Manuscript Collection, the oldest monuments of Hungarian language, 32 Corvina codices of King Matthias and many historical and literary documents are preserved. The Musical Collection possesses both Hungarian and foreign musical documents, e.g. rich collections of manuscripts by Franz Liszt and Joseph Haydn.

Exhibition Areas. There are no special exhibition rooms but there are display cases in various rooms for

National Széchényi Library, Budapest

The first Hungarian-language book printed in Hungary, János Sylvester's translation of the New Testament (1541), in the National Széchényi Library, Budapest

occasional exhibitions. As the Library and the Hungarian National Museum are in the same building, the Museum occasionally places its exhibition rooms at the Library's disposal.

Hours.   General Reading Room: Tues.-Sat. 0900-2100, Mon. 1200-2100. Closed Sun. Research Reading Room and Special Collections: usually daily 0900-1700.

Transport.   The Library is accessible by tram, bus and tube.

Parking.   Behind the Library's central building.

Admission.   *Readers:* Anyone over 18 years of age may use the Library. Readers must register at the Information Service desk. The annual registration charge is 3 forints (1 forint for students).
Visitors: Admission free.

Information.   Next to the Central Reading Room.

Sales.   Library publications (e.g. *Yearbook*) are sold in the Publications Section.

Guidebooks.   Guidebook to the Library in English, French, German, Russian and Hungarian.

Restaurant/Snack Facilities.   Snack bar in the central building, open 0800-1530.

Services.   Cloakroom, lavatory, telephone (in the snack bar), smoking permitted only in the vestibule, typing permitted.

Catalogues.   There are almost 125 different catalogues within the Library. The main catalogues are: alphabetical for books and periodicals and subject for books.

Classification.   Universal Decimal Classification.

Copying/Photography.   Photocopying and dry-copying service. Prepayment required. Readers and visitors must obtain permission before using their cameras.

BUDAPEST
Egyetemi Könyvtár (Central Library of the Loránd Eötvös University)
H-1053 Budapest, V Károlyi u.10
Tel. 185-865

History.   The University was founded in 1635 at Nagyszombat (today Trnava in Czechoslovakia), as a result of the efforts of the Hungarian statesman and ecclesiastic Cardinal Pázmány. The Library opened in 1636, its nucleus being derived from the Jesuit library of Nagyszombat, founded about 1560, and containing much valuable material saved from the Turks. The University and the Library moved to Buda Castle in 1777. In 1780-81 György Pray published the first catalogue of the Library, which moved to Pest in 1784. At the same time the Library was transformed into a state-owned institution and housed in the building of a disused Franciscan monastery (located on the present site of the Library). The present building, designed by Antal Skalnitzky and Henrik Koch, was constructed between 1873 and 1875. The 20th century has seen the gradual modernisation of nearly all the Library's procedures. Current holdings total 1,257,204 volumes and 40,000 MSS.

Special Collections and Treasures. The oldest manuscript in the Library is an 8th century Beda fragment. Other rarities include eleven codices of the Bibliotheca Corviniana; a Greek *Gospel* compiled in Constantinople in the 10th century; a manuscript of Dante's *Divine Comedy* (c.1340); six 14th century antiphonals and 1,222 incunabula. Rich sources of Hungarian historical research are the Pray, Kaprinay and Hevenesi Collections.

Exhibition Areas. The show-cases in the vestibule display recently acquired books as well as occasional, more permanent exhibitions.

Hours. Main Reading Room: Mon.-Sat. 0900-2000, Sun. (at examination times) 0900-1300. Closed the last two weeks of July and the first two weeks of Aug.

Transport. The Library is in the centre of the city and bus, subway and tram stops are within one minute's walk from the Library.

Parking. None.

Admission. Readers: Must be at least 16 years of age. Free admission to members of the University. Other readers must pay 3Ft. for an admission card for one year, if they wish to borrow.
Visitors: Apply to Library Director.

Information. In every Reading Room and in the Catalogue Room.

Sales. None.

Guidebooks. The Budapest University Library, in English.

Restaurant/Snack Facilities. None.

Services. Lavatories behind the Main Reading Room and in the vestibule. Smoking lounge opening into the vestibule.

Catalogues. Basic descriptive (alphabetical) catalogue covers entire Library holdings from 1501 onwards. This is

Loránd Eötvös University, Budapest

in the information service room and is on quarto leaves in cases. Another descriptive (alphabetical) catalogue is in the Lending Room. On cards, this covers all books acquired since 1925 or recatalogued since then. Old subject catalogue (part of) in the Lending Room. Two subject catalogues cover books acquired or recatalogued since 1949: one uses the Universal Decimal system, the other is purely alphabetical. Separate catalogues to cover special collections (e.g. periodicals, reference library, portraits in books, etc.).

Classification. Universal Decimal Classification.

Copying/Photography. There is a copying service but machines are not available for individual use.

BUDAPEST

Fővárosi Szabó Ervin Könyvtár (Ervin Szabó Municipal Library)
H-1371 Budapest, Szabó Ervin-tér 1, Postafiók 487
Tel. 330-580; Information Service, 141-005

History. The Library was founded in 1904, as a result of the amalgamation of several 18th and 19th century collections. The first Librarian was Ervin Szabó, after whom the Library was named in 1945. The first five branch libraries were established between 1910 and 1914. From August 1919 to World War II the development of the Library and its collections was slow, while the Library network suffered heavy damage during World War II. In 1945 the network consisted of 11 units, while today there are 116 units, including the Music Library (founded in 1964) and 18 independent children's libraries. The total number of books in the network currently exceeds 2.5 million volumes, with the Szabó Library containing 750,000 items.

Special Collections and Treasures. Collections include the Budapest Collection, rich in material on the history of Budapest; the Social Science Collection (it is the national special library for sociology); the Vámbéry Oriental Collection; the Ballagi pamphlets; the Hentaller Collection on the Hungarian War of Independence 1848-49; the Szüry and Zichy Collections; and the Hungarian Political Pamphlet Collection (1711-1911) of over 10,000 items. Treasures include 53 incunabula; the *Zichy Codex* (1489-1545), containing architectural drawings by Angelo da Cortino and poems by Gualtiero Sanvitale and Antonio Tebaldeo; and the 9 volume manuscript *Diaries* of Therese Brunswick, the friend of Beethoven.

Exhibition Areas. The vestibule.

Hours. Mon.-Wed. and Fri. 0900-2100, Sat. and Sun. 0900-1300. Closed Thurs. and public hols.

Ervin Szabó Municipal Library, Budapest

Transport. Bus: nos 1, 6, 9, 15, 81. Tram: nos 42, 47,

49, 52. The Metro may also be used to reach the Library.

Parking. Available.

Admission. Readers: Anyone over 16 may use the reading rooms. Registration is in the Lending Room on the first floor. Registration fee 3 Ft. for adults, 1 Ft. for students per annum.
Visitors: Are welcome but it is advisable to give prior notification.

Information. In the Reference Room.

Sales. In the Lending Room.

Guidebooks. Brochures in English, French, German and Russian available, free of charge.

Restaurant/Snack Facilities. None.

Services. Cloakroom, telephone and smoking lounge on the ground floor. Lavatories on the first floor.

Catalogues. Alphabetical, subject and geographical catalogues. Various special catalogues.

Classification. Dewey (slightly modified by Ervin Szabó).

Copying/Photography. Copying facilities available only through Library staff. Prior permission must be obtained for private photography.

BUDAPEST
Magyar Tudományos Akadémia Könyvtára (Library of the Hungarian Academy of Sciences)
H-1361 Budapest p.f.7, V Akadémia u.2
Tel. 126-779, 113-400

History. The Hungarian Academy of Sciences was founded on 3 November 1825 by István Széchényi, son of Count Ferenc Széchényi, founder of the Hungarian National Museum. The Library was founded in 1826 with the 30,000 volume family library of Count József Teleki, then Governor of Transylvania. Lack of space precluded the Library's opening for research until 1844, when it had a stock of 50,000 volumes. From its inception the Library aimed to be a large research library of a general character. It occupied the neo-Renaissance palace of the Academy erected 1862-5. The growth of the collections declined during and after World War I, but in 1929 Count Ferenc Vigyázó left his family wealth to the Academy. The Library and buildings suffered during World War II but benefited from the subsequent re-organisation of the Academy in 1949. The Academy changed from a private learned society into the supreme scientific body of Hungary. Its budget improved proportionately, e.g. the Library staff increased from 29 in 1949 to some 120 in

Hungarian Academy of Sciences, Budapest

1972. Current holdings total 1,377,852 items (Dec. 1973).

Special Collections and Treasures. Collections include the György Ráth Collection of 6,200 volumes printed in Hungary, or about Hungary abroad, up to 1711; the Vigyázó Collection of 17,000 volumes; the Kaufmann Collection of 3,000 volumes of Hebrew and other Oriental languages; the Elischer Goethe Collection; the MSS of István Széchényi, the founder; the complete archive of the pre-1949 Academy; the so-called *Antiqua Collection* of 2,100 books printed 1501-1550; and a good selection of the papers of Ignác Goldzieher and Sir Aurel Stein. Treasures include the *Beszterce Glossary;* the *Guary Codex;* the *Czech Codex;* the *Érsekújvári Codex;* the *Carbo-Corvinus Codex;* and the first book published entirely in Hungarian, *The Epistles of St. Paul* by Benedek Komjáthi (Cracow, 1553). The collection of 1,177 incunabula contains 9 unique items.

Exhibition Areas. The Library has no exhibition rooms.

Hours. Main Reading Room: Mon.-Fri. 0900-2000, Sat. 0900-1700. Manuscript Department: Mon., Wed. and Fri. 0900-1930, Tues. and Thurs. 0900-1700, Sat. 0900-1300. Closed Sun. and public hols.

Transport. By tram no. 2 or buses nos. 2, 4 and 16. By the old underground to Vörösmarty-tér station and by the new underground to Kossuth-tér station. (The Library building is on the Danube embankment near the Suspension Bridge.)

Parking. In front of the Library.

Admission. Readers: Library may be used by the members of the Academy, highly qualified scholars and scientists, research workers, university staff and senior students of universities. Registration is in the Catalogue Room and is free.
Visitors: All visitors should write for the permission of the Directorate.

Information. In the Catalogue Room.

Sales. None.

Guidebooks. Book, *The Library of the Hungarian Academy of Sciences 1826-1961,* and also a pamphlet in Hungarian, English and Russian. The latter is free of charge.

Restaurant/Snack Facilities. Snack-bar in the adjoining corridor of the entrance hall. Open 0800-1530.

Services. Cloakroom and lavatories. Smoking room near the Reading Room.

János Thuróczy, *Chronika hungarorum* (*Augsburg, 1488*), in the Library of the Hungarian Academy of Sciences. Detail

Catalogues.   Alphabetical author catalogue; Universal Decimal Classification. subject catalogue; geographical catalogue based on Universal Decimal Classification; periodical catalogues; alphabetical serials catalogue; union catalogue of the holdings of research libraries of the Academy's research institutes. Special collections have their own catalogues.

Classification.   Universal Decimal Classification.

Copying/Photography.   Dry-copying   and   microfilm machines are available, operated by the staff of the Reprographic Department. Readers may use their own cameras with the permission of the Directorate and heads of departments.

ESZTERGOM

Főszékesegyházi Könyvtár (Library of the Cathedral)
H-2500 Esztergom, Bajcsy Zsilinsky u.28
Tel. Esztergom 527

History.   The Library was founded in the 11th century, the same time as the Archbishopric of Esztergom. It received its first major gift of books in 1397 from its Canon, John de Kükülloi, and in the 15th century received the Latin and Greek books of John Vitéz de Zrednai. During the Turkish occupation of Hungary the Arch-bishopric and Chapter retreated to Nagyszombat (now Trnava in Czechoslovakia). In 1611 the Synod of Nagyszombat decreed that all collections belonging to the Archbishops and Canons of Esztergom were to pass to the Library on their deaths. On 21 May 1820 Sándor Rudnay became Archbishop of Esztergom and his energy facilitated the return of the Primateship from Nagys-zombat to Esztergom. The collections were housed in a new building in 1853, in which the Library has remained to the present day. Present holdings total just over 200,000 volumes, with 290 incunabula and 3,030 pre-1600 books.

Special Collections and Treasures.   Collections include the Joseph Batthyány and Joseph Kopácsy manuscript collections. Treasures include the Jordanszky, Nagys-zombat and Corvin codices, and the *Biblia Pauperum*, block-book dated c. 1450.

Exhibition   Areas.   The   Library   contains   two   small exhibition rooms, whose contents are changed yearly.

Hours.   Daily 1000-1400 except on Mon.

Transport.   By bus and train from Budapest (46 km.). Taxis in the city.

Parking.   Parking available nearby.

Cathedral Library, Esztergom

Admission. Readers: Readers must provide means of identification for permission to use the Library.
Visitors: May see the exhibitions. Adults, 2 forints; students, 1 forint. Readers, free.

Information. The Director will provide any information necessary.

Sales. None.

Guidebooks. There is no guide to the Library but some copies of exhibition catalogues are still available.

Restaurant/Snack Facilities. There is no restaurant on the premises but there are eating places nearby.

Services. Typewriter in the students' room, lavatories and washroom with a smoking area, pay telephone.

Catalogues. Inventory catalogue and also an alphabetical card catalogue of the complete holdings. Catalogues exist for the separate collections, e.g. incunabula, Old Hungarian books, MSS etc.

Classification. Own.

Copying/Photography. Apply through Library staff. The use of cameras is allowed with the Director's permission.

PANNONHALMA
Szent Benedekrend Közp Fökönyvtára
(Library of the Benedictine Abbey)
H-9090 Pannonhalma
Tel. Pannonhalma 5/Vár/
History. The monastery at Pannonhalma was founded by Prince Géza in 969, although its real growth came after 1001 when it had the support of King Stefan I. The Library is the oldest extant library in Hungary and has been called the greatest Benedictine library in the world. It was at Pannonhalma, between 1019 and 1060, that Hungarian history was first set down in literary form. By 1083 the Library possessed 80 codices. A catalogue of 1090 reveals a significant stock of ritual books, Bibles, the writings of the church fathers, etc. During the Tartar invasions and Turkish occupation, Pannonhalma was looted and many of its books destroyed or dispersed. The present library building was built between 1824 and 1832 to a design of the Viennese architects Josef Engel and Johann Packh. Beneath the vaulted chamber of the Library lie the vaults, where the archives of the Benedicine Order and a valuable numismatic collection are stored. Current holdings total 320,000 books and 1,300 modern MSS, with Benedictine material comprising 80 per cent of the total.

Special Collections and Treasures. Pannonhalma houses the finest mediaeval archives of Hungary. It has been

Pannonhalma Library

estimated that almost half of the existing documents of the 11th and 12th centuries are kept here. Treasures include the foundation charter of the Benedictine Order in Tihany (1055), the oldest Hungarian document in existence and the first written document in the history of Finno-Ugrian languages; the *Liber Ruber,* the first Hungarian collection of documents, listing the 60 papal and royal deeds and letters which Pannonhalma possessed at the beginning of the 13th century; a 13th century Latin *Codex;* a 14th century German *Evangelien buch;* the *Pfannberger Missal,* 15th century, from the Salzburg diocese; the *Pannonhalmi-Kodex* and the *Peraldus-Kodex,* 15th century. Among the 230 incunabula are Tacitus, *Germania* (1469); Schedel, *Chronica mundi* (1482); and The Library also possesses a large natural sciences collection, illustrating the geology of the Pannonhalma district and the birds and trees of the area.

Exhibition Areas.   Small temporary exhibitions in the main hall.

Hours.   Mon.-Sat. 0830-1630, Sun. 1030-1630. Closed to Readers, 20 Dec.-7 Jan. and in July and Aug., but visitors are admitted all year round.

Transport.   Pannonhalma is near the Austro-Hungarian border, not far from Györ. By train take the Györ-Veszprém Line or by bus from Györ (route 82). (The Abbey (and the Library) are situated on the top of St. Martin's Hill.)

Parking.   Parking facilities in the village.

Admission.   Readers: On application to the Librarian. Members of the Abbey and its school free of charge. *Visitors:* Guided tours are available in English, French and German for a small charge.

Information.   The Tourist Office in the Abbey buildings.

Sales.   In the Abbey buildings where souvenirs and cards are on sale and refreshments are available.

Guidebooks.   There is a chapter on the Library in the guidebook on Pannonhalma (in Hungarian, German, French and English).

Restaurant/Snack Facilities.   There are two restaurants and a coffee bar in the village, one kilometre away.

Services.   No details available.

Catalogues.   Author, place and subject catalogues.

Classification.   Own.

Copying/Photography.   Apply to the Library staff for copying facilities. Photography of the buildings and their interiors is permitted.

SÁROSPATAK

*Tiszáninneni Református Egyházkerület Nagykönyvtára
(Library of the Cistibiscan Reformed Church District)
Sárospatak, Rákóczy ut 1
Tel. Sárospatak 29*

History. The College of the Reformed Church in Sárospatak was founded in 1531 by Péter Perényi, as the first Protestant college in Hungary having the aim of educating laymen, as well as theological students. Both the College and the Library came under the patronage of the Rákóczy family, whose collection. was given to the Library in 1652. In 1671 the College went into exile, first to Debrecen, and then to Transylvania in order to retain its independence during the religious wars. It returned to Sárospatak in 1703, although most of the Library's collections had been lost. During the 18th century the College maintained many links with Protestant institutes in England and Scotland. By 1800 the collections totalled 30,000 volumes. Today they total 240,487 items, including 11,137 MSS. In 1952 the Library and the College separated, with the Library joined the archive, museum and data (mainly regional history) collection to become the scientific collections of the Cistibiscan district.

Special Collections and Treasures. The greatest treasures of the Library were lost during World War II but even so the Library is still rich in pre-1711 Hungarian books (some 1,250 pieces). A separate collection is the Bretzenheim-Windischgrätz library of 12,000 volumes, bought in 1946. The archives contain important local historical material, as well as nearly 100,000 items on Hungarian Calvinist congregations in Hungary and abroad. A major treasure is Martin Luther's *Bible* bearing his signature.

Exhibition Areas. The Main Hall and the Gutenberg Room.

Hours. Mon.-Sat. 0800-1700, Sun. 1100-1300. Main Hall only.

Transport. Sárospatak is on the main Budapest-Miskolc-Sátoraljaújhely line.

Parking. Available.

Admission. Readers: A small yearly reader's fee is payable.
Visitors: Main Hall and Museum — a small charge, students and soldiers free.

Information. No details available.

Library of the Cistibiscan Reformed Church District, Sárospatak

Sales. No details available.

Guidebooks. No details available.

Restaurant/Snack Facilities. No details available.

Services. No details available.

Catalogues. Author and title catalogue. Since 1935, subject catalogue.

Classification. Dewey.

Copying/Photography. Apply to the Library staff. Private photography with the Director's permission.

Iceland

REYKJAVÍK

Landsbókasafn Íslands (National Library of Iceland)
Reykjavík
Tel. 13375 (Director); 16864 (Staff)

History. The National Library of Iceland was founded on 28 August 1818, with the title Stiftisbókasafn Íslands. It was not until 1825, however, that facilities were obtained in the loft of Reykjavík Cathedral, where it was housed until 1879. Jón Árnason, the well-known collector and editor of Icelandic folklore, became the Library's first remunerated librarian in 1848, a post he held to 1887. In 1881 the Library moved into the newly erected Parliament Building, where it remained until it obtained its own quarters in the Safnahús (Museums Building), erected 1906-8. In 1918, on the Library's centenary, its holdings totalled 100,000 volumes and 7,000 MSS, as against 313,245 books and 12,706 manuscripts at the end of 1973. As a result of a vote of 30 April 1970 by the *Althing,* a new National Library building is to be erected, housing the collections of the National Library and the University Library (see next entry).

Special Collections and Treasures. The Library has assembled a most comprehensive collection of books and manuscripts on Iceland. In 1846 the Library acquired Bishop Steingrímur Jónsson's manuscript collection, in 1877 Jón Sigurðsson's collection and in 1901 the collections of the Icelandic Literary Society.

Exhibition Areas. Exhibitions are held regularly in the entrance hall of the Library.

Hours. Mon.-Sat. 0900-1900. (Sat. at 1200 in June, July and Aug.) Closed Sun. and national hols.

Transport. By bus to the old centre of Reykjavík, where the Library is located.

National Library of Iceland, Reykjavík

Hallgrímur Pétursson, Passius-álmar ('Passion hymns'), holo-graph (1659), in National Library of Iceland

Parking.   Large parking lots in the neighbourhood.

Admission.   *Readers* and *Visitors:* Admission is free to everyone over 16 years old.

Information.   In the cloakroom in the entrance hall.

Sales.   The caretaker sells the publications of the Library, catalogues of manuscripts and its yearbook.

Guidebooks.   Only a guide to the catalogues is currently available. It is free, in Icelandic.

Restaurant/Snack Facilities.   None.

Services.   Typing in the Reading Room of the Manuscript Department. Cloakroom, telephone, lavatories and smoking area in the entrance hall.

Catalogues.   Author and classified subject card catalogues. Printed catalogue for manuscripts.

Classification.   Dewey.

Copying/Photography.   Library has its own photographic department. Machines are only available for individual use in exceptional cases. Cameras are allowed in the Library.

REYKJAVÍK
Háskólabókasafn (University Library)
Reykjavík
Tel. 25088

History.   The University of Iceland was founded in 1911 but the main University Library (Háskólabókasafn) was not formally opened in its present building until 1 November 1940. The origins of the Library can, however, be traced back to 1847, when the Reykjavík Theological School was founded. Its library, plus those of the Medical and Law Schools, founded in 1876 and 1908 respectively, provided a basis for the book collection of the University. When the Library opened in 1940 it had some 30,000 books. As a result of purchase, gifts, copyright deposit and exchange this total has now risen to 170,000 books and 1,200 periodicals. This has placed a severe strain on existing Library accommodation. The decision has, therefore, been taken to amalgamate the National Library (see preceding entry) and the University Library in a new building near the University campus.

Special Collections and Treasures.   The most outstanding collection is the 8,000 volume Benedikt S. Thórarinsson Collection, housed in its own room and containing most of the treasures of Icelandic literature. Other collections include the Finnur Jónsson Collection of 7,500 volumes; books from the libraries of the poet

Einar Benediktsson (d. 1940), Sigfús Blöndal, librarian at the Royal Library in Copenhagen (d.1950), and Axel Nelson, librarian at the University Library in Uppsala (d.1962). In 1970 Stefán Einarsson, former professor at Johns Hopkins University (d.1972), presented the whole of his collection of 4,500 volumes.

Exhibition Areas. No details available.

Hours. Oct.-May: Mon.-Fri. 0900-1900, Sat. 0900-1200. Closed Sun. June-Sept.: Mon.-Fri. 0900-1700. Closed Sat., Sun. and public hols.

Transport. By bus to the University. (The Library is located in the back wing of the main University building.)

Parking. Good parking facilities available on campus.

Admission. Readers: University staff and students and those wishing to pursue serious research are admitted. *Visitors:* Apply to Librarian.

Information. At the main desk.

Sales. None.

Guidebooks. A Guide in Icelandic is available.

Restaurant/Snack Facilities. Available. Open 0900-2000 (University building).

Services. The Library uses the services of the main University building.

Catalogues. Author and classified card catalogues.

Classification. Dewey.

Copying/Photography. Photocopying machine near main desk.

India

ALIGARH
Maulana Azad Library
Aligarh Muslim University,
Aligarh, Uttar Pradesh
Tel. (not available)

History. The Aligarh Muslim University was established in 1920, as a result of the Aligarh Muslim University Act of 1920. Its origins lie in the Muhammedan Anglo-Oriental College, founded in 1877 by Syed Ahmad Khan and his associates, to serve as the springboard of a reformist movement that later came to be known as the 'Aligarh Movement'. The University places a special emphasis on the teaching of Islamic studies. The University Library was originally known as the Lytton Library and housed in a part of the Main Office building. In 1945 the collections totalled 58,098 volumes but since that date growth has been rapid, partly as a result of grants received under the US India Wheat Loan Programme. The Library moved into its present building in March 1960, changing its name at the same time to the Maulana Azad Library. Current holdings include 455,000 volumes.

Special Collections and Treasures. Collections include the private library of Abu Mohammed; the 1,000 volume collection of Ashfaque Hussain; the Muslim Educational Conference of 6,935 volumes, known as the Aftab Collection; the library of Professor Zafral Hasan; the Arabic and Persian MSS collection of Mohammed Saheb Ansari, comprising 1,514 items; 277 Firmans from the Sultanate of Delhi; the 6,000 MSS and printed volume collection belonging to the late Alhaj Maulana Habibur Rahman Khan Sahets Sherwani, Nawab Sadar Yar Jung; 2,000 MSS and 150 Firmans and similar documents from the Jawaharlal Museum established by K.B. Moulvi Bashiruddin Saheb of Etawah.

Exhibition Areas. Regular exhibitions, e.g. on Gandhian literature and the poet Rabindra Nath Tagore, are held. Details of location not available.

Hours. No details available.

Transport. No details available.

Parking. Available.

Admission. Readers: Open to members of the University and serious researchers.
Visitors: Apply to the Librarian.

Information. Reference Section.

Sales. None.

Guidebooks. None.

Restaurant/Snack Facilities. No details available.

Services. Basement used for audio-visual services. Lavatories. Lists compiled for individual scholars on Oriental and Islamic Studies.

Catalogues. Dictionary card catalogue. Various special catalogues detailing the contents of the Manuscripts Section.

Classification. Dewey (modified).

Copying/Photography. Photoduplication service at end

of Research Hall. Apply to Librarian for permission for private photography.

CALCUTTA

National Library of India
Belvedere, Calcutta 27
Tel. 45-5381

History. The National Library has its origins in the establishment in 1836 of a public library in Calcutta, which the municipality of Calcutta agreed to maintain in 1890. In 1903 Lord Curzon effected the amalgamation of the Calcutta Public Library and the Official Imperial Library to form the new Imperial Library, with its first location in the Metcalfe Hall. Since the amount of money for book purchase was quite inadequate, the Library was largely built up by gifts from various sources. In April 1947 the Library contained some 350,000 volumes, of which 60 per cent had been gifts. On 1 February 1953 the Library (re-named the National Library in 1948) moved to a beautiful and spacious site at Belvedere (once a winter residence of the Viceroys of India). In 1954 the Library received copyright deposit privileges. Holdings grew so quickly that a multi-storied annexe was constructed in the 1960s. Holdings of the Library currently include 1,467,914 volumes and 3,000 manuscripts.

Special Collections and Treasures. Collections include the Asutosh Mukhopadhyay Collection, covering most subjects in the humanities and sciences; the Ramdas Sen Collection, with its wealth of fugitive Bengali publications; the Barid Baran Mukherjee Collection on Indian history and culture and Bengali emphemera; the Sir Jadunath Sarkar Collection, famous for its source material on medieval Indian history and books on Portuguese and French India; the S.N. Sen Collection of Indiana; the Vaiyapuri Pillai Collection, with its wealth of palmleaf manuscripts and classics particularly in Tamil and Sanskrit; the Buhar Collection of Arabic and Persian MSS and printed books; and the Tej Bahdur Sapau Correspondence, reflecting the struggle for Indian Independence.

Exhibition Areas. Exhibitions are located in two halls in the main building and in the auditorium of the annexe.

Hours. Mon.-Sat. 0900-2000. Sun. and hols. 1000-1700. The Library is closed on 26 Jan. (Republic Day), 15 Aug. (Independence Day) and 2 Oct. (Mahatma Gandhi's birthday).

Transport. The Library is at Alipore, about three miles south of the Raj Bhawan. It is on several city bus and tram routes. Taxis and minibuses are also available.

Parking. Facilities available.

National Library of India

Admission.   Readers: Admission is free to those over 18 years of age. Tickets are issued on submission of a completed application form and a written reference. A temporary ticket, valid for one day, may be issued to anyone wishing to use the Reading Room for reference purposes only.
Visitors: Anyone who wishes to visit the Library may do so.

Information.   There is a reception/inquiry desk near the Library entrance.

Sales. Library publications, mainly the printed catalogues, are sold.

Guidebooks.   India's National Library by B.S. Kesavan, published in 1961 (Price Rs.10.00).

Restaurant/Snack Facilities.   Canteen on the ground floor of the annexe building, serves tea and snacks. Open 1000-1900.

Services.   Lavatories, lift in annexe building and in main building. Garden. Readers' lounge in main building (at the head of the staircase leading to the Reading Room). Two public telephone booths. There is also a readers' hostel (consisting of single rooms with baths — cost Rs. 2.00 per day).

Catalogues.   Various card and printed catalogues in European and Indian languages.

Classification.   Dewey (since 1958). Prior to 1958 the Library had its own scheme.

Copying/Photography.   The Library has a photocopier but this is not available for individual use. Only authorised personnel may use cameras inside the Library.

CALCUTTA
The Central Library, Calcutta University
Calcutta 700012
Tel. 34-3014-19; 34-7701-04

The Central Library, Calcutta University

History.   The Library of Calcutta University is the oldest of the existing Indian University libraries. The University was founded on 12 December 1856, but since it was only an examining body and not a teaching or research institution, no real library services were inaugurated until 1873. The Library was originally housed in the University Senate House but in 1912 it moved to its own building, constructed in large part as a result of the munificence of the Maharaja of Darbhanga. In April 1935 the University Library and the Postgraduate Lending Library, now known as the University Central Library, moved to the Asutosh building. In this year the collections totalled 100,000 volumes and by 1961 329,000 volumes, a rise partly accounted for by books received under the India-USA Wheat Loan Programme. This growth of the collections necessitated the Library's occupation of its present building in 1966. Current holdings include 460,000 volumes.

Special Collections and Treasures.   Collections include the Pischel Collection of Sanskrit, Pali, philological and ancient Indian historical works; the T.O. Dunn Collection of English Literature; the S.C. Ray Economic Collection; the Das Gupta Collection; the Bagchi Collection of 3,000 volumes on physics, mathematics and French and German literature; the Fine Arts Collection; the collection of books and periodicals on the history and archaeology of Indo-China and Indonesia presented by the Greater India Society of Calcutta; the Rai Sahib Nagendra Nath Basu Collection of Bengali MSS; the Sri Sanat Kumar Chatterjee Collection of 3,000 MSS, including a copy of the *Ramayana of Krithivas,* dated 1580; a collection of Vaishnabha Padavali songs, some of which are unique; the P.C. Ghosh Collection of 5,000 volumes; and the Uma Ghosh Collection of books written by Bengali women writers.

Exhibition Areas.   No details available.

Hours.   Mon.-Fri. 0700-2000, Sat. 0700-1900, Sun. 1100-1700.

Transport.   Public transport available. (The Library is close to Presidency College and the Sanskrit College on College Street. It lies within two kilometres of the seat of the State Government, as well as the business area.)

Parking.   Available.

Admission.   *Readers:* The Library is open to resident registered graduates, University Teachers and bona-fide research workers.
Visitors: Apply to the Library staff.

Information.   At Library staff desks.

Sales.   None.

Guidebooks.   None.

Restaurant/Snack Facilities.   None.

Services.   Lavatories.

Catalogues.   Author and classified card catalogues. Various special catalogues.

Classification.   Dewey (mainly).

Copying/Photography.   Photocopying facilities available.

DELHI
Delhi Public Library
S.P. Mukerji Marg. Delhi 110006
Tel. 26 40 01 (Director) and 26 38 10 (General)

History. The Library was established in 1951 by the government of India and UNESCO, as a part of the UNESCO programme to start model public libraries in developing countries. It was housed in Dalmia Jain House, originally designed as a rest-house for British troops. The Library is controlled by the Ministry of Education through an autonomous Library Board, which is the policy making body. It has been termed the busiest lending library in Asia. The Library system consists of the Central Library, four full-fledged branches and 15 sub-branches. It has also five mobile library vans which provide library service to 57 distant areas. It has 19 Deposit Stations, three of these in local city hospitals and one in the central gaol of the city. The Library also provides special services, notable among which are group activities through the Social Education Department, a Gramophone Records Lending Library and a Braille Library for the Blind. Lending books for home reading is the major activity of the Library. The Library at present serves about a third of the population of Delhi, whose population stands at just over 5 million people. The plans for expansion have been somewhat hampered by the financial difficulties facing the Indian Government. The Library has acquired two plots of land (one in South Delhi and the other in West Delhi) for construction of buildings to house the projected Regional Branches of the Library. Designing of the South Delhi building is in progress and construction will be taken up as soon as funds are made available. Current holdings total 537,885 volumes and about 20 MSS.

Special Collections and Treasures. No specific rare collections or items. Almost all subjects are represented in the Library, although the concentration is on the social sciences and the humanities.

Exhibition Areas. There is no separate exhibition room. The auditorium (which has a flat floor), the foyer and the corridors can be used for exhibitions.

Hours. Summer: daily 0830-2000. Winter: 0900-2000.

Transport. The Library is located outside Delhi Main Railway Station and is accessible by public transport.

Parking. On the road in front of the Library.

Admission. Readers and *Visitors:* Admission is free to all but intending borrowers have to register at the Library.

Information. Registration/Enquiry counter, near main gate of the Library.

Delhi Public Library

Sales. None.

Guidebooks. None at present but one in preparation. In the meantime a descriptive note on the Library is distributed free.

Restaurant/Snack Facilities. The cafeteria on the mezzanine, overlooking the auditorium, is open 0900-2000.

Services. Lavatories in a small annexe. Plays, concerts, competitions, story hours organized in Children's Department.

Catalogues. Classified card catalogue.

Classification. Dewey.

Copying/Photography. It is hoped to provide photocopying facilities in the near future. Permission must be sought for taking photographs of the interior of the Library.

Indonesia

DJAKARTA
Perpustakaan Museum Pusat
Departemen Pendidikan dan Kebudayaan, Merdeka Barat 12, Djakarta
Tel. 40551

History. The Library of the Central Museum was established in 1778 as part of the Bataviaasch Genootschap van Kunsten en Wetenschappen (Royal Batavian Society of Culture and Sciences). The Library specialises in publications in the humanities and social sciences, particularly those related to Indonesia. Its collection of Indonesian publications, published from the beginning of the 19th century to the Japanese occupation, is the most comprehensive in Indonesia. In 1913 the Dutch Government decreed that all publishers had to send two copies of all items published to the Library. The Library did not suffer under Japanese occupation in World War II; indeed it now possesses a valuable collection of official occupation documents. After the proclamation of Indonesian Independence the name of the Bataviaasch Genootschap was retained until 1950, and then in 1962 the Museum, together with its Library, was handed over to the jurisdiction of the Indonesian Ministry of Education and Culture. Today holdings total 100,000 book titles, 12,000 periodicals (titles) and 1,341 newspapers (titles) a collection which is designated as the nucleus of the National Library of Indonesia.

Special Collections and Treasures. The major treasures are the extensive collections of Indonesian publications

Perpustakaan Museum Pusat, Djakarta

published prior to 1945; the 18th century drawings of Johannes Rach; and Indonesian newspapers dating from 1810.

Exhibition Areas. As the Library is still housed in the Museum building, the Exhibition Room is used for the collections of both the Library and the Museum.

Hours. Tues.-Thurs. 0830-1430, Fri. 0830-1100, Sat. and Sun. 0830-1430. Closed Mon. and national hols.

Transport. By bus or 'bemo' (a three-wheeler cab) to the Museum.

Parking. There is parking space for 20 cars in front of the Museum.

Admission. Readers: Students' fee is Rp 350 annually. All must register at the Registration Desk, by filling in a form and submitting two passport-type photographs. *Visitors:* Apply to Library Director.

Information. At the Registration Desk.

Sales. In the entrance hall of the Museum.

Guidebooks. The Library guidebooks are in Indonesian — price Rp 150. A brief mimeographed English guide is available free of charge.

Restaurant/Snack Facilities. None.

Services. Telephone in the Assistant's room. Smoking lounge in the Catalogue Room. Lavatories in the Museum building.

Catalogues. Dictionary, subject and classified catalogues.

Classification. Dewey.

Copying/Photography. There is a copying service but machines are not available for individual use. Permission from the Library Director must be obtained in order to use cameras within the Library. The charge for each page photographed is Rp 25 and one copy of the photograph must be given to the Library. The use of flash bulbs is not permitted.

Friends of the Library. Honorary (free) membership is granted to newspaper agencies and publishers who regularly present their publications to the Library and to those who donate library equipment.

Iran

SHIRAZ
Mulla Sadra Library
College of Arts and Sciences, Pahlavi University, Shiraz
Tel. 22369, 22747, ext. 16, 18, 19, 20

History.   The Library opened in September 1964, taking over the small collection (less than 10,000 volumes) of the former Shiraz University. Through the combined efforts of Pahlavi University, the Iranian oil companies and Pennsylvania University, a project for the development and improvement of library services was begun in the summer of 1965. This enabled, in particular, the fast development of the Library of the College of Arts and Sciences. At present there is no central library of Pahlavi University. Instead there are four faculty libraries, with the largest being that of Arts and Sciences, opened in 1968, with a collection of 80,000 volumes. The growth of the collections has necessitated the current construction of a new library building. Current holdings of the Arts and Sciences Library total some 150,000 books (including 30,000 Persian titles).

Special Collections and Treasures. The Persian Manuscript Collection contains about 200 books and MSS.

Exhibition Areas.   None at present.

Hours.   Sat.-Wed. 0700-2200, Thurs. 0700-1700, Fri. 0800-1200.

Transport.   The University and Library are in the city and are served by several buses that run on the hour, every hour. Taxis are cheap and readily available. Shiraz can be reached by plane or bus from Isfahan, Tehran, Abadan and the Persian Gulf.

Parking.   The University parking lot close to the Library.

Admission.   *Readers:* The Library may only be used by University staff and students.
Visitors: May use the Library if they are working for the University or if the Tourist Office recommends them. There is no charge.

Information.   Circulation Desk, in front of the entrance door.

Sales.   The University bookstore.

Guidebooks.   A Library guidebook in Farsi is distributed to students, free.

Restaurant/Snack Facilities. None on the Library premises but there is a University snackbar close by.

Services. Telephones and smoking lounge. Other facilities will be available in the new building.

Catalogues. Dictionary card catalogue. Catalogues for Latin books and one for Farsi books.

Classification. Dewey, with Library of Congress subject headings.

Copying/Photography. Copying machines close to the entrance door. Readers and visitors may use their own cameras in the Library.

Iraq

BAGHDAD
Central Library of the University of Baghdad
Safi El-Din Al-Hilli Street, PO Box 12, Baghdad
Tel. 64742

History. The Central Library of the University of Baghdad was established in 1960 to serve the needs of the University of Baghdad and is centrally located in the middle of several colleges and higher educational institutions in the Al-Waziriya suburb of Baghdad. It occupies a modern library building erected in 1965 which currently contains over 250,000 volumes and nearly 2,480 periodicals. The Library has been a depository library for Iraqi publications since 1963 and acts as the National Library, International Exchange Centre and a training centre for Iraqi librarians.

Special Collections and Treasures. Among the special collections are theses of Iraqi graduates; United Nations publications; Iraqi Government publications, bibliographies, micro-films, records. In addition, the Library maintains a sizable collection of periodicals, atlases and maps, considered among the best in Iraq.

Exhibition Areas. On the second floor.

Hours. During academic year (Sept.-June): Sat.-Wed. 0800-2000, Thurs. 0800-1800. During summer vacation (July-Aug.): Sat.-Wed. 0800-1800, Thurs. 0800-1600. During the final examination period: Sat.-Wed. 0800-2100, Thurs. 0800-1900. Closed on Fridays and public hols.

Central Library of the University of Baghdad

Transport. Bus station close to the Library. Routes 61, 71, 76, 83, 97 from Bab-Al-Muddham (the central station).

Parking. The Library has no car park but facilities are available nearby.

Admission. Readers: Members of the University may use the Library free of charge. Registration takes place in the Circulation Department.
Visitors: Visitors are admitted to the Library.

Information. The Information Department is just inside the Library entrance.

Sales. None.

Guidebooks. A guide to the Library is available in Arabic, with an English summary.

Restaurant/Snack Facilities. A snack bar is under construction.

Services. Lavatories, public telephones, seminar room, carrels, bindery.

Catalogues. Dictionary card catalogue.

Classification. Dewey.

Copying/Photography. Copying facilities are available on the second floor, including a new microfilm reader printer, micro-film machine, film processor and duplicator. Prior permission must be obtained from the Chief Librarian for private photography.

Ireland, Republic of

DUBLIN
National Library of Ireland
Kildare Street, Dublin 2
Tel. 765521

History. The National Library of Ireland was set up by Act of Parliament in 1877 and was, at first, housed in Leinster House, Kildare Street, Dublin. As the nucleus of its collections it purchased a large selection of books from the Royal Dublin Society Library and received by gift the large Joly Collection of 23,000 printed books, as well as an extensive collection of music and engravings. New accommodation was soon deemed necessary and in 1890 the Library moved to its present premises. The completed block forms an impressive group of buildings with Leinster House and the two modern wings extending to Kildare Street: the left wing comprises the National Library and the College of Art, while the opposite wing is the National Museum. The Library is rich in works relating to Ireland, and every effort is made

National Library of Ireland, Dublin

to make its collections as complete as possible. All books published in Ireland have been acquired under legal deposit arrangements since 1927. Current holdings total just over 500,000 printed books, about 10,000 bound volumes of MSS and 6,000 reels of microfilm, covering Irish MS material throughout the world. The Genealogical Office at present housed in Dulin Castle, Dublin 2, is under the administration of the National Library. That office undertakes research on a fee basis (Tel. 751284).

Special Collections and Treasures.   Special collections, apart from the Joly Collection, include the Thom Collection of 3,900 volumes, mainly Irish in interest; the Dix Collection of books printed in Ireland; the Holloway Collection relating to the theatre in Ireland; the Ormond Archives, 12th to 19th centuries; the Fitzgerald-Lennox Correspondence and the Lismore Castle papers deposited in 1952-3. The Department of Manuscripts contains a collection of over 1,000 Gaelic MSS, the earliest of these, *The Book of Magauran,* a 14th century Gaelic MS, is the oldest known book of bardic poetry.

Exhibition Areas.   Exhibitions are arranged in the main hall on entering the Library.

Hours.   Mon.-Fri. 1000-2200, Sat. 1000-1300. Closed Sun. and three weeks in Aug. and normal public hols.

Transport.   The Library is located in a central city area and readily accessible by public transport.

Parking.   Parking meters in the street.

Admission. Readers: Readers' tickets issued on personal application at Reading Room.
Visitors: Admittance on signing register.

Information.   In Reading Room.

Sales.   None.

Guidebooks.   None.

Restaurant/Snack Facilities.   None.

Services.   Cloakrooms, lavatories, typing accommodation.

Catalogues.   Author and subject catalogues.

Classification.   Dewey.

Copying/Photography.   Facilities available for most forms of photographic reproduction. Visitors may use their own cameras on request.

Friends of the Library.   National Library of Ireland Society. Annual subscription £1.00.

DUBLIN

Chester Beatty Library and Gallery of Oriental Art
20 Shrewsbury Road, Dublin 4
Tel. Dublin 692386

History. The Chester Beatty Library was assembled by Sir Alfred Chester Beatty (1875-1968), who was born in New York but became a naturalised Englishman in 1933. For many years the collections were housed in Baroda House, Kensington Palace Gardens, London, but in 1953 they were moved to a specially built library building in Dublin, where Chester Beatty had taken up residence. In 1957 an additional large exhibition gallery was erected to enable more of the treasures to be displayed. In 1975 a second storey was added to this building. The Library and its collections were left in trust to the Irish people on Chester Beatty's death in 1968. It now contains nearly 5,000 rare books and 10,000 manuscripts.

Special Collections and Treasures. The Library reflects Chester Beatty's great interest in Orientalia. It has been stated that his is the greatest collection of Oriental manuscripts ever assembled by a private collector. The oldest items in the Library are the Babylonian clay tablets dating from 2500-2300 B C. Of the fine collection of papyri, perhaps the most important are the Greek Biblical Papyri dating from the early 2nd to the 4th centuries. Treasures from the Western manuscripts include the volume of *Gospels* from Stavelot Abbey (Flanders, c.1000), the *Walsingham Bible* (English, 12th century) and the Coëtivy *Book of Hours* (executed before 1445). There are nearly 70 illuminated manuscripts from Armenia (12th-18th centuries), and the Arabic texts number over 2,500. Especially precious is a unique MS by Ibn al-Bawwab (Baghdad, c.1001). The Turkish manuscripts number over 100 and the Persian nearly 300. The Chinese Collection contains over 170 painted handscrolls and painting albums, and there are six sections of the famous Chinese encyclopaedia *Yung Lo Ta Tien,* prepared, but never printed, at the beginning of the 15th century.

Exhibition Areas. There are four exhibition rooms.

Hours. Mon.-Fri. 1000-1300, 1430-1700. Closed Sat., Sun. and usual public hols.

Transport. Buses 6, 7, 7a, 8 and 45 from Dublin centre (about 2½ miles).

Parking. Available at Library.

Admission. *Readers* and *Visitors:* Free of charge.

Information. Inside main door.

Sales. A brochure and postcards are available.

Chester Beatty Library, Dublin.
Part of the new gallery (1957)

Guidebooks.   Brochure, price 25p.

Restaurant/Snack Facilities.   None.

Services.   Lavatories.

Catalogues.   Various catalogues to the individual collections in the Library.

Classification.   Own.

Copying/Photography.   Photographs, slides and microfilms can be made on request.

DUBLIN
Library of Trinity College
College Street, Dublin 2
Tel. 772941

History.   Trinity College was founded by Queen Elizabeth I in 1592, although by 1600 the Library only possessed some thirty books. These were housed in an upper-storey room of the original quadrangle, adjacent to the square where today the Library now occupies a building of its own. In 1601 two fellows of the College, James Ussher (later Archbishop) and Luke Challenor, went to London to buy books, with the result that in 1604 the Library had 4,900 volumes. The only other acquisition of importance during the 17th century was the collection of 10,000 items of Archbishop Ussher himself. A new building, now called the Old Library, and designed by Capt. Thomas Burgh, was completed in 1732. It currently houses most of the books received up to 1962. Copyright deposit privileges have been in force since 1801, for books printed in Great Britain and Ireland. The New Library, designed by Paul Koralek, was opened in 1967 and today the Library's total holdings number about 1.5 million items.

Special Collections and Treasures.   Collections include the Quin Collection of first editions, vellum printings and fine bindings; the Fagel Library of over 20,000 volumes, especially rich in the history of the United Provinces (The Netherlands); the Ussher Collection of medieval MSS; and the papers of John Millington Synge, probably the leading playwright of the Irish literary revival. Individual treasures include the *Book of Kells,* an 8th or late 7th century illustrated MS of the Gospels in Latin, which has been called 'the greatest Irish paleographic and artistic monument'; the *Book of Durrow,* late 17th century MS; the *Book of Armagh* (c.807-808); Caxton's *Dicts and Sayengis of the Philosophres* (1477); and Roger Bacon's *Opus Majus.*

Exhibition Areas.   The Long Room of the Old Library (first floor) is used as an exhibition hall. Usually about three major exhibitions are displayed each year.

Library of Trinity College, Dublin

Hours. Reading Rooms: Mon.-Fri. 1000-2230, Sat. 1000-1300. For part of the year the Reading Rooms close at 1700 and they are entirely closed for a fortnight in July (as stated in the *Almanack*). Manuscript Room: open Mon.-Fri. until 1700, Sat. 1000-1300, and remaining open during the general Library closing in July. All parts of the Library are closed on 24-25 Dec. and the three days following, New Year's Day, St. Patrick's Day, Good Fri., Easter Eve, Easter Mon., the first Mon. in June and the first Mon. in August.

Transport. The College is in the centre of Dublin and accessible by public transport.

Parking. Subject to the availablity of parking space for visitors, vehicles may enter by the Lincoln Place gate at the east end of the College.

Admission. Readers: Graduates of the Universities of Dublin, Cambridge and Oxford, undertaking research, and, with the approval of the Librarian, other persons engaged in research may be admitted as readers.
Visitors: Visitors are admitted only to the Long Room of the Old Library, the Library Shop and the entrance hall of the New Library.

Information. In the entrance hall of the New Library.

Sales. The Library Shop is at the east end of the Old Library. A considerable range of books, as well as postcards, slides and gift items available.

Guidebooks. The Library guide, in English, is available to authorised readers.

Restaurant/Snack Facilities. None.

Services. Lavatories and public telephone off the entrance hall of the New Library. Lifts in both Old and New Libraries.

Catalogues. The main Library catalogues are in the Iveagh Hall of the New Library. There are several author and subject catalogues, each covering acquisitions of the Library during a particular period. (It is therefore necessary to consult the catalogues for all periods covering and subsequent to the publication date of a book.)

Classification. Dewey.

Copying/Photography. There is a copying service available through the Library staff, at the counter in the Iveagh Hall, the 1937 Reading Room, the Science Library Hut or in the Biomedical Library. Private photography is prohibited in all Library buildings, except by special arrangement.

Friends of the Library. Subscription £4 per annum, Life membership £40.

Israel

JERUSALEM
Jewish National and University Library
POB 503, Jerusalem
Tel. 38441

History. The Jewish National and University Library
serves a three-fold purpose: it is the National Library of
the Jewish people, the Library of the Hebrew University
and the Central Library of Israel. The nucleus of the
Library was begun in 1884 by a group of scholars in
Jerusalem, whose small collection was later incorporated
into the B'nai B'rith Library in Jerusalem. The idea of a
National Library was conceived in 1890 by Dr. Joseph
Chasanowitz of Bialystok (1844-1919), during a visit to
Jerusalem. Upon his return to Russia, Dr. Chasanowitz
sent his first consignment of 8,800 books, and by 1908
the holdings of the Library totalled 22,000 books. In 1920
the World Zionist Organisation assumed responsibility
for the National Library, and in 1925 it was integrated
into the Hebrew University and renamed the Jewish
National and University Library. From 1930 until 1948 the
Library was located in the Wolffsohn Building on Mount
Scopus. With the severance from Mount Scopus in
1948, only a fraction of its 465,000 volumes were
available in the city and until 1960 the remaining
collections were scattered throughout Jerusalem. Today
the Library is located in the Lady Davis (of Canada)
Building on the Givat Ram campus. Its collections total 2
million volumes (1 million in the Central Library), 8,900
MSS, 200 incunabula and 31,000 microfilmed Hebrew
MSS.

Special Collections and Treasures. Collections include
the Dr. Abraham Schwadron (Sharon) Collection of
Jewish autographs and portraits, dating from the 16th
century. Special efforts have been made to obtain MSS,
autographs and portraits of Jewish Nobel Prize winners.
Particular treasures are the original MSS of Einstein's
general theory of relativity, his 'Simplified Derivation of
the Equivalence of Mass and Energy', 'Generalised
Theory of Gravitation' and 'Theory of Gravitation'. Other
collections include the Dr. H. Friedenwald Collection on
Medicine (3,000 volumes); the private library of the
conductor Serge Koussevitzky; the Jacob Michael
Collection of Jewish Music; the Yahuda and Ignaz
Goldhizer Collections of Orientalia; the Prins Collection
on the History of Dutch Jewry; the Julius Jarcho
medical library; the Johann Dawud Collection of Old
Yiddish Literature; the Otto Warburg Collection of
Botanical Works; the archives of the Hebrew poet
J.L. Gordon, and the Albert Ehrenstein literary estate.

*Jewish National and
University Library*

Exhibition Areas. No permanent exhibition area.

Hours. Circulation, reference, catalogues, music, art and periodicals reading rooms: Sun.-Thurs. 0900-1800, Fri. 0900-1300. General Judaic and Oriental studies reading rooms: Sun.-Thurs. 0900-2200, Fri. 0900-1300. Closed on Jewish holidays.

Transport. Buses to Hebrew University, 9, 24, 28.

Parking. Hebrew University visitors' parking lot (outside main gate).

Admission. Readers: Open to all. Those wishing to borrow must register at the Circulation Desk.
Visitors: Free admission but large groups of visitors are not allowed in the Reading Rooms.

Information. General information may be given at the main entrance. Library information is available in Reference Department.

Sales. At the main entrance. Reproductions from manuscripts available.

Guidebooks. Library guide, in Hebrew and English, available from the Information Desk in the Reference Department.

Restaurant/Snack Facilities. On the lower main floor. Open Sun.-Thurs. 0800-2000, Fri. 0800-1200.

Services. Cloakroom and telephones on lower main floor. Lift at main entrance. Lavatories on first floor (outside Reading Rooms).

Catalogues. Author/title and subject (classified) catalogues.

Classification. Mainly Dewey; some Universal Decimal Classification (Law, Medicine); expanded Dewey for Judaica and Islam.

Copying/Photography. Individuals may use machines on lower main floor and first floor outside reading rooms. The Reprographic Service is in Room 3 of the basement. Private photography permitted but readers must not be disturbed.

TEL AVIV
Elias Sourasky Central Library
Tel Aviv University, POB 39038, Ramat Aviv, Tel Aviv
Tel. 03 416111

History. The University Library was founded in 1954 and today consists of the Elias Sourasky Central Library and various departmental libraries: the Library of Life Sciences (Sakler Building), the Library of Exact Sciences and Engineering (Shenkar Building), the Social Sciences

Elias Sourasky Central Library, Tel Aviv

Library (Peretz Naftali Building), the Business Administration Library (Leon Recaneti Building), the Law Library (Trubowicz Building), the Mehlman Library of Jewish Studies (House of Jewish Communities), the Archaeology Library (Gillman Building), the School of Education Library (Sharet Building) and the Geography Library (Abner House). The Central Library, completed in 1961 in a split-level design, currently contains over 400,000 volumes of the total Library figure of 650,000 volumes.

Special Collections and Treasures. Collections include the Faitlovitch (Jacques) Jacob Collection, an extensive collection of about 6,000 books, periodicals, clippings and MSS on the history and geography of Ethiopia; the Collection of British Parliamentary Papers of 1,100 volumes, donated by Sir Charles Clore; and the General Assaf Simchoni Collection on military history, which was donated by the Israeli Ministry of Defence in memory of the late General Simchoni.

Exhibition Areas. Lobby: general exhibitions. Stands on 1st and 2nd floors: new books.

Hours. Sun.-Thurs. 0900-2200 (Aug. 0900-2000), Fri. and holiday eves. 0900-1300. Closed Sat. and Jewish hols.

Transport. Bus nos. 13, 24, 25, from northern parts of Tel Aviv; bus nos. 74, 79, 27 from southern parts of Tel Aviv.

Parking. General parking area at the main entrance to the campus. There are also parking facilities at the rear entrance of the Library building, near the University swimming pool.

Admission. Readers: The Library is open to all University personnel, teaching staff and students. For borrowing privileges, all readers should register at the main borrowing desk in the Catalogue Room. There is no charge but a student or personnel card must be shown. *Visitors:* Free, but no children allowed in the Library.

Information. General information and reference desk near the entrance of the Catalogue Room.

Sales. None.

Guidebooks. Taped tour of the Library in Hebrew on individual cassette recorders with earphones. Recording lasts 30 minutes and explains building facilities, services, catalogues and collections.

Restaurant/Snack Facilities. Automatic vending machines for hot and cold drinks in the basement.

Services. Cloakroom at the entrance, telephones on basement floor, smoking lounges in the main lobby, lavatories 1st and 2nd floors and basement. Lifts for the handicapped only.

Catalogues.   Alphabetical author catalogue, separate for Western languages, Hebrew, Arabic and Russian. Also classified catalogue. Alphabetical kardex for periodicals. Catalogues are located in the Main Reading Room.

Classification.   Dewey (for books), Library of Congress (for music).

Copying/Photography.   Automatic xerographic copiers on underground floor. Private photography is permitted.

Italy

BOLOGNA
Biblioteca Comunale dell'Archiginnasio
Portici del Pavaglione, Piazza Galvani 1, I-40124 Bologna
Tel. 22 55 09 and 27 95 65

History.   The Library was founded in 1801 by the Departmental Administration of Reno. Its initial stock was based on two collections — the Libreria dei Barnabiti di Santa Lucia (the first public library in Bologna, opened in the middle of the 18th century), and material from the religious bodies suppressed in 1797-8. The Library, occupying the premises of the ex-monastery of San Domenico, began to function actively in 1806. In 1811 it received the rich private library of bibliophile Abbé Antonio Magnani, professor at Bologna University and librarian at the Science Institute, although the two collections were not finally merged until 1824, when they became the Magnani Municipal Library. The growth of the collections occasioned the move in 1838 to the historical building of the Archiginnasio, the original site of Bologna University. At this time the Library also adopted its present name. The systematic organisation of the material in its new home did not begin, however, until 1858. Since that date the collections, which focus on history, literature, art and bibliography, have grown (despite some losses in World War II) to include 609,982 volumes, 12,000 MSS and 2,500 incunabula.

Special Collections and Treasures.   The Magnani Collection (see above) contained 25,000 printed works, including many rare 16th century editions (particularly Aldine) and a series of Greek codices from the 10th to the 16th centuries. Other collections include the library of the poet Severino Ferrari; the Spada Miscellanea (12,000 items); a collection of mediaeval documents gathered by Giuseppe Azzolini; the Atlante del Coppo Collection;

Biblioteca Comunale dell'Archiginnasio, Bologna

the codices of the Company of the Battuti; the Mezzofanti MSS; the historical archives of the Commune; the Rusconi Collection; and the Minghetti Collection. The Bologna Collection covers the life, customs and traditions of Bologna from the earliest times to the present day. Treasures include Aesop, *Fables* (Bologna, 1494); the letters of Frederick the Great, Galileo and Napoleon; and the notebooks kept by Galvani during his experiments.

Exhibition Areas.   There are no specific exhibition areas. Exhibition cases on tops of low bookshelves.

Hours.   Mon.-Sat. 0900-2000. Closed Sun., the whole of Aug. and public hols.

Transport.   The Library is accessible by public transport. The Library occupies rooms at first floor level above a row of shops.

Parking.   No details available.

Admission.   Readers and *Visitors:* Admission free of charge, although this is mainly a library for the serious student. Special permission is required to use the 35,000 volume open access Reference Room.

Information.   Information desk.

Sales.   None.

Guidebooks.   Brochure in English and Italian.

Restaurant/Snack Facilities.   None on premises but available nearby.

Services.   No details available.

Catalogues.   Author, subject and special catalogues. Sheaf catalogue prior to 1961, since that date 7½ x 12½ cm. card catalogue.

Classification.   Own, adapted from Dewey.

Copying/Photography.   Photocopies and microfilm copies can be made through Library staff.

CESENA
Biblioteca Comunale Malatestiana
Piazza Bufalini 1, I-47023 Cesena (Forlì)
Tel. 2 12 97

History.   The Malatesta Library was founded in 1452 in the old convent of the Franciscan Minors, which had been built in the 13th century. The enlightened patronage of Malatesta Novello Malatesti, Lord of Cesena, was responsible not only for the construction of the Library but also for the essential nucleus of its collection. Construction of the famous Library Hall began in 1447 and the building was completed in 1452. Today it can claim to be the only early Renaissance library which preserves its original building, furniture and books. The Hall was planned as a basilica with three naves of eleven spans and lined with two rows of columns bearing the insignia of the Malatesta. 29 stalls, or *plutei,* are disposed along each side of the lateral spans. In 1465, Malatesta Novello died and in 1474 the Library received its last substantial bequest from Giovanni di Marco of Rimini, particularly rich in medical works. The Library subsequently fell into neglect but the supervision of the Communal Council probably saved the collections from dispersal. During the Napoleonic Wars the building was requisitioned as a barracks and the collection put in store. The modern Communal Library, located next to the Malatestiana, took shape at about this time. Today total holdings include 191,438 volumes, 286 incunabula and 2,180 MSS.

Special Collections and Treasures. Next to the Malatesta Library, in the great hall which once served as a dormitory for the friars, is housed the valuable private collection of Pope Pius VII Chiaramonti (commonly called the Biblioteca Piana), acquired in 1941 from the heirs of the Cesena-born Pope. This collection is composed of 2,801 works in 5,057 volumes, including about 100 MSS from the 12th-19th centuries, 26 incunabula and many richly bound rare works dating from the 18th and 19th centuries. The Communal Library contains a notable collection of Duomo illuminated choral MSS; and the Bufalini, Finali, Trovanelli, Allocatelli, Giommi and Comandini Collections. The last of these collections is assembled in the old Franciscan refectory and has been open to the public since 15 March 1970. Treasures include the *Etymologiae* of St. Isidore of Seville, dating from the 9th century; St. Jerome's *Letters and Sermons,* MS c.1451-65, copied by Johannes de Spinalo, a French notary from Épinal; a three volume MS of Plutarch's *Lives* in Francesco Filelfo's Latin translation, copied in Cesena c.1450 by Jacopo da Pergola and illuminated in Ferrara by Taddeo Crivelli; and Cardinal Bessarion's translation of Aristotle's *Metaphysics,* probably a present from the translator to Malatesta Novello, c.1460.

Exhibition Areas. The Biblioteca Malatestiana, Biblioteca Piana, the 'Quaderia', the Morellini Foundation, Biblioteca Comandini and the Museum of Ancient History.

Hours. 1 Oct.-14 June: Mon. 1500-1900, Tues.-Fri. 0900-1300, 1500-1900, Sat. 0900-1300, 1500-1800. 15 June-30 Sept.: Mon. 1600-2000, Tues.-Sat. 0800-1300. The Library is closed to readers for 3 weeks in Aug. Closed Sun. and public hols.

Transport. Bus.

Parking. In neighbouring streets.

Biblioteca Comunale Malatestiana, Cesena

Admission. Readers: Free of charge.
Visitors: Free. Hours for visiting, 15 June-30 Sept.: Mon. 1600-1800, Tues.-Sat. 0830-1230, 1600-1800. Sun. and public hols. 1000-1200.

Information. Information Office.

Sales. None.

Guidebooks. None in print.

Restaurant/Snack Facilities. None.

Services. Lavatories.

Catalogues. Dictionary catalogue up to 1959. Author and subject catalogues since 1960.

Classification. Up to 1954 by material; since that date by the size of book.

Copying/Photography. Photocopies and microfilm copying available through Library staff. Private photography of library material requires the Director's permission. Photographs of the buildings permissible.

FLORENCE
Biblioteca Nazionale Centrale
Piazza Cavalleggeri 1, Firenze
Tel. 287 052; 294 423 (Director)

History. The Library, the most important in Italy, was founded in 1714 by Antonio Magliabechi. Magliabechi, described as 'an eccentric self-tutored scholar', left his collection of 30,000 volumes and 3,000 manuscripts 'to the poor of Florence' and it was opened to the public in 1747, with the title Biblioteca Magliabechiana. Its stock grew from numerous bequests and then from the suppression of the monasteries by the Grand Duke of Tuscany in 1775-1789 and later suppressions in 1810 and 1867. In 1861 when the unity of Italy was constituted, the Magliabechiana and the Palatina (the Library of the Grand Dukes of Tuscany, with a total of 90,000 volumes and 3,000 manuscripts) Libraries were merged to form the Biblioteca Nazionale. In 1870 a second National Central Library (see entry for Biblioteca Nazionale Centrale Vittorio Emanuele II) was established in Rome, but while both libraries have many similarities of purpose and both enjoy copyright deposit, each has its own special responsibilities. In 1885 the Library became the Biblioteca Nazionale Centrale and in 1935 occupied new buildings designed by Cesare Bazzani on the edge of the River Arno. The Library survived World War II but not the floods of 3-4 November 1966, which severely damaged the building, books and periodicals. It has now been estimated that the actual loss of original material may have been 5 per cent of the whole collection, which

Biblioteca Nazionale Centrale, Florence

now totals 4.5 million books, 24,723 MSS, 723,137 documents, 3,769 incunabula and 10,000 microfilms.

Special Collections and Treasures. Collections include the Dante Collection, which was started in 1888; the Guicciardini Collection of over 8,000 volumes relating to the religious reformation in Italy during the 16th century; the Savonarola Collection based on material collected from the Magliabechi and Palatina libraries, with additions from the collection of Count Lorenzo Capponi; the Aldine Collection; the Galileo Collection; the Landau-Finaly Collection of incunabula and rare books; the Giovanni Nencini Collection numbering over 13,000 volumes; the Foscolo MSS; the library of Count Angelo de Gubernatis, acquired in 1886; the 'Pistoiese' Collection of MSS of Rossi-Cassigoli; the theatrical collection of Luigi Suñer; the bio-bibliographical Collection of Diomede Bonamici; the Domenico Tordi MSS on the history of Florence; the correspondence of Lambruschini, Le Monnler, Cambray-Digny, Peruzzi, and other eminent personalities of the nineteenth century; the W. Benn Collection of philosophy and philology; MSS relating to Machiavelli and Lorenzo de Medici; the Gonnelli Collection of 17,000 letters and documents including such figures as Bembo, Guarino, Vasari and Montesquieu. Treasures include a 10th century *Sacramentarium* with miniatures of the Reichenau School; Boccaccio's *Zibaldone magliabechiano* (a collection of material for his *De genealogia deorum*); the MS of Machiavelli's *Arte della guerra*; 35 sonnets and other poems in Tasso's hand; the *Itinerario* of Lodovico Vartema's travels from Venice to India by way of Mecca (1502-8); the apparently unique *Orationi del corpo di Cristo* (Florence?) of Thomas Aquinas; and Andrea da Barberino, *Guerino il Meschino* (Venice, 1480), one of only two known copies in Italy.

Exhibition Areas. None at the present time.

Hours. Mon.-Fri. 0900-1900, Sat. 0900-1300. Closed on Sundays, during Aug. and the week before Easter.

Transport. Autobus 19.

Parking. Limited parking in front of the Library.

Admission. Readers: Open to all over 16 years old. *Visitors:* May visit the Library on application to the Director.

Information. Issue, Catalogue and Reading Room Desks.

Sales. None.

Guidebooks. None

Restaurant/Snack Facilities. Bar open daily from 0900-1800.

Services.   Cloakrooms, lavatories, telephones.

Catalogues. 1886 onwards, author card catalogue. Subject catalogue since 1925. Various specialised catalogues.

Classification.   Dewey.

Copying/Photography. Two photocopy machines are available for the use of students. Micro-filming through the Library staff. Apply to the Director for permission for private photography.

FLORENCE
Biblioteca della Facoltà di Lettere e Filosofia
Università degli Studi di Firenze,
I-Piazza Brunelleschi 4, 50121 Firenze
Tel (55) 260705

History. The Library structure of the University of Florence is essentially plural and autonomous, with a number of faculty libraries scattered through the city and the surrounding region. The Library of the Faculty of Letters and Philosophy is the largest in the University. It has its origins in the creation on 22 December 1859 of the Istituto di Studi Superiori, which was organised in four sections: legal, philosophical and philological, natural sciences and medicine. During 1867-8 the philosophical and philological section became the Faculty of Letters and Philosophy, largely as a result of the efforts of Pasquale Villari. The early collection of the Library largely reflects the interests of the contemporary teachers. Early growth owed much to numerous bequests, which are still largely kept as separate entities. During the 20th century, despite various setbacks from theft and the 1966 flood (with damage to 100,000 items) the Library has grown into what has been termed 'the largest academic library in Italy'. Holdings currently include 1.2 million volumes, 690 microfilms and 1,250 current periodicals.

Facoltà di Lettere e Filosofia, Florence University. Main entrance

Special Collections and Treasures. Collections include the important libraries acquired from the heirs of the Assyriologist Felice Finzi, from the Orientalist Dorn and from the Istituto dei Bardi; the Domenico Comparetti Collection (classical philology, mythology, comparative folklore); Felice Tocco (Greek and mediaeval philosophy); Francesco de Sarlo (philosophy and psychology); E.G. Parodi (dialects, literary criticism, history of language); the papers of Allesandro d'Ancona, Mussafia and part of the Borgese papers; the collection of Giovanni Papini (greatly damaged by the flood); and the collection of Milan Rešetar containing a great part of Bibliotheca Rhacusina. Treasures include Samuel Marochinatus, *Della vera teologia* (Bologna, 1477); Cristoforo Landino, *Quaestiones camaldolenses* (Florence, 1480?); Michele Marullo, *Epigrammaton* (Florence, 1497); a Benedictine

MS codex of the 16th century; and Kant, *Physische Geographie* I-VI (Mainz/Hamburg, 1803).

Exhibition Areas. None.

Hours. Mon.-Fri. 0800-2000, Sat. 0800-1300. Closed Sun., during Aug. and public hols.

Transport. The Library is accessible by bus.

Parking. Facilities for University personnel only.

Admission. Readers: Usually students and members of the University but other applicants may be accepted as readers.
Visitors: Admitted to the Library. Large groups should give prior notice of their visit.

Information. From the loan desk or in the office.

Sales. None.

Guidebooks. None.

Restaurant/Snack Facilities. Open 0800-1930.

Services. Lavatories, lift. Corridors are used as smoking areas.

Catalogues. Typewritten catalogue: author catalogue; subject catalogue 1966; catalogue of periodicals.

Classification. Own.

Copying/Photography. Copying service operated by Library staff. Also two coin-operated photo-copying machines for individual use in the passage to the Reading Room. Prior permission is required for private photography.

FLORENCE
Biblioteca Medicea Laurenziana
Piazza S. Lorenzo 9, Firenze
Tel. 270760

History. The Library is, as its name indicates, the library of the Medici rulers of Florence. It began with the personal collection of manuscripts collected by Cosimo de Medici (the Elder) (1389-1464) and was later enriched by his sons Giovanni and Piero and then by his grandson Lorenzo (1449-92) (il Magnifico), who sent his agents throughout Europe and the Orient for books and MSS. On the expulsion from Florence of the Medici family in 1490, the Library was confiscated by the 'Signoria' of Florence and then acquired by the Convent of San Marco, but was eventually re-sold to Giovanni de Medici. It remained in Rome until 1522, when it was brought

Biblioteca Medicea Laurenziana, Florence

back to Florence to be housed in the Michelangelo designed building in the cloisters of the San Lorenzo Basilica. It was eventually opened to the public in 1571 with some 3,000 printed and manuscript works. It then experienced a long period of stagnation until 1757, when the librarian Angelo Maria Bandini prepared and printed a full catalogue and sought regular accessions. The French Revolution resulted in many manuscripts being acquired from the suppressed monasteries. Now the property of the State, the Library's present holdings total 54,724 volumes, 10,722 manuscripts and 4,389 incunabula.

Special Collections and Treasures. Collections include the D'Elci Collection of 1,220 first editions; the Ashburnham Collection of codices and MSS; the 1,278 Elzevirs; and the collection of papyri from 300 BC to AD 600. Treasures include a famous illuminated MS containing various texts of Greek surgeons of the classical period, owned by the Byzantine surgeon Nicetas; one of the oldest extant Virgil MSS (494); the Syriac *Gospels,* written by Rabula in 586 with decorated canons and 14 large miniatures, among them possibly the earliest representation of the Crucifixion and Resurrection; the *Pandectae* (533) of Justinian; many important MSS of Cicero and of Tacitus and the famous Laurentian Aeschylus; the 10th century Visigothic Hildephonsus, *De virginitate Mariae,* with primitive Mozarabic miniatures; the *Codex Amiatinus* (715), written either at Monkwearmouth or Jarrow; the 13th century *Medici Antiphonary,* one of the best collections of medieval French polyphonic music; the *Squarcialupi Codex* of Italian 14th century songs; an 11th century *Odes* of Horace, with marginal notes in Petrarch's hand; a treatise on architecture by Francesco di Giorgio Martini, with marginal notes by Leonardo da Vinci, to whom the item belonged; Sahagún's *Universal History of New Spain* (1560), one of the chief sources on Aztec civilisation and Spanish colonization of Mexico; astronomical charts by Kepler; Copernicus's signature on the astronomical chart of Alfonso el Sabio; and a collection of notes on geography made by Napoleon as a student.

Exhibition Areas. Exhibitions of a philological nature and of illuminated MSS are held alternately in the Hall of Michelangelo and in various rooms of the Library.

Hours. Mon.-Fri. 0800-1400, Sat. 0800-1300. Closed Sun. and annually from 1-15 Sept., the week before Easter and public hols.

Transport. The Library is housed in rooms in the upper cloisters of the Church of San Lorenzo, which is situated in the centre of the city, near the termini of all the public transport services.

Parking. None.

Admission. Readers and *Visitors:* Admission is free to anyone over 18, particularly students. A letter of recommendation is necessary before manuscripts may be consulted.

Information. Bibliographical information is given to scholars either by letter or personally during their visit.

Sales. None.

Guidebooks. Available in most languages at bookshops but not at the Library.

Restaurant/Snack Facilities. There are none in the Library but many in the immediate neighbourhood.

Services. Usual services available for scholars.

Catalogues. Author and subject card catalogues 1958-. Numerous special catalogues to MSS and books. There are 11 catalogues of the manuscripts and various other specialized catalogues.

Classification. Own (in accordance with national regulations).

Copying/Photography. Apply to the Director. No private photography is permitted, not even of the interior of the building. For photographs of manuscripts, written application should be made to the Director.

FLORENCE
Biblioteca Riccardiana-Moreniana
Via dei Ginori 10, I-50129 Firenze
Tel. (055) 212-586; Administration: 211-379

History. Towards the end of the 16th century, Riccardo Romolo Riccardi (1558-1612), a poet, formed a library, which was added to by later members of the Riccardi family, notably Francesco. With the extinction of the family line, it was bought by the Government in 1812 and given to the State in 1815 on the condition that the Library was opened to the public. In 1942 the Biblioteca Riccardiana was linked with the Biblioteca Moreniana, which focused on the history of the Tuscan state. Domenico Moreni (1763-1835) was a great collector of works on Tuscany and his library occupies two smaller rooms, adjoining the Riccardiana. Current holdings include 38,611 printed works, 15,233 pamphlets, 1,974 microfilms, 4,280 manuscript volumes, and 1,610 manuscripts.

Special Collections and Treasures. Major treasures include a Venetian *Bible* of 1482; a 14th century *Psalter;* early Dante MSS (including one with his portrait, 15th century) and the most complete edition of the *Divina Commedia* (1481), with 21 Botticelli engravings; a 15th century illuminated MS of Virgil; 723 incunabula including the unique copy of the first edition of the

Biblioteca Moreniana, Florence

Erotemata of Chrysoloras; many rare Oriental MSS; the 16th century *Codice Vaglienti;* and an account book of Benvenuto Cellini. Notable collections include those of Vincenzo Capponi, Giovanni Lami, G.B. Fagiuoli, Mario Pieri and the Libri Collection on Florentine history.

Exhibition Areas. Recent accessions are usually exhibited near the entrance.

Hours. Mon.-Sat. 0800-1400. Closed the week before Easter and 15-30 Aug.

Transport. Buses to nearby thoroughfares. The Library is situated at the back of the Palazzo Medici-Riccardi.

Parking. No details available.

Admission. *Readers:* For access to collections readers must present identification papers. Foreigners must present a passport.
Visitors: Conducted tours of the Palace available.

Information. Available at the desks in the Catalogue and Reading Rooms.

Sales. None.

Guidebooks. None.

Restaurant/Snack Facilities. Available nearby.

Services. Cloakrooms, lavatory.

Catalogues. Alphabetical author catalogue in manuscript (book) form. Various special catalogues, e.g. music.

Classification. Own fixed location system.

Copying/Photography. Microfilms, microcards, slides and photocopies can be made.

MILAN
Biblioteca Ambrosiana
Piazza Pio XI, 2, I-20123 Milano
Tel. (02) 800146

History. The Library was founded by Cardinal Federico Borromeo (1564-1631), Bishop of Milan, and named after the patron saint of Milan, St. Ambrose. It was opened to the public on 8 December 1609, the first public library in Italy. Borromeo was an avid bibliophile and it was his donation of his own library that enabled the Ambrosiana to open with 30,000 printed books and 12,000 MSS. The collections were housed in the palace built by Borromeo 1603-1609, on the site of the ancient Scuole Taverna. The Library received many donations, notably from Bobbio monastery, while acquisitions were deliberately sought through agents travelling abroad. This initial flurry of activity did not last, however, and a reduction of funds meant an almost total reliance on gifts for the second half of the 17th and most of the 18th centuries. During the Napoleonic administration the collections were raided for treasures, although most of these were returned by the Bibliothèque nationale in 1815. By 1887 the printed volumes totalled 146,000 and by 1937, 500,000. On 15-16 August 1943 the Library building was severely damaged by bombing and 50,000 volumes lost. The Library has since been restored to its original design. Current holdings include 755,000 volumes, 35,000 MSS and 3,000 incunabula.

Special Collections and Treasures. Collections received during the 20th century include the Griffini Bey Arabic Collection; the Salvioni Dialect Collection; the Casanova Collection, dealing with the history of heraldry and blazonry; the Bonomelli Collection of letters relating to the Italian Risorgimento; the Archives of the Duke Bracciano; and the Rachele Villa Pernice Collection of 20,000 volumes. Perhaps the most valued single MS of the Library is the single volume of the works of Leonardo da Vinci, known as the *Codex Atlanticus* and containing about 1,700 original drawings and MSS. Other treasures include the 5th or 6th century *Iliad,* 58 leaves with text on the verso and pictures on the recto, one of the three great surviving illustrated MSS of antiquity; the 5th century palmpsest of Ulfilas's Gothic translation of the *Epistles,* which with the *Codex argenteus* at Uppsala is the oldest monument of the Germanic languages; the 7th century Syriac *Hexapla,* an important source for the knowledge of the Septuagint text; a 9th-10th century *Missal* from Bobbio; the *Virgil* owned and annotated by Petrarch; the *Codice Resta,* a collection of over 200 drawings, which includes 9 Michelangelos, 2 Dürers, 3 Leonardos, 2 Titians and 3 Raphaels; the *Arabic Portolan* of the 14th century, the only known Arabic loxodromic map; Galileo Galilei's *Il saggiatore* (Rome, 1623), the copy sent by the author to Cardinal Borromeo; and one of two recorded copies of Thomas à Kempis, *Contemptus mundi,* printed in Japanese in 1596 on the Jesuit press at Amakusa.

Exhibition Areas. Sala dell'Incoronazione.

Hours. Mon.-Fri. 0900-1630, Sat. 0900-1200. Closed Sun., during Aug. and public hols.

Transport. The Library is located in the old centre of Milan. Buses to neighbouring thoroughfares. (The Library is on the ground floor of the Palazzo.)

Parking. In nearby streets.

Admission. Readers and *Visitors:* Free admission.

Information. At the Information Desk.

Biblioteca Ambrosiana, Milan

Sales.   No details available.

Guidebooks.   None.

Restaurant/Snack Facilities.   None, but available nearby.

Services.   Lavatories, telephones.

Catalogues.   Author, subject and systematic catalogues, but not complete.

Classification.   Own.

Copying/Photography.   Copying   service   providing photographs and photocopies but there are no machines for individual use. Private photography not permitted inside the Library.

MILAN
Biblioteca Nazionale Braidense
Palazzo di Brera, Via Brera 28, I-20121 Milano
Tel. 872 376, 808 345

History.   The Library owes its foundation to the Empress Maria Theresa. Its initial stock comprised the library of Count Carlo Pertusati (purchased at his death in 1763 by the 'Congregazione di Stato' and made into a public library at the insistence of Maria Theresa) and the Jesuit Library in the Palace of Brera, erected in 1591. The Library was given the name Braidense and formally opened to the public in 1786. The Library enjoys copyright privileges for the Milan province, although it passes on works of music to the Conservatorio 'Giuseppe Verdi' Library. The collections have also expanded in the 19th and 20th centuries through many bequests of material in the humanities. Collections now total 839,515 books, 2,075 MSS and 1,440 microfilms.

Special Collections and Treasures.   Collections include the library of Albrecht von Haller, containing the MSS of the famous doctor, together with 13,000 printed volumes on medicine and natural science; the Gerli Collection of liturgical works; the Castiglioni Collection of romances of chivalry, incunabula and MSS; the History of Lombardy Collection; and works by and about Alessandro Manzoni (this collection is housed in its own room). The Library contains the richest known collection of the works of the printer Bodoni, totalling over 1,000 items and including all known extant works. Treasures include the 13th century del Bescapé poem, the earliest document in the Milanese dialect; the 15th century *Legend of Josaphat,* the property of Bona di Savoia; the 12th century *Benedict Missal,* attributed to a scriptorium in Padua; the *Decretales,* written in 1354 in the style of the Bologna school, with two miniatures by Niccolò di Giacomo; the 11th century *Hexameron* of St. Ambrose, the oldest

Biblioteca Nazionale
Braidense, Milan

MS in the Library; three Dante codices of the 14th century; the *Geografia* of Berlinghieri, written for Lorenzo the Magnificent with miniatures from the school of Attavante; and Gaspare Aselli, *De lactibus sive lacteis venis* (Milan, 1627), the first anatomical work with plates in two colours.

Hours.   Mon., Wed., Fri. 0900-1900, Tues., Thurs., Sat. 0900-1400. Closed Sun., during Easter week and 15-30 Aug.

Transport.   Bus routes: 0, 43. Tram routes: 1, 4, 8, 18, 21. (The Library occupies the first floor of the Brera Palace.)

Parking.   In front of the Library building.

Admission.   *Readers:* Admission free. Readers must be at least 16 years of age.
Visitors: Admission free.

Information.   In the Catalogue Room.

Sales.   None.

Guidebooks.   None.

Restaurant/Snack Facilities.   None.

Services.   Lavatories, telephones.

Catalogues.   Author and subject catalogues. MS catalogue to 1890. Sheaf catalogue 1891-1925. Dictionary card catalogue 1926. Various special catalogues, e.g. periodicals, MSS, incunabula.

Classification.   Generally by size.

Copying/Photography.   There is a copying service providing dry copies and microfilms. Private photography only with the permission of the Librarian.

Roman Missal (16th century), in Biblioteca Nazionale Braidense, Milan. Detail

MILAN
Biblioteca dell'Archivio Storico Civico e Biblioteca Trivulziana
Castello Sforzesco, I-20121 Milano
Tel. 8868, int. 3946, 3960, 3967

History.   The Trivulziana Library shares quarters with the city historical archives in the architecturally impressive Castello Sforzesco, the stronghold built by Francesco Sforza from 1451-66. The Library dates back to the collection founded by Alessandro Teodoro Trivulzio (1694-1763) and his brother Carlo (1715-1789). Material was acquired from the collections of suppressed monasteries and other private libraries. The Trivulzio Collection was continued and extended by Gian Giacomo

Castello Sforzesco, Milan

Trivulzio (1774-1831), who considerably enriched the Dante and Petrarch sections, as did another Gian Giacomo (1839-1902), who finally established the collection as a library of the first order. In April 1935 the Trivulzio family library was acquired by the city of Milan and was added to the City Archives. The official inauguration of the Library in the restored Castello Sforzesco took place on 16 February 1963. Current holdings total nearly 82,000 items, including 1,312 incunabula and 6,500 editions of the 16th century.

Special Collections and Treasures. The most important collection is the Dante Collection, which includes 23 MSS (six of the 14th century), all 15 incunabula (beginning with the first, Foligno, 1472) and nearly all succeeding editions. Other treasures include Lucanus, *De bello pharsalico,* executed in 1373 by Niccolò Giacomo of Bologna, illustrating Lucan's poem on the wars between Caesar and Pompey; the *Breviarium Ambrosianum* (1396), executed by Giovanni de Grassi; the *Aelius Donatus grammaticus* (15th century), a fine example of the Lombard school of illumination; the *Constantine Lascaris,* a Greek grammar in the Lombard style; the *Evangelistarium* (c.1531), written by Benedetto Cremonense for Francesco II Sforza, with miniatures by Agostino Decio; and a notebook of Leonardo da Vinci.

Exhibition Areas. Exhibition Room, 'Sala del Tesoro'.

Hours. Mon.-Fri. 0900-1200, 1430-1730. Closed Sat., Sun., and during August and on public hols.

Transport. Bus to the Castello Sforzesco. (The principal entrance to the Castello is through the portico under the tower of Filarete, while the Library is approached via the Courtyard of the Rocchetta.)

Parking. Available at the Castle. A fee is charged.

Admission. Readers: Free to students and researchers. Access to rare materials on identification of research project.
Visitors: Free entrance to the exhibition areas.

Information. In the entrance hall.

Sales. In the entrance hall.

Guidebooks. No details available.

Restaurant/Snack Facilities. None.

Services. None.

Catalogues. Author and subject catalogues. Separate catalogues for MSS, periodicals, incunabula, etc.

Classification. Own.

Copying/Photography. Photocopies and microfilm copying available through Library staff.

MODENA

Biblioteca Estense e Universitaria
Largo Porta S. Agostino, 309, I-4100 Modena
Tel. 222248 (Centralino); 230195 (Director)

History.   The origin of the Library lies in the private collection of the house of Este, the foundation of which, at Ferrara, dates back to the beginning of the 13th century. A catalogue of 1436 lists 278 codices, many of which are still preserved. The Library moved from Ferrara to Modena in 1598, losing in the process various volumes, now to be found in such libraries as the Vatican and Bibliothèque nationale. Finally installed in the wing of the Ducal Palace, the Library revived under a succession of notable librarians such as Muratori, Zaccaria and Tiraboschi. In the 18th century the suppression of the Jesuit Order brought the Library a large number of accessions, and it also acquired from the Court archives a great number of letters, which form the basis of the present collection. In 1761 the Library was opened to the public but it fell into neglect in the 19th century, under the last Archduke, Francesco V. In 1869 the Library became a state institution and in 1883 it moved to its present premises. The University Library, founded in 1772, suppressed in 1796 and reopened in 1884, was amalgamated with the Estense in 1892. Both libraries have a well defined role, supporting humanistic and scientific studies respectively. Current holdings of the Biblioteca Estense total 400,371 volumes, 1,642 incunabula and 13,389 MSS volumes, while the University Library contains 71,094 volumes, 5 incunabula and 62 volumes of MSS.

Special Collections and Treasures.   Biblioteca Estense: the MSS collection, with the great foundations of the Este and Campori MSS, is one of the richest in Italy. The Marquis Giuseppe Campori Collection contains 6,082 codices and 100,000 autographs. The musical collection, deriving from the Court of Este, contains a fine collection of madrigals and operas of the 16th and 17th centuries. The map collection, especially rich in 14th century material, contains Cantino's map of America. Treasures include the *Borso Bible,* with miniatures by Taddeo Crivelli and Franco Russi (it has been termed the most illuminated book in the world with more than 2,000 illuminations, heraldic emblems and various ornaments); the *Missal* of Anna Sforza; and *De Sphaera,* written by Giovanni di Sacrobosco for the Duke of Milan. Biblioteca Universitaria: contains the foundation of the S. Carlo Congregation; the 8,000 volume collection bequeathed by Antonio Pisani; and some 1,400 volumes of acts and scientific memoirs of the 'Italian Society of Forty'.

Exhibition Areas.   The permanent exhibition of illuminated MSS is situated on the first floor of the Library (Palazzo dei Musei).

Hours.   Oct.-June: Mon.-Fri. 0900-2000, Sat. 0900-1300.

Biblioteca Estense e Universitaria, Modena

June-Sept.:   Mon.-Fri.   0900-1400,   Sat.   0900-1300. Holidays (experimental) 0900-1300. Closed the week before Easter and for 15 days during the winter; the exact dates differ from year to year.

Transport. The Library can be reached by a bus from the railway station or by taxi. (The Library is on the first floor of the 18th century Palace, dominating the right side of the square of Sant Agostino.)

Parking.   Space is available.

Admission.   *Readers* and *Visitors:* Free of charge.

Information.   At Library staff desks.

Sales.   None.

Guidebooks.   None.

Restaurant/Snack Facilities.   None.

Services.   Lavatories, cloakrooms.

Catalogues.   General author catalogue in three parts: (I) General in 24 MS volumes, (2) General accessions since 1890 on cards, (3) General accessions since 1958 on cards by accepted international cataloguing code. Subject card catalogue of accessions since 1890. Various specialist catalogues.

Classification.   Decimal.

Copying/Photography.   Xerox and microfilm copying facilities are available through Library staff. Private photography is forbidden.

NAPLES
Biblioteca Nazionale Vittorio Emanuele III
Palazzo Reale, I-80132 Napoli
Tel. 407921, 40282, 397093, 391212

History.   The Library was founded in 1734 by Charles III of Bourbon, on the basis of the Farnese Library of Parma, and was later enriched by acquisitions from the Jesuits and from the suppressed monasteries. It was opened to the public in 1804 in the Palazzo degli Studi (now the National Museum) under the title of the Royal Library of Naples, later changed to Bourbon Library (1816) and National Library (1860). In 1922 it moved to the Royal Palace, with the Brancacciana, the Provinciale and various other small Neapolitan libraries. The building, situated near the port, suffered considerable damage during World War II and repairs were not completed until 1949. The Library has copyright privileges, receiving all works published in the province and all others in certain fields. Current holdings include over 1.5 million books,

Biblioteca Nazionale Vittorio Emanuele III, Naples

12,955 volumes of MSS and 4,546 incunabula.

Special Collections and Treasures. The basis of the MSS Collection was formed by the Fondo Farnesiano, to which were added the MS holdings of the suppressed monasteries of S. Giovanni a Carbonara, Abruzzi and Terra di Lavoro, followed in 1860 by material from the convents of Monteoliveto, S. Domenico Maggiore, S. Efremo, S. Lorenzo Maggiore and others. Treasures include an illuminated 15th century *Breviary* of Ferdinand I of Aragon on vellum; a 14th century MS of the *Divine Comedy;* and codices of Aquinas, Ariosto, Tasso, Campanella, Leopardi, Spaventa and Settembrini. Printed items include the collections of incunabula (chiefly of Melchiorre Delfico and the Marquis Taccone); the Tasso Collection; the material relating to Vesuvius and volcanos in general; and the Leopardi, Calabra and Lucana Collections. The Lucchesi-Palli Library, offered to the state in 1888 by Count Eduardo Lucchesi-Palli, contains predominantly dramatic literature and is rich in Neapolitan, Italian and French operas, musical MSS, theatre records and important autographs of theatrical and musical writers. The Office of the Herculanean Papyri was established for the investigation of the papyri discovered in 1752 during the Herculaneum excavations.

Exhibition Areas.   No details available.

Hours.   Mon.-Sat. 0900-1930. Closed Sun. and public hols.

Transport.   By 'Filobus' from the Central Station to the Palazzo Reale (entrance via Vittorio Emanuele).

Parking.   No details available.

Admission. Readers and *Visitors:* Free of charge. Lending facilities are available on application.

Information.   Room adjacent to the Catalogue.

Sales.   None.

Guidebooks.   None.

Restaurant/Snack Facilities.   None.

Services.   Lavatories, lifts and telephones.

Catalogues.   Author and subject catalogues. Various special catalogues.

Classification.   Dewey Decimal (for some sections of the Library).

Copying/Photography.   3 coin-operated photostat machines and another machine are available. Microfilms available through Library staff. Readers and visitors are permitted to take photographs of the inside of

Prayer Book named La Flora (15th century), in the Biblioteca Nazionale Vittorio Emanuele III, Naples

the Library.

PARMA
Biblioteca Palatina
Palazzo della Pilotta, Parma
Tel. 22.217

History. The Library was founded in 1762 by Duke Philip of Bourbon and inaugurated on 11 May 1769. It benefited from material received in 1768 after the expulsion of the Jesuits, and also from its active first Librarian, Father Paolo Maria Paciaudi, the Piedmontese archaeologist and philologist, who died in 1785. Under his successor, Father Ireneo Affó, the growth of the collections slowed down, partly as a result of a reduction in government grants. Matters improved with the succession of Maria Louisa, wife of Napoleon I, and the directorship of Angelo Pezzana. At Pezzana's death in 1862 the Library contained 120,000 volumes. In 1865 the Library was amalgamated with, and took the name of, the Biblioteca Palatina, which had been founded in Lucca by Duke Charles II of Bourbon, transferred to Parma, and comprised some 60,000 volumes and a number of very rare MSS. In 1867 the Library acquired 20,000 volumes from the collections of the suppressed Benedictine, Minorite, Capuchin and Reformed Orders. The Library has continued to receive significant donations in the 20th century and, despite losses during World War II, the collections now include over 600,000 volumes, 3,000 incunabula and 5,000 volumes of MSS.

Special Collections and Treasures. Collections include Professor G.B. de Rossi's Collection of Hebraic codices and printed works, received in 1816; the M. Ortalli Collection of 40,000 prints (1828); the Lope de Vega Collection; Bartolomeo Gamba and Michele Colombo libraries; the medical writings of Rasori and Spallanzani; the letters of Gian Battista Bodoni and his collection of die-stamps and matrices; the Mansueto Tarchini Collection of 20,000 literary, historical, and philosophical works, bequeathed in 1928; the Library of the Military Praesidium of Parma, comprising 15,000 volumes and incorporated by government decree in 1935; the Mario Ferrarini Theatrical Collection, received in 1950; and the Micheli-Mariotti Collection of 25,000 pieces received in 1964. A section of the Library, housed since 1889 in the Royal Conservatory of Music, contains 60,000 volumes and prints and 5,000 musical MSS of the 17th-19th centuries, many extremely rare. Treasures include a Greek *Evangelary,* 11th century MS, with rich Byzantine miniatures on gold backgrounds; a French 15th century MS of Petrarch's *Rime Volgari; S. Ildefonse Toletano,* an 11th century tract of the Bishop of Toledo, written in the style of the Cluny school; a book written in 1265 about the art of illumination, by Abraham ben Judah ibn Hayyīm; Aesop, *Fabulae* (Venice, 1470-71); St. Augustine, *De civitate dei* (Subiaco, 1467); Johannes

Biblioteca Palatina, Parma

Balbus, *Catholicon* (Mainz, 1460); Pliny, *Historia naturalis* (Parma, 1476); Battista Guarini, *Il pastor fido* (Verona, 1737-8), and Gian Battista Bodoni, *Manuale tipgrafico* (Parma, 1818).

Exhibition Areas.   No details available.

Hours.   Mon.-Sat. 0900-1200, 1500-2000. Closed Sun. and public hols.

Transport.   Accessible by bus. (The Library is located on the ground floor of the Palazzo della Pilotta, on the bank of the river near the Ponte Verdi bridge.)

Parking.   In nearby streets.

Admission.   *Readers:* Apply to the Librarian.
Visitors: Free of charge.

Information.   At Library staff desks.

Sales.   No details available.

Guidebooks.   No details available.

Restaurant/Snack Facilities.   No details available.

Services.   No details available.

Catalogues.   Author catalogues in volume and sheaf form. Various subject catalogues in sheaf form.

Classification.   Own.

Copying/Photography.   Apply through Library staff.

ROME
Biblioteca Nazionale Centrale Vittorio Emanuele II
Viale Castro Pretorio, 1-00185 Roma
Tel. (06) 4989

History.   The Library was founded in 1875 and opened to the public on 14 March 1876. The initial collection of 120,000 volumes owed much to the 1873 law suppressing the religious houses in Rome. Material was obtained in this way from the Jesuit College collections and 59 confiscated monastic collections, housed in the former Palace of the Jesuit College (designed by the Florentine architect, Bartalommeo Ammannati in 1582). The Library, originally entitled the 'Biblioteca Nazionale Vittorio Emanuele II', received the added title 'Centrale' in 1885. The 20th century has seen the constant growth of the collections, which have received legal deposit material since 1886 (confirmed and modified in 1911, 1945 and 1949). This growth placed an increasing strain

Biblioteca Nazionale Centrale Vittorio Emanuele II, Rome

on the Library's facilities. Plans were drawn up in the late 1950's for a new building but construction did not begin until 1964 and the new building was not officially inaugurated until 31 January 1975. Located in the 'Castro Pretorio' area, the new building contains 2.5 million volumes and 6,181 MSS, with space for 1,200 readers. While the Biblioteca Nazionale Centrale at Florence (see relevant entry) is the main centre for Italian books, the Rome Library is mainly responsible for the acquisition of foreign material, for bibliographical and reference work and for the National Union Catalogue.

Special Collections and Treasures. Collections include the Dante, Petrarch and Boccaccio Collections; the Dina Collection of 11,500 works of a political nature; the Valenti Collection; the collection of material relating to the history of the Society of Jesus; the Theatre Collection; the Bonghi Collection of philological, historical and philosophical works; the Carlo Valenziani Collection of Chinese and Japanese works; the Roman Topography Collection; the Nallino Collection; and the Giorgio Levi Collection on Duelling comprising 5,000 items. The collection of 1,975 incunabula includes St. Augustine, *De civitate Dei* (1470); F. Petrarch, *Vite dei pontefici ed imperatori romani* (1478); Ptolemy, *Cosmographia* (1486); Euclid, *Elementa geometriae* (1482); Vincent de Beauvais, *Speculum naturale* (1485); A. Cornazano, *Vita della Vergine Maria* (Venice, 1475); Jacopo della Marca, *La Confessione* (Cagli, 1475); and *Italia mia di te quanto mi doglio* (Milan, 1485).

Exhibition Areas. On the right hand side of the entrance hall.

Hours. Mon.-Sat. 0900-1330. Closed Sun., Easter Week, 15 days in Aug. and public hols.

Transport. The Library is near the main railway station and is accessible by public transport.

Parking. Space for 400 cars.

Admission. Readers and *Visitors:* Free of charge. No special requirements.

Information. At the entrance. Specialised information desks in the Catalogue Room and in the reading rooms.

Sales. None.

Guidebooks. In preparation.

Restaurant/Snack Facilities. None at present.

Services. Cloakrooms, lavatories, lifts, smoking lounges, telephone, all on ground floor.

Catalogues. Author, subject and specialised catalogues.

Classification.   Universal Decimal Classification in the reference rooms.

Copying/Photography.   Copying facilities not yet available. No restrictions on private photography, provided no trouble is caused to readers or damage to the Library.

ROME
Biblioteca Angelica
Piazza S. Agostino 8, I-00186 Roma
Tel. 65.58.74

History.   The Library was founded in 1605 as the private library of the Augustinian Fr. Angelo Rocca. In 1614 it became the first library in Rome to be opened to the public. To this foundation collection were added the libraries of Cardinal Passionei (rich In rare editions and MSS), Cardinal Noris and the Vatican librarian, Luca Holstenio. In 1669 at the request of Pope Alexander VII the Library moved to its present spacious building. In 1756 the main hall of the Library was completely restored. In 1873 the Library passed into state control. In 1941 the 10,000 volume collection of the Accademia dell' 'Arcadia' and its archives were joined to the Library, whose holdings now include 170,500 books, 2,664 MSS and 1,108 incunabula.

Special Collections and Treasures.   Treasures include a 9th century Necrology; an 11th century gradual of the Bolognese school; the *Divina Commedia* with chapters by Jacopo Alighieri and Bosone da Gubbio; *De Balneis Puteolanis,* 13th century MS, with miniatures of the Sicilian school; Cicero, *De oratore* (Subiaco, 1465); one of three existing copies of the 1521 *Orlando Furioso;* and Blaeu's terrestial and celestial globes of 1599 and 1603. Collections, apart from those mentioned above, include a Dante Collection and collections of confraternity statutes and ecclesiastical works. The Library also contains 954 opera libretti, the gift of the marchese Nicola Santangelo of Naples.

Exhibition Areas.   None.

Hours.   Daily 0830-1330, Wed. and Fri. also 1630-1930 (except during July, Aug. and Sept.). Closed 1-15 Oct. and public hols.

Transport. Buses 26, 64, 70, 60, 62, 56.

Parking.   No details available.

Admission.   *Readers* and *Visitors:* Free of charge.

Information.   In the Reading Room.

Sales.   None.

Biblioteca Angelica, Rome

Guidebooks. Available.

Restaurant/Snack Facilities. None.

Services. None.

Catalogues. Author, subject, special (e.g. incunabula, MSS, periodicals) catalogues.

Classification. Own (fixed location).

Copying/Photography. Photocopying machine in the Reading Room. The use of cameras within the Library is forbidden.

ROME
Biblioteca Musicale Governativa del Conservatorio di Musica S. Cecilia
Via dei Greci 18, Roma
Tel. 6784-552/12

History. The origins of the Library date back to the end of the 16th century, with the Collection of the Congregation of the Musici di Roma, under the aegis of S. Cecilia, this Congregation being definitively established in 1585. Subsequent centuries saw the dispersal of the collection, until in 1875 it was refounded with the Academy of Music of S. Cecilia. The Library, opened to the public in 1878, was in 1911-12 annexed to the Musical Liceo of S. Cecilia, the actual State Conservatory. Purchases, gifts and the State assisted its growth with the purpose of forming a library specifically for musical studies. The formation of the collection was particularly assisted both by the transfer of material formerly preserved in general libraries in Rome, the Angelica (qv), the Alessandrina and the National Central Library (qv), and also by material from dispersed ecclesiastical archives (especially S. Spirito in Saxia and the Chiesa Nuova). From 1879 the Library received the music printed in Italy through the copyright laws. Since 1912 the Library has developed two main sections, the larger being that of the Government Music Library, the smaller belonging to the National Academy of S. Cecilia. Holdings currently total 178,000 printed items, c.7,000 MSS and c.300 microfilms.

Special Collections and Treasures. The Library is, in itself, a special collection. Particular collections incorporated as complete or partial in it are those of the singing master Alessandro Orsini; Queen Margherita of Savoy; prince Paolo Borghese; the tenor Giovanni M. de Candia (the Fondo Mario, rich in English printed editions and musical manuscripts, particularly vocal works of the 17th and most of the 18th centuries); Silvestri (6,000 libretti of 1670-1775 from Milan and Monza theatres); Manoel Pereira Peixoto d'Almeida da Carvalhaes (21,000 libretti of opera, cantata and oratorio); and V. Carotti (4,000 libretti of 17th-19th centuries).

Treasures include two motets attributed to Palestrina's hand; cantatas thought to be in Alessandro Scarlatti's hand; the complete scores of Bellini's *Norma* and *Beatrice di Tenda;* one sketch of Donizetti's *Favorita* ('Nouvelle Stretta' finale Act IIIe); 3 organ preludes by Mendelssohn; and complete scores of Alfredo Casella's *Serenata,* Bloch's *Macbeth* and a harp concerto by Pizzetti.

Exhibition Areas. There are no permanent exhibition rooms but the public are permitted to visit the reading and catalogue rooms with their 17th century frescoes and portraits.

Hours. Mon.-Sat. 0900-1315 and twice a week 1600-1930. Closed Sun., and public hols., and the whole of Aug.

Transport. The Library can be reached by bus. (The Library shares a building with the Conservatory and Academy.)

Parking. The Library is in the Historic Zone of Rome and private cars are restricted or banned, according to the regulations in force at the time.

Admission. Readers: Are asked for proof of identity and their names, addresses and professions are entered in a register in the Reading Room each time a book is issued. Readers who wish to consult rare books or MSS are asked to sign another register and to state the nature of their research. It is advisable for foreign readers to send in advance a letter of recommendation from an institution or an accredited individual.
Visitors: Must apply in advance and are only admitted to rooms used by the public.

Information. At the charging desk, off the entrance corridor.

Sales. None.

Guidebooks. None.

Restaurant/Snack Facilities. Readers may use the Conservatorio snackbar but this is closed in the holidays when lectures at the Conservatorio have ceased.

Services. Lavatories near the Catalogue and Reading Rooms opened on request, telephones, smoking in the entrance corridor.

Catalogues. Author, subject, systematic and special catalogues.

Classification. Own.

Copying/Photography: Photocopying and microfilms by an outside firm. For details apply to the Library staff.

Private photography is not usually permitted.

VENICE

Biblioteca Nazionale Marciana
San Marco 7, I-30124 Venezia
Tel. 041-25001

History. The Library has its origin in the collection of valuable Greek and Latin MSS presented to Venice by Cardinal Bessarione in 1468 and housed in 1553 in the 'Old Library', designed by Jacopo Sansovino. The 17th and 18th centuries saw steady growth in the collections, in particular with material from confiscated monastic libraries. By the 19th century the Library had become the greatest depository of historical and literary sources of ancient Venice and in 1812 it was transferred to the Palace of the Doges. In 1904 the Library was reorganised and arranged in the Palazzo della Zecca, also designed by Sansovino, which it still occupies, together with the original Library building. Current holdings total 1,201,832 books, 12,719 MSS and 3,303 microfilms. The Library enjoys copyright deposit privileges for works published in Venice.

Special Collections and Treasures. Collections include the Zeno Collection of Italian literary works; the library of the Abbot Jacopo Morelli; the Emilio Teza Collection of 40,000 works of classical and Oriental philology, history, literature and comparative religion; the Girolamo Contarini Collection of 17th century Venetian opera; the Pietro Canal Collection of 1,034 books on music; and the collections on the history and culture of Venice. Treasures of the Library include a 14th century Dante *Divina Commedia* MS; Marco Polo's last will and testament, dated 1323; the famous 16th century Grimani *Breviary* of the Flemish School; Fra Mauro's *Mappamundi* of 1459; many examples of early printing by the Speier brothers (who had the first press in Venice in 1467), Sweynheym, Schöffer, Scotus and Aldus Manutius (the Aldine Collection of the Library is particularly fine); and two editions of the Columbus *Letter* (Rome, 1493 and the unique Venice, 1505).

Exhibition Areas. In the 'Sansovino Hall'.

Hours. Mon.-Sat. 0900-1700, Sun. 0900-1400. Closed for the week before Easter, the first two weeks of Aug., and public hols.

Transport. Vaporetti: lines 1, 2, 4, get off at the San Marco, or S. Zaccaria stop; line 3, get off at the San Marco stop; line 5, get off at the S. Zaccaria stop.

Biblioteca Nazionale Marciana, Venice

Parking. None. (The Library is located just off St. Mark's Square.)

Admission.   Readers: Open to all over 16 years of age. Application should be made to the Administration. *Visitors:* Admission free.

Information.   Apply to the Librarian's secretaries.

Sales.   None.

Guidebooks.   M. Luxoro, *La Biblioteca San Marco* (Florence, 1954), in Italian only, a history rather than a guidebook as such.

Restaurant/Snack Facilities.   None.

Services.   Lavatories adjacent to the Reading Room.

Catalogues.   Author, subject and systematic catalogues. Various specialised catalogues, e.g. MSS, music.

Classification.   Own (Reference Room).

Copying/Photography.   Copying machines on the first floor but they are not for individual use. For microfilms, slides, etc. apply to Library staff. Permission for private photography must be sought from the Administration.

Jamaica

KINGSTON
University of the West Indies Library
Mona, Kingston 7
Tel. Librarian, 92-76661 Ext. 294; Reference Desk, 92-76661 Ext. 296 or 92-70923

History.   The Library was established in 1948 to support the research and teaching needs of what was then called the University College of the West Indies (associated with the University of London). The Library was housed in temporary quarters until 1952, when it moved into its present building. In 1957 an extension was completed, doubling the space for readers and allowing for a stock of 180,000 volumes. In 1962 the College was retitled by Royal Charter the University of the West Indies. The expansion of the University brought about by the establishment of the St. Augustine campus in Trinidad in 1960 and the Cave Hill campus in Barbados in 1963, entailed the provision of supporting libraries on both these campuses. On the Mona campus two new branch libraries, one for medicine and one for natural sciences, were opened in 1973, leaving the Main Library to house the arts and social sciences collections, as well as central, technical, and administrative functions. Current holdings total 678,063 bound volumes, unbound parts and microforms.

Special Collections and Treasures. The major special collection is the West Indies Collection comprising printed, archival and manuscript material pertaining to the West Indies (including the Guyanas and Belize). Other collections include the Queen Mary Collection of finely bound 19th and 20th century memoirs, historical and literary works from the library of the late Queen Mary at Marlborough House, and a collection of 16th-19th century medical works from the library of the late Gerald Ovens, Professor of Surgery at the University College of the West Indies, bibliophile and collector of medical books. These collections are located on the second (or top) floor of the Main Library.

Exhibition Areas. The Main Catalogue Hall contains a number of display cases.

Hours. Main Library: Term and Easter Vacation: Mon.-Fri. 0830-2200, Sat. 0830-1600. Other Vacations: Mon.-Fri. 0830-1700, Sat. 0830-1200. Closed Sun. and public hols.

Transport. Jamaica omnibus service routes 72 and 65 pass the main gate of the University and route 6 passes another entrance.

Parking. Free parking is available.

Admission. Readers: Library is open to all registered undergraduate and post-graduate students at the University and to the academic, research and senior administrative staff. Research workers and members of other universities may be granted library privileges on recommendation by a faculty member and at the discretion of the Librarian.
Visitors: Apply to the Librarian in writing.

Information. Main Issue Desk, Periodicals Office, Government Serials Office and the West Indies and Special Collections Office at the Main Library.

Sales. None.

Guidebooks. Guide to the Library is available free.

Restaurant/Snack Facilities. None in the Library but available on campus.

Services. Lavatories (2nd floor), smoking lounge (1st floor).

Catalogues. Author, subject and classified catalogues. Various special catalogues.

Classification. Library of Congress.

Copying/Photography. Coin-operated photocopying machines at the entrance to the Main Library. Readers may not use their own cameras without permission of the Librarian.

Japan

KYOTO

Kyoto University Library
Yoshida Hommachi, Sakyo-Ku, 606, Kyoto
Tel. Kyoto (075) 751-2111 Ext. 2614

History. Kyoto University Library was established in December 1899, soon after the founding of the University. Early growth largely resulted from donations. The construction of the present building began in 1939 but, because of World War II, the original plan was scaled down and the work left unfinished. Although the interior was completed after 1945, a part of the structure still remains unfinished to this day. The University contained 3,359,842 volumes as of May 1975, with approximately 460,000 of these in the Main University Library. The rest are kept in the libraries of the separate faculties and research institutes, the largest of which are the Faculties of Law, Economics, Letters, Medicine and the Institute of Humanistic Studies.

Special Collections and Treasures. Special collections include the Kikutei Collection of 2,357 volumes, rich in antiquarian music; the Nakanoin Collection of 1,192 volumes containing the autograph MSS of Michikatsu (1558-1610) and Michimura (1588-1653); the Seike Collection of 2,654 volumes consisting chiefly of ancient Chinese editions of Sung, Yüan and Ming; the Kawai Collection of 2,160 volumes on the history of Korea; the Meiji Restoration Collection of 2,442 volumes; and the Konoe Collection of 3,148 volumes, mainly of Chinese classics but including some ancient MSS and Kokatsujiban (printed by movable type) in the Keitcho-Genna period.

Exhibition Areas. Exhibition Room in the basement.

Hours. Mon.-Fri. 0900-1900 (temporarily), Sat. 0900-1700. Closed Sun., national hols., Anniversary of Kyoto University (18 June), 1-5 April, 1-15 Aug. (reading rooms open), 25 Dec.-5 Jan.

Transport. The Library can be reached from Kyoto Station by both bus and streetcar.

Parking. In front of the Library.

Admission. Readers: Free but readers are required to show identification cards.
Visitors: Permission of the Librarian should be obtained in advance.

Information. In the Reference Room.

Kyoto University Library

Sales. None.

Guidebooks. Free guidebook and leaflets may be obtained from the service desks.

Restaurant/Snack Facilities. None.

Services. Lavatories, telephones.

Catalogues. Author and title catalogues for Oriental books. Author only for Western books.

Classification. Own.

Copying/Photography. Copying facilities are provided but these are not available for individual use. Private photography only permitted with the permission of the Librarian.

OSAKA
The Osaka Prefectural Nakanoshima Library
1-27 Nakanoshima, Kita-ku, Osaka
Tel. 06-203-0474

History. The Library was built in 1903, with funds contributed by the late Baron Sumitomo, and opened to the public in 1904. It is, effectively, the oldest public library in Japan, since the 'Osaka Shojakukan', the predecessor of the Library, opened in 1876. A stack room was added to the present building in 1915, two large wings in 1922, a further stack room in 1927, the commerce and industry library in 1956 and a restaurant in 1960. The Library has seven subject departments with 50,000 volumes on open shelves. Current holdings include 595,346 volumes and 2,100 reels of microfilm.

Special Collections and Treasures. Collections include the Sumitomo Collection of 21,872 volumes (science and technology); the Ichikawa Collection of 1,044 volumes (English language); the Saitô Collection of 173 volumes (English literature); the Matsushita Collection of 4,600 volumes (electrical engineering); the Ishizaki Collection of 11,478 volumes (Japanese and Chinese classics); the Satô Collection of 5,083 volumes (Korean classics); and the Asahi-Shimbun Collection of 18,523 volumes (Japanese classics).

Exhibition Areas. Exhibition room on the first floor (Floor 2).

Hours. Mon.-Sat. 0900-2100. Closed Sun. and national hols.

Transport. Subway: nearest station is Yodoyabashi, five minutes' walk from the Library. (The Library is located in Nakanoshima Park in the centre of Osaka City, near the Municipal Offices, the Bank of Japan

Osaka Prefectural
Nakanoshima Library

and the Central Public Hall.)

Parking. No facilities.

Admission. Readers and *Visitors:* No special regulations or costs.

Information. Information Desk on the first floor (Floor 2).

Sales. First floor (Floor 2).

Guidebooks. A pamphlet, in Japanese, free of charge.

Restaurant/Snack Facilities. On the first floor (Floor 2), open 0900-1900.

Services. Cloakrooms, lavatories, smoking lounges, telephones.

Catalogues. Title, author and classified catalogues.

Classification. Osaka Prefectural Library Decimal Classification.

Copying/Photography. Microphotography room, ground floor (Floor 1). Photocopying machine on the first floor (Floor 2). Permission is required from the Director for private photography.

SAPPORO
Hokkaido University Library
Kita-8, Nishi-5, Sapporo
Tel. 011-711-2111

History. The University Library was founded in 1876 as a small library attached to Sapporo Agricultural College, which became the Hokkaido Imperial University in 1918. In September 1947 the University was renamed Hokkaido University. With the development of the University, the University Library has made steady progress in its holdings, function and organisation. The University Library consists of the Central Library and nineteen branch libraries attached to each of the faculties and research institutes. In 1965 the Central Library was moved to a new building with a total floor space of 12,519 sq. metres and a seating capacity of 700. Current holdings of all libraries total just over 1.4 million volumes and 10,000 periodicals.

Special Collections and Treasures. Collections include the Uchimura Memorial Library on Christianity; the Nitobe Memorial Library, which is comprised mainly of books relating to agricultural and economic problems in Europe of the late 19th and early 20th centuries; the Northern Areas Collection, which contains books, maps, MSS, records, pictures and portraits concerning

Hokkaido University Library

Hokkaido and North Pacific Coast areas; and the Slavonic Collection which is considered the best in Japan.

Exhibition Areas. General exhibition room and exhibition room for the 'University Memorial Materials'.

Hours. Mon.-Fri. 0830-2100, Sat. 0830-1500. Closed Sun. and public hols.

Transport. 10 minutes' walk from Sapporo Railway Station. 5 minutes' walk from the Kita 12-jo Subway station.

Parking. No details available.

Admission. *Readers:* The Library is open to all members of Hokkaido University. Others wishing to use the Library must obtain permission from the Director and must explain the object of their research to the Circulation Librarian.
Visitors: Apply to the Director.

Information. General Affairs Section (1F), Open-shelf Room (2F), General Reading Room (3F), Reference Room (4F).

Sales. None.

Guidebooks. *Riyo no Shiori* (Guide to use of the Library), in Japanese, free of charge.

Restaurant/Snack Facilities. None in the Library but there are restaurants in the vicinity.

Services. Cloakrooms on the 2nd and 4th floors. Lavatories on each floor. Lift in south-east corner of the Library building. Smoking lounges on the 2nd and 3rd floors. Telephone on the 1st floor.

Catalogues. Author, classified and title catalogues.

Classification. Dewey (16th edition).

Copying/Photography. The photoduplication room is on the 1st floor. No restrictions on private photography.

TENRI
Tenri Central Library
1050 Samanouchi-cho, Tenri City, Nara 632
Tel. 07436-3-1511, extn. 6750

History. The Library was opened in late 1926 on the third floor of the newly established Tenri Foreign Language School, which was then principally aimed at the education of overseas missions of the Tenrikyō Mother Church. The initial stock totalled 26,000 volumes, derived from the libraries of several schools and offices belonging to the Church and the private library of the Reverend Shōzen Nakayama. On 18 October 1930 a new Library building was opened, which combined the functions of school, research and public libraries. In 1947 the Tenri Foreign Language School became Tenri University and the Library's functions changed accordingly. As the number of acquisitions soon exceeded the capacity of the 1930 building, in July 1963 an extension was completed providing a floor space of 10,739 square metres. Current holdings total 1.1 million items.

Special Collections and Treasures. Collections include the Wataya Bunko, a collection of *Renga* and *Haikai* books; the Yoshida Bunko, 7,000 titles, most of which were formerly in the household of Yoshida, head of a once flourishing sect of Shintoism in Kyoto; the Yasui Bunko of 60,000 items pertaining to regional history and geography of Yamato Province, modern Nara Prefecture. Individual treasures include Jesuit Mission printings in Japan, *Kirishitan-ban* including *Contemptus mundi* (1610); a 14th century Japanese manuscript of *Wamyosho,* a dictionary of Japanese common and proper names; the original 17th century manuscript of the diary *Meigetsu-ki* of the courtier poet and politician, Fujiwara no Teika; and, from Edo literature, the original edition of Bashō's *Kai-ōi* (1782) and Saikakū's *Jichū Hyaku-in Emaki,* illustrated and annotated by the author (1729).

Exhibition Areas. Room 13B on the second floor.

Hours. April-Oct.: Tues.-Sat. 0900-1800, Sun.-Mon. 0900-1600. Nov.-Mar.: Tues.-Sat. 0900-1700, Sun.-Mon. 0900-1600. Closed 27 Dec.-4 Jan., 26 Jan., 25-31 Mar., 18, 29 April, 3 May, 1-15 Aug., 18, 26 Oct., 3 Nov., last day of every month except Mar. and Dec.

Transport. By air or national railway (Tokaido Main Line or Shinkansen) and Kinki Nippon Railway, from Tokyo via Kyoto.

Parking. Space available.

Admission. Readers: Open to anyone over 15 years old. Admission free.
Visitors: Must apply in advance.

Information. In Reading Rooms.

Sales. At the General Office. Tenri Central Library publications on sale.

Guidebooks. In English and Japanese. Free of charge, except for postage.

Restaurant/Snack Facilities. None for readers/visitors.

Services. Cloakrooms, lavatories, smoking lounges (on 1st and 2nd floors).

Tenri Central Library

Catalogues. Card and book catalogues. The book catalogues are all published in the Tenri Central Library series. The card catalogues consist of classified and dictionary catalogues.

Classification. Nippon Decimal Classification, 2nd ed.

Copying/Photography. There is a copying service but machines are not available for individual use. The Photographic Department is on the first floor. Private photography prohibited within the Library.

TOKYO

National Diet Library
10-1, 1-chome, Nagata-cho, Chiyoda-ku, Tokyo
Tel. 03 (581) 2331

History. The character of the Japanese Diet went through a radical transformation following World War II to adjust itself to the democratic principles expounded in the new Japanese constitution. This led to the realisation that the establishment of a parliamentary library with an effective research function was of paramount importance for the deliberation of State affairs by Diet members. A National Diet Library Law of 9 February 1948 resulted in the new National Diet Library, opened on 5 June 1948, with a collection of 215,000 volumes. The Library is thus a product of post-war Japan, though it has in its background the long history and tradition of the former Imperial (Ueno) Library, established in 1872, and the libraries formerly attached to both Houses of the Diet. The Library was initially housed in the Akasaka Detached Palace (now remodelled as the State Guesthouse) until it moved in 1961 on completion of Phase 1 of its new building. Phase 2 was completed in 1968. Legal deposit privileges and extensive purchasing have resulted in a current stock of 2,957,594 volumes, 52,750 reels of microfilm, 27,495 current periodicals, 131,508 doctoral theses and 658,077 reports on microcard, fiche or print, as at the end of March 1975.

Special Collections and Treasures. Of the collections, special mention must be made of the 170,000 items on the modern history of Japan, including documents relating to Post-Restoration statesmen such as Sanjo Sanetomi, Iwakura Tomomi, Yamagata Aritomo, Inoue Kaoru, Ito Hirobumi etc. The collection of classic Chinese books has incorporated in it the collections of the former Ueno Library, the Fujiyama Collection and the Chinese Collections of the former Toa Kenkyujo. Other collections include the Kameda Bunko and the Okada Bunko on Japanese language and literature; the Harima Bunko of Russian Czarist books; the Shinjo Bunko on oriental astronomy; and a collection of manuscript records of the Tokugawa Shogunate Government.

National Diet Library, Tokyo

Exhibition Areas. None.

Hours. General Reading Room open Mon.-Sat. 0930-1700. The Library is closed Sun. and the last day of each month, national hols., and during the New Year season from 28 Dec. to 4 Jan.

Transport. Subway: station Nagata-cho, is in front of the National Diet building. (The Library is situated just north of the Diet building.)

Parking. The Library has car-parks for readers and visitors.

Admission. Readers: University students and anyone over 20 years of age may use the Library. Registration takes place at the readers' entrance.
Visitors: No particular regulations. Open to visitors Mon.-Sat. 0930-1700.

Information. The Reference Counter is in the Central Catalogue Hall on the 2nd floor.

Sales. Shop in the basement.

Guidebooks. The National Diet Library/La Bibliothèque nationale de la Diète (in English and French).

Restaurant/Snack Facilities. Dining room (on the 6th floor) open 1130-1800. Snacks (on the 3rd floor) 0930-1700.

Services. Typing room, 2nd floor. Photographic studio for the use of personal cameras, 2nd floor. Lifts at each corner of the building. Smoking lounges around the Central Catalogue Hall on the 2nd floor. Public telephones at one corner of the lounge on the 2nd floor. Locker room for readers by the readers' entrance on the 2nd floor.

Catalogues. The Library's public card catalogue consists of author-title, subject and classified catalogues. The Public Catalogue Hall is on the 2nd floor.

Classification. The Library originally used the Nippon Decimal Classification for Japanese and Chinese books and Dewey for books in European languages. In 1969 the National Diet Library Classification was introduced, and continues to be used.

Copying/Photography. Microfilming and photocopying service. The Photo-duplication laboratory is housed on the 1st floor. Readers may also arrange to use their own cameras to photograph library materials.

TOKYO
The Toyo Bunko
Honkomagome 2-chome, 28-21, Bunko Tokyo 113
Tel. 03-942-0121

History. The Toyo Bunko, as its name implies, is a library specialising in Oriental studies. It was established in 1917 under the name of Morrison Bunko (Morrison Library), on the basis of the Asiatic library established by G.E. Morrison (1862-1920) and purchased by Hisaya Iwasaki (1865-1955). Iwasaki, a leading industrialist of 20th century Japan, widened the scope of the collection to cover all of Asia and incorporated it, in 1924, into a foundation called the Toyo Bunko, which is still located at its original site. After World War II there was a period of difficulty but in 1948 the National Diet Library (see preceding entry) incorporated the Toyo Bunko as a branch and reopened it to the public. In 1961, at the request of UNESCO, the Centre for East Asian Cultural Studies was added to the Toyo Bunko. Today its holdings total 600,000 books, 90 manuscripts and about 3,000 reels of microfilm.

Special Collections and Treasures. Apart from the Morrison Library special collections include the Maema Library on Korea; the Iwasaki Library of 23,700 Japanese and Chinese books, including *Gozan* works, works on Edo literature, on drama and geography; the Fujii Library of Japanese books on Western medicine; the Umehara Sueji Collection on the archaeology of Scythia, China, Korea and Japan; the Kawaguchi Library of Tibetan books; the Nagata Library of Vietnamese books; various Thai language books donated by Yoshihisa Matsuda; Japanese, Chinese and Western books from the library of Junnosuke Inoue; the Masunosoke Odagiri Library; and the Modern Chinese History Collection.

Exhibition Areas. An annual exhibition is based on the rare and specialised items in the Toyo Bunko.

Hours. Mon.-Sat. 0900-1630 (closed 1200-1230). Closed on Sun., Thurs. afternoons, the last day of each month, Foundation Day (19 Nov.) and the last five and first four days of the year.

Transport. The Library is about eight minutes' walk from Komagome Station, Yamate Line (Circular Line), Japan National Railways. Five minutes' walk from Sengoku Station, Rokugosen Line (6th Line), Tokyo Municipal Subway. One minute's walk from Kamifujimae bus stop.

Parking. Available near Library.

Admission. Readers: A reader's permit must be obtained by filling in an application form.
Visitors: The Library is open to the public.

The Toyo Bunko, Tokyo

Information. In Reading Room (1st floor).

Sales. Library publications available from the Kinokuniya Book Store, 17-7 Shinjuku 3-chome, Shinjuku, Tokyo.

Guidebooks. Leaflet, *A Guide to the Toyo Bunko,* in English.

Restaurant/Snack Facilities. None.

Services. Lavatories in the basement, lifts, research rooms (3rd floor), occasional free lectures on Tuesdays (1800-2000) in May or June and Oct. or Nov. of each year.

Catalogues. Various Library catalogues have been published.

Classification. Own.

Copying/Photography. Microfilming and electrostatic copying service. Requests to the staff in the Reading Room. Permission must be obtained for private photography.

TOKYO
University of Tokyo Library
3-1 Hongo 7-chome, Bunkyo-ku, Tokyo 113
Tel. 03 812-2111

History. Tokyo University was established in 1877, with the various faculties setting up their own libraries. The University Library was not founded until 1887, taking the name Tokyo Imperial University Library. The first separate Library building was constructed in 1892 and extended in 1907. By 1923 the collections totalled 800,000 volumes, mainly in the humanities, but the great earthquake of 1 September 1923 (the Kanto Earthquake) and subsequent fire destroyed 750,000 volumes and badly damaged the Library. Reconstruction began almost immediately as a result of numerous donations, notably from John D. Rockefeller, who contributed 4 million yen. The new Library was dedicated in December 1928 and by 1936 its book stock had grown to 1,038,400 volumes. The Library was not damaged during World War II, after which its name reverted to Tokyo University Library. In 1961 the Rockefeller Foundation gave 84 million yen towards the modernisation of the General Library, in accordance with the Reform Project planned by the late Director, Professor Hideo Kishimoto. Current holdings total 3,950,000 items housed in the General Library, 10 Faculty libraries and 13 Institute libraries. The General Library functions as the central bureau for co-ordinating all of the library activities on campus and contains nearly 800,000 volumes.

University of Tokyo Library

Special Collections and Treasures. Collections include

the Agawa Collection on Chinese philosophy and literature (5,000 volumes); the Chiju, Shachiku and Chikurei Collections of books on *haiku* (5,000 volumes in all); the Sir Charles Eliot Collection mainly on Oriental Studies, Buddhism, etc. (6,200 volumes); the Hozumi Collection, consisting of various editions and MSS of the *Goseibai-shikimoku* (1,053 volumes); the Koreaki Kamei Collection of books on European Fine Arts (2,000 volumes); the Watanabe Katei Collection of 1,800 volumes of Japanese fiction of the Edo period; the Edward S. Morse Collection of 12,000 volumes, mainly in the natural sciences; the Nanki Collection of 96,000 volumes given by Tokugawa Yorimichi (the nucleus of this collection was the library of the feudal lords of Kii Province — the books are mainly in the field of Japanese history and literature); the Ogai Collection comprising 16,000 volumes in Chinese and Japanese, mostly in biography and history, and 3,000 foreign works, mainly German literature of the 19th century; and the Seishū Collection comprising Japanese novels of the Edo period and Chinese classics (25,000 volumes). Departmental Collections include the Collection of Newspapers and Magazines of the Meiji Era (Faculty of Law); the Lafcadio Hearn Collection (Faculty of Letters); the Books for Persian Studies (Faculty of Letters); and the Adam Smith Collection (Faculty of Economics).

Exhibition Areas.   Exhibition Hall on 3rd floor.

Hours.   Mon.-Fri. 0830-2130, Sat. 0830-1900. Open on Sun. during examination periods (21 July-31 Aug.: Mon.-Fri. 0830-1700, Sat. 0830-1200). Closed Sun., 28 Dec.-5 Jan. and public hols.

Transport.   Public transport to the University campus, situated in Hongo, Bunkyo-ku, Tokyo.

Parking.   In front of the Library.

Admission.   Readers: Members of the University and visiting research workers may use the Library as readers.

Visitors: Apply to the Librarian.

Information.   Circulation Desk.

Sales.   None.

Guidebooks.   Brochures in English and Japanese.

Restaurant/Snack Facilities.   None.

Services.   Cloakrooms, seminar rooms, lifts.

Catalogues.   Author and classified card catalogues of the General Library and University Union Catalogue housed on main floor.

Classification.   Own.

Copying/Photography. Apply to photo-reproduction room on main floor.

Kenya

NAIROBI
University of Nairobi Library
PO Box 30197, Nairobi
Tel. Nairobi 34244

History. The Library's history began in 1956, when it was the Library of the Royal Technical College of East Africa serving only 215 students. In 1961 the College had its name changed to the Royal College. In 1963 the University of East Africa was formed with the Royal College, now re-named University College, Nairobi, becoming one of the constituent colleges. In 1970 the College became the University of Nairobi. The development of the University Library system has kept pace with the growth of the University, from a small library serving a junior technical college to a system of libraries comprising the Main Library and 6 branch libraries in the Main University, as well as other campuses. Current holdings total 180,000 volumes and 2,000 periodicals, mainly housed in the Gandhi Library, completed in 1962.

Special Collections and Treasures. The Library is a legal depository for books, periodicals and newspapers published in Kenya, although not including government publications. These constitute the core of the East African Collection, housed on the 4th floor, which also includes the publications of other East African governments and library material published elsewhere on East Africa. The Library is also a depository for material issued by the United Nations and the Food and Agricultural Organisation and this material is housed, as the United Nations Collection, under closed access on the 4th floor. The Law Collection is located on the 5th floor of the Library.

Exhibition Areas. None.

Hours. Term: (July-March) Mon.-Fri. 0800-2200, Sat. 0800-1700. Vacation: (April-June) Mon.-Fri. 0800-1700, Sat. 0800-1200. Closed Sun. and public hols.

Transport. Bus stops near the University. (The main campus occupies a site of 18 acres near the centre of Nairobi.)

Parking. Parking facilities on campus.

Admission. *Readers:* Staff and students of University

University of Nairobi. Gandhi Library

admitted free. Approved researchers Kshs. 20/- per annum. Proof of identity must be provided.
Visitors: Free.

Information. Near the entrance to the Library.

Sales. None.

Guidebooks. University of Nairobi, *Guide to University Library Services,* free, in English.

Restaurant/Snack Facilities. None.

Services. Cloakroom at the entrance, lavatories on each floor, study carrels.

Catalogues. Author/title and subject catalogues.

Classification. Library of Congress.

Copying/Photography. Copying facilities available only through Library staff. Permission must be sought for private photography.

Lebanon

BEIRUT

Bibliothèque Nationale du Liban
à la place de l' Étoile, Imm. du Parlement, Beirut
Tel. 256160/256161

History. In 1919 the Lebanese scholar Elviconte Philippe Di Trazi founded a library at his home. In 1922 Di Trazi offered it to the Government (Franco-Lebanese) as a gift. This was accepted by the Ministry of Education and located in the Haouz El Saatieh district. In 1937 the Library moved to its present site in a government building in the centre of Beirut. Today the Library, which has legal deposit privileges, has a total of 300,000 books, 2,000 MSS and 500 microforms.

Special Collections and Treasures. Collections focus on the history of Lebanon and neighbouring countries. The Library has an important collection of Persian and Arabic MSS.

Exhibition Areas. Exhibition Room for manuscripts.

Hours. Daily 0800-2000.

Transport. The Library is in the centre of Beirut and accessible by public transport.

Parking. No facilities.

Admission.   Readers and *Visitors:* Free of charge.

Information.   At the staff desks.

Sales.   None.

Guidebooks.   Guide to the manuscripts only (in Arabic), available free.

Restaurant/Snack Facilities.   None, but many eating places nearby.

Services.   Cloakroom, lavatory, lift, smoking room.

Catalogues.   Title, author, topographical subject catalogues and a catalogue of legal deposit books.

Classification.   Dewey.

Copying/Photography.   A photocopying machine may be used by readers, with the Director's permission. Cameras may be used within the Library.

BEIRUT
Nami C. Jafet Memorial Library
American University of Beirut, Beirut
Tel. 340740, extn. 2205

History.   The Library was founded in 1866 at the same time as the University (then named the Syrian Protestant College). By 1882 it contained 2,300 volumes and by 1903 15,000 volumes. In 1920 the University adopted its present name. In 1951, at which time total collections comprised 73,000 volumes, a new Central Library was opened, and named the Nami C. Jafet Memorial Library, in honour of the Lebanese-Brazilian family which had donated the money to build it. With a capacity of about 250,000 volumes this seemed adequate; but the increase in student numbers and teaching programmes necessitated a reconstruction in 1959, when the building was enlarged to hold about 400,000 volumes. There are separate Medical, Engineering, Science and Agriculture libraries. Civil disorder in the Lebanon in the second half of 1975 led to the temporary closure of the University. Total holdings currently number 362,460 volumes, 2,000 microforms and 2,206 MSS.

Special Collections and Treasures.   Treasures include the first Vulgate Bible printed in Arabic (1671), the first publications of the Dilletanti Society, and 1,250 Arabic MSS.

Exhibition Areas.   An Exhibition Gallery is located on the first floor between the Main Reading Room and the Periodicals Reading Room. It is used for rotating exhibits sponsored by the Library and the Fine Arts Department.

Nami C. Jafet Memorial Library, Beirut

New Testament, manuscript in Syriac by the monk John (probably between AD 700 and 900), in the American University Library, Beirut. Detail

Hours. Reference and Reserve Reading Rooms: Sun. 1400-2200, Mon.-Fri. 0800-2300, Sat. 0800-1700. Opening times vary during summer sessions and vacations.

Transport. Bus route number 1 to the 'University' bus stop, which is at the main gate of the University.

Parking. Facilities are limited but because of its central location the Library is easily accessible.

Admission. Readers: University members and members of the American Community School are eligible to use the Library. Others may apply to the University Librarian. *Visitors:* Apply to the Librarian.

Information. In the lobby at the main entrance to the Library.

Sales. None.

Guidebooks. The *Library Handbook* is provided free to all Library users.

Restaurant/Snack Facilities. None.

Services. Lavatories on the ground floor and third floor, lift, telephones.

Catalogues. Public card catalogue, which contains a union catalogue of the books and journals in the Jafet, Engineering and Architecture, Science and Agriculture and AREC (Farm) Libraries. The catalogue is divided into two parts: author/title, and subject.

Classification. Dewey.

Copying/Photography. In Room 301. No special regulations on private photography.

Luxembourg

LUXEMBOURG
Bibliothèque nationale du Grand-Duché de Luxembourg
37 boulevard F.D. Roosevelt, Luxembourg
Tel. 2-62-55

History. The first public library in Luxembourg was created by decrees of 15 April and 29 June 1798. Its stock of 9,273 printed volumes and 244 MSS came from the libraries of the former Estates of the country and the Provincial Council, together with those formerly belonging to the Jesuit order, which had been suppressed in 1773, and those of the abbeys of Echternach, Orval, Munster and St. Hubert. The Library

Bibliothèque nationale, Luxembourg

was annexed to the École centrale, which was itself suppressed in 1802, coming under the control of the municipality. The reorganisation of secondary education in 1848 led to the amalgamation of the Library with that of the Athenaeum Library which had been founded in 1837. In 1899 it was re-titled the Bibliothèque nationale and today contains 500,000 books and 524 manuscripts.

Special Collections and Treasures. The Library's most important special collection is that devoted to the history and culture of Luxembourg ('Luxemburgensia'). The Library also possesses 136 incunabula and 524 MSS, dating from the 9th-20th centuries. These latter include the *Dialogues* of St. Gregory (9th century); Pliny's *Natural History* (11th century); and two 15th-century *Books of Hours.*

Exhibition Areas. Exhibition Room on the first floor of the Library.

Hours. Reading Room: Tues.-Fri. 1400-1900, Sat. 0900-1200. Closed Sun. and public hols.

Transport. The Library is situated in the centre of the town and can be reached by several bus services.

Parking. In the vicinity of the Library.

Admission. *Readers:* Registration by showing suitable identification. Minimum age 18.
Visitors: May use all Library facilities, except borrowing.

Information. At the entrance.

Sales. None.

Guidebooks. Temporary guidebook available.

Restaurant/Snack Facilities. None.

Services. Cloakroom, lavatories, smoking lounges, telephones.

Catalogues. Alphabetical author and subject catalogues for both the general and Luxembourg collections.

Classification. Own.

Copying/Photography. Copying service only available through Library staff. Permission must be obtained for private photography.

Malta

VALLETTA
Royal Malta Library
36 Old Treasury Street, Valletta
Tel. Central 26585

History. The Royal Malta Library may be considered to owe its origin to a decision taken on 24 May 1555, by a General Chapter of the Order of St. John, whereby the Chapter decreed the establishment of a Library for the use of the Conventual Chaplains. At this time the seat of the Order was at Birgu. The General Chapter passed a statute on 7 May 1612, which forbade the sale of books belonging to deceased knights, and in 1650 the Library was established in the vestry of the conventual church. In 1750 the Library became public and in the second half of the 18th century received several large collections. The present building was built in the last decade of the 18th century but was not officially opened until 4 June 1812. Since then several eminent Maltese citizens have bequeathed, or donated, important collections to the Library, which was given its present designation in 1936 and fulfils the role of the National Library of Malta. Holdings currently total 335,000 volumes and 8,930 MSS.

Special Collections and Treasures. The Archives of the Order of St. John and those of the Università (the medieval autonomous commune) are housed on the first floor of the Library. Collections include those of Cardinal Gioacchino Portocarrero, donated in 1763; and the libraries of the Hospitaller Order of St. Antoine of Vienne and of the Sacred Infirmary. The Library has fine examples of fore-edge paintings; a *Life of St. Anthony the Abbot* with 200 paintings in grisaille by Master Fornier of Avignon (1426); and a collection of incunabula.

Exhibition Areas. Exhibits are located in showcases in the Main Reading Room.

Hours. 1 Oct.-15 June: Mon., Tues., Thurs., Fri. 0815-1300, 1345-1745; Sat. 0815-1315. 16 June-30 Sept.: Mon., Tues., Thurs., Fri. and Sat. 0815-1315. Closed Wed., Sun. and public hols.

Transport. The Library is in the centre of Valletta near the Bus Terminus.

Parking. Parking facilities nearby.

Admission. Readers and *Visitors:* The Library is open, free of charge, to all readers and bona fide research workers.

Royal Malta Library, Valletta

Information.   Main Reading Room.

Sales.   None.

Guidebooks.   None.

Restaurant/Snack Facilities.   No facilities on the Library premises but there are several eating places nearby.

Services.   Lavatories (opened on request).

Catalogues.   Author and subject catalogues of printed works. Catalogues of MSS collections.

Classification.   Books acquired before 1955 are available by call mark; those acquired since are Dewey classified.

Copying/Photography.   Photocopies of Library material can be made on application to the Government Department of Information. Private photography requires prior permission of the Director.

Mexico

MEXICO CITY
Biblioteca Nacional de México
República de El Salvador 70, México 1, D.F.
Tel. 5-12-93-16; 5-10-31-61; 5-12-17-71

History.   After various unsuccessful attempts in 1833, 1856 and 1857, the last suppressing the University of Mexico and allocating its building and books to the new foundation, the National Library of Mexico was established by a Presidential decree of 1867. The basic collection consisted of 10,600 volumes from the University and 80,000 volumes from the suppressed religious orders. The Library was opened in 1861, only to be closed during the period of European intervention in Mexico. After the fall of Maximilian and the restoration of the rule of Juárez in 1867, the Library was reopened in the modernised chu.ch of San Agustín. The formal opening took place on 2 April 1884. Systematic organisation of the collections owed much to the administration of José María Vigil from 1880-1909. Since 1929 the Library has fallen under the administration of the National University (UNAM).   It was intended at one time that the Library should move out to the University campus to become the central library of the University (see next entry), but this change has not been realised. Since February 1958, Mexican publishers have been required to deposit in the National and Congressional Libraries two copies of every book published in Mexico. Current holdings total 1.2 million books, over 100,000 MSS and 200 incunabula.

Biblioteca Nacional de México

Special Collections and Treasures. Collections include the José María Lafragua Collection, an extensive pamphlet collection dating from the end of the 18th century through the first half of the 19th; the Antonio Mier y Celis Collection of 9,350 volumes; the Guillermo Prieto Collection of 4,931 volumes; the Andrés Clemente Vázquez Collection of 5,880 volumes, strong on chess; the Angel Núñez Ortega Collection with 1,170 foreign works on Mexican affairs, mostly concerned with Maximilian; the Mexican Revolution Collection; the papers of Benito Juárez; the Madero Papers; the Archivo Franciscano; the Agustín Rivera Collection of 1,400 volumes; and the María Enriqueta Collection of 506 works, reflecting the work of the Mexican writer and poetess. The Hermeroteca Nacional (El Carmen 31, Mexico 1, D.F.) — the National Periodical Library — contains a comprehensive collection of early and current Mexican periodicals and newspapers. Special collections include a library of Mexican journalism and a file of some 44,000 portraits and photographs of important Mexicans.

Exhibition Areas. Various areas throughout the Library.

Hours. Daily 0900-2200. Closed public hols.

Transport. The Library is situated on Isabel la Católica and República de El Salvador, in the centre of Mexico City. It is within walking distance of bus and metro stops.

Parking. In the surrounding streets.

Admission. Readers: Free. Only accredited researchers, with proof of identification, can use the Rare Books and Manuscript Departments.
Visitors: Free. Guided tours on certain days.

Information. Library staff desks.

Sales. None.

Guidebooks. Reader's guide in Spanish, free of charge. A fuller guide to the Library in preparation.

Restaurant/Snack Facilities. Available on Library premises.

Services. Lavatories, telephones.

Catalogues. Author and subject catalogues. Various special catalogues.

Classification. Dewey.

Copying/Photography. Microfilm and photocopies through Library staff. Private photography only with the permission of section heads.

MEXICO CITY
Biblioteca Central, Entrepiso
Ciudad Universitaria, Villa Obregón, México 20, D.F.
Tel. 548-65-00, ext. 168 (Director); ext. 360 (Public Services)

History. The University of Mexico was dedicated on 25 January 1553 and classes began on 3 June, under both the legal and financial patronage of the Spanish Crown. The Real y Pontifical Universidad de México continued until 1857, when it was suppressed, although to all intents and purposes it had ceased to function as a centre for higher studies in 1810, with the beginning of the War of Independence. It was reopened on 22 September 1910 as the Universidad Nacional de México. The present Library was founded in 1924. In 1929 the Federal Government granted autonomy to the University, and control of the National Library (see preceding entry) passed to the University from the Department of Public Instruction. At one time it was intended that the National Library should occupy the spectacular library building, designed by Juan O'Gorman, Gustavo Saavedra and Juan Martínez de Velasco, on the new University campus. The University Library's exterior walls are covered in mosaics representing the two cultures of Mexico, aboriginal and Spanish. It has space for 1.5 million books. Current holdings total over 300,000 volumes and 12,451 periodicals

Special Collections and Treasures. The Archivo Histórico on the 8th floor (ext. 373. Hours: Mon.-Fri. 0900-1400) contains the Fondo Universidad, documents dating from the 16th century; the Fondo Escuela Nacional Preparatoria, 1,340 volumes (1829-1958); the Fondo Gildardo Magaña, particularly strong on the *zapatistas;* the Fondo Conflicto Religioso, relating to the *cristero* conflict in Mexico in the 20th century; the Fondo Ezequiel A. Chávez; the Jesús Díaz de León Collection; the Alfonso Cornejo Franco Collection on the history of science in Mexico; the Tomás Gurza Collection; the Luján Collection; and the Carlos Basave y del Castillo Negrete Collection (items on Mexican history, 1546-1949).

Exhibition Areas. Exhibition Room.

Hours. Mon.-Fri. 0715-2000. Closed Sat. and Sun. and public hols.

Transport. The University campus is located about 11 miles south of the centre of the city, along Avenida Insurgentes. By bus: buses to the University run along Juárez from the Alameda, then turn into Insurgentes. Some buses are labelled 'Ciudad Universitaria'; others are marked 'San Angel' but usually have a card in the window reading 'CU'. Taxis from downtown will go to the University. By car: along Insurgentes and then take Ciudad Universitaria underpass just after the San Jeronimo turn.

Biblioteca Central, Universidad de México. South and east walls with mural by Juan O'Gorman

Parking. Available on campus, e.g. the far side of the Science Museum.

Admission. Readers: Members of the University and all serious researchers. Members of the University, serious researchers and students in higher education are permitted to read in the reading rooms.
Visitors: Free of charge.

Information. In entrance hall and in the Reading Rooms (first two floors).

Sales. None.

Guidebooks. None.

Restaurant/Snack Facilities. None in the Library but available on campus.

Services. Cloakrooms, lavatories, lifts, telephones (on each floor).

Catalogues. Dictionary Catalogue 1. Central Library Catalogue, 2. Union Catalogue of Branch Libraries of University.

Classification. Library of Congress classification.

Copying/Photography. Microfilm copying available through Library staff. Xerox copying in the Reading Room for readers.

MEXICO CITY
Archivos Históricos y Bibliotecas, Instituto Nacional de Antropología e Historia
Calzada M. Gandhi y Paseo de la Reforma, México 5, D.F.
Tel. 533-59-60, Ext. 15

Museo Nacional de Antropología

History. In 1823 Lucas Alamán, the historian and politician, founded the Museum of Antiquities and Natural History, which in 1825 was renamed the National Museum. Alamán provided the nucleus of the Library by sending the Arthur Wade Collection in 1831 to the Museum Curator, Isidro Ignacio Icaza. The collections grew slowly and it was not until the 1860s that the Library increased its holdings to over 1,000 volumes, as a result of acquisitions from the University and sequestrated religious houses. The Library received its orientation towards the anthropological sciences from 1880 onwards, when Gumersindo Mendoza was Director of the Museum and then subsequently by Francisco del Paso y Troncoso and José María de Agreda y Sánchez. By 1900 the collection totalled 5,000 volumes. In 1919 the Museum was renamed the National Museum of Archaeology, History and Ethnography. In 1939 it affiliated with the new founded Institute of Anthropology and History and became the National Museum of Anthropology. It remained housed in the old Mint (Casa de la Moneda) until late 1964, when it occupied its present building of great architectural distinction, designed by Luis Ramírez Vázquez. The Library which occupies the first floor has space for ½ million books. Holdings currently total 300,000 volumes and documents, covering in particular Mexican history and anthropology.

Special Collections and Treasures. Collections include the libraries of Vicente Lira; Pablo González Casanova, especially important for linguistics; Federico Gómez de Orozco, in history; Luis González Obregón, particularly rich in Mexican Independence pamphlets; Luis Alvarez y Alvarez de la Cadena; Luis Gutiérrez Cañedo; Alfonso Caso, a most valuable collection in Mexican anthropology; and the Paso y Troncoso Collection. Other collections relate to the early history of Mexico; the fight for emancipation; the Jesuits in Mexico (1526-1913); the Hospital Real de Naturales (118 volumes); a set of MSS concerning the Inquisition assembled by Vicente Riva Palacio; and 14 million microfilmed MSS in the *Fondo de Microfilm.*

Exhibition Areas. Vestibule and first floor of the Museum.

Hours. Mon.-Fri. 0900-1400, 1600-2100, Sat. 0900-1400. Closed Sun. and public hols.

Transport. By bus, metro or *pesero* to the Museum of Anthropology, which is situated on the right hand side of the Paseo de la Reforma, about half a mile past the Diana Statute, opposite Chapultepec Park Zoo. The Library is on the first floor above the Vestibule.

Parking. Museum Car Park.

Admission. Readers: Open to all serious researchers. *Visitors:* Apply to the Librarian.

Information. First floor desk.

Sales. In Museum sales area.

Guidebooks. None.

Restaurant/Snack Facilities. The indoor/outdoor restaurant of the Museum.

Services. Lavatories, cloakrooms off the entrance hall (ground floor).

Catalogues. Author and subject card catalogues. Published catalogues by G.K. Hall & Co.

Classification. Own.

Copying/Photography. Most forms of copying available

through Library staff. Apply to the Librarian for private photography.

Mongolian People's Republic

ULAN BATOR
State Public Library of the Mongolian People's Republic
Lenin Prospekt, Ulan-Bator
Tel. 22-3-96 (for the official on duty)

History. The Library was founded on 19 November 1921 with a stock of 2,000 books as part of the Chamber of Books and Manuscripts (the present Academy of Sciences). The Library has since grown to become the largest in the People's Republic, with the MPR Academy of Sciences exercising overall authority. It has also become the centre for library science, bibliographic and scientific-methodical work. Holdings have grown through legal deposit privileges and also exchange agreements with 50 libraries in over 20 countries. The collections currently include 1.5 million books, 30,000 MSS and 500,000 periodical issues.

Special Collections and Treasures. The Library has the following repositories: Mongol repository, Soviet and Western European repository, Oriental repository, Tibetan repository, Newspaper and Magazine repository and Exchange Publication repository. Treasures include the *Golden Clasps* of the 18th century; *Poem in 8,000 Lines (Nayman myangat)* written on palm leaves; the *Kanjur,* 1,260 works in 109 volumes and the *Tanjur,* 3,427 works in 226 volumes, which form the Buddhist encyclopaedia (each volume measures 72.5 x 23.4 x 12 cm). Many works in the library are written in gold, silver, coral, pearl, lapis lazuli, mother of pearl, turquoise, steel and copper, or in powdered mixtures of these materials; they are known as the 'nine treasures' *(yesön erden).* Many of the works are about Mongolian history: *History of the Yüan Dynasty* in 210 volumes; *Secret History of the Yüan Dynasty* in 12 volumes; *Treasure Code of the Origin of Haans, Great Yellow History of the Origin of Haans and Works on the Great Yüan Dynasty,* comprising 15 volumes in all; the *Altan Tobci (Golden Annal),* the only copy of the Mongolian historical chronicle compiled in the 18th century; *Crystal Beads of the Great Yüan Dynasty; History of the Origin of the Ch'ing Dynasty; History of the Subjugation of Dzungaria; Imperial Affirmation of the Biography of the Lords of Outer Mongolia and Turkestan* in several dozen volumes; *Sacred Tales, The Treasured Mirror* and many other items of interest, including xylographs of works in various Mongolian scripts.

State Public Library, Ulan Bator

Exhibition Areas. Exhibitions in the General Reading

Room and the corridors on the 1st and 2nd floors.

Hours. Mon. and Thurs. 0800-1700, Tues., Wed. and Fri.-Sun. 0800-2300.

Transport. Local buses serve the Library.

Parking. In front of the Library.

Admission. Readers and *Visitors:* The Library is open to all without charge.

Information. The Information Department on the first floor.

Sales. None.

Guidebooks. A guidebook is available free in Mongolian, Russian and English.

Restaurant/Snack Facilities. None.

Services. Cloakroom in the vestibule, lavatories on all floors, smoking room on 3rd floor.

Catalogues. Alphabetical and classified catalogues. Separate alphabetical and classified catalogues of 'Mongolica' and classified catalogues of the Tibetan and Chinese collections.

Classification. One Mongolian and two Soviet classification schemes are used.

Copying/Photography. Copying only available through Library staff. Private photography is forbidden.

Netherlands

AMSTERDAM
Universiteitsbibliotheek van Amsterdam
Singel 425, Amsterdam
Tel. 020-5252333

History. The Library of the University of Amsterdam serves both the University and the City. The City Library was founded in 1578. When in 1632 an institution for higher education was founded, the City Library also became the library of the Athenaeum Illustre. Since that time it has maintained its dual nature and has extensive collections of books which are not within the academic curriculum. It is nevertheless a full-scale University Library, the largest in Holland. Holdings currently total over 2 million volumes, about 7,000 MSS, 150,000 letters, 90,000 maps and 45,000 periodicals.

Universiteitsbibliotheek van Amsterdam

Special Collections and Treasures. Collections include the Bibliotheca Rosenthaliana, one of the richest collections in the world in the Hebraistic and Judaistic field; the Vondel Museum; the Frederik van Eeden Museum; the Réveil Archives; the Albert Verwey Archives; and the Provo Archives. Collections on loan include the libraries of the Dutch Booksellers' Association, the Royal Netherlands Society of Medicine and the Royal Netherlands Geographical Society.

Exhibition Areas. No specific area indicated, although exhibitions are held on varying themes.

Hours. Reading rooms: Mon.-Fri. 0930-2400, Sat. 0930-1300. Closed Sun., evenings of 1 July-15 Aug., 5, 24-26 and 31 Dec., 1 Jan., 30 April, 5 May, Good Fri.-Easter Mon., Ascension Day, Whit Sun. and Mon.

Transport. Tramways 1 and 2.

Parking. In nearby streets.

Admission. Readers and *Visitors:* Free entrance for adults. Free lending facilities for students and adults after registration on first floor.

Information. Desk on the first floor.

Sales. Special catalogues may be obtained at the Information Desk.

Guidebooks. Dutch language only, free of charge.

Restaurant/Snack Facilities. Non-alcoholic drinks in coffee bar on ground floor.

Services. Typing-room, cloakroom, lavatories, lift and telephone. Smoking allowed in the coffee bar.

Catalogues. Card catalogues: alphabetical, subject, periodical and pamphlet catalogues.

Classification. Own.

Copying/Photography. There are two photocopiers in the entrance hall. The use of private cameras is forbidden without special permission.

Friends of the Library. Society of Friends of the University Library. Annual subscription Dfl. 5

AMSTERDAM
Internationaal Instituut voor Sociale Geschiedenis
Herengracht 262-266, Amsterdam-C
Tel. (020) 246671

History. The International Institute of Social History

was founded in 1935 with the purpose of preserving the traces of 'social history'. Its first director was Dr. N.W. Posthumus (1880-1960), who began bringing literature out of Nazi Germany to prevent its destruction. The necessary funds came from a Dutch insurance company, whose director, Nehemia de Lieme, a prominent Zionist, took a personal interest in the project. Gradually as the Institute's importance was increasingly recognised, its character gradually changed from a mere 'rescue-company' to a scientific research institution with scholarly objectives. If the main emphasis before 1940 lay in rescuing material and enlarging the collections, after 1945 the stress was put on classifying and publishing. In 1938 most of the valuable collections had been sent to Oxford, the rest being confiscated during World War II, and in 1945 the task of the first Librarian, Mrs. A.A. van Scheltema-Kleefstra, was to reassemble them all again in Amsterdam. The Institute was reorganised as an independent foundation and financial support came both nationally and internationally. Current holdings include 500,000 books and pamphlets, 60,000 periodicals and 2,500 running metres of archives.

Special Collections and Treasures. Collections include the Max Nettlau Collection of 40,000 items, principally on anarchy; the Marx-Engels Archives; the Bakunin Archives; the Lucien Descaves Collection on the Paris Commune; the archives of Karl Kautsky (1854-1938), the Austrian German socialist; the library of Gustav Mayer, the historian of German social democracy in the 19th century; the Leon Trotsky papers, mainly covering the period 1917-1922; the archives of the International Federation of Trade Unions 1914-45; the Socialist International Archives 1921-75; the archives of the Dutch Sociaal-Democratische Arbeiderspartij and the Dutch Labour Party; the archives and MSS of some 300 organizations and individuals prominent in socialist, anarchist, communist and peace movements; and the library of the Wiardi Beckman Stichting (Research Institute of the Dutch Labour Party).

Exhibition Areas. The Ferdinand Domela Nieuwenhuis-Museum.

Hours. Mon.-Fri. 0930-1700, Sat. 0930-1300. Closed Sun. and public hols.

Transport. The Institute is 5 minutes' walk from Dam Square.

Parking. Outside the Institute.

Admission. Readers: Free admission.
Visitors: Free access to the Reading Room, the Loan Desk and the catalogues.

Information. In the Catalogue Room.

Sales. None.

Internationaal Instituut voor Sociale Geschiedenis, Amsterdam

Karl Marx, Das Kapital (first edition), vol. 1 (Hamburg, 1867), in the Library of the Internationaal Instituut voor Sociale Geschiedenis, Amsterdam. This is Marx's own copy with unpublished notes by him, mostly corrections and additions for the second edition and the French translation

Guidebooks. International Institute of Social History. *History and Activities,* 1968; annual reports printed in English (with list of publications).

Restaurant/Snack Facilities. None.

Services. Cloakroom, lavatory, lift, smoking lounge.

Catalogues. Author and subject catalogues of books, pamphlets and periodicals. Published catalogue by G.K. Hall & Co. Inventories of the most important archives.

Classification. Own.

Copying/Photography. The Photographic Department can provide photocopies and microfilms. Cameras may not be used within the Institute.

Friends of the Institute. All donors and contributors to the Institute's Appeal Fund will be considered as 'Friends of the Institute'.

THE HAGUE
Koninklijke Bibliotheek
Lange Voorhout 34, Den Haag
Tel. 070-644920

History. The Royal Library has its origins in the initiative take in 1798 by the First Chamber of the government of the Batavian Republic to turn the library left behind by the last Stadtholder, William V, into a national library. At first the Library was only intended for official Parliamentary use but during the short reign of Louis Napoleon (1806-10) it was re-named the Royal Library. By this, Louis Napoleon confirmed his intention of making it into a truly national library, on the extension of which he spent large sums. In 1819 William I donated part of his ancestral library at Dillenburg Castle. In the same year the Library moved into its present home in the Lange Voorhout, and since then its history has been largely uneventful, except for the evacuation of a considerable number of books and manuscripts during World War II. Holdings currently total over 1 million volumes of books and MSS, housed in the original (extended) building and a new building, added in 1956, on the other side of Kazernestraat, and linked with the old by means of a tunnel and covered bridge.

Special Collections and Treasures. Collections include the MSS and incunabula of J. Visser (acquired in 1809); part of the library of the Abbey of Tongerloo, the seat of the Bollandists (1827); the Spinoza and Chess Collections of Dr. A. van der Linde (1871 and 1876); the Songbook Collection of D.F. Scheurleer (1933); the L.J. Koopman Collection of Modern French Literature (1940); the

Koninklijke Bibliotheek,
The Hague

A.E.H. Swaen Collection of Falconry (1948); the H.A. van Baak Collection of Dutch Literature (1951); and the M.R. Radermacher Schorer Collection of Fine Printing (1956).

Exhibition Areas. There are no specific exhibition rooms in the Library. Exhibitions are often held in the Museum Meermanno-Westreenianum (see next entry), which is administered by the Royal Library.

Hours. Mon.-Fri. 0900-1700 and (except for 15 June-15 Sept.) 1930-2200, Sat. 0900-1200. Closed Sun. and public hols.

Transport. Within walking distance from Centraal Station. From 'Station Hollands Spoor' by tramway no. 8 or 9, or by bus no. 4.

Parking. No special facilities.

Admission. Readers: A reader's permit is required for borrowing. A permit is given on presentation of a passport or other identification. There are no charges. Foreign visitors wishing to borrow should present a passport and an introduction from their country's diplomatic representatives.
Visitors: Admission free.

Information. Near the Lending Desk.

Sales. None.

Guidebooks. Guidebook in Dutch and a limited stock of information booklets in English.

Restaurant/Snack Facilities. Available on the Library premises.

Services. Cloakroom, lavatories, lift, telephone.

Catalogues. Author and classified catalogues.

Classification. Own.

Copying/Photography. A machine available for individual use, near the Reading Room. Otherwise, there is a separate Copying Department. Visitors wishing to use cameras should ask permission at the Information Desk.

Friends of the Library. Friends of the Royal Library — minimum fee of Dfl. 15 per year.

THE HAGUE
Rijksmuseum Meermanno-Westreenianum/Museum van het Boek
Prinsessegracht 30, Den Haag
Tel. 070 462700

History. The first element of the Museum's name commemorates the Meerman Library which was left to the State in 1815 by Johan Meerman (1753-1815). This legacy was refused, however, because of the financial obligations involved in maintaining it. In 1824 the Meerman Library was auctioned when Baron W.H.J. van Westreenen van Tiellandt (1783-1848), a cousin of Johan Meerman, managed to buy a significant portion, which he added to his own library housed in his home on the Prinsessegracht. When van Westreenen died in 1848, he left his house, Library, other collections and family archives to the State, which, this time, accepted the gift on various conditions, e.g. that the Librarian of the Royal Library (see preceding entry) would be the Principal Curator. The Museum was opened in 1852. Current holdings include 15,000 volumes, 300 MSS and 1,233 incunabula. A Museum of Modern Book Design was opened in the same building in 1960.

Special Collections and Treasures. Treasures include, among the MSS, a *Book of Hours* with illumination ascribed to the Master of Catherine of Cleves (purchased 1964); Jacob van Maerlant's *Rijmbijbel,* a rhymed Biblical history, illuminated in 1332 by Michiel van der Borch; the illuminated *Bible* of Charles V, King of France, dated 1371, containing a portrait of the sovereign painted by Jan van Brugge; St. Augustine's *La cité de Dieu,* translated by Raoul de Pralles, and the chronicle *La Bouquechardière,* both dating from the 15th century. Printed books include 415 Elzevirs; 2,200 pamphlets on Dutch history; the Mainz Psalter of 1459; *Die historie van koninck karel ende van elegast* (Delft, c.1487), the only copy known; the *Itinerario* by Jan Huygen van Linschoten (Amsterdam, 1596); Blaeu's *Atlas* (1665); and copies of the entire production of the Kelmscott Press founded by William Morris. There is a collection of drawn type designs by Jan van Krimpen.

Exhibition Areas. Four exhibition rooms.

Hours. Mon.-Sat. 1300-1700. Closed Sun. and public hols.

Transport. The Hague Central Railway Station (Centraal Station) is ten minutes' walk from the Museum. Tram: line 9 from The Hague Station HS (Hollands Spoor) — journey takes 15 minutes. (The Museum is located on the Prinsessegracht, a wide canal.)

Museum van het Boek, The Hague

Parking. Opposite the Museum (on Malieveld), or in the car-park at the Central Station.

Admission. Readers: No special regulations and no charge
Visitors: Free of charge.

Information. In the Reading Room.

Sales. At the Museum entrance. Catalogues, slides and some reproductions available.

Guidebooks. Rijksmuseum Meermanno-Westreenianum, in Dutch/English.

Restaurant/Snack Facilities. None.

Services. Cloakrooms, lavatories.

Catalogues. Printed catalogues: manuscripts, incunabula, archives, books printed on vellum, other books. Card catalogue: index-catalogue of the Museum's holdings of (modern) books. There is a printed subject catalogue of the books in the Museum.

Classification. There is subject-classification of the books in the printed catalogue.

Copying/Photography. There is a copying service but machines are not available for individual use. Private photography only with prior permission of the Keeper.

Friends of the Library. Cost: Hfl. 10.00 per annum, or more.

LEIDEN
Bibliotheek der Rijksuniversiteit te Leiden
Rapenburg 70-74 te Leiden, Postbus 58
Tel. 071-23344

History. The University of Leiden was founded in 1575 and the Library opened in 1587. It was initially housed in a room in the University Building but in 1595 transferred to the upper storey of the Church of the Beguines, which is still part of the library complex. Early growth depended greatly on donations but many important collections were also purchased, e.g. the library of Isaac Vossius (1618-1689) with its important collection of Greek and, in particular, Latin MSS (bought in 1690). In 1872 the Library's holdings developed dramatically with the addition of the entire library of the Maatschappij der Nederlandse Letterkunde (Society for Dutch Literature). Holdings currently total 2 million books, 321,160 MSS and 40,000 maps housed in the main Library building and in various separate Departmental buildings such as those housing the Medical and Law collections.

Special Collections and Treasures. The Vossius Collection (mentioned above) also contains many French MSS dating from the early Middle Ages. Other

Bibliotheek der Rijksuniversiteit te Leiden

collections include the Bodel Nijenhuis Collection of maps received in 1872 and the Leiden Collection of Oriental MSS, renowned for its wealth of Arabic, Hebrew, Persian and Turkish MSS. Although the majority of these items were acquired in the 17th century, the collection has since then been extensively enlarged, e.g. by the addition of numerous MSS from the Indonesian Archipelago. The Map Collection mainly comprises old topographic and cartographic material and, as far as old printed maps are concerned, it can be called the largest collection in the Netherlands.

Exhibition Areas. The Library does not have a permanent exhibition room. Occasionally exhibitions are held in the periodicals reading room on the ground floor.

Hours. Mon.-Fri. 0830-1700, 1915-2200, Sat. 0830-1700, Sun. 1400-1730. In the months of July and Aug. the Library is closed in the evenings and on Sun.

Transport. The Library is only 15 minutes on foot from the railway station though taxis are available. Bus no. 15, 31, 40, 41 or 42 may be taken as far as the Town Hall, and from there the Library is only 10 minutes' walk.

Parking. No parking facilities, as the Library is in a no-parking zone.

Admission. Readers: Admission is free. Readers register at the Lending Desk, after showing proper identification.
Visitors: No special rules for visitors but should they wish to borrow books they can register at the Lending Desk, provided they carry a formal letter of introduction.

Information. General information is given at the window of the room to the right of the entrance. Bibliographical information can be obtained from the Bureau *Bibliografische Inlichtingen,* which is in a room adjoining the Lending Room.

Sales. None.

Guidebooks. Guide to the Library, in Dutch, available free of charge.

Restaurant/Snack Facilities. Tearoom in the basement is open to visitors Mon.-Fri. 1130-1200, 1545-1615.

Services. Cloakroom at the entrance, three lavatories on the ground floor (gentlemen) and three lavatories on the first floor (ladies), lift. Smoking is allowed only in the tearoom.

Catalogues. Alphabetical and systematic catalogues.

Classification. Own.

Copying/Photography. Copying machines on the

The Aratea manuscript in the Bibliotheek der Rijksuniversiteit te Leiden (MS Voss. lat. q 79). Folio 30, verso

ground floor. Professional photographers are sometimes allowed to photograph material belonging to the Library after acquiring special permission from the Librarian.

UTRECHT
Bibliotheek der Rijksuniversiteit te Utrecht
9-11 Wittevrouwenstraat, Utrecht
Tel. (030) 333116

History. The Library was founded in 1584 as a city library, the initial collection consisting mainly of confiscated seminary libraries. In 1636 on the foundation of the University it became the Library of this institution. It moved to its present site in 1820 when it was housed in buildings consisting partly of the palace of Louis, King of Holland, Napoleon's brother. As the collections developed, further buildings were added, the latest being opened in the courtyard in May 1975 and housing the public services and processing department. Current holdings total 1.5 million volumes (books and serials) and 2,500 MSS.

Special Collections and Treasures. Collections include the H.E. van Buchell Collection of works of the Humanists and the forerunners of the Reformation; the E. van de Poll Collection of old Roman-Dutch Law; the T. Janssonius van Almeloveen Collection of Plautus and Quintilianus editions, and the collection of Jansenistica. Treasures include 800 incunabula; the *Psalterium Trajectense* with drawings c.825 from the Rheims School; an MS of St. Augustine from the Bruges School c.1475; and many Dutch illuminated MSS particularly from the Utrecht School.

Exhibition Areas. After the restoration of the old building an exhibition room will be installed.

Hours. Reading rooms: Mon.-Thurs. 0930-1715, 1830-2300, Fri. 0930-1715, Sat. 0930-1215. Closed Sun., public hols. and most academic hols.

Transport. Buses 3, 4, 9 from the Central Station.

Parking. Within 5 minutes' walk of the Library, which is located in the centre of the town.

Admission. Readers: Open to university students and teachers and any person over 18 who has a serious interest in science and/or the humanities.
Visitors: As above.

Information. Information Desk in the Circulation Department. More extensive information is given by the officers of the Bibliography Reading Room. On-line access to several data bases is offered to readers.

Sales. None.

Bibliotheek der Rijksuniversiteite te Utrecht

Guidebooks. Fly-sheets available free of charge.

Restaurant/Snack Facilities. Available 1030-1130, 1330-1400, 1530-1600. Also coffee vending machines near the entrance of the new building.

Services. Cloakroom with individual lockers and lavatories in or around the entrance of the new building.

Catalogues. Author/title and classified catalogues. Shelf list. Chronological catalogue for old and rare books.

Classification. The Library has its own classification scheme based on the German example of the University of Halle.

Copying/Photography. The Library has a fully equipped reproduction department. Two self-service photocopy machines are also available in the entrance hall. The normal use of private cameras is allowed.

New Zealand

AUCKLAND
University of Auckland Library
Private Bag, Auckland
Tel. Auckland 74-740

History. The University Library was established in 1884 with a grant of £37 for books which were to be 'bought in England and uniformly bound in full calf with golden lettering'. Growth was relatively slow until the early 1960's. It took the library 83 years to collect 250,000 volumes but only 7 more years to collect a further 250,000. One of the reasons for slow growth was the inadequate accommodation of the central library. This improved very considerably with the opening of a new building in 1969. The inadequacy of the former main building was partly responsible for the development of a decentralized library system. Over recent years some small libraries have been amalgamated or re-incorporated in the General Library. All divisional libraries are members of the University Library system. Holdings currently total about 650,000 books and 10,000 periodical titles housed in the General Library and 12 divisional libraries.

Special Collections and Treasures. Collections include the collection of Classics and Old Testament Literature bequeathed by the late Professor A.C. Paterson and housed in a special room on Floor 2; the P.W.G. McAra Collection on the Labour movement in New Zealand and elsewhere; the Reverend William Jellie Collection of 1,500 volumes, particularly strong on Dante, and the Sir George Fowlds Collection, documenting his life and

University of Auckland Library

political career. A separate room on the mezzanine floor houses books of New Zealand and Pacific interest.

Exhibition Areas.   None.

Hours.   Mon.-Fri. 0830-2300, Sat. 0900-1700, Sun. (second and third terms), 0900-1700. May Study Break: Mon.-Fri. 0900-1800, Sat. 0900-1300. Summer vacation: Mon.-Fri. 0900-1700, Wed. 0900-2100, Sat. 1000-1200. Closed Sun. (except as stated above), Anniversary Day, New Zealand Day, Good Fri.-Easter Mon., Anzac Day, Queen's Birthday and three weeks from 24 Dec.

Transport.   The Library is 10 minutes' walk from the centre of Auckland.

Parking.   Limited parking is available for visitors.

Admission.   *Readers:* Members of the University and others with special permission of the Librarian may borrow. Enquiries should be made to the Circulation Department. The Library is open to the public for reference purposes.
Visitors: As above.

Information.   The Circulation and Reference Enquiries Desks on Floor 1, General Library.

Sales.   None.

Guidebooks.   Free guide in English available from the Reference Enquiries Desk.

Restaurant/Snack Facilities.   None.

Services.   Pay telephones to the left inside the main entrance of the Library, lavatories on the main staircase and at the far end of the ground floor Reading Room, lifts.

Catalogues.   Author, title, subject and periodical card catalogues.

Classification.   Mainly Dewey.

Copying/Photography.   Self-service photocopying is available in the General Library, ground floor, approached by the staircase at the far end of the Circulation Desk. Microtext reader/printers are also available: enquiries to Reference Department. Permission must be obtained from the Librarian in advance for private photography.

WELLINGTON
Alexander Turnbull Library
44 The Terrace, Wellington, PO Box 8016
Tel. 48 617

History. The Library, since 1966 a part of the National Library of New Zealand, is a State reference and research library, which originated in the bequest in 1918 of the private collection of Alexander Horsburgh Turnbull (1868-1918). Turnbull, the bachelor son of a Wellington merchant, inherited a modest fortune from his father and his uncle, which he used to build up a world class collection, broadly in the fields of English literature and Pacific and New Zealand history and literature. On his death the Library, which was willed to the Crown as the nucleus of a national collection, numbered about 55,000 volumes, as well as many paintings, sketches and MSS. Turnbull's home in Bowen Street was bought by the Crown and housed the Library until the end of 1972. In 1973 the Library moved to temporary premises at 44, The Terrace, pending the building of a National Library (currently planned for completion by 1979). Legislation for the National Library was enacted in 1965, which recognised the urgent need to provide a single library building to house the three major state libraries, namely the Turnbull, the General Assembly Library (see next entry) and the National Library Service. Current holdings of the Turnbull Library include 154,598 books, 1,600 linear feet of MSS and 6,020 reels of microfilm.

Special Collections and Treasures. The Library contains about 30,000 volumes of books and pamphlets on New Zealand in addition to runs of newspapers and periodicals. The Library's notable collection of works on Oceania and Pacific discovery and exploration includes the De Bry, Hakluyt and Linschoten series and a virtually complete range of the folios and atlases of the circumnavigators. Material on British naval history and biography is also a special interest. Full collections on Polynesia, Melanesia and Micronesia are maintained. The rare book collection is strong in first and rare editions of works of English literature, with emphasis on poetry and drama. The Milton Collection is of particular importance. Special collections include the Kinsey (15,000 volumes), the Mantell (1,000 volumes and MSS) and the Trimble, Atkinson, Wright and Hogg Collections. The MSS collection is the main national repository beyond the National Archives for primary source material. The collection includes the papers of such national figures as Katherine Mansfield, the Field family and Frances Hodgkins, Sir Donald McLean, W.B.D. Mantell, Elson Best, Sir Walter Buller, R. McNab and John White.

Exhibition Areas. Exhibition space is limited in the present building to an area inside the main doors consisting of a short lobby opening into a large display area.

Hours. Mon.-Thurs. 0900-2000, Fri. 0900-1700, Sat. 0900-1200. Closed Sun. and public hols.

Transport. The Library is located near the city centre, within easy walking distance of the railway station and the airline centre.

Parking. Parking meter space available.

Admission. *Readers:* The resources of the Library are available to readers and scholars at every level of interest and knowledge.
Visitors: Free of charge. The services of the Library are fully available to visitors within the authority of the rules, copies of which are available at the entrance to the Reading Room.

Information. Enquiry Office in the display area.

Sales. At the Enquiry Office. Prints, greeting cards, colour transparencies etc.

Guidebooks. None.

Restaurant/Snack Facilities. None.

Services. Ladies' and gentlemen's cloakrooms off the display area, passenger lift from ground to 2nd floor. No typing rooms but one microfilm carrel can be used for typing.

Catalogues. The main card catalogue is divided into 2 sections: the Pacific catalogue, divided into author/title and subject, and the general catalogue for English literature, printing and other non-Pacific material which is a dictionary catalogue. All periodicals are recorded in 2 alphabetical card files. A separate rare book catalogue consists of author/title card entries, with 2 indexes, one chronological and one by place of printing. The Library also maintains the New Zealand Union catalogue of pre-1801 imprints and the Union catalogue of New Zealand and Pacific manuscripts in New Zealand libraries. Various special catalogues.

Classification. Dewey.

Copying/Photography. Copying available through Library staff. No restrictions on casual photography of exterior and interior but permission is required for photographing the collections.

Friends of the Library. Friends of the Turnbull Library. Annual subscription of $2.50.

WELLINGTON
General Assembly Library
Parliament House, Wellington 1
Tel. 49-090

History. The Library was founded in 1858 and was initially run jointly with the Auckland Provincial Council Library. When Parliament moved to Wellington in 1865 a wooden building was specially constructed for the Library. The present building was completed in 1899 and occupied in 1901. It is believed to be the finest example of Victorian Gothic architecture in New Zealand. The Library was originally administered by the Library Committee, one of the select committees of the House, but the administration was later shared with the Legislative Department. In 1965, with the passing of the National Library Act, the Library became a constituent division of the National Library of New Zealand (see also preceding entry). Current holdings total 452,000 volumes.

Special Collections and Treasures. The Library has extensive depository collections of documents of the United Nations and its specialised agencies; the only major collections of parliamentary and government documents of the British Commonwealth in New Zealand, and a research collection of New Zealand material, including manuscripts of both former and present political leaders.

Exhibition Areas. The Main Reading Room, on the 1st floor.

Hours. When the House is sitting: Mon. 0830-1700, Tues., Wed. and Thurs. 0830-2300, Fri. 0830-1830, Sat. 0900-1700. During a recess, the Library is closed on Sat. and the days on which Government Offices in Wellington are closed. It is open otherwise 0830-1700.

Transport. Take the train or bus to Wellington Railway Station, then proceed up Molesworth Street. Parliament House and the Library are in the first block on the left.

Parking. Parking for visitors is available in the Parliament House grounds. Turn in at the main entrance to Parliament House on Molesworth Street or the Hill Street entrance to the Library.

Admission. Readers: Admission is free but readers limited in general to MPs and their families, staff of Parliament House, officers of Government departments, special research privilege holders, or holders of recess privileges. The latter are granted at the discretion of the Chief Librarian.
Visitors: Not allowed.

Information. To the left of the entrance.

Sales. None.

General Assembly Library, Wellington

Guidebooks. None.

Restaurant/Snack Facilities. None on premises but available nearby.

Services. Lounge chairs in Main Reading Room, lavatories.

Catalogues. Divided (author-title/subject) card catalogue.

Classification. Dewey.

Copying/Photography. Copying facilities are available, though not for individual use. Permission must be obtained from the Chief Librarian for private photography.

Nigeria

IBADAN
Ibadan University Library
University of Ibadan, Ibadan
Tel. 62550

History. The Ibadan University Library is the most important library in Nigeria in terms of size and resources. It was founded in 1948 at a temporary site along Eleiyele Road, Ibadan. It started with a collection of about 40,000 volumes acquired as gift, by deposit or by purchase. Notable among the various collections that formed the nucleus of the Library collection were 10,000 volumes inherited from the defunct Yaba Higher College; the Henry Carr Library of about 18,000 volumes, which was bought by the Government of Nigeria on Dr. Carr's death and deposited with the University; and the Dyke Collection of about 10,000 books, journals, pamphlets, reprints, etc., presented by Mr. Montague Dyke, an Englishman whose life had been largely devoted to problems of tropical agriculture in West Africa. When the Library moved to its permanent location in 1954, the collection had doubled in size to some 80,000 volumes and the Library was subscribing to 1,300 current serials. In February 1969, a research extension to the Library was formally opened and this new building, completely air-conditioned, added 56,000 square feet to the 46,000 square feet of the existing Library building. It also raised the total capacity of the Library, which was formerly 250,000 volumes and 250 readers, to 500,000 volumes and 1,250 readers. Current holdings total about 275,000 volumes and over 5,000 current serials. The founding Librarian, Professor John Harris, retired in 1968 after twenty years of service.

Special Collections and Treasures. Collections include

Ibadan University Library

Africana of about 40,000 volumes; valuable manuscripts totalling nearly 14,000 and including those of such notable personalities as the late Herbert Macaulay, the celebrated father of Nigerian nationalism, and the late Bishop Samuel Charles Phillips, a notable church dignitary; an Arabic Collection of about 2,500 volumes; and a map collection of 10,960 items.

Exhibition Areas.   Display cases and stands are located in the Public Catalogue Hall.

Hours.   Mon.-Fri. 0800-2200, Sat. 0800-1300, Sun. 1700-2200. First Term and Long Vacations: Mon.-Fri. 0800-1800, Sat. 0800-1300. Closed Sun. and public hols.

Transport.   Bus to University precinct.

Parking.   Parking lot for about 50 cars in the Library courtyard.

Admission.   *Readers:* Students and staff should fill in a registration form at the Circulation Section.
Visitors: Should make personal application to the Librarian.

Information.   The Circulation Desk at the southern entrance to the Library on the ground floor.

Sales.   None.

Guidebooks.   Library guide and brochure available free of charge.

Restaurant/Snack Facilities.   None.

Services.   Typing rooms, cloakroom at entrance, lavatories, lifts in the main entrance hall, pay telephones.

Catalogues.   The catalogue is on the ground floor between the Circulation Desk and the Research Library. It is in four parts — author/title, serials, subject and shelf list. The Africana catalogue was published in 2 volumes in 1973. The Library also maintains a separate card catalogue for the Africana Collection and one for items acquired through depository laws.

Classification.   Bliss. A decision has recently been made to change to the Library of Congress scheme and all new accessions from January 1975 are classified by the new scheme.

Copying/Photography.   Reprographic Unit handles all requests. The photocopy section is located in the basement.

Norway

OSLO
Universitetsbiblioteket i Oslo [Royal University Library]
Drammensveien 42, Oslo 2
Tel. 56 49 80

History. The Library was founded with the University
on 2 September 1811 by a royal decree of King Frederik
VI of Norway and Denmark, but the collections were not
organised by the time of the separation of Norway and
Denmark in 1814. The long union of the two countries,
in effect, deprived Norway of a national library, so the
duties devolved upon the University Library. (Its national
character is recognised by the additional title 'Norges
Riksbibliotek'). The nucleus of the collections was a
stock of 29,000 duplicates from the Royal Library in
Copenhagen (see relevant entry), together with the
smaller collections of two Norwegian officials, Chief
Justice J.E. Colbjørnsen and the Kancelliraad H.
Anderson. Copyright deposit privileges resulted from an
ordinance of 21 February 1815 (although these lapsed
1839-1883). For its first hundred years the Library was
housed in various premises, although for most of this
period (1850-1913) it was in the West Building of the
University. The present building in Solli Plass was
opened on 2 January 1914, the West Wing was added in
1933 and the East Wing completed in 1945. The old
Observatory, 150 metres south, was taken over in 1965
and rebuilt to house the Division for Studies in Education
and the National Music Collection. Current holdings
include 1,950,000 volumes (3 million if institute libraries
are included), 17,000 MSS items and 85,000 maps.

Special Collections and Treasures. The Library's
function as a national library is primarily carried out by
the Norwegian Department, which collects all that is
printed in Norway and also Norvegica printed abroad,
original works by Norwegian writers both in Norwegian
and in translation and works on Norway by foreign
writers. Special collections include the Anton Aure
Collection of new Norwegian literature; the Schweigaard
Collection of 10,000 volumes of Norwegian and older
Danish humanistic literature; the Bjørnsen Archives; the
Collection of Norwegian Graphic Works; the Division for
Norwegian text books from 1800; the Drama Collection;
the Holberg Collection of 2,000 books; the Ibsen
Collection; the National Music Collection; the Map
Collection, a virtually complete collection of maps printed
in Norway; the Norwegian Sound Library; the Norwegian-
American Collection; the Norwegian War Publications
Collection; and the Manuscript Collection, which includes
MSS and letters, mostly from the 19th and 20th
centuries, representing all aspects of Norwegian
intellectual life.

Universitetsbiblioteket i Oslo.
Morning queue for the reading
room

Exhibition Areas.   None at present.

Hours.   Main Reading Room, Study Room, Medical Room: Mon.-Fri. 0830-2200, Sat. 0830-1600. University Vacations: Mon.-Fri. 0900-1900, Sat. 0900-1330. Closed Sun. and public hols. The Main Library opening hours are limited between Christmas and New Year and during Easter Week.

Transport.   Municipal transport is available. (The Library is within walking distance from the city centre.)

Parking.   Available.

Admission.   *Readers:* Readers must sign the attendance register on the desk in the Main Reading Room. Due to lack of space, admission to the Reading Rooms is limited to research workers and to students who have been registered at the University for at least three terms. Readers must pay a subscription. Anyone wishing to borrow books must sign an application form, signed by a Norwegian tax-paying citizen.
Visitors: Free of charge. The public may have access to the special collections by arrangement with the librarian in charge. Applications should be made to the inspectors in the Main Reading Room or Information Department.

Information.   Information Department on the second floor.

Sales.   In the cloakroom on the first floor.

Guidebooks.   In Norwegian and English.

Restaurant/Snack Facilities.   The Andhrimner Café. Open Mon.-Fri. 0830-1800, Sat. 0830-1400. Opening times are limited during vacations.

Services.   All the usual facilities.

Catalogues.   Author, subject and various special catalogues. The Main Catalogue is an alphabetical list of the complete Norwegian and foreign bookstock, excluding Norwegian periodicals. The latter are registered in the bibliography *Norwegian Periodicals up to 1920* and in the Norwegian National Bibliography.

Classification.   Varies: some Dewey, some Universal Decimal Classification, some own.

Copying/Photography.   Photocopier for self-service is placed by the entrance to the Main Reading Room. All other forms of reproduction carried out by Photography Department. Order forms for photocopies, microfilms etc. are available from the Main Reading Room, the Lending Department and in the Reception Room.

OSLO
Deichmanske Bibliotek
Henrik Ibsensgt 1, Oslo 1
Tel. 203543

History. The Library, the largest public library complex in Norway, takes its name from Carl Deichman (1705-80), who in 1780 donated his collection of 6,000 volumes to the free use of the citizens of Oslo. The Library was opened to the public in 1785. In spite of its long tradition as a public institution the Library did not gain real momentum as a free-access library until 1896, when Haakon Nyhuus was appointed Director. His reforms included an open-shelf policy and the use of Dewey and modern cataloguing practices. In 1933 the Library moved to its present building, but growth for the next thirty years suffered as a result firstly of the pre-war financial crises, then of World War II and the severe competition for limited funds after the war. In 1961 a new long term Library development programme was initiated, which included the construction of a new wing, opened in September 1972. Current holdings total just over 1.4 million volumes.

Deichmanske Bibliotek, Oslo

Special Collections and Treasures. Collections include the Carl Deichman Collection of manuscripts and early prints (displayed in the galleries above the Adult Lending Library).

Exhibition Areas. Exhibitions are located in the entrance area.

Hours. Reading Room. 1 Sept.-31 May: Mon.-Fri. 0815-2100, Sat. 0815-1500. 1 June-31 Aug.: Mon.-Fri. 0815-1800, Sat. 0815-1500. Closed Sun. and public hols.

Transport. Tram, bus, underground.

Parking. At the moment short stays only. 11 parking spaces are planned for main library visitors.

Admission. *Readers* and *Visitors:* No regulations.

Information. In all divisions open to the public.

Sales. None.

Guidebooks. In Norwegian only, free of charge.

Restaurant/Snack Facilities. A combined newspaper and relaxation room, with refreshment facilities, is being planned in the entrance area of the main Library.

Services. Cloakrooms, lavatories, lifts, telephones, all in the entrance area.

Catalogues. Dictionary catalogue.

Bible (Flemish, 13th century), in the Deichmanske Bibliotek, Oslo (MS 69). St. Luke's Gospel for Christmas Day. This Bible belonged to the powerful 15th century Norwegian archbishop, Aslak Bolt

Classification.   Dewey.

Copying/Photography.   Facilities are available in the general lending department in the main Library. Tourists are permitted to use cameras inside the Library.

Pakistan

KARACHI
Karachi University Library
Karachi 32
Tel. 418227, 419291/43, 419291/46

History.   The University of Karachi was established in June 1951. The Library was founded on 12 August 1952, opening its doors in the middle of 1953. Its initial stock totalled only a few hundred volumes, housed in temporary premises. In 1954 the Library moved to the third floor of the Chemistry Department building and then, when the University moved to its new campus in 1960, the University Library was temporarily housed on the top floor of the Arts Building. In 1964 the library finally moved to its present seven-storey building centrally located among the teaching departments of the University. The Library has total covered area of 296,000 square feet, space for 700,000 volumes, and a seating capacity of 950. Prior to the opening of the new building, over 30 departmental libraries had been established, partly because of lack of accommodation in the Main Library. Their collections were transferred to the new building. Current holdings now include 208,595 books, 5,000 microforms, 70,000 bound and unbound periodicals and 64 MSS.

Special Collections and Treasures.   Collections include the Shamsul Islam Collection; the Tahra Jameel Memorial Collection; the Haleema Siddiqui Memorial Collection; the A.D. Azhar and Asif Azhar Collection; the Imtiaz Mohd. Khan Collection; the Bilal R. Riaz Collection; the Dr. Zahiruddin Al-Jamaee Collection; the Nazir Ahmed Collection; the Pakistan Collection; the Quaid-e-Azam Collection; and the United Nations Collection.

Exhibition Areas.   The main floor near the main entrance.

Hours.   Daily 0830-2200 (except Fri. 0830-1230, 1500-2200).

Transport.   During working hours (0800-1500) University Buses and omnibuses run from Sabilwali Majid to the University Campus. (The University is situated about ten miles from the centre of Karachi.) From 1500-2200 and

Karachi University Library

on holidays only, University buses run from the Empress Market to the campus at half hourly intervals.

Parking. Facilities available on campus.

Admission. Readers: The Library is open to University teachers and students and others as allowed by authorities. Readers must register to receive a Borrower's Ticket but there is no charge.
Visitors: Welcome.

Information. In the Reference Section on the main floor opposite the Circulation Counter.

Sales. Bookshop on the ground floor of the library. Books and stationery are sold.

Guidebooks. Available.

Restaurant/Snack Facilities. None in Library but available on campus.

Services. Smoking lounge near the main entrance. Telephone booth near main gate. Lavatories by the main staircase on each floor.

Catalogues. Classified catalogue with author index. Dictionary catalogue. Various special catalogues (e.g. for Urdu, Persian, Arabic, and Bengali languages).

Classification. Dewey with the Shafi expansion.

Copying/Photography. Copying machine in the Research Room of the Library. Private cameras are only allowed with the permission of the library administration.

LAHORE
Punjab University Library
1 Kutchery Road, Lahore 2/12
Tel. 52262

History. The Library of the University of the Punjab at Lahore is the oldest and largest library in Pakistan. Its foundation stock derived from the 2,000 volume collection of Sir D.F. McLeod, Lt. Governor of the Punjab 1865-1870, purchased for the Panjab University College, which developed into a university under the Panjab University Act of 1882. The collections languished somewhat, until 1903, when Mr. (later Dr.) A.C. Woolner was appointed Honorary Librarian, a position he held for 25 years. The present building was built on a site acquired in 1910. The foundation stone was laid on 27 February 1911, part of the building was formally opened in April 1912, and the two storied structure was completed in February 1917. At present, the Library is divided into two sections, General and Oriental, and holdings total nearly 270,000 volumes, including more

Punjab University Library, Lahore

than 18,000 MSS. It is intended that the Library should move to a new building on the new University campus in the relatively near future.

Special Collections and Treasures. Collections include the H.M. Percival Collection of 6,500 volumes, presented in 1911, and the collections of Maulana Mohammed Husain Azad, Pirzada Mohammad Husain Arif, Pandit Brij Mohan Datatriya Kaifi, Dr. A.C. Woolner, Sir Shahab-ud-Din, Maulvi Mahboob Alam, Hakim Abdul Majid Attiqi, Professor Mohammad Iqbal, Mian Ahmad Shafi, Hafiz Mahmud Shirani and Professor Siraj-ud-Din Azar.

Exhibition Areas. None.

Hours. Nov.-Feb.: Daily 0800-1800. March-Oct.: Daily 0730-1900.

Transport. The Library is located at the old campus, more than 6 miles from the new campus. Public and University transport available between the two campuses.

Parking. Facilities available at the Library.

Admission. Readers: Membership is free to students, teachers and research scholars of the University and the colleges affiliated to it.
Visitors: Visitors are permitted to study in the Library but permission must be applied for.

Information. In the main halls of the two sections of the Library.

Sales. Sales depot maintained by the University as a separate unit.

Guidebooks. The University Handbooks, published in English, include information on the Library.

Restaurant/Snack Facilities. University Cafeteria next door to the Library (open 0730-1600).

Services. Cloakrooms, lavatories.

Catalogues. Dictionary card catalogue for both General and Oriental sections.

Classification. Dewey Decimal classification. The Oriental Section follows a scheme of its own.

Copying/Photography. The Photographic Section provides microfilms, photostats and enlargements. Cameras may only be used with the permission of the Librarian.

Panama Canal Zone

BALBOA HEIGHTS
Canal Zone Library-Museum
Balboa Heights
Tel. 52-3486

History. The Canal Zone Library was established by General George W. Goethals, chief engineer in the construction of the Panama Canal, through his order signed 24 August 1914, only nine days after the official opening of the Canal. The Library's chief mission at that time was information for those operating the Canal and this continues to be its basic task. Since 1914 the size of the collection has grown steadily, branch libraries have been established in six Canal Zone communities and in 1950 the Museum was added to house the memorabilia of the Canal's construction and history. Current holdings total over 290,000 items.

Special Collections and Treasures. The Panama Collection is the most important special collection of the Canal Zone Library. Beginning with exploration and early voyages, the collection includes early editions of Dampier, Ulloa, Exquemelin, etc. The bulk of the collection, however, covers the planning and construction of the Canal. It totals 5,000 items, including books, US congressional hearings, engineering drawings, maps, diaries and photographs.

Exhibition Areas. Permanent exhibits of the history of the Canal and models of construction equipment line the entrance to the Library.

Hours. Mon.-Sat. 0930-2100. Closed Sun. and public hols.

Transport. Bus every 40 minutes.

Parking. Adequate parking space.

Admission. Readers: Free admission to Library and Museum. Borrowing privileges may require $10 deposit (refundable).
Visitors: No charge and no special regulations.

Information. From the Loan Desk, in the main public room of the Library.

Sales. None.

Guidebooks. A guidebook in English, and possibly in Spanish, is in preparation.

Restaurant/Snack Facilities. Food and drink vending machines on the first floor, available Mon.-Fri. 0700-1600.

Services. Public telephone on first floor, lavatories on first and second floors.

Catalogues. Author/title and subject card catalogues. Book catalogue of the Panama Collection was published in 1964 (by G.K. Hall & Co.).

Classification. Dewey.

Copying/Photography. No facilities. Private photography by special permission.

Peru

LIMA
Instituto Nacional de Cultura, Biblioteca Nacional
Apartado Postal 2335, Lima
Tel. 28-7690

History. The National Library was founded on 28 August 1821 by a decree of General José de San Martín and opened to the public on 8 February 1822. At the time of the official inauguration on 7 September 1822 it had a collection of 11,256 volumes, 762 of which had been given by San Martín himself. By 1879 the Library had 50,000 volumes but in this year war broke out between Chile and Peru. In 1881 the invading Chilean army was quartered in the Library, which lost all but 700 volumes. Ricardo Palma managed, however, to re-open the Library on 28 July 1884 with 27,894 volumes. Disaster struck again in the 20th century, when on the night of 9/10 May 1943 the Library, and the Sociedad Geográfica de Lima, were severely damaged by fire. Only 1,038 items of the 150,000 volume collection were saved. The fire destroyed the original library building. Construction of the first stage of the new library was completed in 1947. Its reorganization owed much to the work of Dr. Jorge Basadre, the new Director and noted Peruvian historian. It currently houses a total collection of 2,072,246 items, comprising 640,690 books, 1,431,556 journals, 180 micro-materials, 5,584 audio-visual materials, 170,701 manuscripts, 11,511 maps and 7,710 music scores.

Special Collections and Treasures. Collections include the 28,000 volume library of Agustín P. Justo, a former President of Argentina, purchased in 1945; the Paz Soldan archives; the collection of Marshal Cáceres and the Ricardo Palma Library. The Library has had copyright privileges since 1945 and is trying to make its collection of Peruvian books as complete as possible. Treasures include the oldest printed Peruvian book, *La doctrina christiana* (Lima, 1584); *Fundamento expedido por el marqués Don Francisco Pizarro* (Lima, 1541); the musical

Biblioteca Nacional del Peru

MS *La purpura de la rosa de Tomás Torrejón de Velasco* (Lima, 1701); and the only incunable to survive the 1943 fire: the *Opus pulcherrimus chiromante* (Venice, 1499), which Ricardo Palma had bought back from a Chilean soldier in 1883.

Exhibition Areas. In the main hall on the first floor.

Hours. Winter: Mon.-Fri. 0900-2300, Sat. and Sun. 0900-1300. Summer: Mon.-Fri. 0900-1315, 1600-2250, Sat. and Sun. 0900-1250. Closed on public hols.

Transport. Numerous buses pass close to the Library.

Parking. In the nearby lots.

Admission. Readers: Registration on the 2nd floor. Identification documents must be produced. A small fee is charged.
Visitors: Free of charge.

Information. At the entrance to the main hall.

Sales. In the administration office.

Guidebooks. In preparation.

Restaurant/Snack Facilities. None.

Services. Typing rooms, washrooms, lifts, telephones.

Catalogues. Author, title and subject catalogues.

Classification. Modified Dewey.

Copying/Photography. Microfilm and photocopying. Apply to the office on the 2nd floor. No regulations regarding private camera photography.

Doctrina christiana, y catecismo para instrucción de los indios (Lima, 1584), in the Biblioteca Nacional, Lima. This was the second book to be printed in Lima and the first major work to be published in Peru

Philippines

MANILA
Ang Pambansang Aklatan (The National Library)
T.M. Kalaw, Ermita, Manila
Tel. Filipiniana 48-55-19; Reference 48-55-88; Public Documents 49-11-14

History. The Library has its origins in two libraries, the Museo-Biblioteca de Filipinas, created in 1887, and the American Circulating Library, established after the fall of Spain and the occupation of the Philippines by the United States. In 1905 the Circulating Library came under government control and became a division of the Bureau of Public Education, which subsequently brought

National Library, Manila

together all libraries belonging to any branch of the Philippines Insular government under the name of the Philippines Library. In 1928 the Library was renamed the National Library and growth was steady until World War II, which drastically affected library development throughout the Philippines. The National Library managed to save only 36,000 volumes out of a pre-war collection of 733,000. Of the 72,000 volumes comprising the Filipiniana Collection, only 2,996 books and 150 MSS survived. The post-war development has seen the inauguration in June 1961 of the present six-storey building, with a floor space of 198,700 square feet and space for over 1 million volumes. Earthquakes in 1967 and 1970 caused temporary internal disarray to this new building, which currently contains 131,481 volumes. The public library function of the National Library is carried out by the Extension Division, with the 446 branch libraries currently containing just over 714,346 volumes.

Special Collections and Treasures. Collections include the Presidential Collection, which, to date, includes the papers of the following past Philippine presidents: General Emilio Aguinaldo (embedded in the Philippine Revolutionary Papers, better known as the Philippine Insurgent Records); President Manuel L. Quezon, Sergio Osmeña, Manuel Roxas and Carlos P. Garcia. The latest acquisition — the papers and memorabilia of the late President Carlos P. Garcia — are contained in some 200 boxes and composed of printed and handwritten materials; the Rizal Collection, including not only the works written by Dr. Jose Rizal (e.g. *Noli Me Tangere* and *El Filibusterismo*) but also works about him; the Julian C. Balmaseda Collection with books and type-scripts on Tagalog language and literature; the Lope K. Santos, Nicanor K. Abad, Alvaro Alir, Maura Nepomuceno, Santiago Cuino and Roman Ozaeta Collections of Filipiniana; the Carlos Ronquillo Collection of 2,000 items, largely on linguistics and different Philippine dialects; the Serials Collection, with rare periodicals such as the *Gaceta de Manila* (1869-1897) and *Lipang Kalabaw* (1907-09); the Music Collection of about 400 pieces of sheet music printed both in the Philippines and abroad, including Alfredo Serapios' *Lumagot ng Tanikalang Inang Bayan* (Manila, 1896); the A. Samson and Jamir Zobel Picture Collections; and the Insurgent Records (1899-1903), 200,000 documents captured from Filipino leaders of the Revolution by the American forces.

Exhibition Areas. Presidential Exhibition Hall. Exhibit areas on all six floors.

Hours. Mon.-Sat. 0900-1800. Closed Sun. and public hols. (Extension libraries: Mon.-Fri. 0800-1700, Sat. 0800-1200).

Transport. Public transport is available. (The Library is located on the south-east side of Rizal Park facing

Teodoro M. Kalaw St.)

Parking. Facilities available.

Admission. Readers: Free of charge. The Filipiniana Division maintains a reading room to serve researchers, scholars, college students etc., who must obtain an identification card to be admitted. The extension libraries are open to all.
Visitors: Free of charge.

Information. General Reference Reading Room.

Sales. Publications Division, whose task includes republishing documents owned by the Library that seem of value and interest to the general public.

Guidebooks. Your National Library (Manila, 1974), 62p.

Restaurant/Snack Facilities. Facilities available. Cantoon managed by the Bureau of Vocational Education.

Services. Cloakroom, lavatories and auditorium.

Catalogues. Author-title and subject card catalogues for the Filipiniana Division. In the Reference Division the card catalogue is arranged in dictionary form but conversion to author-title and subject catalogues is planned in the near future.

Classification. Dewey, with expansions for the Philippine language, literature and history sections.

Copying/Photography. Microfilm and photocopying available through Library staff. Apply to the Librarian for permission for private photography.

MANILA
The Library, University of Santo Tomas
España, Manila
Tel. 21-00-81, loc. 234

History. The College of Santo Tomas was founded by the Superiors of the Dominican Province of the Most Holy Rosary on 11 April 1611. It was raised by Pope Innocent X on 20 November 1645 to the status of a university for ecclesiastical and civil studies. Its Library, the oldest in the Philippines, is an outgrowth of the donations of Fr. Miguel de Benavides and Fr. Diego de Soria. The growth of the collections up to the 20th century depended largely on donations and purchases. In 1927 the University Main Building and the Library moved from Intramuros to the present campus, which was used during World War II as a prisoner-of-war camp. The Library's collections survived the war, however, and today holdings total about 260,000 volumes, as well as

University of Santo Tomas, Manila. Main building where the Central Library is located

thousands of other items in the form of maps, microforms, etc.

Special Collections and Treasures. The Library has reputedly the best Filipiniana Collection in the Philippines (occupying 4 rooms on the ground floor of the main building, right wing). Treasures include the original edition and the photo-offset edition of *The Philippine Islands* (55 volumes) by E.H. Blair and J.A. Robertson; *Vocabulario de la Lengua Tagala,* written by F. Domingo de los Santos in 1835; *Arte y Reglas de la Lengua Tagala,* written by Fray Francisco de San Josef in 1832; a facsimile of *Doctrina Cristiana,* the first book printed in the Philippines (1593); *Catálogo sistemático de toda la fauna de Filipinas* by F. Castro de Elera (Manila, 1895), 3 volumes; *Suma de una junta que se hizo a manera de concilio el año 1582,* an 18th century MS copy of the proceedings of the first Synod of Manila summoned by the first Bishop of the Philippines, Domingo Salazar, in 1582; and runs of rare Philippine journals such as *La Independencia, Gaceta de Manila* and *Kalayaan.* The Rizaliana Collection contains 1,000 books including first editions of *Noli Me Tangere* and *El Filibusterismo,* with Jose Rizal's own notations.

Exhibition Areas. Exhibitions are held in the Main Library and usually consist of new books received from the different embassies in Manila, or items of special interest in connection with significant events.

Hours. Mon.-Sat. 0800-2000. Closed Sun., except for two Sun. before Preliminary and Final Examinations, when the Library is open 0800-1200 and 1300-1700.

Transport. Any public vehicle (jeepneys or buses) passing España Street. (The campus is in the Sampaloc area of Manila.)

Parking. There are three colour codes for parking on campus but for outsiders and visitors there is a free parking zone under a white colour code.

Admission. Readers: Free admission for non-UST students, provided they can present credentials such as an Identification Card and a letter from the school, college or office where the researcher studies or works. *Visitors:* Apply to the Librarian.

Information. In the main lobby of the Library.

Sales. None.

Guidebooks. Forthcoming.

Restaurant/Snack Facilities. None on the Library premises but snack facilities are available nearby.

Services. Lifts, pay telephones, lavatories.

Catalogues. Classified catalogue.

Classification. Library of Congress.

Copying/Photography. Copying facilities are located at the Main Library. Cameras are allowed but permission must be obtained first from the Prefect of Libraries or the Chief Librarian.

QUEZON CITY
University of the Philippines Library
Gonzalez Hall, Diliman, Quezon City 3004
Tel. 97-60-61 to 68, local 284

History. The Library was formally established in 1922. The major factor in its early history was World War II, when it lost all its holdings except 3,000 volumes which were shelved in branch libraries outside Manila. Today the University of the Philippines Library is a centrally administered library system consisting of a Main Library and 35 college and departmental libraries. It is the largest library in the Philippines, with current holdings of over 725,000 volumes, 17,200 serial titles and 9,300 microfilms. The Main Library contains the bulk of the collection in the social sciences, humanities and natural sciences.

Special Collections and Treasures. The Filipiniana Collection includes the Faustino Aguilar Papers, covering his life as a labour leader and novelist; the original MSS of the novels of Magdalena Jalandoni, noted Hiligaynon writer; the Andres Cristobal Cruz Collection relating to Philippine literature and society; the Hermogenes E. Ilagan Collection consisting mainly of his original three-act and one-act zarzuelas written in the Tagalog language; Japanese Occupation Papers, in Tagalog, Ilocano, Bicol, Cebuano, Hiligaynon, Spanish, Nippongo and English; the Jose Llanes Collection, important historical materials for the study of resistance movements under the Japanese; the Luther Parker Collection on the history and government of various provinces in the Philippines; the H.W. Harnish Collection of historical prints and glass negatives dating from 1898-1907; and the Marcelo T. Garcia Collection of 4,000 items, of which 2,000 deal with Philippine linguistics and literature in Tagalog, Pampango, and other Philippine languages.

Exhibition Areas. Occasional exhibits are housed in the Main Library.

Hours. Mon.-Sat. 0800-1700. Closed Sun. and public hols.

Transport. Bus from Rizal Park, Manila, to UP Balara. (The Library occupies Gonzales Hall centrally located on the Diliman campus.)

Parking. Parking area for Library users in the Library grounds.

University of the Philippines Library, Quezon City

Admission. Readers: Registration at the South Corner in the Main Lobby. Free use for the first two days, then a payment of about $13 must be made for a term's use, or for a part of a term. Students and personnel of the University may use the Library free of charge.
Visitors: Free admission. Visitors should apply at the Librarian's Office for permission to use the Library, or for a conducted tour.

Information. Desk in the Main Lobby.

Sales. Library publications are on sale in the Librarian's Office.

Guidebooks. Guides to the Library in English. A small charge is made.

Restaurant/Snack Facilities. Snack facilities on Library premises, open 0700-1800. There are also restaurants on the University campus.

Services. Some carrells are available to researchers, graduate students and faculty members. Cloakrooms, lavatories, lifts. Extensive indexing and bibliographic services are undertaken by the Bibliography, Indexing and Publication Section.

Catalogues. Author, title and subject card catalogues for the entire University Library system, supplemented by departmental divided catalogues, printed catalogues for special collections etc. The card catalogue is located on the first floor lobby near the General Loan Desk.

Classification. Library of Congress. Law classified by the Los Angeles County Law Library classification.

Copying/Photography. Copying service, operated by staff, on the second floor (Room 203). Permission must be obtained from the Librarian's Office for private photography.

Poland

Biblioteka Jagiellońska, Cracow

CRACOW
Biblioteka Jagiellońska
Aleja Mickiewicza 22, 30-059 Kraków
Tel. 335-05; 335-00; 309-03 (Secretary); 319-71 (Director)

History. The Library was established simultaneously with the foundation of Cracow University in 1364 by King Casimir the Great. It was re-established by Queen Hedwig and her husband Władysław Jagiełło (hence the name Jagiellońska) in 1400. It is the oldest non-private secular book collection in Poland. Its early growth owed much to numerous gifts from professors, alumni, bibliophiles and book dealers. In 1515, Professor Tomasz Obiedziński left an endowment, which allowed the construction of a large library room in the newly built wing of the Collegium Maius building. During the 17th and 18th centuries the Library reflected the general decline of the town and the University. In the 19th century, however, it revived under Librarians such as J.S. Bandtke, J. Muczkowski and particularly Karol Estreicher, who directed the Library 1868-1905. The Library received legal deposit privileges in 1932 and occupied its present building in 1939 (extended in 1963). At the present time, the Library functions as the University Library, as a public research library and as a back up to the National Library in Warsaw (see entry for Biblioteka Narodowa). In accordance with the profile of collections accumulated from the beginning of its existence, the Library is attempting in the first place a complete collection of pre-1800 Polish books and periodicals. Holdings at the end of 1974 totalled some 1,818,836 items.

Special Collections and Treasures. Treasures in the MSS Department include: Jan Długosz, *Banderia Prutenorum* (1448); Baltazar Behem, *Codex picturatus* (Cracow, 1505), containing privileges and statutes of the town of Cracow; Copernicus, *De revolutionibus orbium coelestium* (c. 1530); and autograph letters of Tadeusz Kościuszko, Adam Mickiewicz, Stanisław Wyspianski, Henryk Sienkiewicz and Józef Ignacy Kraszewski. The pre-1800 printed books number 95,324 volumes, including 3,397 incunabula. Treasures include unique fragments of printer's proofs, probably from Gutenberg's shop; *Almanach Cracoviense* (Cracow, 1474), the first printing in Poland; old Church Slavonic incunabula printed in Cracow in 1491 by Szwajpolt Fiol in the world's first Cyrillic printing shop; and Copernicus, *De revolutionibus orbium coelestium* (Nürnberg, 1543, Basel, 1566, and Amsterdam, 1617).

Exhibition Areas. Exhibition Room situated on the ground floor. Entrance from the hall, which has 4 show-cases illustrating the history of the Library.

Hours. Mon.-Sat. 0800-2100. Closed Sun. and public hols.

Transport. Buses: numbers 103, 114, 119. Trams: numbers 17, 18.

Parking. Permitted in the Library drive-way and in the adjoining streets.

Admission. Readers: Unrestricted use of the reading rooms for study. Books may be borrowed by the students and scientific staff of the academic schools in Cracow. Those wishing to read on the premises should register in the Main Reading Room on the first floor. Borrowers should register in the Lending Room on the

Nicolaus Copernicus, holograph of De revolutionibus (c. 1520-41), in the Biblioteka Jagiellońska, Cracow (MS 10.000). Book 1, folio 9, verso, with diagram of the heliocentric system

ground floor.

Visitors: Those wishing to visit the Library may do so on weekdays only between 0800-1400 and must make prior application.

Information. The Department of Scientific Information (with the Bibliographic Reading Room) is open on weekdays 0800-2100 (on the first floor). Enquiries may also be addressed to all librarians on duty in the reading rooms.

Sales. None.

Guidebooks. The *Guidebook to the Biblioteka Jagiellońska* by Irena Bar (in Polish, with English, French and Russian summaries) may be obtained free from the management office of the Library.

Restaurant/Snack Facilities. 'Breakfast' snack bar, on the first floor, open 1000-1300, 1600-1900.

Services. Lavatories on every floor, lift from hall to first and second floors, smoking permitted in the hall on the ground flor and in the corridors of the first and second floors, typing rooms on the first and second floors (typewriters not provided), public telephone in the hall on the ground floor, cloakroom in the hall.

Catalogues. Card catalogues: alphabetical, classified, subject (since 1950-, Polish books only). Union catalogue of institute libraries of the Jagiellonian University. Printed catalogues of incunabula and manuscripts.

Classification. Own, partly based on the scheme of *Przewodnik Bibliograficzny* (the general current bibliography of Poland).

Copying/Photography. No machines for individual use but the Library's copying service can provide microfilms, photocopies and xerographic copies of Library materials. This service operates in the phototechnical workroom, in the basement. Prior permission must be obtained for private photography.

Silesian Library, Katowice

KATOWICE
Biblioteka Śląska (Silesian Library)
ul. Francuska 12, 40-015 Katowice
Tel. 5164-41

History. The Library was founded in 1922 as a reference library of the Sejm Śląski (the Silesian Parliament). At first it was essentially a collection of books on law, the social and economic sciences, later supplemented by regional publications. Library assistance was given not only to members of the Silesian Sejm but also to many readers outside it. In 1936 it did, in fact, become a public library, entitled to receive a free copy of all books published in Silesia. In 1939, at the outbreak of World War II, the Library contained some 100,000 volumes and was affiliated with the collections of the so-called Oberschlesische Landesbibliothek in Bytom. Between 1939-45 the Library lost 10 per cent of its stock, as well as its catalogues. On 31 January 1945, after the liberation of Katowice, the administration of the Library was assumed by the Office of the Silesian Province in Katowice. Since 1945 the Library has increasingly specialised in publications in the scientific field and is now directly dependent on the Polish Ministry of Culture and Arts. Since 1969 the Library has been entitled to receive a free copy of every book published in Poland. Current holdings total 773,819 items.

Special Collections and Treasures. Collections include the Szembek of Poręba Library, including rare works in literature, history, law and religion; the Oppersdorff of Głogówek Library, with extensive material on Silesia; the Silesian Collection of 60,000 volumes; the Konstanty Zaleski Collection including Joachim Lelewel's letters; the Joseph I. Kraszewski Library; and the John Leopold Szersznik Collection of 18th century printed books. Treasures include N. Copernicus, *De lateribus et angulis triangulorum* (Wittenberg, 1542); Persius Aulus Flaccus, *Satirae* (Venice, 1494); Jan Kochanowski, *David's Psalter* (Cracow, 1606), and *Officia de Beata Maria Virginae,* illuminated gradual from 1526.

Exhibition Areas. No exhibition rooms. Show-cases in the hall on the ground floor.

Hours. Main Reading Room: Mon.-Fri. 0900-2100, Sat. 1000-2000. Closed Sun., 15 July-15 Aug. and public hols.

Transport. The Library can be reached by bus, tram and train.

Parking. Facilities available.

Admission. Readers: Free to registered adult readers. *Visitors:* Free admission.

Information. On the ground floor, room 5.

Sales. None.

Guidebooks. Available in Polish, free of charge.

Restaurant/Snack Facilities. Ground floor, rooms 2-3. Open 1100-1800.

Services. Telephone in the hall on the ground floor, two cloakrooms on the ground floor, two lavatories on each floor.

Catalogues. Alphabetical author and systematic subject

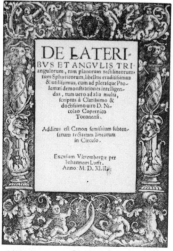

Nicolaus Copernicus, *De lateribus et angulis triangulorum* (*Wittenberg, 1542*)

catalogues.

Classification. 'Close' classification.

Copying/Photography. Microfilm and xerographic copying provided. Cameras may be used in the Library with the permission of the Director.

WARSAW
Biblioteka Narodowa
ul. Hankiewicza 1, 00-973 Warszawa
Tel. Main Building: 22-46-21; Special Collections: 31-32-41

History. The origins of the Library lie in the public library founded in Warsaw in 1747 by Józef Andrzej Załuski, Bishop of Kiev and Andrzej Stanisław, his brother, Bishop of Cracow. The end of Poland's existence as an independent state (1795) resulted in a confiscation of the Załuski Library by the Tsarist authorities and its removal to St. Petersburg. Part of it was returned to Poland after the Treaty of Riga (1921) to form the nucleus of the present Library. It was supplemented by material assembled during the 19th century by Polish political exiles, the most important being the collections of the Polish Museum in Rapperswyl Castle, Switzerland and the Polish School at Batignolles in Paris. Legal deposit privileges were received in 1927 and the Library officially opened on 24 February 1928 under its first Director, Stefan Demby. In 1939 the Library had about 770,000 volumes but many were lost, including nearly the whole of the Manuscript Collection, as a result of Nazi destruction in 1944. Work on rebuilding and reorganising what was left (mostly 19th and 20th century publications) began after the liberation of Warsaw in January 1945. A temporary reading room was opened in April 1946. Current holdings total nearly 3 million volumes and single items, which are housed in three separate buildings. The new National Library building is scheduled for completion in 1981, with 1,000 seats, storage space for 5 million volumes, exhibition and lecture halls, and a museum of the book.

Special Collections and Treasures. Special Collections (MSS, pre-1801 books, music, maps, prints and drawings, microforms) are kept in the Palace of the Republic (Plac Krasińskich 3/5). Collections include Polonica in general and, in particular, on such themes as the November Uprising (1830), Polish emigration 1831-70, the Peasant Movement at the turn of the 20th century and socialism in Poland. The collection of letters, posters and other ephemeral material now numbers about 800,000 items, including rare pamphlets issued during 1848 and World War I. The pre-1801 book collection numbers over 100,000 volumes and is strong in material relating to the history of the Polish Diet of 1788-1792 and the Kościuzko Insurrection (1794). Treasures include the only known copy of Mikołaj Rej's

Biblioteka Narodowa, Warsaw

Short Discourse (1543); Jan Kockhanowski, *Odprawa posłow greckich* (The Dismissal of the Greek Envoys) (Warsaw, 1578); and the so called *St. Cross Sermons*, the oldest monument of the Polish language (13th century text copied in early 14th century). The Manuscript Collection has been largely acquired since 1945. Treasures include the 14th century *St. Florian Psalter;* the *Catalogus Archiepiscoporum Gnesnensium* by Jan Długosz, the famous Polish 15th century historian; the *Missal* of Erazm Ciołek (c. 1515); the MSS of Chopin's compositions; and the autograph MS of Henryk Sienkiewicz, *Quo Vadis?.*

Exhibition Areas. No permanent exhibition area. Occasional displays in the Special Collections Department: Plac Krasińskich 3/5.

Hours. Main Reading Room (Hankiewicza 1): Mon.-Sat. 0800-2100, Sun. 1500-2100. Closed 25 Dec.-1 Jan., 15-31 July. Special Collections (Plac Krasińskich 3/5): Mon.-Sun. 0830-2030. In July and Aug. 0830-1430. Closed 25 Dec.-1 Jan., 1-15 Aug.

Transport. Main Building: Hankiewicza 1. Buses, 154, 157, 167, 184, 187, 359 and fast buses C, H, and K stopping at the corner of Grójecka and Wery Kostrzewy. Trams, 2, 7, 9, 14 stop at the corner of Grójecka and Wery Kostrzewy; 8, 20, 25, 29 stop at the corner of Banacha and Metrykantów. Special Collections: Plac Krasińskich 3/5. Buses, 116, 122, 135, 132, 171 and 179 stop at Krasiński Square.

Parking. Free parking space available at both buildings.

Admission. Readers: The General Reading Room in the Main Building is open to everyone over 18 years of age. Registration is not necessary. Application should be made to the Librarian at the desk and some sort of identification must be presented. The Special Collections Reading Room is restricted to research scholars.
Visitors: Visitors are freely admitted to all rooms open to the public. Librarians wishing to be shown around should go to the Reference Service Department, preferably having arranged the visit in advance. Group visits must be arranged beforehand with the above named Department.

Information. Information can be obtained in the reading rooms and catalogue areas. The Reference Service Department is located in the Main Building (2nd floor, room 1017).

Sales. None.

Guidebooks. The National Library in Warsaw (1974) in English. *Biblioteka Narodowa* in Polish. A larger guide in Polish, plus shortened foreign language versions.

Psalter (14th century), in Biblioteka Narodowa, Warsaw. Detail

Restaurant/Snack Facilities. Snack bar serving tea, coffee, sandwiches and sweets located in the basement of the Main Building, open 0800-1200.

Services. Main Building: cloakroom and lavatories, smoking lounge on the second floor landing, public telephone in the vestibule. Special Collections: cloakroom and lavatories, smoking allowed only in the corridors.

Catalogues. Alphabetical catalogues. Classified catalogue but only covering post-war acquisitions with pre-1970 imprints. Alphabetical subject catalogue: post-war Polish books and foreign publications issued after 1969. Various published catalogues.

Classification. Own.

Copying/Photography. Machines are not available for individual use. Orders for microfilms, xerographic copies etc. should be placed with the Department of Reprography (Zakład Reprografi), Plac Krasińskich 3/5, 00-973 Warsaw. The Director's permission must be obtained for private photography.

WARSAW
Biblioteka Uniwersytecka w Warszawie
Krakowskie Przedmieście 26/28, Warszawa
Tel. 26-41-55 (Chief Librarian); 26-40-47 (Department of Scientific Information)

History. Warsaw University Library was founded with the University in 1817. Its nucleus was the Library of the Warsaw Lyceum, the Library of the Court of Appeals and the collection of the School of Law and Administration. In 1819 the Library received legal deposit privileges. At the time of the November 1830 uprising it contained 134,067 volumes and 2,000 MSS. The collapse of the uprising led to the greater part of the Library's being removed by the Russians to St. Petersburg. It was not until 1860, with a series of liberal reforms by the Tsarist government, that the Library began to expand and to assume the character of a national library. In the 1890s the Library received two large collections: the 15,000 volume library of the Russian civil servant Arkadi Tolotchanov in 1893, and then in 1899 the 12,000 volume collection of the former Polish Bank. The Tolotchanov collection placed an intolerable strain on the already overcrowded Kazimierzowski Palace, so in 1894 the Library, then totalling 440,000 volumes, moved to its present building on campus. Copyright deposit privileges were renewed in 1919. The Nazi occupation of Poland during World War II proved as disastrous to the University Library as it was to the National Library, with 95 per cent of the MSS and 60 per cent of the Cabinet of Engravings being destroyed. The building, however, managed to survive even though it was seriously damaged. The growth of the Library since 1945 has

Biblioteka Uniwersytecka w Warszawie

necessitated the creation of numerous seminar libraries and some outhousing. Current holdings include 1,720,000 books and periodicals, 2,346 MSS and 12,000 microfilms.

Special Collections and Treasures. Collecting trends are basically in the humanities, with special interest in *Varsoviana.* The Library contains the greatest collection in Poland of materials pertaining to Russia, particularly of 19th century material. The Music Collection contains among others the letters and autographs of Polish musicians and composers such as Karol Szymanowski, Ludomir Rózycki and Jan Maklakiewicz. Treasures include the *Breviarum Alarici,* a parchment MS of the 9th century; a 15th century *Book of Hours* of the Blessed Virgin; a MS prayer book of Queen Anna Jagiellonka of Poland, finely bound, end of 16th century; Jan Łaski, *Commune inclyti Regni Poloniae privilegium* (Cracow, 1506), the first Polish legal code in print; Jacobus Vitelo, *Opticae libri decem* (Basel, 1572), a famous work of one of the earliest Polish scientists; Abraham Ortelius, *Theatrum orbis terrarum* (Antwerp, Plantin, 1575); and Joannes Hevelius, *Machinae coelestis pars prior* (Gdańsk, 1673), with a MS dedication by the astronomer to King Jan III Sobieski.

Exhibition Areas. No permanent exhibition areas.

Hours. Mon.-Sat. 0900-2100, Sun. 1500-2000. Closed for the month of Aug.

Transport. By city bus.

Parking. In the University forecourt.

Admission. Readers: Reading rooms open to all. Loans only to members of the University and research workers. *Visitors:* No charge.

Information. Information desk at catalogues; Department of Scientific Information; special information on library and information sciences at Reading Room of Bibliology.

Sales. None.

Guidebooks. A student's Guide in Polish is available.

Restaurant/Snack Facilities. Café in the building next to the Library.

Services. Cloakroom, lavatories and telephones on the ground floor.

Catalogues. Author and subject catalogues for books. Titles catalogues for periodicals, catalogues of special collections and card indexes containing materials on the history of the Reformation in Poland.

Classification. Own.

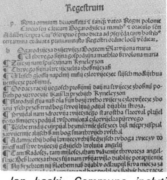

Jan Łaski, Commune inclyti Regni Poloniae privilegium constitutionum... (Cracow, 1506), in Biblioteka Uniwersytecka w Warszawie. Including a fragment in Polish, Bogurodzica (song, 'Mother of God') — the third piece of printed Polish

Prayer Book (in Polish) (16th century), in Biblioteka Uniwersytecka w Warszawie. Tan-coloured calf-leather binding with gold decoration representing the eagle arms of Poland and the letters AKP (Anna Królowa Polska — Anna, Queen of Poland). The Prayer Book was made for Queen Anna Jagiellońska

Copying/Photography. There are no machines for individual use but microfilms and xerographic copies can be ordered through the staff. Permission to use cameras should be obtained from the Library administration.

WROCLAW

Zakład Narodowy im. Ossolińskich, Biblioteka Polska Akademia Nauk (Library of the Ossoliński National Institute of the Polish Academy of Sciences)
ul. Szewska 37, Wrocław
Tel. 444-71, 444-72; Director: 343-04

History. The Library with the Publishing House was established as part of the Ossoliński National Institute (Zakład Narodowy im. Ossolińskich) in Lvov in 1817 by the writer and scientist, Józef Maksymilian Ossoliński (1748-1826). In 1823 the Library was enriched by the collection of Prince Henryk Lubomirski of Przeworsk. The true opening of the Library could properly be stated to date from 1827, when the last of the Vienna collections arrived in Lvov, or 1832 when the Reading Room was opened to the public. The Library's holdings, primarily in the humanities, grew steadily during the 19th century. In 1921 the Library received the Pawlikowski family library, which included 35,000 printed books and 289 MSS. By 1939 the Library's holdings totalled 500,000 volumes, although losses were sustained during World War II. In 1946-7, on the basis of an agreement between Poland and the USSR, part of the Library's collection was moved to Wroclaw and transferred to the Polish Academy of Sciences (PAN). The Library is now an independent scholarly institute of PAN providing services in the research and scientific fields, although, of course, the Library's collection is still representative in the humanities and is of nationwide importance in this field. The Library occupies an historic late 17th century building in Szewska Street, superbly restored after World War II damage. Current holdings total 903,695 volumes.

Special Collections and Treasures. The Library specializes in the collection of Polonica and learned literature concerning the Slavonic and Eastern European area. Collections include the Wodzicki, Lubomirski and Mniszech Family Archives; the Kozlowski, Badeni, Fredro and Skarbek Libraries; the Jablonowski Archives and Library; a large collection of Polish publications published abroad; and the Marx-Lenin 'Cabinet', covering over 5,000 books and several dozen periodicals depicting the course of revolutionary struggle, particularly Polish. Treasures include the *Exameron Beati Ambrosü,* 12th century MS, the oldest in the Library; a 15th century Burgundian *Missal;* Jan Łaski, *Statuts* (Cracow, 1506); Marcin Bielski, *Kronika Polska* (Cracow, 1597); Ptolemy, *Cosmographia* (Ulm, 1482); Joachim Lelewel, *Geographie du Moyen Age* (Brussels, 1850), dedicated by the author to the Library; and periodicals *Dekada Polska, Przegląd Naukowy, Nowa Polska, Konfederatka, Walka Klas,*

Zakład Narodowy im. Ossolińskich, Biblioteka Polska Akademia Nauk, Wroclaw

Przedświt, Praca, Równość, Kronika Ruchu Rewolucyj-nego, Głos Wolny and *Niepodległość,* illustrating the growth of democratic socialism.

Exhibition Areas. Exhibition Room.

Hours. Mon.-Sat. 0800-2000, Sun. 0900-1400. The Library closes in July. During Aug. and Sept. the Library hours are Mon. 1100-1800, Tues.-Sat. 0800-1430.

Transport. No details available.

Parking. Nearby.

Admission. Readers: Admission to all serious research workers.
Visitors: Apply to the Librarian three days before visit.

Information. Information desk in the Public Catalogue Room and separate Department of Information.

Sales. None.

Guidebooks. A free guide is available in Polish and French. A new edition in Polish and German is in preparation.

Restaurant/Snack Facilities. Mess hall.

Services. Cloakrooms and lavatories near the main reading rooms.

Catalogues. Alphabetical and subject card catalogues.

Classification. Own.

Copying/Photography. The Reproductions Department can provide microcopies and xerographic copies.

Portugal

COIMBRA
Biblioteca Geral da Universidade
Universidade de Coimbra, Coimbra
Tel. (0039) 230 15 or 255 41

History. The University of Coimbra, the oldest university in Portugal, was founded in Lisbon in 1290. It moved between Lisbon and Coimbra until finally settling in Coimbra in 1537. Of the Library at Lisbon no official records remain and it is possible that only five small faculty libraries existed. The first specific mention of the Library is a letter of 17 June 1541 in which King João III directed the University Rector to acquire book-cases

Biblioteca da Universidade, Coimbra

and to choose a building in which to instal the Library. The first Librarian was Fernão Lopes de Castanheda, the chronicler of the Indies. Growth of the collections was steady during the 16th century but the 17th century, as in Spain, marked a period of decline. By the beginning of the 18th century the Library building was in virtual ruins and the books stored in the Registry. The present building has as its founder King João V, also the benefactor of Malta (see entry for Biblioteca do Palácio Nacional de Mafra). Building began on 17 July 1717 and virtually completed during the Rectorship of Francisco de Carneiro de Figueiroa (1722-25). The Library, built in the baroque style, consists of a chamber, divided into three parts each opening into each other. It constitutes one of the most beautiful library buildings of the 18th century. In 1835 the Library received the sequestrated libraries of S. Bento, Santo Cruz (printed books only), Santa Rita and Graça. In 1920 the Library had 200,000 volumes and now, with the aid of legal deposit, has over one million items housed in the original 18th century building, in a new Central Library building completed in 1958 and in various faculty libraries (notably those of Science, Law and Letters).

Special Collections and Treasures. Collections include the Hasse Collection of fine and rare books acquired in 1806 and important collections of material in Law, Theology, Medicine and Literature dating from the 16th-18th centuries. Treasures include a giant 12th century Bible in an 18th century Parisian binding; Ludolph of Saxony's *Vita Christi* (Lisbon, 1495), conceivably the finest Portuguese publication prior to 1500; H. Schedel, *Liber chronicarum* (Nürnberg, 1493); Florian de Ocampo, *Las quatro partes enteras de la cronica de España* (Zamora, 1541); Luis de Camões, *Os lusíadas* (Lisbon, 1572), the first edition of this most important Portuguese poem; Antonio Galvão, *Tratado que compôs o nobre e notavel capitão Antonio Galvão* (Lisbon, 1563), the first edition of the famous geographic compendium; Alonso de Ercilla y Zuñiga, *Primera, segunda y tercera partes de la Araucana* (Antwerp, 1597); Pedro Murillo Velarde, *Historia de la provincia de Philipinas de la Compania de Jesus* (Manila, 1749); and manuscript works of Pedro da Esperança, Francisco de Santa Maria, Marcos Portugal, Heliodoro de Paiva and Pedro de Cristo.

Exhibition Areas. Old Library.

Hours. Mon.-Fri. 0923-1230, 1400-2245. Closed Sat., Sun. and public hols.

Transport. Car, bus or train to Coimbra. If the latter, those arriving at the main station Coimbra B, which is a mile from town, can either take the local train to Coimbra A station or taxi or tram from the station yard. The Library stands at one end of the three-sided University square.

Parking. Available on campus.

Admission. Readers: Members of the University and other researchers with proof of identity.
Visitors: Free of charge.

Information. At Library staff desks.

Sales. No details available.

Guidebooks. None.

Restaurant/Snack Facilities. None.

Services. No details available.

Catalogues. Author and subject catalogues.

Classification. Own.

Copying/Photography. Microfilm and photocopying available through Library staff. Apply to the Librarian for permission for private photography.

LISBON
Biblioteca Nacional de Lisboa
Rua Ocidental do Campo Grande 83, Lisboa 5
Tel. 76-77-86

History. The Library was founded by royal charter on 29 February 1796, as the Real Biblioteca Pública da Corte. Its establishment owed much to the initiative of Manuel do Cenáculo, Bishop of Beja. The foundation collections included the library of the Mesa Censória (of which Cenáculo was President), formed in 1768 to examine works scheduled for publication. A copy of each work published had also to be deposited with the Mesa and these books, together with those formerly belonging to the Jesuit order, formed its library, which, in turn, was the nucleus of the Public Library (a title altered to National Library in 1836). The Library opened its doors on 13 May 1797, with António Riberio dos Santos as its first Director. Legal deposit privileges were introduced on 24 May 1798. In 1841, the Library received 176,699 books and MSS, as a direct result of the order of 28 May 1834 suppressing the religious orders. The Library was originally housed in a building in the Praça do Comércio (which had earlier contained the Mesa Censória library). It then moved in 1836 to the Convent of San Francis and finally in 1969 to its present building, on a site adjoining the University of Lisbon campus. Current holdings total over 1 million volumes, 1,450 incunabula and 20,000 MSS.

Special Collections and Treasures. Collections include the Manuel do Cenáculo Collection of books and MSS; the Francisco Vieira Collection of Bodoni printed works;

Biblioteca Nacional, Lisbon

the Fontinelli Collection of coins and rare books; the D. Tomás Caetano do Bem Collection of MSS and medals; the Alcobaça Collection of MS codices dating from the 11th-17th centuries; the Pombalina Collection including 759 codices; the Camoneana Collection of 1,373 volumes; the de Câmara Collection of 6,350 ecclesiastical items; the Fialho de Almeida Collection; the library of Ivo Cruz, former Director of the Conservatório Nacional; and the library of musicologist Mario Sampayo Ribeiro (died 1967). Treasures include a MS copy of the *Codex Calixtinus* (the original is in Santiago de Compostela) and MSS and prints by Marcos Portugal, Rebello, Silva Leite, Giovanni Giorgi and Manuel Mendes. Printed books include the *Gutenberg Bible* (Mainz, 1455); Guy de Cauliaco, *Cirugia* (Seville, 1493); Juan Pastrana, *Grámatica* (Lisbon, 1497); and Fernão de Oliveira, *Grámatica da linguagem portuguesa* (Lisbon, 1536).

Exhibition Areas.   4 exhibition rooms within the Library.

Hours.   General Reading Room: Mon.-Fri. 1000-2100, Sat. 1000-1300. Closed Sun., 1 Jan., Good Fri., 25 April, 1 May, 10 June, 15 Aug., 5 Oct., 1 Nov., 1, 8, 25 Dec.

Transport.   By bus: routes 35, 44 and 45. By car: take the road through Campo Grande, a long narrow public park. To the west is the campus of Lisbon University. Underground railway station: Entre-Campos.

Parking.   Available at the Library.

Admission.   *Readers:* Portuguese nationals must present identity card. Foreigners need to provide passport or identity card.
Visitors: Free of charge.

Information.   At Library staff desks.

Sales.   None.

Guidebooks.   None.

Restaurant/Snack Facilities.   Available, Jan.-July and Oct.-Dec. 1000-1900, Aug. and Sept. 1000-1730.

Services.   Cloakrooms, lavatories, lifts, smoking lounge, telephones on ground floor.

Catalogues.   Author, subject and title catalogues.

Classification.   Universal Decimal Classification in various sections but largely arranged in legal deposit order.

Copying/Photography.   Microfilm and photocopying available through Library staff. Private photography forbidden.

LISBON
Biblioteca da Ajuda
Palácio da Ajuda, Lisboa 3
Tel. 63 85 92

History. The Library replaced the Biblioteca da Corte Portuguesa (Royal Library) which had been destroyed in the famous Lisbon earthquake of 1755. Known as the 'Real Biblioteca da Ajuda', it was initially housed in rooms next to the Ajuda Palace and was transferred to the Palace itself in 1880. Between 1770 and 1773 the Library received the collection of the famous bibliographer Diogo Barbosa Machado and subsequently books from the Jesuit colleges of Portugal and the Azores, which had been closed by order of the Marquis de Pombal. With the move of the Portuguese royal family to Brazil in 1807, the Library lost a significant proportion of its holdings, including the Barbosa Machado library (see entry for Biblioteca Nacional, Rio de Janeiro, the National Library of Brazil). Since that date the Library's collections have grown slowly to the present total of 110,000 items, including 213 incunabula and 13,000 MSS.

Special Collections and Treasures. Collections include a 62 volume manuscript collection of the Jesuits in Asia; the 'Rerum Lusitanicarum' collection of 222 volumes; and collections on music and Portuguese colonisation. Treasures include the *Missal de Chartreux,* 13th century MS; the *Cancioneiro da Ajuda,* 12th-13th centuries; Francisco de Holanda, *Da fábrica que falece ha cidade de Lysboa,* 16th century MS; *Missal Bracarense* (Lisbon, 1498); Garcia de Resende, *Cancioneiro Geral* (Lisbon, 1516); *Relaçam verdadeira dos trabalhos que ho Governador dom Fernando de Souto* (Evora, 1557), the rare first edition describing de Soto's travels in the southern United States; João Bonifácio, *Christiani pueri institutio* (Macao, 1588), one of the few surviving copies; João de Barros, *Grammatica da lingua Portuguesa* (Lisbon, 1540); and G.A. Cavazzi da Montecuccolo, *Istorica descrizione de 'tre' regni Congo, Matamba et Angola* (Bologna, 1687).

Exhibition Areas. None.

Hours. Mon.-Fri. 1030-1700, Sat. 1030-1400. Closed Sun. and public hols.

Transport. Bus: nos. 14, 27, 29, 32 and 40. Tram: 15, 18 from the Terreiro do Paço along the Rua da Junqueira. (The Palace is set on a hillside behind Belém, in the extreme west of Lisbon. The Library is on the ground floor, right hand side of the Palace.)

Parking. Next to the Palace.

Admission. Readers: Portuguese or Brazilian readers should present their identity card or passport. Other

Palácio Nacional da Ajuda, Lisbon

nationalities must present their passports and suitable letter of recommendation (e.g. from government official). *Visitors:* Apply to the Librarian.

Information. At the Library staff desks.

Sales. None.

Guidebooks. None.

Restaurant/Snack Facilities. None.

Services. Cloakrooms, lavatories.

Catalogues. Alphabetical, special (e.g. MS, iconographical) card catalogues.

Classification. Own.

Copying/Photography. Microfilm and photocopying with Director's authorisation. Private photography requires written permission of the Director.

MAFRA
Biblioteca do Palácio Nacional de Mafra
Terreiro de João V, Mafra
Tel. 52398

History. The Mafra Library is housed in a spectacular vaulted room, 88 metres long, constructed between 1717 and 1730 by Johann Friedrich Ludwig. It forms part of the Mafra Palace/Monastery, which was built for João V on the model of the Spanish Escorial. The Library did not realise its full potential, however, until after May 1771, when the Augustinian order replaced the Franciscans. Although the new Library was planned in 1771, work was interrupted soon after the bookcases had been fitted. When the Augustinians left in 1792, to be replaced once more on 12 May by the Franciscans, there had been no opportunity to gild the woodwork. By 1794, however, the books, 38,000 in all, were in place. Today they remain exactly as arranged by the first Librarian of the restored Franciscans, Fr. João de Santa Anna, whose manuscript catalogue, which is still used, was completed in 1819. After the expulsion of the religious orders in 1834, the Library languished until it was opened to the public in 1937. The books are still shelved by subject, folios in the lower cases, smaller books in the gallery. The total impact of the white bookcases, the rich marble floor, the vaulting and the old bindings provides, as one commentator has stated, 'one of the unforgettable sights in any of the major Portuguese monuments'.

Special Collections and Treasures. Treasures include G. López Madera, *Excelencias de la monarchia y reino de España* (Valladolid, 1537); Florián de Ocampo, *Chronica general de España* (Alcalá, 1578); Rodrigo Méndez

Palácio Nacional de Mafra

Silva, *Población general de España* (Madrid, 1645); Pomponius Mela, *De orbis situ* (Basel, 1516); A. Ortelius, *Thesaurus geographicus* (Antwerp, 1596); A. Montanus, *De nieuwe en onbekende weereld* (Amsterdam, 1671); and Sebastián de Miñano, *Diccionario geográfico y estadístico de España y Portugal* (Madrid, 1826-8), 9 volumes.

Exhibition Areas. Vestibule and Library rooms.

Hours. Mon.-Sat. 1100-1700. Closed Sun. and public hols.

Transport. Mafra is within easy distance of Sintra by bus or car and can be reached from Lisbon by bus. (NB. The railway station at Mafra is some miles from the town itself.)

Parking. Available.

Admission. Readers: Free of charge. Citizens of Portugal must present their identity cards, while foreigners must present their passports.
Visitors: A small entrance fee is charged.

Information. In the Reading Room.

Sales. At the Palace.

Guidebooks. None.

Restaurant/Snack Facilities. None in the Library, but café opposite the Palace.

Services. Lavatory.

Catalogues. Author catalogue.

Classification. Own.

Copying/Photography. Apply to the Director of the Library. For private photography, permission is required from the Direcção Geral da Fazenda Pública.

Rhodesia

SALISBURY
University Library, University of Rhodesia
PO Box MP 45, Mount Pleasant, Salisbury
Tel. Salisbury 36635

History. The University Library was founded in 1956. It was first located in premises on Baker Avenue in the centre of Salisbury. It then moved into various buildings on the University campus until it occupied its present building on 29 February 1960, which was given to the University by the British South Africa Company, the Anglo American Corporation and the Rhodesian Selection Trust. The Library consists of the Main Library and four branches: the Medical Library (1963), the Education Library (1967) and the Law and Map Libraries (1971). Holdings currently total 152,043 volumes, 75,361 periodical volumes, 4,881 maps and 98 sets of micro-publications.

Special Collections and Treasures. The Special Collections Department, housed on the third floor of the Main Library, includes the William Godlonton Collection of Rhodesiana, which also contains an extensive coverage of the history of Central Africa. It includes books by and about the early explorers, missionaries and pioneers in British Central Africa. There are also many works on Portuguese colonists and a collection of official documents. The C.M. Doke Collection of African languages comprises some 3,000 items, while the Government Publications Collection specialises in Rhodesian, South African and British government documents.

Exhibition Areas. Exhibitions are normally displayed in the main hall or foyer of the Library.

Hours. Main Library and Medical Library: Term: Mon.-Fri. 0800-2200, Sat. 0800-1200. Vacation: Mon.-Fri. 0800-1245, 1400-1700, Sat. 0800-1200. Closed Sun. and public hols.

Transport. Public bus service and ₁a University bus service.

Parking. Adequate space.

Admission. Readers: No charge. The Library is open to all members of the University. Others who wish to use the Library may be allowed to do so on producing satisfactory recommendation or identification.
Visitors: No charge. Visitors may view the surrounding district from the Library Tower.

Information. In the Library main hall.

Sales. University publications are available from the Publications and Exchanges Department.

Guidebooks. In English. Available, without charge, to staff and students, in the main hall.

Restaurant/Snack Facilities. None.

Services. Lifts, study carrells, cloakrooms (lower ground floor).

Catalogues. Author and classified card catalogues.

University Library, University of Rhodesia

Classification. Library of Congress.

Copying/Photography. Photo-copiers in the Main Library, Law Library and Medical Library, Microfiche, microfilm copying facilities also available. The Photographic Department is housed on the lower ground floor. Private photography permitted.

Romania

BUCHAREST
Biblioteca Centrală de Stat a Republicii Socialiste România
Bucureşti, Str. Ion Ghica nr. 4
Tel. 16.12.60; 50.70.63; 14.07.46

History. The Library, founded in 1955, is one of the two national libraries in Romania, the other being the Library of the Academy of Sciences (see next entry). Since the Library of the Academy had responsibility, first and foremost, to scientific researchers, it was felt that a large public library of an encyclopaedic nature with free general access was needed in Bucharest. The Library's initial stock derived from the Biblioteca Atheneum Romana (which had had legal deposit privileges), the 'Nicolae Bălcescu' Library and the Dimitrie Sturza Collection. Many other collections were donated and, with legal deposit privileges, growth was rapid. The Library receives 9 copies of each Romanian publication; it retains 3, sends 3 to the Academy Library and one each to the University libraries of Bucharest, Cluj and Iaşi (see relevant entries). At present the State Central Library's collections are housed in the former stock exchange building in the centre of Bucharest but plans are in hand for a new building to combat existing overcrowding. Holdings currently include 6,175,816 volumes.

Special Collections and Treasures. Collections include a complete collection of Romanian publications issued since 1952, while the Manuscripts Section includes the papers of Tudor Arghezi, G. Călinescu, E. Lovinescu, Titu Maiorescu, Ion Minulescu, I. Nădejde, Al. Odobescu, Ion Pillat, Sextil Puşcariu, Liviu Rebreanu, Mihail Sadoveanu, Ionel Teodoreanu, Vlad de la Marina, Al. Vlahuţă and Duiliu Zamfirescu. The Library's collection of 104 incunabula includes Boniface VIII, *Liber sextus decretalium* (Mainz, 1471) and H. Schedel, *Liber chronicarum* (Nürnberg, 1493). Other treasures include Sebastian Münster's *Cosmographia* in various editions; Guagninus, *Rerum Polonicorum* (Frankfurt, 1584); the *Slav Liturgy* (1508), the first book printed in Romanian territory; Dimitri Lyubavich's *Molitvelnic* (Prayer-book) of 1547; the first book printed in Moldavia, the *Homilies of Metropolitan Varlaam* (1643); and the first full Romanian

Biblioteca Centrală de Stat, Bucharest. Reading Room

language edition of the Bible (Bucharest, 1688).

Exhibition Areas. At the premises of the central headquarters (Strada Ion Ghica 4) and at the Special Collections Section (Strada Fundaţiei 2).

Hours. Mon., Tues., Wed., Fri. and Sat. 0800-2200; Thurs. and Sun. 0800-1500.

Transport. City bus services pass close by the Library.

Parking. Available in adjacent streets.

Admission. *Readers:* Open to all over 18 years of age. *Visitors:* Free of charge following a previous notification.

Information. In the 16 reading rooms. Bibliographic and information services are offered.

Sales. None.

Guidebooks. No details provided.

Restaurant/Snack Facilities. None.

Services. No details provided.

Catalogues. Author and subject catalogues. Various special catalogues such as MSS, music etc. Union catalogue of books in the principal libraries of the country, except for those of the Academy of the RSR.

Classification. Universal Decimal Classification.

Copying/Photography. Photocopies and microfilms can be supplied. Apply to the Librarian for permission for private photography.

Biblioteca Academiei, Bucharest

BUCHAREST
Biblioteca Academiei Republicii Socialiste România
Bucureşti, Calea Victoriei 125
Tel. 50.30.43

History. The Academy Library was founded in 1867. It is one of the two national libraries in Romania (see also preceding entry). Its early growth owed much to private donations, notably from B.P. Haşdeu, Timotei Cipariu, Ion Ghica and Alexandru Obobescu, and from legal deposit privileges received in 1885. The Library benefited from the Directorship of Ion Bianu, who effectively managed the Library for 56 years (1879-1935). In 1901, the Library took over the books of the Central State Library (founded 1864), which had been deprived of state support. In 1948 the reorganization of the old Romanian Academy and its conversion to an Academy of the RSR, the highest scientific and cultural authority in Romania, also brought about the transformation of the

Library. Until 1948 the collections had been restricted almost exclusively to the realm of the humanities and social sciences, but after this date collecting embraced the medical and scientific fields. The present building is inadequate but a new building, on land adjacent to the existing building, is expected to be completed in the late 1970s. Current holdings total 7,157,517 volumes.

Special Collections and Treasures. Printed book treasures include the *Slav Liturgy* (1508), the first book printed on Romanian territory; Thomas Aquinas, *Questiones disputatae de veritate* (Cologne, 1475); 4 of the 5 copies of the *Octoèque* printed in Venice 1536-7 by Bojidar Vucovici; Ciro Spontani, *Historia della Transilvania* (Venice, 1638), the copy of the Romanian historian Nicolae Bălcesco; and the first complete edition of the *Bible* in Romanian (Bucharest, 1688). Manuscript treasures include Durand's *Rationale divinorum officiorum* written on parchment, 1370; late 15th century copies of the *Codicele Voroneţean,* the *Psaltirea Scheină* and the *Psaltirea Voronoţeană,* the oldest texts in the Romanian language; 46 MSS of the Romanian national poet Eminescu; the 11th century Byzantine *Canon of Penitence,* with miniatures of the Cretan school; the MSS of the writers V. Alecsandri, Ion Creangă, I.L. Caragiale, G. Coşbuc and L. Rebreanu; 300,000 letters and autographs of such people as Darwin, Lincoln, Einstein, R. Rolland and Valéry outside Romania, and B.P. Haşdeu, Al. Odobescu, Ion Ghica, Prince Al. I. Cuza, D.A. Stourdza, N. Iorga, Dr. I. Cantacuzino, Dr. V. Babeş, H. Vacaresco, Marthe Bibesco, G. Tocilescu and S.O. Iosif within Romania. The Music Section contains manuscript scores by George Enescu, Mozart, Rossini and a notebook of Richard Strauss with unpublished compositions and notes.

Exhibition Areas. Various within the Library.

Hours. Mon.-Fri. 0800-2200, Sat. and Sun. 0800-1400. Closed public hols.

Transport. The Library, which is on the right hand side of the Calea Victoriei, can be reached by bus and tram.

Parking. The Library is situated in the Academy Park, where there are ample parking areas.

Admission. Readers: Members of the Academy and all serious researchers.
Visitors: Apply to Director of the Library.

Information. Entrance hall desk, Catalogue Room and Reading Room.

Sales. None.

Guidebooks. La Bibliothèque de l'Académie de la République Socialiste de Roumanie, in French.

Restaurant/Snack Facilities. Snack facilities are available in the Library, Mon.-Sat. 0800-1400.

Services. Cloakrooms, lavatories, lifts, smoking lounges and telephones.

Catalogues. Author and subject card catalogues. Various special catalogues, e.g. periodicals.

Classification. Universal Decimal Classification.

Copying/Photography. Copying facilities are available through the Library staff.

BUCHAREST
Biblioteca Centrală Universitară
Bucureşti, Str. Oneşti nr. 1, Sectorul 1
Tel. 13.25.57

History. The University of Bucharest was founded in 1865 and the Central University Library was inaugurated on 14 March 1895. The Library, which has copyright privileges, made steady growth until World War II, when the building was partly destroyed, as were some of the special collections. The present administrative organisation dates from a decree of 12 July 1948, which established the present Central University Library as a central unit with 20 branch libraries. Since 1948 the collections have grown to the present total of over 2 million volumes. The Library has assumed responsibility for the supply of all Romanian higher education libraries with foreign books and for supplying Romanian language and literature departments abroad with Romanian publications.

Special Collections and Treasures. The Library contains an important collection of old Romanian books dating from the beginning of printing in Romania, 1508, up to 1830. Other collections include those of Titu Maiorescu (about 8,000 volumes), Ioan Bogdan, N. Iorga, Panait Cerna. I.A. Cantacuzino, Em. Grigorovitza, C. Balmuş, E. Pangratti, Arem Frenkian, Mircea Florian, Al. Popovici-Bîznoşanu and P.P. Panaitescu. Treasures include Vicentius Serrerius Sanctus, *De sine mundi* (Treviso, 1475); the *Slav Liturgy* (1508), the first book printed in Romania; and *Sapte Taine* (Iasi, 1644).

Exhibition Areas. Main Hall.

Hours. Daily 0730-2100. Opening times are extended during students' examination periods.

Transport. Buses: Nos. 31, 32, 34, 35, 36, 37, 74, 78, 113. Trolleybuses: Nos. 82, 83, 87, 94. (The Library is located in the centre of Bucharest.)

Biblioteca Centrală
Universitară, Bucharest

Parking. Space available near the Library.

Admission. Readers: Members of the University are granted free admission. The registration office is in the central Library unit. To register, students must produce an identity card and proof of enrolment at the University or at any other college. Teaching staff must also prove their identity.
Visitors: Free admission Mon.-Sat. 0730-1500. Visitors are not admitted on Sun.

Information. The Library has an information service. General information may be obtained from the Secretariat in the central unit of the Library.

Sales. In the central Library unit. Library publications, indexes, handbooks etc. are available.

Guidebooks. The Library guide, in Romanian, published 1975. Booklets, issued annually, also in Romanian. Free of charge.

Restaurant/Snack Facilities. None.

Services. Cloakrooms, lavatories, public telephones.

Catalogues. Alphabetical and systematic catalogues. The branch libraries have bibliographical catalogues.

Classification. Universal Decimal Classification.

Copying/Photography. No facilities for copying indicated. The Director's permission must be obtained for private photography.

CLUJ
Biblioteca Centrală Universitară Cluj
Cluj, Str. Clinicilor 2
Tel. 1.50.92; 1.50.95; 2.10.92

History. The Central University Library of Cluj was founded in 1872, in the same year as the University. Its initial stock was formed from the collections of the Law Academy of Sibiu, the Medical Institute of Cluj, the Provincial Archives and the collection of Josef Benigni, the latter rich in history, geography and illuminated MSS. Soon after the holdings were enriched by the collections of the Society 'Muzeul Ardelean' (Transylvanian Museum), the total number of holdings in the Library then reaching 31,000 volumes. After the creation of the Romanian national unitary state in 1918, the holdings of the Library were considerably increased by important donations made by the Romanian Academy, by a series of Romanian and foreign scientific institutions, and by personalities of Romanian science and culture, among the most valuable was the collection of books of Gheorghe Sion. By 1939 holdings totalled 500,000 volumes, while today the Library, which has copyright deposit privileges, contains 2,600,000

Biblioteca Centrală Universitară, Cluj

volumes, housed in the Central Library and 26 branch libraries.

Special Collections and Treasures. Collections include those of Gh. Sion (4,500 volumes of rare Romanian books); Al. Lapedatu (8,000 volumes); Gh. Bogdan-Duică (3,500 volumes); Ion Bianu; Hossu Longin Francisc (400 volumes); Emil Petrovici (490 volumes); N. Bănescu; Ion Breazu (1,000 volumes); Alexandru Borza (3,000 volumes); I. Vasculescu (25,000 volumes); and Ion Crețu (6,630 volumes).

Exhibition Areas. No details available.

Hours. No details available.

Transport. No details available.

Parking. No details available.

Admission. Readers: Open to the public as well as members of the University.
Visitors: Apply to Librarian.

Information. Entrance hall and Service of Documentation and Bibliography.

Sales. None.

Guidebooks. No details available.

Restaurant/Snack Facilities. None in the Library but available nearby.

Services. Lavatories, cloakrooms, conference hall.

Catalogues. Alphabetical and subject card catalogues. Various special card catalogues.

Classification. Universal Decimal Classification.

Copying/Photography. Microfilm and photocopying available through Library staff. Permission for private photography must be obtained from the Librarian.

IASI
Biblioteca Centrală Universitară 'Mihail Eminescu'
Str. Păcurari nr. 4, Iaşi
Tel. 40709

History. The Library was founded in 1839 as the library of the Academia Mihăileană, the first Academy of Sciences in Romania. It enjoyed legal deposit privileges from 1839 and for much of the 19th century fulfilled the functions of a public as well as an academic library. The Library's initial stock derived from the collection donated by the Wallachian Prince, Mihail Sturza, to which other collections were subsequently added. In 1860 when the University was inaugurated at Iasi, the Library became the University Library. The present administrative set-up dates from 1932 and the present building was opened in 1934. It is named after Mihail Eminescu, the famous poet, who was Director of the Library from 1874-5. Current holdings total 1,506,027 items, of which 972,551 are held in the Central Library and the rest in the 19 branch libraries.

Special Collections and Treasures.   Collections include those of V.A. Alecsandri, M. Kogălniceanu, S. Bărnuţiu, B.P. Haşdeu (a former Director 1859-63 — 4,000 volumes), Gh. Asachi, C. Bolliac, C. Hurmuzaki (7,461 volumes), T. Maiorescu, Ion Ionescu de la Brad, V. Adamachi, Teodor Burada, G. Ibrăileanu and T. Simensky. Treasures include the oldest Romanian book, the *Slav Liturgy* (1508); the first book printed in Moldavia, *Cartea romanêască de învăţătură/Cazania lui Varlaam* (Iasi, 1643); the first New Testament printed in Romania (1648); and the first full Romanian language edition of the Bible (1688).

Exhibition Areas.   No special exhibition rooms.

Hours.   Mon.-Sat. 0900-1400, 1500-2100. Sun. 0900-1300. Closed two weeks for cleaning at the beginning of the summer holidays.

Transport.   Iasi is located in the NE corner of Romania, a few kilometeres from the border with the USSR. The Library can be reached by public transport.

Parking.   No facilities at the Library.

Admission.   *Readers* and *Visitors:* Admission is free of charge.

Information.   At Library staff desks.

Sales.   None.

Guidebooks.   None indicated.

Restaurant/Snack Facilities.   None.

Services.   None indicated.

Catalogues.   Books: alphabetical and classified catalogues. Periodicals: alphabetical, topographical, geographical, chronological catalogues.

Classification.   Dewey.

Copying/Photography.   One photocopying machine is available for individual use.

Biblioteca Centrală Universitară 'Mihail Eminescu', Iaşi

Singapore

SINGAPORE
National Library
Stamford Road, Singapore 6
Tel. 327355-58 (4 lines)

History. The Library traces its development back to 1823 when Sir Stamford Raffles founded the Singapore Institution, now called the Raffles Institution. The small school library grew into a subscription library, known as the Singapore Library, in 1844. In 1873 the collections totalled 3,000 books, which were merged into the Raffles Library and Museum in September 1874. In 1887 the Library was taken over by the government and moved to a new Library and Museum building. During the Japanese Occupation of Singapore in World War II the Library was closed. The collection remained largely intact under the charge of a Japanese professor who did not allow books to be taken out of the Library even by the Japanese themselves without his permission. In 1957 the Raffles National Library Ordinance was enacted and on 1 April 1958 it became the National Library, moving to its present quarters in November 1960. In addition to the Central Library in Stamford Road, there are two full-time branch libraries, two part-time branch libraries and ten mobile library service points. Current holdings (as of June 1975) include 829,003 books, 8,151 reels of microfilm and 10,071 music sheets and scores.

Special Collections and Treasures. The South East Asia Collection, housed on the first floor, is substantial and contains over 20,000 books and about 6,000 periodical titles and 8,100 reels of microfilm relating to the region, as well as 900 maps and over 600 prints. Many of the books and journals date back to the last century and have close links with the Library of the Singapore Institution. The Collection also contains local publications deposited with the Library by copyright law since 1955. The 10,000 volume library of Mr Tan Yeok Seong, donated in 1964, focuses on the influence of the Chinese in South East Asia. Treasures include Thomas Bowrey's *A Dictionary English and Malayo, Malayo and English* (London, 1701) and *Journal of a tour along the coast of Java and Bali & c. with a short account of the island of Bali particularly of Bali Baliling* (Singapore, printed at the Mission Press, 1830).

Exhibition Areas. Display cases are found in all public service areas. Major exhibits are held in the Lecture Hall of the Central Library and of the Toa Payoh Branch and in the foyer of the Queenstown Branch.

National Library, Singapore.
Central Library

Hours. (Central Library) Adult and Young People's Section: Mon.-Sat. 0830-2000. Children's Section: Mon.-

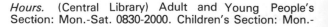

Sat. 0830-1730. Reference Services Division: Mon.-Sat. 0900-2000. Closed Sun. and public hols.

Transport. Public transport passes the Library. (The Library is on a main road in the heart of the city near the National Museum and the Cultural Centre.)

Parking. Within the Library grounds.

Admission. *Readers:* Membership is open to all adults and children. Readers over 15 years of age are required to pay and deposit of S$5, refundable when membership ceases. A non-Singapore citizen will need a Singapore citizen as guarantor.
Visitors: Free.

Information. Desks in all public service areas.

Sales. None.

Guidebooks. Various guides to the Central and branch libraries available in English and Chinese. Booklists and accessions lists are also available on request.

Restaurant/Snack Facilities. None.

Services. Typing room in the South East Asia Room for use of research workers. Lavatories on each floor. Public telephones on the ground floor near the main entrance at Central and branch libraries.

Catalogues. Separate classified catalogues are maintained for books in Malay, Chinese, Tamil and English, as well as separate catalogues for music, maps, microfilms, etc.

Classification. Dewey (16th edition). The Library is reclassifying its collection by the 18th edition.

Copying/Photography. Microfilming and electrostatic copying services are available in the Reference Services Division. Permission for private photography must be obtained from the Librarian.

Abdullah bin Abdul Kadir, Munshi, Hikayat Abdullah ('The story of Abdullah'), lithographed at the Mission Press, Singapore (1849), in the South East Asia Collection of the National Library, Singapore. First of the two introductory pages. Abdullah was secretary to Sir Stamford Raffles and his book is the first Malay autobiography

SINGAPORE
University of Singapore Library
Bukit Timah Road, Singapore 10
Tel. 50451

History. The University of Singapore has its roots in two earlier institutions of higher learning: the King Edward VII College of Medicine, founded in 1905, and the Raffles College, formally opened in 1929. These institutions were amalgamated to form the University of Malaya in 1949. In January 1959 the University split into two largely autonomous divisions of equal status, one in Singapore and the other in Kuala Lumpur. On 1 January 1962

University of Singapore Library

the former became the University of Singapore, while the latter continued under the old name of the University of Malaya. The University Library system now comprises six libraries: the Main Library, the Chinese Library and the Law Library (which are located in the Main Library building at the Bukit Timah campus of the University), the Medical Library at Sepoy Lines, the Architecture Library at the Lady Hill campus and the Engineering Library at the Prince Edward campus. The Main Library had approximately 22,859 volumes and 300 current journals in 1950, the majority inherited from Raffles College. Today, total collections comprise 602,900 volumes, and 130,888 microforms, most of which are housed in the Main Library, built in 1953 and expanded in 1958, 1963, 1967 and 1971.

Special Collections and Treasures. The Singapore/ Malaysia Collection contains approximately 13,350 catalogued items. It is particularly strong in source material tracing the various aspects of development of the Malayan States, Singapore and the Bornean regions (excluding Brunei and Indonesian Borneo) from their founding to independence and after. Microfilm holdings include the Java, Sumatra and Straits Settlements Factory Records and Colonial Office correspondence relating to the Malay Peninsula 1872-1895. The Chinese Library, which was established in 1953, is particularly rich in the classics and the commentaries, in bibliography, archaeology, language and literature. Treasures include rare editions handwritten or printed in the Yüen (1280-1368) and Ming (1368-1644) dynasties, academic and scholarly periodicals published in the early Republican period (after 1911), as well as works on Buddhism.

Exhibition Areas. Wall display cases in corridors.

Hours. Term: Mon.-Fri. 0800-2300, Sat. 0800-2200, Sun. and public hols. 0900-1900. Vacation: Mon.-Fri. 0900-1700, Sat. 0900-1300. Closed Sun. during vacation, 25 Dec., 1 Jan., Chinese New Year's Day and National Day.

Transport. Buses provide transport to the Library.

Parking. Certain areas are designated for student parking and facilities are provided for visitors' parking.

Admission. Readers: Library membership is open to University graduates, government officers, senior staff of commercial firms and industries, researchers and others on application. A refundable deposit of S$50/- is required.
Visitors: Temporary membership is open to visitors for reference purposes only. No charge.

Information. In the Reference Department.

Sales. None.

Issue of the newspaper Lat Pau for 19 August 1887, in the University of Singapore Library. Lat Pau was the first Chinese newspaper published in Southeast Asia and this is the earliest issue held by the Library

Handbooks. Library handbooks in English, free on application.

Restaurant/Snack Facilities. None.

Services. Typing rooms in the study cubicles. Lavatories at each end of the Library building. Telephones outside the Library. Cloakroom — pigeon holes provided at Library entrance.

Catalogues. Author/title card catalogues. Subject card catalogue, arranged alphabetically by Library of Congress subject headings. Various published catalogues, e.g. of the Singapore/Malaysia Collection.

Classification. Library of Congress. The Chinese Library is classified according to the Harvard-Yenching system.

Copying/Photography. Facilities provided in the corridor, Reserve Book Reading Room and in the Microfilm Services Department. Permission must be obtained from the Librarian for private photography.

South Africa, Republic of

CAPE TOWN
South African Library
Queen Victoria Street, Cape Town 8001
Tel. 43-1132; 43-3829; 43-2486

History. The Library, the oldest in South Africa, has its origins in a decree of 20 March 1818, which allowed the proceeds of a tax on wine to be used for the formation of a public library. Its foundation collection comprised the 4,565 volumes left by Joachim Nicolaas von Dessin, Secretary to the Orphan Chamber. The Library opened to the public on 2 January 1822, in a building erected for the purpose not far from the present site. In 1828 it moved to the north wing of the Commercial Exchange and in the same year the proceeds of the tax on wine were withdrawn. The Library was accordingly transformed in March 1829 into a subscription and circulating library. In 1858, Sir George Grey, the Governor, laid the foundation stone of the neo-classical building which was completed in 1860, and in 1861 he gave his personal collection to the Library. In 1910, at the time of Union, the South African Government took responsibility for the Library's somewhat precarious finances. In 1916, it received legal deposit privileges for the Union (it had received them for the Cape Colony in 1873). In 1954, the Cape Town City Libraries assumed full responsibility for book circulating functions in Cape Town, leaving the South African Library free to develop as a national reference library. On 18 December 1967 the Library officially changed its title from the South African

South African Library, Cape Town

Public Library to that of South African Library. Extensions to the building were carried out in 1922, 1926 and 1959 and it currently houses some 510,000 books.

Special Collections and Treasures. The Library's principal strengths lie in the fields of humanities and biological sciences. Apart from the Dessinian and Sir George Grey Collections it includes the J.H. Hofmeyr Collection on historical and general subjects; the M.L. Wessels Collection on classics in foreign languages; the Sir Thomas Muir Collection of mathematics; the Charles Aken Fairbridge Collection covering English literature, travel and history and works on Southern Africa (the gift of Sir Abe Bailey); the F.F. Churchill Collection on genealogy and topography; the G. Travers-Jackson Collection on mountaineering; the C.L. Leipoldt Collection on cookery and nutrition; the Alain White Collection on chess problems; the Springbok Memorial Collection; the I. Schapera Collection on etiquette; the John Armstrong Collection of vocal music; the Hilda Gerber Collection of cookery; and the Marischal Murray Collection of ships and shipping. The Africana Collections (including the relevant sections of the Grey, Fairbridge and Hofmeyr Collections) constitute one of the most complete collections of literature in existence dealing with Southern Africa. The MSS section includes the private papers of J.H. Hofmeyr ('Onze Jan'), J.X. Merriman, Sir Graham Bower, Sir James Rose Innes, Roy Campbell, Sir J.C. Molteno, W.P. Schreiner and Lady Anne Barnard.

Exhibition Areas. Central: periodic exhibitions of different subjects. Grey Collection: medieval MSS, incunabula, first editions (including Shakespeare's first and second Folios).

Hours. Mon.-Fri. 0900-1930, Sat. 0900-1800. Closed on Sun. and public hols.

Transport. Trains and buses from suburbs. (The Library is situated in the centre of Cape Town.)

Parking. Meters in neighbouring streets.

Admission. Readers: No registration for general readers but readers' tickets required for Africana Department. No admission fee. A sponsored application form is necessary in order to use MSS, rare books and newspapers. *Visitors:* Admitted free to exhibitions. Tours by arrangement.

Information. In main building.

Sales. In main building. Library's own publications on sale.

Guidebooks. A new guidebook is in preparation.

Restaurant/Snack Facilities. None in the Library but

Four Gospels, in Latin, School of Tours (c. 900), in the Grey Collection of the South African Library, Cape Town

public facilities nearby.

Services. Lavatories, telephone, cloakroom, study carrels.

Catalogues. Author and subject card catalogues. Periodicals catalogue. Printed catalogues of Dessinian, Grey and Fairbridge Collections.

Classification. Dewey and Perkins (modified).

Copying/Photography. Photocopies and microfilming available through Library staff. The use of cameras by readers is only permitted on application to the Librarian.

Friends of the Library. Friends of the South African Library: Annual subscription R. 4.50. Family subscription R. 6.00.

CAPE TOWN
J.W. Jagger Library
University of Cape Town, Private Bag, Rondebosch 7700
Tel. 69-8531

History. The South African College, which became the University of Cape Town, was founded in 1829 but the collection of books which gradually accumulated was not organised until 1905. The first University Librarian in South Africa, the Reverend G.F. Parker, was appointed in 1920 and in 1931 the Library moved into its present main building. The subsequent expansion is reflected in the increase of seats for readers from the initial 230 to 600 in 1974, and the staff has grown from 5 to 133. Current holdings total 620,000 volumes housed in seven libraries: the J.W. Jagger Library (nearly 400,000 volumes), the Architectural Library, the Brand van Zyl Law Library and the Carlton Harrison Education Library, Rondebosch; the Medical Library, Observatory; the Music Library, Rosebank; and the Hiddingh Hall Library, Cape Town.

Special Collections and Treasures. Most of the rarer items in the Library are kept in the Special Collections Department in the Jagger Library, which has its own reading room. Collections include the Africana Collection; the Ballot Collection, a typical 'gentleman's library' of the late 18th and early 19th centuries in South Africa; the Bowle-Evans Collection of English literature, history, topography etc.; the Cameron-Swan Collection of Scottish literature, history etc; the Crawford Collection of monographs on mathematics; the McGregor Collections on Kipling and modern English poetry; the J. McLean Memorial Collection; the D. MacMillan Collection of illustrations of South African interest; the Sibbett Collection of pictures; the Bertha and Ellis Silverman Collection of Hebraica; the H.C. Willis Collection on naval and aeronautical history; the Medical History

J.W. Jagger Library, Cape Town. Original building without extensions

Collection; the Music Africana Collection; and the van Zyl Bequest, 2,500 books chiefly on Roman-Dutch law. The Manuscripts and Archives Division administers the various MSS collections, the Leo Marquard Collection and the University Archive.

Exhibition Areas.   None.

Hours.   March-June and Aug.-mid Nov.: Mon.-Thurs. 0830-2200, Fri. 0830-1800, Sat. 0830-1230. Mid Nov.-mid Dec.: Mon. — Fri. 0830-1700, Sat. 0830-1200. Jan., Feb. and July: Mon.-Fri. 0830-1700, Sat. 0830-1200. Rest of Dec.: Mon.-Fri. 0830-1300, Sat. 0830-1200. Closed Sun. and public hols.

Transport.   Bus from suburban station to the campus.

Parking.   Parking for visitors can be arranged.

Admission.   *Readers* and *Visitors:* Admitted at the discretion of the University Librarian. No charge.

Information.   In the Main Reading Room on the ground floor.

Sales.   None.

Guidebooks.   Guidebooks in English are available free of charge.

Restaurant/Snack Facilities.   None in the Library but available on campus.

Services.   Cloakrooms, lavatories, lifts.

Catalogues.   Separate author and subject card catalogues. Classified catalogue (McColvin) for music.

Classification.   Dewey.

Copying/Photography.   Photocopying machines for readers' use are available in the following locations: 5 in Jagger Library, 1 in Music Library, 1 in Medical Library and 1 in Hiddingh Hall Library. The Printing and Photographic Department, located in the annex of Jagger, provides photographic reproduction of printed or documentary material, including microfilming. Readers should ask the permission of the University Librarian before using their own cameras.

PRETORIA
State Library
PO Box 397, 239 Vermeulen Street, Pretoria 0001
Tel. 48-3920

History. This Library is one of the three national libraries of the Republic of South Africa — the others being the South African Library, Cape Town (see relevant entry), and the South African Library for the Blind, Grahamstown. In general the South African Library concentrates on reference functions and the preservation of library treasures, while the State Library acts as bibliographic centre and as centre of the national inter-library loan service. The State Library was founded in 1887 by President Paul Kruger as 'De Staatsbibliotheek der Zuid-Afrikaansche Republiek'. It had a dual function as a lending and reference library. In fact it only ceased to act as a general lending library for the City of Pretoria in 1964, when the Minister of Education allowed the Library to concentrate on its national task only by separating the Pretoria Public Library from the State Library. In 1903 the name was changed to 'Government Library' and in 1910 it became known as the State Library (Afrikaans: Die Staatsbibliotheek) when the Government of the newly established Union of South Africa assumed responsibility for it. After Union, with the Copyright Act of 1916, the State Library was recognized as one of the two national libraries of South Africa and was also given legal deposit privileges. In 1933 the Carnegie Corporation of New York made a grant of $125,000 in terms of an agreement between the Corporation and the Union Government, which was intended to establish the Library as the centre of the South African library system. The State Library acts today as inter-library lending centre for South Africa and maintains the joint catalogue on monographs (1.25 million entries plus 150,000 on microfiche). Since 1972 the joint catalogue has been published in microfiche form with the ISBN as the key. The State Library also publishes various bibliographies, the most important of which is the *SANB* (*South African National Bibliography*), since 1959, and the *Bibliography of Overseas Publications about South Africa,* since 1972. The *Retrospective SANB* (1926-1958) is under preparation. Current holdings include 700,000 books, 11,000 periodical titles and 2,000 reels of microfilms.

Special Collections and Treasures. The Library's collections during its early years consisted almost entirely of works in Dutch and the present collection of Dutch literature is probably the largest in South Africa. Other collections include the Smithsonian Collection, the largest library in Africa of United States official documents; the Legal Deposit Collection; the United Nations Publications Collection; the Library Science Collection; and the Printing Collection.

Exhibition Areas. The McFadyan Hall: permanent exhibition on the history, aims and functions of the

State Library, Pretoria

State Library.

Hours. Mon.-Fri. 0800-1245, 1330-1615. Closed Sat., Sun. and public hols.

Transport. Any form of public transport to the centre of town, 239 Vermeulen Street.

Parking. Parking garage opposite the Library.

Admission. Readers and *Visitors:* The Reference Division is open to all.

Information. Reference Division.

Sales. Reference Division.

Guidebooks. Pamphlets on the aims and functions of the Library are available.

Restaurant/Snack Facilities. Not in the Library but many in the vicinity.

Services. Lavatories, cloakrooms.

Catalogues. Joint catalogue of books in South African libraries. Author/title and classified catalogues.

Classification. Dewey.

Copying/Photography. Copying facilities are available in the Reference Division. Readers and visitors may use their own cameras in the Library.

Spain

Biblioteca Central de la Diputación de Barcelona. Main Reading Room

BARCELONA
Biblioteca Central de la Diputación de Barcelona
(Biblioteca de Cataluña y Central de Bibliotecas Populares)
Apdo 1077, Calle del Carmen 47, Barcelona 1
Tel. 21 70 86 (Director); 21 46 39 (General)

History. With the foundation in 1907 of the Institut d'Estudis Catalans came the establishment of a library collection. The holdings grew so rapidly that on 24 May 1914 the Library, with the title Biblioteca de Cataluña, was opened to the public. In 1923 the Library passed under the administrative control of the town council and adopted its present title. The collections soon outgrew the available space in the Palacio de la Diputación, so on 20 February 1940 the Library officially opened in the old restored Hospital de la Santa Cruz y San Pablo (constructed in the 15th and 16th centuries). The distinctive reading rooms were restored in 1936 and 1972 respectively. Current holdings include 640,000 volumes.

Special Collections and Treasures. The Catalan Collection remains affiliated with the Institut d'Estudis Catalans. Other collections include the Aguiló Collection of printed works of Catalonia, Valencia and Majorca; the Jacinto Verdaguer Collection of 1,390 volumes and 33 MSS; the Bonsoms y Sicart Cervantes Collection; the Music Collections of Carreras Dagas, Pedrell, Pena, Anglés and Massana; the Janer Collection of Thomas à Kempis; the Bonsoms-Chacón Collection of books of chivalry; the Soler Collection of San Juan de la Cruz; the Miralles Collection of bindings; the Elzevir Collection; the Santiago y Brunet Collection, rich in MSS, incunabula and first editions; the Paluzie Collection of books of chess; the Samaranch Collection of books on sport; the Archivo Carbo-Marin; and the Proter-Moix Collection on 'Spain in the world'.

Exhibition Areas. No details available.

Hours. Mon.-Sat. 0900-1400, 1530-2030. Closed Sun. and public hols.

Transport. Bus. (The Library is located in the old centre of Barcelona.)

Parking. Available in Calle Cervelló.

Admission. Readers: Free of charge, after obtaining reader's ticket in the vestibule.
Visitors: Apply to Director.

Information. Reading rooms or Loan Service in vestibule.

Sales. No details available.

Guidebooks. Guía de las bibliotecas de la Diputación Provincial de Barcelona, in Spanish only.

Restaurant/Snack Facilities. 'Bar' available. No details of hours of opening.

Services. Cloakroom.

Catalogues. Author, systematic and subject catalogues. Various special catalogues (including printed catalogues). Union catalogue of holdings of Barcelona libraries. The catalogues are located in the Main Reading Room.

Classification. Universal Decimal Classification.

Copying/Photography. Microfilm and photocopying available through Library staff.

MADRID

Biblioteca Nacional
Calvo Sotelo 20, Madrid 1
Tel. 2756800

History. On 29 December 1711, King Philip V (1700-46) approved a scheme put forward by Father Pedro Robinet, of the Society of Jesus, for the establishment of a library in Madrid. Accordingly on 1 March 1712, the Library was opened in the Royal Palace, with Father Robinet as the first Director. Philip V donated some 8,000 volumes, MSS and prints, a good proportion of which came from the collection which in 1637 had been brought together in the tower of the Alcazar and was known as the *Librería de la Reina Madre.* The Library received copyright privileges in 1716, which were subsequently amended in 1896, 1938 and 1957. During the French invasion of Spain, 1808-14, the Library went for a while into semi-storage. In 1836, the Royal Library came under the control of the State and took the name National Library which it still bears. It grew steadily during the rest of the 19th century, and when in 1896 it moved into its present building, it contained over 500,000 volumes. Growth was again suspended during the Spanish Civil War (1936-39), although now it contains over 3 million items, including 2,670 incunabula and 35,000 codices and volumes of MSS.

Special Collections and Treasures. Collections include those of Luis de Usoz y del Río of 11,357 volumes, including a large collection of Bibles and many 16th century Spanish works; the Juan Nicolás Böhl de Faber Collection of rare Spanish printings; the Agustín Durán dramatic Collection; the José Carlos Mejia Mexicana Collection; the Antonio López de Córdoba Collection of Turkish, Armenian and Arabic works; the library of Cardinal Arquinto, strong in early Italian books; the 19,630 volume library of the Marquis de la Romana, and the Cervantes Collections of José María Asensio y Toledo and Juan Sedó Peris-Mencheta (the total Cervantes Collection of the Library is the most comprehensive in the world). Manuscript treasures include the original codex of *El Cid; Biblia Sacra Hispalense* (*Codex Toletanus*) (988 AD); *Etimologias de San Isodoro,* 10th century; *Biblia Sacra* (*Biblia de Avila*), late 11th-early 12th centuries; Jean Scylitzes, *Sinopsis historiarum,* 12th-13th centuries; two Beato de Liéban codices and autographed comedies of Spanish authors. Printed book treasures include the *Biblia Latina* (Fust and Schoeffer, 1462); *Suma de geografía* of Fernández de Encisco (Seville, 1519); and Francisco de la Rocha Burguen, *Geometría y traza perteneciente al oficio de sastre* (Valencia, 1618).

Exhibition Areas. Exhibitions are regularly held in the three main exhibition rooms. New acquisitions are displayed in show-cases in each department and in the entrance hall.

Biblioteca Nacional, Madrid

Hours. Reading Room: Mon-Fri. 0900-2200, Sat. 0900-2100. Closed Sun., 1, 5 and 6 Jan., 1 and 15 May, 29 June, 18 and 25 July, 15 Aug., 12 Oct., 1 Nov., 8, 24, 25, 31 Dec., Thurs.-Mon. of Easter Weekend.

Transport. Metro: to Colón, Cibeles or Serrano. Buses: 1, 2, 5, 9, 14, 19, 27, 45, 53. (Starting from Cibeles and following the Paseo de Calvo Sotelo towards the Plaza de Colón, the Palacio de Bibliotecas y Museos is on the right. The ground and principal floors to the left house the Library.)

Parking. Pay parking in nearby streets.

Admission. *Readers:* Must obtain a Library card, free of charge. A Spanish citizen has only to prove his identity and job affiliation to receive a card. A foreign researcher, for special researches, must provide a letter of introduction (preferably from an embassy) and two passport-type photographs.
Visitors: Free of charge but limited to certain parts of the Library. Saturdays, conducted tours.

Information. At the entrance, in the Catalogue Hall and the Reading Room.

Sales. The Library only sells catalogues of its exhibitions. (Available from the Servicio de Publicaciones del Ministerio de Educación y Ciencia, Ciudad Universitaria, Madrid 3).

Guidebooks. No current guide book but several pamphlets, *Folletos de uso,* available free of charge.

Restaurant/Snack Facilities. The cafeteria and restaurant services on the 2nd floor are available during the hours the Library is open.

Services. Cloakroom at the entrance; smoking areas at the entrance to each reading room/study area; telephones at the lower entrance, next to the Bibliographical Information Section and at the entrance to the special sections; typing rooms; microfilm readers; and audio-visual units.

Catalogues. Printed books: author catalogue closed at 1956. Dictionary card catalogue since 1956. Manuscripts: various published general and special catalogues.

Classification. Universal Decimal Classification after 1954 (prior to that, own).

Copying/Photography. Microfilm and photocopying through staff. No private camera photography without permission.

MADRID
Biblioteca de Palacio
Palacio de Oriente, Calle Bailén, Madrid 13
Tel. The central line of the Patrimonio Nacional

History. The common belief that Philip V created a private library in the Royal Palace at the same time as he founded the Royal Public Library (i.e. the Biblioteca Nacional, see preceding entry) has no solid foundation. In fact, the private Royal Library was only really installed in the Palacio de Oriente during the reign of Charles III (1759-88). In 1760 he possessed 824 works in 2,153 volumes; by 1782 there had been only 453 additions, giving a rate of accession of only about twenty books a year. By 1801, 13 years after Charles III's death, the Library contained over 20,000 works, thanks to the interest of Charles IV. The Library languished after the latter's death until the reign of Isabella II (1833-68), when Miguel Salvá was Director. The collections gradually grew under a succession of able directors, notably Manuel Ramón Zarco del Valle. During the Spanish Civil War the holdings had to be evacuated but they were restored in 1940. Current holdings total 300,000 printed works, 4,000 MSS, 3,000 musical works and 3,500 maps.

Special Collections and Treasures. Treasures include the 15th-century MS, *Libro de horas con las armas de Aragón y Enríquez,* possibly the most beautiful example of Flemish art in Spain; Durandus, *Rationale divinorum officiorum* (Mainz, 1459), the oldest printed book in the Library; Alfonso de Cartegena, *Genealogía de los reyes de Espana,* MS (c.1460); Fray Bernardino de Sahagún's autographed *Historia de Nueva Espana* (1577); Francisco López de Caravantes, *Historia del Perú,* MS, 17th century; J.A. Vera y Figueroa, *Fracmentos históricos de la vida de Don Gaspar Phelipe de Guzmán, Conde de Olivares,* MS (1638), in a decorative 17th century Spanish binding; Juan José de Eguilara y Eguren, *Biblioteca Mexicana* (Mexico, 1755); and Antonio de Capmany y Montpálau, *Memorias históricas sobre la marina, comercio y artes de la ciudad de Barcelona* (Madrid, 1779-1792), 3 volumes. Collections include the Cervantes Collection and the Americana Collection of Jaime Baltasar Martínez Compañón, Bishop of Trujillo, in Peru. The collection of bindings is exceptional, particularly for the 18th and 19th centuries.

Exhibition Areas. Eight rooms of the Library display the most interesting and valuable books, MSS, and fine bindings.

Hours. Mon.-Sat. 1000-1330. Closed Sun., public hols. and the whole of Aug.

Transport. Buses and metro to the Isabel II square. (The Library occupies 24 rooms on the lower floor in the north-east corner of the Palacio de Oriente.)

Parking. In front of the Palace.

Palacio de Oriente, Madrid

Admission.   Readers: Free admission on presentation of proof of identity.
Visitors: Free admission 1000-1300, 1600-1800. (Mornings only on public hols.)   Guided tours of the Palace available.

Information.   At the Library desks.

Sales.   In the Library itself, in the vestibule of the Palacio Real and in the shop of the Patrimonio Nacional, Plaza de Oriente.

Guidebooks.   M. Lopez Serrano, *Palacio Real de Madrid* (Madrid, 1972), in German, French and English as well as Spanish. Includes a small section on the Library. Also guide to the Library in Spanish.

Restaurant/Snack Facilities.   Cafeteria in the foyer of the Palace.

Services.   Cloakrooms, lavatories and telephones.

Catalogues.   Various published catalogues.

Classification.   Own.

Copying/Photography.   Apply through Library staff for microfilm and photocopies.

MADRID
Biblioteca de San Lorenzo el Real del Escorial
Monasterio de San Lorenzo del Escorial, Real Biblioteca, Madrid
Tel. 2960984

History.   The monastery-palace of El Escorial, situated some thirty miles outside Madrid, dates from 1562. It was built at the order of Philip II to commemorate the Spanish victory over the French at St. Quentin in 1557. The structure was not completed until 1584 but the first books arrived in 1565. By 1593 over 10,000 volumes, classified and organised by the humanist Benito Arias Montano, were installed in the Exhibition Hall of the Laurentian Library. During the reign of Philip III further acquisitions were made, notably 4,000 manuscripts from the library of Muley Zidán, the Sultan of Morocco. Setbacks, however, came first in 1671 when more than 4,000 manuscripts and incunabula were destroyed by fire; many volumes were despoiled during the Napoleonic invasion, and again between 1820-3 losses were sustained. By 1859 the Library had 30,000 volumes, while today holdings total over 60,000 volumes and nearly 5,000 MSS.

Biblioteca de San Lorenzo el Real del Escorial.

Special Collections and Treasures.   Among the Library's

treasures are the *Etymologies* of St. Isidore, 10th century; the *Albeldense* and *Emilianense* codices, 10th century; the *Codice Aureo* (c. 1033-39), presented by Philip II; four autograph manuscripts of Saint Teresa of Avila; the *Libro de las cantigas* by Alfonso X (el Sabio); the *Breviaries* of Charles V and Philip II; the 1594 *Koran* of Muley Zidán; *De civitate Dei* of St. Augustine (Rome, 1468); Sánchez de Arévalo's *Speculum vitae humanae* (Rome, 1468); the *Fábulas de Esopo* (Zaragoza, 1489) and the *Relación de Michoacán* (c. 1540-41), possibly the work of Fr. Maturino de Gilberti.

Exhibition Areas. The Exhibition Hall/Library is located above the main entrance to the monastery. It is entered through the angle formed by the lesser cloisters on the third floor between the west and north wings. Exhibits are housed in seven cabinets with the surrounding bookcases designed by Juan de Herrera in the Tuscan order.

Hours. Summer: daily 1000-1300, 1500-1900. Rest of year 1000-1300, 1500-1800.

Transport. By train from the Estación del Norte or bus from Madrid. By car drive west on N6 to Las Rozas, where a turn onto C505 leads directly to the monastery. (The Escorial lies 43 km north-west of Madrid.)

Parking. Facilities available.

Admission. Readers: Open to qualified students. Registration takes place in the Reading Room.
Visitors: The Library is part of the monastery tour, costing 60 pesetas.

Information. In the Reading Room.

Sales. In various parts of the monastery.

Guidebooks. Gregorio de Andres, *Real Biblioteca de El Escorial,* in Spanish only.

Restaurant/Snack Facilities. Not available in the monastery.

Services. Lavatories, cloakrooms, telephones.

Catalogues. Printed manuscript catalogue. Author card catalogue for printed books.

Classification. Own.

Copying/Photography. Photocopying and microfilm facilities available through library staff. Special permission required for private photography.

SALAMANCA
Biblioteca Universitaria
Universidad Pontificia de Salamanca, Calle de Libros,
Salamanca
Tel. 213964

History. The University of Salamanca and its Library were founded by Alfonso IX of León in 1218, but it was the charter of Alfonson X (Alfonso the Wise) of 8 May 1254 that gave the University a permanent endowment. He stipulated that it should have a professional Librarian with a fixed salary, the first of the kind in Spain. The Library did not have its own quarters until 1479, and it is possible that up to this time books were kept in chests. Building began in 1509 of the Main Hall of the Library, whose gothic arches were destroyed in 1664 and were reconstructed, in the baroque style, in 1749. The Library's history has reflected that of the University. At the end of the 16th century Salamanca had 8,000 students and 70 chairs, but it suffered a period of severe decline during the 17th and most of the 18th centuries. Recovery took place during the 19th century, partly as a result of the educational reforms of the mid-century. Various subsidiary libraries were added in the 1950s, such as the Library of the Faculty of Philosophy and Letters, which has a significant MSS collection. The Main University Library now houses about 130,000 volumes, with 2,771 MSS and 462 incunabula.

Special Collections and Treasures. Treasures amongst the manuscripts include *Liber mozarabicus canticorum et horarum* (1059), which belonged to Doña Sancha, wife of Ferdinand I; the autographed copy of Friar Luis de León's *Book of Job; Claras mujeres* of Don Alvaro de Luna; the autographed *Batallas y quinquagenas* of Gonzalo Fernández de Oviedo; and the *Salamanca Codex,* the most complete of the three manuscript copies of the *Libro del Buen Amor,* by Juan Ruiz the Archpriest of Hita, one of the classics of medieval literature.

Exhibition Areas. Exhibitions are occasionally held in the Main Library Hall.

Hours. Mon.-Fri. 0930-1400, 1530-2130, Sat. 0930-1400 only. Closed Sun. and public hols.

Transport. The Library is near the Plaza Mayor, which is served by buses. The University is reached from the cathedral via Calles Calderón and Libreros, or approaching from any other direction following the signs marked Universidad.

Parking. There are parking spaces in the vicinity of the Library.

Admission. *Readers* and *Visitors:* On application to the Library Director.

Biblioteca Universitaria, Salamanca

Information.   At the staff desks.

Sales.   None.

Guidebooks.   None.

Restaurant/Snack Facilities.   None on the Library premises but available nearby.

Services.   The Library is housed in the main building of the University, which has the usual services.

Catalogues.   Alphabetical author catalogue. Various special catalogues.

Classification.   Own.

Copying/Photography.   Microfilm and photocopies only available through Library staff.

Sri Lanka

COLOMBO

National Museum Library
Department of National Museums (PO Box 854), Sir Marcus Fernando Mawatha, Colombo-7
Tel. 93314

History.   The Library was opened in January 1877, following the establishment of the Colombo Museum in 1877. Its initial stock was formed from the libraries of the Royal Asiatic Society (Ceylon Branch), founded in 1845, and the Government Oriental Library, opened in 1870. At its inauguration the Library was the only library in Ceylon open to the public. In 1885 the Library obtained the right to receive one copy of every book, periodical, and pamphlet published in Ceylon. By 1910 the collections totalled 15,000 volumes, with the Royal Asiatic Society Library containing 10,000 volumes. In 1942, following the change of name of the Museum, the Library became known as the National Museum Library. In the same year the Royal Asiatic Society Library was restored to the Society. In 1970 with the extension of the Library premises, the science collections were centralised and housed in a separate unit as the Science Division. Current holdings total 80,000 volumes and 3,516 MSS.

National Museum Library,
Colombo

Special Collections and Treasures.   The Library was established as a centre for research studies with special emphasis on Oriental studies, natural history and Ceylon studies. It now has, perhaps, the best collection on Sri Lanka in the world, while its resources on zoology and anthropology rank among the best in the East.

Exhibition Areas.   None.

Hours.   Sun.-Thurs. 0900-1700. Closed Fri., Sat., and public hols.

Transport.   Buses nos. 177, 155, 193, 138 operate along the Marcus Fernando Mawatha.

Parking.   Parking is available in the Museum grounds.

Admission. Readers: Application to use the Library should be made to the Director, Department of National Museums, on provided forms at least one week in advance. All applications must be supported by a scholar, or institution, verifying the statements on the application form. A Readers' Ticket will then be issued, valid only until 31 Dec. of the year of issue. Short-term tickets of a maximum of six months can also be obtained on application in writing to the Librarian on a provided form. Annual registration fee Rs 5/-.
Visitors: Must ask the permission of the Librarian.

Information.   At the entrance to the Reading Room.

Sales.   None.

Guidebooks.   None.

Restaurant/Snack Facilities.   Restaurant on the Museum premises.

Services.   Lavatories and telephones.

Catalogues.   Card catalogue.

Classification.   Universal Decimal Classification.

Copying/Photography. Photocopies are provided through the Public Library, Colombo. Private photography is allowed with the Director's permission.

Sudan

KHARTOUM
University of Khartoum Library
PO Box 321, Khartoum
Tel. 72185

History. The Library was established in 1945 with a foundation collection of 13,000 volumes. Some 3,000 volumes were donated by the administrative secretariat of the Sudan Government and another 3,000 were taken over from the old Higher Schools. The Library is not only the most important academic library in the Sudan, but

Khartoum University. Main building

also the most important of any kind any, in effect, acts as the national library. It is currently in receipt of legal deposit privileges. The main section of the Library is housed in the Old Gordon Memorial College building, while separate branch libraries exist for Medicine, Engineering, Law and Agriculture. Holdings currently total 255,000 books and 3,000 MSS.

Special Collections and Treasures.   All books and other publications about the Sudan are kept in a special room (the Sudan Library), which is perhaps the most comprehensive on the area in the world.

Exhibition Areas.   None.

Hours.   Sat.-Wed. 0700-2230 (except April and May: 0700-1400), Thurs. 0700-1400, Fri. and public hols. 0800-1200.

Transport.   Buses to the Library.

Parking.   Space available.

Admission. Readers: Open to all members of the University of Khartoum and also to non-members wishing to read in the Library.
Visitors: Admitted.

Information.   In the Catalogue Hall.

Sales.   None.

Guidebooks.   A guide is published in the *University of Khartoum Annual Calendar.* Off-prints are available free on request.

Restaurant/Snack Facilities.   None in the Library but available in the vicinity.

Services.   Lavatories, telephones.

Catalogues.   Author and classified catalogues.

Classification.   Bliss.

Copying/Photography.   Very limited service. Apply to Reading Room staff. Permission must be obtained for private photography.

Sweden

GOTHENBURG
Göteborgs Universitetsbiblioteket
Centralbiblioteket, Box 5096, S-402 22 Göteborg 5,
Renströmsgatan 4
Tel. 031/81 04 00

History. The Library traces its existence as an independent institution from 1890, when it was known as the Göteborgs Stadsbiblioteket (Gothenburg City Library). Its origins, however, can be dated back to 1774 when the library of the Royal Society of Science and Letters was founded. The Society's collection was incorporated in the Gothenburg Museum Library in 1861 and, in turn, the latter became the basis of the Stadsbiblioket in 1890. It received partial legal deposit privileges in 1921 and full rights in 1950. The growth of the collections soon placed a severe strain on the Library building, occupied in 1900. The present building was constructed 1951-4 on a solid granite basis and can be likened to an iceberg in that only the 6th-8th floors are visible, the rest being below ground. In 1961, the Library adopted its present title to avoid confusion with the current city public library. Current holdings, which include those of the Bio-Medical, Botanical, Economics and Karlstad branch libraries, as well as the Central Library, total well over 1 million volumes (about 35,000 metres of shelving).

Special Collections and Treasures. Collections include the 4,000 volume library of the Swedish poet and librarian, Carl Snoilsky (1841-1903); the Tranemåla Collection of over 25,000 items; the Chinese Collection of 1,500 volumes; the Armenian Collection; and the Ludvig Holberg Collection. Treasures include the MSS of Hjalmar Söderberg, Birger Sjöberg, August Strindberg, Selma Lagerlöf and Viktor Rydberg.

Exhibition Areas. Show-cases in the entrance hall of the Central Library.

Hours. Mon.-Fri. 0800-2100, Sat. 0900-1800, Sun. 1300-1700. Closed public hols.

Transport. The Library is within easy reach of tram and bus lines.

Parking. Space available but may be crowded during term.

Admission. Readers: No fees. Those wishing to borrow must deposit a warrant signed by a resident of Gothenburg, or submit evidence of being an enrolled student in an academic institute in Gothenburg.

Göteborgs Universitetsbiblioteket

Visitors: Free admission.

Information: In the Catalogue Hall and in the Lending Department.

Sales. None.

Guidebooks. None.

Restaurant/Snack Facilities. Cafeteria at the Library entrance, open Mon.-Fri. 0930-1600.

Services. Typing room, cloakroom, lavatories, smoking lounge, telephones.

Catalogues. For books printed before 1958: author catalogue on cards, systematic catalogue on slips. For books printed after 1958: author and systematic catalogues on cards.

Classification. Pre-1958: Library's own system. Post-1958: Swedish Library Association scheme.

Copying/Photography. Photo-copier available in the entrance hall. No restrictions on private photography.

LUND
University Library of Lund
Box 1010, S-221 03 Lund
Tel. 046/12 4100

University Library of Lund

History. Lund University was founded in 1668 and the Library three years later, when the old cathedral library was handed over to the University. In 1684 King Charles XI presented the 6,000 volume library of his former tutor Edmund Gripenhielm. In 1698 the Library received legal deposit privileges for all Swedish publications. Growth was slow in the 18th century and accessions came mainly in the form of gifts, such as the Falkenberg Collection of 1,372 books and 21 MSS, received in 1780. In 1800 the collections totalled some 20,000 volumes, but grew rapidly from this date onwards, partly as a result of extensive foreign exchange agreements inaugurated in 1818. The Library had occupied its own building since 1690 (the Old Library) but this became increasingly inadequate. In 1907 the present Library building was occupied; in 1936 a book stack was added, with further extensions in the 1950s. The Library, which acts as the main research library of southern Sweden, has current holdings of over 2 million volumes and 12,000 MSS.

Special Collections and Treasures. Collections include the Franz Schubert Collection, donated by the late Otto Taussig, with autographs of the composer and original editions of his works; manuscript collections of Swedish authors, e.g. of Esaias Tegnér, the poet; the original Cathedral Library of 371 items, the *Bibliotheca antiqua;*

the de la Gardie Archives (about 1,500 volumes and fascicles); the bulk of the University Archives and of the Akademiska föreningen (the Academic Society); the 5,000 volume library of C.M. Collin, including works of Goethe and Dante; and a collection of old music belonging to the Akademiska kapellet (the Academic Orchestra). Treasures include two 12th century MSS on vellum, the *Necrologium Lundense* and the *Liber daticus Lundensis vetustior,* which are the oldest records of Lund Cathedral that have been preserved.

Exhibition Areas. Exhibition Room at the entrance. Rotating exhibitions.

Hours. Mon.-Fri. 0800-2100 (vacations 0800-1900), Sat. 0800-1500. Closed Sun. and public hols.

Transport. Bus no. 1 from Central Station.

Parking. Limited parking facilities available.

Admission. *Readers:* Apply at the Information Desk. *Visitors:* Free entrance to the Exhibition Room.

Information. Information Desk.

Sales. None.

Guidebooks. Available in Swedish.

Restaurant/Snack Facilities. In basement, Mon.-Fri. 0930-1700. (Vacations 1000- 1530.)

Services. Cloakrooms, lavatories and telephones at the entrance. Smoking lounges in the basement.

Catalogues. Author and classified catalogues for both books and MSS. Separate card index of foreign dissertations.

Classification. Before 1958: the Library's own classification; after 1958: the classification system of the Swedish Library Association; for mathematics, science and technology: Universal Decimal Classification.

Copying/Photography. Photocopying and microfilm facilities are available. Apply to staff in the Reading Room.

Necrologium Lundese, in the University Library of Lund. A list of the most ancient Christian kings of Denmark

STOCKHOLM
Kungliga Biblioteket
Box 5039, S-102 41 Stockholm 5
Tel. 08/24 10 40

History. The Kungliga Biblioteket (Royal Library) is the national library of Sweden. It is also the principal library in Stockholm for humanistic studies and serves as the main library of the Stockholm University Faculties of Arts, Law and Social Sciences. Its origins lie in the private collections of the Swedish kings. The earliest catalogues still preserved date from 1564 and 1571. Real growth came during the reign of Queen Christina (1632-54), although on her abdication in 1654 a great many of the treasures went with her to Rome (where they are still kept together in the Vatican Library as the 'Bibliotheca Alexandrae Reginae'). Her successor Charles X helped rebuild the collections and in 1661 legal deposit privileges were received. In 1697, however, the Royal Palace, where the collections were housed, was destroyed by fire and 75 per cent of the MSS and books were lost, only 6,826 books and 283 MSS being saved. It was not till the late 18th century that the Library recovered, moving into the new Royal Palace in 1768, and receiving several collections, notably that of the dissolved College of Antiquities in 1780. The 19th century also witnessed a number of important donations such as that, in 1873, of the private library of Charles XV (including the library of Charles XIII assembled at Rosersberg), altogether about 30,000 volumes. By 1800 the collections had totalled 30,000 volumes, whereas in 1900 the total was 300,000 volumes. In 1877 the Library moved into its present building, reconstructed in the 1920s and the 1950s. The completion of this rebuilding programme was followed by the construction of an underground stack, opened in 1971. Current holdings include about 1.5 million books and 14,000 MSS.

Special Collections and Treasures. Collections include C.G. Tessin's Collection of feast books, emblem books and libretti; A.E. Nordenskiöld's Japanese Collection (5,380 volumes); G. Berghman's Collection of Elzevir books (about 2,650 volumes); F. Vult von Steyern's Collections of Goethe and Wagner literature (more than 2,500 volumes); G. Martin's Collection of Chinese and Japanese literature (about 1,650 volumes); the Sohm Collection of type specimens; Dag Hammarskjöld's private library; the E. Gellerstedt Collection of maps; the E. Hellman Collection of bibles and biblical literature (more than 4,000 volumes); and the George Stephens Collection. The Department of MSS includes a large collection of medieval Swedish and foreign manuscripts, many early Norwegian and Old Icelandic manuscripts, and the papers of Swedish writers, such as Georg Stiernhielm, Olof von Dalin, Carl Michael Bellman, Viktor Rydberg, August Strindberg and Selma Lagerlöf. The Engeström Collection (mainly history and biography) and the Rålamb Collection of manuscripts (mostly historical) are kept as separate units. Among the treasures are the *Codex Aureus Holmiensis,* a beautiful English vellum manuscript, 8th century, containing the four Gospels in a Latin translation which in some parts differs from the Vulgate version; and the *Gigas Librorum* or 'Devil's Bible', a large Bohemian vellum manuscript which dates from the beginning of the 13th century and which contains, among other things, the Old Testament in a version which is partly unique. The collection of maps

Kungliga Biblioteket,
Stockholm

and prints includes, apart from cartographical literature and maps in book form, about 40,000 separate maps and 150,000 plates. The De la Gardie Collection, a separate unit, contains a number of views of towns, etc., some of which are unique, and of ornament engraving with several unique items.

Exhibition Areas. Exhibition Room, adjoining cloakroom.

Hours. Reading rooms: Mon.-Thurs. 0845-2200, Fri. 0845-2100, Sat. 0845-1800, Sun. 1100-1700. (Midsummer until approx. 20 Aug. Mon.-Fri. 0845-2000, Sat. 0845-1400, closed Sun.).

Transport. Underground: nearest station Östermalmstorg. (The Library is in Humlegården Park in the centre of Stockholm.)

Parking. No facilities.

Admission. *Readers* and *Visitors:* Free of charge.

Information. Catalogue Room.

Sales. In the cloakroom. The Library's own publications and postcards for sale.

Guidebooks. None

Restaurant/Snack Facilities. Available 1000-1600.

Services. Typing rooms, cloakrooms, lavatories, telephones.

Catalogues. Alphabetical, systematic, dictionary and special catalogues.

Classification. After 1955: the Swedish Library Association system.

Copying/Photography. Copying facilities are provided. Private photography only allowed in exceptional circumstances.

Friends of the Library. *Föreningen för bokhantverk* acts as Friends of the Library. Membership: Sw.Kr. 25 per annum.

UPPSALA
Uppsala Universitetsbiblioteket
Box 510, S-751 20 Uppsala
Tel. (018) 139440

History. The Royal University Library of Uppsala is the largest and oldest library in Sweden. The University was founded in 1477 on the initiative of Archbishop Jacob Ulfsson, but the Library was not really established until

13 April 1620, when Gustavus Adolphus presented to the University most of what remained of Sweden's principal medieval libraries, e.g. from Vadstena Abbey, the Franciscan Monastery in Stockholm, and the Dominican Monastery in Sigtuna, as well as the library of King John III (1568-92). By 1700 the Library had some 30,000 volumes, mostly foreign works, but copyright deposit privileges received in 1692 and 1707 ensured the continuing intake of Swedish books. During the 18th century a succession of able librarians, such as Eric Benzelius (1702-23) and Pehr Aurivillius (1789-1829), and above all a number of large donations, brought the Library into the front rank of European libraries. Until 1841 the Library was inadequately housed in the University building, the Gustavianum, but in that year it moved into its present neo-classical building, the *Carolina Rediviva* (in memory of an older University building, the *Academia Carolina*). Between 1934 and 1945 and again from 1964, the building was greatly enlarged to accommodate the intake of material, which now includes over 2 million books, 40,000 MSS and a great number of pamphlets and small prints.

Special Collections and Treasures. Collections include the Wahlund Collection of 2,500 volumes on Romance, philology, literature etc; the Waller Collection of 25,000 volumes on the history of medicine; the papers of King Gustavus III (reigned 1771-92); the De la Gardie Collection; the Palmskiöld Collection of MSS and printed source material for Swedish history, genealogy and topography; the Nordin Collection of MSS for Swedish history (over 2,000 volumes), the Westin Collection (about 25,000 items) and the Ihre Collection on Swedish history, literature, philology etc; the Count Gyllenborg Map Collection; the Bodoni Collection; the Düben and Gimo Collections of old manuscript music; and the Gösta Oldenburg Collection of American books. Treasures include the *Carta marina* (Venice, 1539), the earliest map to present a fairly accurate picture of the Scandinavian countries, drawn by Olaus Magnus, one of only two copies known to exist; the *Codex Argenteus* or 'Silver Bible', a beautiful vellum MS, c.500 AD, containing fragments of the four Gospels in the Gothic translation of Bishop Ulfila; Snorre Sturlason's *Edda,* an Icelandic MS, c.1300 AD; the *Codex Caesareus* or 'Imperial Bible', a gospel book in Latin, written in Germany about 1050 for the Emperor Henry III; the MS of Linnaeus's *Sponsalia plantarum;* the first dated book printed in Sweden, *Dialogus creaturarum moralizatus* (Stockholm, 1483); and Mozart's original draft for the finale of the first act of *The Magic Flute.*

Exhibition Areas. Ground floor, near main entrance. Exhibition Room is open Mon.-Fri. 0900-2100 (between 16 June and 15 Aug. 0900-2000), Sat. 0900-1800, Sun. 1230-1500 (15 May-15 Sept. only).

Hours. Mon.-Fri. 0830-2100, Sat. 0900-1800. Closed Sun. and public hols.

Uppsala Universitetsbiblioteket

Transport. Bus stop outside the Library (for several bus routes).

Parking. Available in the vicinity of the Library.

Admission. Readers: No charge and no registration rules.
Visitors: No charge, except a small entrance fee to the Exhibition Room on Sun. from 15 May-15 Sept.

Information. In Catalogue Room on ground floor.

Sales. On ground floor in entrance hall. Guides, brochures, postcards and slides are sold.

Guidebooks. Guide to the Library available in Swedish, English, French, German, Russian, Spanish (Sw.Kr. 1.50).

Restaurant/Snack Facilities. cafeteria, with automats (for coffee etc.) and snacks. Open: Mon.-Fri. 0930-2100, Sat. 0930-1800.

Services. Typing rooms in basement, cloakroom, lavatories, smoking room in cafeteria, telephone booths on ground floor around main hall.

Catalogues. Printed catalogue for books acquired before 1796. Catalogue (handwritten or typed) in bound volumes up to and including 1962. Card catalogue from 1963 onwards. Catalogues of the MSS collections. Various special catalogues.

Classification. The Swedish Library Association system.

Copying/Photography. Copying facilities are provided. Cameras may be used with special permission.

Switzerland

BASEL
Öffentliche Bibliothek der Universität Basel
Schönbeinstrasse 18-20, CH-4056 Basel
Tel. (061) 252250

History. The Library was founded in 1460 at the same time as the University. The Library's early development was hampered by lack of funds. It received some assistance from the monastic and endowment libraries of the city, and after the Reformation was enriched by the acquisition of a number of sequestrated monastic collections, notably of the Carthusians. The Amerbach and Dr. Remigius Faesch museums, with their libraries, were incorporated in 1661 and 1823 respectively. The

Öffentliche Bibliothek der Universität Basel

collections in 1800 totalled 16,000 volumes and 4,000 MSS. The Library was from the beginning under the care of a Professor of the University, the first official Librarian being appointed in 1866. In 1896 the Library moved into its own building, designed by Emanuel La Roche and built in the baroque style. An extension was built from 1962-68. Current holdings include 2,068,000 books and 32,000 maps.

Special Collections and Treasures. Collections include the Faesch Collection (mentioned above) of 5,000 volumes including medieval MSS from the Fulda monastery; an Ex-Libris Collection of 50,000 items; the private library of Johannes de Lapide; the libraries of the Basel Naturalist Society and of the Historical and Antiquarian Society of Basel; the 'Zieglersche Kartensammlung' (the Map Collection); the Church Library; the older holdings of the Basel Reading Society; the library of the Swiss Music Research Society (which includes the 18th century collection of Lucas Sarasin); the archive of the General Music Society; the library of the Frey-Grynäisches Institut; and a Portrait Collection of 90,000 items covering Swiss and foreign personalities.

Exhibition Areas. Exhibition Hall.

Hours. Reading and Catalogue Rooms: Mon., Tues., and Thurs. 0900-2200, Wed. and Fri. 0900-1900, Sat. 0900-1700. Closed Sun., public hols. and 2 or 3 weeks in July/Aug.

Transport. Trams and buses serve the Library.

Parking. None.

Admission. Readers: Students at the University may use the Library on production of a student's identity card. Schoolchildren over 16 and local residents have free access. Non-residents of the Canton, or temporary residents in Basel, must either obtain a local guarantor, or pay a deposit, which will be returned on conclusion of their use of the Library. Persons known to the Library, or whose standing is deemed sufficient, may be excused this condition.
Visitors: Apply to the Librarian.

Information. The Catalogue Room and the Reading Room.

Sales. No details available.

Guidebooks. No general guide is issued but *Extracts from the Rules for the Users of the Library* is available in German, and an illustrated description of the new building with plans (1968).

Restaurant/Snack Facilities. Restaurant on the top floor, open daily from 0845-1845.

Services. Typing room, microfilm reading room, cloakroom in the entrance hall, Conference Hall, lavatories, lifts and pay telephones.

Catalogues. Author, keyword and dissertation catalogues. Union catalogue of Basel libraries.

Classification. Own.

Copying/Photography. 5 automatic copiers are located in the Studio for Photoreproduction. Permission to photograph books and MSS is granted only in exceptional circumstances and must be done under proper supervision. Other photography is freely permitted.

BERN
Schweizerische Landesbibliothek
Hallwylstrasse 15, CH-3003 Bern
Tel. (031) 618921 (Secretary), (031) 618931 (Lending Department)

History. The centralisation of Swiss culture was only possible after the Federal Constitution of 1848 and it was not until the end of the century that general national institutes were established, as was the National Library in 1895. The Library was charged with the duty of collecting all works on Switzerland published since 1848 (the Bürgerbibliothek at Lucerne had responsibility until 1950 for earlier works). The first Librarian was Dr. Johannes Bernoulli, who operated from five rooms in a house at 7 Christoffelgasse in Bern. Larger premises soon became essential and in 1900 the Library reopened in a new building, designed to house also the National Archives. There it remained until 1931, when it moved into its present building, formally opened on 31 October. The collections had benefited from the 1916 agreement with Swiss publishers and printers, who agreed to deposit their books in the Library in return for a listing in *Das Schweizer Buch.* Holdings currently include 1.5 million books, 16,000 MSS, 120,000 microforms and 130,000 maps.

Special Collections and Treasures. The major collection is, of course, Helvetica. The Library attempts to secure books, pamphlets, dissertations, articles etc., published anywhere in the world, which deal with Switzerland or the Swiss in any way, or contain the work of Swiss translators, editors or illustrators. Collections include the Friedrich Staub Collection of Swiss dialects; the Hörmann Library of Rheto-Romance; the F.J. Lüthi Collection of Bibles in over 300 languages; the Gerster and Kundig Poster Collection; the Liebeskind Music Collection including works by Gluck and Haydn; over 400 letters of R.M. Rilke, with additional material relating to him (received in 1950 from Mme N. Wunderly-Volkart); the Rossat Collection of Swiss popular songs; and the

*Schweizerische
Landesbibliothek, Bern*

collections of the Schweizerisches Gutenbergmuseum deposited in 1931.

Exhibition Areas. The Lending Department.

Hours. Reading Room: Mon.-Fri. 0800-1200, 1300-1800 (open Wed. to 2100), Sat. 0800-1200, 1400-1700. Closed Sun., public hols. and for 1 week in Aug.

Transport. Tramway no. 3 or 5 from the station to Helvetiaplatz.

Parking. Facilities next to the Library.

Admission. Readers and *Visitors:* Free of charge.

Information. Information desk in the Catalogue Room. Information Department (separate).

Sales. None.

Guidebooks. Available in German and French. No charge.

Restaurant/Snack Facilities. On the ground floor. Open 0915-1015, 1130-1330, 1500-1600.

Services. Typing rooms, cloakrooms, lavatories, lifts, smoking lounges, telephones.

Catalogues. The author card catalogues are divided by chronological divisions: publications before 1900; 1901-1950 and 1948 onwards (the years 1948-50 are duplicated). Subject catalogue. Various special catalogues. Swiss union catalogue.

Classification. Universal Decimal Classification.

Copying/Photography. In the Lending Department. Private photography requires the permission of the Director.

Friends of the Library. Single members S.Fr. 10 per year. Collective members S.Fr. 25 per year.

Bibliotheca Bodmeriana, Cologny/Geneva

COLOGNY/GENEVA
Fondation Martin Bodmer, Bibliotheca Bodmeriana
Case postale 7, CH-1223 Cologny/Genève
Tel. (022) 362370

History. The Library has its origins in the private library of the late Dr. Martin Bodmer, who began collecting in Zürich in the 1920s. At the outbreak of World War II, Dr. Bodmer moved to Geneva but the Library remained in Zürich until 1951. On 6 October 1951 the Bibliotheca Bodmeriana was formally inaugurated at Cologny, occupying the library building constructed 1948-1950. The Library's holdings, which total 140,000 volumes, 300 manuscripts, and 300 incunabula, reflect Bodmer's concept of 'Weltliteratur', a concept exemplified by the Library's opening exhibition devoted to what Bodmer regarded as its most seminal elements: the Bible, Homer, Dante, Shakespeare and Goethe — his 'Pentagon'. A little before Bodmer's death on 22 March 1971 the Library was transformed into a Foundation, to which the canton of Geneva contributes.

Special Collections and Treasures.   Manuscript treasures include a Greek papyrus, 2nd century, of the Gospel of St. John; Hippocrates, *De observatione ciborum,* MS 1st half 9th century, Fulda; the 14th century *Kalocza Codex,* containing nearly 200 Middle High German poems; René d'Anjou, *Le mortifiement de vaine plaisance,* a 15th century MS with 8 full page illuminations; 3 MSS of Dante of which the *Codex Guarneri* (c. 1350) is the most important; Jalāl ul-Dīn Rūmī, *Masnawī,* Persian MS, 1562-3; an unpublished autograph of Newton's *On the Church;* a large section of the *Kinder- und Hausmärchen* of the brothers Grimm, 43 tales on 66 leaves (c.1808-10); and an important early MS of the *Nibelungenlied.* Printed treasures include the former Leningrad copy of the *Gutenberg Bible;* what is thought to be the only extant complete copy of an edition of the *Celestina* (Toledo, 1500); Ptolemy, *Cosmographia* (Ulm, 1482); one of the three recorded copies of Luther's *Disputatio pro Declaratione Indulgentiarum* (Wittenberg, 1517); Machiavelli, *Il Principe* (1532); Cervantes, *Don Quixote,* the extremely rare 1st ed. of 1605 (vol. I) and 1615 (vol. II); Redouté, *Les Roses* (Paris, 1817-24); Goethe's thesis *Positiones juris* (Strassburg, 1771) and about 400 autograph verses of *Faust II.* The Rosenbach Collection of Shakespeare folios and quartos, acquired in 1952, includes perfect copies of all four folios and more than 50 quartos, eight of them first editions.

Exhibition Areas.   4 exhibition rooms within the Library.

Hours.   Open to the public Thurs. 1400-1800 only. Closed: usually 4 weeks from the end of July for annual revision.

Transport.   Bus: route 'A', starting from Rond Point de Rive to 'Temple de Cologny'.   (The library is at 19-21 Chemin du Guignard, 10 minutes' drive from the centre of the city.)

Parking.   Parking spaces are available at the 'Lion d'Or' Restaurant, 50 metres from the Library.

Admission.   Readers: Must write asking for permission to use the Library.
Visitors: Must pay S.Fr. 2.50 and students S.Fr. 1.50 (note restricted hours of opening above).

Information.   Information desk at the entrance.

Sales. Postcards and the publication series of the Library may be bought at the information desk.

Guidebooks. Une source capitale pour la recherche à Genève. La Fondation Martin Bodmer.

Restaurant/Snack Facilities. None in the Library but available nearby.

Services. No details available.

Catalogues. Author and subject printed card index.

Classification. Own.

Copying/Photography. Microfilm facilities and photocopiers may be used only by special previous permission. Private photography not permitted.

GENEVA
Bibliothèque publique et universitaire de Genève
promenade des Bastions, CH-1211 Genève 4
Tel. (022) 208266

History. The origins of the Library coincide with the spread of the Reformation to Geneva and the foundation of Calvin's College and Academy in 1559. Its first collections derived from the 1539 legal deposit law, which obliged printers to deposit copies of their works in the 'librarie de la Seigneurie'. This stock was transferred to the College in 1562. The Library was enlarged and reorganised at the beginning of the 18th century, when it was opened to the public for two hours a day. From this time dates the legacy of various 14th and 15th century illuminated MSS. In the middle of the 19th century the ecclesiastical administrators were replaced by a professional staff, the Library became the property of the municipality and received a cantonal subsidy. In 1872 it was installed in a wing of the University building and received its present title of Public and University Library in 1907. Current holdings include 1.2 million volumes and pamphlets, 23,000 maps, 45,000 engravings and 10,000 MSS.

Bibliothèque publique et universitaire, Geneva

Special Collections and Treasures. The MSS Department houses the Ami Lullin legacy (80 illuminated MSS of the 14th-15th centuries) which is the most valuable part of its stock. Its other treasures include a collection of Greek papyri, correspondence of the Reformers and the scholars of the Genevan school of the 18th-19th centuries, as well as the archives of Töpffer, Amiel and Henri Dunant. Other collections include works on Genevensia; the history of the French Reformation; 18th century literature; the history of French revolutionary movements; Egyptology; and Arabic archaeology and epigraphy. The Sociéte du Musée historique de la Réformation was founded in 1897 to collect documents on the Reformation, which since 1921 have been housed in the Library. The Rousseau Museum in the Salle Ami-Lullin contains Rousseau MSS and letters, first editions, pictures, engravings and the death mask of the 'Citoyen de Genève'.

Exhibition Areas.   The main Exhibition Hall is the 'Salle Ami-Lullin' which is on the ground floor facing the main entrance. Visits on request to the Salle Ami-Lullin, Musée historique de la Reformation, Musée Rousseau (please contact housekeeper): 0900-1200, 1400-1800. Closed Sat. afternoon and Sun.

Hours.   Reading Room: During University term (Oct.-June): Mon.-Fri. 0900-2200, Sat. 0900-1300, 1400-1700. During vacations (July-Sept., 3 weeks at the New Year and 3 weeks at Easter): Mon.-Fri. 0900-1210, 1400-1700, Sat. 0900-1210. Closed Sun. and public hols.

Transport.   From the Gare de Cornavin: trolleybuses, nos. 3 and 33. Tram line no. 12 passes near the Library (stopping at Place Neuve).

Parking.   Permitted on the Plaine de Plainpalais.

Admission.   Readers: No charge. Minimum age 18. A reader's ticket is issued in the Reading Room on presentation of proof of identity.
Visitors: Free admission to the Exhibition Room (Salle Ami-Lullin).

Information.   In the Secretary's Office and in the Catalogue Information Office.

Sales.   In the Porter's Lodge in the entrance hall on the ground floor.

Guidebooks.   Reader's guide, in French, *Museums and Libraries of Geneva,* available in French, German or English. *La Bibliothèque publique et universitaire de Genève* (pamphlet). All free of charge.

Restaurant/Snack Facilities.   Unibar (snack-bar) in the central University building, open during University opening hours.

Services.   1 public telephone in the entrance hall on the ground floor. Lavatories, cloakrooms, microfilm readers in the Salle Moynier.

Catalogues.   General catalogue (alphabetical by authors' names and by titles of anonymous works). Alphabetical subject, bio-bibliographic, topo-bibliographic and Cyrillic catalogues.

Classification.   Own.

Copying/Photography.   Photocopying machines for use

Jean Calvin, holograph letter to M. de Fallais (dated 5 August 1545), in the Bibliothèque publique et universitaire, Geneva (MS fr. 194, folio 15)

Jean-Jacques Rousseau, holograph MS of Profession de foi du Vicaire Savoyard, in the Bibliothèque publique et universitaire, Geneva (MS fr. 224). Rousseau's book attacked revealed religion and he had to flee from arrest when it was published

by readers on the 1st floor (next to the Reading Room) and the 2nd floor (at the entrance to the Salle des Sciences de l'Antiquité). Microfilm copying available through staff. Private photography permitted in the Exhibition Room but not in the Library workrooms.

ST. GALLEN

Stiftsbibliothek
Klosterhof 6, CH-9000 St. Gallen
Tel. (071) 225719

History. The Stiftsbibliothek is the library of the former Benedictine Abbey of St. Gallen, which dates back to AD 612, when an Irish missionary Callech (Gallus in Latin) founded a cell there. In about 719, the cell developed under St. Otmar into an Abbey, which by the 9th century had reached the height of its religious, intellectual and economic fame. A period of decline began after the year 1000 but the Renaissance period of the Abbey witnessed a revival. In 1758 the present Library was built, the architect being Peter Thumb of Constance. The interior decoration was completed in 1767 under Prince-Abbot Coelestin II, Gugger von Staudach. It has been called the most beautiful rococo interior in Switzerland. In 1805 the Abbey was secularised but the Library remained intact, one of the few examples to do so. Current holdings total 100,000 printed books, 2,000 MSS and 1,700 incunabula, providing an almost unrivalled source of information for both historians and paleographers of the earlier and later Middle Ages.

Special Collections and Treasures. Most of the 2,000 MSS date back to the early and late Middle Ages, when St. Gallen was at its creative zenith. Among the treasures are the Irish *Evangelary* (AD 750); the *Evangelistarium* of Wolfcoz (820); the *Benedictine Regula* (810-20), its Latin text written in black ink and a German translation written between the lines; the *Psalterium Aureum* (875); the *Folcardus Psalter* (864-872); the *Evangelium Longum,* written by Sintram c. 900 and encased in a binding of ivory panels, banded in gold and encrusted with jewels, executed by the monk Tuotilo; and Notker Balbulus's manuscripts of the hymns, in copies of the 11th century. Collections include the private libraries of the Abbots Grimald (841-872) and Hartmut (872-883), and the MSS of Matthias Burer von Lindau (1427-85).

Exhibition Areas. Exhibits are contained in display cases and in the baroque 18th century Library Hall. Exhibitions are held twice a year.

Hours. Summer (May-October): Mon.-Sat. 0900-1200, 1400-1700, Sun. 1030-1200. Winter (December-April): Mon. morning, Tues.-Sat. 0900-1200, 1400-1600. Closed on Sun., Mon. afternoon, and during the month of Nov.

Stiftsbibliothek, St. Gallen

Transport. The Abbey is encircled by the town of St. Gallen.

Parking. None in the Abbey complex.

Admission. Readers: Free of charge. Apply in writing to the Librarian.
Visitors: S.Fr.1.00

Information. No details available.

Sales. Postcards available.

Guidebooks. Stiftsbibliothek St. Gallen, by J. Duft (3rd edition, 1974), S.Fr. 2.50, in German only. Also leaflets in English, French, Italian, Swedish, Danish, German, free of charge.

Restaurant/Snack Facilities. None in the Library, but available in the town.

Services. None.

Catalogues. Author and subject card catalogues.

Classification. Own.

Copying/Photography. Copying facilities not available. Permission must be sought for private photography.

ZÜRICH
Eidgenössische Technische Hochschule, Bibliothek
(Library of the Swiss Federal Institute of Technology)
Rämistrasse 101, CH-8006 Zürich
Tel. (01) 326211

History. The Library was founded in 1855 as part of the Swiss Federal Institute of Technology (SFIT). It was, at first, housed in several temporary locations, and then in 1863 moved into its present building, which was subsequently enlarged and rebuilt in 1899-1900, 1921, 1948-9, 1956-7 and 1965-73. Since 1921 the Library has been established on the third floor of the above building, designed by Gustav Semper and enlarged by Gustav Gull. The Documentation Department was founded in 1931 and the subsequent enlargement of the circle of users led to the establishment of the Library's function as a State technical library. In 1968 the 1 millionth book was acquired. Holdings currently total 1.85 million units, of which 500,000 are microfiches. Subjects covered correspond to the faculties of the Swiss Federal Institute of Technology, i.e. architecture, art, civil engineering, mechanical engineering, electrical engineering, chemistry, pharmacy, forestry, agriculture and food, rural engineering and surveying, mathematics, physics, natural sciences and military science.

Eidgenössische Technische Hochschule, Bibliothek, Zürich

Special Collections and Treasures. The Library has many early prints on astronomy, mathematics, architecture and fortification. The Microtexts Room (H23), founded in 1964, has 464,400 scientific and technical reports and 30,000 US dissertations on microfiche. The Map Collection has 100,000 maps and 1,500 books and atlases. The Archive Records of the History of Science (H29.4) contain 39,600 MSS, 9,800 portraits and 1,600 biographical dossiers. This section include MSS on the history of science and administration of the 'Bürgerhaus' archives and the archives of architects.

Exhibition Areas. In the foyers of the Library (H30 and 29.5) displaying alternating exhibitions on technology and history and new acquisitions.

Hours. Reading rooms: Mon.-Fri. 0800-2200, Sat. 0800-1700. The Library is closed Sun., 1-2 Jan., one week during Spring holiday, Good Fri.-Easter Mon., 1 May, Ascension Day, Whit Sat., Whit Mon., 1 Aug., 25-31 Dec. and the afternoons of 'Sechseläuten, Knabenschiessen, Day of the Polyball' and 24 Dec.

Transport. Trams: no. 6 or 10, stopping at Hochschule or Kantonsspital. Cog-railway from the city centre to the Swiss Federal Institute of Technology.

Parking. Visitors may obtain permission to park from the Caretaker's Office (Main Building E39).

Admission. Readers: Registration takes place either at the information desk or by mail. Readers must show proof of identity and pay the appropriate fee. User's-card must be shown on request.
Visitors: Apply to Library Director.

Information. Desk H26, or by telephone and mail.

Sales. None.

Guidebooks. Information sheets available in German, English, French and Italian, free of charge.

Restaurant/Snack Facilities. Restaurant in main building (F32); Polybar (F27).

Services. Foyers of the Library (H30 and H29.5) have smoking lounge, telephones, lifts, lavatories, washrooms.

Catalogues. Author/title, subject and systematic catalogues.

Classification. Keywords and Universal Decimal Classification.

Copying/Photography. Photocopies, photostatic semitone and microfilm copying available. Prior permission must be sought for private photography.

ZÜRICH

*Zentralbibliothek Zürich, Kantons-, Stadt- und
Universitätsbibliothek
Zähringerplatz 6, Postfach, CH-8025 Zürich
Tel. (01) 477272*

History. The Library, as presently constituted, was
founded in 1914, but its origins date back to several
earlier foundations, notably the Stadtbibliothek (founded
in 1629); the libraries of the Society of Natural Sciences
(1746), the Medico-Surgical Society (c.1780), the Juristic
Society (1780) and the Society of Antiquaries (1833); and
the libraries of the various cantonal educational establish-
ments, including that serving the University (1835). In
1903 a commission was established to consider the
amalgamation of the various libraries. Statutes were
drawn up in 1914 and in 1917 the Library opened in a
building, constructed at a cost of over 800,000 francs,
raised by subscription. Current holdings total 1.9 million
items, including 1.35 million monographs and 18,500
MSS.

Special Collections and Treasures. Collections include
the central library of the Swiss Alpine Club; the library of
the Zürich Musical Society; the archives of the former
Rascher Publishing Company; the 4,000 item autograph
collection of Emil Bebler (1883-1954); the Mozart
Collection of the Zürich conductor and composer Ernst
Hess; and over 100 letters and cards from the composer
Heinrich Sutermeister to his librettist Albert Rösler.
Treasures include MSS of the world chronicle of Rudolf
von Ems; the *Berne Chronicles* of Diebold Schilling and
Benedikt Tschachtlan; a number of the MSS of
Paracelsus; the MS of J.S. Bach's *Aria* in A Minor, with
15 variations (acquired in 1972); and letters and notes
from Heinrich Pestalozzi to Laue and Co. in 1785.

Exhibition Areas. Exhibition Room: Predigerchor,
Predigerplatz 33. Recent accesions are also displayed in
the vestibule of the main building.

Hours. Reading Room: Mon.-Fri. 0800-2000, Sat. 0800-
1700. Closed Sun. and public hols.

Transport. Tram: nearest stops Rudolf-Brun-Brücke,
Central, Neumarkt. Bus: nearest stops Central,
Neumarkt.

Parking. No details available.

Admission. Readers: Registration with valid identification (cost: S.Fr. 2) takes place at the Loans Desk.
Visitors: May consult Library materials.

Information. General information at the vestibule desk.
Reference, subject and bibliographical information in the
Catalogue Room.

Zentralbibliothek, Zürich

Sales. None.

Guidebooks. None.

Restaurant/Snack Facilities. Hot and cold drinks available from automatic vending machines. Snacks are sold at the cloakroom counter.

Services. Lavatories, telephones, cloakroom.

Catalogues. Central author/title catalogue of Zürich libraries. Dissertation catalogue. Subject catalogue of Zentralbibliothek holdings.

Classification. Own.

Copying/Photography. Photocopies may be ordered at the desk in the Reading Room. Two self-service photocopying machines are situated opposite the cloakroom. A microfilm reader-copier is available in the Catalogue Room. Those wishing to use cameras within the Library should first consult the Public Relations Section (internal telephone number — 65).

Friends of the Library. Gesellschaft von Freunden der Zentralbibliothek, annual subscription S.Fr. 40.

Taiwan

TAIPEI
National Central Library
43 Nan Hai Road, Taipei
Tel. Office of the Director: 313981; Reference and Readers' Service Department: 314601

History. The Library was established in Nanking in 1933 (see entry for Nanking Library), but only one year after the Library began its services to the public in 1936, the Sino-Japanese War broke out, forcing the Library to evacuate to Chungking, the wartime capital. It returned to Nanking in 1945, only to move once more in 1949 to Taipei, as the Chinese communists gained control of the mainland. Of the more than 1 million volumes that comprised its holdings at Nanking, only 120,000 arrived in Taiwan, but these were in many cases the rarest items. The Library finally reopened in 1954 in its present building, located in the Botanical Gardens in the south central part of Taipei. Current holdings total over 500,000 volumes, including 143,998 rare Chinese books, the largest collection in the world.

National Central Library, Taipei. Main reading room

Special Collections and Treasures. Treasures include Pao Ch'ieh Yin T'o Lo Ni Ching, printed by Wu Yueh Wang Chien Shu in T'ai Tso K'ai Pao year 8 (975) of the Sung Dynasty; *The History of Han Dynasty,* edited by the Imperial Academy during the period of Shao Hsing (1131-1162) of the Sung Dynasty; the block printings of the Yüan Dynasty such as *Biographies of Famous Court Officials, Lu Shih Spring* and *Autumn Annals, The Collection of Manuscripts from Yun Shan. The Commentary of the Poems* by Su Tung Po is one of only four copies in the world (the Library has vols. 7, 10, 15 and 20, which no other collector possesses). MSS include *Nan Yu Tang Chi* by Wang Chih Teng of the Ming Dynasty and *Ching Shih K'un Ch'ung Ts'ao Mu Chuang,* with coloured illustrations by Wen Shu of the Ming Dynasty. Its collections include some 290 Sung imprints (AD 960-1279), 11 Chin imprints (AD 111-1234), 360 Yüan imprints(AD 1260-1368), and over 8,000 Ming imprints (AD 1368-1644). The Library also contains 747 pieces of fragmentary 'oracle bones', 30 pieces of Han Dynasty wooden tablets, 153 rolls of ancient MSS and 5,999 sets of bronze and stone inscriptions.

Exhibition Areas. Two exhibition rooms.

Hours. General Reading Room: 0900-2100 daily. Periodicals, Newspapers, Chinese and Western Languages Rooms: 0900-1700 daily (including Sun.). Closed Sun. and national hols.

Transport. City buses serve the Library.

Parking. No details available.

Admission. Readers: All readers must be over 20 years of age and enrolled at a university or college.
Visitors: Apply to Librarian.

Information. At Library staff desks.

Sales. None.

Guidebooks. General Introduction to the National Central Library (in Chinese), *Booklet of the National Central Library* (in Chinese and English). Available free of charge.

Restaurant/Snack Facilities. None.

Services. Lavatories, cloakrooms.

Catalogues. Classified card catalogue of Oriental books and dictionary catalogue of Western books.

Classification. Dewey Decimal and Library of Congress.

Copying/Photography. Copying facilities are provided by the Library. A microfilm service is provided by the Microfilm Centre within the Library.

Thailand

BANGKOK
National Library of Thailand
Samsen Road, Bangkok 3
Tel. 815449, 810263

History. The National Library of Thailand is composed of three libraries, namely the Vajirayana Library, the Vajiravudh Library and the Damrongrajanupharb Library. The first of these three, the Vajirayana National Library, was established by King Rama V on 12 October 1905 in the Royal Palace, when three royal libraries were amalgamated. In 1925, King Rama VII donated the valuable collections of MSS and books, assembled by his brother Rama VI, and named the building which housed them, the Vajiravudh Library. In 1947, the heiress of his Royal Highness Krom Phraya Damrongrajanupharb entrusted to the National Library the valuable collections of his Royal Highness. The building housing these collections was termed the Damrongrajanupharb Library. The Library occupied a new building in May 1966, construction having started in October 1964. The building at Ta Vasukri, Bangkok, was designed in the Thai architectural style with five floors and a large auditorium. The Library has legal deposit privileges and currently contains 802,925 volumes, 144,865 MSS, 340 microfilms and 3,398 maps.

Special Collections and Treasures. Major collections include those of King Vajiravudh (Rama VI), Krom Phraya Damrongrajanupharb and Phraya Anumanrajadhon. The Manuscript Department has a fine collection of writings on palm-leaves and locally-made paper and stone-inscriptions, the royal editions being gilded and marked with royal emblems of each reign. The Library posseses extensive collections on Buddhism in Thai, Pali, Sanskrit, Mon, Burmese, Chinese, Japanese and Singhalese and books on a variety of subjects published for distribution at cremation ceremonies. (Each volume contains the biography of the person cremated and thus constitutes a unique biographical source on the Thai people.)

Exhibition Areas. Two display cases in the main entrance, plus exhibition rooms in the auditorium sections of the ground and second floors.

Hours. Daily 0830-2030. Closed public hols.

Transport. Bus: nos. 3, 9, 16, 19, 23, 30-33, 51-2, 55-6, 63-6, 90-1.

Parking. Parking area, at the front of the main entrance and the auditorium section, will hold 100 cars.

National Library of Thailand

Admission. Readers: Must register at the first time of entry and subsequently show their identification card (issued by the Library) every time they want to use the Library. The cards are free of charge.
Visitors: Free of charge.

Information. In the entrance hall.

Sales. Sales of books printed by the Division of History and Literature at the entrance hall.

Guidebooks. Mimeographed sheets in Thai and English, free of charge.

Restaurant/Snack Facilities. In separate building at back of main Library building. Opening times correspond with those of the Library.

Services. Lavatories, telephone in the main hall on the ground floor, lift, cloakrooms at the entrance.

Catalogues. Author, subject and title card catalogues.

Classification. Dewey.

Copying/Photography. Photocopies and microfilm copying available through Library staff. The Reprography Services are located on the 3rd floor. Cameras are not allowed in the Library.

Turkey

ANKARA

Millî Kütüphane Genel Müdürlüğü (General Directorate of the National Library)
Kumrular sokak, Kizilay, Ankara
Tel. 12 31 30; 12 31 32; 12 32 96; 12 32 97.

History. The National Library was opened to the public on 16 August 1948. Preparation for the establishment of the Library had begun towards the end of April 1946 in a small room of the Directorate of Publications at the Ministry of Education, which had accumulated over the previous 15 years copyright copies of Turkish books, periodicals and newspapers. By 1950 the Library possessed a collection of 132,000 volumes, a figure which owed much to the early support of the 'Society to Aid the National Library'. The increase in the collections, aided by copyright deposit privileges, necessitated the building of a five floor annexe in 1954, to supplement the existing two floor building (originally built as a social club). A further annexe of six floors was completed in 1963 and it is hoped that a new National Library building will be erected in the near future. Current holdings include 573,547 volumes,

National Library, Ankara

3,659 MSS, 99,785 periodical volumes and 9,209 reels of microfilm.

Special Collections and Treasures. The Library has 20,000 books written in the old Turkish script. This number represents the majority of the books printed in Turkey from 1729 (the first printing in Turkey) to 1928 when the Latin alphabet was adopted. Missing volumes in this collection are gradually being added. The collection of newspapers published since 1934 is almost complete. Other collections include the Atatürk Collection; the Pröetorius Music Collection; the Üsküdarli Ali Riza Bey Collection of oil paintings, water colours, black and white drawings; and the Hayali Küçük Ali Collection on Turkish puppetry. The Microfilm Archive contains 9,209 microfilmed MSS.

Exhibition Areas. Two exhibition rooms.

Hours. Mon.-Sat. 0830-2230 (Wed.-1230). Closed Sun. and public hols.

Transport. The Library is situated at Kizilay, the city centre of Ankara, very close to the main street which is served by buses and taxis.

Parking. A park for 5-6 vehicles only, just inside the entrance gate of the Library.

Admission. Readers: Application for membership card should be made to the Reference Department. No charge.
Visitors: Free of charge.

Information. From the staff located just inside the main entrance, in the Reading Room and in the Periodicals Reading Room.

Sales. The Library's publications can be obtained from the Accessions Department.

Guidebooks. Brochures in Turkish and English, free of charge.

Restaurant/Snack Facilities. None at present but the new National Library building will contain such facilities.

Services. Cloakrooms, lavatories, smoking areas.

Catalogues. Alphabetical card catalogues for foreign language books, Latin Script, Turkish and Arabic Script Turkish books. Various special catalogues. Systematic subject catalogue. Union card catalogue of works in foreign languages (cards supplied by 220 libraries).

Classification. Dewey.

Copying/Photography. Copying available through the Microfilm and Photocopy Section. Apply to the Librarian for private photography.

Friends of the Library. Friends of the Library, *Millî Kutüphane ye Yardim Derneği* (Society to Aid the National Library).

ISTANBUL

Süleymaniye Kütüphanesi Müdürlüğü (*Library of the Süleymaniye Mosque*)
Süleymaniye Mahallesi, Ayşe Kadin Sokak Nu 30: 35, Beyazit, Istanbul,
Tel. 220186, 278708

History. The Süleymaniye Mosque was built by the famous Turkish architect Mimar Sinan for the Sultan Süleyman the Magnificent. Building commenced in 1549 and the mosque was opened to the public in 1557. It was both mosque and *madraseh* (religious college). Since 1918 it has been used only as a library. Manuscripts from Istanbul and all the important provincial centres have been collected in the Library. Today there are no less than 94 of these collections each of which has preserved its own separate identity. Current holdings include 63,905 Turkish, Arabic and Persian MSS, 32,215 printed books, 4,381 microfilms and 222 photocopies.

Special Collections and Treasures. The Library is renowed for its collections of Turkish, Arabic and Persian MSS.

Exhibition Areas. Exhibition Hall, where selected manuscripts are regularly on show.

Hours. Mon.-Sat. 0830-1630. Closed Sun. and public hols.

Transport. City trams pass near the Library.

Parking. Available near the Library.

Admission. *Readers* and *Visitors:* Free of charge.

Information. At Library staff desks.

Sales. None.

Guidebooks. A guide to the Library in Turkish is available free of charge.

Restaurant/Snack Facilities. None in the Library but there are restaurants and cafés nearby.

Services. Telephones, cloakroom, smoking room, microfilm readers.

Catalogues. An alphabetical and systematic catalogue is

Library of the Süleymaniye Mosque, Istanbul

available on cards by author and title. Various special manuscript catalogues.

Classification. Dewey.

Copying/Photography. The photographic services will undertake to make photocopies and microfilms.

ISTANBUL
Istanbul Üniversitesi Merkez Kütüphanesi (Istanbul University Central Library)
Istanbul-Beyazit
Tel. 22 21 80

History. The Library was established in 1924, following a decree of Atatürk, authorising the transfer of the book collection at Yildiz Palace to the University. This collection of 50,000 volumes, with the books from what were then the libraries of the various faculties of Istanbul University, formed the basis of the University Central Library. A 1935 law designated the Library a national depository, thus enhancing its status as a specialised library for Middle Eastern studies and as a national library. The Library is housed in a building originally erected as a school in 1912. A new building is now under construction to relieve the present accommodation problems. Current holdings total 250,000 volumes and 18,600 MSS.

Special Collections and Treasures. The manuscripts transferred from the Yildiz Palace constitute perhaps the most outstanding collection of Orientalia in Turkey. Manuscripts are in Turkish, Arabic and Persian. The Library has an almost complete collection of Turkish incunabula. Treasures include albums belonging to the Abdülhamit II period, and Müteferrika books (the first ever to have been printed in Turkey). Among the most famous MSS are Loqmân ibn Hosein al-Ashûrî al Hoseinî, *Qiyafet al-insaniyeh Si Shemâ 'il'othmâniyeh,* Turkish MS, T.6087; Khavaja Sa'd ad-dîn, *Taj at-tavârikĥ,* T.5970, doçumenting the history of the Ottoman empire to the end of the reign of Selîm I (1520); and Nasuh as-Silahî al-matrâqî, *Beyân-i menâzil-i sefer-i 'Irageyni Sultan Suleiman Khán* (16th century), T.5964.

Exhibition Areas. Six glass show-cases throughout the Library.

Hours. Mon.-Fri. 0830-1200, 1300-1730. Closed Sat., Sun. From 15 July-15 Sept., open only on Tues. and Thurs.

Transport. Buses leave from all parts of the city to Beyazit, from which point the Library is a five minute walk.

Istanbul University, Central Library

Parking.   On the street in front of the Library.

Admission.   Readers: Admission is free but restricted to undergraduate students of the Faculty of Letters, members of the Faculty, assistants of the University and people of any nationality doing scholarly research.
Visitors: Apply to the Librarian.

Information.   At Library staff desks.

Sales.   None.

Guidebooks.   None.

Restaurant/Snack Facilities.   None.

Services.   Cloakrooms and lavatories.

Catalogues.   Alphabetical,   subject   and   manuscript catalogues.

Classification.   Currently being reclassified according to Universal Decimal Classification.

Copying/Photography.   Apply to the Librarian for both copying and private photography.

Uganda

KAMPALA
Makerere University Library
PO Box 16002, Kampala
Tel. Kampala 42471, Extns. 411-414, Kampala 31041-2

History.   Makerere College was founded in 1922 as a Uganda Government technical school. The report of the De la Warr commission (1937) recommended its development to university college and later university status, a recommendation which became a fact after World War II. On 1 July 1970 the college became Makerere University, Kampala, with the largest general library in the country. At the centre of the University Library system is the Main Library, built in 1959 and extended in 1962. Early in 1972 a large new wing, which doubled the previous space, was opened to house the rapidly expanding Periodicals and Special Collection Departments. Five sub-libraries are now in operation, the largest being the Albert Cook Library serving the Faculty of Medicine on the adjacent hill of Mulago. The Library, which has legal deposit privileges, has current holdings of over 400,000 volumes.

Special   Collections   and   Treasures.   The   Special Collections Section is located on Level 4 of the Library. Collections include the Africana Collection of material

Makerere   University   Library, Kampala

relating to East Africa; the Law Collection (Level 2), rich in laws and law reports of Africa, India and the UK; the Government Documents Collection; the Uganda Legal Deposit Collection; and the University Collection of material emanating from or about Makerere. The Albert Cook Medical Library contains books dating from 1545 and the Cook Special Collection, named after Sir Albert Ruskin Cook (1870-1951), who organised the first medical library in Uganda.

Exhibition Areas. None.

Hours. Term: Mon.-Fri. 0800- 1930, 2030-2300, Sat. 0800-1800, Sun. 0930-1230, 1400-1700. Vacation: Mon.-Fri. 0830-1230, 1400-1800, Sat. 0830-1200. Closed Sun. and public hols.

Parking. Facilities available.

Admission. Readers: Present and former members of the University are entitled to use the Library. Others wishing to use the Library should obtain the Librarian's permission. Those wishing to borrow must sign a Library registration card.
Visitors: Visitors are welcome to visit the Library and may be issued with a Library pass if they are not conducted round.

Information. Desk opposite the main entrance to the Library. There are also enquiries windows in each section of the Library and in each departmental library.

Sales. There is no sales desk but University publications are available from the Reference and Circulation Section.

Guidebooks. Library guide and *Library regulations* are available, in English, free of charge. Separate guides to the Medical and Education Libraries are available.

Restaurant/Snack Facilities. None.

Services. Research carrels, cloakroom (on the right hand side of the main entrance), lavatories, microreaders.

Catalogues. Card catalogue in two sections: one containing author, name and title cards, the other consisting of subject cards. There is also a union catalogue of all East Africana holdings of the University Libraries of Nairobi and Dar-es-Salaam. This is maintained in the Special Collections section on Level 4.

Classification. Dewey in all libraries, except the Medical Sub-library, which uses the National Library of Medicine scheme and Barnard classification.

Copying/Photography. Work done by the Photographic Section includes photocopying, enlargements, microfilming and slide-making.

USSR

BAKU

Azerbaidzhanskaya gosudarstvennaya Respublikanskaya Biblioteka im M.F. Akhundova (M.F. Akhundov State Republic Library of the Azerbaidzhan)
37061 Baku, Tsentr ul. Khagani 29
Tel. 93-68-01; (Reference and Bibliography Department: 93-60-04)

History. The Azerbaidzhan SSR was founded on 28 April 1920. The proposal for a national library was first raised after the 1917 Russian Revolution and the Library was eventually opened on 5 June 1923. The rapid growth of the collections, stimulated by legal deposit privileges for material printed in the Republic, necessitated the building of a new purpose-built Library. This was completed in 1960 and recently the second stage of the bookstack, with capacity for 2 million books, has been added. The Library's staff now serve some 25,000 readers per annum and holdings total 3,036,035 items.

Special Collections and Treasures. Treasures include M.F. Akhundov, *Comedies* (Tiflis, 1853); M. Fizuli, *Divan* (Tabriz, 1849); *Divan Adzhiz* (Tabriz, 1857); *Sovremennik* (*The Contemporary*), edited by Pushkin and Nekrasov (1836-66); *Otechestvennye Zapiski,* another important 19th century journal; Karl Marx, *Das Kapital* in the first Russian translation: Tome I in 1872 ed., Tome II in 1885 ed.: and the journal *Molla Nasreddin* (1906-30). A major collection is that on Azerbaidzhan, covering all aspects of the history, geography, economy and culture of the Republic. Where original material is not available microfilms and copies have been made from the collections of other libraries.

Exhibition Areas. Hall on the 2nd floor.

Hours. Tues.-Sun. 1000-2200. Closed Mon. and public hols.

Transport. Metro, motor bus, trolley bus.

Parking. In the street adjoining the Library.

Admission. Readers: Free admittance after obtaining reader's ticket.
Visitors: Free of charge.

Information. On the 2nd floor.

Sales. None.

Guidebooks. Library guide in Russian (1971).

M.F. Akhundov State Republic Library of the Azerbaidzhan, Baku

Restaurant/Snack Facilities. Buffet, open 1200-1700.

Services. Cloakrooms, smoking room, public telephones.

Catalogues. Author and classified catalogues. General author catalogue for staff use (i.e. fuller than that used by readers). Bibliographic card indexes on special topics.

Classification. Universal Decimal Classification; Bibliotechno-bibliograficheskaya klassifikatsiya (standard system in the USSR).

Copying/Photography. Microfilm and photocopying service available through staff.

KIEV

Tsentral'naya nauchnaya biblioteka AN USSR
(*Central Scientific Library of the Academy of Sciences of the Ukrainian SSR*)
252601 Kiev 601, Vladimirskaya ul. 62
Tel. 24-31-26 (Director); 21-32-31 (Reference/ Bibliography Section)

History. Following the Russian Revolution and the re-establishment of Ukrainian statehood under the Central Rada, steps were taken to establish a large Ukrainian National Library as early as 1917. The Government of Hetman Paul Skoropadsky issued an act on 2 August 1918 establishing the National Library of the Ukrainian State in Kiev. During the Bolshevik occupation of the Ukraine, the committee changed the name to the All-People's Library of Ukraine on 2 May 1919. In August 1919 stocks totalled 40,000 volumes and by June 1923 1 million volumes. Growth in the 1920s was rapid as large book collections were received from dispersed or reorganized libraries, notably the bulk of the library of Kiev University (nearly 500,000 volumes in 1927). Legal deposit privileges for Ukrainian works were received in 1917 and for USSR publications in 1922. By 1932 holdings totalled 2,503,500 books in Kiev and 125,000 in the branch library at Vinnytsa. In the 1930s, following the reorganization of the All-Ukrainian Academy of Sciences, the Library was merged with the libraries of the departments, chairs, commissions and institutions of the Academy into a single entity. During World War II some 700,000 books were shipped to Germany, although some were returned after 1945. In 1948 the Library was renamed the State Public Library of the Ukrainian SSR, only to be renamed the Central Scientific Library of the Academy of Sciences in 1965, when it was no longer required as a general public library. In 1964 some 5 per cent of the Library's holdings were lost or damaged by an act of arson. Current holdings include 7.5 million books, 7 million newspapers and over 200,000 MSS.

Central Scientific Library of the Academy of Sciences of the Ukrainian SSR, Kiev

Special Collections and Treasures. Collections received

include the libraries of the Kiev Theological Academy (150,000 volumes in 1923), of Saint Sophia Cathedral and of the Kiev monasteries (52,000 volumes in 1925). The Library is particularly strong in works printed in, and about, all aspects of the Ukraine, and in official and personal MSS and archives relating to the area. Treasures include Aristotle, *Libri de animalibus* (Venice, 1476); Copernicus, *De revolutionibus orbium coelestium* (Nürnberg, 1543); first editions of works by the Ukrainian writer and patriot Ivan Franko; MSS by Gogol (including *Taras Bulba*) and Turgenev; the first Russian editions of works by Marx, Engels and Lenin; rare works by M.V. Lomonosov, A.N. Radishchev, I.P. Kotlyarevsky and T.G. Shevchenko; 516 incunabula; and examples of works from the presses of the Aldine Press, Plantin, Elzevier and Estienne.

Exhibition Areas.   An exhibition of new acquisitions is maintained off the entrance foyer.

Hours.   Mon.-Fri. 0915-2145, Sat. and Sun. 0915-1745.

Transport.   Metro. Buses stop in front of the Library.

Parking.   Available.

Admission.   Readers: Admission, free of charge to scholars, specialists and advanced students.
Visitors: No details provided.

Information.   Readers' Service Section.

Sales.   None.

Guidebooks. Available in Russian with English summary.

Restaurant/Snack Facilities.   No details provided.

Services.   Conference Hall. Lavatories.

Catalogues.   Alphabetical catalogues for books, journals, newspapers, maps, etc. Classified catalogue for books, maps and atlases. Special indexes to popular vocal music, iconographic material, etc.

Classification.   General systematic classification.

Copying/Photography.   Photocopying and microfilming requests to be handed to Library staff in External Services Section (Tel. 21-32-80).

LENINGRAD
*Gosudarstvennaya Publichnaya biblioteka im M.E.
Saltykowa-Shchedrina (M.E. Saltykov-Shchedrin
State Public Library)
Leningrad D-69, Sadovaya ul. 18
Tel. 15-28-56*

History. The Library was formally opened on 2 (14) January 1814 but its origins lie in the late 18th century with Catherine the Great. Catherine planned to establish a national library using as its basis a collection of all Russian books published since 1564 with the addition of the Załuski Library (see entry for the Biblioteka Narodiva, Warsaw). Various collections were also placed at the disposal of the new institution. Catherine died in 1796 and this delayed the Library's opening, as did the Napoleonic invasion, until January 1814. Legal deposit privileges had been granted in 1810 and the collections were housed in a domed building, erected at the angle of Nevski Prospekt and Sadovaya Street between 1795 and 1801 (extended 1828-1830). The Library's growth was slow until the administration of Count M.A. Korf from 1849-1862. The Library occupied its present main building in 1901 and by 1917 holdings totalled 3.2 million volumes. Growth has been rapid in the 20th century. The Library assumed its present name on 27 April 1932 (after the Russian writer M.E. Saltykov-Shchedrin) and then on 14 January 1939 it was awarded the Order of the Red Banner of Labour, the first Russian library to receive it. Despite the Siege of Leningrad the Library managed to survive World War II. In 1949 the pressure on space necessitated the occupation of an annex building at Fontanka 36. Current holdings total over 20 million items and the Library is ranked second in national importance to the Lenin Library in Moscow (see relevant entry).

Special Collections and Treasures. The most important collection is the Russian Book Collection. It is the most complete in the world, particularly for the pre-Revolutionary period, and contains nearly 5 million items. Treasures include first editions of the works of Marx, Engels and Lenin. Other collections include the Pushkin Collection; the Free Russian Press Collection, the complete Collection of Russian publications published abroad or 'underground' in Russia from 1854-1917; and a complete file of the Russian revolutionary periodical *Kolokol* (1857-1867). The Library holdings of Slav books printed in the Cyrillic alphabet before 1800 number 4,500 volumes. Among them are a great many Moscow editions, including one of the five surviving copies of Ivan Fedorov's *Chasovnik* (1565). There are also fairly full collections of Kiev books and Skorina's Prague and Vilna editions. The Rare Books Department contains the largest collection in the world of printed Russian books in the modern alphabet published in Peter the Great's time, from 1 January 1708 to 28 January 1725. Treasures include an almost exhaustive collection of calendars; a large number of edicts; the only complete copies of the first book in the modern alphabet

*M.E. Saltykov-Shchedrin
State Public Library, Leningrad*

Geometria slavenski zemlemerie (1708); and a complete set of the first Russian newspaper *Vedomosti* for 1703-1727. Treasures of manuscripts include the *Ostromir Gospel* (1056-57), the oldest extant Russian, i.e. Church Slavonic, MS; the *Laurentian Chronicle* codex (1377); the *Pravda Russkaya*, the first Russian code of laws; the Pogodin Collection of old Russo-Slavonic MSS; the archives of G.V. Plekhanov; the music archives of Glinka, Rimsky-Korsakov, Mussorgsky, Borodin and Scriabin. Other collections include the 'Rossica' Collection of a quarter of a million foreign printed books dealing with Russia and its culture. Collections in other fields include the private library of Voltaire, purchased by Catherine the Great in 1778, consisting of 7,000 volumes, many with MS notes by Voltaire; the Paris Commune Collection; the Incunabula Collection, over 5,000 volumes; the Aldine and Elzevir Collections, numbering over 7,000 volumes; the Bible Collection; the outstanding MSS Collections of Dubrovsky, Sukhtelen and the Vaxel Collection of autographs and others.

Exhibition Areas.   Permanent exhibitions in Department of Manuscripts and Rare Books. Exhibition room for new acquisitions. Various exhibitions in specialised reading rooms.

Hours.   Daily 0900-2200 (except the last Tuesday of the month).

Transport.   Metro: Nevski Prospekt or Gostiny Dvor. Trolleybus: 1, 3, 5, 7, 10, 14, 22. Bus: 2, 3, 6, 7, 14, 22, 44-5, 47, 70.

Parking.   At the main entrance.

Admission.   *Readers:* Open to all free of charge, including children of school age (beginning from the 8th form) who produce suitable identification. Admission for non-Russians is obtained on presentation of passport or tourist visa and completion of the requisite forms. An individual Library Card is issued upon registration to every reader. Admission to the Manuscript and Rare Books Departments requires special entrance tickets. *Visitors:* Free of charge. Apply to Library staff for details of organised tours.

Information.   Tel. 15-57-10 (General Secretary).

Sales.   None.

Guidebooks.   Currently out of print.

Restaurant/Snack Facilities.   Canteen and snack bar available.

Services.   Typing rooms, cloakrooms, lavatories, lifts, smoking lounges, telephones.

Catalogues.   Alphabetical, systematic and subject card

catalogues. Various special catalogues.

Classification. Bibliotechno-bibliograficheskaya klassifikatsiya (the standard USSR system).

Copying/Photography. Microfilm and photocopies available. For private photography prior permission must be obtained.

LENINGRAD

Biblioteka Akademii Nauk SSSR (Library of the Academy of Sciences of the USSR)
199164 Leningrad V-164, Birzhevaya liniya 1
Tel. Director's Office: 18-35-92 and 18-40-91. Information and Bibliographical Department: 18-39-91

History. The Library is the oldest scientific library in the Soviet Union. Founded in 1714, it has been the main library of the Academy of Sciences since its establishment in 1725. During the whole of the 18th century the Library remained the only large national repository in Russia. Early supporters of the Library repository in Lomonosov, S. Kotelnikov, G. Miller and V. Tatishchev. The first printed catalogue appeared in 1742 and legal deposit privileges were received in 1783. From the beginning of the 19th century libraries began to be attached to the research institutes of the Academy. Following the Russian Revolution and the 1934 move of the headquarters of the USSR Academy of Sciences from Leningrad to Moscow, the Library's position has been redefined. At present there are 36 affiliated libraries in Leningrad and 55 in Moscow. The Leningrad Library now acts as the enquiry, loan and reference centre for the network of 153 libraries in the Academy's departments and institutes. The stocks of the Central Library and those of the academic libraries in Leningrad are regarded as one whole, current holdings totalling nearly 14 million volumes (with the collection of the Central Library totalling 7.6 million volumes).

Library of the Academy of Sciences of the USSR, Leningrad

Special Collections and Treasures. The Library contains a virtually complete collection of everything that the Academy of Sciences has published since its foundation. Other collections include V. Mikhalkov's Collection of 18th and 19th century Western European authors; the personal library and manuscript book collections of Peter the Great, his family and his son Aleksei Petrovich; the manuscript collection of the historian V.N. Tatishchev; the holdings of the Antoniev Siiskii and Alexsandr-Svirskii monasteries; the Arkhangel'sk Collection; and the collections of I.I. Sreznevskii, A.I. Iatsimirskii and P.A. Syrku. Treasures include Szwajpolt Fiol's *Book of Hours* and *Lenten Triodon,* both 15th century; Frantsisk Skorina's *Russian Bible* (Prague, 1517-19); Ivan Fedorov's *Acts of the Apostles* (1564), the first dated Moscow-printed book; the 15th century *Radziwill Chronicle;* and the Voskresenskii, Novgorod, Tver and Pskov

Chronicles.

Exhibition Areas.   No details available.

Hours.   Main Reading Room: Mon.-Sat. 0900-2200, Sun. 1000-1800. Specialised reading rooms have slightly shorter hours.

Transport.   Metro: station Vassileostrovskaya. Bus: 70, 10, 30, 44-5, 47, 60. Tram: 21, 26, 31. Trolleybus: 1, 7, 9, 10.(The Library is located on Vassilievskii Island, near many of the Academy facilities and Leningrad University.)

Parking.   In adjacent streets.

Admission.   Readers: Admission is restricted to members and associates of the Academy and serious researchers. For foreign readers, admission is through the Foreign Division of the Academy of Sciences, or through the Academy-related institution with which the foreign scholar is affiliated.
Visitors: Apply to Librarian.

Information.   In Main Reading Room. There is an Information and Bibliographical Department. Specialist assistance is available in using the catalogues.

Sales.   None.

Guidebooks.   *Biblioteka Akademii Nauk SSSR* (1974), in Russian, with summaries in English, German and French.

Restaurant/Snack Facilities.   None.

Services.   No details available.

Catalogues.   General alphabetical card catalogue which records holdings for the entire network of the Academy; readers' alphabetical catalogue; official classified catalogue; ten special catalogues.

Classification.   Bibliotechno-bibliograficheskaya klassifikatsiya, modified.

Copying/Photography.   Microfilm and photocopies are available through Library staff. Microfilms can be ordered from abroad through the Exchange Division of the Library.

LENINGRAD

*Nauchnaya biblioteka imeni A.M. Gor'kogo
Leningradskogo gosudarstvennogo universiteta imeni
A.A. Zhdanova (A.M. Gor'kii Scientific Library of the
A.A. Zhdanov State University of Leningrad)
Leningrad 199164, Universitetskaya nab. 7/9
Tel. 18-27-41 (Director); 18-95-55 (Reference and
Information Dept.)*

History. The Library was founded in 1819, simultaneously with Leningrad University. Growth of the Library was aided by the receipt of various collections, such as those of the Polotsk Jesuit College, the Censorship Committee and the Leningrad Oriental Institute. The Library receives a deposit copy of USSR editions in accordance with the profile of educational and research activity of the University, buys books and journals by means of the sales network of the city and is in active book exchange within the USSR and abroad. Acquisition of foreign books and journals is co-ordinated with the other large libraries of Leningrad. Since 1958 the whole network of the University libraries, faculty libraries, research institute libraries, etc. has been organized as a unified system with centralized acquisition and cataloguing of literature. Current holdings of the Library include 4,800,000 storage units. The number of books lent yearly is 2.5 million volumes with the number of readers 29,000. Since 1968 the Gor'kii Scientific Library has played an important part as a methodical centre for libraries of educational institutions of the North-West region of the RSFSR (Russian Socialist Federal Soviet Republic).

Special Collections and Treasures. The Division of Rare Books and MSS contains a collection of early Slavic and Russian MSS, dating from the 14th-20th centuries and totalling about 11,000 storage units. The medieval items are mostly of religious and legal interest. Perhaps the single most valuable collection is the archive of the early 19th century literary society *Arkhiv Vol'nogo obshchestva liubitelei slovesnosti, nauk i knudozhestv.* The collection of Mendeleev Papers is housed in the separate Mendeleev Museum and Archive. The Oriental Division of the Library, attached to the Oriental Faculty of the University, keeps its MSS as a separate subdivision. The largest collections are those in Chinese and Japanese studies, while there are also significant East Asian MSS holdings in Manchurian, Tibetan, Mongolian and Korean languages.

Exhibition Areas. Permanent exhibition of new accessions to the Library. Planned subject exhibitions.

Hours. Lending Department 1100-1900 (except Sat. and Sun.). Reading rooms: 1000-2200 (except Sun.).

Transport. Metro: station Vassileostrovskaya. Bus: nos. 7, 10, 30, 44, 45, 47, 60. Trams: 8, 21, 26, 31. (The University is located on Vassilievskii Island.

Parking. Available.

Admission. *Readers:* Open to members of the University and all serious researchers with proof of identification. *Visitors:* Free of charge.

Information. Reference Department.

Sales. No details available.

Guidebooks. No details available.

Restaurant/Snack Facilities. No details available.

Services. No details available.

Catalogues. Alphabetical catalogue of books and journals. Classified catalogue of books and journal articles. Card indexes on the history of Leningrad and the history of the University.

Classification. Bibliotechno-bibliograficheskaya klassifikatsiya.

Copying/Photography. Copying facilities available through Library staff.

MOSCOW
Gosudarstvennaya Ordena Lenina biblioteka SSSR imeni V.I. Lenina (V.I. Lenin State Library of the USSR)
Moscow, Tsentr, pr. Kalinina 3
Tel. 202-40-56

History. The Lenin State Library is the largest and most significant library in the USSR. Its history can be traced back to the private collection of Count N.P. Rumyantsev, and, subsequently, to the library of the Rumyantsev Museum, which opened its doors in 1862. During the pre-Revolutionary period, growth was slow and its collections were relatively inaccessible to the general public. Major growth came, however, after 1917. The Library owed much to the support of Lenin, who attached great importance to libraries. After the Soviet Government moved to Moscow, in 1918, it became the country's central library, with copyright deposit privileges and the pick of the nationalised book collections. Thus between 1918 and 1921 it received over 1½ million volumes, more than doubling its holdings. On 6 February 1925 the Rumyantsev Library was renamed after Lenin and reorganised as the national State Library of the USSR. The growth of the collections demanded more space than was available in the original Pashkov House. The first part of the new building was opened in 1939 and work continued, occupying a whole city block, up to completion in 1960. The main building houses the catalogues, the acquisition, cataloguing and classification departments, together with 19 reading rooms. Behind it

Lenin Library, Moscow

is the nineteen storey bookstack. Holdings currently total 27 million items, including 12 million volumes, 10,658,000 issues of periodicals, 432,000 volumes of newspapers, 344,000 units of MSS, 600,000 reels of microfilm and 3,158,000 sheets of maps etc.

Special Collections and Treasures. Collections include over 40,000 volumes of the works of Marx, Engels and Lenin; the 40,000 volume library of the Sheremetyevs; the 25,000 volume library of the Baryatinskiis; the 18,000 volumes of rare 18th and 19th century editions from the Yusupov estate at Arkhangelskoye; and 30,000 Russian and Slavonic MSS of the 11th-18th centuries. Especially rich MSS collections include those from the Troitsko-Sergievskii monastery; the Moscow Ecclesiastical Academy; the 19th century Society of Russian History and Antiquities; V.I. Grigorovich, V.M. Undol'skii, E.E. Egorov and I. Lukashevich. The MSS division also houses major portions of the papers of such figures as Gogol, Nekrasov, Dostoevskii, Ostrovskii, Turgenev, Tiutchev and Chekhov. Papers of artists include those of the painters A.A. Ivanov and A.A. Kiselev, the composer M. Iu Vel'gorskii and the music critic S.S. Krugliakov. The Library possesses the largest collection in existence of the extremely rare first editions of Giordano Bruno (20 out of 26 recorded), all in contemporary bindings, among them being an inscribed copy — one of two extant — of *Oratio valedictoria* (Wittenberg, 1588). This collection was made by A.S. Norov, the statesman and bibliophile, in the early 19th century and passed at his death to the Rumyantsev Museum. Treasures include the *Archangel Gospels* of 1092; the MS of Gogol's unfinished novel *The Hetman;* and first editions of the works of such notable figures as Rabelais, Descartes, Voltaire, Rousseau, Spinoza and Machiavelli.

Exhibition Areas. Five exhibition rooms, notably the one housing the permanent exhibition on the history of the Russian book. In addition all reading rooms have exhibition areas.

Hours. Daily 0900-2200. Closed last Mon. in each month for cleaning.

Transport. Metro stations: Biblioteka im. V.I. Lenina; Arbatskaya; Kalininskaya. Bus routes: 3, 5, 6, 'K'. Trolley bus routes: 33, 1, 8. (The Library is situated near the Kremlin, in downtown Moscow.)

Parking. Car park available.

Admission. Readers: Readers' tickets can be obtained on completion of forms and presentation of passport, at the office to the right of the main entrance. Tickets for foreigners are usually issued for the period of the visa and can be renewed. Admission to the Manuscript Department requires a special additional stamp and can often involve a more complicated admissions procedure.

The first printed Russian newspaper, Vedomosti (issue of 2 January 1703), in the Lenin Library, Moscow

Visitors: Free of charge.

Information. Information Office at the main entrance. The Central Reference and Information Office answers personal, telephone and written enquiries.

Sales. None.

Guidebooks. Guide in Russian (1959). Description of the Library, in 5 languages (1962). Booklet in Russian, English, German, French and Spanish (1974).

Restaurant/Snack Facilities. Dining-rooms and buffets.

Services. Cloakroom, lifts, smoking rooms, telephones.

Catalogues. Author, classified, subject, and union catalogues. A large gallery outside the Main Reading Room and surrounding the staircase, houses the catalogues.

Classification. Bibliotechno-bibliograficheskaya klassifikatsiya (mostly).

Copying/Photography. Apply to the Microcopying Department. Prior permission must be obtained for private photography.

MOSCOW

Gosudarstvennaya publichnaya istoricheskaya biblioteka RSFSR (State Public Historical Library of the RSFSR)
101839 Moscow, ul. Bogdana Khmel'nitskogo, Starosadskii per., d.9
Tel. 295-65-14 (Director); 228-05-82 (Information)

History. The Library was founded on 20 December 1938 to act as the central historical library of the Russian Federation, to form a state repository of domestic and foreign historical literature in printed or MS form, and to serve as a research institute in historical bibliography and library science. The basis of the Library's pre-Revolutionary holdings was the collection of the Historical Museum, much of which consisted of the private libraries of historians, archaeologists and bibliophiles. The Library now collects, besides material on history, publications dealing with archaeology, ethnography, philosophy and the history of literature and art. Current holdings total 1.6 million book titles, 1.95 million journal issues and 8,000 microfilms.

Special Collections and Treasures. The Department of Rare Books has about 100 incunabula and collections of early Russian printed books, MS books of the 16th-17th centuries, and Western European books of the same period. The Library's holdings are richest in the modern period of Soviet history.

State Public Historical Library of the RSFSR, Moscow

Iñigo López de Mendoza, Marqués de Santillana, Proverbios (Seville, 1500), in the State Public Historical Library of the RSFSR, Moscow

Exhibition Areas. New accessions are displayed each week in a room on the 2nd floor.

Hours. Daily 0900-2200. Closed: 1 Jan., 8 March, 1-2 May, 7-8 Nov. and 5 Dec. Closed on the last Friday of each month for cleaning.

Transport. Metro station: Ploshchad Nogina. Bus route: 3. Trolley bus routes: 41, 25, 45.

Parking. In the Library courtyard.

Admission. Readers: No charge. Anyone aged 18 or over may register as a reader, if the Library's holdings are essential to his scholarly or practical work. Registration takes place on the ground floor (Russian 1st floor). Foreign readers should present their passports and visas.
Visitors. Free of charge. Apply to the Librarian.

Information. Information Desk on the ground floor (Russian 1st floor) in the hall of the Library (for orientation purposes).

Sales. None.

Guidebooks. Guide to the Library, in Russian, free of charge.

Restaurant/Snack Facilities. Dining room/buffet, open daily 1200-1900.

Services. Cloakrooms, lavatories, smoking rooms and telephones, on the 1st floor.

Catalogues. Author catalogue. Classified catalogue supplemented by a subject catalogue. Card indexes (notably one for articles on history from journals and article collection published since 1877).

Classification. The classified catalogue is based on a scheme which is itself based on the Bibliotechno-bibliograficheskaya klassifikatsiya (the standard USSR system).

Copying/Photography. The Library has a copying service. Apply to the Librarian for private photography.

MOSCOW
Gosudarstvennaya publichnaya nauchno-tekhnicheskaya biblioteka SSSR (State Public Scientific and Technical Library of the USSR)
Moscow K-31, Kuznetskii most 12
Tel. K 5-92-88 (Director); B 8-73-79 (Reference-Bibliography Department)

History. The Library is at the head of the technical

library network in the USSR, set up in 1958 by Soviet government decree. The Library covers all fields of science and technology except medicine. Its role is to act as a diversified scientific and technical library of state importance, to serve as an All Union source of information on engineering and related sciences, to operate as a scientific and methodic centre for the technical library network of the USSR and to act as the co-ordinating centre of the USSR for scientific and technical translations, technical bibliography, inter-library loans and the acquisition of foreign technical literature. It has been claimed that, since its main field of interest is engineering, there are few strictly comparable libraries in foreign countries. The Library now co-ordinates the bibliographical activities of 20,000 technical libraries in the USSR. Four copies are received of every technical publication published in the USSR, except for some minor items which are received in either one or two copies. Current holdings of the Library total 6,800,000 books, periodicals and documents, housed in some six buildings.

Special Collections and Treasures. The Library contains several specialised collections of national significance, such as the collection of industrial firm catalogues (2 million units) and the collection of translations of technical literature (200,000 units).

Exhibition Areas. No details available.

Hours. Mon.-Sat. 1000-2200.

Transport. Metro: stations Ploshchad Sverdlova, Ploshchad Revolutsii, Marx Prospekt (then take underground passage). Bus: nos. 3, 5, 18, 24, 87, 107, 111, 213.

Parking. No details available.

Admission. Readers: Open only to suitably qualified researchers, e.g. engineers, technicians and students of higher technical education.
Visitors: Apply to Library Director.

Information. Reference Department, which provides special bibliographies on request.

Sales. None.

Guidebooks. In Russian.

Restaurant/Snack Facilities. No details available.

Services. Lavatories, cloakrooms.

Catalogues. Author, subject and UDC classified catalogues. Various special card catalogues, e.g. for periodicals, foreign literature, translations and patents.

Classification. Universal Decimal Classification (previously the Lenin Library classification was used).

Copying/Photography. All forms of photographic reproduction are available through Library staff. No private photography allowed without permission of the Library Director.

MOSCOW
Institut nauchnoi informatsii po obschestvennym naukam AN SSSR (Institute of Scientific Information in the Social Sciences of the Academy of Sciences of the USSR)
117418 Moscow V-418, ul. Krasikova 28/45
Tel. 128-89-30

History. The Library of the Institute was founded in 1918, as the collection of the Socialist Academy of Social Sciences (which was subsequently renamed the Communist Academy in 1924). It was the first major special library to be established by the Soviet government. In 1936 it became a library of the Academy of Sciences, following the re-organisation of the Academy library complex (see p. 374). Named the Fundamental Library of Social Sciences of the Academy of Sciences, the Library's holdings grew rapidly after World War II. The pressure on space caused severe overcrowding and necessitated the construction of a new three-storey building, completed in 1974, in south-west Moscow. The Library became a division of the Institute of Scientific Information in the Social Sciences in 1969. The present title (abbreviated as INION AN SSSR) reflects the Library's role as a centre of scientific information in the social sciences. It can be said to differ from other social science libraries in that it is the centre of a social science network which also covers the study of language and literature. Holdings at the Institute and its branches in Moscow totalled 9,760,000 units at 1 January 1975, with foreign publications constituting more than half of this total.

Special Collections and Treasures. The Library specialises in the social sciences and its special strength lies in economics, international relations, modern history and philosophy. Marxism-Leninism founders' works, works dealing with activities of the CPSU and foreign communist and progressive organisations are represented on a large scale. The Institute possesses one of the best collections in the USSR of parliamentary reports and diplomatic reports. There is a complete set of international diplomatic conferences' reports, publications of the League of Nations, of the UNO, ILO, UNESCO and other similar organisations. The Institute has a well-selected bibliographical and reference publications section. Other collections relate to the republics and regions of the USSR. It contains the libraries of many older institutions, e.g. the Institute of Red Professors,

Institute of Scientific Information in the Social Sciences, Moscow

the Moscow Book Chamber, the Moscow Zemstvo, etc. The more important institute libraries affiliated with INION include those of the Institute of Material Culture, the Gorkii Institute of World Literature, the Institute of History, the Institute of Philosophy and the Institute of Oriental Studies.

Exhibition Areas.   Numerous exhibitions in the various lobbies, e.g. new scientific literature.

Hours.   Mon.-Fri. 0100-2100, Sat. 1000-1800.

Transport.   The Library is accessible by bus and underground. The Library is located in south-west Moscow, not far from the University, in the centre of a complex of educational buildings, which include the Central State Medical Library.

Parking.   Facilities available.

Admission. Readers: Members of the Academy of Sciences, of institutions of learning and government representatives. Various free admission areas.
Visitors: Apply direct to the Institute.

Information.   Reference-Bibliographic Hall. The preparation of bibliographic and abstracted information on all aspects of the social sciences is the principal task of the Institute.

Sales.   No details available.

Guidebooks.   In Russian and English (the latter entitled *Institute of Scientific Information on Social Sciences,* Moscow, 1975).

Restaurant/Snack Facilities.   Available.

Services.   Two conference halls.

Catalogues. Alphabetical catalogue for books and journals. Subject catalogue for books. Many card indexes on special subjects. Various published bibliographical indexes.

Classification.   No details available.

Copying/Photography.   Orders for copying are accepted by Library staff. Private photography forbidden without prior permission.

MOSCOW

*Nauchnaya biblioteka im A.M. Gor'kogo Moskovskogo
gos. universiteta im. M.V. Lomonosova (Gor'kii Scientific
Library of the Lomonosov State University of Moscow)
Moscow K-9, Marx Prospekt 20
Tel. Director's Office 203-65-25, Service Department
203-37-51*

History. The Library was founded, with Moscow
University, in 1756 by the great Russian scientist Mikhail
Lomonosov. The holdings were originally assembled on
the basis of lists drawn up by members of the Russian
Academy of Sciences, subsequently supplemented by
Russian and foreign scholarly publications, as well as
works of fiction. The Library was, for more than a
hundred years, prior to the establishment of the
Rumyantsev Museum (now the Lenin Library), Moscow's
only accessible public library. After the 1917 October
Revolution the number of students and staff in the
Moscow State University began to increase rapidly and
this involved a comprehensive re-organisation of the
Library's work. In 1920 legal deposit privileges were
received and this ensured a rapid growth of the
collections. In 1950 the Library was entrusted with the
organisation of branch libraries for the new University
buildings on the Lenin Hills, several kilometres from the
city centre. To aid these libraries a sum of 7 million
roubles was spent on acquiring a comprehensive
collection of natural science literature. The Library's
holdings currently total over 6 million volumes, housed in
the Main Library building at Marx Prospekt 20, elsewhere
in Moscow, and in the Lenin Hills complex.

Special Collections and Treasures. Collections include
those of the Muravev family; the Turgenevs (father and
son), including the whole series of publications issued by
the Moscow University Press in the 18th century; the
well-known Russian bibliophile Ostroglazov, whose
collection included those works banned by the Imperial
Russian censorship and Professors Kovalevsky and
Granovsky. Treasures include the Greek MS *Apostol,*
which was written at the order of the Byzantine emperor
Michael Ducas in 1072; a Latin *Bible* of the 13th century;
the censorship MSS of Gogol's *Dead Souls* and
Turgenev's *Sportsman's sketches;* the Russian first
edition of Marx's *Das Kapital* (St. Petersburg, 1872); and
complete files of Lenin's *Iskra* and Herzen's *Kolokol.*

Exhibition Areas. Main vestibule of the building in Marx
Prospekt.

Hours. No details available.

Transport. For Marx Prospekt: metro stations,
Kalininskaya or Biblioteka im. Lenina. For Lenin Hills:
metro station, Universitet. Also various bus services.

Parking. Available close to both locations.

*Moscow University Library.
Main building*

Admission.   Readers: Readers' tickets entitle the holder to use all departments of the Library but only teaching staff and advanced students may use special reading rooms.
Visitors: Apply to the Librarian.

Information.   In reading rooms and in Catalogue Hall.

Sales.   None.

Guidebooks.   Booklet in Russian, 1972.

Restaurant/Snack   Facilities.   None   in   Library   but available nearby at both Marx Prospekt and Lenin Hills.

Services.   Cloakrooms, lavatories.

Catalogues.   Author, classified and subject catalogues.

Classification.   Own.

Copying/Photography.   Copying   facilities   available through Library staff. Permission must be obtained for private photography.

MOSCOW
Vsesoyuznaya gosudarstvennaya ordena Trudovogo Krasnogo Znameni biblioteka inostrannoi literatury (All-Union State Library of Foreign Literature)
Moscow 109240, Uljyanovskaya 1
Tel. 297-28-39

History.   The Library was founded as the 'Neophilological Library' in 1921, with a modest stock of a few hundred volumes in three languages. It is a public library and central book depository of foreign literature and Russian translations in the natural sciences, social and political sciences, philology, literature, fiction and the arts. Prior to World War II the collections were housed in several locations and even after the war they were housed in a comparatively small building in the Ulitsa Razina. In March 1948 the Library was given the status of an All Union Central Library. In 1955 it was granted the legal right to receive one copy of the most significant foreign publications obtained by the Central agencies of the USSR government and one copy of each catalogue card prepared by any Soviet library for newly acquired foreign material. By 1966 the stock of the Library had grown to 3 million items, serving 40,000 readers, and it was this expansion which led to its occupation in 1967 of a new building, not far from the centre of Moscow, on the bank of the Yauza River. In 1972 the Library was awarded the Order of the Red Banner of Labour for its work. In 1973 it was given the status of a Research Institute, which gave a new impetus to diversified research activities in the field of library science. By the end of 1974 the number of readers surpassed the level of

All-Union State Library of Foreign Literature, Moscow

50,000. Holdings currently total more than 4 million items in 132 foreign languages.

Special Collections and Treasures. The Library is itself a special collection, as the USSR's largest depository of books in foreign languages. Collections include the collection of books on Spanish history and culture donated by Spanish opponents of fascism in 1938; a large Shakespeare Collection of over 6,000 items; more than 50,000 volumes on world art; and a large collection of material relating to the anti-fascist struggle and resistance movements in various European countries.

Exhibition Areas. 4 exhibition rooms in the Library. The principal exhibition area is on the 3rd floor (Russian 4th floor).

Hours. Mon.-Sat. 1000-2200, Sun. 1000-2000. Closed for cleaning on the last Thurs. of each month.

Transport. Metro: station Taganskaya, then trolleybus no. 16 to Yauzskaya bol'nitsa bus-stop.

Parking. In front of the Library.

Admission. Readers: No charge. Registration at the desk in the entrance hall. Passport and certificate of higher education must be shown for registration in the scientific (i.e. scholarly) reading room. Only a passport is required for registration in the general reading room. The scientific reading room is open to scholars and researchers and to final-year students. The general reading room is open to Soviet citizens aged 18 or over. *Visitors:* Single visits are permitted.

Information. Registration Desk. Librarians in the Catalogue Hall and the reading rooms may be consulted.

Sales. None.

Guidebooks. A guide in Russian and other languages.

Restaurant/Snack Facilities. Dining room and buffet.

Services. Cloakrooms (ground floor), lavatories, two lifts, lounges (2nd floor), occasional lectures, film shows, etc., audio-visual aid rooms (1st floor).

Catalogues. Alphabetical (i.e. author) and classified catalogues. Catalogues housed on the 1st floor.

Classification. Own.

Copying/Photography. Microfilm and dry-copying facilities available. Apply to Inter-Library Loan Department. Permission must be obtained from the Director's Office for private photography.

NOVOSIBIRSK

Gosudarstvennaya publichnaya nauchno- tekhnicheskaya biblioteka Sibirskogo otdeleniya AN SSSR, (State Public Scientific and Technical Library of the Siberian Department of the Academy of Sciences of the USSR)
630200 Novosibirsk, ul. Voskhod 15
Tel. 66-18-60 (Director); 66-19-91 (Reference and Bibliography Department; 66-80-71 (Reader Registration)

History. The Library was founded on 17 October 1958, when the State Scientific Library of the Ministry of Higher Education in Moscow was transferred to the Siberian Department of the All Union Academy of Sciences and became its State Public Scientific and Technical Library in Novosibirsk. The Ministry stock of almost 4 million specialised items of Soviet and foreign literature on technology and natural sciences meant that the Siberian division, with its increasing demand for scientific material, suddenly acquired a collection of impressive proportions. A statute was granted to the Library in 1960, which expanded the scope of acquisitions according to those divisions of natural sciences and the humanities which were poorly represented in the stocks of the existing state scientific library. In 1966 a new building was opened for the Library, with space for 10 million volumes. The Library received legal deposit privileges for the whole of the USSR in 1968. Current holdings total over 6 million items, 2½ million coming from outside the USSR.

Special Collections and Treasures. The Library has a large collection (over 1 million items) of specialised technical and foreign documentation.

Exhibition Areas. Reading Room no. 8 is devoted entirely to the exhibition of new acquisitions and current periodicals.

Hours. Mon.-Fri. 0900-2100, Sat. and Sun. 1000-1800. Closed on public hols. and the last Thurs. of each month.

Transport. Bus routes: 10, 39, 112. Trolleybuses: 5, 8, 10, 12, 15. Trams: 7, 12, 13.

Parking. Behind the Library.

Admission. Readers: 2 general reading rooms are open to the public and various specialised reading rooms for scholars. Passports must be produced at the Registration Office.
Visitors: An entry permit may be obtained from the Registration Office.

Information. Information desks in all reading rooms. There is a Reference-Bibliography Department.

Sales. None.

State Public Scientific and Technical Library, Novosibirsk

Page from the Drutskoe Gospels (1st half of 14th century), in the State Public Scientific and Technical Library, Novosibirsk

Guidebooks.   Guide in Russian.

Restaurant/Snack Facilities.   No details available.

Services.   Bibliography and translation service, cloak-rooms, lavatories.

Catalogues.   Author, subject and classified catalogues. (The subject catalogue covers natural sciences and technology only.)

Classification.   Partly decimal, partly Bibliotechno-bibliograficheskaya klassifikatsiya.

Copying/Photography.   Microfilms and photocopies can be obtained from the External Services Department.

TARTU

Tartu Riikliku Ülikooli Teaduslik Raamatukogu (Scientific Library of Tartu State University)
202 400 Tartu, Toomemägi, Estonian SSR
Tel. Tartu 341-21/286

History.   The Library was founded in 1802 with the reopening of the University in Tartu. Its initial stock totalled about 4,000 volumes, most of which were donated. The first Director of the Library was Karl Morgenstern (1770-1852), a professor of elocution and classical philology, aesthetics and history of literature and art, who held the post for 37 years. In 1806, the Library occupied its present premises, the main building of the Library at Toomemägi, the restored and converted old Dome Cathedral, whose foundation dates back to the 13th century. Books were initially ordered from Germany and St. Petersburg but later also from England and Italy. Through membership of the University Publications Exchange Association (Akademischer Tauschverein), founded in Germany in 1818, the Library was able to negotiate exchanges with a number of German universities. By 1835 Tartu had 60,473 volumes, the third largest collection in Russia at that time. In 1917 the total had risen to 400,000 volumes, half of which were dissertations. Holdings in 1975 totalled 3.3 million books and periodicals and 16,000 MSS. The Library receives a deposit copy of all the printed books published in the Estonian SSR and since 1946 has received copies of all the publications in Russian in the fields of science studied at Tartu University. At present the Library is exchanging publications with more than 350 institutions abroad. The Library has a readership of over 10,000 who borrow over 900,000 books per annum. Plans are in hand for a new library building which will house over 5 million volumes and seat over 1,000 readers.

Scientific Library of Tartu State University

Special Collections and Treasures.   The stock of Estonian Literature (over 90,000 volumes) includes

Estonian books and periodicals from the 17th century to the present time. The oldest Estonian book in the Library is H. Stahl, *Hand und Haussbuch* (1632). Other treasures include the first complete Estonian bible *Piibli-Ramat* (1739); the first Estonian newspaper, O.W. Masing's *Marahwa Näddala-Leht* (1821-23, 25); and the first two editions of the national epic *Kalevipoeg* (1857-61 and 1862). The Library's other collections include the publications of famous printers (e.g. Plantin, Elzevir and Feodorov); and first editions of classics in the fields of science and literature, e.g. Thomas More's *Utopia* (1516), A. Vesalius, *De humani corporis fabrica* (1543), Karl Marx, *Das Kapital* I-III (1867-94) and F. Engels, *The Condition of the Working Class in England* (1845). The stock of theses now comprises over 400,000 items dating from the 16th century to the present. It includes the theses of such outstanding scientists as M. and P. Curie, A.H. Becquerel, M. Faraday, M. Planck, P. Langevin, N. Bohr, I. Pavlov, N. Burdenko, etc.

Exhibition Areas. Exhibitions are held in the Main Library and in the Branch Library in Vanemuine Street.

Hours. Reading rooms: Mon.-Fri. 0800-2200, Sat. 0800-2000, Sun. 1000-1700. During summer vacation the Library hours are shortened. Closed public hols.

Transport. Library is situated in the old part of town near the bus terminal.

Parking. Free parking facilities are available at the Library.

Admission. Readers: All students and research workers may read in the Library and should register in the Loan Division of the main Library building.
Visitors: Everyone may visit the Library and the reading rooms free of charge.

Information. In the Catalogue Room, on the ground floor of the main building.

Sales. None.

Guidebooks. There are English and German summaries of the current Estonian Guidebook (cost 19 copecks). A new guidebook in Estonian with Russian and English summaries appeared in 1975.

Restaurant/Snack Facilities. None.

Services. Cloakrooms, lavatories, smoking lounges and telephones.

Catalogues. Alphabetical, systematic and subject catalogues.

Classification. Universal Decimal Classification.

Hippocrates, Omnia opera (Venice, 1523) in the Scientific Library of Tartu State University

The first edition of Lenin's works to be published legally in Russia (Moscow, 1899), in the Scientific Library of Tartu State University

Copying/Photography.   Copying facilities are provided.
For private photography consult the Librarian.

TASHKENT

*Gosudarstvennaya biblioteka UzSSR im Alishera Navoi
(Alisher Navoi State Public Library of the Uzbek SSR)
Tashkent 700000, GSP, Alleya Paradov, 5
Tel. 398658, 394341, 394440, 394450*

History.   The Alisher Navoi Library is the centre of a
public library system of 10,600 libraries whose total
holdings amount to 44 million volumes. The history of
the Library dates back to 1870 when the Tashkent Public
Library, the first public library in Central Asia, opened. In
1919 it was renamed the Turkestan People's Library, in
May 1920 it became the Turkestan State Library and in
1924 a Central Asian State Library. In 1948 it was named
after the famous Uzbek poet and statesman, Alisher
Navoi, during the Navoi 500th anniversary celebrations.
The Library has a yearly average of 40,000 readers,
served by a staff of over 300. In addition to the routine
functions of a Soviet national library, the Library sponsors
the Tashkent Popular University of Music and issues
bibliographical indexes to the literature on Uzbekistan.
Holdings currently include 4,004,914 items with 3,350,336
in Russian and 353,905 Uzbek books.

Special Collections and Treasures.   The Library has a
unique Turkestan Collection, which provides an in-
valuable research source on pre-Revolutionary Central
Asia. Especially precious are the first books to be
published for the Uzbek population in their own
language: *Kalendar* by S.M. Ibragimov (Tashkent, 1872);
Amir Timur (Tashkent, 1890) and *Skazanie o gorode
Oshe* (Tashkent, 1885) by N.P. Ostrovinov. The Library
has copies of the first newspapers published in
Turkestan, such as *Turkistan vilojatining gazeti* (1870-
1917); *Todžar* (1907); and *Turon* (1919); and in Russian,
such as *Turkestanskie vedomosti* (1870-1917) and
Russkij Turkestan (1898-1917). Treasures amongst the
old Russian books in the Library are the *Ostrog Bible*
(1581), a work of the first Russian printer Ivan Fedorov;
the first secular book printed in Russia, *Učenie i hitrost'
ratnogo stroenija pehotnyh usudej* (1647); and the
Arifmetika of Leonty magnitskii. The Library has a valuable
collection of satirical magazines for the period 1905-06 and
the collection of I.P. Liprandi, on history, geography,
religion and philosophy.

Exhibition Areas.   Over 100 exhibitions are held each
year, both inside and outside the Library.

Hours.   Mon.-Fri. 1000-2200, Sat. and Sun. 1000-1800.

Transport.   Public transport available.

Parking.   Available.

Admission.   Readers and *Visitors:* Free of charge.

Information.   At Circulation Desk. Over 60 bibliographic, instructional and information publications issued each year.

Sales.   No details provided.

Guidebooks.   In Russian and Uzbek (1970).

Restaurant/Snack Facilities.   Restaurant, snack bars.

Services.   Lavatories, cloakrooms. The Library organises readers' conferences, literary evenings, lectures and talks by writers, composers etc.

Catalogues.   Alphabetical and classified catalogues. Various special card indexes, including a major one for 'Uzbekistanica'.

Classification.   Bibliotechno-bibliograficheskaya klassifikatsiya and Universal Decimal Classification.

Copying/Photography.   Most forms of copying are available through Library staff. Apply to the Librarian for permission for private photography.

TBILISI
Gosudarstvennaya Respublikanskaya biblioteka Gruzinskoi SSR im K. Marksa (State Republican Karl Marx Library of the Georgian SSR)
Tbilisi 380007, ul. Ketskhoveli, no 5
Tel. Director's Office, 93-12-33, 99-92-86

History.   The Library was founded in 1846 as the Tiflis Public Library. Its initial stock was based on the collections of the Chancellery of the Governor-General of the Caucasus. In 1923 it was combined with the Central Academic Library of the Council of People's Commisars of Georgia to become the state public library of Georgia. The Library has made steady growth since then, partly as a result of its right to receive a copy of every publication issued in the Georgian SSR and of every item in Russian published in the Soviet Union as a whole. Current holdings total 11,724,372 items, including 2,719,125 book volumes.

Special Collections and Treasures.   The Georgian Collection of 3,850,476 items is possibly the best in the world. Other collections include the library of the former 'Society for the Promotion of Literacy among the Georgian Population' and the libraries of various Caucasian scholars. Treasures include Stefano Paolini, *Dizzionario Giorgiano e Italiano* (Rome, 1629); Francisco-Maria Maggi, *Syntagmaton linguarum orientalium quae in Georgiae regionibus audiuntur* (Rome, 1670) and early Armenian books of the 17th and 18th centuries.

State Republican Karl Marx Library of the Georgian SSR, Tbilisi

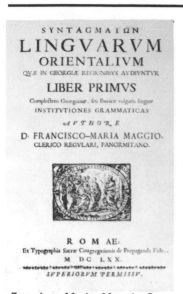

SYNTAGMAIΩN
LINGVARVM
ORIENTALIVM
QVÆ IN GEORGIÆ REGIONIBVS AVDIVNTVR
LIBER PRIMVS
Complectens Georgianæ, seu Ibericæ vulgaris linguæ
INSTITVTIONES GRAMMATICAS
AVTHORE
D· FRANCISCO–MARIA MAGGIO·
CLERICO REGVLARI, PANORMITANO.

R O M AE·
Ex Typographia Sacræ Congregationis de Propaganda Fide..
M DC LXX.

SVPERIORVM PERMISSV.

Francisco-Maria Maggi, Syntagmaton linguarum orientalium quae in Georgiae regionibus audiuntur (Rome, 1670), in the State Republican Karl Marx Library of the Georgian SSR, Tbilisi

Vincas Kapsukas State University, Vilnius. The Sarbievius (Faculty of Philology) Quadrangle

Exhibition Areas. All the reading rooms, and the entrance hall in both Library buildings, contain a variety of displays and exhibitions.

Hours. Daily (except Mon.) 0900-2300. Closed public hols.

Transport. From the railway station by underground to 'Ploshchad Lenina' Station, trollybus no 2 or taxi. From the airport by bus no 8.

Parking. No details available.

Admission. Readers: Open to all citizens aged 18 or over and there is also a special department for older schoolchildren. Admission free of charge.
Visitors: Apply to Library Director.

Information. Reference and Information Department. Information points in all reading rooms.

Sales. None.

Guidebooks. A free guidebook is available in Russian and Georgian.

Restaurant/Snack Facilities. Buffet available.

Services. Cloakrooms, smoking rooms and public telephone available.

Catalogues. Author, geographical and chronological catalogues. Union catalogue of foreign publications in libraries in Georgian SSR.

Classification. Bibliotechno-bibliograficheskaya klassifikatsiya and Universal Decimal Classification.

Copying/Photography. The Photographic Laboratory accepts orders for photocopies. Cameras may be used with the permission of the Director's Office.

VILNIUS
Scientific Library of the Vilnius Vincas Kapsukas State University
Universiteto gatvé 3, 232633 Vilnius
Tel. 2-63-87; 2-63-89

History. The Scientific Library of Vilnius V. Kapsukas State University is the oldest library in Soviet Lithuania. It was founded in 1570 as the library of the Jesuit College, established in the same year. Its original stock derived from the collections of Duke Sigismund Augustus of Lithuania and Georgius Albinus, suffragan of Vilnius. In 1579, on the edict of Stefan Batory, the College was reorganised into an academy and university on the Western European pattern. From the end of the 16th to the middle of the 17th century, the Library was known as one of the largest book collections in Eastern Europe. In 1773 with the repression of the Jesuit Order, the Academy was renamed the Principal School of Lithuania and in 1780 it received compulsory copy privileges for Lithuania. In 1803 it was named the Library of the Imperial University of Vilnius. This period of expansion was cut short in 1832, when the Tsarist Government closed the University and dispersed a considerable part of the Library's collections. (It was not until 1945 that some of these collections were returned to Vilnius.) In 1867 the Vilnius Public Library was opened in the former University buildings and then in 1919 it was renamed with the re-establishment of Vilnius University. The Library and its collections suffered damage during World War II. However, with help from other libraries of the Soviet Union it was able to rebuild its stock and it was also given the right to receive on payment a compulsory deposit copy of all Soviet books. In 1957 the Library adopted its present title. Current holdings total 3,200,000 items, including 1.6 million books.

Special Collections and Treasures. The Library has the world's richest collection of Lithuanian printed books (over 11,000 items). Other collections include the J. Lelewel Collection, which consists of atlases, books and MSS; the archives of the linguists K. Buga and J. Jablonskis and the writers J. Tumas-Vaižgantas and B. Pranskus-Žalionis; and the Vilnius Medical Society Collection, built up in the 19th and early 20th centuries, to which has been added the libraries of prominent medical men. Treasures include 307 incunabula, notably the oldest book in Lithuania, Rhabanus Maurus's *Opus de universo* (Strasbourg, 1467); the first book in the Lithuanian language, the *Catechismusa Prasty Szadei* by M. Mažvydas (Karaliaučius, 1547); and the unique *Grammatica Litvanica* by D. Klein (1653).

Exhibition Areas. The Museum of Progressive Scientific Thought; the Adam Mickiewicz Memorial Museum; the Smuglevičius Hall; the Old Observatory; the Lelewel Hall; and the departmental branches of the Library.

Hours. Reading halls in the central building: Mon.-Sat. 0900-2300, Sun. 0900-1700. Closed on state holidays: 1 Jan., 8 March, 1, 2, 9 May, 7-8 Nov., 5 Dec. and the last day of every month.

Transport. Trolley-bus: no.2 from the railway station; buses: nos. 6 and 10.

Parking. At the central building.

Admission. Readers and *Visitors:* Free of charge.

Information. On the ground floor of the central building.

Sales. None.

The first Lithuanian book, *Catechismusa Prasty Szadei,* by M. Mažvydas *(1547),* in the Scientific Library of Vincas Kapsukas State University, Vilnius. This is the only copy of the book in the USSR

Guidebooks. Booklets in Lithuanian, Russian, English and German (published in 1970).

Restaurant/Snack Facilities. A students' cafeteria on the ground floor, open 1200-1600.

Services. Lavatories, cloakroom, telephone, smoking lounge on the ground floor.

Catalogues. Author and systematic catalogues. Various special catalogues.

Classification. Universal Decimal Classification.

Copying/Photography. Copying service available but machines are not available for individual use. The use of private cameras within the Library is permitted.

United States of America

ANN ARBOR
University Library, University of Michigan
Ann Arbor, Michigan 48104
Tel. 313-764-9356 (Director's Office)

University Library, University of Michigan, Ann Arbor

History. The University of Michigan maintains 30 libraries on the Ann Arbor campus. Of these, 26 are organized administratively as the University Library. The largest of the 26, which contains the administrative office of the Library, is the Harlan Hatcher Graduate Library. The University of Michigan was founded in Detroit in 1817. The year 1837 marks it establishment on the Ann Arbor campus. The effective history of the Library can be said to have begun in 1838 when the Regents appropriated $6,500 so that Dr. Asa Gray could travel to Europe and purchase a library. Dr. Gray delegated the task of purchasing a collection of 3,401 volumes, which arrived in Ann Arbor in 1840. In 1841 the books were placed in Mason Hall, the University's combination classroom, dormitory, chapel and library building. By 1863 the Library had 10,000 volumes and by 1890, 90,000. The first building built especially for the Library was opened in 1883, to be replaced in 1920 by the present North Building of the Harlan Hatcher Graduate Library. Current holdings of the University Library complex now include 4,799,499 volumes, 97,691 reels of microfilm, and 1,036,800 sheets of microforms.

Special Collections and Treasures. Collections include the Papyrus Collection, consisting of about 6,000 papyri dating from the 3rd century BC to the 8th century AD; the Shakespeare Collection of 9,200 volumes; the

Hubbard Collection of Imaginary Voyages of 2,800 volumes, of which nearly half are various editions, translations and versions of *Robinson Crusoe* and *Gulliver's Travels;* the Stephen Spaulding Collection of 5,500 volumes, strong in history and military science; the Labadie Collection of 17,000 books, MSS, etc., on political and social protest movements, civil liberty, monetary reform and economic and labour history; the Myers Collection on German history of the Weimar Republic and Nazi period; the Worcester Philippine Collection; the Woytinsky Collection on Economic and Political Science; and the Van Volkenburg-Browne and the Sanders Theater Collections. The William L. Clements Library, which is administered separately, is in itself a special collection of material on early America to 1866. It specializes in materials relating to the discovery and exploration of the American continent and to the American Revolution. Its collections contain 43,000 rare books, 350 MSS collections numbering about 500,000 items, 36,000 maps, 41,000 volumes of newspapers and thousands of pieces of sheet music. The Bentley Library contains 30,000 volumes, 14,000,000 MS items, and 150,000 photographs relating to Michigan history.

Exhibition Areas. 7th floor of the Harlan Hatcher Graduate Library.

Hours. Mon.-Thurs. 0800-2400, Fri. 0800-2200, Sat. 1000-1800, Sun. 1300-2400. Closed public hols.

Transport. Buses to the University campus. (The Harlan Hatcher Graduate Library is located in the centre of the main campus.)

Parking. Available both in the city and on campus.

Admission. *Readers:* All readers should register at the Circulation Desk, Harlan Hatcher Graduate Library, North Building.
Visitors: Admitted free of charge.

Information. First floor, North Building, Harlan Hatcher Graduate Library.

Sales. None.

Guidebooks. A free brochure is available in English.

Restaurant/Snack Facilities. None in the Library but available on campus.

Services. Typing rooms, lavatories, lifts, smoking rooms and telephones. Study carrels are located throughout the stack areas and are assigned to graduate students and faculty members.

Catalogues. Dictionary union catalogue of all library holdings.

Classification. Library of Congress, except for *belles lettres,* which is classified by Dewey.

Copying/Photography. An extensive photoduplication service is available in the basement of the Harlan Hatcher Graduate Library, North Building. Over 20 coin-operated copying machines are available in the various libraries. Private cameras may only be used with permission.

Friends of the Library. The William L. Clements Library and the Bentley Historical Library have organisations of Friends.

AUSTIN
The Library, University of Texas at Austin
Austin, Texas 78712
Tel. (512) 471-3811

History. Classes began at the University of Texas in 1883. In 1884 the collections totalled 1,200 volumes. The growth of the University and the Library has been dramatic, however, in the 20th century. In 1935 holdings reached 500,000 volumes, a figure which grew to 1 million in 1952, to 2 million in 1967 and to 3 million in 1973. The General Library was housed in rooms in the University Building until 1910 and in the Cass Gilbert designed Library Building, until it moved to the present Main Building in 1933. Portions of the Main Building, the Harry Ransom Center, Sid Richardson Hall, and the Undergraduate and Academic Center Building now contain the Main Library, the Latin American and Texana Collections, Rare Books and 20th century collections and the Undergraduate Library. A contact awarded early in 1974 provides for approximately 480,000 square feet of space in a Social Sciences and Humanities Library Building, named the Perry-Castaneda Library, scheduled for completion in 1977. Current holdings of the University of Texas Library include 3,518,690 books, 596,000 microforms and in excess of 12 million leaves of MSS.

Special Collections and Treasures. Separately housed collections include the Harry Ransom Center, which reflects the inspired purchasing of the University in the late 1950s and early 1960s. The HRC has important research collections in English and American literature, bibliography, history of science, photography and theatre arts. Collections in English and American literature include the Lee Samuels Hemingway Collection; the Jerome Zipkin Collection of Somerset Maugham; the George Lazarus Collections of H.G. Wells and Arthur Rackham; the Frederick Dannay Collection of material by and about Ellery Queen; the Eric Gill Collection; the T.E. Hanley Library with its extensive MS collections of D.H. Lawrence, Dylan Thomas, Samuel Beckett and G.B. Shaw; the Library of Sir Compton Mackenzie; the Edmund Blunden Collection; the Sitwell Collection; the Edgar Lee Masters Collection; the J.B. Pinker Collection;

The University of Texas at Austin

and the John Lehmann Collection. The Latin American Collection, housed in Unit 1 of Sid Richardson Hall, dates from about 1900. It was greatly enlarged and its future shaped, by the acquisition of the Mexican Genaro García Library in 1921. It is now among the top three Latin American collections in the world. The Barker Texas History Center, housed in Unit 2 of Sid Richardson Hall, contains a comprehensive library of books and archives dealing with the development of Texas since the days of French and Spanish exploration. The Undergraduate and Academic Center Building includes the library of the Texas folklorist J. Frank Dobie; the Tinker Collection concentrating on the horsemen of the Americas; the study of the late Erle Stanley Gardner; the Blanche and Alfred Knopf Collection; and the History of Aviation Collection.

Exhibition Areas. The Undergraduate and Academic Center Building; the Harry Ransom Center; Michener Art Gallery (1st and 2nd floors); and the Sid Richardson Hall (Units 1 and 2).

Hours. Library schedules vary. When the University is in session, all libraries observe daytime hours with some observing additional evening and Saturday morning hours. Intersession hours are posted. Libraries are closed on major holidays observed by the University.

Transport. City buses to the campus. For the Main Library go to the University Tower. The Harry Ransom Center is located at the southwest corner of the campus, at 21st and Guadalupe Streets.

Parking. Available but often crowded. Those using the Library facilities of the Sid Richardson Hall are perhaps best served by parking lots.

Admission. Readers: Readers are admitted to any library to use materials within the Library. Borrowing privileges vary, according to type of material. Visiting scholars wishing to borrow must pay a $15.00 deposit plus $2.00 charge for a borrower's card. Apply for borrower's card at the loan desk of the Main Library, second floor of the Main (Tower) Building. Advance application should be made by those wishing to use research collections, especially those in the Harry Ransom Center.
Visitors: Apply to individual library units.

Information. At the main desk of the individual Library units, or at the Central Information Desk of the Main Library, second floor of Main Building.

Sales. No actual sales desk but the Harry Ransom Center offers a limited number of publications.

Guidebooks. Available at Library desks, or on written application.

Restaurant/Snack Facilities. None in the Libraries but many available around the University campus.

Services. Lavatories, elevators, public telephones, smoking areas, ramps for the disabled, conference rooms (including facilities for blind students), typing facilities.

Catalogues. The Main Catalogue and most departmental catalogues are in card format with author and subject entries. Also published catalogues: *Catalog of the Latin American Collection* (G.K. Hall), and the *University of Texas Archives, a guide to the historical manuscripts collections in the Texas Library, Vol. 1* (Univ. of Texas Press).

Classification. Dewey until May 1972; Library of Congress after May 1972.

Copying/Photography. Coin-operated machines in most Library units. Requests for microfilm copy are considered in light of prevailing restrictions. Permission must be obtained to use cameras.

Friends of the Library. A contribution (of not less than $10) entitles membership.

AUSTIN
Lyndon Baines Johnson Library
2313 Red River, Austin, Texas 78705
Tel. (512) 397-5137

History. The Library was founded as a depository for the 31 million papers which relate to the four decades of public service of the late Lyndon Baines Johnson (1908-73). The Library, which is one of six presidential libraries administered by the US Federal Government, is located on the eastern part of the campus of the University of Texas at Austin. In August 1965, the then President reached an agreement with the University of Texas to build the first Presidential Library on a University campus. The building, designed by Gordon Bunshaft, was formally dedicated by former President Richard Nixon on 22 May 1971. Construction costs totalled just under $14 million, mostly financed by the University of Texas. The building is eight stories tall, the Library walls are slightly concave and unrelieved by windows, except on the top floor. On the roof is a helicopter pad. The Library represents a three-way partnership, uniting the contributions of President Johnson, whose papers and other materials form the Library's collections, the University of Texas, which built and owns the building, and the Federal Government, which will operate the building in perpetuity, as part of the Presidential Library system. Current holdings include 31 million pages of MSS, 262,389 clippings, 36,476 government document publications, 2,490 books and 500,000 negatives in still photo.

Lyndon Baines Johnson Library, Austin

Special Collections and Treasures. The major collection is that of the papers of Lyndon B. Johnson as Congressman, Senator, Vice President and President. The most used collection within the papers is the 'White House Central Files', which consists of materials generated by, or flowing into, the White House. Other collections include Government Records: selected records from departments and agencies on microfilm; Personal Papers: papers of personal friends and associates of President Johnson; Oral History: interviews with over 600 individuals who knew Johnson, participated in the Administration, or influenced his programmes; and the Supplementary Book Collection: trade books and government publications concerning Lyndon Johnson and his administration.

Exhibition Areas. Museum exhibits a collection of documents, photographs, art objects and memorabilia surrounding the Presidency. Exhibits also on 1st, 2nd and 8th floors.

Hours. Research Room: Mon.-Fri. 0900-1700. Museum: Mon.-Sun. 0900-1700.

Transport. By bus: Austin Transit System. By car: Take L.B.J. Library, Manor Road — Memorial Stadium exit, off 1H35.

Parking. Large parking lot available.

Admission. Readers: The public use of donated historical materials is subject to the following restrictions: (1) use is subject to all conditions specified by the donor or transferor of such materials or by the Archivist of the United States and (2) use must be related to a study requiring the unique resources of the depository. *Visitors:* Free admission.

Information. At the main entrance.

Sales. Sales desk located at the main entrance. Books, busts, campaign buttons, postcards, bookends, medallions and engravings are sold.

Guidebooks. Free brochure in English is available.

Restaurant/Snack Facilities. Vending machines are located in the building next to the Library, which is reached through an underground connection.

Services. Restrooms on the ground and 8th floors, smoking area on ground floor, telephones on ground floor, outdoor patio on 8th floor.

Catalogues. Card catalogue for book collection. Unpublished finding aids for manuscripts and records in the Reading Room.

Classification. Library of Congress.

Copying/Photography.   Copying facilities are available. Photographs may be taken without flashlight.

Friends of the Library.   Friends of the L.B.J. Library. Cost of membership $50 per annum.

BELTSVILLE
National Agricultural Library
US Department of Agriculture, 10301 Baltimore Blvd,
Beltsville, Maryland
Tel. (301) 344-3726

History.   The National Agricultural Library is one of the principal agencies in the US Department of Agriculture dealing with scientific and technical information. It provides information services in support of all Department agencies, as well as other governmental activities supporting Department missions. Moreover, it serves as one of three national libraries in the United States (the National Library of Medicine and the Library of Congress [see relevant entries] being the other two) to provide researchers, other libraries, and the general public with specialised information in the fields of agriculture and related sciences. Although the present Library began with the establishment of the Department in 1862, the book and journal collection actually derives from the Agricultural Division of the Patent Office, which was created in 1839. Its stock of 1,000 volumes became the nucleus of the new Library in 1862. Appropriation for Library materials began in 1864 and by 1871 the 8,000 volumes in the Library constituted the most complete collection of agricultural books in the US. The Library, however, although functioning as a national library from its inception, was not designated as the National Agricultural Library until 1962, the 100th anniversary of its founding. Its holdings currently total 1.5 million volumes.

Special Collections and Treasures.   While the Library as a whole is a special collection in the sense that its holdings cover the entire field of agriculture and related sciences, within this highly specialised collection there are several outstanding subcollections. For example, the Herd Book Collection, about 9,000 books of records of purebred registration of domestic animals, is one of the largest, most carefully selected collections of blooded stock, herd, flock and stud books in the world. The Horticultural Trade Catalogues Collection comprises some 125,000 catalogues, price lists and broadsides. The Bee Culture Library contains over 5,000 volumes, 1,400 pamphlets and 120 periodicals to form probably the largest apicultural collection in the US. Most of the Library's rare books are in the field of botany and include fine specimens of lithographs, as well as a strong collection of the original works of Linnaeus. The James M. Gwin Poultry Collection was donated in 1971 and contains books on poultry from every State in the US and from 42 foreign countries.

National Agricultural Library, Beltsville

Exhibition Areas.   Exhibits are in the main lobby on the first floor. A rare book exhibit area is housed in a glassed enclosure, also in the main lobby.

Hours.   Main Library and Bee Culture Library: Mon.-Fri. 0800-1630. Closed Sat., Sun. and public hols.

Transport.   The Library is located at the intersection of US Route 1 and Interstate Route 495 (Beltway Exit, 27 North). Beltsville, Md. is 15 miles northeast of Washington DC. A shuttle service is available between downtown Washington and the Library. Transportation from there is also available by Greyhound bus or taxi.

Parking.   The visitors' parking area is accessible from Route 1 and from Rhode Island Avenue.

Admission.   *Readers:* Free to all serious researchers.
Visitors: Library services are available within limits to the general public. Guided tours are available on Tues. at 1500 and Wed. at 1400 and at other times by appointment through the Director's Office (34-43779).

Information.   Main Reading Room.

Sales.   None.

Guidebooks.   None.

Restaurant/Snack Facilities.   None in the Library.

Services.   Cloakrooms and pay telephones in the lobby, lavatories adjacent to lobby and also to Periodicals Reading Room, lifts in the lobby, smoking lounge adjacent to Periodicals Reading Room.

Catalogues.   Dictionary card catalogue 1862-1965 (available in printed volumes also). Card catalogue by author and title, and subject since 1966.

Classification.   Library of Congress.

Copying/Photography.   Pay copier in the lobby. An electrostat service is available at 10 cents per page with a minimum charge of $1 per order. Order forms and price lists are available from the Lending Division. Microfilm service also available. Private cameras may be used with the permission of Library officials.

Friends of the Library.   Associates of the National Agricultural Library Inc. Personal membership $10 per annum, institutional $100 per annum, business $500 per annum.

BERKELEY

General Library, University of California at Berkeley
University of California, Berkeley, California 94720
Tel. Office of the University Librarian 415-642-3773,
General reference service 415-642-2374

History. The University Library at Berkeley, the eighth largest library in the United States, began with a collection of slightly more than 1,000 volumes inherited from the College of California in 1869. The Library numbered 11,800 volumes when, in 1873, it was moved to South Hall, one of the University's two buildings on the new Berkeley campus. An early offer of private funds for a university building came in 1877 when Henry D. Bacon, an Oakland banker, donated $25,000, matched by a legislative appropriation, for a separate library facility. The Bacon Art and Library Building was occupied in 1881 with a collection of 17,000 volumes. In the summer of 1911 the collections moved into the white granite Charles Franklin Doe Memorial Library, also in part a private gift. The Doe Library, known as the 'University Library', or the 'Main Library', has became the centre of the campus library system, which now includes twenty-one branches and the recently constructed Moffitt Undergraduate Library. Growth of the Library's collections in the 20th century has been rapid. In 1902 it had only 100,000 volumes, but by 1940 it reached 1 million items, 2 million in 1955 and 3 million in 1965. It now contains 4,476,759 volumes, 98,408 serials, 827,499 pamphlets, 717,091 microforms, 216,412 maps and 19,145,844 MSS (most of the latter being housed in the Bancroft Library, see next entry).

Special Collections and Treasures. Special Collections include the Bancroft Library (see entry below), East Asiatic Library and Music Library. The East Asiatic Library houses the Asami Library, Yi Dynasty Korean books and MSS; the Murakami Library, Japanese literature of the Meiji Period; and the John Fryer Chinese Library. The Library maintains a distinguished collection of rare materials, comprising, for instance, bronze inscriptions, stone rubbings, scrolls, Tang Dynasty MSS, and fine editions from the Sung, Yüan, Ming and Ching Dynasties. The Music Library houses the Alfred Cortot, Connick, and Sigmund Romberg Collections of opera scores; the Taddei Collection of Italian opera libretti; the Alfred Einstein and Manfred Bukofzer Collections of musicology; the Irving F. Morrow Collection of sheet music and chamber music; the Aldo Olschki and Alfred Cortot Collections of early Italian music theory and vocal music; 18th century Italian instrumental music; the Sidney R. Cowell Collection of California folk music recordings; the Ansley Salz Collection of rare string instruments; and items from the Marc Pincherle Collection of violin music and methodology.

Exhibition Areas. Nine cases in the Main Library lobby and two on the second floor contain changing exhibits.

University of California,
Berkeley, General Library

Hours. Term: Mon.-Thurs. 0800-2200, Fri. 0800-1700, Sat. 0900-1700, Sun. 1300-2200. Vacation: Mon.-Fri. 0800-1700 except: 1 Jan., 4 July, first Mon. in Sept., third Thurs. in Nov., 25 Dec. and two other days during Christmas recess, and one day during spring recess. (The University is closed on these days.)

Transport. There are buses and a rapid transit system 'BART' from San Francisco and other surrounding cities directly to the University. Maps of the campus are located at the entrances to the campus.

Parking. Prior arrangement can be made to park on the University campus. Otherwise visitors may use 'fee lot' parking facilities to the north and south of the campus, without a permit and for a nominal fee.

Admission. Readers: Those wishing to use the Library for an extended period but who do not need to borrow books can obtain a Reference Card, free of charge. Readers needing to borrow books for home use may buy a General Card, for a nominal fee.
Visitors: All visitors are welcome to use the Library, free of charge.

Information. General reference service, second floor, north side, Main Library.

Sales. None.

Guidebooks. The Library publishes 16 'orientation leaflets' as an aid to users of the Main Library. They are in English and are free of charge.

Restaurant/Snack Facilities. None in the Library but facilities available near the Library (to the north and south).

Services. Coin-operated typewriters (including electric ones) in Moffitt Undergraduate Library. Smoking areas in the Main Library and in some of the branches.

Catalogues. Author/title and subject card catalogues.

Classification. Library of Congress, also locally devised systems.

Copying/Photography. Photography laboratory in basement. Rapid copy service available first floor, south lobby of Library Annexe. Other photocopying service points are available in many other library locations. Visitors may use cameras in most departments of the Library.

Friends of the Library. None, but see entry for Bancroft Library below.

BERKELEY

Bancroft Library, University of California at Berkeley
University of California, Berkeley, California 94720
Tel. (415) 642-3781; 642-6481

History. The Bancroft Library is named after Hubert Howe Bancroft, a San Francisco bookseller and publisher, who built up an extensive collection of manuscript and printed material on the history of California, Mexico, Central America and the American West. His collection was used as the source of information for the voluminous *Works* of Bancroft, published between 1874 and 1890. In 1905 the University of California bought Bancroft's library, which subsequently formed the core collection of the Bancroft Library at the Berkeley campus. In recent years the collecting focus has expanded beyond western North America with the merging of the University's Rare Book Collection, University Archives, Regional Oral History Office and Mark Twain Papers with the Bancroft Collection. Current holdings total 257,600 volumes, 19,130,000 MSS, 1,084,600 pictorial materials, 66,100 pamphlets, 32,100 microcopies and 14,600 maps and atlases.

Special Collections and Treasures. Treasures include Horace, *Opera* (Milan, 1474), the first printed edition of the works of Horace to be dated; Blaeu's *Le grand atlas* (Amsterdam, 1663), one of the twelve recorded sets; Sigüenza y Góngora, *Libra astronomica* (Mexico City, 1690); *Amadís de Gaula,* early 15th century, four separate leaves of the third book, all that remain of the oldest known text; D.H. Lawrence, *Sons and Lovers,* the holograph MS of an early draft; the *Codex Fernández Leal,* a pre-Cortesian Mexican pictograph MS, one of only two such records belonging to the Mixtecan-Zapotecan linguistic stock known to exist in the Western hemisphere. Collections include the Mark Twain Papers constituting the most complete personal archive of a major American writer now available in a research library; the Silvestre Terrazas (1873-1944) Collection on the Mexican Revolution; the Tebtunis Papyri Collection (primarily Ptolemaic era); the José Marcos Mugarrieta Collection comprising correspondence and papers (1835-78) relating to Mexico and Baja California.

Exhibition Areas. An exhibition gallery has changing displays of books, manuscripts, pictures and other items in the Library's collections. On permanent display are the Wimmer Gold Nugget and Sir Francis Drake's Plate of Brass claiming California for Queen Elizabeth I.

Hours. During regular academic sessions: Mon.-Fri. 0900-1700, Sat. 1300-1700. Hours vary between sessions and during holidays. Prospective visitors should write beforehand to avoid disappointment.

The Bancroft Library,
Berkeley

Transport. The A.C. Transit Bus line serves the Berkeley campus area. BART (Bay Area Rapid Transit) trains serve downtown Berkeley, which is within walking distance of the Library.

Parking. Parking is available in several pay lots on the north and south of the campus.

Admission. Readers: Regular students of the University of California and other qualified readers may use the collections. They must fill out permanent Readers' Cards on their first visit and will be asked to furnish identification.
Visitors: Apply to the Library Director.

Information. The Registration Desk at the entrance to the Heller Reading Room and the Reference Desk in the Heller Reading Room.

Sales. None.

Guidebooks. Brochure: *The Bancroft Library.*

Restaurant/Snack Facilities. None in the Library but available on campus.

Services. A cloakroom with lockers, lavatories, public telephones; special arrangements can be made for wheel chairs or for lame patrons to enter the Heller Reading Room.

Catalogues. Dictionary card catalogue for printed material. Author/subject and some title entries in an alphabetical file for MSS.

Classification. Library of Congress (modified).

Copying/Photography. No copying machines are available for individual use; all copying is done by the staff. The use of private cameras within the Library is forbidden.

Friends of the Library. The Friends of the Bancroft Library.

BETHESDA
National Library of Medicine
8600 Rockville Pike, Bethesda, Maryland 20014
Tel. (301) 496-6308

History. The National Library of Medicine was originally established in 1836 as the Library of the Army Surgeon General's Office. Its basic role was to serve the needs of military medical officers. Under the direction of John Shaw Billings (1865-95), the Library's mission was expanded and its services made available to physicians generally. The collections expanded from 1,800 volumes in 1865 to 50,000 volumes and 60,000 pamphlets in 1880. In 1956, after 120 years of sponsorship by the armed

National Library of Medicine, Bethesda

forces, the Library was designated the National Library of Medicine by an Act of Congress, and placed within the Public Health Service. The Library occupied its present building in April 1962 and holdings currently total over 1,500,000 units, making it the world's largest research library in a single scientific and professional field.

Special Collections and Treasures.   The Library has one of the largest medical history collections in the USA, with contents dating from the 11th to the mid-19th century. Treasures include Rolando Capelluti, *Tractatus de curatione pestiferorum apostematum* (Rome, 1486/1500); Johann Tollat von Vochenberg, *Ein gut Erczney-buchlin* (Augsburg, 1499); the first edition of Robert Burton's *The Anatomy of Melancholy* (Oxford, 1621); the collected works of Galen published in Lyon in 1528, hitherto known to exist as a complete three volume set only in Leningrad; and the first English translation of Fracastoro's *Syphilis* (London, 1686).

Exhibition Areas.   Changing exhibits on various aspects of medical literature are held in the entrance foyer.

Hours.   Mon.-Fri. 0830-2100, Sat. 0830-1700. (Summer hours: Mon.-Sat. 0830-1700.) Closed Sun. and public hols.

Transport.   Any Washington DC area Metrobus operating from the District of Columbia to Rockville Pike.

Parking.   Visitors may park at the front entrance and in the side parking lot.

Admission.   Readers: Must register in the Reading Room. No admission charge. The Library is open to all health science students, professionals and others wishing to consult the collection.
Visitors: Must register at the front guard's desk. Public tours are conducted at 1300, Mon.-Fri., starting at the guard's desk. Call 301 496 1030 or write to the Public Information Office for advance registration or special arrangements.

Information.   In the lobby. Enquiry Office in room M-121.

Sales.   Apply to the Office of Enquiries and Publications Management.

Guidebooks.   National Library of Medicine, *Brochure* and *Programs and Services* are available free of charge from the Office of Enquiries and Publications Management.

Restaurant/Snack Facilities.   Cafeteria on A-level, open 0730-1330, 1400-1600.

Services.   Cloakroom, lavatories and public telephones all available on main floor near Reading Room.

William Harvey, De motu cordis ... (Frankfurt, 1628), in the National Library of Medicine, Bethesda

Catalogues.   Card catalogue. A book catalogue is issued quarterly, with annual cumulations.

Classification. Own.

Copying/Photography.   Microfilm   and   photocopies available only for inter-library loan. Private photography only allowed with prior approval of the Chief, Office of Enquiries and Publications Management.

BLOOMINGTON
Indiana University Libraries
10th and Jordan Streets, Bloomington, Indiana 47401
Tel. 812/337-3403

History.   The Indiana University Libraries have grown from a small collection, established in an instruction building in 1824, into a system comprising three separate divisions and encompassing 8 campuses. The first Librarian was appointed in 1837 but until 1942 only one trained librarian had occupied the post. In 1854, the then 5,000 volume collection was completely destroyed by fire. Again in 1883, a new building, of which the Library occupied one wing, was struck by lightning and 12,000 volumes and 3,000 pamphlets were destroyed. The Library moved into the first building of its own in 1890 and moved once more in 1907. In the summer of 1969 it occupied its present building which is possibly, in terms of space, the largest university library in the United States. The Main Library, which was officially dedicated on 10 October 1970, houses the Undergraduate Library, the General Collections and the Graduate Library School, a separate academic unit. Current holdings of the total library system include 3,672,848 bound volumes of books and journals, 726,511 microforms, 2,593,098 MSS, 224,781 slides and 353,401 maps.

Special Collections and Treasures.   Special mention should be made of the Lilly (Rare Books and Special Collections) Library, which occupies a building of its own and contains the libraries of such famous collectors as Josiah Lilly, Bernardo Mendel, George A. Poole Jr., and Ian Fleming. Among the (roughly) ¼ million volumes and 2.5 million MSS in the Lilly are such treasures as the *Gutenberg Bible* (Mainz, c.1455); Chaucer, *The Canterbury Tales* (Westminster, Caxton, c. 1478); *The trewe encountre,* a newsbook (c. September 1513), the earliest surviving English news pamphlet, of which this is the only copy in America; *Biblia sacra* (Antwerp, Plantin, 1569-73), the second of the great polyglot Bibles; J.J. Rousseau, *Principes du droit politique* (Amsterdam, 1762); Louis Pasteur, *Les corpuscules organisés* (Paris, 1862); W.C. Röntgen, *Eine neue Art von Strahlen* (Würzburg, 1895) — the discovery of X-rays in this first issue, Robert, Lord Baden-Powell, *Scouting for Boys* (London, 1908), in original parts, the only such copy

Indiana   University   Main Library, Bloomington

recorded; and A. Hitler, *Mein Kampf* (Munich, 1925, 27).

Exhibition Areas. The main exhibition area is the Lilly Library, which has eight exhibition rooms, e.g. the Mendel Room, which houses a portion of the Mendel Collection on voyages, exploration and European expansion.

Hours. Term: Mon.-Sat. 0815-2400, Sun. 1100-2400. Between terms open only to 1700. Closed public hols.

Transport. Bloomington is 51 miles south of Indianapolis and may be reached by both Greyhound Bus Line and Allegheny Airline.

Parking. Paid parking spaces for visitors are immediately south of the Library.

Admission. Readers: No charge for the admission of readers; no registration.
Visitors: Always welcome.

Information. Information desks in the Main Lobby, the Undergraduate Library, and the Reference Department.

Sales. None.

Guidebooks. Indiana University Libraries, Bloomington, a 14-page pamphlet, in English, free.

Restaurant/Snack Facilities. A large cafeteria on the ground floor of the Library. Open: 0800-2230; between terms or during summer sessions: 0800-1700.

Services. One typing room in Government Publications Department. Facilities to hang coats on all levels of the Undergraduate Wing. Lifts, entrance for the handicapped, lockers, seminar rooms. Lounges for smoking and talking on each floor of the General Collections. Telephones and lockers just off the Main Lobby.

Catalogues. The General Collections has a split catalogue: author-title on one side of a large aisle, subject on the other side. Undergraduate Library has a dictionary catalogue. Media Center, 2nd floor, Undergraduate Library has a separate catalogue. Lilly has its own special catalogue.

Classification. Library of Congress.

Copying/Photography. There are coin-operated photocopying machines on the fourth floor, General Collections. Requests for private photography to be made to Departmental Heads.

BLOOMINGTON

*Institute for Sex Research, Library and Archive
Collections
416 Morrison Hall, Indiana University, Bloomington,
Indiana 47401
Tel. 812/337-7686*

History.   The Library dates from 1947 when Dr. Alfred
C. Kinsey established the Institute for Sex Research and
donated his personal collection to the new organisation.
Kinsey, whose two works *Sexual Behaviour in the
Human Male* and *Female* aroused enormous publicity,
died in 1956 but the Institute, a non-profit Indiana
corporation located at Indiana University, continued
its growth under Dr. Paul H. Gebhard, the present
Director. The Library aims to collect anything which
has been written about and has some value in
the understanding of human sexuality. It is unique
in several respects, not only because its collects
erotica but also because of its ephemeral sexual
materials, which are rarely, if ever, systematically
preserved in libraries. The Institute's collections are the
largest of their kind in the world and holdings currently
include 33,000 books, 25 drawers of ephemeral material,
156 audio tapes, 1,300 three-dimensional art objects,
50,000 photographs and 1,800 films.

Special Collections and Treasures.   Many of the
individual items in the Library are either rare or unique
and taken as a whole the collections represent the only
comprehensive and sustained attempt to collect materials
relating to all aspects of sexuality. The photographic
collection dates from 1855 and most are erotic, ranging
from art photography to pornography. The film collection
consists of scientific documentary films, commercial
pornographic films and a small sample of experimental
avant-garde films, which are of value in terms of
censorship studies as well as art studies.

Exhibition Areas.   None.

Hours.   Mon.-Fri. 0830-1700. Closed Sat., Sun. and
during national hols.

Transport.   Morrison Hall is on the University campus,
which is serviced by campus and city buses.

Parking.   No visitor parking is available at Morrison Hall
but there are parking areas in several other parts of the
campus, within walking distance of the building.

Admission.   Readers: Use of the collections is legally
restricted to 'qualified scholars with demonstrable
research needs'. Prospective readers should submit an
outline of their credentials and research project. Upon
approval, an appointment will be scheduled.
Visitors: Only researchers working on projects may
visit the collections. No casual visitors are admitted

*Morrison Hall, Indiana University, which currently
houses the library and collections of the Institute for
Sex Research*

and no conducted tours can be arranged. Use of the collections, general information, bibliographic searching and other services are available to any individual or organisation in the world by mail through the Information Service.

Information.   Only available by telephone or by post.

Sales.   None.

Guidebooks.   None.

Restaurant/Snack Facilities.   None in the building but many eating places available within walking distance.

Services.   Users of the collections share staff facilities.

Catalogues.   The Catalog of the Social and Behavioral Sciences Monograph Section of the Library of the Institute for Sex Research, Indiana University (published by G.K. Hall in 1974). Subject bibliographies are available on specific research areas (by mail request).

Classification.   Own.

Copying/Photography.   Copying machines are operated by staff members only. Private photography only with prior approval of the Institute.

BOSTON
Boston Public Library
666 Boylston Street, Boston, Massachusetts 02117
Tel. 536-5400

History.   The Boston Public Library was founded in 1852 and opened to the public on 20 March 1854. (Boston was the first city in the United States to establish a public library for its citizens.) The Library's foundation was due primarily to the initiative of leading citizens, who had been stimulated by the visit of Alexandre Vattemare, a Frenchman, who arrived in Boston in 1841 to promote literary exchanges. The Library was initially located in two rooms on Mason Street and then in 1858 it occupied the Boylston Street Building with 70,000 volumes and 17,938 pamphlets. Important early donors were Joshua Bates, Edward Everett and Mayor Bigelow. In 1895, the Library moved into its present main building in Copley Square, with the central court almost an exact replica of the Palazzo della Cancelleria in Rome. By 1911-12, holdings had topped the million mark and increasing pressure during the 20th century necessitated the opening, in December 1972, of the new Central Library addition, linked on two levels to the old building. Current holdings include 5,003,205 units, including 3,623,608 volumes and 1,140,482 microforms.

Boston Public Library

Special Collections and Treasures.   Collections include

the Patent Collection, based on a British Government gift of 1858; the Bowditch Library of mathematics and astronomy; the Ticknor Library of Spanish and Portuguese books; the Barton Library, including a collection of Shakespeareana; the Hunt Library of West Indian material; the John A. Lewis Library of Americana; the Allen A. Brown Music Library; the Galatea Collection of works on the history of women; the Bentley Collection of American Accounting to 1900; the Longfellow Memorial known as the Artz Collection; and the Trent Collection of Defoe and Defoeana (the collection of Defoe writings in the Rare Book Department is numerically the second largest in the world).

Exhibition Areas.   The General Library: Boston Room (first floor), material on the history of Boston. Research Library: Exhibition cases lining the walls of the first floor corridors; Sargent Gallery, third floor.

Hours.   Winter (Oct.-May): Mon.-Fri. 0900-2100, Sat. 0900-1800, Sun. 1400-1800. Summer (June-Sept.): Mon.-Fri. 0900-2100, Sat. 0900-1800. Closed Sun. and public hols.

Transport.   Subway station: Copley, just outside the Library, which is located on the corner of Boylston and Dartmouth Streets, in Copley Square.

Parking.   Limited street parking and several garages in the area.

Admission.   *Readers* and *Visitors:* The Library is open to all free of charge.

Information.   Desks at the entrances to the General Library and the Research Library.

Sales.   Sales Office in the Research Library.

Guidebooks.   *A Casual Tour: Boston Public Library,* in English, available free at Sales Office.

Restaurant/Snack Facilities.   None in the Library but available in the neighbourhood.

Services.   Research Library: telephones on first floor, lifts. General Library: telephones and lavatories on concourse level, lift.

Catalogues.   Dictionary and various special catalogues.

Classification.   Library of Congress

Copying/Photography.   Research Library: 3 copiers 1st floor (in Newspaper Room, Government Documents, Microtext), 2 copiers 2nd floor, 1 copier 3rd floor. General Library: 1 copier on concourse and 5 copiers on 2nd floor. Permission must be obtained from the officer in charge for private photography and the photographs must not be used for commercial purposes.

Friends of the Library.   Associates of the Library $25, or more, annually. Other types of honorary membership: Benefactors, who have contributed $1,000 or more; Donors, who have given collections of material; Honorary Curators, who have contributed in some significant way to the Library.

CAMBRIDGE
Harvard University Library
Cambridge, Massachusetts 02138
Tel. (617) 495-2401

History.   Harvard University Library is the oldest library in the United States and the largest university library in the world. Harvard College was founded by a vote of the General Court of the Colony of Massachusetts Bay on 28 October 1636. John Harvard, who died 14 September 1638, left half of his estate and his 400 volume library to the College, which was named after him by vote of the General Court on 13 March 1639. The Library, dependent at first almost entirely on gifts, grew relatively slowly. The first printed catalogue of 1723 listed some 3,500 volumes. In 1764 when the Library had 5,000 volumes, fire destroyed Harvard Hall, causing the loss of all but 404 volumes. By 1800 the Library contained some 13,000 volumes and from then it began to more or less double its stock approximately every 20 years. In 1841 the Library occupied its own building for the first time. Gore Hall, designed on the lines of King's College Chapel, Cambridge, was subsequently improved and extended in 1877 and 1895. By the early 20th century the pressure on space had become acute and was relieved by the opening in 1915 of the Widener Library building, given to Harvard by the mother of Harry Elkins Widener, who died in the *Titanic* disaster. Subsequent developments in the 20th century have been the opening in 1942 of the Houghton Library (for rare books and MSS) and the New England Deposit Library (for infrequently used material), and of the Lamont Undergraduate Library (in 1949), connected by tunnel with Widener and Houghton. The Pusey Library to be opened in 1976 will provide the fourth central unit. The University Library now constitutes over 90 separate units with total holdings currently including 9,028,385 volumes and 1,117,149 microforms.

Special Collections and Treasures.   Major research units of the Harvard University Library complex include the Andover-Harvard Theological Library; the Francis A. Countway Library of Medicine; the Baker Library of Business Administration, which includes the Kress Library on historical aspects of business and economics prior to 1850 and the Bancroft Collection on the South Sea Bubble; the Chinese-Japanese Library of the Harvard-Yenching Institute; the Dumbarton Oaks

Harvard University Library

Research Library with special reference to Byzantine History and Culture; the Eda Kuhn Loeb Music Library; the Gordon McKay Library of Engineering and Applied Physics; the Frances L. Loeb Library of the Graduate School of Design; the Law School Library; the Lucien Howe Library of Opthalmology; the Geological Sciences Library; the Museum of Comparative Zoology Library; the Tozzer Library of the Peabody Museum of Archaeology and Ethnology; the Biblioteca Berenson at Villa I Tatti near Florence; the Milman Parry Collection of Oral Literature; the Rubel Asiatic Research Bureau Library; the Monroe C. Gutman Library-Research Center of Education; the John G. Wolbach Library of the Harvard College Observatory; and the Littauer Library of the John Fitzgerald Kennedy School of Government. Special collections within Harvard College Library include John Keats and his circle (Keats Memorial Collection); the Theatre Collection; Printing and Graphic Arts; the Theodore Roosevelt Collection; the Winsor Memorial Map Room; the Woodberry Poetry Room; the Harry Elkins Widener Memorial Collection; and the Trotsky Archive. Notable author collections relate to Ariosto, Bacon, Beerbohm, Bossuet, Byron, Caldecott, Camões, Carlyle, Carman, Carroll, Cervantes, Chaucer, Coleridge, Walter Crane, Cruikshank, Dante, Dickens, Donne, Dreyfus, Dryden, T.S. Eliot, Faulkner, Galsworthy, John Gay, Hearn, Heine, Herbert, Hofmannsthal, Jeanne d'Arc, Kipling, Lear, Lincoln, Masefield, Milton, Molière, Montaigne, Napoleon, Petrarch, Alexander Pope, Rilke, Rousseau, Schiller, Shakespeare, Shelley, Steinbeck, Stevenson, Strindberg, Tasso, Thackeray, Villard family, Gilbert White and Thomas Wolfe.

Exhibition Areas. The main exhibition area is in the Houghton Library, with other exhibitions in the Widener and the various sections of the Harvard Library complex.

Hours. (Widener Library) Term: Mon.-Fri. 0900-2200, Sat. 0900-1700. Vacation: Mon.-Fri. 0900-1700, Sat. 0900-1300. Closed Sun., 1 Jan., 4 July, Labor Day, Thanksgiving, the afternoon of 24 Dec. and Christmas.

Transport. Harvard Square (on the Boston subway line) is one block away from the Widener Library.

Parking. Parking meters in the vicinity of the Library.

Admission. Readers: The Library is open to members of Harvard University. Other scholars living near the Library may use the Library free of charge for 6 days and those wishing to borrow books or use the Library for more than 6 days must pay a fee. These rules also apply to scholars from other universities. Application forms are available at the Library Privileges Desk on the second floor of Widener Library.
Visitors: Are admitted to Widener building. Persons who wish, without applying for a formal card, to see a specific book not found in other libraries accessible to

them should ask for this privilege at the Library Privileges Desk.

Information. On the second floor of Widener building.

Sales. A sales desk in Houghton Library sells Library publications.

Guidebooks. Several available, in English.

Restaurant/Snack Facilities. None in the Library but available nearby.

Services. Lavatories, lifts, telephones.

Catalogues. Card catalogues in Widener building: main-entry catalogue for the whole University Library (first floor). Dictionary catalogue of central collections (second floor). There are printed catalogues (in book form) of many portions of the collections.

Classification. Own.

Copying/Photography. Copying service on the ground floor of the Widener Library. Private photography not permitted without prior permission.

Friends of the Library. $35.00 per year.

CHICAGO
Chicago Public Library
Administration and Central Library, 425 North Michigan Avenue, Chicago, Illinois 60611
Cultural Center, 78 East Washington Street, Chicago, Illinois 60602
Tel. 312-269-2900

History. A subscription library which was the predecessor to the Chicago Public Library was established in 1834, only one year after the founding of the city. Over the next four decades, the collection grew to 30,000 volumes, all, however, being destroyed by the Chicago Fire of 1871. An appeal in support of a new 'Free Library of Chicago' was made in the British Parliament and eventually 8,000 volumes were shipped to Chicago. On 3 April 1872 a city ordinance established the Chicago Public Library, which opened for service on 1 January 1873, with William Frederick Poole as its first Librarian. By 1875 card holders numbered 24,000 and books 40,000, the circulation outstripping every other US library except Boston's. In 1895 the Library entered into an informal agreement with the John Crerar and Newberry Libraries (see relevant entries) and, as a result, the Chicago Public Library assumed the responsibility of fulfilling the diverse reading and informational requirements of its reading public. During the 20th

Chicago Public Library.
Cultural Center Building

century the Library has developed an extensive collection in the Social Sciences. Holdings currently include 5,193,616 books, 1,120,040 pamphlets and 27,373 microfilm reels. In 1975, the Central Library and Administrative Offices were moved to leased quarters at 425 North Michigan Avenue. The original Central Library building, renamed the Library's Cultural Center, was renovated and remodelled during 1975-6. This building, first opened in 1897, is a combination of Renaissance, Neo-Greek and Roman forms. Designated a Landmark Structure by the Landmark Preservation Council, the Cultural Center Building is noted for decorative mosaic work and two leaded glass domes by Tiffany. The Chicago Public Library consisted of the Central Library, Cultural Center, Woodson Regional and seventy-six branches at the end of 1976.

Special Collections and Treasures. Collections include the Vivian G. Harsh Collection of Afro-American History and Literature; the James Ellsworth Papers, relating to the Columbian Exposition; the Goodman Theatre (of Chicago) Collection of programmes, photographs and scrapbooks; and the GAR museum of Civil War relics.

Exhibition Areas. Major exhibits are presented year round in the Cultural Center's Exhibition Hall (5,300 square feet). Other areas of the Center are also available for smaller exhibits.

Hours. Mon.-Fri. 0900-2100, Sat. 0900-1730. Closed Sun. and the following days: Dr. Martin Luther King's birthday, 12 and 18 Feb., Memorial Day, 4 July, Labor Day, Thanksgiving, 25 Dec. and 1 Jan.

Transport. Both the Central Library and Cultural Center are located in the Loop (downtown Chicago) and are easily accessible to rapid transit, commuter railways, city and suburban bus lines.

Parking. Nearest public parking is the Grant Park Underground Garage off Michigan Avenue.

Admission. Readers and *Visitors:* Admission free of charge. To obtain a Library card readers must provide proof of residence.

Information. Information Desks are located in both downtown buildings.

Sales. Friends of the Library operate gift shop in Cultural Center.

Guidebooks. Pamphlets describing the Cultural Center and Central Library services, hours and locations of departments, available free of charge.

Restaurant/Snack Facilities. None in the Library but many such facilities available nearby.

Services.   Cloakrooms, restrooms, telephones and lifts available in both buildings.

Catalogues.   Dictionary card catalogue.

Classification.   Until 1 Feb. 1974 modified Dewey, after that date Library of Congress.

Copying/Photography.   Photo-copiers and reader-printers are located in most public service areas (departments). All photographers must obtain a pass from the office. Permission is readily granted to private individuals. Commercial photography is allowed by special permission.

Friends of the Library.   Minimum subscription of $10 per annum.

CHICAGO
John Crerar Library
35 West 33rd Street, Chicago, Illinois 60616
Tel. (312) 225-2526

History.   The Library was established in 1894 by an endowment of John Crerar, a leading Chicago industrialist. In a co-operative arrangement with the Newberry Library and the Chicago Public Library (see relevant entries) it was decided that the Crerar Library would specialise in Science and Technology. The Library opened to the public on 1 April 1897 and in 1906 its subject field was extended to include medicine. Until 1920, the Library was located in the Marshall Field building in the centre of Chicago and from 1920 until 1962 it occupied its building at Randolph Street and Michigan Avenue. In 1962 the Library entered into a contract with the Illinois Institute of Technology to administer the Institute's Library and, in effect, to become an academic library, as well as a free public library. In 1962, therefore, it moved to its present location on the IIT campus. Holdings currently include 1,110,180 volumes, 11,478 current periodicals and journals, 5,885 reels of microfilm, 80,000 microcards and 312,380 microfiche.

Special Collections and Treasures.   Collections include the 40,000 volume collection covering the complete works of most figures of early importance to the history of science, technology and medicine; the Technical Reports Collection; the Standards Collection; the Building Codes Collection; the Map Collection; and the Telephone Directory Collection.

Exhibition Areas.   Six exhibit cases in Reading Room; 30 feet of special exhibit area in 'Crerar Room'.

Hours.   Mon.-Sat. 0830-1700. Closed Sun. and public hols. (Reading room is open but unstaffed in Winter

The John Crerar Library, Chicago

until 2200; in Summer to 1900).

Transport. From Chicago's Loop, take CTA train marked Jackson B, or Englewood A, from the State Street subway south and get off at 35th St. Station. From other locations use CTA bus and other transit lines and transfer to subway as above. Bus: CTA bus lines with stops on the IIT campus: Garfields Ltd. (via Dan Ryan Expressway), Garfield-Indiana 6, Hyde Park 2, Indiana 38, Jeffrey 5. By car: Make closest convenient connection with the Dan Ryan Expressway and take the 35th Street or the 31st Street exit.

Parking. Free off-street parking is available to IIT campus visitors.

Admission. *Readers* and *Visitors:* No registration or admission requirements for use of materials within the building. Sliding scale of fees for borrowing privileges.

Information. Desk at the top of the stairs on the second floor.

Sales. None.

Guidebooks. A general account and guides to special services, available in English, free.

Restaurant/Snack Facilities. Cafeterias of IIT open at 1200, Mon.-Fri.

Services. Lavatories and public telephones in first floor hall behind entrance lobby. Smoking permitted only in lobby.

Catalogues. Author, title and classified subject catalogues.

Classification. Dewey, highly modified by Universal Decimal Classification and the Library.

Copying/Photography. Self-service coin-operated copiers on second (public) floor. Photo-duplication Service Department (ground floor at left) provides full range of copying services. No restrictions on private photography provided that other readers are not subjected to disturbance or distraction.

Friends of the Library. Crerar Library Associates. Subscription $50 p.a.

CHICAGO

The Newberry Library
60 West Walton Street, Chicago, Illinois 60610
Tel. (312) 943-9090

History. The Newberry Library was established in 1887,

through the bequest of Walter Loomis Newberry (1804-68), a pioneer Chicago business man. The first Librarian was William Frederick Poole (1821-1894) and the present Romanesque building on West Walton Street was occupied in 1893 (renovated in 1961). Designed by Poole in a running battle with the Trustees and the architect Henry Ives Cobb, only the front section of the projected quadrangle was ever finished. Originally established as a free public reference library, the Newberry has over the course of the years tended to specialise in the humanities, this direction growing out of an 1895 agreement with the Chicago Public Library and the John Crerar Library (see relevant entries). In meeting the needs of a growing humanistic research community, the Library's collections have also come to concentrate in rare research materials and the scholarly works and periodicals necessary to use them. Continuing operations are almost totally privately supported, by the original bequest of Mr. Newberry, by various subsequent gifts and grants and now by the continuing programme of the Newberry Library Associates. Current holdings include 1.3 million volumes and approximately 5 million MSS.

Special Collections and Treasures. Collections include the Edward E. Ayer Collection focussing on the American Indian and his relations with the white man; the Everett D. Graff Collection of Western Americana; and the John M. Wing Foundation on the History of Printing. William B. Greenlee Collection of Portuguese History and Literature; and the general library collection, which includes the Louis H. Silver Library of English and Continental History and Literature; the Frank Deering Collection of Indian captivity narrative; the papers of Sherwood Anderson; and the Franco Novacco Collection of early maps. Individual treasures include a fine 15th century French MS *Speculum humanae salvationis* (c. 1480); a block book of the *Apocalypsis Johannis* (c.1470); the score of the first opera ever performed, Peri's *Euridice* (Florence, 1600); the Thomas Jefferson-Julia Clarke copy of the first edition of the *History* of the Lewis and Clark expedition; and the first edition of *Don Quixote* (1605).

Exhibition Areas. Exhibitions are shown in cases in the Main Lobby and the Fellows Lounge on the second floor.

Hours. Mon.-Sat. 0900-1800, Tues., Thurs., 0900-2130 (Special Collections Dept. closes at 1800 daily). Closed on Sun., 1 Jan., Memorial Day, 4 July, Labor Day, Thanksgiving, and at Christmas.

Transport. Subway: nearest stops Chicago and State Street, and Clark and Division Streets. Bus: CTA buses pass by the Library and also run regularly on the neighbouring main routes such as State Street, Dearborn Street, Clark Street and Michigan Avenue.

The Newberry Library, Chicago

Parking. Available in nearby garages and lots for a fee, or nearby meters.

Admission. Readers: Identification with signature and address required. Apply to Admissions Secretary in the lobby.
Visitors: Should apply to kiosk in lobby.

Information. General information in the main lobby, detailed information in the Reading Rooms.

Sales. Postcards, prints and facsimiles and publications are on sale in the bookshop.

Guidebooks. An Uncommon Collection of Uncommon Collections: the Newberry Library, price $2.00.

Restaurant/Snack Facilities. Restaurant/snack bars available in the neighbourhood.

Services. Limited typing space, lockers for coats and parcels off the lobby, lavatories (women 2nd floor, men 3rd floor), smoking lounge on 2nd floor, public pay telephones on 1st and 3rd floors, automatic lifts, microfilm readers.

Catalogues. Dictionary card catalogue off Main Reading Room. Several published catalogues by G.K. Hall and Co.

Classification. Cutter. Fixed location from November 1967, with some exceptions.

Copying/Photography. By Library staff only, fees according to type of work.

Friends of the Library. The Newberry Library Associates. Minimum contribution $50.00 per year.

CHICAGO
University of Chicago Library
1100 East 57th Street, Chicago, Illinois 60637
Tel. (312) 753-2977

History. The University of Chicago is a private, non-denominational, coeducational, primarily graduate institution of higher learning and research. It was chartered on September 1890 and by the time the University opened its doors in 1892, the Library already had 120,000 volumes. The initial absence of adequate space for a central Library collection resulted in locating most of the book collections with the appropriate academic departments. In 1912 the building of the Harper Memorial Library relieved the pressure on the overcrowded departmental collections. From 1912 to 1970, the University of Chicago Library consisted of Harper Library, containing the administrative, technical

Model of the University of Chicago Library

and general service departments and the book collections in the general social sciences and humanities, and some 20 departmental libraries servicing the other half of the Library's collections. In 1970-71, the books in Harper, together with those in almost all of the departmental libraries in the social sciences and humanities, moved into the new Regenstein Library, where they were merged into a single collection. The Regenstein Library honours the memory of Joseph Regenstein (1889-1957), the Joseph and Helen Regenstein Foundation having provided 10 million dollars towards the cost of the Library. Current holdings include 3,485,140 volumes, 3.5 million MSS and 382,980 microforms.

Special Collections and Treasures. Collections include the Helen and Ruth Regenstein Collection of Rare Books in English and American Literature; the William Vaughn Moody Collection of American Authors; the 13,000 volume Harriet Monroe Collection, particularly strong in poetry and 'little magazines'; the Celia and Delia Austrian Collection covering 18th century drama; and the Atkinson, Morton, Beyer and Briggs Collections of American Drama. American history is covered by the Reuben T. Durrett Collection (Kentucky and the Ohio River Valley), the William H. English Collection (Indiana), the 15,000 letters in the Stephen A. Douglas Collection, the William E. Barton Collection and the Carter H. Harrison Collection on early voyages and the American frontier. Early printed Bibles from the Continent are found in the Hengstenberg and American Bible Union Collections, while practically all the great English Bibles in many of their major editions are found in the Grant Collection. Collections in German language and literature include the Hirsch-Bernays, Kossman and Lincke Collections. The history of science is represented by the Morris Fishbein Collection, while the history of anatomy and physiology is covered by the Mortimer Frank Collection, and gynaecology and obstretrics by the Fehling, Ahlfeld and Adair Collections.

Exhibition Areas. The corridor leading to the Department of Special Collections contains wall and floor-mounted cases. Other display facilities are located within the Department.

Hours. Autumn, Winter and Spring Terms: Reading Areas and Bookstack, Mon.-Thurs. 0830-0100, Fri. 0830-2200, Sat. 0900-2200, Sun. 1200-0100. For rest of year times of opening vary. Closed 1 Jan., Easter Sun., 23 June, 4 July, Labor Day, Thanksgiving and various days over the Christmas holidays.

Transport. By rail: Illinois Central Railroad, via 57th or 59th Street stations. By bus: Chicago Transit Authority Bus Lines, routes 4, 55, 59 and 28. Campus bus service. By car: Via Lake Shore Drive and the Midway Plaisance.

Parking. On Midway Plaisance, both sides. 'Pay parking' behind the Center for Continuing Education and on 60th Street between Kimbark and Kenwood Avenues. Metered parking on both sides of Ellis Avenue, 57th-59th Street.

Admission. Readers: The Library is for the use of University members, who must produce their University identification card or Library privilege card at the main entrance.
Visitors: Visiting scholars may use the Library but must provide references from their home libraries (preferably in advance). Hours for visitors: Mon.-Fri. 0930-1630, Sat. 0930-1300. Access to any Department of the Library is by pass issued by the Cashier-Privilege Office (Regenstein Library 120b), which is only open during the above hours.

Information. At Reference Desk, main floor, Regenstein Library.

Sales. The Department of Special Collections has exhibition catalogues for sale.

Guidebooks. The *Library Handbook* and various brochures, in English, available free of charge.

Restaurant/Snack Facilities. The student canteen is located on the A-level beside the elevators. Otherwise services in the Center for Continuing Education, Hutchinson Commons, International House and Woodward Commons.

Services. Telephones on all floors except the B-level, restrooms on each floor, adjacent to main elevators and in the bookstack. Typing rooms on each floor except B-level, coin-operated typewriters, lifts on the left of the main staircase and in hallway entrance in bookstack, seminar rooms, lockers.

Catalogues. Union catalogue of all library collections (in dictionary form). Separate catalogues of various special collections.

Classification. Library of Congress.

Copying/Photography. Coin-operated copying machines for individual use throughout the Library. A photo-copier available for self-service (in north hallway on B-level). Photoduplication Department provides copying services, including microfilming and microfiche production. No formal restrictions on private photography but persons wishing to take interior photographs should do so with minimum disruptions to others.

Friends of the Library. Currently being formed.

DETROIT
Detroit Public Library
5201 Woodward Avenue, Detroit, Michigan 48202
Tel. (313) 833-1000

History. Detroit Public Library was founded in 1865 and it began circulating books in the same year. By the end of the 19th century it had separate departments for children, medical books and pamphlets and the beginnings of a department for the blind. By 1910 the Library was operating 9 branch libraries on a full time basis. In 1921 the Library moved into its present Italian Renaissance style building, designed by Cass Gilbert. The growth of the Library during the 20th century necessitated the addition in 1963 of two wings, more than doubling the size of the original buildings. Holdings currently total 2.5 million books (1,175,000 in the Main Library), 6,804 feet of MSS and 220,000 microforms.

Special Collections and Treasures. Collections include the Clarence M. Burton Historical Collection (1st floor) relating to the history of Detroit, Michigan, the old Northwest Territory and adjacent Canadian areas; the National Automotive History Collection, with unique records of all aspects of the development of the motor car (2nd floor); an extensive Kate Greenaway Collection; and the E. Azalia Hackley Memorial Collection on Afro-Americans in Music and the Performing Arts (3rd floor). The Rare Book Department, on the 2nd floor, houses many treasures that illustrate the history of the book and provide background material in all subject fields.

Exhibition Areas. Exhibitions are located in the Adam Strohm Hall and the corridor of the 3rd floor.

Hours. Mon. and Wed. 0930-2100, Tues., Thurs., Fri. and Sat. 0930-1730, Sun. 1300-1700. Closed on Sun. from May to Oct., and normal public hols.

Transport. Bus: the Woodward Avenue, Dexter or Crosstown buses.

Parking. Available on Woodward or Cass Avenue at Putnam. There are parking garages across the street.

Admission. Readers and *Visitors:* No admission charges. There is a $10 charge for borrowing by non-residents of Detroit.

Information. Desk at the entrance.

Sales. Postcards are sold at the loan desks.

Guidebooks. None.

Detroit Public Library

Restaurant/Snack Facilities. None.

Services. Lavatories and cloakrooms on first and second floors, typing room and smoking lounge on second floor, lifts, telephones on all floors near stairs and lifts.

Catalogues. Author, title and subject catalogues.

Classification. Dewey.

Copying/Photography. Coin-operated copying machines in each department. Private cameras allowed with prior authorisation.

Friends of the Library. Friends of the Detroit Public Library, annual fee $10.00.

EVANSTON

Northwestern University Library
Evanston, Illinois 60201
Tel. (312) 492-7658

History. Northwestern University is an independent private institution founded in 1851. The Library dates from 1856 when a $1,000 fund enabled the University to acquire 1,977 books and 37 pamphlets, which were housed in a room in Old College Hall. By 1869 the collection had outgrown its quarters and moved to the third floor of University Hall. Early growth owed much to Orrington Lunt, who donated land to the University in 1865, the sale of which provided an endowment fund for book purchases. In 1894, the Lunt Library was built but the collections eventually outgrew this also, as they did its successor the Charles Deering Library, opened in 1933. Therefore in January 1970 the spectacular 12 million dollar Northwestern University Library, designed by Walter Netsch, was opened with seats for 3,000 users and shelving capacity of 2 million volumes. The Deering Library has been renovated and is connected with the three tower Main Library building. Together they contain 1.4 million of the 2.4 million volumes owned by the University.

Special Collections and Treasures. Collections have been developed in History on the French Revolution, Woodrow Wilson, Franklin D. Roosevelt, the Spanish Civil War and underground movements in World War II; in Literature, on English chapbooks, Johnson and Boswell, Spanish Plays, Twentieth Century Literature and Private Press production; on Architecture on Frank Lloyd Wright and on Transportation problems in all their aspects. The Melville J. Herskovits Library of African Studies of 60,000 volumes is one of the best in the United States.

Exhibition Areas. Exhibitions are held in the main concourse, at the entrance to the Library.

Model of Northwestern University Library, Evanston

Hours. Mon.-Fri. 0830-2400, Sat. 0830-1700, Sun. 1000-2400. Hours vary during summer and inter-sessions. Closed most public hols. Enquire in advance.

Transport. Elevated train from Chicago to Foster Avenue in Evanston. Walk 2 blocks east along Foster to University campus.

Parking. Limited parking facilities for visitors on the campus.

Admission. Readers: A letter of introduction is necessary from an academic school, public or special library for use of Library during evenings or the weekends, autumn to spring quarters. Application for 'access privileges' should be made to the Library Privileges Desk, in the Reference Department of the Main Library during weekday hours. It is advisable to telephone (492-7617) or write in advance to determine qualifications and required identification and authorisation.
Visitors: Guided tours each weekday 0830-1700. Prior arrangements should be made with Public Services Offices (492-7628). A visitor's pass, valid for one entrance only, may be obtained in advance by those unable to visit during weekday hours.

Information. Desk in front of the card catalogue on main floor.

Sales. None.

Guidebooks. Available free of charge at the Information Desk.

Restaurant/Snack Facilities. Vending machines in the student lounge on the second floor in the South Tower. Cafeteria in Norris University Center, directly east of Library.

Services. Typing rooms throughout Library. Typewriters for rent at 25¢ per 2 hours, in Reference Department, Periodicals Room, Reserve Room, Core Collection, Curriculum Collection and Africana. Coathooks near readers' spaces and lavatories on every floor. Elevators on every floor in the centre of the building with telephones nearby. Limited locker space available for $5 key deposit. Smoking lounge on second floor in South Tower.

Catalogues. Divided card catalogue, author-title/subject.

Classification. Dewey.

Copying/Photography. Self-service copy machines and staffed copy service available. Written permission may be obtained for private photography from the Assistant University Librarian for Public Services.

Friends of the Library.   Northwestern University Library Council.

HANOVER
Dartmouth College Library
Hanover, New Hampshire 03755
Tel. (603) 646-2235

History.   The Library, as part of Dartmouth College, was founded in 1769 by Elezear Wheelock, who had migrated north from Connecticut to start a missionary school for the Indians and others who might be interested. Financial backers included the Earl of Dartmouth, who gave the school its name. The Library's early stock totalled about 300 volumes, mostly of a theological nature, but by 1800 the collection had approximately 3,000 volumes. By 1861 the total was 15,000 volumes and by 1885, 60,000 volumes, a rise produced by the incorporation of two student literary society libraries. In 1928 the Library occupied the Baker Memorial Library, a Georgian colonial structure, and in the same year it received the Sanborn endowment for the purchase of books. The growth of the collections has been rapid since this date and several extensions have been erected to house them. The Library, which has been called 'the greatest college library' in the United States, now has a total collection of over 1 million volumes.

Special Collections and Treasures.   The Special Collections section is in the Treasure Room of Baker Library, main floor, northwest. It comprises three main sections: the Archives, the Rare Books Department and the Stefansson Collection. The Archives Collections relate primarily to the history of the College and the town of Hanover. The Rare Books Department includes various collections, notably on New Hampshire imprints, New England book illustration 1769-1869, famous presses and the theatre. Author collections total over 30 separate collections, notably on Erskine Caldwell, Robert Frost, H.L. Mencken, Eugene O'Neill and Kenneth Roberts. The Rupert Brooke Collection is considered possibly the finest in America, while the Robert Burns Collection of 1,500 items is also outstanding. The Stefansson Collection consists of 60,000 books, periodicals, pamphlets and MSS, most of which were gathered by the Arctic explorer Vilhjalmur Stefansson (1879-1962) over a period of more than 35 years. It is unique for its comprehensive coverage of the early history of polar exploration and for the large amount of unpublished material such as diaries, correspondence and tape recordings.

Exhibition Areas.   No details available.

Hours.   Mon.-Fri. 0830-2400, Sat. 0800-1700, Sun. 1400-2400.

Baker Library, Dartmouth College, Hanover

Transport. By bus or taxi. By car: Hanover and Lebanon exit of Route 189 North, or the Hanover and Norwich exit of Route 191 North.

Parking. Meter parking is available.

Admission. Readers: The Library is maintained for the use of students and faculty members of the College. However, limited services are available to local, non-affiliated scholars, with an appropriate need for access to research materials not available elsewhere. Borrowing privileges are also available on payment of an annual fee of $100 or $10 per month. Application forms for guest borrowers may be obtained from the Circulation Desk in Baker Memorial Library.
Visitors: Welcome.

Information. Desk at centre of main floor in the Baker Memorial Library. A self-guided, tape-recorded tour of the Library is available at the Information Desk.

Sales. None indicated.

Guidebooks. Handbook of the Libraries (in English) available free but very limited distribution.

Restaurant/Snack Facilities. None.

Services. Study carrels in northeast and northwest wings of the top floor, lavatories on upper and lower floors, typing room on the upper floor, and public telephones and cloakrooms on the lower floor.

Catalogues. Author/title and subject catalogues.

Classification. Mainly Library of Congress, some Dewey.

Copying/Photography. Photocopying machines in the main Library are in the Reserve corridor and on stack level 4.

Friends of the Library. Friends of Dartmouth College Library. Membership by voluntary contributions.

ITHACA
Cornell University Libraries
Cornell University, Ithaca, New York 14850
Tel. (607) 256-3322

History. In October 1868, when Cornell University received its first intake of students, the Library contained about 18,000 volumes, temporarily housed in two rooms of Morrill Hall. The Library in its early years owed much to the two principal founders of the University, Ezra Cornell and Andrew D. White. White, the first President of the University, not only donated large segments of his private collection but also bought extensively in Europe

Cornell University Library

on the Library's behalf. In October 1891 a Library building was dedicated. This building has now been renovated and renamed the Uris Library (serving undergraduates), while the John M. Olin Library, opened in 1961, is devoted more specifically to graduate and faculty scholarship. The Libraries' holdings passed one million in 1937-8, two million in 1958, three million in 1967, four million in 1973, and today total 4,200,564 volumes, 1,260,769 microform units and 49,667 periodicals.

Special Collections and Treasures. Collections include the Dante Collection, one of the largest and most complete to be found outside Italy; the Petrarch Collection including 65 15th century printed editions of Petrarch; the Wordsworth Collection claimed to be the most complete library of Wordsworthiana in the world; the Adelmann Collection on the history of embryology and human and comparative anatomy; the Lavoisier Collection on the history of chemistry; the Hollister Collection on the history of engineering; the Wason Collection on China; and the Fiske Collection of Icelandic material. Other collections relate to witchcraft and magic, slavery and abolition, the French Revolution, Theodore Roosevelt, Rudyard Kipling, Bernard Shaw, James Joyce, Wyndham Lewis, Daniel and Philip Berrigan and the Marquis de Lafayette.

Exhibition Areas. No special exhibition area. Special exhibits, changed routinely, appear in various libraries, notably in the Rare Book Department (Olin Library, First Floor, Room 106).

Hours. Olin Library: Mon.-Thurs. 0800-2400, Fri. 0800-2200, Sat. 0900-2200, Sun. 1300-2400. Closed 1 Jan., 24-26 Dec. and normal public hols.

Transport. Limousine service from the airport. Local buses cross the University campus.

Parking. Very restricted. Visitors should apply at the Traffic Bureau, Rand Hall, for parking permits and for information.

Admission. *Readers:* Regulations differ according to the different libraries. Non-Cornell personnel must produce suitable identification from their home institution.
Visitors: 'Responsible adults' may use materials within the individual libraries. Visitors are advised to write before visiting the Libraries to make sure of regulations and opening times, especially in the case of special collections.

Information. Circulation or reference desk in each library.

Sales. None.

Guidebooks. Guides in English are available, free of

charge, from each library.

Restaurant/Snack Facilities.   None in the libraries but facilities available on the Ithaca campus.

Services.   Cloakrooms, lavatories, lifts, telephones, etc. in nearly all library units.

Catalogues.   The John M. Olin Library has a union card dictionary catalogue. Individual collections have their own card catalogues.

Classification.   Almost entirely Library of Congress.

Copying/Photography.   Most library units have self-service copying machines. In the John M. Olin Library coin-operated machines are located in the Lower Lobby; microfilm reader-printers and photo-copiers in Room 012. Cameras may be used in all areas open to visitors.

LOS ANGELES
University Library, University of California at Los Angeles
405 Hilgard Avenue, Los Angeles, California 90024
Tel. (213) 825-1323

History.   The Library's history dates back to 1881 and the founding of the Los Angeles Normal School but its real beginnings as a university library date only to 1919, when the University of California took over the Normal School as the Southern Branch of the University. The Library at this time had only 28,000 volumes. In 1929, when the university campus was moved from Vermont Avenue to Westwood, the stock had risen to 154,000 volumes, and by 1944, 462,000 volumes. Growth was rapid under the librarianship of Dr. L.C. Powell, so much so that by 1961 the collection totalled 1.5 million volumes and a new building was needed to house them. In 1964 the first unit of the University Research Library was opened, with the second unit being completed in 1971. The original Main Library Building, completed in 1929, with an addition in 1948, has been converted into an undergraduate library, named in 1966 the Powell Library. The UCLA Library comprises a campus-wide system of libraries, containing 3,395,948 volumes, 1,172,022 MSS, 1,069,616 microcards, 305,004 maps, 505,440 pamphlets and 49,944 periodicals.

Special Collections and Treasures.   The major special collection is the William Andrews Clark Memorial Library (see next entry). Other collections include the 10,000 volume Michael Sadleir Collection of Nineteenth Century Fiction, (housed in the Bradford Booth Memorial Room); the Robert E. Cowan Collection of Californiana and Western Americana; the Arthur B. Spingarn Collection of Negro Literature and History; the Ralph Steele Boggs Folklore Collection; the Abraham Wolf Collection on Spinoza; the Elmer Belt Collection on Leonardo da Vinci;

University Research Library, University of California, Los Angeles

the Frederick T. Blanchard Collection of English Literature; the Robert E. Gross Collection of rare books in business and economics; the John A. Benjamin Collection of Medical History; the Walter E. Clark Sanskrit Collection of Indic mythology and folklore; the Dr. M.N. Beigelman Collection of classics in opthalmology; and the Albert Boni Collection on photography. Important manuscript collections include the literary papers of Norman Douglas, Henry Miller and Kenneth Rexroth; the historical correspondence files of Civil War General William S. Rosecrans and former US Senator Cornelius Cole; and from the entertainment world the papers of Eddie Cantor, Jack Benny, Charles Laughton, King Vidor and Stanley Kramer. (The Department of Special Collections is located on Floor A of the University Research Library.)

Exhibition Areas. The University Research Library Lobby; the Department of Special Collections; the Clark Library; and the Biomedical Library.

Hours. Mon.-Thurs. 0745-2300, Fri. 0745-1800, Sat. 0900-1700, Sun. 1300-2200. During summer sessions, intersessions, and holidays, hours of service are reduced.

Transport. By bus to campus. From airport take bus to Westwood Village.

Parking. There are fee paying parking facilities on campus.

Admission. *Readers:* A free library card can be obtained at the Library Card Window in the University Research Library.
Visitors: Free of charge.

Information. All Library and public service departments provide an information service. The Main Information Desk is situated in the Lobby near the turnstile entrances.

Sales. The Library Card Window in the University Research Library sells Library publications, postcards and correspondence stationery. Postal requests for Library publications should be addressed to the Gifts and Exchange Division.

Guidebooks. UCLA Library Guide describes entire Library system. Special guides to Department of Special Collections and the Clark Library (see next entry).

Restaurant/Snack Facilities. None on the Library premises but available elsewhere on campus, e.g. the snack area near the entrance to the Research Library.

Services. Typing rooms, lockers, public telephones, lifts and rest rooms on each floor of the book stacks. Blind Students Reading Room in Room 181 on 1st floor of the Powell Library.

Catalogues.   Union card catalogue for all libraries in University Research Library. (It is an alphabetical dictionary catalogue.) Computer produced book catalogues for newspapers, current serials, and recently acquired books not yet catalogued.

Classification.   Library of Congress.

Copying/Photography.   Audio-visual and photographic services on the ground floor of the west wing of the Powell Library Building. Coin-operated photocopying machines are available in most parts of the Library. In the Research Library these are located on the second floor. Non-commercial private photography permitted in the Library.

Friends of the Library.   Friends of the UCLA Library, open to all. Membership fees p.a.: UCLA Student $10; Regular Member $15; Associate Member $35; Corporate Member $100; Patron Member $100-$1,000.

LOS ANGELES
William Andrews Clark Memorial Library, University of California at Los Angeles
2520 Cimarron Street at West Adams Boulevard, Los Angeles, California 90018
Tel. [213] 731-8529

History.   The William Andrews Clark Memorial Library came to the University of California in 1934, its first and greatest gift. In 1926 its founder, William Andrews Clark Jr., provisionally deeded the Library to the University in memory of his father US Senator W.A. Clark, the Montana 'copper king'. On the death of the younger Clark in 1934, the Library with its buildings and grounds became wholly the property of UCLA, with the stipulation that the books were never to be moved, merged or consolidated with any other institution. An endowment of $1.5 million was provided for maintenance and development of the property and the collection. The Library occupies a Renaissance-style building, designed by R.P. Farquhar, and surrounded by four acres of formal gardens and lawns. Since 1935 holdings have more than tripled to over 70,000 volumes and 5,000 MSS. Principal acquisitions have been English books published 1640-1750 and the production of modern fine presses.

William Andrews Clark Memorial Library, Los Angeles

Special Collections and Treasures.   Within the period 1640-1750 the Library's holdings reflect all aspects of the life and thought of Dryden's England and the half century following his death. Extensive holdings have been built up of such authors as Bunyan, Milton, Prynne, Boyle, Evelyn, Newton, Congreve, Behn, Defoe, Swift, Dennis, Pope and, pre-eminently, Dryden. A collection of 8,500 religious and political tracts of the period provides background depth. Other collections include the Oscar Wilde Collection, which with over

1,500 books and 3,000 original MSS, typescripts and association pieces is . possibly unsurpassed, and the Charles Kessler Collection on Montana and the West of 2,000 bound volumes and 4,000 unbound pamphlets, etc. The Fine Printing Collection ranges from Gutenberg to the present day, with emphasis on California presses, particularly those of the Los Angeles area. Almost every publication of the Kelmscott and Dove Presses is included, the complete production of the Ward Ritchie Press, and the collection of Eric Gill which is believed to be the most varied and numerous in existence.

Exhibition Areas.   Throughout the Library.

Hours.   Mon.-Sat. 0800-1700. Closed Sun., University and public hols.

Transport.   The Library is approximately ten miles from the UCLA campus, three blocks west of Western Avenue and three blocks south of the Santa Monica Freeway. By bus: RTD Coach no. 44 from downtown Los Angeles, going south on Hill Street, to West Adams Boulevard at Cimarron Street. A bus service is also provided, on request, from the UCLA campus: contact the Administrative office.

Parking.   Available in the grounds.

Admission. Readers: The Library is open to all who need to consult its collections. Readers' cards may be obtained by application to the Librarian in person, or by mail.
Visitors: Free of charge. No regular tours are scheduled but visitors are invited to telephone the Library to arrange for a tour at a convenient hour.

Information.   At the entrance to the Library.

Sales.   None.

Guidebooks.   Brochure available, free of charge.

Restaurant/Snack Facilities.   None on the premises but readers may bring lunches, or prepare light meals in the Common Room, which has kitchen facilities.

Services.   All the usual facilities are available.

Catalogues.   Dictionary catalogue; chronological file by date of publication of printed books to 1800; provenance files (incomplete); shelflist of printed books; dictionary catalogue of general MSS; dictionary catalogue and chronological file of Oscar Wilde and Wildeiana MSS; G.K. Hall printed catalogue.

Classification.   Library of Congress, with adaptations. Books in the Fine Printing Collection are arranged by press.

Copying/Photography. Olivetti copier in the Library is available for use with MSS, reference works and unbound pamphlets. Older bound volumes are not copied in this fashion but, if condition permits, will be sent to the UCLA Library Photographic Department for microfilming.

Friends of the Library. See preceding entry.

MINNEAPOLIS
University of Minnesota Libraries
University of Minnesota, Minneapolis, Minnesota 55455
Tel. (612) 373-3097

History. The University of Minnesota Libraries, located at Minneapolis and St. Paul, comprise a library system that includes over 30 service units of varying size, function and subject orientation. These units include the O. Meredith Wilson Library on the West Bank of the Mississippi and the Walter Library on the East Bank. The history of the Libraries goes back to 1851 when the University was founded. The University Library developed not as a single collection of books but rather as a group or system of libraries, these being the General Library, the College Libraries and the Departmental Collections. In 1910 these libraries contained 185,000 volumes and in 1931, 650,000 volumes. By the late 1950's the growth of the collections had placed an immense strain on the existing buildings and a new library building was planned. The O. Meredith Wilson Library (named after the President of the University 1960-67), was accordingly opened on 23 September 1968 to serve the Social Sciences and the Humanities on the West Bank of the Mississippi. The old General Library, the Walter Library, now houses a number of library units, notably in the science field. Current holdings total over 3.5 million items.

University of Minnesota Library, Minneapolis

Special Collections and Treasures. The major special collection is the James Ford Bell Library, housed on the 4th floor of the Wilson Library. It became part of the University of Minnesota Library on 30 October 1953 and is an outstanding collection of sources on the history of world commerce from the time of Marco Polo to the end of the 18th century. It currently contains some 9,000 items including the Waldsemüller Globe Map of 1507; numerous editions of Ptolemy's *Geographia;* the first editions of Marco Polo's *Travels* in German, Latin, French and English; the defence brief for the trial of Warren Hastings, and extensive holdings on various European overseas trading companies. Special Collections in the Main Library include the W.H. Charters Collection on Paul Bunyan; the Kerlan Collection on Illustrated Children's Books; the George H. Hess Collection of Novels and Boys Adventure Series; and the Sinclair Lewis Collection. The Ames Library of South Asia is an extensive collection relating to the histories and cultures of India, Pakistan, Sri Lanka, Afghanistan and Nepal in English, and other languages.

Exhibition Areas. The 4th floor of the Wilson Library, the Rare Books Section and the James Ford Bell Library.

Hours. Wilson Library: Mon.-Thurs. 0800-2200, Fri. 0800-1800, Sat. 0900-1800, Sun. 1200-2200. Closed normal public hols. Walter Library: Mon.-Thurs. 0800-2200, Fri. 0800-1800, Sat. 0900-1800, Sun. 1200-1800. Closed normal public hols.

Transport. Metropolitan Transit Corporation buses go to within 1 block of the Wilson Library and to the East campus, University of Minnesota.

Parking. Adjacent to the Wilson Library on the South and West sides.

Admission. Readers: No special regulations for University Members.
Visitors: Apply to the Director of Libraries.

Information. Desk at the Reference Department on the 1st floor.

Sales. None.

Guidebooks. A Guide to the University of Minnesota Libraries, available free in English.

Restaurant/Snack Facilities. There are restaurants in Blegen and Anderson Halls.

Services. (Wilson Library) Facilities for conferences and short term group study are available in the centre area of the 2nd and 3rd floors. There are separate, glass enclosed, study rooms where smoking is permitted on the east and west sides of the building on 2nd and 3rd floors, as well as on the east side of the 4th floor, basement, Reserve Division and Periodicals Division. Study carrels available. Public telephones are located in the lobbies both on the 1st floor and in the basement and directly across from the elevators on the 2nd, 3rd and 4th floors. Typing rooms are located in the Reserve Room, Periodicals Division on the east and west sides of 2nd and 3rd floors and on the east side of the Documents Division. Lavatories, lifts. Coin-operated typewriters are available in the Reserve Room and Periodical Division typing rooms.

Catalogues. The main card catalogue, situated on the 1st floor of the Wilson Library, is, in fact, a union catalogue of the holdings of all the libraries on the Twin Cities Campus. It lists books by author, title and subject, in one alphabet. There are separate catalogues for Government publications and phonograph records.

Classification. Dewey.

Copying/Photography. A coin-operated copy service is available in locations throughout the Library system. A staffed photocopy service is available in the basement of the Wilson Library, in the Reserve Room, 1st floor of the Walter Library, and the Bio-Medical Library. Apply to the Library staff for private photography.

Friends of the Library. Associates of the James Ford Bell Library. $5.00 per annum.

NEW HAVEN
Yale University Library
Box 1603 A, Yale Station, New Haven, Connecticut 06520
Tel. Information: 203-436-8335; University Librarian: 203-436-2456

History. Yale University Library is the generic title for the libraries of Yale University. The system includes the Sterling Memorial Library, Beinecke Rare Book and Manuscript Library, Medical Library, Law Library and some 40 other school, departmental and college libraries. Yale College, or the Collegiate School of Connecticut, as it was first called, was founded in 1701 by a group of ministers. The Library was formed from their books, which migrated, with the new college, from Branford to Killingworth to Saybrook, and then finally to New Haven in 1718. Important gifts of books were made by such men as Bishop Berkeley and Governor Elihu Yale, for whom the college was named in 1718. For the next hundred years and more, Yale's books were kept in a room in one of the college buildings and it was not until 1846 that the first separate library building (now occupied by Dwight Chapel) was finished. By 1918 the book storage problem was acute, and when John W. Sterling left the major part of his fortune to Yale, it seemed fitting that a new Library building should serve as his memorial. The Sterling Memorial Library, modern Gothic in style, was accordingly opened in 1930. In October 1963 the Beinecke Rare Book and Manuscript Library, the gift of Edwin J., Frederick W. and Walter Beinecke and their families, was opened. This building, of striking architectural design, is located at the northeast corner of Wall and High Streets. Holdings currently include 6,350,824 volumes, over 1 million literary MSS, 18,216 linear feet of historical MSS and 871, 235 microforms.

Special Collections and Treasures. Collections include the O.F. Aldis Collection of American *belles-lettres;* the Elizabethan Club library of Shakespeare quartos and folios and early editions of other Elizabethan writers; the Henry R. Wagner Collection of British and Irish economic and political tracts; the Henry M. Dexter library of Congregational history; the Edward E. Salisbury Collection of Oriental books and MSS; the Count Landberg Arabic MSS; the Alexander Kohut Collection

Sterling Memorial Library, Yale University

of Judaica; the deposited library of the American Oriental Society; the Penniman library of education; the Francis P. Garvan Collection of Irish and sporting works; the Collection of the Literature of the American Musical Theatre; the Babylonian Collection; the Bookplate Collection; the Crawford Collection on the Modern Drama; the Benjamin Franklin Collection; the German Literature Collection, including the William A. Speck Collection of Goetheana and the Von Faber du Faur Collection; the Graphic Arts Collection; the Edward M. Hause Collection; the James Weldon Johnson Memorial Collection of Negro Arts and Letters; the Theatre Guild Collection; and the Western Americana Collection.

Exhibition Areas. Sterling Memorial Library: Nave, Cloister and Arts of the Book Room have exhibitions changing every two to three months. Beinecke Rare Book Library: changing and permanent exhibits of rarities. Medical Library: history of medicine library.

Hours. Term: Sterling Memorial Library: Mon. Thurs. 0830-2400, Fri.-Sat. 0830-1700, Sun. 1400-2400. Term: Beinecke Rare Book Library: Mon.-Fri. 0830-1645, Sat. 0830-1215, Sun. closed. Summer Vacation: Sterling Memorial Library: Mon.-Sat. 0830-2200, Sun. closed. Beinecke Rare Book Library: Mon.-Fri. 0830-1645, Sat., Sun. closed. Closed 1 Jan., 4 July, Labor Day, Thanksgiving Day, 25 Dec. and Memorial Day (when this holiday occurs during vacations).

Transport. Train: Penn Central and Amtrak railroads from New York and Boston. Bus: Greyhound and Continental Trailways from many points. Air: Allegheny and Pilgrim Airlines from New York and Boston. Taxis available at hotels and public transportation stations.

Parking. Meters in nearby streets.

Admission. Readers: Free to all Yale students and faculty members and their spouses. Identification card required. Non-members of the University may obtain borrowing privileges at a set fee. Registration takes place at the Circulation Desk in Sterling Memorial Library. *Visitors:* Open to the public for visiting, free of charge.

Information. Sterling Memorial Library: Reference Desk, main floor. Beinecke Rare Book Library: Information Desk at main entrance.

Sales. Publications of the Library may be obtained from Publications Office, Room 310, Sterling Memorial Library.

Guidebooks. Detailed guide of Special Collections on sale at $3.50 in Beinecke Rare Book Library. Guides to other Libraries distributed free at Sterling Memorial Library Reference Desk.

Restaurant/Snack Facilities. Snack facilities are available on the lower level, Sterling Memorial Library.

A page from the Book of Hours used by Sir Thomas More during his imprisonment in the Tower of London before his execution in 1535. In the margins, More wrote a prayer in English bidding farewell to the world

Open all Library hours.

Services. Lavatories, washrooms, lifts, smoking lounges, telephones, typing room. For locations apply at Reference Desk.

Catalogues. Dictionary card catalogue in the Sterling Memorial Library covering all branches of the system.

Classification. Special Yale classification until 1971 when Library of Congress was adopted for new accessions. Some reclassification.

Copying/Photography. Photocopy machines to the right of Circulation Desk, SML Microfilm, photostats and photographic prints are prepared in the Photographic Services Department (Room 53, basement of SML). Private photography permitted. For use of special equipment other than personal cameras, apply at the Office of the Associate University Librarian, Room 152, Sterling Memorial Library.

Friends of the Library. Yale Library Associates. Annual subscription minimum of $25.

NEW YORK
Columbia University Libraries
Columbia University, New York, NY 10027
Tel. 212-280-3533 (Information Office); 212-280-2241 (Reference Department)

History. The present Library is the lineal descendant of the Library of King's College, founded by royal charter in 1754. It is believed that by the beginning of the American Revolution the Library contained 2,000 volumes. During this War, however, fire and depredations of the armies occasioned the loss of a large proportion of the books, only about 200 surviving. In 1784, the College re-opened under the aegis of the Regents of the University of the State of New York, having loyally changed its name to Columbia. In 1838, the College acquired the library of Professor N.F. Moore, rich in classics and classical philology and the services of Professor Moore as its first full-time librarian. Although in 1857 the College left the Park Place building, where it had been located for 100 years, and moved to a site on 49th Street, it was not until 1883 that the Library was adequately accommodated in its own building. With the removal of the campus to its present Morningside Heights location, the collections occupied the Low Memorial Library in 1897. With the growth of holdings in the 20th century (1,092,343 books and periodicals by 1928) the nine storey Butler Library, the gift of Edward periodicals by 1928) the nine storey Butler Library, the gift of Edward Harkness, was opened for service in 1934. Holdings of Columbia University Libraries in 1974 total 4,572,676 volumes, 4,030,000 letters and MSS and

Butler Library, Columbia University, New York

1,212,706 microforms.

Special Collections and Treasures. Collections include the Engel Collection of English and American literature; the Seligman Library on the history of economics; the Library of the American Typefounders Association; the Plimpton and Smith Collections of school textbooks and mediaeval MSS; the Lodge Collection of Greek and Roman authors; the Dale Collection on weights and measures; the Brander Matthews Collection on drama and the history of the theatre; the Park Benjamin Collection on New York literature; the Kilroe Collection on New York City politics; the Epstean Collection on the history of photography; the Phoenix Collection of general literature and travel; the Montgomery Collection on accounting, and the Spinoza Collection on philosophy. Treasures include a *Canon Missae* (Mainz, Fust and Schoeffer, 1458), printed on vellum, one of three recorded copies in the world; the first printed edition of Marco Polo's *Voyages* (1477), of which only 11 copies are known to exist; the MS of Washington Irving's *Bracebridge Hall;* the MS draft of Herman Wouk's *The Caine Mutiny*, and a portfolio of original sketches done by Arthur Rackham for the stage production of *Hansel and Gretel,* the artist's only work for the theatre.

Exhibition Areas. The third floor, Butler Library and Rotunda, Low Library.

Hours. Term: Mon.-Thurs. 0830-2300, Fri. 0830-2200, Sat. 1000-1800. For information on opening times in the Vacations apply to the Information Office, Room 234, Butler Library. Closed Sun. and public hols.

Transport. By underground: Broadway Seventh Avenue IRT Subway to 116th Street and Broadway. By bus: New York buses 4, 104, 11, 5.

Parking. Metered parking in neighbouring streets.

Admission. Readers and *Visitors:* All applications should be made to the Information Office, Room 234, Butler Library.

Information. Room 234, Butler Library.

Sales. The miscellaneous publications of the Libraries may be obtained from the Gifts and Exchange Department, Room 103, the Butler Library.

Guidebooks. Guides to the Collections are available at the Information Office, usually free of charge.

Restaurant/Snack Facilities. None in the Library but many in the immediate neighbourhood.

Services. Restrooms off the east corridor on all floors. Cloakroom, main floor of the Butler Library. Telephones off the northeast and northwest corridors on the entrance floor of Butler Library. Typewriters, coin-operated typewriters in the Burgess-Carpenter Library, the College Library and some of the other libraries.

Catalogue. Three card catalogues are located in the Reference Room, 325 Butler; the name-titles catalogue, the topical subject catalogue and the serials catalogue.

Classification. Library of Congress and Dewey.

Copying/Photography. Several types of photographic processes are available. Quick-copies are available from the machines in Butler and most of the other libraries. Reader printers are available for making copies of microfilm or microfiche in the Engineering, International Affairs and Medical Libraries and in the Microform Reading Room, 501 Butler. The Photographic Services Department, 110 Butler, in addition to filling requests for quick-copies, can supply microfilms, photographic negatives and contact prints.

Friends of the Library. Friends of the Columbia Libraries, minimum subscription $35 per year.

NEW YORK
The Library, Hispanic Society of America
Broadway between 155th and 156th Streets, New York, NY 10032
Tel. 212-926-2235 (during Reading Room hours)

History. The Hispanic Society of America is the creation of its founder, Archer Milton Huntington (1870-1955). Huntington's Spanish studies and travels in Spain, culminating in excavations at Itálica, and in the translating and editing of the *Poem of the Cid,* resulted in a plan for an institution which would present the culture of the Hispanic peoples. The Society was accordingly founded on 18 May 1904 and Huntington placed in its care his library of MSS and about 40,000 books assembled over a period of some 20 years, as well as paintings and other works of Spanish art. The location for the Society was a then suburban section of New York City, known as Audubon Park. Construction of the main building began in the spring of 1905, and it was opened to the public in January 1908. The growth of the collections necessitated a new west wing in 1915, an east wing in 1920 and the opening of the north building in 1930. The original holdings have been enlarged by extensive purchases and gifts and now include 150,000 printed books and 200,000 MSS.

Special Collections and Treasures. Printed books include some 250 Hispanic incunabula, including several by Lambert Palmart of Valencia, and 8,000 volumes of first and early editions of important Spanish authors such as Cervantes, Góngora and Lope de Vega. 36 editions of the *Celestina,* mainly from the famous collection of the

Hispanic Society of America, New York.

Marquis of Jérez de los Caballeros, cover the period from 1499 to 1635. Among the Portuguese volumes are rare books of discovery, as well as the first and other 16th century editions of *Os Lusíadas* by Camões. The Library's greatest treasure is perhaps one of the four known 'black' books, the *Book of Hours* of Queen María, consort of Alfonso V of Aragon. This MS (c.1458) is written partially in silver and gold on black stained vellum.

Exhibition Areas. Two display cases in the Reading Room; library materials are occasionally exhibited in the Museum.

Hours. Tues.-Fri. 1300-1630, Sat. 1000-1630. Buildings closed: Mon., 1 Jan., 12 Feb., Easter Sun., 30 May, 4 July, Thanksgiving Day, 24, 25, 31 Dec. Reading Room also closed during the month of Aug., from 24 Dec. to 1 Jan. inclusive, 22nd Feb., Good Fri. and 12 Oct.

Transport. By bus: Uptown Bus No.4 or 5 to West 155th Street and Broadway. By subway: Eighth Avenue, Washington Heights local train, to West 155th Street, 2 blocks east of Broadway; West Side IRT local train to 157th Street and Broadway. (Visitors' entrance is at Broadway between 155th and 156th streets.)

Parking. Limited street parking.

Admission. Readers: No fees. No loans. Readers register at the Reading Room desk. Those wishing to use early printed books must present scholarly identification. Those wishing to use MSS must also do so and must make an appointment.
Visitors: No formalities.

Information. In the Reading Room.

Sales. In the Sorolla Room (part of the Museum). Society publications include library catalogues, postcards showing library items, etc.

Guidebooks. None, but an acoustic guide available for the Museum.

Restaurant/Snack Facilities. None.

Services. General cloakroom between the main entrance and the Small Sculpture Gallery, on the way to the Reading Room. Lavatories at the foot of the stairs leading down from the main entrance. Smoking permitted in the Ironwork Gallery on the second floor of the Museum.

Catalogues. Dictionary card catalogue in Reading Room (published version with supplement by G.K. Hall, Boston).

Classification. 'Remnants' of Dewey, Library of

Congress and other classifications. Books are shelved by accession number.

Copying/Photography. No machines for public use. The Society will microfilm or photograph manuscripts and early books, if they are not restricted.

Friends of the Library. The Society is an honorary one and membership is by election in recognition of a person's outstanding accomplishments.

NEW YORK
Library of the Jewish Theological Seminary of America
3080 Broadway, New York, NY 10027
Tel. 212-R19-8000, Ext. 320-327, 329

History. The Seminary Library, founded in 1890, with a few thousand volumes and three manuscripts, has since developed into the largest single collection of Jewish books and MSS ever assembled. The rapid growth of the Library owed much to the work of Professor Alexander Marx, who was Director from 1903 until his death in 1953. Under his administration the Library acquired a number of outstanding private collections, which soon made it a major centre of Jewish research. The first such acquisition was the private library of Judge Mayer Sulzberger of Philadelphia (acquired in 1903), and then in 1907 the collection of Professor Moritz Steinschneider established the Library as one of the main centres of Jewish bibliographical information. The greatest single addition was the collection of Elkan Nathan Adler (acquired in 1923), while the generosity of Mortimer Schiff was largely responsible for the rapid growth during the rest of that decade. On 18 April 1966, however, a fire raged for five hours in the Library tower and 70,000 volumes were lost. Today holdings include over 250,000 printed books, 10,000 MSS codices, 30,000 Genizah fragments and 3,500 microfilm reels.

Special Collections and Treasures. Collections include the Sulzberger Collection of 3,000 rare books and 500 MSS (to which Sulzberger added the Halberstam Library of 5,000 books and 200 MSS); the Ottinger Collection of reference books on biblical subjects; the Solomon Schechter Collection; the Israel Solomons Collection; the Elkin N. Adler Collection, which includes about 4,000 Hebrew MSS and 100 Hebrew incunabula; the Solomon Goodman Collection of some 10,000 titles; the Enelow Memorial Collection of some 1,100 MSS; the Judah A. Joffe Collection on early Yiddish Literature dating from 16th-18th centuries; the Felix Levy Collection comprising rich material in Egyptology; the Brooklyn Jewish Centre Library of almost 5,000 volumes; the Harry G. Friedman Collection; the Louis Ginzberg Microfilm Memorial Library and the Lewis L. Strauss Microfilm Collection.

Jewish Theological Seminary of America, New York

Exhibition Areas. The lobby contains four showcases,

while the Reading Room has two long cases, primarily for display of books. In addition the Jewish Museum (under the auspices of the Jewish Theological Seminary) arranges exhibitions from the Library's collection from time to time.

Hours. Mon.-Thurs. 0900-2200, Fri. 0900-1700. (In winter 0900-sundown). Sun. 1000-1800. Closed Sat. and all Jewish Hols.

Transport. By bus: Broadway bus to 122nd Street NE corner. By subway IRT uptown local 1 to 116th Street then walk up Broadway to 122nd Street.

Parking. Two garages available in the area but parking is usually very difficult.

Admission. Readers: The Reading Room is open to the public. No identification required. Scholars who wish to consult rare books and MSS should ask permission at Room 403, 4th floor.
Visitors: Guided tours are available upon application.

Information. General Collections: 2nd floor Reading Room. Rare Books and MSS: 4th floor Room 403.

Sales. Postcards and other items are on sale at the Bursar's Office and at the Jewish Museum (5th Avenue and 92nd Street).

Guidebooks. Booklet, *How to Use the Library.*

Restaurant/Snack Facilities. A Kosher cafeteria is open to the public for breakfast, lunch and dinner during the academic year. At other times, open for lunch only.

Services. Lavatories (women 4th floor, men 5th floor), lift, a pay telephone in the Teachers' Institute Building.

Catalogues. Card catalogue of printed collections on 2nd floor. Book and card catalogues of the MS collection are available on the 4th floor.

Classification. Library of Congress for printed books. Own system for MSS.

Copying/Photography. A copier is available for general use in the 2nd floor. Catalogue Room. A photo-copying service for rare books and MSS is provided by the research assistant on the 4th floor. Permission must be sought from the Librarian for private photography.

The Rothschild siddur (Jewish prayer book), written in Florence (1492), in the Jewish Theological Seminary Library, New York. Detail

NEW YORK

*New York Public Library
Research Libraries, 5th Avenue and 42nd Street,
New York, NY 10013
Tel. 790-6262*

History. The Library was founded in 1895 by the consolidation of the Astor and Lenox Libraries and the Tilden Trust. The first of these was founded in 1848 under the will of John Jacob Astor and opened to the public in 1854 with a stock of 80-90 volumes; the second comprised the books and paintings collected by James Lenox (1800-1880), and opened in 1870; and the third established from the bequest of Samuel Jones Tilden (d. 1886), former Governor of New York State. The City of New York undertook to erect a building for the new Library, which was placed under the direction of Dr. John Shaw Billings. It was largely through his influence that Andrew Carnegie (1837-1919) gave $5.2 million for the establishment of Branch Libraries throughout the city (now totalling some 84 branches in the Bronx, Manhattan and Staten Island). The Central Building was opened on 23 May 1911 with a stock of 1.2 million volumes. Although the Library's name implies that it is supported by the public, this is true only in part. The Research Libraries depend primarily on endowment and contributions, while the Branch Libraries are maintained for the most part by the City and State of New York and to some extent by the Federal Government. Holdings in 1973 totalled 16,475,213 items, including 3,937,854 volumes and 10,254 MSS.

Special Collections and Treasures. Collections include the Arents Tobacco Collection of over 8,000 items in 28 languages; the Arents Collection of Books in Parts; the Albert A. and Henry W. Berg Collection of English and American Literature; the Jewish Collection of roughly 110,000 volumes; the History of the Americas Collection; the Spencer Collection of Illustrated Books, MSS and Fine Binding; the Drama and Theatre Collections; the World War I Collection; the Dance Collection; the Schomburg Center for Research in Black Culture; the Local History and Genealogy Collection; the Wilberforce Eames Collection of Babylonica; the George Bancroft and Thomas Addis Emmet Collections on the American Revolutionary Period; the William J. Maloney Irish Historical Collections; the Radin Collection of Western European bookplates; the Lenox Collection, particularly strong in the treasures of exploration and discovery; the Elliott Shapiro Collection of sheet music; the Drexel Library, Rare Book and MSS Collection; the Julian Edwards Collection of opera scores, and the Rodgers and Hammerstein Archives of Recorded Sound.

Exhibition Areas. Main entrance hall and corridors. First floor: permanent exhibit on the art of printing and Benjamin K. Miller Collection of US postage stamps.

The New York Public Library

Third floor: the Phelps Stokes Collection of Historical Prints, and Room 318, the Berg Exhibition Room.

Hours.   Opening hours are in the process of change. Please check in advance.

Transport.   Buses: 5th Avenue bus lines (downtown), Madison Avenue bus lines (uptown), 42nd Street crosstown bus lines. Subway: 6th Avenue IND line, IRT Lexington Avenue line and IRT 7th Avenue line. (The Library entrances are on 5th Avenue and 42nd Street.)

Parking.   No facilities available.

Admission.   Readers: Anyone over 18 years of age may use the Library. The Arents, Berg and Spencer Collections and the Manuscript, Prints and Rare Book Divisions require admittance cards issued by the Administrative Office, Room 214. Personal identification and proof of qualification for research must be furnished, while student applicants must be engaged in graduate study for admittance to the Special Collections.
Visitors: Welcome to all public areas of the central building.

Information.   Inquiry Desk, just inside the 5th Avenue entrance. Floor plans and a building directory are at both 5th Avenue and 42nd Street entrances.

Sales.   Sales Shop, inside the 5th Avenue entrance, on the right. Library publications, books, cards, posters, games and souvenirs are sold.

Guidebooks.   Guide to the Research Libraries ($0.25); *Beyond the Lions: a guide to the Libraries of the New York Public Library* ($1.00).

Restaurant/Snack Facilities.   None in the Library but many available nearby.

Services.   Cloakrooms, at 42nd Street entrance. Women's rest rooms, Room 77 (ground floor) to the right of the lifts at the 42nd Street entrance and Room 306 at the south end of the third floor. Men's rest room, Room 325 at the north end of the third floor. Lifts, at the north end of the building. Telephones, to the left of the 42nd Street entrance; off the north corridor leading to the Map Division from the 5th Avenue entrance; at the north end of the 2nd and 3rd floors; in the centre corridor of the 2nd floor and inside the archway to the Main Reading Room. Typing room, Room 310 (restricted use).

Catalogues.   Dictionary card catalogue, closed on 31 Dec. 1971, with about 30 million cards in Room 315. 'The Public Catalog': From 1 Jan. 1972 all titles with 1972 imprint dates, all other materials being added for the first time irrespective of publication date, have been included in the new book catalogue and do not appear in the card catalogue. A researcher must use both catalogues simultaneously. Separate catalogues for special collections. Various published catalogues (e.g. G.K. Hall and Co.).

Classification.   Billings System and Fixed Order System.

Copying/Photography.   The Photographic Service (Room 316) provides a complete copying service. Photocopying is available as well as microfilming etc. Permission to use personal photocopying equipment in reproducing materials may be requested by making written application in the Research Libraries Administrative Office, Room 214. When the Photographic Service is closed, the supervisor of the Main Reading Room may allow a reader to use a simple camera device in the balcony provided that, in his judgement, the material will not come to harm. (Simple camera devices would be limited to cameras that use no lights other than the existing room lighting.)

Friends of the Library.   Friends of the New York Public Library: Friend, $25-$99 annual contribution; Associate, $100-$499 annually; Fellow, $500 or more annually.

The Pierpont Morgan Library, New York

Gospels, in Latin (9th century) in the Pierpont Morgan Library, New York. Back cover

NEW YORK
Pierpont Morgan Library
29 East 36th Street, New York, NY 10016
Tel. 212-685-0008

History.   The Library, opened to the public in 1924, has its origins in the private library of Pierpont Morgan (1837-1913) and J.P. Morgan (1867-1943). Pierpont Morgan began collecting when he was a boy, in the 1850s. By 1902 his books and manuscripts had become so numerous as to require a special building, and the firm of McKim, Mead and White was commissioned to design it. The Library, constructed next to the Morgan house on 36th Street, was completed late in 1906. During the remainder of his life, Morgan added substantially to the collections. At his death in 1913 the building and its contents passed to his son, J.P. Morgan, who continued collecting with the same vigour. In 1924, J.P. Morgan transferred the Library to a Board of Trustees with an endowment to provide for its maintenance. Soon afterwards it was incorporated by a special act of the legislature of New York State as a public reference library. The increasing use of the collections and the large additions to them made it essential to enlarge the Library. J.P. Morgan therefore built an annex in 1928 on the site of his father's house. This more than doubled the size of the Library and provided an exhibition hall, a reading room for scholars, staff offices and stack space for reference books. At the same time, he added generously to the endowment. Further enlargement of the buildings, which included a meeting room, was made in 1960-1962. The continued vigour of the Library has owed much to the three Directors, Belle Da Coşta Greene (1905-48), Frederick B. Adams Jr. (1948-1969) and Dr. Charles Ryskamp (1969-). Current holdings include 60,000 volumes and an unspecified number of MSS.

Special Collections and Treasures. Among the ancient and written records, the Assyrian and Babylonian seals collection is the largest and finest in the United States. Seymour de Ricci has termed the Mediaeval and Renaissance MS collection as 'the most extensive and the most beautifully selected series of manuscripts existing on the American Continent'. The collection includes the *Lindau Gospels* (9th century), the *Berthold Missal,* considered by Morgan 'quite possibly the finest and most luxurious 13th century manuscript produced in Germany', the *Manāfi al-Hayawan* (late 13th century), the *Hours of Catherine of Cleves* (Utrecht, c.1435), the *Hours of Cardinal Alessandro Farnese* (16th century) and the *Maciejowski Bible'.* Concentrating on artists born before 1800, the old master drawing collection consists of approximately 4,500 drawings and is unexcelled within its chronological limits in America. The collection of incunabula surpasses that of any other American library in the number of important early books and in the remarkable condition of most of the volumes. The bookbinding collection is the most comprehensive in America, ranging from the 9th to the 20th century. The later printed books number about 60,000, selected for importance in literature, and the other arts, history and printing. Included are 3 copies of the *Gutenberg Bible* and 45 different texts by Caxton. The early children's books collection includes the unique copy of the earliest known printed children's book (c.1487), the original text of Perrault's *Mother Goose,* and concentrates on 17th and 18th century English and Continental children's literature. The autograph MSS, letters, and documents number in tens of thousands with hundreds of volumes of authors' original MSS. Special concentration is in the Italian Renaissance, the Reformation in Germany, the Tudor and Stuart periods in England and the American Revolution. The total music collection with the Mary Flagler Cary Music Collection forms one of the two finest collections of musical autographs in America. The Reginald Allen Gilbert and Sullivan Collection is the most extensive anywhere.

Exhibition Areas. The exhibition rooms are located on the main floor of the building and include the study and library of J. Pierpont Morgan. Hours (Exhibition) Tues.-Sat. 1030-1700, Sun. 1300-1700. Closed Mon., Sun. during July, whole of Aug. and public hols.

Hours. Reading Room: Weekdays 0930-1645. Closed Sun. and public hols.

Transport. By bus: Buses running along 5th Avenue and Madison Avenue are convenient to the Library with stops close to 36th Street. By subway: closest subway

Life of St. Edmund (12th century), in the Pierpont Morgan Library, New York (MS 736). Folio 22, verso

Bible, illuminated at St. Swithin's Priory, England (1175-1200), in the Pierpont Morgan Library, New York

Book of Hours of Catherine of Cleves (Netherlands, 15th century), in the Pierpont Morgan Library, New York (MS 917). Folio 120

station is on the Lexington IRT line (local), stopping at 33rd Street.

Parking. Metered parking near the Library.

Admission. Readers: The study rooms are open to bonafide scholars, graduate research students, curators and librarians, dealers in books and MSS, etc.
Visitors: Free of charge.

Information. At Library staff desks and entrance vestibule.

Sales. Sales Desk, located in the cloister area, displays greeting and Christmas cards, postcards and various facsimiles and exhibition catalogues.

Guidebooks. Brochure, *The Pierpont Morgan Library,* in English, free of charge.

Restaurant/Snack Facilities. None.

Services. Cloakrooms, lavatories.

Catalogues. Author and subject catalogues.

Classification. Own.

Copying/Photography. Microfilms, photographs, colour slides and Ektachromes available through Library staff. Private photography forbidden.

NEW YORK
Dag Hammarskjold Library
United Nations Headquarters, New York, NY 10017
Tel. (212) 754-1234

Dag Hammarskjold Library, UN Headquarters, New York

History. When the United Nations came into being in 1945 the need for a library was quickly realized. Indeed, at the UN Conference on International Organization in San Francisco in 1945, a library service was organized by the co-operative efforts of the Library of Congress and other American libraries. Thereafter while the temporary headquarters of the United Nations were situated in London, at Hunter College in New York and at Lake Success, the Library grew, notably by addition of the collections of the Economic and Transit Division of the League of Nations, which had been developed at Princeton throughout World War II. In 1950 the Library's collections were enriched by the gift of the Woodrow Wilson Foundation Collection. In early 1951, the Library moved to the permanent site of the Secretariat and was housed in the so-called 'Manhattan Building', which was quite unsuitable for the preservation of books and for the organization of library services. The dedication, therefore, in November 1961, of the Dag Hammarskjold Library building (named after the late Secretary-General) was a great boon to the use of the collections. It is a six-storey and penthouse structure, three of the floors lying above ground and three below, built of white marble, glass and aluminium. Current holdings total some 380,000 volumes and 80,000 maps.

Special Collections and Treasures. The Library can be characterized as a specialized international library which combines the functions of an international affairs information bureau with those of a research library in the social sciences. The specific needs of the United Nations have determined the policy governing the development of its collections. Thus the Library maintains a complete collection of documents and publications of the United Nations and a comprehensive collection of those of the specialized agencies and other organizations and programmes within the United Nations system. It also collects — on a worldwide basis — books, pamphlets and periodicals about all aspects of United Nations activities. A special collection called the Woodrow Wilson Collection numbers about 8,500 volumes of documents of the League of Nations and of its affiliated organizations, together with some 6,500 books and pamphlets dealing with the activities of these organizations and with peace movements and international relations during the period 1918-39. The Library receives some 7,000 official government serials from Member States and some 8,000 other serials, including documents and publications of major inter-governmental organizations outside the United Nations system, e.g. EEC, League of Arab States, OAS, OAU, OECD, and most of those of non-governmental organizations in consultative status with the United Nations. The Library's general collection is strongest in subjects such as international law and relations, economic and social affairs, human rights and other subjects with which the United Nations is concerned.

Exhibition Areas. Display cases are maintained in the main floor lobby and in the Periodicals Reading Room at the concourse level.

Hours. Weekdays 0930-1800, Summer schedule 0900-1730.

Transport. By bus: Crosstown 42nd Street bus. By subway: to Grand Central Station and then a short walk to 1st Avenue and 42nd Street. (The Library building is on the south west corner of the Headquarters site and can be entered either directly from First Avenue or through the Secretariat building).

Parking. Meter parking nearby.

Admission. Readers: The Library is not open to the general public. It is a special Library open to the staff of permanent missions and delegations to the United

Nations and of the Secretariat, and to accredited members of the media. Admission of researchers and students at the PhD level may be granted upon request request.
Visitors: Visitors in groups or individually are admitted only on advance request.

Information. Library desks, e.g. in the General Reference Room and the Woodrow Wilson Reading Room.

Sales. None.

Guidebooks. Dag Hammarskjold Library, Collections and services. Free, in English, French and Spanish.

Restaurant/Snack Facilities. None.

Services. Two lifts, east and west in the building; lavatories near the lifts on all floors.

Catalogues. Special card catalogues of the documents and publications of the League of Nations, the United Nations and the specialized agencies are located in the Woodrow Wilson Reading Room (L-201); most of the materials located in the General collection and the departmental collections are listed in the card catalogue located in the General Reference Room (L-105). Catalogues consist of author (or name) and subject parts.

Classification. Universal Decimal Classification with special modifications.

Copying/Photography. A coin-operated copier is located in the Periodicals Reading Room. No restrictions on private photography.

PHILADELPHIA
The Library Company of Philadelphia
1314 Locust Street, Philadelphia, Pennsylvania 19107
Tel. (215) KI6-3181

The Library Company of Philadelphia

History. The Library Company of Philadelphia was founded on 1 July 1731 by Benjamin Franklin and his friends who wished to establish a library for their common use. The Proprietors of Pennsylvania granted the Company an official charter in 1742. Shares were issued to each member upon the payment of a lump sum which was used to buy books. Annual dues were assessed upon the shares to maintain the Library and its services. The first books were received from London in 1732 and the growth of collections, by purchase and donation, was steady throughout the 18th century. In 1792 the Library occupied a building facing Independence Square, where it remained until 1880. It occupied its present building on Locust Street in early 1966, next door to and connected with the Historical Society of Pennsylvania. Current holdings include over 400,000 volumes.

Special Collections and Treasures. Collections include the library of James Logan (1674-1741), perhaps the finest library of colonial America; the library of the Rev. Dr. Samuel Preston (d. 1803); the collection of William Mackenzie (d. 1828); and the library of James Cox, 6,000 volumes of a literary nature. Individual treasures include W. Blaeu, *Le théâtre du monde* (Amsterdam, 1644-6), the atlas still bound in the original gilt vellum; the first edition of Boswell's *Life of Samuel Johnson* (London, 1791); Diderot's *Encyclopédie* (Paris and Amsterdam, 1751-80); Benjamin Franklin, *A modest enquiry into the nature and necessity of a paper currency* (Philadelphia, 1729), the finest copy known of Franklin's first published book; Galileo, *Discorsi e dimonstrazioni* (Leiden, 1638), which has been called the first modern textbook on physics; Francis Hopkinson, *A pretty story written ...2774* (Philadelphia, 1774), the first American work of fiction; Ruy Lopez, *Libro de la invencion liberal y arte del juego de axedrez* (Alcala, 1561), generally considered to have been the most important work in the history of modern chess; and Walt Whitman's *Leaves of Grass* (Brooklyn, 1855), the first edition (actually purchased in 1855).

Exhibition Areas.   The Logan and Rush Rooms, adjacent to the Reading Room.

Hours.   Mon.-Fri. 0900-1645. Closed Sat., Sun., 4 July, Memorial Day, Labor Day, Thanksgiving Day, Christmas and Good Fri.

Transport.   Subway: From 30th Street Station, 30th and Market Streets, take the Market Street subway east to 13th Street. The Library is on Locust Street, 4 blocks south along 13th Street. Car: From the Schuylkill Expressway (Route 76 or 376) follow signs to 'Center City', take the 15th Street exit and follow 15th Street to its intersection with Locust Street. Turn left (east) and the Library is on the right soon after the intersection of Broad and Locust Streets.

Parking.   Many parking lots in the area.

Admission. Readers: The Library can be used by any qualified scholar without charge.
Visitors: Apply to the Librarian.

Information.   Desk in Reading Room.

Sales.   In Reading Room (Information Desk). Illustrated exhibition catalogues and other publications are sold.

Guidebooks.   None.

Restaurant/Snack Facilities.   None.

Constitution of the USA, first private printing. Copy belonging to John Dickinson, with his annotations, in the collection of the Library Company of Philadelphia

Services. Lavatories, lifts to second floor when authorised, typing area if needed, telephones for local calls.

Catalogues. Card catalogue (details not specified).

Classification. Own.

Copying/Photography. Photocopying by staff. Photography by researchers is permitted.

Friends of the Library. Any interested person may become a member of the Library Company for an initial contribution of $20 and then $8 annually.

PRINCETON
Princeton University Library
Post Office Box 190, Princeton, New Jersey 08540
Tel. Librarian: 609-452-3170; Information: 609-452-3181

History. In 1750 the Trustees of the four-year-old College of New Jersey voted to purchase a bookcase. This is the first record in Princeton's annals of provision for the printed word. The Library's first home was a 2nd floor room above the centre entrance to Nassau Hall. By 1800 the Library had 3,000 volumes, but a fire of 1802, which gutted Nassau Hall, destroyed all but 100 of them. Sympathetic donors restored the collection to 4,000 volumes by 1805, housed in a new building, successively known as the 'Library', 'Geological Hall' and 'Stanhope Hall'. Following another fire in 1855, Nassau Hall was remodelled. Princeton's first professional librarian, Frederick Vinton, was appointed in 1873, an act which coincided with the opening of the new Chancellor Green Library. By 1888, however, this was jammed to capacity with 65,000 volumes, so the rectangular Pyne Library was constructed in 1897. The growth of the collections in the 20th century led to the opening of the Firestone Memorial Library in 1948, the first large university library building designed originally as an 'open stack' library. The Firestone Library, named after Harvey S. Firestone, the rubber pioneer, was substantially enlarged in 1972. Its holdings generally relate to the humanities and social sciences, with other disciplines being housed in a variety of libraries on campus. Current holdings of Princeton University Library include 2,615,317 printed volumes, 838,507 microforms and 258,578 maps.

Special Collections and Treasures. The East Asian Collections in Palmer-Jones Halls, including the Gest Oriental Library, total more than 250,000 volumes and comprise one of the largest and richest Chinese collections in the country. The Robert Garrett Collection of Arabic, Persian, Turkish, Indic and other Oriental MSS is apparently unmatched in the United States. Other collections include the Junius S. Morgan Vergil Collection; the Robert W. Patterson Horace Collection;

Firestone Library, Princeton University

the Morris L. Parrish Collection of Victorian Novelists; the Grenville Kane Collection of early Americana; the Philip A. Rollins Collection of Western Americana; and the John S. Pierson Civil War Collection. The Manuscript Division has the papers of such notable American personalities as S.L. Southard, J.V. Forrestal, J.F. Dulles, A.E. Stevenson and B.M. Baruch, as well as extensive collections of MSS relating to Aaron Burr, Elias Boudinot, Woodrow Wilson, Otto H. Kahn and others.

Exhibition Areas. The main Exhibition Gallery is on the ground floor of the Firestone Library adjoining the Rare Book Department. Smaller changing exhibits are held elsewhere in the building, in the Graphic Arts Room, the Theatre Collection etc.

Hours. Main Library (Firestone): Term: Mon.-Sat. 0800-2400, Sun. 1000-2400. Rare Books and Special Collections Reading Room: Mon.-Fri. 0900-1700. Exhibition Gallery: Mon.-Sat. 0900-1700, Sun. 1400-1700. Summer Vacation: Mon.-Fri. 0800-2400, Sat. 0900-2300, Sun. 1400-2300. Rare Books and Special Collections: Mon.-Fri. 0900-1700. Exhibition Gallery: Mon.-Fri. 0900-1700. The Library closes 1 Jan., 4 July, Labor Day weekend (Sat.-Mon.), Thanksgiving Day, 25 Dec. and the (business) day preceding.

Transport. By rail: Penn Central Railroad. By bus: Suburban Transit buses from New York City. (The Firestone Library is located at Nassau Street and Washington Road.)

Parking. University visitors' car park in William Street near the Firestone Library.

Admission. *Readers:* Anyone may use the Library but schoolchildren and students from elsewhere must apply in writing. Members of the University and certain other people may borrow books without charge. Scholars and professional people not connected with the University must pay a borrower's fee. Students from other colleges and universities are not usually granted borrowing privileges. A Library identification card is issued to everyone who registers as a borrower.
Visitors: Free admission.

Information. Desk in the main lobby.

Sales. In the Rare Book Department and Bookkeeping Office. Library publications available.

Guidebooks. Library handbook, free of charge.

Restaurant/Snack Facilities. Snack facilities on the third floor, open whenever the Library building is open.

Services. Study carrels for senior and graduate

students (500 available). Smoking permitted in the lounges, offices, seminars and graduate study rooms (prohibited elsewhere in the Library). Two public telephones on the main floor near the entrance and another at the rear of the Public Catalog, a telephone for local calls near the Circulation Desk. Typing area near the south stairs (typewriters not provided).

Catalogues.   Dictionary catalogue in card form.

Classification.   Library of Congress and the Library's own system (Richardson).

Copying/Photography.   There is a photographic service, located on C floor of Firestone, providing photostat and microfilm copies. Coin-operated photocopying machines are available in the cloakroom on the first floor and on A, B and C floors. Permission for private photography must be obtained from the Librarian's Office or from the Assistant University Librarian for Buildings and Technical Services.

Friends of the Library.   Friends of the Princeton University Library. Varying rates from student $5.00 to Patron $500.00.

PROVIDENCE
John Carter Brown Library
Brown University, Providence, Rhode Island 02912
Tel. 401-863-2725

History.   The John Carter Brown Library began in about 1824 as the private library of the Providence merchant of that name. In 1846 Brown started systematically to collect early Americana with the first of a series of major purchases from the bookseller Henry Stevens. On John Carter Brown's death in 1874, the Library remained in the family until the death in 1900 of his son, John Nicholas Brown, who had been an equally enthusiastic collector. The Library came to Brown University in 1904 and is housed in the building erected for it under the will of J.N. Brown. The Library is currently part of Brown University but not of its Library system. The holdings in 1904 totalled 20,000 books, maps and broadsides, while today they contain about 40,000 books and 400,000 MSS. The Library is now established as one of the leading research libraries, devoted to collecting primary printed source materials relating to the Americas during the colonial period.

Special Collections and Treasures.   The Brown Papers consisting of some 350,000 MS documents dating from 1726 to 1913 constitute a rich source for the study of American business practices. The Library has an outstanding collection of some 10,000 early maps, ranging in date from 1450 to 1820. Individual treasures include Christopher Columbus, *Epistola de insulis de novo*

John Carter Brown Library, Brown University, Providence, Rhode Island

repertis (Paris, 1943); Amerigo Vespucci's *Mundus novus* (Antwerp, 1508), a unique copy of the Dutch edition; Francisco López de Gómara's *Historia de las Indias* (Zaragoza, 1553); the collections of Ramusio, De Bry, Hulsius, Hakluyt and Purchas; Captain John Smith's *A true relation ... Virginia* (London, 1608); Champlain's *Les voyages* (Paris, 1613); *The whole booke of Psalmes* (Cambridge, 1640), the only perfect copy in a contemporary binding of the 'Bay Psalm Book'; Adam Smith, *The Wealth of Nations* (London, 1776); the 29 volumes of *Correio Braziliense* (1808-22); and Viscount Kingsborough's nine volume *Antiquities of Mexico* (London, 1830-48).

Exhibition Areas.   The main room of the Library is its exhibition room.

Hours.   Academic year: Mon.-Fri. 0830-1700, Sat. 0830-1200. Summer and holiday periods: Mon.-Fri. 0830-1630. Closed Sun. and public hols.

Transport.   Cab or bus to Brown University campus. (The Library is at the corner of George and Brown Streets.)

Parking.   In nearby streets.

Admission.   *Readers* and *Visitors:* The Library is open, free, to all.

Information.   Secretary's Office.

Sales.   Secretary's Office.

Guidebooks.   *Opportunities for Research in John Carter Brown Library* (Brown University, Providence, 1968).

Restaurant/Snack Facilities.   None.

Services.   Lavatories.

Catalogues.   Dictionary catalogue; chronological file; imprint file (partial); map catalogue (partial); manuscript catalogue (partial); print catalogue (partial); various published catalogues.

Classification.   Own for rare books, Library of Congress for reference books.

Copying/Photography.   Photocopying by the Library staff only. Private cameras may not be used in the Library without the permission of the Librarian.

Friends of the Library.   Associates of the John Carter Brown Library (suggested minimal annual contribution $15.00).

SAN MARINO
Huntington Library, Art Gallery, and Botanical Gardens
1151 Oxford Road, San Marino, California 91108
Tel. 213-792-6141

History. The Huntington Library is a research centre with important collections of MSS and rare books for the scholarly study of British and American history and literature. It has its origins in the private collection of Henry Edwards Huntington (1850-1927), the businessman who made a fortune in the development of California. Huntington began collecting in the first decade of the 20th century, but his major acquisitions were made between his retirement in 1910 and his death in 1927. In April 1911 he acquired the E.D. Church Library of 2,133 volumes for about 1 million dollars; in 1911-12 5,500 lots from the Robert Hoe sales went to Huntington, while he was a consistent bidder at the Huth sales (1911-20) in London. In 1914 he acquired the Kemble-Devonshire Collection of 4,000 plays and 40 volumes of playbills. In 1917 he purchased the Bridgewater House library *en bloc.* In August 1919, Huntington signed the deed of trust whereby his treasures would be given to the people of California. A self-perpetuating board of trustees was formed and ground was broken for the Library Building to which his books and MSS were finally brought from New York in 1920 and housed in the new Library completed in 1923. The period from Mr Huntinmgton's death in 1927 until 1939 was almost entirely taken up in equipping the Library to fulfil its current research position. Holdings now include 305,000 rare books including 5,400 incunabula, 220,000 reference books, over 5 million MSS and over 16,000 reels of microfilm.

Special Collections and Treasures. Collections include, in the field of British history, the Battle Abbey papers, the Hastings papers, the Ellesmere collections from Bridgewater House, the Stowe collection (Temple, Brydges and Grenville papers), and the Loudoun papers (18th C. Scottish and American). In English and American literature, the Huntington has some 230 Middle English MS texts, including the Ellesmere Chaucer, the Towneley Plays, the Chester cycle, 4 MSS of *Piers Plowman,* 4 of *Pricke of Conscience;* and an outstanding collection of MSS of printed English and American authors, including the MS of Thoreau's *Walden* and the Wallace Stevens archive. American history collections include important early maps and Portalan charts, the Brock collection, the Samuel L.M. Barlow papers, Jefferson drawings and papers, Francis Lieber papers, the Frederick Jackson Turner archive, the Albert Bacon Fall archive, strong Mormon collections, the Galvez papers, Cave Couts papers, and Abel Stearns papers. Treasures include the *Gutenberg Bible* on vellum, the original MS of Benjamin Franklin's *Autobiography,* the largest collection of Shakespeare quartos, and Robert Hunter's *Androboros,* the unique copy of the first play printed in America.

The Huntington Library, San Marino

Exhibition Areas.   Some of the oustanding works in the collections are on permanent display for the public in the Main Exhibition Hall and west foyer. Special exhibits in adjoining halls.

Hours.   Readers: Mon.-Sat. 0830-1700. Closed major holidays. *Visitors:* Tues.-Sun. 1300-1630. Closed to visitors every Monday, major holidays, and the entire month of October.

Transport.   Bus service on a regular schedule, at about hourly intervals, is available between both the Los Angeles International Airport and the Burbank Airport and the Huntington-Sheraton and the Pasadena Hilton Hotels. The Library is about 12 miles from downtown Los Angeles. Free shuttle bus daily between the University of California at Los Angeles; University of Southern California; California Institute of Technology; and the Huntington.

Parking.   In the official parking area.

Admission.   Readers: Application to be made to the Registrar, Reader Services Department. Reading privileges are for specified subjects and periods but they are renewable under appropriate circumstances. An applicant who is not a regular faculty member or the like should bring letters of recommendation from two persons of recognized standing. Before 1300 readers should enter the grounds at the Service Entrance; after this time they may use the Main Gate. The Library offers a number of small grants to scholars.
Visitors: Free Art Gallery, Museum and Botanical Gardens. Groups are requested to make advance reservations. Guided tours of the Main Exhibition Hall on Tuesdays at 1300.

Information.   Readers: Reader Services Department. *Visitors:* Public Services Department.

Sales.   The Bookstore at the public entrance to the grounds (open 1300-1630 Tues.-Sun.) sells Huntington publications and also collotypes, postcards, notepaper and other reproductions of Huntington treasures.

Guidebooks.   Visitors' Guide to the Exhibitions and Gardens of the Henry E. Huntington Library and Art Gallery. Readers' Guide to the Huntington Library. The Huntington Art Collection. Various subject brochures also available.

Restaurant/Snack Facilities.   Readers and staff only: lunchroom open 1130-1230. Situated in the small building west of the Shakespeare Garden and Art Gallery. Vending machines for readers in the basement of the Library.
Visitors: Beverage vending machines are located at the entrance.

Geoffrey Chaucer. Detail from The Canterbury Tales, the Ellesmere manuscript (late 14th century), in the Huntington Library, San Marino, California

Services. Public telephones (in the Readers' Entry Hall and outside the Bookstore). Restrooms: Men — on main floor in corridor adjoining Manuscript Catalog and in the basement at the bottom of the stairs leading from the Readers' Entry Hall. Women — on the south side of the Reference Room and in the corridor adjoining the Manuscript Catalog. Typewriters can be hired from the Reader Services Department. Mail service for readers (for sending and receiving mail). The Library makes every effort to assist readers who need housing. Readers are invited to write to the Reader Services Department for information.

Catalogues. Author-title card catalogue of printed material. Separate catalogues for prints, photographs, portraits. Subject catalogue to the reference collection. Manuscript catalogue (3 divisions: alphabetical, chronological, and by collection).

Classification. Reference books use Library of Congress classification system.

Copying/Photography. Photoduplication department has a photocopying, photographic, and microfilming service. Readers are not permitted to make their own copies.

Friends of the Library. The Friends of the Huntington Library. Members donate a minimum of $25 annually.

STANFORD
Stanford University Libraries
Stanford, California 94305
Tel. 415/497-2016, TWX 910 373-1787

History. Stanford University was founded by Senator and Mrs. Leland Stanford in memory of their only child, Leland Jr., who died in 1884 at the age of 15. The University opened on 1 October 1891, with the Library containing 3,000 volumes. It was housed in the Quadrangle until 1919, when the present Main Library building was occupied. By this date the main collection had grown to about 200,000 volumes and the volumes in the entire Library complex to 300,000. A number of important special collections had also been established, notably the Hopkins Transportation Library and the Levi Cooper Lane Medical Library, which came to the University in 1910 following the transformation of the Cooper Medical College into the Stanford University School of Medicine. Growth has been dramatic during the 20th century and the Stanford Library complex now contains over 100 miles of linear shelving capacity. The term 'University Libraries' refers to all libraries which are the responsibility of the Director of Libraries but excludes six special libraries called 'Co-ordinate Libraries': the library of the Hoover Institution on War, Revolution and Peace (see next entry); the Law Library; the Lane Medical Library; the J. Hugh Jackson Library of

Stanford University Main Library, Stanford

Business; the Library of the Food Research Institute and the library of the Stanford Linear Accelerator Center, which are under the jurisdiction of individual academic schools or facilities within the University. Current holdings of all libraries (including co-ordinate libraries) include over 4 million volumes; 18,254,914 MSS, 1,184,226 microforms and 132,466 maps.

Special Collections and Treasures. Collections include the Thomas Rowlandson Collection of 18th and 19th century illustrated books (housed in the Art and Architecture Library); the Archive of Recorded Sound and the Harry R. Lange Collection of Historical Musical Instruments and Books (housed in the Music Library); the G.M. Smith Algae Reprint Collection and the F.M. MacFarland Opisthobranchiate Molluscan Library (housed in the Hopkins Marine Station Library) while the following can be consulted in the Bender Room, the service centre for the Special Collections Department: the Charlotte Ashley Felton Library (British and American literature of the 19th and 20th centuries); the Frederick E. Brasch Collection on Sir Isaac Newton and the History of Scientific Thought; the Morgan A. and Aline D. Gunst Memorial Library (history of the book, etc.); the Memorial Library of Music, and the Elmer E. Robinson Collection on American history and government. Manuscript collections include the Antoine Borel Collection of Californiana; the Ernesto Galarza Papers on California Farm Labor, and the Newton Collection, which includes documents by Newton and Einstein.

Exhibition Areas. Exhibitions, usually three a year, are held in the Albert M. Bender Room on the top floor of the Main Library. (The room is accessible by the lift from the lower lobby, or by the stairway near the Loan Desk.)

Hours. Main Library. Regular Sessions: Mon.-Fri. 0800-2200, Sat. 0900-1700, Sun. 1300-2200. Recess Periods: Mon.-Fri. 0800-1700, Sat. 0900-1200. Sun. Closed. Summer Session: Mon.-Thurs. 0800-2100, Fri. 0800-1700, Sat. 0900-1200, Sun. 1300-1700. Closed 1 Jan., Independence Day, Labor Day, Thanksgiving, 24-25 Dec.

Transport. Southern Pacific Railroad or Greyhound Bus to Palo Alto. By bus: Santa Clara County Transit District operates bus routes serving Palo Alto and Stanford University. There are no Sunday services. By car: either north from San José, or south from San Francisco, on Highway 101, take Embarcadero West to Stanford Campus, at which point it becomes Galvez.

Parking. Parking lots for visitors, signposted at campus entrances.

Admission. Readers: Apply to Loan Desk. Any individual doing research who does not quality as an Alumnus or as an 'Associated and Visiting Scholar' and who wishes to borrow, may purchase a library card for a fee of $25.00 p.a., for each card issued.

Visitors: Apply to the Director's Office, Main Library, in advance.

Information. Reference Desk, General Reference Department, Main Library. All major branch and co-ordinate libraries also have desks.

Sales. None.

Guidebooks. Guide to Stanford University Libraries, available free. Various departmental library guides.

Restaurant/Snack Facilities. Several eating facilities on campus.

Services. Restrooms available at all library locations. Main Library offers typing facilities. Telephones available at many points on the campus. In most cases there are areas designated for smokers.

Catalogues. The card catalogue in the Main Library, second floor, records practically all the books in the Main Library, departmental libraries and in the co-ordinate libraries. Author, subject and title cards are interfiled in one alphabetical sequence.

Classification. Dewey and Library of Congress. Since 1965 a changeover from Dewey to LC has been taking place. Some of the newer libraries, and the General Reference Department, are entirely in LC classification.

Copying/Photography. Photocopying facilities are available in the main library and major library branches. Application should be made to the Director's Office for private photography.

Friends of the Library. Associates of the Stanford University Libraries. Regular Membership Fee $25 p.a. Various other memberships available.

Hoover Institution on War, Revolution and Peace, Stanford

STANFORD
Library of the Hoover Institution on War, Revolution and Peace
Stanford, California 94305
Tel. 415-497-2062, Ext 2062

History. Since its founding by Herbert Hoover in 1919 as a special collection dealing with the causes and consequences of World War I, the Hoover Institution has become a national and international centre for documentation and research on problems of political, economic and social change in the 20th century. The collections today include government documents, files of newspapers, MS memoirs, diaries and personal papers of men and women important in world affairs, publications of ephemeral societies and of resistance and underground movements, etc. Mr. Hoover's desire that the Institution should 'promote peace' was coupled with a concern for the preservation and enhancement of individual liberty. Accordingly renewed attention is being given to issues of domestic importance as well as to international problems. The 285 feet high Hoover Tower was completed in 1941, while the Lou Henry Hoover Building, named for the founder's wife, which adjoins the Tower on the east, was dedicated in 1967. Current holdings total over 1 million books and periodicals, 3,700 archival units, 30,000 newspaper and periodical titles and 20,000 microfilms.

Special Collections and Treasures. The Library's holdings comprise area collections on Western Europe, Eastern Europe, Africa, the Middle East, East Asia and Latin America, and material on revolutionary movements, peace movements, communism and international relations. The Western European Collection includes the diary of Joseph Goebbels, some office files of Himmler, microfilmed archives of the Nazi party and documents of the International Military Tribunal at Nuremberg. In the Russian Collection are the Okhrana Archives, files of the Paris office of the Russian secret police (which were given secretly to the Hoover Institution after World War I by Maklakov, the last pre-Soviet Russian Ambassador to France). The Herbert Hoover Archives document the career of Hoover as a humanitarian and administrator.

Exhibition Areas. The Herbert Hoover and Lou Henry Hoover Rooms on either side of the Tower rotunda contain memorabilia of the 31st President and his wife. In the lobby of the Lou Henry Hoover Building are displays of Chinese paintings and other art objects.

Hours. Western Language Collections: Mon.-Fri. 0815-1730, Sat. 0800-1300. Closed Sun. East Asian Collection: Mon.-Fri. 0800-1700, Sat. 0900-1300. Closed Sun. Closed 1 Jan., Washington's Birthday, Memorial Day, 4 July, Labor Day, Thanksgiving Day and the following Fri., 24-25 Dec.

Transport. (See preceding entry.)

Parking. Parking facilities available within one block.

Admission. Readers: Readers should register at Loan Desks. Facilities of the Library are available to all scholars and students of college level and above, and to others doing serious research. Western Language Collection in the Tower. East Asia Collection in the Lou Henry Hoover Building.
Visitors: Tour to the top of the tower, 25 cents. Hours: Mon.-Fri. 1000-1155, 1300-1555, Sat. 1000-1200, 1300-1555, Sun. 1200-1620.

Information. In the front lobby.

Sales. Tourist guides to Stanford University sold in the lobby.

Guidebooks. Guide to the Library of the Hoover Institution on War, Revolution and Peace, and a small brochure on *The Hoover Institution on War, Revolution and Peace.* Both free of charge.

Restaurant/Snack Facilities. None in the Library but available on campus.

Services. Typing rooms, lavatories, telephones, lift to observation platform.

Catalogues. Dictionary card catalogue; author, title and subject. Various special catalogues. The catalogues are located in two rooms to the left and right of the Tower's inner lobby, and in inner lobby of the Lou Henry Hoover Building.

Classification. Library of Congress.

Copying/Photography. Microfilm, copyflo prints from microfilm, direct copy and other types of reproduction are available. Information may be obtained from a reference librarian or at the Photographic Service Desk, Room 113, Tower. The Library does not maintain facilities for photocopying or similar forms of reproduction. Limited copying may be done at the Stanford University Library or at other campus facilities. Readers are permitted to use their own cameras for both picture taking and copying of non-archival material.

Friends of the Library. (See preceding entry.)

URBANA
University of Illinois Library at Urbana-Champaign
University of Illinois, Urbana, Illinois 61801
Tel. (217) 333-0790

University of Illinois Library, Urbana

History. The University of Illinois began instruction in 1868 as the Illinois Industrial University, a name it retained until 1885. The original book collection was kept in a room behind the office of the first Regent, Dr. J.M. Gregory, who had purchased 644 volumes in New York in 1868. As the collection grew, it was moved successively into a former dining room in the original University Building and then into its own room in University Hall, when that building was erected in 1874. By 1897 the Library still only contained some 30,000 volumes but growth was stimulated by the occupation in that year of the first separate library building, later named Altgeld Hall. The Library remained there until 1929, when it occupied the first three modules of the present building. It has since expanded six times, four of the additions being stack and storage areas, the last being completed in 1969. In addition, 35 departmental libraries are in existence, 15 within the Main Library building and 20 in other buildings on campus. Total holdings now include 5,072,962 volumes, 1,084,938 microforms, 7,585 MSS and 425,307 maps and aerial photographs.

Special Collections and Treasures. Collections include the Franklin J. Meine Collection of American Humour and Folklore; the Baskette Collection on Freedom of Expression; the Muierhead Collection on William Cobbett; the Richard B. Harwell Collection of Confederate Imprints; the Hollander Library of Economic History; the Nickell Collection of 18th century English Literature; the William Bentley and Grant Richards Collections on 19th century publishing; the Ernost Ingold Shakespeare Collection; the T.W. Baldwin Elizabethan Library; and collections focussing on Abraham Lincoln, John Milton, Carl Sandberg, H.G. Wells, Thomas Hardy, Somerset Maugham, Winston Churchill and Daniel Defoe.

Exhibition Areas.   16 exhibit cases in Rare Book Room, 346 Main Library. On the first floor corridor of the Main Library there are also six exhibit cases on various themes, plus one permanent exhibit case of Lincoln material.

Hours.   Mon.-Fri. 0800-2200, Sat. 0900-2200, Sun. 1300-2200. Shorter hours or closed during major hols. and semester breaks.

Transport.   Air, rail and bus service to Urbana-Champaign.

Parking.   Metered parking available on campus.

Admission.   Readers and *Visitors:* No regulations.

Information.   Main Library, rooms 200 and 203.

Sales.   None.

Guidebooks.   Available in English, free of charge.

Restaurant/Snack Facilities.   Vending facilities in tunnel between Main and Undergraduate libraries, accessible during all hours when Library is open.

Services.   Typing rooms in Undergraduate Library, lavatories in all locations, lifts in Main and Undergraduate libraries, smoking area in tunnel between Main and Undergraduate libraries, pay telephones available in several locations.

Catalogues.   Dictionary card catalogue (located on 2nd floor). Central serial record (in card form). Public shelf list (in card form).

Classification.   Dewey (in most locations).

Copying/Photography.   Coin-operated copiers available in several locations. Photographic Service located in

Room 66, Main Library. Private photography usually allowed. Photography of Library material, however, must be cleared with the Library Office, Room 230, Main Library.

Friends of the Library. University of Illinois Library Friends at Urbana-Champaign. Membership subscription varies, according to type.

WASHINGTON
Folger Shakespeare Library
201 East Capitol Street, Washington, DC 20003
Tel. (202) 546-4800

History. The Library is the bequest of Henry Clay Folger and his wife, Emily Jordan Folger. Mr. Folger's interest in literature, particularly in Shakespeare, developed during his student days at Amherst College and continued throughout his lifetime. He and his wife collected books, manuscripts, paintings and other materials related to Shakespeare, Shakespeare's contemporaries, and the history of the Elizabethan theatre. The Folger Collection forms the basis of the Library's holdings. Subsequent acquisitions have expanded the collection so that it reflects all aspects of civilisation of the 16th and 17th centuries. Folger was associated throughout his business career with the Standard Oil Company of New York and became president of the company in 1911. Although a resident of the New York City area, Folger elected to build the Library in the nation's capital, close to the Capitol Building itself and adjacent to the Library of Congress. The cornerstone was laid in May 1930, two weeks before Folger's death. The building was completed in April 1932. To ensure adequate maintenance and expansion of the collection, Folger provided for a generous endowment which was later supplemented by a similar bequest by Mrs. Folger who died in 1936. By the terms of Folger's will, the Library is administered by the Trustees of Amherst College, Amherst, Massachusetts. Current holdings include just over 250,000 volumes, 40,000 MSS and 4,800 microfilms.

Special Collections and Treasures. No other library has a collection of Shakespeare's work larger than that in the Folger. Folger's acquisitions included, for example, 79 copies of the first folio edition of 1623, 58 copies of the second folio of 1632, 24 copies of the third folio of 1663-4 and 36 copies of the fourth folio of 1685. The Library's coverage of Tudor-Stuart English civilisation was greatly augmented by the purchase in 1938 of the Sir Leicester Harmsworth Collection of over 11,000 items, strong in Elizabethan history, exploration and theology. Other collections include the Dobell Collection of Dryden and Drydeniana; the Loseley House MSS, consisting of the extant records of the Office of the Revels in England from the reign of Henry VIII through

The Folger Shakespeare Library, Washington, DC

the early years of Elizabeth I; the Bacon-Townshend Collection; the Bagot Collection; and the Newdigate newsletters.

Exhibition Areas. The Exhibition Gallery houses a permanent display of Shakespearean items and changing topical exhibits of books, manuscripts and items from the Library's collections. The Exhibition Gallery and Elizabethan Theatre are open Mon.-Sat. 1000-1630 (Sun. from 15 April to Labor Day).

Hours. Reading Room: Mon.-Sat. 0845-1645. Closed Sun. and public hols.

Transport. Metrobus: 30, 31, 32, 34, 36, 39, 40 (marked 'Stadium'), 52 or 54 (marked 'Navy Yard'), 96 or 98 (marked 'D.C. General').

Parking. Street parking available.

Admission. Readers: Open to advanced scholars and holders of a doctoral degree or equivalent. Identification from an academic institution or other acceptable source is required. Space limitations exclude undergraduate or beginning graduate students.
Visitors: Admitted to the Exhibition Gallery and Elizabethan Theatre, free of charge.

Information. Guard in 2nd Street lobby and/or Registrar in Front Office.

Sales. In 2nd Street lobby. Posters, maps, books, cards, slide sets available.

Guidebooks. In preparation.

Restaurant/Snack Facilities. Afternoon tea available for readers in the tea room.

Services. Reading and smoking lounge for readers in Founder's Room.

Catalogues. Published catalogues: catalogue of printed books (1970-) 28 volumes, catalogues for manuscripts (1971-) 3 volumes. Card catalogues: former owner catalogue, chronological catalogues 1455-1800, art catalogue, catalogue of prompt books, catalogue of playbills.

Classification. Library of Congress.

Copying/Photography. Coin-operated photocopier in the Periodicals Reading Room. Other forms of reproduction available through Library staff. Private cameras may not be used in the Library.

Friends of the Library. Friends of the Folger Library. Membership by invitation. Fee $50.00 p.a.

William Shakespeare, Comedies, Histories and Tragedies, first folio edition (London, 1623), in the Folger Shakespeare Library, Washington, DC

WASHINGTON
Library of Congress
10 First Street, SE, Washington, DC 20540
Tel. (202) 426-5000

History. The Library was founded in 1800 on the transfer of Congress to Washington. Today its services have been extended to other branches of the Government, to the library community and to the public at large. It still serves as the research arm for Congress, while also carrying out the functions of the national library of the United States. The first Library collection of 3,000 volumes was totally destroyed in 1814 when, during the Anglo-American War, the Capitol was fired by British troops. It was reconstituted with much private assistance and the purchase of Thomas Jefferson's library of 6,000 volumes for $23,950. Except for law books and public documents, growth was slow and it took another fire in 1851, which reduced the stock to 20,000 volumes, to awaken public interest. In 1852 Congress voted $10,000 for immediately needed books, and then later another $75,000. It was, however, the librarianship of Ainsworth R. Spofford (1864-1897), which effectively transformed the Library from a legislative into a national institution. In 1865 a new act strengthened the copyright system (in force since 1848) and then in 1866 the Smithsonian Institution's collection of proceedings and publications of learned societies, amounting to 40,000 volumes, was transferred to the Library. In 1867 Congress bought for $100,000 the Peter Force Collection of 60,000 volumes of Americana. The present Main Building designed in Italian Renaissance style was occupied in 1897 and an annexe was added in 1939. The Librarian from 1899-1939 was Herbert Putnam, whose achievements could be compared to those of Panizzi for the British Museum (British Library). The massive growth in both the collections and the importance of the Library of Congress in national and international bibliographical systems has placed an increasing strain on the Library's physical resources. It is hoped that the James Madison Memorial Building will be completed in 1977 and will allow the consolidation of the Library's facilities now located in and around the Washington D.C. area. Current holdings total 73,932,425 items including 16,761,198 books, 31,498,669 MSS and 3,531,304 maps.

Special Collections and Treasures. The Library is particularly rich in material on Social and Political Science; History, especially American History and Civilisation; Science and Technology including probably the world's largest collection of Aeronautical Literature; Bibliography; Music, and Japanese, Chinese and Russian Collections (the largest outside the Orient and the Soviet Union respectively). Special Collections include Books for the Blind; the Cartographic Collection; the Law Library; the Manuscripts Collection, including papers of most of the Presidents from George

Library of Congress,
Washington, DC

Washington through Calvin Coolidge, of many other statesmen, military, scientific and literary leaders of numerous enterprises and institutions; Records of the Virginia Company of London; the American Colonization Society; the League of Women Voters; the National Association for the Advancement of Colored People; Russian Church Records from Alaska; the Harkness Collection (Mexican and Peruvian); and the Herndon-Weik Collection (Lincolniana). The Music Collection is probably the largest collection (more than 3 million items) of music and music literature in the world. It includes autograph MSS and letters of Bach, Haydn, Mozart, Beethoven, Weber, Schubert, Mendelssohn, Schumann, Liszt, Brahms, Wagner, Delibes, Schoenberg, Bartók, Hindemith and others; also of MacDowell, Herbert, Sousa, Chadwick, Taylor, Carpenter, Copland, Barber, Rodgers, Sowerby, Piston, Bernstein and other notable Americans. Separate and distinct collections of great value are included in the holdings of the Elizabeth Sprague Coolidge Foundation; Gertrude Clarke Whittall Foundation; Serge Koussevitzky Music Foundation; Rachmaninoff Archives, and the Fritz Kreisler Collection. Other collections include the Microfilm Collection; the Motion Picture Film Collection; the Prints and Photographs Collection; the Serials Collection, and the Technical Reports Collection. The Rare Books Collection includes the Lessing J. Rosenwald Collection of Incunabula and Rare Books; the Miniature Collection of Books (less than 10cm. in height); the Frederic W. Goudy Collection of Type Design; the Charles Edward Banks Collection of American Genealogy; the Jean Hersholt Collection of Hans Christian Andersen; the Dime Novels Collection circa 1860-1900; the John Boyd Thacher Collection of Incunabula, Early Americana and History of the French Revolution; Adolf Hitler's Library; the Harry Houdini and McManus-Young Collections of Magic; Spanish American Imprints 1543-1800; the Winter Palace Collection of Russian Military, Administrative and Social History, and the Woodrow Wilson Library.

Exhibition Areas. Permanent exhibits of the 'Treasures of Early Printing' are on view in the first floor exhibits area in the Main Building; some historic documents and presidential papers can be seen in the 2nd floor exhibit area. Changing exhibits of a variety of items from the Library's collections are shown in the corridor galleries of the Main Building, on the 5th floor of the Annex Building and, on a small scale, in exhibit cases in individual reading rooms. Hours of exhibitions: Mon.-Fri. 0830-2130, Sat., Sun. 0830-1800.

Hours. Main Reading Room: Mon.-Fri. 0830-2130, Sat. 0830-1700, Sun. 1300-1700. Closed 25 Dec., Memorial Day, 4 July, Labor Day and Thanksgiving Day. Only the Main Exhibition Halls are open.

Transport. The Library is on First Street, SE between Independence Avenue and East Capitol Street and can

Abraham Lincoln, manuscript of the Gettysburg Address, in the Library of Congress, Washington, DC

be reached by bus nos. 30, 54, 37. Current information may be obtained from the Washington Metropolitan Area Transit Authority.

Parking. No parking spaces at the Library or in nearby streets.

Admission. Readers: Readers of college age and over may use the Library without restriction. However registration is required in certain reading rooms, such as the Manuscript and Rare Book Rooms, in order to protect the source material.
Visitors: Visitors of all ages are welcome. Free guided tours of approximately 45 minutes, every hour from 0900-1600, Mon.-Fri. Arrangements for group tours should be made in advance with the Tour Office.

Information. Desk in the west lobby of the Main Building (open Mon.-Sat. 0830-1645, Sun. 1300-1700).

Sales. At the Information Desk. Library of Congress publications including books, facsimiles, greeting cards, slides, postcards and posters are sold.

Guidebooks. Information leaflets in English are available free of charge. Translations in French, German, Spanish and Japanese are also available.

Restaurant/Snack Facilities. The Library Cafeteria serves breakfast and lunch from Mon.-Fri. (reached via the tunnel connecting the Main Building with the Annex); open to the public but for a portion of the lunch hour only Library staff may use it. Concession stands and vending machines are in snack bars in both buildings, open all week.

Services. Typewriters are permitted in some of the special reading rooms but not in the general reading rooms. Permits for typewriters and tape-recorders are issued by the Stack and Reader Division. Checkstands, lavatories, lifts and telephones in both the Main and Annex Buildings. Smoking permitted in the Cafeteria, snack bars, rest rooms and certain other designated areas.

Catalogues. Card catalogue housed in the Main Reading Room and adjoining corridors and rooms in the Main Building. Printed book catalogues available at a number of locations throughout the Library. There are also catalogues for special collections of the Library.

Classification. Library of Congress.

Copying/Photography. Coin-operated machines are available in several of the reading rooms. The Photo-duplication Service of the Library in the Annex Building is open Mon.-Fri. 0830-1630. Cameras are allowed in the Library but signs indicate restricted areas. The use of personal copiers is discouraged. Flash bulbs must not be used in the Visitors' Gallery.

WORCESTER
American Antiquarian Society Library
185 Salisbury Street, Worcester, Massachusetts 01609
Tel. (617) 755-5221

History.   The American Antiquarian Society is a learned society which was founded in 1812, largely through the activities of Isaiah Thomas, who had been the leading printer, editor, publisher and bookseller in the United States after the American Revolutionary War. Thomas gave $20,000 and his library of 8,000 volumes to the Society, which was established at Worcester because of its inland site (and hence safety from the guns of the British fleet). The aims of the Society included 'the collection and preservation of the antiquities of our country.' The activities of the Society covered a wide field in its early years. It was while on his way west to begin the scientific exploration of Indian mounds that one of its early librarians was killed in Ohio. The growth of anthropology and related sciences at the Smithsonian Institution and like organisations, made it obvious that more could be accomplished by specialisation and in 1910 the Society abandoned active anthropological work, broke up its museum, and constructed a building, its third, specifically designed as a research library. This library building contains twenty miles of bookshelves, currently holding 610,000 books and pamphlets, 5,160,000 newspapers, 300,000 graphic and ephemera units, 1,500 boxes and 3,400 volumes of MSS. The Society regularly publishes its *Proceedings* as well as monographs and bibliographies.

Special Collections and Treasures.   The Library as such preserves the largest single collection of printed source material relating to the history, literature and culture of the first 250 years of what is now the United States. A notable special collection is the Mather Library, which was built up by three of the most learned of early Anglo-Americans and was the largest private library in the colonies during the colonial period. In 1816 what remained of it came to the Society where it is preserved, largely in its original bindings, in the Council Room. Treasures include one of the eleven extant copies of the *Bay Psalm Book*; the unique copy of Franklin's printing of *Pamela: or virtue rewarded* (Philadelphia, 1742); and Richard Mather's MS of the *Cambridge platform, a model of church-government* (1649).

Exhibition Areas.   The main Exhibit Room is to the right of the main entrance. The display changes six times a year. Other exhibition areas are on the Rotunda Balcony and in the Graphics Office.

Hours.   Mon.-Fri. 0900-1700. Closed Sat., Sun. and public hols.

Transport.   Taxi from the airport, railway station and bus depot in Worcester. (The Library is located at the

American Antiquarian Society, Worcester, Massachusetts

corner of Park Avenue and Salisbury Streets (Routes 9 and 12).

Parking. Carpark at the rear of the building, Regent Street side.

Admission. Readers: Must sign in at the Library entrance and consult the Director or Associate Librarian. No charges.
Visitors: Must sign in at the entrance. No charges.

Information. At the main entrance.

Sales. Sales at the Main Control Desk in the Reading Room. (All publications are distributed by the University Press of Virginia, Charlottesville).

Guidebooks. None. Brochure in English available, free.

Restaurant/Snack Facilities. None.

Services. Typing may be done in the Reading Room, cloakrooms and lavatories at the main entrance, ramp available for wheelchairs, smoking lounge in the Exhibition Room at the main entrance, public telephone in the workroom of the Reading Room.

Catalogues. Card catalogue. Book catalogue published 1971 by Greenwood Publishing Co.

Classification. Own.

Copying/Photography. Photocopies may be ordered at the Main Desk. Readex-Dennison copying in the Microform Room. Private photography only allowed with the Director's permission.

Friends of the Library. Membership of the Society is by election only (limited to a total of 300).

Vatican City

VATICAN CITY
Biblioteca Apostolica Vaticana
00120 Città del Vaticano
Tel. 698 33 23

History. The Vatican Library is the library of the Popes. In 1295, under Pope Bonifacius VIII, the Library is known to have contained 443 works. A number of volumes were dispersed after 1345, while many were transported to Avignon on the establishment there of the Holy See. The origins of the present collection lie with Pope Nicholas V, who took office in 1447. In the short

Biblioteca Apostolica Vaticana

period until his death in 1455 the Library's stock rose from 340 to 1,200 volumes. The Library grew so rapidly under successive Popes that the old Floreria beneath the Borgia Apartment was no longer capable of holding it. Sixtus V (1585-90) therefore commissioned Domenico Fontana to design the Salone Sistina, erected 1587-9. The 17th century brought many collections to the Library, including the Palatine Library, the library of the Dukes of Urbino and the MSS and books which had belonged to Queen Christina of Sweden. In the late 19th century under Leo XIII the archives were opened to scholars of all nations and some 60,000 reference books assembled in the vast new Sala di Consultazione. Further modernisations and enlargements have taken place in the 20th century. Current holdings include 700,000 printed works, 61,697 MS volumes, 100,000 separate autograph items and 100,000 maps and prints.

Special Collections and Treasures. The Library possesses twelve 'core' collections: the *Vaticani* (pre-1622); the *Palatini* (presented in 1622 by Maximilian I); the *Urbinates* (purchased by Alexander VII); the *Reginenses* (formerly the property of Queen Christina and including Greek and Latin MSS of Pius II); the *Capponiani* (bequeathed 1745 by the Marquis A.G. Capponi); the *Ottoboniani;* the *Borghesiani;* the *Barberiniani;* the *Chisiani* (collected by Fabio Chigi and later by Alexander VII); the *Ferrajoli* (bequeathed 1926); the *Ruoli* and *Introiti e esiti,* both from the offices of the Roman Curia. Incunabula number about 6,000, besides several hundred duplicates. Treasures include the *Codex B Vaticanus* (4th century), the best representative of the Alexandrine text of the Greek Bible; the only manuscript of Cicero's, *De republica;* the *Vatican Virgil* (4th century) and the *Roman Virgil* (5th century), the oldest surviving Roman illustrated manuscripts; the *Vatican Gospels,* an 8th century Anglo-Saxon manuscript; the *Lorsch Gospels* (9th century) of the school of Trier; the *Homilies* of Jacobus Monachus of Kokkinobaphos, a 12th century copy of earlier Gospel illustration; Frederick II's illustrated book of falconry of the 13th century; the Ferrarese *Divina Commedia* (15th century) illuminated by Guglielmo and Alessandro Giraldi and Franco de'Russi; a vellum copy of the *editio princeps* of Homer (Florence, 1488); and a copy of the *Directorium Horarum Canonicarum,* printed by Juan Luschner at the monastery of Montserrat in 1500.

Exhibition Areas. The exhibition rooms of the Library are the Museum of Pagan Antiquities, the Clementine Gallery, the Alexandrine Room, the Pauline Rooms, the Sistine Hall, the Sistine Rooms and the Gallery of Urban VIII. The Sistine Hall contains a display of some of the most valuable MSS and printed books.

Hours. Mon.-Sat. 0830-1330. Closed: Sun., 16 July-15 Sept., and public hols.

Transport. City of Rome transportation system to the

Vatican.

Parking.   Facilities available.

Admission. Readers: Only qualified scholars at a middle/high level of research, in the fields of humanities, history, philology, philosophy, theology, paleography. Foreign scholars/students will need their passport, letters of introduction and two passport-type photographs. These should be presented at the Porta S. Anna in the Via de Porta Angelica and the Segretaria of the Library.
Visitors: Apply to the Librarian.

Information.   In the Reading Room.

Sales.   No sales desk but a Sales Department with many Library publications available.

Guidebooks.   La Biblioteca Apostolica Vaticana (1970), in Italian.

Restaurant/Snack Facilities.   None.

Services.   Cloakroom, lavatories, lifts (for invalids), telephones.

Catalogues.   Various card catalogues. Catalogues of manuscripts, catalogues of exhibitions, catalogues of printed books, all published.

Classification.   Local schemes, except for Bibliographical Information Centre, which uses Class Z of the Library of Congress system.

Copying/Photography.   Photocopies, microfilm and other forms of photographic reproduction available through Library staff. Private photography not permitted.

Venezuela

CARACAS
Biblioteca Nacional
Apartado 6525, Caracas 101
Tel. (not available)

History.   The Library opened to the public on 19 April 1841, after previous attempts at establishing a National Library had failed in 1811, 1831 and 1833. It owed its foundation to the activity of the literary society Liceo Venezolano, which had begun collecting books some years earlier. The Liceo eventually handed over 2,000 volumes to the Library, which was initially located in the

Biblioteca Nacional, Caracas

San Francisco Convent. By 1857 it possessed 9,830 volumes. On 17 December 1852 it was relocated in the Universidad Central, where it remained until 1903 when it moved into a separate building. It occupied its present building in 1912 and was extended by an annex in 1938. A new building has been planned since 1958 and the present extensive development plans call for the Library to serve as a public and school library, in addition to fulfilling its national responsibilities. When the public and school libraries develop their own systems they will move out, providing expansion space for the National Library. The Library now constitutes one of the departments of the Instituto Nacional de Cultura y Bellas Artes, with current holdings totalling 800,000 volumes and 4,000 periodicals.

Special Collections and Treasures. Collections include the Rudolph Dolge Collection of 20,000 volumes, purchased in 1941, rich in Venezuelan material, including a large collection of newspapers and periodicals dating from about 1810; the Pedro M. Arcaya Collection of more than 70,000 volumes donated by his descendants; the 'Venezuelan Incunabula' Collection (printed 1808-21); the Aristides Rojas Collection of 1,000 volumes; the Dr. Lucio Arocha Collection, primarily literary works; the Dr. José L. Andarra Collection, with a set of the famous liberation journal *El Correo del Orinoco* (Angostura, 1818-22); the Music Archive incorporating the José Angel Montero Collection; and the Official Paper Collection.

Exhibition Areas. Planned for the new building.

Hours. Mon.-Sat. 0800-2200. Open Sun. but no details available about hours. Closed public hols.

Transport. Buses pass close to the Library. Details not available.

Parking. In front of the Library.

Admission. Readers and *Visitors:* Open to students of all kinds and the public in general. (The Library may, however, be closed during the projected rebuilding and reorganisation.)

Information. Reference Section.

Sales. None.

Guidebooks. Planned for the new building.

Restaurant/Snack Facilities. Planned for the new building.

Services. No details available.

Catalogues. No details available.

Classification.   Library of Congress.

Copying/Photography.   Photocopies   and   microfilm copying available through Library staff.

Friends of the Library.   In existence but no details available.

Viet-Nam, Democratic Republic of

HANOI
Thu Viên Quōc Gia Viet Nam (National Library of the Democratic Republic of Viet-Nam)
31 Tràng Thi, Hanoi
Tel. 2643

History.   The Library was founded in 1918 as the Central Library, Hanoi, although subsequently it became known as the Pierre Pasquier Library and the General Library, Hanoi. Thanks to numerous gifts and the system of legal deposit the collections grew steadily and by 1954, before the partition of Viet-Nam, they totalled over 155,000 books and 2,300 journals. Most of the books were in French, about 17,000 were in Vietnamese and half the periodicals were published in Indo-China. The total after partition is now put at only 120,000 volumes, as the French, on withdrawing from Viet-Nam, are reputed to have taken with them 851 boxes of books and manuscripts belonging to the Library. From 1954 to 1957 the Library functioned as the Central Library and it was not until June 1957 that a directive from the Ministry of Culture changed the name to National Library. The Library is the largest public library in Viet-Nam and acts as a centre for library science and methodology, for the storage and preservation of national publications and for bibliographical activities. Current holdings total more than 1 million books and MSS, 7,000 periodicals and newspapers and more than 2,000 rolls of microfilm.

Special Collections and Treasures.   Despite the losses suffered in 1954 the Library is rich in materials dealing with Indo-China in general and Viet-Nam in particular.

Exhibition Areas.   New books and periodicals are displayed in a small room off the General Reading Room. Special displays, to coincide with lectures, are mounted in the Conference Hall.

Hours.   Open daily: 0800-2100. Closed National Day, 25 Dec., 1 Jan., May Day and Tét (1st of Lunar Year, which often falls in the latter half of Jan. or earlier half of Feb.).

National Library of the Democratic Republic of Viet-Nam, Hanoi

Transport.   Trams and buses run to the Library.

Parking.   No parking facilities available.

Admission.   Readers: Must have a University degree or its equivalent and undergraduates are only admitted temporarily for research purposes.
Visitors: Welcome, but they should give advance notice of their date of visit.

Information.   In the General Reading Hall.

Sales.   None.

Guidebooks.   A guide to the Library is available, free of charge, in Vietnamese. A more detailed guide is planned.

Restaurant/Snack Facilities.   None.

Services.   Readers can request to use the typing room and the telephone booth in the Library. Lavatories are only a few minutes' walk from the reading rooms.

Catalogues.   Author-title and systematic catalogues. Subject catalogue 1918-1960.

Classification.   1918-1960, subject classification. Since 1960, modified Universal Decimal Classification.

Copying/Photography.   The Library is equipped with microfilm cameras and photocopiers. Permission must be sought for private photography.

Yugoslavia

BELGRADE
Narodna biblioteka Socijalističke Republike Srbije
(National Library of the Socialist Republic of Serbia)
11000 Beograd, Skerlićeva 1
Tel. 451-242 to 9

History.   The Library was founded as the town library of Belgrade in 1832 and took on national responsibilities when, in the same year, it began to receive deposit publications. In the 1850s the Library adopted the title 'Narodna biblioteka', under the librarianship of Duro Daničić. During the last thirty years of the 19th century the Library was, at different times, a department of the Ministry of Education, the Museum and the Serbian Academy of Sciences. The National Library Act of 1901 adapted the functions and organization of the Library to the requirements of contemporary librarianship. In 1915 the Library was sacked by enemy troops. Damages, losses and lack of space made reconstruction after 1918

National Library of Serbia, Belgrade. New building under construction

difficult, but thanks to the endeavours of the Librarian, J. Tomić, a part of the Library's collection was repatriated from Sofia, and a new building was opened to the public in 1925. In 1928 the Library began receiving legal deposit copies of works published in Yugoslavia, thus gradually building up a considerable collection, only once more to lose over half a million volumes during the bombing of Belgrade on 6 April 1941, which entailed the destruction of over 1,300 Cyrillic manuscripts from the 15th to the 18th centuries as well as the inestimable loss of the whole collection of works published between 1832 and 1941. In 1945 the Ministry of Education decided that all public libraries should donate their rarities to the National Library. By the end of 1946 the Library had 133,574 items, made available to the public in an adapted hotel on 30 April 1947. Construction of a new Library began only in 1966, the official inauguration taking place on 6 April 1973. Current holdings total 1.5 million volumes.

Special Collections and Treasures. Collections include the libraries of Dr. Tihomir Djordjević (18,000 books and 6,000 archivalia); Dr. Peter Kolendić (6,000 books); Milan Rakić, the poet (2,000 books), and Professor Veselin Čajkanović (20,000 books); Treasures include an early 13th century MS, *Paroemien;* the 14th century *Four Gospels* from Dovolja Monastery; the *Biographies of Serbian Saints* (c., 1370); the *Four Gospels* written by Silvestar (1570); and the original MS of *Karageorge,* an unpublished tragedy in 3 parts by Simo Milutinović-Sarajlija, dating from 1847.

Exhibition Areas. Two exhibition rooms in the Lounge and the Gallery.

Hours. Mon.-Sat. 0800-2000. Closed Sun. and public hols.

Transport. Buses: 12 and 13. Trams: 9 and 10.

Parking. Available at the Library.

Admission. Readers: Adults over 18 may use the Library. A small charge is made. A Library card is issued on the basis of identity papers.
Visitors: Free of charge.

Information. Desk near the catalogues on the 1st floor.

Sales. Foreign bookshop and second hand bookshop within the Library.

Guidebooks. Guides available in English, French, German and Russian. Free of charge.

Restaurant/Snack Facilities. None.

Services. Cloakroom, telephone and lavatories on the ground floor. Smokers' lounge and lavatories on 1st floor and the Gallery.

Catalogues. Various author catalogues. Subject and periodical catalogues. Classified catalogue near completion, as is the Central Catalogue of the Serbian Socialist Republic. The catalogues are located on the 1st floor.

Classification. Universal Decimal Classification.

Copying/Photography. Photocopier in front of the Reading Room available to readers. Photo-laboratory in the basement. Private photography only with the permission of the Library authorities.

Friends of the Library. The Society of National Library Friends.

LJUBLJANA
Narodna in univerzitetna knjižnica (National and University Library)
61011 Ljubljana p.p. 259, Turjaška 1
Tel. 23 197 (Central); 22 045 (Information)

History. The Library was founded in 1774 from the stock remaining after the fire of the Jesuit Collegium. In 1790 holdings totalled 19,000 volumes, a figure achieved by material received 1784-86 from the secularised monasteries. In 1791 the Library was handed to the Lyceum of Ljubljana and in 1794 opened to the public. In 1807 it was given the right to receive deposit copies from the Duchy of Carniola. When the Lyceum was abolished in 1850, the Library took the name Studienbibliothek until 1918, when the Yugoslav State was formed and it assumed the name of State Library. After the foundation of the Slovenian University, the Library took over the functions of the University Library, which title was not conferred until 1938. In 1941 the Library moved into new buildings, which were partly damaged when a German plane crashed into them on 29 January 1944 destroying 60,000 books. By February 1947 the Library was fully restored and given its present title. The National and University Library is the only Yugoslav deposit library in Slovenia (since 1919) and currently contains 1,053,000 items.

Special Collections and Treasures. The Library's collections relate to all fields of the humanities and the sciences but the materials of greatest importance are classified as Slavica and Slovenica and are based on materials left by J. Japelj, Ž. Zois and J. Kopitar and on the writings of M. Čop, E. Korytko, F. Prešern, M. Kastelić, S. Vraz, F. Levstik, S. Gregorčič, I. Cankar, A. Aškerc, I. Prijatelj, M. Murko, F. Finžgar and others. The Music Collection (over 50,000 volumes) includes numerous works from the Renaissance period (e.g. those of the Slovenian composer Jakob Gallus Carniolus), as well as sheet music and phonograph records. The Manuscript Collection includes Istrian Glagolitic texts as well as

National and University Library, Ljubljana

material for the study of the Slovenian history and the Slovenian literary past (including documents from World War II). The Reference Collection is rich in Slovenian reference works, notable examples of which are F. Simonič, *Slovenska bibliografija, I. del. Knjige* (1550-1900) (Ljubljana, 1903-05), and its continuation by J. Slebinger, *Slovenski časniki i časopisi: bibliografski pregled od 1797-1936* (reprint from *Razstava slovenskega novinarstva v Ljubljana*, Ljubljana, 1937).

Exhibition Areas. Exhibition Room, small permanent exhibition of rare books and MSS. Various temporary exhibitions.

Hours. Main Reading Room: Mon.-Fri. 0700-2100, Sat. 0700-1400. Closed Sun. and public hols. During July and Aug. the Library is closed in the afternoons.

Transport. Bus or trolley-bus. The bus station is outside the railway station. (The Library is situated in the centre of Ljubljana.)

Parking. Available.

Admission. Readers: Adults over 18 with proof of identity. A small fee is charged.
Visitors: Apply to the Library Director. Free admission.

Information. First floor, Room 63.

Sales. None.

Guidebooks. A new edition is in preparation. The former guidebook is out of print.

Restaurant/Snack Facilities. None.

Services. Cloakrooms, lavatories, smoking areas, telephones.

Catalogues. Author, subject and classified catalogues. Various special catalogues.

Classification. Universal Decimal Classification.

Copying/Photography. Copying machines available. Permission required from Library Director for private photography.

SKOPJE
Narodna i univerzitetska biblioteka 'Kliment Ohridski'
(*'Kliment Ohridski' National and University Library*)
91000 Skopje, Ul. 'Goce Delčev' bb
Tel. 34360; 50301; 50303

History. The Library was founded on 23 November 1944, with holdings inherited from the former library of the

Faculty of Philosophy in Skopje. Deposit privileges, for material published throughout Yugoslavia, were received in 1945 and these have ensured a steady growth of the collections. In 1958 the Library's name was changed from 'National' to 'National and University Library' and it now constitutes the central library of the library network of the Socialist Republic of Macedonia (SRM). The earthquake which devastated Skopje on 26 July 1963 destroyed most of the Library buildings. After the earthquake the Library occupied prefabricated buildings, while the collections were partly housed in the Art Gallery. The new Library building was completed in 1971 and formally opened in 1972. Holdings currently include 800,000 volumes, 1,527 microfilms and 4,587 MSS.

'Kliment Ohridski' National and University Library, Skopje

Special Collections and Treasures. The Rare Book Collection includes 33 Slavic, nine Latin and two Greek manuscripts. The oldest Cyrillic MS is a fragment of the *Posen triod* in its 13th-century Macedonian version. Other treasures include *Časoslov* (1566), printed in Venice by Jakov from Kamena Reka; *Četirijazičnikot* (1802), by D. Moskopoljac; *Ogledalo* (1816) and *Utešenie grešnim* (1840), by K. Pejčinović. The graphic and cartographic material stresses works relative to Macedonia and the art of D. Avramski-Gute, D. Perčinskovski and P. Hadzi-Boskov, while the Music Collection has over 100 MSS, the legacy of S. Mihajlov and V. Nikolovski, and posters and programmes of the Skopje Philharmonic Orchestra (1946-72).

Exhibition Areas. Apart from the Main Exhibition Room on the ground floor, the entrance hall is also used to display material.

Hours. Mon.-Fri. 0730-2000, Sat. 0730-1900. Closed Sun. and public hols.

Transport. Buses: 1, 2, 6, 8, 9, 11, 12, 16, 19, 45, 57, 59, 61. Bus stop in front of the Library.

Parking. In front of the main entrance to the Library.

Admission. Readers: Readers must register at the Library entrance. The fees are: ND30 for scholars, ND10 for students, ND20 for others.
Visitors: No admission charge.

Information. On the first floor.

Sales. None.

Guidebooks. Available in Macedonian language with summaries in English, Russian, French and German. Free of charge.

Restaurant/Snack Facilities. On the ground floor, open 0700-1900.

Services. Cloakroom on ground floor near the main entrance, lavatories on ground floor and first floor near

Book of Hours (Kamena Reka, 1566), in the 'Kliment Ohridski' National and University Library, Skopje. This was published by the first Macedonian publisher, Jakov. Detail

the reading rooms, smoking lounge on ground floor near the snack bar.

Catalogues. Author and classified catalogues.

Classification. Universal Decimal Classification.

Copying/Photography. Copying machines are available for individual use, in the basement (Mon.-Fri. 0700-1500). Permission must be obtained from the Director for private photography.

Friends of the Library. A society is in the process of formation.

ZAGREB
Nacionalna i sveučilišna biblioteka (National and University Library)
41001 Zagreb, Marulićev trg 21, POB 550
Tel. Director 445-440; Secretariat 446-725; Information Office 446-525

History. The Library's origins can be traced back to the Jesuit Collegium founded in Zagreb in 1606. After the expulsion of the Jesuit Order in 1773, some of the Collegium's books were given to the Academia Scientiarum, a college for law and philosophy, in 1776. In the same year the Academia also received the books of Canon Baltazar Krčelič on the condition that they should be made available to scholars. By the first half of the 19th century the Library had become known as the 'Biblioteca Publico-Nationalis' and in 1837 it was granted legal deposit privileges for present-day northern Croatia. The foundation of the University of Zagreb in 1874 raised the status of the Library and in 1875 the library of the National Museum was added. The present Library building was erected in 1911-13 and today contains nearly 1.1 million volumes, 5,184 manuscripts, 15,097 maps and 3,500 microfilms. Since 1919 the Library has received one legal deposit copy of works published in all of Yugoslavia, and since 1946 an additional deposit copy of works published in Croatia. In 1960 the Library, which is administratively independent of the University, assumed the legal functions of the bibliographic centre of Croatia.

Special Collections and Treasures. The Manuscript Collection includes *Vinodolski zakon* (1288) and the 15th century *Istarski razvod* (both in 16th century copies); a Glagolitic missal of 1483, the first Croatian book printed in Church Slavonic (but under the influence of Croatian); MSS of the 16th and 17th century Croatian writers, e.g. D. Zlatarić, I. Bunić Vučić, I. Gundulić, and J. Palmotić; documents of the Illyrian movement in the first half of the 19th century, including the writings of L. Gaj, J. Drašković, A. and I. Mažuranić; and the legacies of the

National and University Library, Zagreb

philologists F. Miklošić,. V. Jagić, and J. Kopitar. The Rare Book Collection includes many works in the Glagolitic script, particularly of the 15th and 16th century Senj printers, in Latin (hrvatski latinisti), e.g. I. Česmički (Janus Pannonius), Mathias Flacius Illyricus, R. Bošković; Croatian Protestant works printed in Urach, Germany, in the 16th century; the collection of the Croatian ban Nikola Zrinski (1620-64); and documents from the national liberation struggle (1941-45). The Graphic Collection of 6,000 drawings, 1,200 bookplates, 20,000 posters and 50,000 postcards includes several original drawings of the 18th century Austrian architect J.B. Fischer von Erlach, as well as drawings and watercolours by I. Meštrović, J. Račić and V. Radaus. The Music Collection includes *Liber antifonarium* (1489), the 17th century *Passionale Croaticum* by Peršić and *Fundamentum cantus gregoriani* (1760) by M. Šilobod-Bolšić.

Exhibition Areas. There is a permanent exhibition of books and MSS in the Rare Books Department and an occasional exhibition room on the first floor.

Hours. Mon.-Fri. 0800-2100, Sat. 0800-1500. Reading room for rare books and manuscripts: Mon.-Sat. 0800-1300. Closed Sun., 1-2 Jan., 1-2 May, 4 July, 1-15 Aug., 29-30 Nov.

Transport. All forms of city transport pass close by.

Parking. Free parking places available near the Library.

Admission. *Readers:* Students of Zagreb University: 5.00 Din per term. Other researchers: 10.00 Din per term. *Visitors:* Not charged unless they work in the reading rooms.

Information. Information Office close to the entrance hall.

Sales. None.

Guidebooks. None.

Restaurant/Snack Facilities. None.

Services. Cloakrooms, lavatories, telephones.

Catalogues. Alphabetical, classified, shelf and special catalogues. Union catalogue of foreign books and periodicals in the libraries of the Socialist Republic of Croatia.

Classification. Own.

Copying/Photography. Photocopying facilities are available but machines are not available for individual use. Permission is required for private photography.

The first Croatian printed book, a Glagolitic Missal (1483), in the National and University Library, Zagreb. Detail